# BREWER'S BOOK OF
# MYTH AND LEGEND

### edited by J.C. Cooper

Quality Paperbacks Direct
London

Cassell Publishers Limited
Villiers House, 41/47 Strand
London WC2N 5JE, England

This edition published 1992 by QPD by arrangement
with Cassell.

First published 1992

CN 6713

Printed and bound in Great Britain by
Mackays of Chatham PLC, Chatham, Kent

# Contents

Introduction iv

Key to Pronunciation vii

Abbreviations ix

Cross-References ix

Brewer's Book of Myth and Legend 1

# INTRODUCTION

The present volume is essentially the work of Brewer, relevant subjects having been taken from his *Dictionary of Phrase and Fable*. No one can study this earlier work without admiring his immense erudition and meticulous scholarship and although most of the great number of books which stand to his name have passed into oblivion, his dictionaries remain classics. Brewer's work, however, was the fruit of the Victorian era when education and culture were grounded on the Greek and Roman classics and but a cursory interest was shown in the texts, religions and mythology of the Eastern and Far Eastern cultures which were largely dismissed as 'heathen' or 'pagan'. For example, while the highly erotic antics of Zeus came within the 'classical', the similar activities of Krishna were 'pagan' and their mythological and symbolic significance largely misunderstood or ignored.

Even less were the tribal cultures of Oceania, Africa and the American Indians accepted; they, in the estimation and works of the early anthropologists, were 'savage' or 'primitive'. The rich and fruitful heritage of their philosophies and mythologies had not yet been fully and sympathetically explored. It is in these provinces that additions have been made to Brewer's original text. Since his time the world has shrunk, East and West have met and, in inter-cultural exchanges, have discovered the importance and the significance of their mythologies and legends, and have a deeper understanding of their unity in diversity.

Myth was, for the early anthropologists, that which was untrue, a figment of the imagination, that which was dreamed up by elementary, uncultured minds, whereas it is now recognized as a serious expression of some sacred truth. This century has seen at first an awakening of interest in mythology and the realization of its value and now a full appreciation and interest in its value. As Thomas Mann said: 'Something timeless has once more emerged into the light and become present.' He also asserts that mythology is 'the legitimization of life; only through and in it does life find self-awareness, sanction, consecration' and that although the mythical is an early stage for the race, for the individual it is a late and mature one. It is this late and mature stage we are now seeing.

Notable scholars such as Mircea Eliade and Joseph Campbell have brought a wealth of myth and legend into the present day, revealing a breadth and depth in ancient traditions, particularly in the hitherto neglected tribal lore of people who identify with nature and present a whole mythology of their own which fills the gap in the over-rational European experience. A discerning and keen interest in these mythologies is now everywhere apparent.

To quote examples of the awareness of the importance of myth and legend, Schorer says that 'myths are the instruments by which we continually struggle to make our experiences intelligible to ourselves. A myth is a controlling image that gives philosophical meaning to the facts of ordinary life; that which has organizing value for experience ... without such images experience is chaotic, fragmentary and merely phenomenal. Myths unify experience in a way that is satisfactory to the whole culture and to the whole personality.'

Eliade wrote that 'we are at last beginning to know and understand the value of myth and to appreciate the heritage from societies where myth is the very foundation of social life and culture, in which, being real and sacred, it becomes exemplary.' While current language confuses myth with fable, traditional societies see myth as the only valid revelation of reality, dealing with the sacred, while fable is concerned with the secular or profane.

Joseph Campbell maintains that the fullness of life stands in direct ratio to the range of mythological response rather than to rational thought. He says that 'no human society has yet been found in which mythological motives have not been rehearsed in liturgies, interpreted by seers, poets, theologians or philosophers, presented in art, magnified in song and ecstatically expressed in life-empowering visions.' This theme is echoed by Wheelwright who says that 'the very essence of myth is the haunting awareness of transcendental forces peering through the cracks of the visible universe'.

Many myths are universal, such as those of initiation, birth-death-and-rebirth, the trials and triumphs of the hero or heroine and the heroic slaying of evil monsters; descent into the underworld or ascent to the heavens. Creation myths and the Deluge appear world-wide as do myths of the Golden Age when all dwelt together in amity; then came the loss of Paradise and the longing for return to the primordial perfection. There are amazing similarities in the myths from widely separated and different parts. These myths are the fundamental responses of the people to their environment, to the existential situation and experiences as well as the embodiment of their longings; some are quasi-historical, others the response to religious beliefs and to cultural, psychological urges, both social and personal. They have been handed down by word of mouth, in rituals, festivals, religious drama and in literature, becoming a creative force, perpetuating the powers of which they are an expression.

In the wide range covered by the present volume there are naturally different interpretations and versions of similar myths and legends, depending on their geographical, climatic, historical and cultural back-grounds and the term 'myth' must be held to cover these extensive fields which involve the traditional, the universal, the old and the new, the social and the personal. Myth is essential to all peoples' beliefs, also there is no great literature separable from mythology. As Malinowski says, 'it is an indispensable ingredient of all culture.'

J.C. Cooper

# KEY TO PRONUNCIATION

Vowel sounds:

| | | | | | | |
|---|---|---|---|---|---|---|
| ah | far | (fah) | o | not | (not) | |
| a | fat | (fat) | ō | note | (nōt) | |
| ā | fate | (fāt) | | sower | (sō'ə) | |
| aw | fall | (fawl) | oo | blue | (bloo) | |
| | north | (nawth) | ŭ | sun | (sŭn) | |
| | paw | (paw) | u | foot | (fut) | |
| | soar | (saw) | | bull | (bul) | |
| e | bell | (bel) | ū | muse | (mūz) | |
| ē | beef | (bēf) | ə | again | (əgen') | |
| œ | her | (hœ) | | current | (kŭ'rənt) | |
| | fur | (fœ) | | sailor | (sā'lə) | |
| i | bit | (bit) | | publicity | (pəblis'iti) | |
| ī | bite | (bīt) | | | | |

Note: the neutral sound of many unstressed vowels is represented, as shown above, by the symbol ə; some unstressed vowels in this dictionary are (more correctly) transcribed as (-i-), as in (ilek'trik).

Consonants:

| | | | | | | |
|---|---|---|---|---|---|---|
| p | pit | (pit) | s | sit | (sit) | |
| b | bit | (bit) | v | van | (van) | |
| t | tin | (tin) | w | win | (win) | |
| d | dance | (dahns) | y | yet | (yet) | |
| k | kit | (kit) | z | haze | (hāz) | |
| m | man | (man) | ng | sing | (sing) | |
| n | nut | (nŭt) | th | thin | (thin) | |
| l | lid | (lid) | dh | this | (dhis) | |
| f | fit | (fit) | sh | ship | (ship) | |
| h | hit | (hit) | zh | measure | (mezh'ə) | |
| g | get | (get) | kh | loch | (lokh) | |
| j | just | (jŭst) | ch | church | (chœch) | |
| r | run | (rŭn) | | | | |

Note: where a sound represented by two consonants *e.g.* (-ng-) is followed by another syllable which begins with the second consonant (-g-) and where the stress mark falls elsewhere, a centred dot is used to show where the syllable break occurs, for example as in (ling·gwis'tiks).

'Diphthongs'

(i) Vowel sounds incorporating the final unpronounced 'r' of standard British English:

| eə | fair  | (feə)  |
|    | mare  | (meə)  |
|    | mayor | (meə)  |
| iə | fear  | (fɪə)  |
|    | seer  | (siə)  |
| īə | fire  | (fīə)  |
| ūə | pure  | (pūə)  |
| uə | poor  | (puə)  |

(ii) Others:

| ow | bout | (bowt) |
|    | cow  | (kow)  |
| oi | join | (join) |

Foreign vowels not dealt with by the main system:

(i) Nasalized:

| ā | (āsyen′) | a̲n̲cienne |
| ē̃ | (ēfä′)   | e̲n̲fant   |
| ī | (līfam′) | (écraser) |
|   |          | l'i̲n̲fâme  |
| ō | (kō′zhā) | (co̲n̲gé)  |
| ū | (verdū′) | (Verdu̲n̲) |

(ii) Other:

| ü | (ētēdü′) | entendu̲ |
|   | (ü′bə)   | ü̲ber    |

**Stress**

Stress (′) is shown in pronunciations immediately *after* the syllable which is stressed, *e.g.* (tī′gə) = **tiger**. Stress is *not* given on compounds composed of two or more separate words, nor on idioms.

# ABBREVIATIONS

| | | | |
|---|---|---|---|
| Arab. | Arabic | L. Lat. | Late Latin |
| Austr. | Australian | M.E. | Middle English |
| c. | *circa* (about) | Med. Lat. | Mediaeval Latin |
| cp. | compare | Mod. Fr. | Modern French |
| Dan. | Danish | O.E. | Old English |
| Dut. | Dutch | O.Fr. | Old French |
| e.g. | *exempli gratia* (for example) | O.H.Ger. | Old High German |
| | | O.Slav. | Old Slavonic |
| Fr. | French | O.W. | Old Welsh |
| Gael. | Gaelic | Pers. | Persian |
| Ger. | German | Port. | Portuguese |
| Gr. | Greek | q.v. | *quod vide* (which see) |
| Heb. | Hebrew | Russ. | Russian |
| Hind. | Hindustani | Sans. | Sanskrit |
| Icel. | Icelandic | Scot. | Scottish |
| i.e. | *id est* (that is) | Sp. | Spanish |
| Ital. | Italian | Swed. | Swedish |
| Jap. | Japanese | Turk. | Turkish |
| Lat. | Latin | viz. | *videlicet* (namely) |

# CROSS-REFERENCES

These are indicated in the text by the use of SMALL CAPITALS unless *q.v.* is used.

# NOTE

All biblical references are to the *Authorized Version* unless otherwise stated. Entries concerning liturgical customs of the Church of England refer to those associated with the *Book of Common Prayer*. Ecclesiastical usages are those of the Church of England except where otherwise indicated.

# A

**Aalu** (ah'loo), or **Aaru.** In ancient Egyptian religion the fields of Aalu, where food was grown for the dead to supplement the votive offerings of their descendants, correspond roughly with the ELYSIAN FIELDS of Greek mythology.

**Aarvak.** *See* HORSE.

**Abaddon** (əbad'ən). The angel of the bottomless pit (*Rev.* ix, 11), from Heb. *abad*, he perished. Milton used the name for the pit itself:

> In all her gates Abaddon rues
> Thy bold attempt.
> *Paradise Regained*, IV, 624.

**Abaris** (ab'əris). **The dart of Abaris.** A mythical priest of APOLLO mentioned by Herodotus, Pindar, etc. and surnamed 'the Hyperborean'. Apollo gave him a magic arrow which rendered him invisible and on which he rode through the air. He cured diseases and spoke oracles. Abaris gave the dart to Pythagoras.

**Abbot of Misrule.** *See* KING OF MISRULE.
**Abbot's Bromley Horn,** or **Antler Dance.** One of the rare European animal dances surviving from remote times. Originally danced on Twelfth Day at Abbot's Bromley, Staffordshire, it now takes place on the first Monday after 4 September. The six dancers, all male as in MORRIS DANCES, hold antlers (three of which are painted blue or red and three white) to their heads as they dance. It may originally have been a form of fertility rite since the dancers go the round of neighbouring farms before the dance.

**Abdallah** (abdal'ə). The father of Mohammed. He was so beautiful that when he married Amina 200 virgins broke their hearts from disappointed love. He died before his son was born. *See* Washington Irving's *Life of Mahomet*.

**Abdals** (ab'dəlz). The name given by Muslims to certain mysterious persons whose identity is known only to God and through whom the world is able to continue in existence. When one dies another is secretly appointed by God to fill the vacant place.

**Abdera** (abdē'rə). A maritime town of Thrace, mythically founded by HERCULES in memory of ABDERUS. The *Abderites* or *Abderitans* were proverbial for stupidity, said to be caused by the air, but among them were Democritus, the laughing philosopher (hence *Abderitan laughter* = scoffing laughter, and *Abderite* = scoffer); Protagoras, the sophist; Anaxarchos, the philosopher friend of Alexander; and Hecataeus, the historian.

**Abderus.** A friend of HERCULES, who was devoured by the horses of DIOMEDES when keeping guard over them.

**Abdiel** (ab'dēl). In Milton's *Paradise Lost* (V, 805, 896 etc.) the faithful seraph who withstood SATAN when he urged the angels to revolt.

**Abif.** *See* HIRAM ABIF.

**Abominable Snowman.** Name, popularized by Shipton's Everest Expedition of 1951, for the yeti, a rare, elusive, and supposedly bear-like (some say ape-like) animal of the Himalayas.

**Abou Hassan** (aboo has'ən). A rich merchant (in the ARABIAN NIGHTS, *The Sleeper Awakened*), transferred while asleep to the bed of the Caliph Haroun Al-Raschid. Next morning he was treated as the Caliph and every effort was made to make him forget his identity. The same trick was played on Christopher SLY in the Induction of Shakespeare's *The Taming of the Shrew*; and according to Burton (*Anatomy of Melancholy*, 1621) by Philip the Good, duke of Burgundy, on a drunken rustic, the sub-

1

ject of *The Frolicsome Duke, or the Tinker's Good Fortune* found in Percy's *Reliques*. Calderón's play, *Life's a Dream* (*c.* 1633), contains another version.

**Ab ovo** (ab ō'vō) (Lat. from the egg). Laboriously from the very beginning. Stasinus in his *Cypria*, an introduction to the ILIAD, begins with the eggs of LEDA, from one of which HELEN was born. If Leda had not laid this egg Helen would never have been born, therefore PARIS could not have eloped with her, therefore there would have been no TROJAN WAR etc. The English use of the phrase probably derives from the line in Horace's *De Arte Poetica*:

Nec gemino bellum Troianum orditur ab ovo.

**Abracadabra.** A cabbalistic charm, said to be made up from the initials of the Hebrew words Ab (Father), Ben (Son), and Ruach ACadsch (Holy Spirit), and formerly used against ague, flux, toothache etc. The word was written on parchment as shown and hung from the neck by a linen thread.

```
A B R A C A D A B R A
  A B R A C A D A B R
    A B R A C A D A B
      A B R A C A D A
        A B R A C A D
          A B R A C A
            A B R A C
              A B R A
                A B R
                  A B
                    A
```

**Abraham.** In addition to the Bible stories about the Hebrew patriarch, Muslim legend adds the following: His parents were Prince Azar and his wife Adna. As King Nimrod had been told that one shortly to be born would dethrone him, he proclaimed a 'massacre of the innocents'. Adna retired to a cave where Abraham was born and was nourished by sucking two of her fingers, one giving milk and the other honey. At fifteen months the boy was the size of a lad of fifteen, and so wise that Azar introduced him to Nimrod's court. Further, legend says that Abraham and his son 'Ismail' rebuilt for the fourth time the KAABA; that Abraham destroyed the idols made and worshipped by his father Terah; and that the mountain on which he offered up his son ('Mount Moriah' in the Bible) was 'Arfaday'.

The Ghebers say that the infant Abraham was thrown into the fire by Nimrod's order

but it turned into a bed of roses on which he went to sleep.

**Abraxas** (əbrak'səs). A cabbalistic word used by the Gnostics to denote the Supreme Being, the source of 365 emanations, the sum of the numbers represented by the Greek letters of the word. It was often engraved on gems (*Abraxas stones*) used as TALISMANS. By some authorities the name is given as that of one of the horses of AURORA.

**Abyla.** *See* CALPE.

**Acadine** (ak'ədīn). A Sicilian fountain mentioned by Diodorus Siculus as having magic properties. Writings were thrown into it to be tested; if genuine they floated, if spurious they sank to the bottom.

**Acanthus** (əkan'thəs). The representation of the leaf of *Acanthus mollis* used to decorate the capitals of Corinthian and composite columns. The story is that an acanthus sprang up around a basket of flowers that Callimachus had placed on his daughter's grave. This so struck the fancy of the architect that he introduced the design into his buildings.

**Accius Naevius** (ak'iəs nē'viəs). A legendary Roman augur who forbade TARQUIN the Elder (616–579 B.C.) to increase the number of centuries (*i.e.* divisions of the army) instituted by ROMULUS, without consulting the augurs. Tarquin asked him if, according to the augurs, the thought then in his (Tarquin's) mind was feasible of accomplishment. 'Undoubtedly', said Accius after consultation. 'Then cut through this whetstone with the razor in your hand'. The priest gave a bold cut and the block fell in two (Livy, I, 36). *See* AUGURY.

**Acestes** (əses'tēz). **The arrow of Acestes.** In a trial of skill Acestes, the Sicilian, shot his arrow with such force that it took fire (*Aeneid*, V, 525).

**Achates** (əkā'tēz). **A fidus Achates** is a faithful companion, a bosom friend. Achates (in Virgil's *Aeneid*) was the chosen comrade of AENEAS.

**Achemon** (əkem'on). According to Greek legend, Achemon and his brother Basalas were two Cercopes (a people of Ephesus) for ever quarrelling. One day they saw

HERCULES asleep under a tree and insulted him, so he tied them by their feet to his club and walked off with them, heads downwards. Everyone laughed at the sight, and it became a proverbial cry among the Greeks, when two men were seen quarrelling—'Look out for Melampygos!' (*i.e.* Hercules):

Ne incidas in Melampygum.

**Acheri.** The ghost of a little girl, who, according to folk tradition of India, comes down at night from her mountain haunts to bring sickness to children in human habitations. A bright-red thread worn round the neck is believed to be a protection against such molestation.

**Acheron** (ak'eron). The 'woeful river' of the underworld into which flow the PHLEGETHON and COCYTUS. Also HADES itself. *See* CHARON; STYX.

> They pass the bitter waves of Acheron
> Where many souls sit wailing woefully.
> SPENSER: *Faerie Queene* I, v, 33.

*See also* Virgil's *Aeneid*, Bk. VI.

**Acherontian Books.** *See* TAGES.

**Acherusia** (akeroo'zia). A cavern on the borders of Pontus, through which HERCULES dragged CERBERUS from the infernal regions to earth.

**Achillea** (akilē'a). A genus of plants of the aster family, including common yarrow (*Achillea millifolium*), so called from ACHILLES. The tale is that the Greeks, on the way to TROY, landed in Mysia and were opposed by Telephus, son of HERCULES. DIONYSUS caused Telephus to stumble and he was wounded by Achilles with his spear. Told by the ORACLE that Achilles (the wounder) would be the healer (meaning milfoil or yarrow), Telephus sought out the Greek leader, promising to lead him to Troy in return for his help. Achilles agreed, scraped some rust from his spear from which sprang the plant milfoil, and this healed the wound. It is called carpenters' wort by the French (*herbe aux charpentiers*) because it is supposed to heal wounds made by carpenters' tools.

**Achilles** (əkil'ēz). Hero of the ILIAD, the son of Peleus, King of the MYRMIDONS in Thessaly, and grandson of Aeacus. Brave and relentless, his quarrel with AGAMEMNON, the Greek commander-in-chief, caused him to withdraw from the struggle. The TROJANS prevailed and Achilles allowed PATROCLUS to lead the Myrmidons back. Patroclus was killed by HECTOR. Achilles then returned, routed the Trojans, and slew Hector. According to later poems Achilles was killed by PARIS at the Scaean gate. *See* ACHILLES TENDON.

**Achilles and the tortoise.** Alludes to a paradox by Zeno. In a race Achilles, who can run ten times as fast as a tortoise, gives the latter 100 yards start; but cannot win the race because while he is running the first 100 yards, the tortoise runs ten, while Achilles runs that ten the tortoise runs one, while Achilles is running one, the tortoise runs one-tenth of a yard, and so on *ad infinitum*.

**Achilles of the West.** ROLAND the Paladin, also called 'the Christian THESEUS'.

**Achilles tendon** (*tendo Achillis*). A strong sinew connecting the heel and calf frequently strained by athletes. The tale is that THETIS took her son Achilles by the heel, and dipped him in the river STYX to make him invulnerable, but the heel in her hand remained dry. The hero was slain by an arrow wound in the heel—the one weak spot (a post-Homeric story).

**Achilles's horses.** Balios and XANTHUS. *See* HORSE.

**Achilles's mistress in Troy.** Hippodamia, surnamed BRISEIS.

**Achilles's spear.** *See* ACHILLEA. Shakespeare and Chaucer allude to its powers.

> Whose smile and frown, like to Achilles's spear,
> Is able with the change to kill and cure.
> SHAKESPEARE: *Henry VI, Part II*, V, i.

> And of Achilles with his queynte spere,
> For he coude with it both hele and dere [harm].
> CHAUCER: *Squire's Tale*, 238.

**Achilles's tomb.** In Sigeum, over which no bird ever flies. *Pliny*, X, 29.

**Achilles's tutors.** PHOENIX, who taught him the arts of war and rhetoric, and CHIRON, the CENTAUR, the art of healing.

**Achilles's wife.** DEIDAMIA.

**The heel of Achilles.** The vulnerable spot in the character of a man or a nation. *See* ACHILLES TENDON.

**Achor** (ā'kaw). Said by Pliny to be the deity prayed to by the Cyreneans for the averting of insect pests.

**Acis** (ā′sis). The son of FAUNUS, in love with GALATEA, crushed to death with a rock by his rival, POLYPHEMUS the CYCLOPS, and changed into the river Acis (Ovid, *Metam.* xiii, 750–968).

**Aconite** (ak′ənīt). The herb Monkshood or Wolfsbane. According to classic fable when HERCULES, at the command of Eurystheus, dragged CERBERUS from the infernal regions, the poisonous aconite grew from the foam which dropped from his mouths.

**Acrasia** (əkrā′ziə). The personification of intemperance, the name signifying 'lack of self control'. In Spenser's *Faerie Queene* (II, xii) *Acrasia*, an enchantress, mistress of the 'Bower of Bliss', transformed her lovers into monstrous shapes and kept them captive. Sir Guyon destroyed her bower, freed her victims, and sent her in chains of adamant to the Faerie Queene.

**Acrostic** (Gr. *akros*, outermost; *stichos*, line of verse). Verse in which the initial letters of each line read downwards to form a word; if the final letters also form a word it is a double acrostic; if the middle letters also, it is a triple acrostic. The term was first applied to the obscure prophecies of the Erythraean SIBYL written on loose leaves, which made a word when sorted into order (*Dionys.* IV, 62).

**Actaeon** (aktē′on). In Greek mythology a huntsman who, having surprised DIANA bathing (or according to Euripides boasted his superiority in the chase) was changed into a stag and torn to pieces by his own hounds. Thus (as a stag) he became representative of men whose wives are unfaithful.

**Actian Games** (ak′tiən). The games celebrated at Actium in honour of APOLLO, renewed by Augustus after his naval victory over Antony off Actium (31 B.C.).

**Adam.** The Talmudists say that Adam lived in PARADISE only twelve hours before he was thrust out. Muslim legend says that:

God sent GABRIEL, MICHAEL, and ISRAFEL in turn to fetch seven handfuls of earth from different depths and of different colours for the creation of Adam (hence the varying colours of mankind), but they returned empty-handed because Earth foresaw that the creature to be made from her would rebel against God and draw down his curse on

her. AZRAEL was then sent and he fulfilled the task, and so was appointed to separate the souls from the bodies, hence becoming the ANGEL of Death. The earth he fetched was taken to Arabia to a place between Mecca and Tayef, kneaded by angels, fashioned into human form by God and left to dry for either 40 days or 40 years. The tradition holds that Adam was buried on Aboucais, a mountain in Arabia.

For the Bible story of Adam, see *Gen.* i-v.

**Adam Bell.** *See* CLYM OF THE CLOUGH.

**Adam's bridge.** *See* RAMA.

**Adam's Peak.** A mountain in Sri Lanka where, according to Muslim legend, ADAM, after his expulsion from PARADISE, expiated his crime by standing on one foot for 200 years until GABRIEL took him to Mount Ararat, where he found Eve. In the granite there is a large impression resembling a human foot. Hindus assert that it was made by Buddha when he ascended into heaven.

**Adamastor** (adəmas′taw). The spirit of the Cape of Storms (Good Hope), described by Camoëns (1524–1580) in the LUSIADS, who appeared to Vasco da Gama and foretold disaster to all attempting the voyage to India.

**Add insult to injury.** To wound by word or deed someone who has already suffered an act of violence or injustice. Phaedrus quotes the fable of AESOP about a bald man who, in attempting to kill a fly which had bitten his head, missed and dealt himself a sharp smack. Whereupon the fly said: 'You wished to kill me for a mere touch. What will you do to yourself since you have added insult to injury?'

**Adept.** One who has attained (Lat. *adeptus*). The alchemists applied the term *vere adeptus* to those who professed to have found out the ELIXIR OF LIFE or the PHILOSOPHER'S STONE.

**Aditi** (ədē′tē). The great earth mother of Hindu mythology, sometimes an abstract concept of limitless space and time. Variously described as the mother, wife, and daughter of VISHNU.

**Adityas.** In the Vedas they are the divine sons of ADITI, the chief being VARUNA, sustainer of the moral law, who is often called *Aditya*. Originally seven, the sons were later increased to twelve as the months of the year and the passage of the sun.

**Adonia** (ədō′niə). An eight-day feast of ADONIS, celebrated in Assyria, Alexandria, Egypt, Judaea, Persia, Cyprus, Greece and Rome. The women first lamented the death of ADONIS then wildly rejoiced at his resurrection—a custom referred to in the Bible (*Ezek*. viii, 14), where Adonis appears under his Phoenician name, Tammuz. *See* THAMMUZ.

**Adonis** (ədō′nis). In classical mythology, a beautiful youth, son of MYRRHA (or Smyrna), he was beloved by APHRODITE (Venus) and killed by a boar while hunting. Hence, usually ironical, any beautiful young man. Leigh Hunt was sent to prison for libelling the Prince Regent by calling him 'a corpulent Adonis of fifty' (*Examiner*, 1813).

**Adonis Flower,** the rose, once white, but coloured red by the blood of APHRODITE when pricked by a thorn rushing to help the fallen ADONIS; the anemone which sprang from his blood or the tears of Aphrodite; and more commonly Pheasant's Eye (*Adonis autumnalis*), which arose from the hunter's blood.

**Adonis garden.** A worthless toy; very perishable goods.

> Thy promises are like Adonis' gardens.
> That one day bloomed and fruitful were the next.
> SHAKESPEARE: *Henry VI, Pt. I*, 1, vi.

At the Greek festival of the ADONIA, pots of earth stuck with flowers, and called Adonis gardens, were made symbolizing the revival of vegetation with the coming rains.

**Adonis River,** the stream near Byblos which ran red with the soil brought down from Lebanon.

> Thammuz came next behind,
> Whose annual wound in Lebanon allured
> The Syrian damsels to lament his fate
> In amorous ditties all a summer's day,
> While smooth Adonis from his native rock
> Ran purple to the sea, supposed with blood
> Of Thammuz yearly wounded.
> MILTON: *Paradise Lost*, I, 446.

**Adoption. Adoption by hair.** Boso, King of Provence (879–889), is said to have cut off his hair and given it to Pope John VIII (872–882) as a sign that the latter had adopted him.

**Adrammelech** (ədram′elek). A Babylonian deity to whom infants were burnt in sacrifice (II *Kings* xvii, 31). Possibly the sun god worshipped at Sippar (Sepharvaim).

**Adrastus** (ədras′təs). (i) A mythical Greek king of Argos, leader of the expedition of the SEVEN AGAINST THEBES. (ii) An Indian prince, slain by RINALDO (in Tasso's *Jerusalem Delivered*, Bk. XX), who aided the king of Egypt against the crusaders.

**Adriatic.** *See* BRIDE OF THE SEA.

**Adversary, The.** SATAN or the DEVIL (from I *Pet.* v, 8).

**Adytum** (ad′itəm) (Gr. *aduton*, not to be entered). The Holy of Holies in Greek and Roman temples, into which the public was not admitted; hence a sanctum.

**Aegeus** (ē′jūs). A mythical king of Attica, who sent his son THESEUS to Crete to deliver ATHENS from the yearly tribute of seven youths and seven maidens exacted by MINOS. If successful, Theseus was to hoist white sails (in place of black) on his return, as a signal of his safety. He omitted to do so. Aegeus, thinking his son was lost, threw himself into the sea. The story is repeated in the tale of TRISTRAM and Isolde.

**Aeginetan Sculptures** consist of two groups of figures from the east and west pediments of the temple of ATHENE, on the island of Aegina, representing exploits of the Greek heroes at TROY. They date from *c.* 500 B.C., being found in 1811, and are preserved in the Glyptothek, in Munich.

**Aegir** (ē′jir, ē′gir). In Norse mythology the god of the ocean, husband of Ran. They had nine daughters (the billows), who wore white robes and veils.

**Aegis** (ē′jis) (Gr. goat skin). The shield of ZEUS, made by HEPHAESTUS and covered with the skin of the goat AMALTHEA, who had suckled the infant Zeus. With the GORGON'S head in the centre, it was also carried by his daughter ATHENE. By shaking his aegis Zeus produced storms and thunder. In relation to Athene it is usually represented as a cloak fringed with serpents and the Gorgon's head. It is symbolic of divine protection, hence *under my aegis*, under my protection.

**Aegyptus** (ējip′tus). In Greek legend a son of Belus and twin brother of Danaus who was king of that part of Africa named after him (Egypt).

**Aeneas** (ēnē′as). In Greek mythology the son of Anchises, King of Dardanus, and APHRODITE. According to HOMER he fought in the TROJAN WAR, and after the sack of TROY withdrew to Mount IDA and reigned in the Troad. The post-Homeric legends are largely embodied in the AENEID.

**Aeneid** (ē′nēid or ēnē′id). Virgil's epic poem in twelve books, accounting for the settlement of AENEAS in Italy, thus claiming Trojan origins for the Roman state. The story tells how Aeneas escaped from the flames of TROY carrying his father Anchises to Mount IDA. With his Trojan followers he sailed to Crete but learnt in a vision that he was destined for Italy, and eventually reached Sicily where his father died. Heading for the mainland, he was wrecked on the coast of Carthage. He left secretly, at JUPITER'S behest, whereupon the lovelorn queen DIDO of Carthage killed herself. Reaching Latium he was betrothed to LAVINIA, daughter of king LATINUS; but war arose with Turnus, king of the Rutuli, who also wished to marry Lavinia. Turnus was finally killed by Aeneas.

**Aeolus** (ē′ōlәs), in Homeric legend, was appointed ruler of the winds by ZEUS, and lived on his Aeolian island.

**Aeon** (ē′on) (Gr. *aiōn*). An age of the universe, an infinite length of time. Also the personification of an age, a god, any being that is eternal. Basilides, in the early 2nd century, held that there had been 365 such Aeons but Valentinus, the 2nd-century Gnostic, restricted the number to 30.

**Aeschylus** (ēs′kilәs) (525–456 B.C.), the main father of Greek tragic drama. Only seven plays, of over seventy known titles, are extant. Fable says he was killed by a tortoise dropped by an eagle (to break the shell) on his bald head (mistaken for a stone).
**Aeschylus of France.** Prosper Jolyot de Crébillon (1674–1762).

**Aesculapius** (ēskūlā′piәs). The Latin form of the Greek *Asklēpios*, god of medicine and of healing, son of APOLLO and father of HYGEIA. The usual offering to him was a cock, hence 'to sacrifice a cock to Aesculapius'—to give thanks (or pay the doctor's bill) after recovery from an illness.

When men a dangerous disease did scape,
Of old, they gave a cock to Aesculape.
BEN JONSON: *Epigram.*

Introduced to ROME (293 B.C.), in the form of a snake, during a pestilence, the SERPENT entwined round a staff became his attribute.

**Aesir** (ē′zēr). The collective name of the mythical gods of Scandinavia, who lived in ASGARD. (1) ODIN the chief; (2) THOR; (3) TIU; (4) BALDER; (5) BRAGI, god of poetry; (6) VIDAR, god of silence; (7) Hoder the blind (slayer of Balder); (8) Hermoder, Odin's son and messenger; (9) Hoenir, a minor god; (10) Odnir, husband of FREYJA; (11) LOKI; (12) Vali (Odin's youngest son).

**Aeson's Bath** (ē′son).

I perceive a man may be twice a child before the days of dotage; and stands in need of Aeson's Bath before three score.
SIR THOMAS BROWNE: *Religio Medici, Section* xlii.

The reference is to MEDEA rejuvenating Aeson, father of JASON, with the juices of various magic herbs. After Aeson had absorbed these juices, Ovid says:

Barba comaeque,
Canitie posita, nigrum rapuere, colorem.
*Metamorphoses*, VII, 288.

**Aesop's Fables** (ē′sop). These popular animal fables are traditionally the work of Aesop, a deformed Phrygian slave (*c.* 620–560 B.C.), but many are far older, being found on Egyptian papyri of 800–1,000 years earlier. Socrates, in prison, began committing them to verse. A collection made in choliambic by Babrius (early 3rd century A.D.), was found in a monastery on Mount Athos in 1844.
**Aesop of England.** John Gay (1685–1732).
**Aesop of France.** Jean de la Fontaine (1621–1695).
**Aesop of India.** Pilpay has been so called.

**Aetites** (āētī′tēz) (Gr. *aetos*, an eagle). Eagle stones, also called *gagites*: according to fable found in eagle's nests, possessing magical and medical properties.

The stone in question is big with another inside it, which rattles, as if in a jar when you shake it.
PLINY: *Natural History*, X, iv (*see also* XXX, xliv).

Lyly's *Euphues* (1578–1580) says:

The precious stone Aetites which is found in the filthy nests of the eagle.

**Afreet, Afrit** (af'rēt). In Muslim mythology the second most powerful of the five classes of JINN or devils. They were of gigantic stature, malicious and inspiring great dread.

**African Sisters, The.** The HESPERIDES, who dwelt in Africa.

**Agamemnon** (agəmem'non). In Greek legend, the King of Mycenae, son of Atreus, grandson of PELOPS, brother of MENELAUS, and leader of the Greeks at the siege of TROY. He married CLYTEMNESTRA. ORESTES was their son. Their daughters were IPHIGENIA and/or Iphianassa, Laodice (in later legend ELECTRA), and Chrysothemis. He returned from Troy with CASSANDRA (daughter of King PRIAM) and both were murdered by his wife Clytemnestra and her paramour Aegisthus. The guilty pair were killed by Orestes, called Agamemnonides.
**Vixere fortes ante Agamemnona,** a quotation from Horace (*Od.* IV, ix), paraphrased by Byron in *Don Juan* (i, 5);

Brave men were living before Agamemnon
And since, exceeding valorous and sage,
A good deal like him too, though quite the same
none;
But then they shone not on the poet's page,
And so have been forgotten.

In general, we are not to suppose our own age or locality monopolizes all that is good.

**Aganippe** (agənip'i). In Greek legend a fountain of BOEOTIA at the foot of Mount HELICON, dedicated to the MUSES because it imparted poetic inspiration. Hence the Muses are sometimes called *Aganippides.* Also the NYMPH of this fountain.

**Agape** (ag'əpi). A love-feast (Gr. *agapē,* love). The early Christians held a love-feast in conjunction with the Lord's Supper when the rich provided food for the poor. Eventually they became a scandal and were condemned by the Council of Carthage, 397. *Agape* was the mother of Priamond, Diamond, Triamond and Cambina in Spenser's *Faerie Queene* (IV, ii, 4188).

**Agate** (ag'ət). So called, says Pliny (XXXVII, 10), from Achates or Gagates, a river in Sicily, near which it is found in abundance. It was supposed to render a person invisible, and to turn the sword of foes against themselves.

A diminutive person has been called an *agate* from the custom of carving small figures on seals made from agate. Thus Shakespeare speaks of Queen MAB as no bigger than an agate-stone on the forefinger of an alderman.

**Agdistes** (agdis'tēz). The god who kept the 'Bower of Bliss' in Spenser's *Faerie Queene.*

**Agdistis** (agdis'tis). A Phrygian mother goddess sometimes identified with CYBELE the goddess of fertility. Originally hermaphrodite, she was made female by castration.

**Age,** a word used in mythology, geology, archaeology, history etc. to denote a period of time marked by particular characteristics, *e.g.* Golden Age, Ice Age, Stone Age, Dark Ages, Middle Ages, Elizabethan Age, Augustan Age, Machine Age, Atomic Age, etc.

Hesiod (? 8th century B.C.) names five ages: the Golden or patriarchal; the SILVER or voluptuous; the Brazen, warlike and violent; the Heroic or renaissant; the Iron or present, an age of misery and crime when justice and piety have vanished.

Lucretius (*c.* 94–55 B.C.) distinguishes three ages, stone, bronze and iron, according to the material from which implements were made (V, 2128).

Varro (116–27 B.C.) recognizes three—from the beginning of mankind to the DELUGE; from the Deluge to the first OLYMPIAD, called the mythical period; from the first Olympiad to his own time, called the historic period (*Fragments*, p. 219 Scaliger's edition, 1623).

Ovid (B.C. 43–A.D. 18) describes four ages—Golden, Silver, Bronze and Iron (*Metamorphoses* I, 89–150).

St. Augustine specifically mentions Seven Ages in the history of man in *de Civitate Dei XX11: 30,* derived from the Days of Creation in Genesis (i, ii).

Thomas Heywood (*c.* 1572–1650) has a series of plays based on classical mythology called *The Golden Age, The Silver Age, The Brazen Age,* and *The Iron Age.*

Shakespeare's seven ages of man are described in *As You Like It,* II, vii.

In Hinduism there are four ages, *Yugas*, roughly corresponding to the Gold, Silver, Brass and Iron Ages, the *Krita, Treta, Dvapara* and *Kali*. Law and virtue, perfect in the Golden Age, gradually decline until the *Kali Yuga*, the Iron Age and the present state, sees their dissolution. In the life of man there are three stages: the student, the householder and, when the social duties are completed, the forest dweller or contemplative.

**Age of Animals.** According to an old Celtic rhyme:

Thrice the age of a dog is that of a horse;
Thrice the age of a horse is that of a man;
Thrice the age of a man is that of a deer;
Thrice the age of a deer is that of an eagle.

**Age hoc** (ah'jē hok). 'Attend to this.' In sacrifice the Roman crier perpetually repeated these words to arouse attention. Somewhat similar is the frequent use of the exhortation 'Let us pray' in the Church of England services.

**Agelasta** (ajelas'tə), (Gr. joyless). The stone on which CERES (Demeter) rested when wearied in the search for her daughter, PERSEPHONE.

**Agenor** (ajen'aw). King of Tyre, son of POSEIDON (Neptune). His descendants Europa, CADMUS, PHOENIX, Cilix, etc., are known as Agenorides.

**Aglaia** (əglī'ə). One of the three GRACES.

**Aglaonice** (aglāōnī'si), the Thessalian, being able to calculate eclipses, claimed power over the MOON and to be able to draw it from HEAVEN. Her vaunting became a laughing-stock and gave rise to the Greek proverb cast at braggarts, 'Yes, as the Moon obeys Aglaonice.'

**Agnes, St.,** patron saint of young virgins, possibly martyred in the Diocletian persecution (*c.* 304) at the age of 13. There are various unreliable and conflicting accounts on the manner of her death; some say she was burnt at the stake and others that she was beheaded or stabbed. She vowed that her body was consecrated to Christ and rejected all her suitors. Her festival is on 21 January. Upon St. Agnes's night, says Aubrey in his *Miscellanies* (1696), you take a row of pins, and pull out every one, one after another. Saying a Paternoster, stick a pin in your sleeve, and you will dream of him or her you shall marry. In Keats' *The Eve of St. Agnes*, we are told:

how upon St. Agnes' Eve,
Young virgins might have visions of delight,
And soft adorings from their loves receive
Upon the honey'd middle of the night,
If ceremonies due they did aright;
As, supperless to bed they must retire.

Tennyson has a poem called *St. Agnes' Eve*.

**Ahmed, Prince** (ah'med), in the ARABIAN NIGHTS, is noted for the tent given him by the fairy Paribanou, which would cover a whole army, but might be carried in one's pocket; and for the apple of Samarkand (*see* APPLE, PRINCE AHMED'S), which would cure all diseases. Similar qualities to those of the tent are common to many legends. *See* BAYARD; CARPET; SKIDBLADNIR.

**Ahriman** (ah'rimən). In the dualism of later Zoroastrianism, the spirit of evil, also called Angra Mainyu. He is in eternal conflict with Ahura Mazda or ORMUZD. The spirit of deceit and wickedness was earlier personified as Druj.

**Ahura Mazda.** *See* ORMUZD.

**Ajax** (ā'jaks). (1) *The Greater*. A famous hero of the TROJAN WAR. Son of Telamon and King of Salamis, a man of giant stature, daring and slow-witted. In the ODYSSEY, when the armour of ACHILLES was awarded to Odysseus (ULYSSES), as the champion, Ajax killed himself.

(2) *The Lesser*. In Homer, son of Oileus, King of Locris, in Greece, and of small stature. In consequence of his attack on PRIAM'S daughter CASSANDRA he was drowned by POSEIDON after being shipwrecked.

**Aladdin** (əlad'in), in the ARABIAN NIGHTS, obtains a magic lamp and has a splendid palace built by the genie of the lamp. He marries the daughter of the Sultan of China, who disposes of the lamp, and his palace is transported to Africa. He subsequently recovers the lamp and returns with both wife and palace to China to live happily for many years.

**Aladdin's lamp.** The source of wealth and good fortune. After his good luck and marriage Aladdin neglected his lamp and allowed it to rust.

**To finish Aladdin's window**—*i.e.* to attempt to complete something begun by a master hand or genius. The palace built by the genie of the lamp had a room with twenty-four windows, all but one being set in precious stones; the last being left for the Sultan to finish but his resources proved unequal to the task.

**Al Araf** (al ar'af) (Arab. the partition). In the Koran, a region between PARADISE and Jahannam (HELL), for those who are neither morally good nor bad, such as infants, lunatics and idiots. Also where those whose good and evil deeds are equally balanced can await their ultimate admission to HEAVEN—a kind of LIMBO.

**Alasnam** (əlas'nam). In the ARABIAN NIGHTS Alasnam had eight diamond statues, but was required to find a ninth more precious still, to fill the vacant pedestal. The prize was found in the woman who became his wife, at once the most beautiful and perfect of her race.
**Alasnam's mirror.** The 'touchstone of virtue', given to him by one of the genii. If he looked into this mirror and it remained unsullied so would the maiden he had in mind; if it clouded she would prove faithless.

**Alastor** (əlas'taw). The evil genius of a house; a NEMESIS, the Greek term for an avenging power who visits the sins of the fathers on their children. Shelley has a poem entitled *Alastor; or the Spirit of Solitude*.

**Albatross.** A legendary weather prophet, forecasting winds and bad weather. It was said to brood its eggs on a floating raft and to sleep motionless on the wing. Killing one brings a curse, as related by Coleridge in his poem of the *Ancient Mariner*. The albatross is a sacred bird among the Ainu of Japan; it is the servant of the Chief God of the Sea and seeing one is a good omen.

**Alberich** (al'bərikh). In Scandinavian mythology, the all-powerful King of the DWARFS. In Wagner's version of the NIBELUNGENLIED he appears as a hideous GNOME and steals the magic gold guarded by the Rhine Maidens but is later captured by the gods, and forced to give up all he has in return for freedom.

**Albion.** An ancient and poetical name for Great Britain, probably from the white (Lat. *albus*) cliffs that face Gaul, but possibly from the Celtic word *alp*. Albion or Albany originally may have been the Celtic name of all Great Britain.

One legend is that a giant son of NEPTUNE, named Albion, discovered the country and ruled over it for forty-four years. Another such derivation is that the fifty daughters of the King of Syria (the eldest of whom was named Albia), were all married on the same day, and murdered their husbands on their wedding night. They were set adrift in a ship as punishment and eventually reached this western isle where they duly married natives.

In *Poly-Olbion* (1613) Michael Drayton says that Albion came from Rome and was the first Christian martyr in Britain.
**Perfide Albion.** Although the sentiment is often traced back to a mid-17th-century sermon by Bossuet, where the phrase 'la perfide Angleterre' is used, he is referring to England's adoption of Protestantism, and there is no real connection with the subsequent expression which is first noticed in a poem of 1793 by the Marquis de Ximenez—'Attaquons dans ses eaux la perfide Albion'. It attracted no particular attention and next appears in 1809 in both a poem by Henri Simon and a song. Its popular currency stems from its wide use in the Napoleonic recruiting drive of 1813 and it was well established by the end of the war in 1815.

**Al Borak.** *See* BORAK.

**Alcestis.** In Greek legend the daughter of Pelias and wife of Admetus, King of Pherae in Sicily to whom the FATES agreed to grant deliverance from death if his mother, father or wife would die for him instead. Alcestis thus sacrificed her life but was restored to her husband from the lower world by PERSEPHONE (another version says by HERCULES).

**Alchemy** (al'kəmi). The derivation of this word is obscure; *al* is the Arabic article the, and *kimia* the Arabic form of the Greek *chemeia*, which seems to have meant 'Egyptian art'; hence 'the art of the Egyptians'. Its main objects were the transmutation of base metals into gold, and the search for the PHILOSOPHER'S STONE, the universal solvent or Alkahest, the PANACEA, and the ELIXIR OF LIFE. It was the forerunner of the science of chemistry. Ben

Jonson wrote a play called *The Alchemist* (1610).

**Alcina** (alsē'nə). In Ariosto's *Orlando Furioso* (1516) the personification of carnal pleasure; the CIRCE of fable and Labe of the Arabians. Handel's opera *Alcina* appeared in 1735.

**Alcinoo poma dare** (al'sinō·ō pō'mə dah're) (to give apples to Alcinous). 'To carry coals to Newcastle.' The gardens of Alcinous, legendary king of the Phaeacians, by whom ULYSSES was entertained, were famous for their fruits.

**Alcmena** (alkmē'nə). In Greek mythology, daughter of Electryon (King of Mycenae), wife of AMPHITRYON, and mother (by ZEUS) of HERCULES. The legend is that at the conception of Hercules, Zeus (in the guise of Amphitryon), for additional pleasure with Alcmena, made the night the length of three ordinary nights.

**Alecto** (əlek'tō). In Greek mythology 'she who rests not', one of the three ERINYES, goddesses of vengeance, the Latin FURIES.

**Alectorian Stone** (alektaw'riən) (Gr. *alector*, a COCK). A stone, fabled to be of talismanic power, found in the stomach of cocks. Those who possess one are strong, brave and wealthy. MILO of Crotona owed his strength to one.

**Alectryomancy** (əlek'triōmansi). DIVINATION by a COCK. Draw a circle, and write in succession round it the letters of the alphabet, on each of which lay a grain of corn. Then put a cock in the centre of the circle, and watch what grains he eats. The letters will prognosticate the answer. Libanus and Jamblicus thus discovered who was to succeed the emperor Valens. The cock ate the grains over the letters t, h, e, o, d = Theod (orus).

**Alexander.** So PARIS, son of PRIAM, was called by the shepherds who brought him up.
**Alexander and the Robber.** The pirate Diomedes, having been captured, was asked by Alexander how he dared to molest the seas. 'How darest thou molest the earth?' was the reply. 'Because I am the master of a single galley I am termed a robber; but you who oppress the world with huge squadrons are called king.' Alexander

was so struck by this reasoning that he made Diomedes a rich prince, and a dispenser of justice.
**Only two Alexanders.** Alexander said, 'There are but two Alexanders—the invincible son of Philip, and the inimitable painting of the hero by Apelles.'

**Alfadir** (ahlfah'der) (father of all). In Scandinavian mythology, one of the epithets of ODIN.

**Alfana.** *See* HORSE.

**Alfar.** The elves of the northern mythology. In German legend the *döckalfar* frequent dark underground caverns and mines. The O.E. *Aelfric* means 'ruler of the elves'.

**Alfred the Great** (849–899), King of Wessex, especially noted for his resistance to the Danish invaders who in the winter of 877–8 occupied much of Wessex. Alfred withdrew to his base at Athelney and it is to this period that the story of Alfred and the cakes belongs—the first known version probably dating from the 11th/12th century. The story is that the king, unrecognized, took refuge in a cowherd's hut. He was sitting by the fire seeing to his equipment and allowed the housewife's loaves to burn. For this he was vigorously scolded. The story is not found in Asser's *Life of Alfred* (written in 893). After the defeat of the Danes Alfred commanded the building of a monastery at Athelney.

The beautiful gold enamelled relic, known as *Alfred's Jewel*, and bearing his name, was dug up at Athelney in 1693. It is now in the Ashmolean Museum, Oxford.

**Ali** (ah'lē). Mohammed's cousin and son-in-law, famed among Persians for the beauty of his eyes, hence *Ayn Hali* (eyes of Ali) as the highest expression for beauty.
**Ali Baba** (al'ē bah'bah). The hero of a story in the ARABIAN NIGHTS ENTERTAINMENTS, who sees a band of robbers enter a cave by means of the magic password 'Open SESAME'. When they have gone away he enters the cave, loads his ass with treasure and returns home. The Forty Thieves discover that Ali Baba has learned their secret and resolve to kill him, but they are finally outwitted by the slave-girl MORGIANA.

**Alice in Wonderland.** *Alice's Adventures in Wonderland* (1865) and *Through the Look-*

*ing Glass* (1871), widely read children's classics, originally illustrated by Sir John Tenniel, were written by C. L. Dodgson, an Oxford mathematician, under the pseudonym of Lewis Carroll. The original of Alice was Alice Liddell, daughter of Dean Liddell, famous as joint author of Liddell and Scott's Greek Lexicon. The Alice stories are noted for their whimsical humour and the 'nonsense' verse included in them.

'Alice in Wonderland' schemes, projects, ideas etc., are those which are unreal, totally impractical, things which can only exist in the realm of fantasy.

**Alifanfaron** (alifahn'fəron). Don QUIXOTE attacked a flock of sheep, and declared them to be the army of the giant Alifanfaron. Similarly AJAX, in a fit of madness, fell upon a flock of sheep, mistaking them for the sons of Atreus.

**Al Kadr** (al kadr') (the divine decree). A particular night in the month Ramadan when Muslims say that angels descend to earth and GABRIEL reveals to man the decrees of God. — *Al Koran*, ch. xcvii.

**All. All-Hallows' Eve** or **Hallowe'en** (31 October), also called 'NUTCRACK NIGHT' and 'Holy Eve', is associated with many ancient customs including bobbing for apples, cracking nuts (mentioned in *The Vicar of Wakefield*), finding one's lover by various rites, etc. Burns portrays the Scottish customs in his poem *Hallowe'en*, and Scottish tradition says that those born on HALLOWE'EN have the gift of second sight. Thus Mary Avenel, in Scott's *The Monastery* (1820), is made to see the WHITE LADY.

**All Heal.** The common Valerian, formerly supposed to have many medicinal virtues, also called *Hercules Woundwort*, because HERCULES is supposed to have learned its virtues from CHIRON. Spikenard, mentioned in the Bible (*Mark* xiv, 3), and extracted from a Himalayan member of the family, was used in perfumes by the ancient Egyptians, Greeks and Romans.

**All Souls' Day** (2 November). The day which Roman Catholics devote to prayer and almsgiving on behalf of the faithful departed. According to tradition, a pilgrim returning from the Holy Land took refuge on a rocky island during a storm. There he met a hermit, who told him that among the

cliffs was an opening to the infernal regions, through which flames ascended, and where the groans of the tormented were distinctly audible. The pilgrim told Odilo, abbot of Cluny, who appointed the day following (2 November 998) to be set apart for the benefit of those souls in Purgatory.

**Allan-a-Dale.** A minstrel in the ROBIN HOOD ballads who also appears in Scott's *Ivanhoe*. Robin Hood helped him to carry off his bride when she was on the point of being married against her will to a rich old knight.

**Alma** (al'mə) (Ital. soul, spirit, essence). In Matthew Prior's poem *Alma, or The Progress of the Mind*, the name typifies the mind or guiding principles of man. Alma is queen of 'Body Castle', and is beset by a rabble rout of evil desires, foul imaginations and silly conceits for seven years. In Spenser's *Faerie Queene* (II, ix-xi) Alma typifies the soul. She is mistress of the House of Temperance, and there entertains Prince Arthur and Sir Guyon.

**Almesbury.** It was in a Sanctuary at Almesbury that Queen GUINEVERE, according to Malory, took refuge after her adulterous passion for LANCELOT was revealed to King ARTHUR. Here she died; but her body was buried at GLASTONBURY.

**Alnaschar's Dream.** Counting your chickens before they are hatched. In the ARABIAN NIGHTS, Alnaschar, the Talkative Barber's fifth (and deaf) brother, spent all his money on a basket of glassware, on which he was to make a profit which was to be invested to make more, and so on until he grew rich enough to marry the vizier's daughter. Being angry with his imaginary wife he gave a kick, overturned his basket and broke all his wares.

**Alpheus and Arethusa** (alfē'əs, arithū'zə). Greek legend says that the river-god Alpheus fell in love with the nymph Arethusa, who fled from him in affright to Ortygia, an island near Syracuse, where ARTEMIS changed her into a fountain. Alpheus flowed under the sea from Peloponnesus to rise in Ortygia and so unite with his beloved. The myth seems to derive from the fact that the Alpheus, in places, does flow underground.

**Alruna-wife, An** (alroo'nə). The Alrunes were the LARES or PENATES of the ancient

Germans; and an Alruna-wife, the household goddess.

> She looked as fair as the sun, and talked like an Alruna-wife.
> KINGSLEY: *Hypatia* (1853), ch. xii.

**Al-Sirat** (Arab. the path). In Muslim mythology, the bridge leading to PARADISE; a bridge over a mid-HELL, no wider than the edge of a sword, across which all who enter HEAVEN must pass.

**Althaea's Brand** (althē'ə), a fatal contingency. Althaea's son MELEAGER was to live just so long as a log of wood, then on the fire, remained unconsumed, so she snatched it from the fire. Years later, to avenge her brothers (slain by Meleager) she threw the brand into the fire, and her son died as it was consumed (Ovid: *Metamorphoses*, viii).

> As did the fatal brand Althaea burned.
> SHAKESPEARE: *Henry VI, Part II*, 1, i.

**Altis.** The sacred precinct of ZEUS at OLYMPIA combining the altar of Zeus, the temples of Zeus and HERA, the Pelopion (grave of PELOPS), etc. It was connected by an arched passage with the STADIUM, where the games were held.

**Amadis of Gaul** (əmah'dis). The hero of the famous prose romance of the same title. The oldest extant edition (1508) is in Spanish by Montalvo but is probably an adaptation of a 14th-century Portuguese or Spanish original with his own additions. Many details are derived from ARTHURIAN legend, and subsequent writers increased the romance to fourteen books by adding other exploits. It long enjoyed popularity and exerted a wide influence on literature.

Amadis, called the 'Lion-Knight', from the device on his shield, and 'Beltenebros' (darkly beautiful), was a love-child of Perion, King of Gaula (Wales), and Elizena, Princess of Brittany. He was cast away at birth and became known as the Child of the Sun. After many adventures he secured the hand of Oriana. He is represented as a poet and musician, a linguist and a gallant, a knight-errant and a king, the very model of Chivalry.

Other names by which Amadis was called were the *Lovely Obscure*, the *Knight of the Green Sword*, the *Knight of the Dwarf*, etc.
**Amadis of Greece.** A supplemental part of the romance *Amadis of Gaul* supposedly added by the Spaniard Feliciano de Silva in 1530.

**Amaimon** (əmī'imon). A DEVIL, king of the eastern portion of HELL in mediaeval demonology. He might be bound or restrained from doing hurt from the third hour till noon, and from the ninth hour till evening. ASMODEUS is his chief officer. *See* LUCIFER.

> Amaimon sounds well; Lucifer well; Barbason well; yet they are devils' additions, the names of fiends.
> SHAKESPEARE: *Merry Wives of Windsor*, II, ii.

**Amalthea** (əmalthē'ə). In Greek mythology a NYMPH, the nurse of ZEUS; (alternatively the she-goat which suckled him). In Roman legend a SIBYL of Cumae who offered the SIBYLLINE BOOKS to Tarquin II.
**Amalthea's horn.** The cornucopia or HORN OF PLENTY. The infant ZEUS was fed with goat's milk by Amalthea, daughter of Melisseus, King of Crete. Zeus, in gratitude, broke off one of the goat's horns, and gave it to Amalthea, promising that the possessor should always have in abundance everything desired. *See* AEGIS.

> When Amalthea's horn
> O'er hill and dale the rose-crowned flora pours,
> And scatters corn and wine, and fruits and flowers.
> CAMOËNS: *Lusiad*, Bk. II.

**Amaranth** (am'əranth) (Gr. *amarantos*, everlasting). In Pliny the name of some real or imaginary fadeless flower. Clement of Alexandria says:

> Amarantus flos, symbolum est immortalitatis.

It is so called because its flowers retain to the last much of their deep blood-red colour. The best-known species are 'Love lies bleeding' (*Amarantus caudatus*), and 'Prince's feather' (*Amarantus hypochondriacus*). Wordsworth has a poem called *Love lies Bleeding*, and Milton refers to 'Immortal amarant' in *Paradise Lost* (III, 353). Spenser has 'sad Amaranthus' (*Faerie Queene*, III, vi, 45), one of the flowers 'to which sad lovers were transformed of yore', but there is no known legendary basis for this.

In 1653 Queen Christina of Sweden instituted an order of *Knights of the Amaranth* which lapsed on her death.

**Amasis, Ring of** (əmā'sis). Herodotus tells us (III, iv) that Polycrates, tyrant of Samos, was so fortunate in everything that Amasis, King of Egypt, fearing such unprecedented luck boded ill, advised him to part with something which he highly prized. Polycrates accordingly threw into the sea an extremely valuable RING, but a few days afterwards a fish was presented to him, in which the ring was found. Amasis now renounced friendship with Polycrates, as a man doomed by the gods; and not long afterwards the latter was crucified by his host, the satrap Oroetes.

**Amaurote** (amawrō'tā) (Gr. the shadowy or unknown place). The chief city of Sir Thomas More's *Utopia*. Rabelais introduces Utopia and 'the great city of the Amaurots' into his *Pantagruel* (Bk. II, ch. xxiii).

**Amazon** (am'əzon). A Greek word meaning *without breast*. In Greek mythology a race of female warriors living in Scythia, although some writers mention an older nation of Amazons in Africa. There were no men in the nation, but any sons born of their union with their neighbours were killed or sent to their fathers. The girls had their right breasts burnt off, that they might better draw the bow. The term is now applied to any strong brawny woman of masculine habits.

> She towered, fit person for a Queen
> To lead those ancient Amazonian files;
> Or ruling Bandit's wife among the Grecian isles.
> WORDSWORTH: *Beggars*.

**Amber.** A yellow, translucent, fossilized vegetable resin, the name of which originally belonged to ambergris. Legend says that amber is a concretion of the tears of birds who were the sisters of MELEAGER and who never ceased weeping for the death of their brother (Ovid: *Metamorphoses*, viii, 170).

**Ambrosia** (ambrō'ziə) (Gr. *a*, not, *brotos*, mortal). The food of the gods, so called because it made them immortal. Hence anything delicious to the taste. *See* NECTAR.

**Amen-Ra** (ah'men rah), or **Amon-Ra.** The King of the gods during the ancient Egyptian Empire, a development from *Amon* ('the hidden one'), patron of Thebes. Usually figured as human-headed, with two long ostrich plumes rising above his head, sometimes with a ram's head. The ram was sacred to him and his ORACLE was at the

oasis of Jupiter AMMON. The Greeks identified him with ZEUS.

**Amenthes** (amen'thēz). The HADES of the ancient Egyptians, the abode of the spirits of the dead where judgment was passed by OSIRIS.

**Amethea.** *See* FAMOUS HORSES *under* HORSE.

**Amis and Amiles.** *See* AMYS.

**Ammon,** or **Hammon.** The Greek form of the name of the Libyan and Egyptian god Amun or Amon. *See* AMEN-RA.
**Son of Ammon.** Alexander the Great was thus greeted by the priests of the Libyan temple of JUPITER Ammon.

> Ammon's great son one shoulder had too high.
> POPE: *Epistle to Dr. Arbuthnot*, 117.

**Amoret** (am'əret), in Spenser's *Faerie Queene* (Bk. III), is the type of female loveliness—young, handsome, gay, witty and good; soft as a rose, sweet as a violet, chaste as a lily, gentle as a dove, loving everybody and by all beloved.
Also a love-song, love-knot, love-affair, or love personified.

> He will be in his amorets, and his canzonets, his pastorals and his madrigals.
> THOMAS HEYWOOD: *Loves Maistresse* (1633).

**Amphion** (amfī'on). The son of ZEUS and Antiope who, according to Greek legend, built Thebes by the music of his lute, which was so melodious that the stones danced into walls and houses of their own accord.

**Amphisbaena** (amfisbē'nə), (Gr. *amphis*, both ways; *baino*, go). A fabulous venomous serpent with a head at each end and able to move in either direction. The name is applied to a genus of South American lizards.

**Amphitrite** (amfitrī'ti). In classical mythology, the goddess of the sea, wife of POSEIDON, daughter of NEREUS and Doris (Gr. *amphi-trio* for *tribo*, rubbing or wearing away [the shore] on all sides).

**Amphitryon** (amfit'rion). Son of Alcaeus and husband of ALCMENA.

> Le véritable Amphitryon
> Est l'Amphitryon où l'on dine.
> MOLIÈRE: *Amphitryon*.

That is, the person who provides the feast (whether master of the house or not) is the real host. The tale is that ZEUS

13

assumed the likeness of Amphitryon, in order to visit Alcmena, and gave a banquet; but Amphitryon came home and claimed the honour of being master of the house. As far as the servants and guests were concerned 'he who gave the feast was to them the host'.

**Amphrysian Prophetess** (amfriz'iən). The Cumaean SIBYL; so called from Amphrysus, a river of Thessaly, on the banks of which APOLLO fed the herds of Admetus.

**Amram's Son.** Moses (*Exod.* vi, 20). Milton's reference in *Paradise Lost*, I, 338–40:

> As when the potent rod
> Of Amram's son, in Egypt's evil day,
> Waved round the coast,

is to *Exod.* x, 13.

**Amrita** (amrē'tə). In Hindu mythology the ELIXIR of immortality, corresponding to the AMBROSIA of classical mythology. It is the Water of Life, sometimes described as the drink of the gods and demons produced when they churned the sea of milk, or it can be the sacred SOMA juice used in sacrifices.

**Amulet** (Lat. *amuletum*, a charm). Something worn, usually round the neck, as a preventive charm. The word was formerly connected with the Arabic *himalah*, the name given to the cord that secured the Koran to the person.

The early Christians used to wear amulets called *ichthus*. *See also* TALISMAN.

**Amun**, or **Amon.** *See* AMEN-RA.

**Amyris plays the Fool** (əmī'ris). An expression used of one who assumes a false character with an ulterior object like JUNIUS BRUTUS. Amyris was a Sybarite sent to DELPHI to consult the ORACLE, who informed him of the approaching destruction of his nation; he fled to Peloponnesus and his countrymen called him a fool; but like the madness of David, his 'folly' was true wisdom, for thereby he saved his life.

**Amys and Amylion** (am'is, amil'yən), or **Amis et Amiles.** A late 12th-century French romance telling the story of the friendship of two knights in the reign of CHARLEMAGNE. At the end of the story Amylion slays his children to cure his friend of leprosy.

**Anaclethra.** Another name for the AGELASTA.

**Anadyomene** (anədīom'ənē) (Gr. rising). In ancient Greece a name given to APHRODITE in allusion to her having risen from the sea as portrayed in the famous painting by Apelles.

**Anastasia, St.** (anəstā'ziə), a Roman matron said to have been beheaded with St. Basilissa for having buried the bodies of St. Peter and St. Paul.

**Anathema** (ənath'imə). A denunciation or curse. A Greek word meaning 'a thing set up or hung up', an offering to the gods. Thus Gordius (*see* GORDIAN KNOT) hung up his yoke and beam; the shipwrecked hung up their wet clothes; retired workmen hung up their tools, cripples their crutches, etc. Later it came to mean a thing devoted to evil since animals offered up were destined for death.

In the Catholic and Calvinistic churches it became a more extreme form of denunciation than Excommunication.

**Ancaeus** (ansē'əs). Helmsman of the ship ARGO, after the death of Tiphys. He was told by a hard-pressed slave that he would never live to taste the wine of his vineyards, and when wine, made from his own grapes, was set before him he sent for the slave to laugh at the latter's prognostications; but the slave made the answer 'there's many a slip 'twixt the CUP and the lip'. At this very instant a messenger informed Ancaeus that the Calydonian BOAR was devastating his vineyard, whereupon he set down his cup, went out against the boar, and was slain in the encounter.

**Anchises** (angkī'sēz). In Greek mythology, ruler of DARDANUS. APHRODITE became enamoured of his beauty and bore him AENEAS, the Trojan hero. According to one legend Anchises was blinded or killed by lightning for naming his son's mother. Virgil gives a different legend.

**Ancile** (an'sīl). The PALLADIUM of Rome; the sacred buckler said to have fallen from heaven in the reign of Numa. To prevent its being stolen, as the safety of the state depended on it, he caused eleven others, exactly similar, to be made, and entrusted them to twelve priests called SALII.

**Androcles and the Lion** (an'drōklēz). Androcles was a runaway slave who took refuge in a cavern. A lion entered and, instead of tearing him to pieces, lifted up his forepaw that Androcles might extract from it a thorn. The slave, being subsequently captured, was doomed to fight with a lion in the Roman arena. It so happened that the same lion was led out against him, and recognizing his benefactor, showed towards him every demonstration of love and gratitude.

The tale is told by Aulus Gellius (*c.* 130–180) and similar stories are found in AESOP'S FABLES and the *Gesta Romanorum.* Bernard Shaw's *Androcles and the Lion* (1916) is based on the story.

**Andromache** (androm'əki). In Greek legend she was the wife of HECTOR, on whose death she was given to Pyrrhus (Neoptolemus). The latter was killed by ORESTES and she became the wife of Helenus, Hector's brother. It is the title of a play by Euripides.

**Andromeda** (androm'idə). Daughter of CEPHEUS and CASSIOPEIA. Her mother boasted that her beauty surpassed that of the NEREIDS; so the Nereids induced NEPTUNE to send a sea-monster to the country, to which the oracle of Jupiter AMMON declared ANDROMEDA must be surrendered. She was accordingly chained to a rock but was delivered by PERSEUS, who married her and slew Phineus, her uncle, to whom she had been promised. After death she was placed among the stars.

**Angel.** In post-canonical and apocalyptic literature angels are grouped in varying orders. The commonly used hierarchy of nine orders is that popularized by the Pseudo-Areopagite or Pseudo-Dionysius (early 5th century) in his *De Hierarchia Celesti,* which arranges them in three triads:

(1) Seraphim, Cherubim, and Thrones in the first circle.
(2) Dominions, Virtues, and Powers in the second circle.
(3) Principalities, Archangels, and Angels in the third circle.

The names are taken from the *Old Testament* and *Eph.* i, 21 and *Col.* i, 16.

The seven holy angels are MICHAEL, GABRIEL, RAPHAEL, URIEL, Chamuel, Jophiel and ZADKIEL. Michael and Gabriel are mentioned in the Bible, Raphael in the Apocrypha and all appear in *Enoch* (viii, 2).

Milton in *Paradise Lost,* Bk. I, 392, gives a list of the fallen angels.

Muslims say that angels were created from pure bright gems; the genii from fire, and man from clay.

**Angelica** (anjel'ikə). This beautiful but fickle young woman was the heroine of Boiardo's *Orlando Innamorato* and Ariosto's *Orlando Furioso.* Orlando's unrequited love for her drove him mad. The name was used by Congreve for the principal character in *Love for Love* and by Farquhar in *The Constant Couple* and *Sir Harry Wildair.* Also the name of a plant (*Archangelica officinalis*) cultivated for its aromatic stalks which when candied are used in decorating cakes and confectionery. Called the **angelic herb** from a belief in its medicinal virtues, especially against plague and pestilence, it was also used as an ingredient of Absinthe, of gin and of 'bitters'.

**Angles. Non Angli, sed angeli** (Not Angles, but angels). The legend is that when Pope Gregory the Great (590–604) saw some fair-complexioned youths in the slave-market he asked whence they had come. He was told that they were Angles and also heathen. 'Not Angles, but angels' was his comment and on becoming Pope he sent St. Augustine to effect their conversion.

**Angurvadel.** FRITHIOF'S sword, inscribed with runic letters, which blazed in time of war, but gleamed with a dim light in time of peace. *See* SWORD.

**Animals. Animals in Heaven.** According to Muslim legend the following ten animals have been allowed to enter paradise: Jonah's whale; Solomon's ant; the ram caught by ABRAHAM and sacrificed instead of Isaac; the lapwing of BALKIS; the camel of the prophet Saleh; Balaam's ass; the ox of Moses; the dog KRATIM of the SEVEN SLEEPERS; AL BORAK, Mohammed's steed; and Noah's dove.

**Animals sacred to special deities:**

To Aesculapius, the serpent; to Apollo, the wolf, the griffon, and the crow; to Bacchus, the dragon and the panther; to Diana, the stag; to Hercules, the deer; to Isis, the heifer; to Juno, the peacock and the lamb; to Jupiter, the eagle;

15

to the Lares, the dog; to Mars, the horse and the vulture; to Mercury, the cock; to Minerva, the owl; to Neptune, the bull; to Tethys, the halcyon; to Venus, the dove, the swan, and the sparrow; to Vulcan, the lion, etc.

**Annwn** (an'oon), or **Annwyfn** (anoi'vən). In Welsh legend, the land of the departed, the Celtic HADES.

**Antaeus** (antē'əs), in Greek mythology, a gigantic wrestler, son of Earth and Sea (GAEA and POSEIDON), who became stronger whenever he touched the earth. HERCULES lifted him from the ground and slew him.

**Antediluvian.** Before the DELUGE. Colloquially used for anything hopelessly outdated.

**Anthony the Great, St.** (*c.* 250–356), the patron saint of herdsmen and hermit of Upper Egypt; also the father of Christian monasticism. The story of his temptations by the devil was a popular subject in literature and art. His day is 17 January.
**St Anthony's fire.** In mediaeval times a pestilential disease, so called from the belief that those who sought the intercession of St. Anthony recovered from this epidemic or sacred fire. It was commonly supposed to be erysipelas (Gr. red skin) but in fact the disease was ergotism, a poisoning due to eating rye bread with fungal infection. *Cp.* ST. VITUS'S DANCE *under* VITUS.

**Antigone** (antig'əni). The subject of a tragedy by Sophocles: she was the daughter of OEDIPUS by his mother, Jocasta. She slew herself to avoid being buried alive for disobeying an edict of Creon. She was famed for her devotion to her brother Polynices, hence the Duchess of Angoulême (1778–1851) was called *the Modern Antigone* for her attachment to her brother Louis XVII.

**Anu.** Chief God of the Akkadians and Babylonians, king of heaven and ruler of destiny and counterpart of the Sumerian god An. The centre of his cult was at Erech, mentioned in *Genesis* (x, 10) as part of Nimrod's kingdom.

**Anubis** (ənū'bis). An Egyptian god similar to HERMES of Greece with whom he was sometimes identified. His office was to take the souls of the dead before the judge of the infernal regions. The son of OSIRIS, the judge, he was represented with a human body and a jackal's head.

**Aonian** (āō'niən). Poetical, pertaining to the MUSES. The Muses, according to Greek mythology, dwelt in Aonia, that part of Boeotia which contains Mount HELICON and the MUSES' fountain. Milton speaks of 'the Aonian mount' (*Paradise Lost*, I, 15), and Thomson calls the fraternity of poets:

> The Aonian hive
> Who praised are, and starve right merrily,
> *Castle of Indolence*, ii, 2.

**Aphrodite** (afrōdī'ti) (Gr. *aphros*, foam). The Greek VENUS; so called because she sprang from the foam of the sea. In Homer she is the daughter of ZEUS and DIONE.
**Aphrodite's girdle.** The CESTUS.

**Apis** (ā'pis). In Egyptian mythology, Hap, the bull of Memphis, sacred to Ptah (later associated and identified with OSIRIS) of whose soul it was supposed to be the image. SERAPIS was the dead Apis. The sacred bull had to be black with special markings. Sometimes it was not suffered to live more than twenty-five years, when it was sacrificed and embalmed with great ceremony. Cambyses, King of Persia (529–521 B.C.), and conqueror of Egypt, slew the bull of Memphis, and is said to have been punished with madness.

**Apollo** (əpol'ō). In Greek mythology, son of ZEUS and Leto (LATONA), and sometimes identified with HELIOS the sun god. He was the brother of Artemis (*see* DIANA), half-brother of HERMES, and father of AESCULAPIUS. He was the god of music, poetry, archery, prophecy and the healing art. His plant was the LAUREL and he is represented as the perfection of youthful manhood.

> the fire rob'd god,
> Golden Apollo.
> SHAKESPEARE: *A Winter's Tale*, IV, iii.

*A perfect Apollo* is a model of manly beauty, referring to the Apollo Belvedere.

**Apollonius of Tyana** (apəlō'niəs). A Pythagorean philosopher (born shortly before the Christian era), accredited with exceptional powers of magic. It was he who discovered that the Phoenician woman whom Menippus Lycius intended to wed was in fact a serpent or LAMIA. This story was noted by Robert Burton in his *Anatomy of Melancholy*, and it forms the subject of Keats' *Lamia*.

**Apollyon** (əpol'yən). The Greek name of ABADDON, King of HELL. It is used by Bunyan in *The Pilgrim's Progress*.

**Aposiopesis.** *See* QUOS EGO.

**Appiades** (ap'iədēz). Five divinities whose temple stood near the Appian aqueduct in Rome. Their names are VENUS, PALLAS, Concord, Peace and VESTA. They were represented on horseback, like AMAZONS. Also a name for the courtesans of this locality.

**Apple.** The apple appears more than once in Greek legend; *see* APPLE OF DISCORD; ATALANTA'S RACE; HESPERIDES.

There is no mention of an apple in the Bible story of Eve's temptation. She took 'the fruit of the tree which is in the midst of the garden' (*Gen.* iii, 3).

The apple, the Silver Bough, is the fruit of the Celtic otherworld and has magical powers.

For the story of William Tell and the apple, *see* TELL.

**Apple, Prince Ahmed's,** a cure for every disorder. In THE ARABIAN NIGHTS story of Prince Ahmed, the Prince purchased his apple at Samarkand.

**Apple of Discord.** A cause of dispute; something to contend about. At the marriage of THETIS and Peleus, where all the gods and goddesses assembled, Discord (Eris), who had not been invited, threw on the table a golden apple 'for the most beautiful'. Hera (JUNO), Pallas Athene (MINERVA), and Aphrodite (VENUS) put in their claims and PARIS, as referee, gave judgment in favour of Aphrodite. This brought upon him the vengeance of Hera and PALLAS, to whose spite the fall of TROY was attributed.

**Apples, Isle of.** *See* AVALON.
**Apples of Iduna.** *See* IDUNA.
**Apples of perpetual youth.** *See* IDUNA.
**Apples of Pyban,** says Sir John Mandeville, fed the pygmies with their odour only.
**Apples of Sodom.** Possibly the *madar* or *oschur* (*Caloptris procera*). The fruit of trees reputed to grow on the shores of the Dead Sea 'which bear lovely fruit, but within are full of ashes'. Josephus, Strabo and Tacitus refer to them.

*Like an apple of Sodom*, signifies disappointment and disillusion. 'Dead Sea fruit' has a similar meaning.

> Like to the apples on the Dead Sea shore,
> All ashes to the taste.
> BYRON: *Childe Harold*, III, 34.

**April fool,** called in France *un poisson d'avril*, and in Scotland a *gowk* (cuckoo), a person befooled or tricked on *All Fools' Day* (1 April). In India similar tricks are played at the Holi Festival (31 March), so that it cannot refer to the uncertainty of the weather, nor yet to a mockery of the trial of Christ, the two most popular explanations. A better solution is this: as 25 March used to be New Year's Day, 1 April was its octave, when its festivities culminated and ended.

It may be a relic of the Roman CEREALIA, held at the beginning of April. The tale is that PROSERPINA was sporting in the Elysian meadows, and had just filled her lap with daffodils, when PLUTO carried her off to the lower world. Her mother, CERES, heard the echo of her screams, and went in search of the voice; but her search was a fool's errand, it was 'hunting the gowk', or looking for the 'echo of a scream'.

**Aqua Tofana** (ak'wə tofah'nə). A poisonous liquid containing arsenic, much used in Italy in the 18th century by young wives who wanted to get rid of their husbands. It was invented about 1690 by a Greek woman named Tofana, who called it the *Manna* of St. Nicholas of Bari, from a widespread notion that an oil of miraculous efficacy flowed from the tomb of that saint.

**Aquarius** (əkweə'riəs) (Lat. the water-bearer). The eleventh sign of the ZODIAC (21 January to 18 February). Its symbol is a man pouring water from a vessel, its sign ≈ representing a stream of water.

**Aquiline.** *See* FAMOUS HORSES *under* HORSE.

**Arabian. Arabian Bird, The.** The PHOENIX; hence, figuratively, a marvellous or unique person.

> All of her that is out of door most rich!
> If she be furnish'd with a mind so rare,
> She is alone the Arabian bird.
> SHAKESPEARE: *Cymbeline*, I, vi.

**Arabian Nights Entertainments, The,** or **The Thousand and One Nights.** These ancient Oriental tales were first introduced into western Europe in a French translation by Antoine Galland (12 vols., 1704–1717), derived from an Egyptian text probably of 14th- or 15th-century origin.

English translations based on Galland were made by R. Heron (1792) and W. Beloe (1795). The later English translations by Henry Torrens (1838), E.W. Lane (1839–1841), John Payne (1882–1884), and Sir Richard Burton's unexpurgated edition published at Benares (16 vols., 1885–1888) are based on a late 18th-century Egyptian text. The standard French translation by J. C. Mardrus (1899–1904) has been severely criticized.

The framework of the tales is that they were told by SCHEHERAZADE, bride of Sultan Schahriah, to stave off her execution.

**Arachne's Labours** (ərak′ni). Spinning and weaving. The story is that Arachne challenged ATHENE to a weaving contest and hanged herself when the goddess destroyed her web. Athene then changed her into a spider, hence Arachnida, the scientific name for spiders, scorpions and mites.

**Arawn** (ar′own). King of ANNWN.

**Arcadia** (ahkā′diə). A district of the Peloponnesus named after Arcas, son of JUPITER, chiefly inhabited by shepherds and the abode of PAN. According to Virgil it was the home of pastoral simplicity and happiness. The name was used by Sidney for the title of his romance (1590) and soon became a byword for rustic bliss.

**Arcades ambo** (ah′kədēz am′bō) (Lat.). From Virgil's seventh Eclogue: 'Ambo florentes aetatibus, Arcades ambo' (Both in the flower of youth, Arcadians both), meaning 'both poets or musicians', now extended to two persons having tastes or habits in common. Byron gave the phrase a whimsical turn:

> Each pulled different ways with many an oath,
> 'Arcades ambo'—id est, blackguards both.
> Don Juan, iv, 93.

**Arcadian beasts.** An old expression to be found in Plautus, Pliny, etc. See Persius, iii, 9:

> Arcadiae pecuaria rudere credas,

and Rabelais, V, vii. So called because the ancient Arcadians were renowned as simpletons. Juvenal (vii, 160) has arcadicus juvenis, meaning a stupid youth.

**Arcas.** See CALLISTO.

**Archangel.** In Christian story the title is usually given to MICHAEL, the chief opponent of SATAN and his angels, and to GABRIEL, RAPHAEL, URIEL, Chamuel, Jophiel and ZADKIEL. See ANGEL.

According to the Koran, there are four archangels; Gabriel, the angel of revelations, who writes down the divine decrees; Michael, the champion, who fights the battle of faith; AZRAEL, the angel of death; and ISRAFEL, who is commissioned to sound the trumpet of the resurrection.

**Archers.** The best archers in British legend are ROBIN HOOD, and his two companions LITTLE JOHN and Will Scarlet.

The famous archers of Henry II were Tepus, his bowman of the guards, Gilbert of the white hind, Hubert of Suffolk, and Clifton of Hampshire.

Nearly equal to these were Egbert of Kent and William of Southampton, and CLYM OF THE CLOUGH.

Domitian, the Roman emperor, we are told, could shoot four arrows between the spread of the fingers of a man's hand.

The story of TELL reproduces the Scandinavian tale of EGIL, who at the command of King Nidung performed a precisely similar feat.

**Archimago** (ahkimā′gō). The enchanter in Spenser's Faerie Queene (Bks. I and II), typifying hypocrisy.

**Arcite** (ahsī′ti, ah′sīt). A Theban knight made captive by Duke THESEUS, and imprisoned with Palamon at ATHENS. Both captives fell in love with Emily, the duke's sister (or daughter in some versions), and after gaining their liberty Emily was promised by the duke to the victor in a tournament. Arcite won but was thrown from his horse and killed when riding to receive his prize. Emily became the bride of Palamon. Chaucer, in his Knight's Tale, borrowed the story from Boccaccio's Teseide (1341), and it is told by Fletcher in his Two Noble Kinsmen (1634), and Dryden in his Fables (1699).

**Arcos Barbs.** War steeds of Arcos, in Andalusia, famous in Spanish ballads.

**Areopagus** (ariop′əgəs) (Gr. the hill of Mars or Ares). The seat of a famous tribunal in ATHENS; so called from the tradition that

MARS was tried there for causing the death of NEPTUNE'S son Halirrhothius.

**Ares** (eə'rēz). The Greek god of war, son of ZEUS and HERA and identified with the Roman MARS.

**Arethusa.** *See* ALPHEUS AND ARETHUSA.

**Argo** (Gr. *argos*, swift). The galley of JASON in which he sailed in search of the GOLDEN FLEECE and finally succeeded with the rhelp of MEDEA. Hence a sailing ship on any particularly adventurous voyage; also the name of a Southern constellation (the Ship).
**Argonauts.** The sailors of the ship Argo, who sailed from Iolcos to Colchis in quest of the GOLDEN FLEECE. Apollonius of Rhodes wrote an epic poem on the subject. The name is also given to a family of cephalopod molluscs (cuttlefish).

**Argus-eyed.** Jealously watchful. According to Grecian fable, Argus had 100 eyes, and JUNO set him to watch the priestess IO, of whom she was jealous. MERCURY, however, charmed him to sleep with his lyre, and slew him. Juno then set the eyes of Argus on the peacock's tail.

> So praysen babes the Peacocks spotted traine,
> And wondren at bright Argus blazing eye.
> SPENSER: *The Shepheards Calendar*, October.

**Argyle. God bless the Duke of Argyle,** a phrase supposed to have been used by Scottish Highlanders when they scratched themselves. The story is that a Duke of Argyle (now Argyll) had posts erected on a treeless part of his estates so that his cattle might rub against them to ease themselves of the 'torment of flies'. The herdsmen saw the value of the practice, and as they rubbed their itching backs against the posts they thankfully uttered the above words.

**Ariadne** (ariad'ni). In Greek mythology, daughter of the Cretan King, MINOS. She helped THESEUS to escape from the LABYRINTH, and later went with him to Naxos where he deserted her. Here DIONYSUS found her and married her.

**Ariel** (eə'riəl). A Hebrew name signifying 'lion of God'. In *Isaiah* xxix, 1–7, it is applied to Jerusalem; in astronomy a satellite of URANUS; in demonology and literature, the name of a spirit. Thus Ariel is one of the seven angelic 'princes' in Heywood's *Hierarchie of the Blessed Angels*

(1635); one of the rebel angels in Milton's *Paradise Lost*, VI, 371 (1667); a SYLPH, the guardian of Belinda, in Pope's *Rape of the Lock* (1712); but best known as 'an ayrie spirit' in Shakespeare's *Tempest*. According to the play Ariel was enslaved to the witch Sycorax (I, ii) who overtasked him, and in punishment for not doing what was beyond his power, shut him up in a pine-rift for twelve years. On the death of Sycorax, Ariel became the slave of Caliban, who tortured him most cruelly. Prospero liberated him and was gratefully served by the fairy until he set Ariel free.

**Aries** (eə'riēz). The RAM. The first sign of the ZODIAC in which the sun is from 21 March to 20 April. The legend is that the ram with the GOLDEN FLEECE, which bore Phrixus and Helle on its back, was finally sacrificed to ZEUS, who set it in the heavens as a constellation.

**Arimaspians** (arimas'piənz). A one-eyed people of Scythia constantly at war with the GRIFFINS who guarded a hoard of gold. They are mentioned by Lucan (*Pharsalia*, iii, 280), Hcrodotus (iii, 116; iv, 13, 27), Pliny, Strabo etc. Rabelais (IV, lvi, and V, xxix) so names the peoples of northern Europe who had accepted the Reformation, the suggestion being that they had lost one eye—that of faith.

> As when a gryphon, through the wilderness
> With winged course, o'er hill or moory dale
> Pursues the Arimaspian, who by stealth
> Had from his wakeful custody purloin'd
> The guarded gold.
> MILTON: *Paradise Lost*, II, 943–7.

**Arioch** (ar'iok). The name means 'a fierce lion' and was used for one of the fallen angels in *Paradise Lost* (VI, 371); Milton took it from *Dan.* ii, 14, where it is the name of the captain of the guard.

**Arion** (ərī'on). A Greek poet and musician (7th century B.C.) reputed to have been cast into the sea by mariners but carried to Taenaros on a dolphin's back. *See* FAMOUS HORSES *under* HORSE.

**Armida** (ahmē'də). In Tasso's *Jerusalem Delivered*, a beautiful sorceress, with whom RINALDO fell in love and wasted his time in voluptuous pleasure. After his escape from her, Armida followed him, but being unable to lure him back, set fire to her palace, rushed into a combat, and was slain.

In 1806 Frederick William III of Prussia declared war on Napoleon, and his young queen rode about in military costume to arouse popular enthusiasm. When Napoleon was told of it, he said, 'She is Armida, in her distraction setting fire to her own palace.'

**Arondight** (ah'rondīt). The sword of Sir LANCELOT OF THE LAKE.

**Artegal,** or **Arthegal, Sir** (ah'tigəl). The hero of Bk. V of Spenser's *Faerie Queene*, lover of BRITOMART, to whom he was made known by means of a magic mirror. He is emblematic of Justice, and in many of his deeds, such as the rescue of Irena (Ireland) from Grantorto, is mirrored on Arthur, 14th Lord Grey de Wilton, who became lord deputy of Ireland in 1580 with Spenser as his secretary. *See* ELIDURE.

**Artemis.** *See* DIANA.

**Arthegal.** *See* ARTEGAL.

**Arthur.** As a shadowy 'historical' figure he is first mentioned under the Latin name Artorius in the late 7th-century *Historia Britonum* (usually known by the name of Nennius, its 9th-century editor). Arthur, as *Dux Bellorum*, not king, is said to have led the Britons against the Saxons in twelve great battles culminating in the great victory of *Mons Badonicus* (fought between 493 and 516). He is mentioned again by William of Malmesbury (early 12th century), but ARTHURIAN ROMANCES owe most to Geoffrey of Monmouth. *See* CAMELOT.

**Arthur's Seat.** A hill overlooking Edinburgh from the East. The name is a corruption of the Gaelic *Ard-na-said*, the height of the arrows, a convenient shooting ground.

**Arthurian Romances.** The stories which have King Arthur as their central figure appear as early as 1136 in Geoffrey of Monmouth's mainly fabulous *Historia Regum Britanniae*, which purported to be a translation (in Latin) of an ancient Celtic history of Britain, lent to him by Walter Map, Archdeacon of Oxford. Geoffrey's *Historia* was dedicated to Robert, Earl of Gloucester, a natural son of Henry I. This was versified in French in Wace's *Roman de Brut* or *Brut d'Angleterre* (1155), which is the first to mention the ROUND TABLE. These were used by Layamon, the Worcestershire priest, whose BRUT (in English) was completed in about 1205, with additions such as the story of the fairies at Arthur's birth, who transported him to AVALON at his death. In France, in the late 12th century, Robert de Borron introduced the legend of the GRAIL and gave prominence to MERLIN; Chréstien de Troyes brought in the tale of ENID and GERAINT, the tragic loves of LANCELOT and GUINEVERE, the story of PERCIVAL and other material which was probably drawn from Welsh sources including the MABINOGION. Thus Walter Map and the Arthurian writers introduced the romantic spirit of Chivalry and courtly manners into European literature and King Arthur became the embodiment of the ideal Christian Knight. Many other Welsh and Breton ballads, lays and romances popularized the legend and the whole corpus was collected and edited by Sir Thomas Malory (d. 1471), whose great prose romance *Le Morte d'Arthur* was produced by Caxton in 1485. Tennyson's *Morte d'Arthur* and *Idylls of the King* (1857–1885) were based upon it. *See* ALMESBURY, ARONDIGHT, ASTOLAT, BALIN, BAN, BEDIVERE, CAMELOT, CAMLAN, DAGONET, DIAMOND JOUSTS, ELAINE, EXCALIBUR, GLASTONBURY, LAUNFAL, LYONESSE, MODRED, MORGAN LE FAY, TRISTRAM, YSOLDE, etc.

**Arundel.** *See* HORSE.

**Arval Brothers** (*Fratres Arvales*). An ancient Roman college of Priests, revived by Augustus. It consisted of twelve priests (including the Emperor), whose sole duty was to preside at the festival of *Dea Dia* in May. Ceremonies took place in Rome and in the grove of the goddess, who seems to be identical with *Acca Larentia*, goddess of cornfields.

**Ascalaphus** (askal'əfəs). In Greek mythology, a son of ACHERON who said that PROSERPINA had partaken of a pomegranate when PLUTO had given her permission to return to the upper world if she had eaten nothing. In revenge Proserpina turned him into an owl by sprinkling him with the water of PHLEGETHON.

**Ascendant.** In casting a HOROSCOPE the point of the Ecliptic or degree of the ZODIAC which is nearest the eastern horizon at the time of birth is called the ascendant, and the easternmost star represents the house of life (*see* HOUSES, ASTROLOGICAL; STAR), because it is in the act of ascending. This is a person's strongest star, and when his outlook is bright, we say *his star is in the ascendant.*

**The house of the Ascendant,** includes five degrees of the ZODIAC above the point just rising, and twenty-five below it. Usually, the point of birth is referred to.

**The lord of the ascendant,** is any planet within the 'house of the Ascendant'. The house and lord of the ascendant at birth were said by astrologers to exercise great influence on the future life of the child. Deborah referred to the influence of the stars when she said 'the stars in their courses fought against Sisera' (*Judges* v. 20).

**Asgard** (as'gahd) (*As*, a god; *gard*, or *gardh*, an enclosure, garth or yard). The realm of the AESIR or the Northern gods, the OLYMPUS of Scandinavian mythology. It is said to be situated in the centre of the universe, and accessible only by the rainbow bridge, BIFROST. It contains many regions, and mansions such as Gladshcim and VALHALLA.

**Ash Tree,** or **Tree of the Universe.** *See* YGGDRASIL.

**Ashtaroth,** or **Ashtoreth.** The goddess of fertility and reproduction among the Canaanites and Phoenicians, called by the Babylonians ISHTAR (VENUS) and by the Greeks ASTARTE. She is referred to in I *Sam.* xxi, 10; I *Kings* xi, 5 and II *Kings* xxiii, 13; and she may be the 'queen of heaven' mentioned by *Jeremiah* (vii, 18; xliv, 17, 25). Formerly she was supposed to be a moon-goddess, hence Milton's reference in his *Hymn on the Nativity.*

And moonèd Ashtaroth,
Heav'ns Queen and Mother both.

**Ashur.** *See* ASSHUR.

**Asir.** *See* AESIR.

**Askance at, To look.** To regard obliquely, with suspicion or disapproval. Of uncertain origin, but the expression of ill will sometimes used by gypsies 'May the Lord look upon you sideways' probably stems from the same root idea.

**Asmodeus** (asmŏdē'əs, asmŏ'diəs). The evil demon who appears in the Apocryphal book of *Tobit* and is derived from the Persian *Aeshma.* In *Tobit* Asmodeus falls in love with Sara, daughter of Raguel, and causes the death of seven husbands in succession, each on his bridal night. He was finally driven into Egypt through a charm made by Tobias of the heart and liver of a fish burnt on perfumed ashes, as described by Milton in *Paradise Lost* (IV, 167–71). Hence Asmodeus often figures as the spirit of matrimonial jealousy or unhappiness. Le Sage gave the name to the companion of Don Cleofas in his *Le Diable Boiteux* (1707).

**Asmodeus flight.** Don Cleofas, catching hold of his companion's cloak, is perched on the steeple of St. Salvador. Here the foul fiend stretches out his hand, and the roofs of all the houses open in a moment, to show the Don what is going on privately in each respective dwelling.

Could the reader take an Asmodeus-flight, and, waving open all roofs and privacies, look down from the roof of Notre Dame, what a Paris were it!
CARLYLE: *French Revolution* II, vi.

**Asphodel** (as'fŏdel). A plant genus of the lily family, particularly associated with death and the underworld in Greek legend. It was planted on graves, and the departed lived their phantom life in the *Plain of Asphodel.* The name DAFFODIL is a corruption of asphodel.

**Ass. Ass-eared.** MIDAS had the ears of an ass. The tale says APOLLO and PAN had a contest, and chose Midas to decide which was the better musician. Midas gave sentence in favour of Pan; and Apollo, in disgust, changed his ears into those of an ass.

Avarice is as deaf to the voice of virtue, as the ass to the voice of Apollo.
ARIOSTO: *Orlando Furioso*, xvii.

**Wrangle for an ass's shadow.** To contend about trifles. The tale told by Demosthenes is that a man hired an ass to take him to Megara; and at noon, the sun being very hot, the traveller dismounted, and set himself down in the shadow of the ass. Just then the owner came up and claimed the right of sitting in this shady spot, saying that he let out the ass for hire, but there was no bargain made about the ass's shade. The two men then fell to blows to settle the point in dispute. While they were wrangling the ass took to its heels and ran away, leaving them both in the glare of the sun.

**Feast of Asses.** *See under* FOOL.

**Asshur** (ash'uə) Originally the local god of Asshur, the capital of Assyria, he became the chief god of the kingdom, taking the place of Marduk. His symbol was the winged sun disc enclosing a male figure wearing a horned cap, often with a bow in his hand, but he could also be represented mounted on a bull. His name was frequently linked with Ninlil, goddess of fertility and with ISHTAR of Nineveh. *See* ASHTAROTH.

**Astarte** (əstah'ti). The Greek and Roman name for the supreme goddess of the Phoenicians, ASHTAROTH. She was also a moon goddess and was depicted with the horns of the new moon or a crescent.

Byron gave the name to the lady beloved by Manfred in his drama, *Manfred*. It has been suggested that Astarte was drawn from the poet's half-sister, Augusta (Mrs. Leigh).

**Astolat** (as'tōlat). This town, mentioned in the ARTHURIAN ROMANCES, is generally identified with Guildford, in Surrey.

**The Lily Maid of Astolat.** ELAINE.

**Astoreth.** *See* ASHTAROTH.

**Astraea** (astrē'ə). Justice, innocence. During the Golden Age this goddess dwelt on earth, but when sin began to prevail, she reluctantly left it, and was metamorphosed into the constellation VIRGO.

**Astral Body.** In theosophical parlance, the phantasmal or spiritual appearance of the physical human form, that is existent both before and after the death of the material body, though during life it is not usually separated from it; also the 'Kamarupa' or body of desires, which retains a finite life in the astral world after bodily death.

**Astral spirits.** The spirits animating the stars. According to occultists, each star had its special spirit; and Paracelsus maintained that every man had his attendant star, which received him at death, and took charge of him until the great resurrection.

**Astrology.** The pseudo-science of the ancient and mediaeval world, concerned with DIVINATION etc., based on the stars and heavenly bodies. *Natural Astrology* dealt with the movements and phenomena of the heavenly bodies, time, tides, eclipses, the fixing of Easter, etc., and was the forerunner of the science of astronomy (*cp.* ALCHEMY); *Judicial Astrology* dealt with what is now known as astrology, the influence of the stars upon human affairs. *See* ASCENDANT; HOROSCOPE; HOUSES, ASTROLOGICAL; STAR.

**Asur** (as'ə). *See* ASSHUR.

**Asynja** (əsin'yə). The goddesses of ASGARD; the feminine counterparts of the AESIR.

**Atalanta's Race** (atəlan'tə). In Greek myth the daughter of Iasus or of Schoenus. She took part in the hunt of the Calydonian BOAR and, being very swift of foot, refused to marry unless the suitor should first defeat her in a race. Milanion (or HIPPOMENES) overcame her by dropping at intervals during the race three golden apples, the gift of VENUS. Atalanta stopped to pick them up, lost the race and became his wife.

**Atargatis** (atahgat'is). The 'Syrian Goddess', the 'fish goddess'. A fertility goddess represented at Ascalon as half woman, half fish.

**Ate** (ā'tē). In Greek mythology, the goddess of vengeance and mischief; she was cast down to earth by ZEUS.

> With Ate by his side come hot from hell...
> Cry 'Havoc' and let slip the dogs of war.
> SHAKESPEARE: *Julius Caesar*, III, i.

In Spenser's *Faerie Queene* (IV, i, iv, ix, etc.), the name is given to a lying and slanderous hag, the companion of Duessa.

**Athene,** or **Pallas Athene** (əthē'nē). The patron goddess of ATHENS and patroness of arts and crafts; the goddess of wisdom and subsequently identified with MINERVA by the Romans.

**Athens.** When ATHENE and POSEIDON disputed for the honour of being the city's patron, the goddess of wisdom produced an olive branch, the symbol of peace and prosperity, and the sea-god created a horse, symbolic of war. The gods deemed the olive the better boon, and the city was called Athens.

**Athens of Ireland.** Belfast.

**Athens of the New World.** Boston.

**Athens of the West.** Cordoba, in Spain, was so called in the Middle Ages.

**The Modern Athens.** Edinburgh.

**Athenian Bee.** Plato (*c.* 429–347 B.C.), a native of ATHENS, was so called from the tradition that a swarm of bees alighted on his mouth when he was in his cradle, consequently his words flowed with the sweetness of honey. The same tale is told of St. Ambrose, and others. *See* BEE. Xenophon (*c.* 430–*c.* 354 B.C.) was also called 'the Athenian Bee' or 'Bee of Athens'.

**Atlantean Shoulders** (atlantē'ən). Shoulders able to bear a great weight, like those of ATLAS.

> Sage he stood,
> With Atlantean shoulders fit to bear
> The weight of mightiest monarchies.
> MILTON: *Paradise Lost*, II, 305–7.

**Atlantis.** According to ancient myth, an extensive island in the Atlantic Ocean, mentioned by Plato in the *Timaeus* and *Critias*. It was said to have been a powerful kingdom before it was overwhelmed by the sea. The story was brought from Egypt by Solon. In the 16th century it was suggested that America was Atlantis and there have been a number of other implausible identifications. More recently, and more likely, the work of archaeologists and scientists has placed it in the Eastern Mediterranean. The centre of the former island of Stronghyle (Santorini) collapsed after catastrophic volcanic action and was submerged (*c.* 1500 B.C.). The civilization of the island was Minoan and the Minoan Empire suffered overwhelming disaster at this time. The general conclusion equates Atlantis with Stronghyle-Santorini and Minoan Crete. *Cp.* LEMURIA; LYONESSE.

**The New Atlantis.** An allegorical romance by Francis Bacon (written in 1624) in which he describes an imaginary island where was established a philosophical commonwealth bent on the cultivation of the natural sciences. *See* UTOPIA.

**Atlas.** In Greek mythology, one of the TITANS, condemned by ZEUS for his part in the war of the Titans to uphold the heavens on his shoulders. His abode became the Atlas mountains in Africa, which accorded with the legend that they supported the heavens.

**Atli.** *See* ETZEL.

**Atropos** (at'rōpos). In Greek mythology the eldest of the Three FATES, and the one who severs the thread of life.

**Attic. The Attic Boy.** Cephalos, beloved by AURORA or Morn; passionately fond of hunting.

> Till civil-suited Morn appeer,
> Not trickt and frounc't as she was wont,
> With the Attick Boy to hunt,
> But chercheft in a comly Cloud.
> MILTON: *Il Penseroso*.

**Attila.** *See* ETZEL.

**Attis** (at'is), or **Atys.** A youth beloved by AGDISTIS (Cybele). Driven mad by her jealousy he castrated himself with a sharp stone. According to Ovid's *Metamorphoses* Cybele changed him into a pine tree as he was about to commit suicide.

**Aubry's Dog.** *See* DOG.

**Auburn.** The hamlet described by Goldsmith in *The Deserted Village*, said to be Lissoy, County Westmeath, Ireland.

**Audley. We will John Audley it.** A theatrical phrase meaning to abridge, or bring to a conclusion, a play in progress. It is said that an 18th-century travelling showman named Shuter used to lengthen out his performance until sufficient newcomers were waiting for the next house. An assistant would then call out, 'Is John Audley here?' and the play was ended as soon as possible.

**Augean Stables** (awjē'ən). The stables of Augeas, the mythological King of Elis, in Greece, which housed his great herd of oxen. They were never cleaned and it was one of the labours of HERCULES to cleanse them, which he did by diverting the course of a river through them. Hence *to cleanse the Augean stables* means to clear away an accumulated mass of rubbish or corruption, physical, moral, religious or legal.

**Augury** (aw'gūri) (etymology uncertain), means properly the function of an augur, a Roman religious official. The duty of members of the college of Augurs was to pronounce, by the observation of signs called AUSPICES, whether the gods favoured or disfavoured a proposed course of action, and they were consulted before any important public action. *See* DIVINATION; OMENS; SINISTER.

23

**Auld Hornie.** After the establishment of Christianity, the heathen deities were degraded by the Church into fallen angels; and PAN, with his horns, crooked nose, goat's beard, pointed ears, and goat's feet, was transformed to his Satanic majesty, and called Old Hornie.

O thou, whatever title suit thee,
Auld Hornie, Satan, Nick, or Clootie.
BURNS.

**Aulis** (aw'lis). The port in BOEOTIA where the Greek fleet assembled before sailing against TROY. Becalmed by the intervention of ARTEMIS, because AGAMEMNON had killed a stag sacred to her, she was propitiated by the sacrifice of his daughter IPHIGENIA. This is the subject of Gluck's opera *Iphigénie en Aulide* (1774), based upon Racine's *Iphigénie* (1675).

**Aurora** (awraw'rə). Early morning. According to Greek mythology, the dawn-goddess Eos (Lat. *Aurora*) called by Homer 'rosy-fingered', sets out before the sun to proclaim the coming of day.
**Aurora's tears.** The morning dew.

**Ausonia** (awsō'niə). An ancient name of Italy; so called from Auson, son of ULYSSES, and father of the Ausones.

**Auspices** (aw'spisēz) (Lat. *avis*, a bird; *specere*, to observe). In ancient Rome the name for the interpreters of signs from birds, animals, and other phenomena, who were later called augurs.
AUGURY depended on the observation and interpretation of signs which were known as auspices. Only the chief in command was allowed to take the auspices of war, thus if a subordinate gained a victory he won it 'under the good auspices' of his superior. *Cp.* DIVINATION.

**Autolycus** (awtol'ikəs). In Greek mythology, son of MERCURY, and the craftiest of thieves. He stole his neighbours' flocks and altered their marks; but SISYPHUS outwitted him by marking his sheep under their feet. Delighted with this device, Autolycus became friends with Sisyphus. Shakespeare uses his name for a rascally pedlar in *The Winter's Tale* (IV, ii).

My father named me Autolycus; who being, as I am, littered under Mercury, was likewise a snapper-up of unconsidered trifles.

**Automedon** (awtom'idon). A coachman. He was the charioteer of ACHILLES.

**Avalon** (av'əlon). Called *Avilion* in Tennyson's *Morte d'Arthur*, a Celtic word meaning the 'island of apples', and in Celtic mythology the *Island of Blessed Souls*. In the ARTHURIAN ROMANCES it is the abode and burial place of ARTHUR, who was carried thither by MORGAN LE FAY. Its identification with GLASTONBURY is due to etymological error. OGIER THE DANE and OBERON also held their courts at Avalon.

**Avatar** (Sans. *avatara*, descent; hence incarnation of a god). In Hindu mythology the advent to earth of a deity in a visible form. The ten avatars of VISHNU are the most celebrated. He appeared as (1) the fish (Matsya); (2) the tortoise (Kurma); (3) the boar (Varaha); (4) half-man, half-lion (Nrisinha); (5) the dwarf (Vamana); (6) RAMA with the Axe (Parasurama); (7) again as Rama (Ramachandra); (8) KRISHNA; (9) Buddha; the tenth advent is to occur at the end of the four ages and will be in the form of a white horse with wings (Kalki), to destroy the earth and bring in a new age.
The word is used metaphorically to denote a manifestation or embodiment of some idea or phrase:

I would take the last years of Queen Anne's reign as the zenith, or palmy state of Whiggism, in its divinest avatar of common sense.
COLERIDGE: *Table-talk.*

**Avernus** (əvœ'nəs) (Gr. *a-ornis*, without a bird). A lake in Campania, so called from the belief that its sulphurous and mephitic vapours caused any bird that attempted to fly over it to fall into its waters. Latin mythology made it the entrance to Hell; hence Virgil's lines:

Facilis descensus Averno;
Noctes atque dies patet atri janua Ditis;
Sed revocare gradum, superas que evadere ad auras,
Hoc opus, hic labor est.
*Aeneid,* vi, 126.

Rendered in Dryden's *Virgil* as:

Smooth the descent and easy is the way
(The Gates of Hell stand open night and day);
But to return and view the cheerful skies,
In this the task and mighty labour lies.

**Awar.** One of the sons of EBLIS.

**Axinomancy** (aks'inōmansi). DIVINATION by the axe, practised by the ancient Greeks with a view to discovering crime. An agate or piece of jet was placed on a red-hot axe which indicated the guilty person by its motion.

**Ayesha,** or **A'isha** (īyesh'ə). Favourite wife of Mohammed, daughter of Abou Bekr. He married her when she was only a child, soon after the Hegira, and ultimately died in her arms. Sir Henry Rider Haggard (1856–1925) wrote a novel called *Ayesha.*

**Aymon, The Four Sons of** (ā'mon). The *geste* of *Doon de Mayence* (13th century) describes the struggle of certain feudal Vassals against CHARLEMAGNE, including Doon of Mayence and Aymon of Dordone. The exploits of the four sons of Aymon— Renauld or RINALDO, Alard, Guichard, and Richard with their famous horse BAYARD is a central feature. They appear in many other poems and romances including Boiardo's *Orlando Innamorato,* Pulci's MORGANTE MAGGIORE, Ariosto's *Orlando Furioso,* Tasso's *Rinaldo* and *Jerusalem Delivered,* etc.

**Azazel** (əzaz'el). In *Lev.* xvi, 7–8, we read that Aaron, as an atonement, 'shall cast lots' on two goats 'one lot for the Lord, and the other lot for the scapegoat' (Azazel). Milton uses the name for the standard-bearer of the rebel angels (*Paradise Lost,* I, 534). In Muslim demonology Azazel is the counterpart of the DEVIL, cast out of HEAVEN for refusing to worship ADAM. His name was changed to EBLIS (Iblis), which means 'despair'.

**Azaziel** (əzāz'iel). In Byron's *Heaven and Earth,* a seraph who fell in love with Anah, a granddaughter of Cain. When the flood came he carried her under his wing to another planet.

**Azoth** (az'oth) (Arab.). The alchemists' name for mercury; also the PANACEA or universal remedy of Paracelsus. In Browning's *Paracelsus* (Bk. V), it is the name of Paracelsus' sword:

> Last my good sword; ah, trusty Azoth, leapest
> Beneath thy master's grasp for the last time?

**Azrael** (az'rāl). The Muslim ANGEL of death. He will be the last to die, but will do so at the second trump of the ARCHANGEL. *See* ADAM.

> The bitter cold stole into the cottages, marking the old and feeble with the touch of Azrael.
> MRS. HUMPHRY WARD: *Marcella,* II, i.

**The Wings of Azrael.** The approach of death; the signs of death coming on the dying.

**Azrafil.** *See* ISRAFEL; ADAM.

# B

**Ba.** The SOUL, which according to more primitive Egyptian belief roamed the burial places at night. Later belief held that it travelled to the realm of OSIRIS, after a harrowing journey, where its happiness was assured. It was depicted as a bird or as a human-headed bird.

**Baalbek.** *See* CHILMINAR.

**Baalzebub.** *See* BEELZEBUB.

**Baba Yaga.** A cannibalistic ogress of Russian folk-lore who stole young children and cooked them. She lived in the remote forest, sailed through the air in an iron cauldron raising tempests on her way, and swept with a broom all traces of her passing. She bears a strong resemblance to BERCHTA of S. German folk-lore.

**Babe. Babe the Blue Ox.** A legendary and indeed remarkable beast that belonged to Paul BUNYAN.
**Babes, Protecting deities of.** According to Varro (116–27 B.C.), Roman infants were looked after by Vagitanus, the god who caused them to utter their first *cry*; FABULINUS, who presided over their *speech*; CUBA, the goddess who protected them in their cots; and Domiduca, who brought young children safe *home*, and guarded them when out of their parents' sight. In the Christian Church St. NICHOLAS is the patron SAINT of children.
**Babes in the Wood.** *See* CHILDREN.

**Bacbuc** (bak'bŭk). A Chaldean or Assyrian word for an earthenware pitcher, cruse, or bottle, taken by Rabelais as the ORACLE of the Holy Bottle (and of its priestess). PANURGE consulted the Holy Bottle on the question whether or not he ought to marry and it answered with a click, like the noise made by glass snapping. Bacbuc told Panurge the noise meant *trinc* (drink), and that was the response, the most direct and positive ever given by the oracle. Panurge

might interpret it as he liked, the obscurity would always save the oracle.

**Bacchus** (bak'əs). In Roman mythology, the god of wine, the Dionysus of the Greeks, son of ZEUS and SEMELE. The name 'Bacchus' is a corruption of the Gr. *Iacchus* (from *Iache*, a shout) and was originally merely an epithet of Dionysus as the noisy and rowdy god. First represented as a bearded man, he later appears as a beautiful youth with black eyes and flowing locks, crowned with vine and ivy and carrying the THYRSUS. In peace his robe was purple, in war a panther's skin. According to some accounts he married ARIADNE after her desertion by THESEUS.

Bacchus, in the LUSIAD, is the evil demon or antagonist of JUPITER, the lord of destiny. As MARS is the guardian power of Christianity, Bacchus is the guardian power of Islam.
**Bacchus sprang from the thigh of Zeus.** The tale is that SEMELE, at the suggestion of JUNO, asked JUPITER to appear before her in all his glory, but the foolish request proved her death. Jupiter saved the child, which was prematurely born, by sewing it up in his thigh till it came to maturity.
**What has that to do with Bacchus?** *i.e.* What has that to do with the matter in hand? When Thespis introduced recitations in the vintage songs, the innovation was suffered to pass, so long as the subject of recitation bore on the exploits of BACCHUS; but when, for variety's sake, he wandered to other subjects, the Greeks pulled him up with the exclamation, 'What has that to do with Bacchus?'
**Bacchus a noyé plus d'hommes que Neptune** (Fr.). The ale-house has overwhelmed more men than the ocean.
**A priest,** or **son of Bacchus.** A toper.
**Bacchanals** (bak'ənəlz), **Bacchants, Bacchantes.** Priests and priestesses, or male and female votaries of BACCHUS; hence

26

drunken roysterers. *See also* BAG O' NAILS *under* PUBLIC HOUSE SIGNS.

**Badoura** (badoo'rə). 'The most beautiful woman ever seen upon earth', heroine of the story of Camaralzaman and Badoura in the ARABIAN NIGHTS.

**Baker, The.** Louis XVI was so called and his Queen 'the baker's wife', and the Dauphin the 'shop boy'; because they gave bread to the starving men and women who came to Versailles on 6 October 1789.

> The return of the baker, his wife, and the shop-boy to Paris had not the expected effect. Flour and bread were still scarce.
> A. DUMAS: *The Countess de Charny*, ch. ix.

**Bakha.** The sacred bull of Hermonthis in Egypt, an incarnation of Menthu, a personi-fication of the heat of the sun. He changed colour every hour of the day.

**Balan** (bā'lən). A strong and courageous giant in many old romances. In FIERABRAS the 'Sowdan of Babylon', father of Fiera-bras, ultimately conquered by CHARLEMAGNE. In the Arthurian cycle, brother of BALIN.

**Balance, The.** LIBRA, an ancient zodiacal constellation between VIRGO and SCORPIO representing a pair of scales, the 7th sign of the ZODIAC, which the sun enters a few days before the autumnal equinox.

According to Persian mythology, at the Last Day there will be a huge balance as big as the vault of HEAVEN. The two scale pans will be called that of light and that of dark-ness. In the former all good will be placed, in the latter all evil; and everyone will be rewarded according to the verdict of the balance.

The Scales of Justice represent balance and equality. In Christianity they are an emblem of the Archangel Michael. In Egyptian mythology Osiris weighs the soul of the departed in the balance against the feather of truth in Amenti. *See* SCALES.

**Balder** (bawl'də). A Scandinavian god of light, son of ODIN and FRIGG who dwelt at Breidhablik, one of the mansions of ASGARD. One legend says that Frigg bound all things by oath not to harm him, but accidentally omitted MISTLETOE, with a twig of which he was slain. Another tells that he was slain by his rival Hoder while fighting for the beauti-ful Nanna. His death was the final prelude to the overthrow of the gods.

**Baldwin.** (1) In the CHARLEMAGNE romances, nephew of ROLAND and the youngest and comeliest of Charlemagne's PALADINS.

(2) First King of Jerusalem (1100–1118), brother of Godfrey of Bouillon, the previous ruler, who declined the title of king. He figures in Tasso's *Jerusalem Delivered* as the restless and ambitious Duke of Bologna, leader of 1,200 horse in the allied Christian army.

**Bale. When bale is highest, boot is nigh-est.** An old Icelandic proverb appearing in Heywood and other English writers. It means, when things have come to the worst they must needs mend. *Bale* means 'evil', *boot* is the M.E. *bote*, relief, remedy, good.

**Balin** (bā'lin). In the ARTHURIAN ROMANCES devoted brother of BALAN. They accident-ally slew one another in ignorance of each other's identity and were buried in one grave by MERLIN. The story is told by Mal-ory in Bk. II and an altered version appears in Tennyson's *Idylls of the King*.

**Balios.** *See* HORSE.

**Balisarda.** *See* SWORD.

**Balkis** (bol'kis). The Muslim name of the Queen of Sheba, who visited Solomon.

**Balthazar** (balthaz'ər). One of the three kings of COLOGNE. *See* MAGI.

**Ban, King.** In the ARTHURIAN ROMANCES, father of Sir LANCELOT DU LAC. He died of grief when his castle was taken and burnt through the treachery of his seneschal.

**Banbury Cross** of nursery rhyme fame was removed by the Puritans as a heathenish memorial in 1646. Another CROSS was erec-ted on the site in 1858.

**Banks's Horse.** A horse called Marocco, belonging to one Banks about the end of Queen Elizabeth I's reign, and trained to do all manner of tricks. One of his exploits is said to have been the ascent of St. Paul's steeple. A favourite story of the time is of an apprentice who called his master to see the spectacle. 'Away, you fool,' said the shopkeeper, 'what need I go to see a horse on the top when I can see so many horses at the bottom!' The horse is mentioned by

Ralegh, Gayton, Kenelm Digby, Ben Jonson and others.

**Banner of the Prophet, The.** What purports to be the actual standard of Mohammed is present in the Eyab mosque of Istanbul. It is twelve feet in length and made of four layers of silk, the top-most being green, embroidered with gold. In times of peace it is kept in the hall of the 'noble vestment' as the Prophet's garb is styled, along with his stirrup, sabre, bow and other relics.

**Banner of France, The Sacred.** The Oriflamme.

**Baphomet** (baf'ōmet) (Fr. *Baphomet*; O.Sp. *Matomat*). A corruption of Mahomet, the imaginary idol which the Templars were said to worship with licentious rites.

**Baptes** (bap'tēz). Priests of the goddess COTYTTO, the Thracian goddess of lewdness, whose midnight orgies were so obscene that they disgusted even the goddess herself. The name is derived from the Greek verb *bapto*, to wash, because of the so-called ceremonies of purification connected with her rites (*Juvenal*, ii, 91).

**Barataria.** Sancho Panza's island-city, in Don QUIXOTE, over which he was appointed governor. The table was presided over by Doctor Pedro Rezio de Aguero, who caused every dish set upon the board to be removed without being tasted—some because they heated the blood, and others because they chilled it, some for one ill effect, and some for another; so that Sancho was allowed to eat nothing. The word is from Sp. *barato*, cheap.

Barataria is also the setting of Act II of *The Gondoliers*. Cp. BARMECIDE'S FEAST.

**Barber of Seville.** The comedy of this name (*Le Barbier de Séville*) was written by Beaumarchais and produced in Paris in 1775. In it appeared as the barber the famous character of FIGARO. Paisello's opera appeared in 1780 but was eclipsed by Rossini's *Barbiere di Siviglia*, with words by Sterbini. The latter was hissed on its first appearance in 1816 under the title of *Almaviva*.

**Bard.** The minstrel of the ancient Celtic peoples, the Gauls, British, Welsh, Irish and Scots. They celebrated the deeds of the gods and heroes, incited to battle, acted as heralds, and sang at festivities. The oldest extant bardic compositions are of the 5th century.

**Barisal Guns.** The name given to certain mysterious booming sounds which occur at Barisal (Bangladesh) and seem to come from the sea. Similar phenomena at Seneca Lake, New York, are called *Lake guns*; on the coast of the Netherlands and Belgium *mistpoeffers*; and in Italy *bombiti, baturlio marina* etc.

**Barlaam and Josaphat** (bah'ləm, jō'səfat). An Indian romance telling how Barlaam, an ascetic of the desert of Sinai, converted Josaphat, a Hindu prince, to Christianity. Probably translated into Greek by the 6th century, and put into its final form by St. John of Damascus, a Syrian monk of the 8th century, in part it corresponds closely with the legendary story of Buddha's youth. It became a widely popular mediaeval romance. The Story of the Three Caskets was used by Shakespeare in *The Merchant of Venice*.

**Barmecide's Feast.** An illusion, particularly one containing a great disappointment. In the ARABIAN NIGHTS, *The Barber's story of his sixth Brother*, a prince of the great Barmecide family in Baghdad, desirous of sport, asked Schacabac, a poor starving wretch, to dinner. Having set before him a series of empty plates, the merchant asked, 'How do you like your soup?' 'Excellently well,' replied Schacabac. 'Did you ever see whiter bread?' 'Never, honourable sir,' was the civil answer. Illusory wine was later offered, but Schacabac excused himself by pretending to be drunk already, and knocked the Barmecide down. The latter saw the humour of the situation, forgave Schacabac, and provided him with food to his heart's content.

**Bartholomew Fair.** A fair opened annually at Smithfield on St. Bartholomew's Day, from 1133 to 1752; after the reform of the Calendar it began on 3 September. It was removed to Islington in 1840 and was last held in 1855. One of the great national fairs dealing in cloth, livestock etc., accompanied by a variety of amusements and entertainments, it long held its place as a centre of London life. The Puritans failed to suppress it. Ben Jonson's *Bartholomew Fair*, a comedy of manners, was first acted in 1614.

Here's that will challenge all the fairs,
Come buy my nuts and damsons and Burgamy pears!
Here's the *Woman of Babylon, the Devil and the Pope.*
And here's the little girl just going on the rope!
Here's *Dives and Lazarus,* and the *World's Creation;*
Here's the Tall Dutchwoman, the like's not in the nation.
Here is the booths where the high Dutch maid is,
Here are the bears that dance like any ladies;
Tat, tat, tat, tat, says little penny trumpet;
Here's Jacob Hall, that does so jump it, jump it;
Sound trumpet, sound, for silver spoon and fork.
Come, here's your dainty pig and pork!
*Wit and Drollery* (1682).

**Basilisk** (baz'ilisk). The fabulous king of serpents (Gr. *basileus*, a king), also called a Cockatrice and alleged to be hatched by a serpent from a cock's egg. It was reputed to be capable of 'looking anyone dead on whom it fixed its eyes'.

The Basiliske...
From powerful eyes close venim doth convay
Into the lookers hart, and killeth farre away.
SPENSER: *The Faerie Queene,* IV, vii, 37.

Also the name given to a genus of Central American lizard and to a large brass cannon of Tudor times.

**Bast.** *See* BUBASTIS.

**Bat.** In the Old Testament bats are 'fowls that creep, going upon all four' (*Lev.* xi, 20); they are unclean and an abomination. The *Book of Baruch* says that they sat on the heads of Babylonian idols (vi, 22). Bats' heads were charms in Egypt and were hung on dovecotes to prevent the doves leaving them.

The bat is important in Amerindian lore in initiation ceremonies, representing rebirth as emerging from the dark cave of the womb of Mother Earth.

A sacred bat figures as a totem in Australian Aboriginal myth in Queensland, but it is unlucky in New Zealand.

In parts of Africa bats are sacred as embodying the souls of the dead.

Western legend associates the bat with vampires, witches, death and the Devil. It was supposed to be a hybrid of bird and rat and as such represented duplicity and hypocrisy. *See* VAMPIRE.

**Bathyllus** (bath'iləs). A beautiful boy of Samos, greatly beloved by Polycrates the tyrant, and by the poet Anacreon (Horace: *Epistle* xiv, 9).

**Bat-Kol** (bat-kol') (daughter of the voice). A heavenly or divine voice announcing the will of God. It existed in the time of the Jewish prophets but was also heard in post-prophetic times. The expression 'daughter of a voice', meaning a small voice, differentiated it from the customary voice. Bat-Kol also denoted a kind of omen or augury. After an appeal to Bat-Kol the first words heard were considered oracular.

**Battle of the Giants.** *See* GIANTS.

**Baucis.** *See* PHILEMON.

**Bavieca.** *See* FAMOUS HORSES (under HORSE).

**Bay.** A shrub of the laurel family, *Laurus nobilis*, used for flavouring, was the bay of the ancients. As the tree of Apollo (*see* DAPHNE) it was held to be a safeguard against thunder and lightning. Hence, according to Pliny, Tiberius and other Roman emperors wore a wreath of bay as an amulet.

Reach the bays—
I'll tie a garland here about his head;
'Twill keep my boy from lightning.
WEBSTER: *Vittoria Corombona,* V, i.

The withering of a bay tree was supposed to be an omen of evil or death. Holinshed's reference to this superstition is used by Shakespeare in *King Richard II* (II, iv).

'Tis thought the King is dead; we will not stay.
The bay trees in our country all are wither'd.

In another sense *bay* is a reddish-brown colour, generally used of horses. The word is the Fr. *bai*, from Lat. *badius*, a term used by Varro in his list of colours appropriate to horses. Thus BAYARD means 'bay-coloured'.

**Bayard** (bā'yahd). A horse of incredible swiftness, given by Charlemagne to the four sons of Aymon. If only one of the sons mounted, the horse was of ordinary size; but if all four mounted, his body became elongated to the requisite length. He is introduced in Boiardo's *Orlando Innamorato* and Ariosto's *Orlando Furioso*, Tasso's *Rinaldo* etc. It is the name given to Fitz-James's horse in Scott's *The Lady of the*

*Lake*. The name is used for any valuable or wonderful horse. *See* BAY.

**Bayardo.** The famous steed of Rinaldo, which once belonged to Amadis of Gaul. *See* BAYARD.

**Bayardo's Leap.** Three stones, about thirty yards apart, near Sleaford. It is said that Rinaldo was riding on his favourite steed, when the demon of the place sprang up behind him; but Bayardo took three tremendous leaps and unhorsed the fiend.

**Bean. Jack and the bean-stalk.** *See* JACK.

**Bean-king.** *Rey de Habas*, the child appointed to play king on Twelfth Night, the Bean-king's festival. The allusion is to the custom of hiding a bean in Twelfth Night cakes. When the cake is cut up, he who gets the bean is Bean-king.

**Bear.** The cult of the bear has existed from earliest times, Neanderthal man having bear shrines with bear skulls and bones ritually interred with human remains. The bear is one of the oldest, if not the oldest, of sacrificial animals. All Siberian shamanistic cultures, together with the Ainus, regard the bear as a mythological ancestor; it is also the Animal Master, instructing shamans.

Bears played an important part in early Mediterranean myth. Arcadians were descended from bears; they were sacred to Artemis and DIANA, lunar goddesses. In the cult of Artemis attendant girls were dressed in yellow robes and called 'bears' and imitated their actions in the rites of the festival of Brauronia. The goddess Artio was a she-bear. One classical fable is that the nymph CALLISTO had a son by ZEUS called Arcas; she was changed into a bear by the jealous HERA. Callisto and her son were then set in the sky as constellations by Zeus.

In Scandinavian myth the bear is sacred to THOR and to the lunar goddess of the waters. The she-bear Atla represents the feminine principle with Atli as the masculine.

In Celtic myth the bear is a lunar power and an emblem of the goddess Berne.

Old Testament legend depicts the bear as ferocious and used to punish wrong-doers. In Christianity it typifies the DEVIL.

The phrase 'licked into shape' is derived from the ancient belief that bear cubs were born amorphous and were licked into shape by the mother. Aristotle, Pliny, Aelian, Oppian and Isadore all use this fable.

In mediaeval Mummers' Plays in England the bear pursues little boys dressed as lambs who are rescued by the Shepherd Hero.

**The bear and ragged staff.** Crest of the Nevilles and later, Earls of Warwick, attracting particular note through the activities of Warwick the Kingmaker and used as a PUBLIC HOUSE SIGN.

Now by my father's badge, Old Nevil's crest,
The rampant bear chain'd to the ragged staff.
SHAKESPEARE: *Henry VI, Pt. II*, V, i.

Legend has it that the first earl was Arthgal of the Round Table, whose cognizance was a bear through having strangled one. Morvid, the second earl, slew a giant with a club made of a young tree stripped of its branches. To commemorate this victory he added the 'ragged staff'.

**The bear and the tea-kettle.** Said of a person who injures himself by foolish rage. The story is that one day the bear entered a hut in Kamchatka, when a kettle was on the fire. Master Bruin smelt at it and burnt his nose; greatly irritated he seized it and squeezed it against his breast, scalding himself terribly. He growled in agony till some neighbours killed him with their guns.

**Bear-leader.** In the 18th century denoted the tutor who conducted a young nobleman or youth of wealth and fashion on the Grand Tour. It is taken from the old custom of leading muzzled bears about the streets and making them show off to attract notice and money. (This practice was only made illegal in 1925.)

Bear! (said Dr. Pangloss to his pupil). Under favour, young gentleman, I am the bear-leader, being appointed your tutor.
G. COLMAN: *Heir-at-Law* (1797).

**Beard.** Among the Jews, Turks, Persians and many other peoples the beard has long been a sign of manly dignity and to cut it off wilfully is a deadly insult. Muslims swore by the beard of the Prophet and to swear by one's beard was an assurance of good faith. To pluck or touch a man's beard was an extreme affront, hence the phrase *to beard one*, to defy or insult or contradict flatly.

**Beauty. Beauty and the Beast.** A handsome woman with an uncouth or uncomely male companion.

The heroine and hero of the well-known fairy tale in which Beauty saved the life of her father by consenting to live with the Beast; and the Beast, being disenchanted by Beauty's love, became a handsome prince, and married her. The story is found in Straparola's *Piacevoli Notti* (1550), and this is probably the source of Mme. le Prince de Beaumont's popular French version (1757). It is the basis of Grétry's opera *Zémire et Azor* (1771). The story is of great antiquity and takes various forms. *Cp.* LOATHLY LADY.

**Beauty of Buttermere.** *See* MAID OF BUTTERMERE.

**Beauty sleep.** Sleep taken before midnight. Those who habitually go to bed after midnight, especially during youth, are supposed to become pale and haggard.

**Beddgelert** (bethgel'ət). The name of a village in Gwynedd (the grave of Gelert). According to Welsh folklore, Prince Llewelyn returned to his castle to find his dog Gelert's jaws dripping with blood. His son had been left in Gelert's care but the baby was not to be found. In his distress, Llewelyn slew the faithful hound and found his son, close to the body of a wolf, which the hound had killed. This story has many variants in other ancient literatures.

**Bedivere,** or **Bedver**. In the ARTHURIAN ROMANCES, a knight of the ROUND TABLE, butler and staunch adherent of King ARTHUR. It was he who, at the request of the dying king, threw EXCALIBUR into the lake, and afterwards bore his body to the ladies in the barge which was to take him to AVALON.

**Bednall Green.** *See* BEGGAR.

**Bee.** In ancient Egypt the Lower Egypt was that which 'belongs to the bee' and the earliest known reference occurred about 3550 B.C. at the union of the two kingdoms, Upper and Lower Egypt, when they had 'joined the Reed to the Bee'. Bees were the tears of RA, the sun god: 'when Ra weeps again the waters which flow from his eyes upon the ground turn into working bees'. The bee is the giver of life and resurrection.

In India KRISHNA, as an AVATAR of VISHNU, has a blue bee on his forehead.

SOMA, the moon, is called a bee and a bee surmounting a triangle represents Siva. Kama, god of love, has a bow-string of bees and is followed by them.

Both Plato and Aristotle say that bees have something divine about them. The Great Mother was known as the Queen Bee and her priestesses were Melissae, the Bees. Pindar says that the Pythian priestess at DELPHI was known as the Delphic Bee. Sophocles, Plato, Virgil and Lucan were supposed to have been fed by bees or had their lips touched with honey in infancy. Pindar, Sappho and Homer were all referred to as having the gift of honeyed words. There are various myths associating both ZEUS and DIONYSUS with bees; both were said to have been fed by them. PAN and Priapus were said to be protectors and keepers of bees which were also an emblem of EROS/CUPID, DEMETER, CYBELE, DIANA, RHEA and the Ephesian Artemis.

In Celtic mythology bees have a secret wisdom derived from the otherworld.

The Apocryphal New Testament has numerous legends of bee-creation by God or Jesus; Christ was called the 'aethereal bee' and the belief that the bee was parthenogenic made it an apt symbol of virginity and the Virgin Queen of Heaven, and hence of the Virgin Mary.

In Australia and Africa bees are found as tribal totems and among the Kung Bushmen they are the carriers of supernatural power. **To have your head full of bees,** or **to have a bee in your bonnet.** To be cranky; to have an idiosyncrasy; to be full of devices, crotchets, fancies, inventions and dreamy theories. The connection between bees and the soul was once generally maintained; hence Mohammed admits bees to PARADISE. Porphyry says of fountains, 'they are adapted to the NYMPHS or those souls which the ancients called bees.'

**Beelzebub** (biel'zibŭb). Other forms are *Beelzebul, Baalzebub*. Baalzebub was the god of Ekron (II *Kings* i, 3), and the meaning is obscure although it has been popularly held to mean 'lord of FLIES'. In any event it was probably a derisory title. The most likely explanation so far is that Baalzebul means 'lord of the lofty dwelling' and refers to the Syrian Baal. This was altered to Baalzebub by the Jews, as the former title seemed only proper to Jahweh. To the Jews he came to be the chief representative of the false gods. In *Matt.* xii, 24, he is referred to as 'the prince of the devils' and similarly in *Mark* iii, 22, and *Luke* xi, 15. Hence Milton places him next in rank to SATAN.

> One next himself in power, and next in crime,
> Long after known in Palestine, and named
> Beelzebub.
> *Paradise Lost,* I, 79.

**Befana** (befah'nə). The good fairy of Italian children, who is supposed to fill their stockings with toys when they go to bed on Twelfth Night. Someone enters the children's bedroom for the purpose and the wakeful youngsters cry out, *'Ecco la Befana.'* According to legend, Befana was too busy with house affairs to look after the MAGI when they went out to offer their gifts, and said she would wait to see them on their return; but they went another way, and Befana, every Twelfth Night, watches for them. The name is a corruption of *Epiphania.*

**Beggar. Beggar's daughter of Bednall Green, Bessee the.** An old ballad given in Percy's *Reliques*; the subject of a play by Chettle and Day (1600) and also one by Sheridan Knowles (1834). The beautiful Bessee had four suitors—a knight, a gentleman of fortune, a London merchant and the son of the innkeeper at Romford. She told them that they must obtain the consent of her father, the poor blind beggar of Bethnal Green, whereupon they all slunk off except the knight, who went to ask the beggar's leave to wed the 'pretty Bessee'. The beggar gave her £3000 for her dower, and £100 to buy her wedding gown. At the wedding feast he explained to the guests that he was Henry, son of Sir Simon de Montfort.
**To go by beggar's bush,** or **Go home by beggar's bush**—*i.e.* to go to ruin. Beggar's bush is the name of a tree which once stood on the left hand of the London road from Huntingdon to Caxton; so called because it was a noted rendezvous for beggars.

**Bel.** The name of the Assyrio-Babylonian gods En-lil and MARDUK. It has the same meaning as Baal. The story of Bel and the Dragon, in which we are told how Daniel convinced the King that Bel was not an actual living deity but only an image, was formerly part of the book of *Daniel,* but is now relegated to the Apocrypha.

**Bel-fires.** *See* BELTANE.

**Bell.** As the bell clinks, so the fool thinks, or **As the fool thinks, so the bell clinks.** The tale says that when Dick WHITTINGTON ran away from his master, and had got as far as Highgate Hill, he was hungry, tired, and wished to return. Bow Bells began to ring, and Whittington fancied they said, 'Turn again, Whittington, Lord Mayor of London.' The bells clinked in response to the boy's thoughts.

**Belladonna.** The Deadly Nightshade. The name is Italian and means 'beautiful lady'. Its power of enlarging the pupils was put to use by would-be glamorous females. This is the usual explanation of the name but another is that it was used by an Italian poisoner named Leucota to poison beautiful women.

**Bellerophon** (beler'ōfon). The Joseph of Greek mythology; Antaea, spouse of Proetus, being the 'Potiphar's Wife' who tempted him and afterwards falsely accused him. Proetus sent Bellerophon with a letter to Iobates, King of Lycia, his wife's father, narrating the charge, and praying that the bearer might be put to death. Iobates, reluctant to slay Bellerophon himself, gave him many hazardous tasks, including the killing of the CHIMAERA, but as he succeeded in all of them Iobates made him his heir. Later Bellerophon attempted to fly to heaven on PEGASUS, but ZEUS sent a gadfly to sting the horse, and the rider was thrown.

**Bellerus** (belē'rəs). A Cornish giant invented by Milton to account for 'Bellerium', the Roman name for the Land's End area.

> Sleep'st by the fable of Bellerus old.
> *Lycidas,* 160.

**Bellona** (belō'nə). The Roman goddess of war, wife (or sometimes sister) of MARS.

**Belly. The belly and its members.** The fable of Menenius Agrippa to the Roman people when they seceded to the Sacred Mount. 'Once upon a time the members refused to work for the lazy belly; but, as the supply of food was thus stopped, they found there was a necessary and mutual dependence between them.' The fable is given by AESOP and by Plutarch, whence Shakespeare introduced it in his *Coriolanus*, I, i.

**Belomancy** (bel'ōmansi) (Gr.). DIVINATION by arrows. Labels being attached to a given number of arrows, the archers let them fly, and the advice on the label of the arrow which flies farthest is accepted. It was anciently practised by the Babylonians, Scythians etc. Sir Thomas Browne describes it in *Pseudodoxia Epidemica*, v, 23, and it is also mentioned in *Ezekiel* xxi, 21.

**Belphegor** (bel'fegaw). The Assyrian form of *Baal-Peor*, the Moabitish god to whom the Israelites became attached in Shittim (*Numb.* xxv, 3), which was associated with licentious orgies (*Hos.* ix, 10).

The name was given in mediaeval Latin legend to a demon sent into the world by his fellows to test rumours concerning the happiness of married life on earth. After a thorough trial, he fled to the happy regions where female companionship was non-existent. Hence the name is applied to a misanthrope and to a nasty, obscene, licentious fellow. The story is found in *Machiavelli*, and occurs in English in Barnabe Rich's *Farewell to the Militarie Profession* (1581) and is used in *Grim, The Collier of Croyden* (1600), Jonson's *The Divell is an Asse* (1616), and John Wilson's *Belphegor, or the Marriage of the Devil* (1691).

**Belphoebe** (belfē'bi). The Huntress-goddess in Spenser's *Faerie Queene*, daughter of Chrysogone and sister of AMORET, typifies Queen Elizabeth I as a model of chastity. She was of the DIANA and MINERVA type; cold as an icicle, passionless, immovable and, like a moonbeam, light without warmth.

**Beltane** (bel'tān) (Gaelic, *bealltainn*). The derivation is uncertain but it is not connected with *baal*. In Scotland, May Day (O.S.); also an ancient Celtic festival when *bel-fires* were kindled on the hill-tops and cattle were driven between the flames, either to protect them from disease, or as a preparatory to sacrifice.

**Bendy, Old.** The DEVIL; who is willing to bend to anyone's inclination.

**Bengodi** (ben·gō'di). A 'land of COCKAIGNE' mentioned in Boccaccio's *Decameron* (viii,

3), where 'they tie the vines with sausages, where you may buy a fat goose for a penny and have a gosling into the bargain; where there is also a mountain of grated Parmesan cheese, and people do nothing but make cheese-cakes and macaroons. There is also a river which runs Malmsey wine of the very best quality,' etc., etc.

**Beowulf** (bā'ōwulf). The hero of the Old English epic poem of the same name of unknown date and authorship, but certainly originally written before the Saxons came to England and modified subsequent to the introduction of Christianity. In its present form, it probably dates from the 8th century. It is the oldest epic in English and also in the whole Teutonic group of languages.

The scene is laid in Denmark or Sweden; the hall of King Hrothgar is raided nightly by GRENDEL, whom Beowulf mortally wounds after a fierce fight. Next night Grendel's mother comes to avenge his death. Beowulf pursues her to her lair under the water and slays her with a magic sword. He eventually becomes king and fifty years later is killed in combat with a DRAGON, which had ravished the land.

**Berchta** (bœkh'tə). A goddess of South German mythology akin to the HULDA of North Germany, but after the introduction of Christianity she was degraded into a BOGY to frighten children. She was sometimes represented with a long iron nose and one large foot. *See* BERTHA; WHITE LADY.

**Berecynthian Hero** (berisin'thiən). MIDAS, the mythological king of Phrygia; so called from Mount Berecynthus in Phrygia.

**Berenice** (berinī'si). The wife of Ptolemy III Euergetes (246–221 B.C.). She vowed to sacrifice her hair to the gods, if her husband returned home the vanquisher of Asia. She suspended her hair in the temple, but it was stolen the first night and Conon of Samos told the king that the winds had wafted it to heaven, where it still forms the seven stars near the tail of LEO, called *Coma Berenices*.

**Bergomask** (bœ'gōmahsk). A rustic dance (*see Midsummer Night's Dream*, V, i); so called from Bergamo, a Venetian province, whose inhabitants were noted for their clownishness. Also a clown.

**Bermoothes** (bœmō·ooth'ēz). The name of the island in *The Tempest*, feigned by Shakespeare to be enchanted and inhabited by WITCHES and DEVILS. He almost certainly had the newly discovered Bermudas in mind.

**Bermudas** (bœmū'dəz). An old name for a district of Westminster, probably the narrow alleys in the neighbourhood of Covent Garden, St. Martin's Lane and the Strand whose residents had certain privileges against arrest. Hence **to live in the Bermudas,** to skulk in some out-of-the-way place for cheapness or safety.

**Bermuda Triangle.** The triangular sea area between Bermuda, Florida and Puerto Rico where the currents are very strong. It gained notoriety in the 1960s on account of the disappearance of numerous ships and aircraft without any trace of wreckage.

**Bernard. St. Bernard Soup.** *See* STONE SOUP.

**Bernardo del Carpio.** A semi-mythical Spanish hero of the 9th century and a favourite subject of minstrels. Lope de Vega wrote several plays around his exploits. He is credited with having defeated ROLAND at Roncesvalles.

**Berserk, Berserker.** In Scandinavian mythology, the sons of Berserk, grandson of the eight-handed Starkadder and Alfhilde. The name probably means bear-sark, or bear-coat. Berserk always fought ferociously and recklessly, without armour. Hence *berserk* for a savage and reckless fighter, one with the fighting fever on him.

**Bertha.** A German impersonation of the EPIPHANY with some of the attributes of BERCHTA, and corresponding to the Italian BEFANA. She is a WHITE LADY, who steals softly into nurseries and rocks infants to sleep, but is the terror of all naughty children.

**Berthe au Grand Pied** (bert ō grã pyã). Mother of CHARLEMAGNE, and great-granddaughter of Charles Martel; she had a club-foot and died in 783. Many of her qualities, as described in the Charlemagne romances, appear to be derived from BERCHTA.

**Bess. Black Bess.** Dick Turpin's mythical but celebrated mare, created by Harrison Ainsworth in his romance *Rookwood* (1834), particularly known for Dick's famous ride to York. *See* TURPIN.

**Bessee of Bednall Green.** *See* BEGGAR.

**Bessie Bell and Mary Gray.** A ballad relating how two young women of Perth, to avoid the plague of 1666, retired to a rural retreat called the Burnbraes, near Lynedock, the residence of Mary Gray. A young man, in love with both, carried them provisions, and they all died of the plague and were buried at Dornock Hough.

**Bestiaries,** or **Bestials.** Books which had a great vogue between the 11th and 14th centuries, describing the supposed habits and peculiarities of animals both real and fabled, with much legendary lore and moral symbolism. They were founded on the *Physiologi* of earlier centuries and those in English were mostly translations of continental originals. Among the most popular were those of Philippe de Thaun, Guillaume le Clerc, and Richard de Fournival's satirical *Bestiaire d'Amour* (*c.* 1250).

> The unicorn represents Jesus Christ, who took on him our nature in the virgin's womb, was betrayed to the Jews, and delivered into the hands of Pontius Pilate. Its one horn signifies the Gospel truth, that Christ is one with the Father, *etc.*
> GUILLAUME: *Le Bestiaire Divin.*

**Beth Gelert.** *See* BEDDGELERT.

**Bevis of Hampton.** Sir Bevis was the hero of this popular English mediaeval romance slightly connected with the CHARLEMAGNE cycle. Bevis sought to avenge his father's death, which had been contrived by his mother. As a result he was sold to heathen merchants, and after many adventures he married Josian, daughter of King Ermyn, eventually returning to England to avenge his father. Hampton is usually interpreted as Southampton. The English version (14th century) is based on an earlier French version, but it is possible that the story had previous English origins. Drayton tells the story in his *Poly-Olbion*, Song ii, lines 260–384.

**Bhagavad Gita** (bah'gəvəd gē'tə) (The Song of the Blessed). One of the great religious and philosophical poems of India which occurs in the sixth book of the MAHABHARATA. In it, KRISHNA, in the form of a charioteer, instructs Arjuna, chief of the Pandus, in his duties and elaborates his ethical and pantheistic philosophy, finally revealing himself as the Supreme Being.

**Bibliomancy.** DIVINATION by means of the Bible. *See* SORTES.

**Bicorn** (bī'kawn). A mythical beast, fabled by the early French romancers to grow very fat through living on good and enduring husbands. It was the antitype of CHICHEVACHE.

**Bifrost** (bēf'rost). (Icel. *bifa*, tremble; *rost*, path). In Scandinavian mythology, the bridge between HEAVEN and earth, ASGARD and MIDGARD. The rainbow may be considered to be this bridge, and its various colours are the reflections of its precious stones. HEIMDALL is its keeper.

**Big-endians.** In Swift's *Gulliver's Travels*, a party in the empire of Lilliput who made it a matter of conscience to break their eggs at the *big end*; they were looked on as heretics by the orthodox party, who broke theirs at the *little end*. The *Big-endians* typify the Catholics and the *Little-endians* the Protestants.

**Bimini.** A legendary island of the Bahamas where the fountain of youth gave everlasting life to all who drank from it.

**Bird.** In mythology birds, with their powers of flight, universally represent the spirit, the soul, ascent to the heavens and communication between gods and men. In many traditions the soul takes flight in the form of a bird when it leaves the body. In myth and fable the hero is often accompanied and guided by a bird and he understands the language of birds. 'A little bird told me.' In shamanism birds are the obvious vehicle for the spiritual flight for visiting other worlds.

Birds are of two classes, the heavenly and the demonic, those that help and work good for humanity and those that are inimical and evilly intended; the clean and the unclean.

There are also many fabulous birds representing spiritual or elemental powers, such as the THUNDERBIRD of the Amerindians and the ROC of Arabian legend etc.
**The Arabian bird.** The PHOENIX.
**The bird of Juno.** The peacock. MINERVA'S bird is either the COCK or the OWL; that of VENUS is the DOVE.

**Birds Protected by Superstitions:**
**The Chough** was protected in CORNWALL because the soul of King ARTHUR was fabled to have migrated into one.

The arms of Cornwall contain 'over the crest on a wreath Argent and Azure a chough proper resting the dexter claw upon a ducal coronet Or'.

**The Falcon** was held sacred by the Egyptians because it was the form assumed by RA and HORUS; and the **Ibis** because the god THOTH escaped from the pursuit of TYPHON disguised as an Ibis.

**Mother Carey's Chickens,** or Stormy Petrels, are protected by sailors from a superstition that they are the living embodiment of the souls of dead mariners. *See also* MOTHER.

**Bird of Paradise.** Also called the **Bird of God**, was reported by travellers from the Far East as having brilliant plumage but no wings or feet, it suspended itself from the boughs by wire-like feathers on its tail. It was about the size of a goose. Malaysian legend said that the bird dropped its egg from the air and on reaching the ground the egg burst and released a fully-fledged bird.

The Bird of Paradise was also spoken of as the **Bird of the Nile**, but the myth was widespread.

**The Robin** is protected on account of Christian tradition and nursery legend. *See* ROBIN REDBREAST.

**The Stork** is held sacred in Sweden, from the legend that it flew round the cross crying, 'Styrka, Styrka!' when Jesus was crucified. *See* STORK.

**Swans** are protected in Ireland from the legend of the FIONNUALA (daughter of LIR) who was metamorphosed into a swan and condemned to wander the waters until the advent of Christianity. Moore wrote a poem on the subject. *See* SWAN.

**Bistonians** (bistō'niənz). The Thracians; after Biston, son of MARS, who allegedly built Bistonia on Lake Bistonis.

**Black.** *See* COLOURS for its symbolism. Its use for mourning was a Roman custom (*Juvenal*, x, 245), borrowed from the Egyptians. At funerals mutes who wore black cloaks were sometimes known as the *blacks*, and sometimes as *Black Guards*.

> I do pray ye
> To give me leave to live a little longer.

You stand about me like my Blacks.
BEAUMONT and FLETCHER: *Monsieur Thomas*,
III, i.

In several of the Oriental nations it is a badge of servitude, slavery and low birth. Our word *blackguard* seems to point to this meaning, and the Lat. *niger*, black, also meant bad, impropitious.

**Blackamoor. Washing the blackamoor white**—*i.e.* engaged upon a hopeless and useless task. The allusion is to one of AESOP'S FABLES of that name.

**Black art, The.** Magic, NECROMANCY. The name seems to have derived from Med. Lat. *nigromantia* used erroneously for Gr. *nekromanteia*. The devil was also portrayed as black.

**Black Dwarf.** *See under* DWARF.

**Blackfoot.** A Scottish term for a match-maker, or an intermediary in love affairs; if he chanced to play traitor he was called a *whitefoot*. Also the name of one of the Irish agrarian secret societies of the early 19th century.

And the Blackfoot who courted each foeman's
approach,
Faith! 'tis hot-foot he'd fly from the stout Father
Roach.
LOVER.

**Black Mass.** A sacrilegious Mass in which the DEVIL is invoked in place of God and various obscene rites performed in ridicule of the proper ceremony.

It is also a Requiem Mass from the custom of wearing black vestments.

**Black ox. The black ox has trod on his foot,** *i.e.* misfortune has come to him. Black oxen were sacrificed to PLUTO and other infernal deities.

**Black sheep.** A disgrace to the family or community; a *mauvais sujet*. Black sheep are not as valuable as white and in times of superstition were looked on as bearing the devil's mark. A black sheep in a white flock is the Odd Man Out.

**Black Stone.** The famous stone kissed by every pilgrim to the KAABA at Mecca. Muslims say that it was white when it fell from heaven but it turned black because of the sins of mankind. The stone was worshipped centuries before Mohammed. In Persian legend it was an emblem of SATURN.

**Bladud** (blā'dəd). A mythical English king, father of King Lear. According to Geoffrey of Monmouth he built Bath and dedicated the medicinal springs to MINERVA, studied magic, and was dashed to pieces when he fell into the temple of APOLLO whilst trying to fly.

**Blanchefleur** (blonsh'flœr). The heroine of the Old French metrical romance, *Flore et Blanchefleur*, used by Boccaccio for his prose romance, *Il Filocolo*. It is substantially the same as that of Dianora and Ansaldo in the *Decameron* and that of Dorigen and Aurelius by Chaucer. The tale is of a young Christian prince who is in love with the Saracen slave-girl with whom he has been brought up. They are parted, but after many adventures he rescues her unharmed from the harem of the Emir of Babylon.

**Blarney.** Soft wheedling speeches to gain some end; flattery or lying with unblushing effrontery. Legend has it that Cormac Macarthy in 1602 undertook to surrender Blarney Castle (near Cork) to the English, as part of an armistice. Daily the Lord President Carew looked for the fulfilment of the terms, but received nothing but soft speeches, till he became the laughing-stock of Elizabeth's ministers, and the dupe of the Lord of Blarney.

Among American criminals 'to blarney' means to pick locks.

**To kiss the Blarney Stone.** In the wall of Blarney Castle about twenty feet from the top and difficult of access is a triangular stone inscribed, 'Cormac Macarthy *fortis me fieri fecit*, A.D. 1446'. Tradition says that whoever kisses it is endowed with wonderful powers of cajolery. As it is almost impossible to reach, a substitute has been provided, which is said to be as effective as the original.

**Blatant Beast.** In Spenser's *Faerie Queene* (Bks. V, VI) 'a dreadful fiend of gods and men, ydrad'; the type of calumny or slander. He was born of CERBERUS and CHIMAERA, and had a hundred tongues and a sting; with his tongues he speaks things 'most shameful, most unrighteous, most untrue'; and with his sting 'steeps them in poison'. Sir CALIDORE muzzled him and drew him with a chain to Fairyland but the beast escaped. The word *blatant* seems to have been coined by Spenser and is probably from the provincial word *blate*, to bellow.

**Blefuscu** (blefūs′kū). An island in Swift's *Gulliver's Travels*. In describing it he satirized France.

**Blemmyes** (blem′iz). An ancient Ethiopian tribe mentioned by Roman writers as inhabiting Nubia and Upper Egypt. They were fabled to have no head, their eyes and mouth being placed in the breast. *Cp.* CAORA.

**Bloody-bones.** A HOBGOBLIN; generally 'Raw-head and Bloody-bones'.

**Blue. Bluebeard.** A BOGY, a murderous tyrant in Charles Perrault's *Contes du Temps* (1697). In this version Bluebeard goes on a journey leaving his new wife the keys of his castle, but forbidding her to enter one room. Curiosity overcomes her and she opens the door to find the bodies of all Bluebeard's former wives. On his return he finds a blood spot on the key which tells him of his wife's disobedience. He is about to cut off her head when her two brothers rush in and kill him. The tale is of an internationally widespread and ancient type and it is unprofitable to regard Gilles de Rais or Henry VIII as the historical Bluebeard.

**Blue-eyed Maid.** MINERVA, the goddess of wisdom, is so called by Homer.

> Now Prudence gently pulled the poet's ear,
> And thus the daughter of the Blue-eyed Maid,
> In flattery's soothing sounds, divinely said,
> 'O Peter, eldest-born of Phoebus, hear.'
> PETER PINDAR: *A Falling Minister.*

**Blunderbore.** A nursery-tale giant, brother of CORMORAN, who put JACK THE GIANT KILLER to bed and intended to kill him; but Jack thrust a billet of wood into the bed, and crept under the bedstead. Blunderbore came with his club and broke the billet to pieces and was amazed to see Jack next morning at breakfast. He asked Jack how he had slept. 'Pretty well,' said the Cornish hero, 'but once or twice I fancied a mouse tickled me with its tail.' This increased the giant's surprise. Hasty pudding being provided for breakfast, Jack stowed away such a bulk in a bag concealed within his dress that the giant could not keep pace. Jack cut the bag open to relieve the 'gorge' and the giant, to effect the same relief, cut his throat and thus killed himself.

**Boar.** The Golden Boar is one of the great solar animals, while the White Boar, dwelling in the swamps, and thus associated with the watery element, is lunar.

In Vedic times the storm god Ruda was the Boar of the Sky. The boar was also an emblem of Vajravrahi, goddess of the dawn.

The boar is the animal of the hunt par excellence; it is also an important sacrificial animal. There are various legends of the hero slain by a boar while out hunting. In Sumero-Semitic myth THAMMUZ was so killed; the Greek and Phoenician ADONIS met a similar fate and the same legend occurs in Celtic lore with Diarmaid. The boar holds an important place in Celtic and Gallic mythology.

In the Far East, in China, the boar represents the wealth of the forest; in Japan it depicts courage and the warrior qualities.

**Buddha and the boar.** A Hindu legend relates that BUDDHA died from eating dried boar's flesh. The third AVATAR of VISHNU was in the form of a boar, and in the legend 'dried boar's flesh' probably typifies Esoteric knowledge prepared for popular use. None but Buddha himself must take the responsibility of giving out occult secrets, and he died while preparing for the general esoteric knowledge.

**The Calydonian boar.** In Greek legend, Oeneus, King of Calydon in Aetolia, having neglected the sacrifices to ARTEMIS, was punished by the goddess sending a ferocious boar to ravage his lands. A band of princes collected to hunt the boar, which was wounded by Atalanta (*see* ATALANTA'S RACE), and killed by MELEAGER.

**Boar's Head.** The old English custom of serving this as a Christmas dish is said to derive from Norse mythology. FREYR, the god of peace and plenty, used to ride on the boar Gullinbursti: his festival was held at Yuletide, when a boar was sacrificed to his honour. The English custom is described in Washington Irving's *Sketch Book* (*The Christmas Dinner*). The Boar's Head was brought in ceremoniously to a flourish of trumpets and a carol was sung. The following is the first verse of that sung before Prince Henry at St. John's College, Oxford, at Christmas, 1607:

> The Boar is dead
> So, here is his head;
> What man could have done more
> Than his head off to strike,
> Meleager like
> And bring it as I do before?

Irving gives the Boar's Head Carol of Queen's College, Oxford.

**Boeotia** (bēō'shə). The ancient name for a district in central Greece, probably so called from its abundance of cattle. The fable is that CADMUS was conducted thence by an ox (Gr. *bous*) to the spot where he built THEBES.

**Boeotian** (bēō'shən). Rude and unlettered, a dullard. The ancient Boeotians were an agricultural and pastoral people, so the Athenians used to say that they were as dull and thick as their own atmosphere; yet Hesiod, Pindar, Corinna, Plutarch, Pelopidas, and Epaminondas were Boeotians.

**Boeotian ears.** Ears unable to appreciate music or rhetoric.

> Well, friend, I can assure thee thou has not got Boeotian ears (because you can appreciate the beauty of my sermons).
> LE SAGE: *Gil Blas*, vii, 3.

**Boggard** or **Boggart**. A North of England name for a GOBLIN or spectre, especially one haunting a particular place. It is the same as a BROWNIE or KOBOLD and the Scottish *bogle*. When a horse took fright it was said to have seen a boggart. In the Isle of Man a *buggane* was an evil creature with a great head and body, with long teeth and nails.

**Bogey.** *See* BOGY.

**Bogy.** A HOBGOBLIN; a person or object of terror; a bugbear. The word first appeared in the 19th century and is perhaps connected with the Scottish *bogle* and so with the obsolete BUG. There was also an evil creature in Manx folklore called a *buggane* (*see* BOGGARD). A more recent suggestion is that *bogy* derives from the *Boogie* tribesmen's privateering and piratical activities in S.E. Asian waters.

**Bold. Bold as Beauchamp.** It is said that Thomas Beauchamp, Earl of Warwick, with one squire and six archers, overthrew 100 armed men at Hogges, in Normandy, in 1346. This exploit is not more incredible than that attributed to Captal-de-Buch, who, with forty followers, cleared Meaux of the JACQUERIE in 1358, slaying some 7000!

**Bona Dea** (bon'ə dā'ə) (Lat. the good goddess). A Roman goddess supposed to preside over the earth and all its blessings. She was worshipped by the VESTALS as the goddess of chastity and fertility. Her festival was 1 May and no men were allowed to be present at the celebration.

**Book. The Book of the Dead.** A collection of ancient Egyptian texts, both religious and magical, concerned with guidance for the safe conduct of the soul through Amenti (the Egyptian HADES). The Egyptians called it *The Book of Going Forth by Day* and copies, or parts of it, were buried with the mummy. There is a variety of texts.

**Boot. Puss in Boots.** *See under* PUSS.

**Boötes** (bō·oo'tēz). Greek for 'the ploughman'; the name of the constellation which contains the bright star, Arcturus. According to ancient mythology Boötes invented the plough, to which he yoked two oxen, and at death was taken to HEAVEN with his plough and oxen and made a constellation. HOMER calls it 'the wagoner', *i.e.* the wagoner of Charles's Wain, the Great Bear. *See* BEAR.

**Borak,** or **Al Borak** (baw'rak) (the lightning). The animal brought by GABRIEL to carry Mohammed to the seventh HEAVEN, and itself received into PARADISE. It had the face of a man but the cheeks of a HORSE; its eyes were like jacinths, but brilliant as the stars; it had the wings of an EAGLE, spoke with the voice of a man, and glittered all over with radiant light.

**Boreas** (baw'rias). In Greek mythology, the god of the north wind, and the north wind itself. He was the son of Astraeus, a TITAN, and Eos, the morning, and lived in a cave of Mount Haemus, in Thrace.

Hence *boreal*, of or pertaining to the north.

> In radiant streams,
> Bright over Europe, bursts the Boreal morn.
> THOMSON: *Autumn*, 98.

**Bosporus** (bos'pərəs), or less correctly **Bosphorus** (-fərəs), is a Greek compound meaning 'ox-ford'. The Thracian Bosporus unites the Sea of Marmara with the Euxine or Black Sea. Greek legend says that ZEUS, enamoured of Io, changed her into a white heifer from fear of Hera, to flee from whom Io swam across the strait, which was thence called *bos porus*, the passage of the cow. Hera discovered the trick, and sent a gadfly to torment Io, who was made to wander, in a state of frenzy, from land to land, ultimately finding rest on the banks of the Nile. The wanderings of the Argive princess were a favourite theme among ancient writers.

**Botanomancy** (bot'ənōmansi). DIVINATION by leaves. One method was by writing sentences on leaves which were exposed to the wind, the answer being gathered from those which were left; another was through the crackling made by leaves of various plants when thrown on the fire or crushed in the hands.

**Bo-tree.** The pipal tree or *Ficus religiosa* of India, allied to the banyan and so called from Pali *Bodhi*, perfect knowledge, because it is under one of these trees that Gautama attained enlightenment and so became the Buddha. At the ruined city of Anuradhapura in Ceylon is a bo-tree reputed to have grown from a cutting sent by King Asoka in 288 B.C.

**Bottomless Pit, The.** Hell is so called in *Revelation*, xx, 1. *See* ABADDON. William Pitt, the younger (1759–1806), was humorously called **the bottomless Pitt,** in allusion to his thinness.

**Bower of Bliss.** In Spenser's *Faerie Queene* (Bk. II), the enchanted home of Acrasia. In Tasso's *Jerusalem Delivered*, ARMIDA'S garden.

**Bowing** (bow'ing). We uncover the head when we wish to salute anyone with respect; but the Jews, Turks, Thais etc., uncover their feet. The reason is that with us the chief act of investiture is crowning or placing a cap on the head, but in the East it is the putting on of slippers.

**Bowyer God.** The 'archer god', usually applied to CUPID.

**Boy. The Gazelle Boy.** *See* GAZELLE.

**Braggadocio** (bragədō'siō). A braggart; one who is valiant with his tongue but a great coward at heart. *Cp.* ERYTHYNUS. The character is from Spenser's *Faerie Queene* and a type of the 'Intemperance of the Tongue'. After a time, like the jackdaw in borrowed plumes, Braggadocio is stripped of all his glories; his shield is claimed by Sir Marinell; his lady is proved by the golden girdle to be the false Florimell; his horse is claimed by Sir Guyon; Talus shaves off his beard and

scourges his squire; and the pretender sneaks off amidst the jeers of everyone. It is thought that the poet had the Duke of Alençon, a suitor of Queen Elizabeth I, in mind when he drew this character (*Faerie Queene*, II, iii; III, v, viii, x; IV, ii, iv; V, iii, etc.).

**Bragi** (brah'gi). In Norse mythology, the god of poetry and eloquence, son of ODIN and husband of IDUNA. He welcomes the slain heroes who arrive in VALHALLA.

**Brahma** (brah'mə). In Hinduism Brahma, properly speaking, is the Absolute, or God conceived as entirely impersonal. This theological abstraction was later endowed with personality and became the Creator of the universe, the first in the divine Triad, of which the other partners were VISHNU the maintainer, and SIVA, the destroyer. As such the Brahmins claim Brahma as the founder of their religious system.

**Brandan, St.,** or **Brendan.** A semi-legendary Irish saint, said to have been born at Tralee in 484. He founded the abbey of Clonfert and died in 577. The *Rule of St. Brendan* was dictated to him by an angel and he is said to have presided over 3000 monks in the various houses of his foundation.

He is best known for the mediaeval legend, widespread throughout Europe, of his seven-year voyage in search of the 'Land of the Saints', the Isle of St. Brendan, reputed to be in mid-Atlantic. The very birds and beasts he encountered observed the Christian fasts and festivals. The earliest surviving version of the story is the *Navigatio Brendani* (11th century). *See* MAELDUNE.

And we came to the isle of a saint who had sailed
    with St. Brendan of yore,
He had lived ever since on the Isle and his winters
    were fifteen score.
    TENNYSON: *Voyage of Maeldune.*

**Brass. The Man of Brass.** Talus, the work of Hephaestus (VULCAN). He was the guardian of Crete and threw rocks at the ARGONAUTS to prevent their landing; he used to make himself red-hot, and then hug intruders to death.

**Brawn. The test of the brawn's head** (boar's head). In *The Boy and the Mantle* (Percy's *Reliques*), a little boy came to the court of King ARTHUR and brought in a

boar's head saying 'there never was a cuckold's knife that could carve it'. No knight in
the court except Sir Cradock was able to
accomplish the feat.

> He brought in the boar's head,
> And was wondrous bold
> He said ther was never a cuckold's knife,
> Carve itt that cold.

**Brazen. Brazen head.** The legend of the
wonderful head of brass that could speak
and was omniscient, found in early
romances, is of Eastern origin. Ferragus in
VALENTINE AND ORSON is an example but the
most famous in English legend is that fabled
to have been made by the great Roger
Bacon. It was said if Bacon heard it speak
he would succeed in his projects; if not, he
would fail. His familiar, Miles, was set to
watch, and while Bacon slept the Head
spoke thrice: 'Time is'; half an hour later it
said, 'Time was'. In another half-hour it
said, 'Time's past', fell down and was
broken to atoms. Byron refers to this
legend.

> Like Friar Bacon's head, I've spoken,
> 'Time is', 'Time was', 'Time's past'.
> *Don Juan*, i, 217.

References to Bacon's brazen head are
frequent in literature. Most notable is
Robert Greene's *Honourable History of
Friar Bacon and Friar Bungay*, 1594.
Other allusions are:

> Bacon for his brazen head.
> POPE: *Dunciad*, III, 104.

> Quoth he, 'My head's not made of brass,
> As Friar Bacon's noddle was.'
> BUTLER: *Hudibras*, II, i.

*See also* SPEAKING HEADS.

**To brazen it out.** To stick to an assertion
knowing it to be wrong; to outface in a
shameless manner; to disregard public
opinion.

**Break. Breaking a Stick.** Part of the marriage ceremony of certain North American
Indians, as breaking a wineglass is part of
the marriage ceremony of the Jews.

One of Raphael's pictures shows an unsuccessful suitor of the Virgin Mary breaking his stick. This alludes to the legend that
suitors were each to bring an almond stick
to be laid up in the sanctuary overnight.
The owner of the stick which budded was
to be accounted the suitor approved by
God. It was thus Joseph became the husband of Mary.

**Brèche de Roland** (bresh). A deep defile in
the crest of the Pyrenees, some three
hundred feet wide. The legend is that
ROLAND, the PALADIN, cleft the rocks in two
with his sword DURANDAL, when he was set
upon by the Gascons at RONCESVALLES.

**Br'er Fox, he lay low.** A hint that silence in
speech or action is the wise course. The
expression was in fairly common use in the
early 1900s and was derived from the
popular stories, largely concerning Br'er
Fox and Br'er Rabbit, by the American
writer Joel Chandler Harris (1848–1908).
These animal stories in the Negro dialect,
which began to appear in 1879, were
supposedly told to a plantation owner's little
boy by Uncle Remus, a kindly old Negro.

**Briareus** (brīeə'riəs), or **Aegeon.** A giant
with fifty heads and a hundred hands.
Homer says the gods called him Briareus,
but men called him Aegeon (*Iliad*, I, 403).
He was the offspring of HEAVEN and Earth
and was one of the race of TITANS, against
whom he fought in their war with ZEUS.

> He [Ajax] hath the joints of everything, but every-
> thing so out of joint that he is a gouty Briareus,
> many hands and no use, or purblind Argus, all
> eyes and no sight.
> SHAKESPEARE: *Troilus and Cressida*, I, ii.

**Bride. Bride of the Sea.** Venice; so called
from the ancient ceremony of the wedding
of the sea by the Doge, who threw a ring
into the Adriatic saying, 'We wed thee, O
sea, in token of perpetual domination.' This
took place annually on Ascension Day, and
was enjoined upon the Venetians in 1177 by
Pope Alexander III, who gave the Doge a
gold ring from his own finger in token of the
Venetian fleet's victory over Frederick
Barbarossa, in defence of the Pope's
quarrel. At the same time his Holiness
desired the event to be commemorated
each year.

**Bridge. Bridge of Gold.** According to a
German tradition, CHARLEMAGNE's spirit
crosses the Rhine on a golden bridge at
Bingen, in seasons of plenty, to bless the
vineyards and cornfields.

> Thou standest, like imperial Charlemagne,
> Upon thy bridge of gold.
> LONGFELLOW: *Sonnets, Autumn*.

**Bridge of Jehennam.** Another name for
AL SIRAT.

**Brinvilliers, Marquise de** (brinvē'yā) (*c.* 1630–1676), a notorious French poisoner. She married the Marquis in 1651 and became the mistress of the Seigneur de Sainte Croix in 1659. Her father secured the latter's consignment to the Bastille by *lettre de cachet*, where Sainte Croix learnt the use of poison (probably AQUA TOFANA). Together they plotted revenge and she poisoned her father in 1666 and two brothers in 1670. Her crimes were discovered when Sainte Croix died of accidental poisoning in 1672, and the Marquise was duly beheaded and burned.

**Brioche** (brēosh'). A kind of pâtisserie made with flour, butter and eggs. The French phrase *Qu'ils mangent de la brioche*, popularly translated as 'Let them eat cake', has been commonly, but apocryphally, attributed to Queen Marie Antoinette. The remark was said to have been occasioned at the time of the bread riots at Paris (October 1789) when she was told that the starving populace could not afford bread. The saying in various forms has also been attributed to Yolande, duchesse de Polignac; the Princess Victoire; Queen Maria Theresa and others, but seems to have a considerably earlier ancestry. It is also said that Princess Charlotte (1796–1817), daughter of the then Prince Regent (later George IV), avowed that she would for her part 'rather eat beef than starve' and wondered why the people should insist on bread when it was so scarce.

**Briseis** (brī'sēis). The patronymic name of Hippodamia, daughter of Briseus. She was the cause of the quarrel between AGAMEMNON and ACHILLES, and when the former robbed Achilles of her, Achilles withdrew from battle and the Greeks lost ground daily. Ultimately, Achilles sent his friend PATROCLUS to supply his place; he was slain, and Achilles, towering with rage, rushed to battle, slew HECTOR, and TROY fell.

**Britomart** (brit'ōmaht). In Spenser's *Faerie Queene*, a female knight, daughter of King Ryence of Wales. She is the personification of chastity and purity; encounters the 'savage, fierce bandit mountaineer' without injury, and is assailed by 'hag and unlaid ghost, goblin and swart fairy of the mine', but 'dashes their brute violence into sudden adoration and blank awe'. She finally marries ARTEGAL.

Spenser which means 'sweet maiden', from Britomartis, a Cretan NYMPH of Greek mythology, who was very fond of the chase. King MINOS fell in love with her, and persisted in his advances for nine months, after which she threw herself into the sea.

**Brobdingnag** (brob'dingnag). In Swift's *Gulliver's Travels*, the country of the giants, to whom Gulliver was a pigmy 'not half so big as a round little worm plucked from the lazy finger of a maid'. Hence the adjective, *Brobdingnagian*, colossal.

**Brontes** (bron'tēz). A blacksmith personified; in Greek mythology, one of the CYCLOPS. The name signifies *Thunder*.

**Brownie.** The home spirit in Scottish superstition. He is called in England ROBIN GOODFELLOW. At night he is supposed to busy himself on little jobs for the family over which he presides. Brownies are brown or tawny spirits and farms are their favourite abode.

**Bruin. Sir Bruin.** The bear in the famous mediaeval beast-epic, REYNARD THE FOX.

**Brunhild** (broon'hild). Daughter of the King of Islant, and of superhuman physique, beloved by GUNTHER, one of the two great chieftains in the NIBELUNGENLIED. She was to be won by strength, and SIEGFRIED contrived the matter but Brunhild never forgave him for his treachery.

**Brut** (broot). A rhyming chronicle of British history beginning with the mythical Brut, or BRUTE, and so named from him. Wace's *Roman de Brut*, or *Brut d'Angleterre* is a rhythmical translation of Geoffrey of Monmouth's *History*, with additional legends. Wace's work formed the basis of Layamon's *Brut* (early 13th century), a versified history of England from the fall of TROY to A.D. 698. (*See* ARTHURIAN ROMANCES.)

**Brute** (broot), or **Brutus.** In the mythological history of Britain the first king was Brute, the son of Sylvius (grandson of Ascanius and great-grandson of AENEAS). Having inadvertently killed his father, he first took refuge in Greece, and then in Britain. In remembrance of TROY he called the capital of his kingdom Troy Novant, now London.

**Brutus, Junius** (broo′təs, joo′niəs). In legend, the first consul of ROME, fabled to have held office about 509 B.C. He condemned to death his own two sons for joining a conspiracy to restore the banished TARQUIN. *See* JUNIUS.

**Bubastis.** The ancient capital of Lower Egypt named after Bast, the local cat-headed goddess. The Greeks identified her with ARTEMIS and the CAT was sacred to her.

**Bucca** (bŭk′ə). A GOBLIN of the wind, once supposed by Cornish people to foretell shipwrecks; also a sprite fabled to live in the tin mines.

**Bucephalus** (būsef′ələs) (bull-headed). A HORSE. The famous charger of Alexander The Great.

**Buckler.** *See* SHIELD.

**Bug.** An old word for GOBLIN, SPRITE, BOGY; probably from the Welsh *bwg*, a ghost. The word is used in the Bug Bible and survives in *bogle, bogy*, and in *bugaboo*, a monster or goblin, and *bugbear*, a scarecrow, or sort of HOBGOBLIN in the form of a bear.

> Warwick was a bug that feare'd us all.
> SHAKESPEARE: *Henry VI, Pt. III*, V, ii.

In common usage the word *bug* is applied to almost any kind of insect or germ, especially an insect of the creeping crawling sort, and notably the *bed bug*. Also it is colloquially used to refer to anyone 'bitten' with a particular craze or obsession, from the *love-bug* to the *money-bug*.
**Bug-eyed Monster.** Generic for the creatures of the science-fiction writers' imaginations, inhabitants of, or visitors from, outer space; from the American slang 'bug' (*i.e.* bulging) eyes. It is known as BEM to science-fiction addicts.

**Buggane.** *See* BOGGARD.

**Bull.** The bull is the primary mythological and sacrificial animal of pastoral and agricultural communities as the BEAR was of the hunters, and was worshipped from earliest times. It was a symbol of strength and virility and was often regarded as a divine incarnation.

The bull cult appears extensively in Sumero-Semitic religions as a sacred fertilizing power. The Celestial Bull

ploughed the furrow of the sky. Sky gods ride on the Bulls of Light.

The bull was the most venerated animal in Egypt; early kings called themselves bulls and later the Pharaoh was called 'the bull of his mother'. *See* APIS.

The bull sacrifice was central in Mithraic rites and Mithras is represented as either carrying, mastering or slaying the bull, releasing the sacred and fertilizing blood which was also used at baptism.

The roar and stamping of the bull represents thunder gods such as the Sumerian Dumuzi whose voice was the thunder, and the Phoenician and Canaanite Baal or Bel.

In Zoroastrianism the bull was the first created animal, from its soul came the germ of all later creation.

Jupiter Dolichenus and Dionysus Zagreus were associated with the bull in Greek and Roman myth. The Cretan bull was sent from the sea by Poseidon for King MINOS.

In Hinduism Agni is the Mighty Bull and INDRA takes the form of a bull in his fertile aspect. Siva rides the bull Nandin and the bull is the vital breath of Aditi. In the Vedas Rudra, both destructive and beneficent, is called a bull.

Celtic and pre-Celtic cults ascribed great power and importance to the bull and the animal was ritually killed for divination. For the DRUIDS the white bull was the chief sacrifice.

The Scandinavian THOR, as thunder god, has the bull as an attribute and the animal was also sacred to FREYJA as goddess of fertility.

The Hebrew Yahveh (Jahveh?) is the Bull of Israel and in Christianity the bull depicts brute force and is the emblem of the martyr St. Eustace.

**Bun.** Hot cross buns on Good Friday were supposed to be made of the dough kneaded for the HOST, and were marked with a cross accordingly. As they are said to keep for twelve months without turning mouldy, some persons still hang up one or more in their house as a 'charm against evil'. Hot cross buns are associated with the sacred cakes or consecrated bread in the rites of ISIS, and cakes offered to ARTEMIS were also marked with a cross.

The Greeks offered cakes with 'horns' on them to APOLLO, DIANA, HECATE and the

MOON. Such a cake was called a *bous*, and (it is said) never grew mouldy. The round bun represented the full moon, and the cross symbolized the four quarters.

> Good Friday comes this month: the old woman runs.
> With one a penny, two a penny 'hot cross buns',
> Whose virtue is, if you believe what's said,
> They'll not grow mouldy like the common bread.
> *Poor Robin's Almanack*, 1733.

**Bunch, Mother.** A noted London ale wife of the late 16th century, on whose name have been fathered many jests and anecdotes, and who is mentioned more than once in the drama of the period.

> Now, now, Mother Bunch, how dost thou? What dost frowne, Queen Gwyniver, dost wrinkle?
> DEKKER: *Satiromastix*, III, i.

*Pasquil's Jests, mixed with Mother Bunches Merriments* was published in 1604 and she is humorously described in the 'Epistle to the Merrie Reader':

> ... She spent most of her time in telling of tales, and when she laughed she was heard from Aldgate to the monuments at Westminster, and all Southwarke stood in amazement, the Lyons in the Tower, and the Bulls and Beares of Parish Garden roar'd louder than the great roaring Megge... She dwelt in Cornhill neere the exchange, and sold strong ale...and lived an hundred and seventy and five yeares, two days and a quarter, and halfe a minute.

Other books were named after her, such as *Mother Bunch's Closet newly Broke Open, containing rare secrets of art and nature, tried and experienced by learned philosophers, and recommended to all ingenious young men and maids, teaching them how to get good wives and husbands.*

**Bundle of Sticks.** AESOP, in one of his fables, shows that sticks one by one may be readily broken; not so when several are bound together in a bundle. The lesson taught is that 'Union gives strength'.

The bundle of rods with an axe or *Fasces*, the Roman symbol of absolute authority, was adopted by Mussolini's party. Hence the name FASCIST.

**Bungay.** *See* FRIAR BUNGAY.

**Bunyan, Paul.** A legendary hero of the lumber camps of the north-western U.S.A. His feats—such as cutting the Grand Canyon of the Colorado by dragging his pick behind him—are told and retold with embellishments by the lumbermen; some of them were collected in a curious volume entitled, *Paul Bunyan Comes West.*

**Bunyip.** According to Australian aboriginal folk-lore, a man-eating bellowing monster who drags his victims down to the bottom of the lake or swamp that he inhabits. It is also used to mean an 'impostor'.

**Burke.** To murder by smothering. So called from William Burke, an Irish navvy, who with his accomplice William Hare, used to suffocate his victims and sell the bodies to Dr. Robert Knox, an Edinburgh surgeon. Aided by their wives they lured fifteen people to their deaths before discovery. Hare turned King's Evidence and Burke was hanged in 1829.

**Burns' Night.** The evening of 25th January, the birthday of the Scottish poet Robert Burns (1759–1796). In Scotland it is a celebration for many accompanied by feasting and drinking, the haggis being a prominent dish on the bill of fare.

**Bursa** (Gr. a hide). So the citadel of Carthage was called. The tale is that when DIDO came to Africa she bought from the natives 'as much land as could be encompassed by a bull's hide'. The agreement was made, and Dido cut the hide into thongs so as to enclose a space sufficient for a citadel.

The following is a similar story: The Yakuts granted to the Russian explorers as much land as they could encompass with a cow's hide; but the Russians, cutting the hide into strips, obtained land enough for the port and town of Yakutsk.

The Indians have a somewhat similar tradition. The fifth incarnation of VISHNU was in the form of a DWARF called Vamen who obtained permission to have as much land as he could measure in three paces to build a hut on. The request was laughed at but granted; whereupon the dwarf grew so prodigiously that with three paces he encircled the world.

**Bury the Hatchet.** Let bygones be bygones. The 'GREAT SPIRIT' commanded the North American Indians, when they smoked their calumet or peace-pipe, to bury their hatchets, scalping-knives and war clubs, that all thought of hostility might be put out of sight.

> Buried was the bloody hatchet.
> Buried was the dreadful war club;

Buried were all warlike weapons,
And the war-cry was forgotten.
There was peace among the nations.
LONGFELLOW: *The Song of Hiawatha*, xiii.

**Bus. Busman's holiday.** There is a story that in the old horse-bus days a driver spent his holiday travelling to and fro on a bus driven by one of his pals. From this has arisen the phrase, which means to occupy one's spare or free time on the same or similar work to one's everyday occupation, *i.e.* a holiday in name only.

**Bush. Good wine needs no bush.** That which has real worth, quality or merit does not need to be advertised. An ivy-bush (in the ancient world sacred to BACCHUS) was once the common sign of taverns and ale and wine vendors.

Some ale-houses upon the road I saw,
And some with bushes showing they wine did draw.
*Poor Robin's Perambulations* (1678).

The proverb is a Latin one, and shows that the Romans introduced the custom into Europe. *Vino vendibili hedera non opus est* (Columella). It is also common to France (*Au vin qui se vend bien, il ne faut point de lierre*).

If it be true that good wine needs no bush, 'tis true that a good play needs no epilogue.
SHAKESPEARE: *As You Like It*, Epilogue.

Shakespeare does continue with words more encouraging to the modern advertiser: 'Yet to good wine they do use good bushes; and good plays prove the better by the help of good epilogues.'

**Bushido** (booshē'dō). The code of conduct of the Samurai of Japan. Courage, self-discipline, courtesy, gentleness and keeping one's word were among the virtues enjoined.

**Business tomorrow.** When the SPARTANS seized upon Thebes they placed Archias over the garrison. Pelopidas with eleven others banded together to put Archias to the sword. A letter giving full details of the plot was given to Archias at the banquet table but he thrust the letter under his cushion, saying 'Business tomorrow.' But long ere the sun rose he was dead.

**Busiris** (būsī'ris). A mythical king of Egypt who, in order to avert a famine, used to sacrifice to the gods all strangers who set foot on his shores. HERCULES was seized by him; and would have fallen a victim, but he broke his chain and slew the inhospitable king.

**Buttons.** A page whose jacket in front is remarkable for a display of small round buttons, as close as they can be fixed, from chin to waist. In the pantomime of CINDERELLA, Buttons, the page, is a stock character.

So at last Mrs. Casey, her pangs to assuage,
Having snapped off his buttonses, curried the page.
WALTER DE LA MARE: *Buttons.*

**Buzfuz** (bŭz'fŭz). Sergeant Buzfuz was the windy, grandiloquent counsel for Mrs Bardell in the famous breach of promise trial described in *Pickwick Papers*. He represented a type of barrister of the early 19th century, seeking to gain his case by abuse of the other side and a distortion of the true facts.

**Bycorne.** *See* BICORN.

**Byrsa.** *See* BURSA.

# C

**Caaba.** *See* KAABA.

**Cabbalist.** From the later MIDDLE AGES the cabbalists were chiefly occupied in concocting and deciphering charms, mystical anagrams, etc., by unintelligible combinations of letters, words and numbers; in searching for the PHILOSOPHER'S STONE; in prognostications, attempted or pretended relations with the dead, and suchlike fantasies.

**Cabiri** (kahbī'ri). Certain deities, probably of Phrygian origin, worshipped in Asia Minor, Greece and the islands. Samothrace was the centre of their worship, which involved scandalous obscenities. The traditional four deities are Axierus, Axiocersa, Axiocersus and Cadmilus who promoted fertility and safeguarded mariners.

**Cacodaemon** (kakōdē'mon) (Gr. *kakos daimon*). An evil spirit. Astrologers gave this name to the Twelfth House of HEAVEN, from which only evil prognostics proceed.

> Hie thee to hell for shame, and leave this world,
> Thou cacodemon.
>
> SHAKESPEARE: *Richard III*, I, iii.

**Cacus** (kā'kəs). In classical mythology, a famous robber, son of VULCAN, represented as three-headed and vomiting flames. He lived in Italy and was strangled by HERCULES for stealing some of his cattle. The curate of La Mancha says of Lord Rinaldo and his friends, 'They are greater thieves than Cacus' (*Don Quixote*).

**Cader Idris** (kad'er id'ris). *Cader* in Welsh means chair, and *Idris* is the name of one of the old Welsh giants. The legend is that anyone who passes the night in this 'chair' will either be a poet or a madman.

**Cadmus.** In Greek mythology, the son of AGENOR, King of Phoenicia and Telephassa, founder of THEBES (Boeotia) and the introducer of the alphabet into Greece. Legend says that, having slain the dragon which guarded the fountain of Dirce, in BOEOTIA, he sowed its teeth, and a number of armed men sprang up with intent to kill him. By the counsel of ATHENE, he threw a PRECIOUS STONE among them and they killed each other in the struggle to gain it, except five who helped to build the city. *See also* JASON.

**Cadmean letters** (kadmē'ən). The sixteen simple Greek letters, which CADMUS is supposed to have introduced from Phoenicia. *See also* PALAMEDES.

**Cadmean victory.** A victory purchased with great loss. The allusion is to the armed men who sprang from the dragon's teeth sown by CADMUS.

**Caduceus.** A white wand carried by Roman heralds when they went to treat for peace; the wand placed in the hands of MERCURY, the herald of the gods, with which, poets feign, he could give sleep to whomsoever he chose; wherefore Milton styles it his 'opiate rod' (*Paradise Lost*, XI, 133). It is generally pictured with two SERPENTS twined about it (a symbol thought to have originated in Egypt), and—with reference to the serpents of AESCULAPIUS—it was adopted as the badge of the Royal Army Medical Corps.

**Caerleon** (kah'lēən). The Isca Silurum of the Romans, about three miles N.E. of Newport in South Wales. It is the traditional residence of King ARTHUR, where he lived in splendid state, surrounded by hundreds of knights, twelve of whom he selected to be KNIGHTS OF THE ROUND TABLE. *See* CAMELOT.

**Calainos** (kəlī'nos). The most ancient of Spanish ballads. Calainos the Moor asked a damsel to wife; she consented on condition that he should bring her the heads of the three PALADINS of CHARLEMAGNE—RINALDO, ROLAND and OLIVER. Calainos went to Paris and challenged them. First Sir

Baldwin, the youngest Knight, accepted the challenge and was overthrown; then his uncle Roland went against the Moor and smote him.

**Calchas** (kal'kas). The famous Greek soothsayer in the TROJAN WAR who told the Greeks that the aid of ACHILLES was essential for the taking of the city, that IPHIGENIA must be sacrificed before the fleet could sail from AULIS, and that the siege would take ten years. He died of disappointment when beaten in a trial of skill by the prophet Mopsus.

**Caliburn** (kal'ibœn). Same as EXCALIBUR, King ARTHUR's well-known sword.

> And onward Arthur paced, with hand
> On Caliburn's resistless brand.
> SCOTT: *Bridal of Triermain*, xv.

**Calidore, Sir** (kal'idaw). In Spenser's *Faerie Queene* (Bk. VI) the type of courtesy, and the lover of 'fair Pastorella'. He is described as the most courteous of all knights, and is entitled the 'all-beloved'. He typifies Sir Philip Sidney or the Earl of Essex.

**Calliope** (kəlī'ōpi) (Gr. beautiful voice). Chief of the nine MUSES; the muse of epic or heroic poetry, and of poetic inspiration and eloquence. Her emblems are a stylus and wax tablets.

The name is also applied to a steam organ, making raucous music on steam whistles.

**Callisto and Arcas.** Callisto was an Arcadian NYMPH metamorphosed into a she-bear by JUPITER. Her son Arcas having met her in the chase, would have killed her, but Jupiter converted him into a he-bear, and placed them both in the heavens, where they are recognized as the Great and Little Bear. *See* BEAR.

**Calpe** (kal'pi). Gibraltar, one of the PILLARS OF HERCULES; the other, the opposite promontory in Africa (Jebel Musa, or Apes' Hill), was anciently called Abyla. According to one account these two were originally one mountain which HERCULES tore asunder; but some say he piled up each mountain separately.

The pack of hounds introduced into the peninsula by Wellington's officers is the *Calpe Hunt*.

**Calydon** (kal'idon). In classical geography, a city in Aetolia, near the forest which was the scene of the legendary hunt of the CALYDONIAN BOAR (*see* BOAR). Also in Arthurian legend, the name given to a forest in northern England.

**Calypso** (kəlip'sō). In classical mythology, the queen of the island Ogygia on which ULYSSES was wrecked. She kept him there for seven years and promised him perpetual youth and immortality if he would remain with her for ever. She bore him two sons and was inconsolable when he left. Ogygia is generally identified with Gozo, near Malta.

A **calypso** is a type of popular song developed by the people of Trinidad, improvised on topical subjects.

**Camacho** (kəmah'chō). A rich but unfortunate man in one of the stories in *Don Quixote*, who is cheated of his bride just when he has prepared a great feast for the wedding; hence the phrase **Camacho's wedding** to describe useless show and expenditure.

**Camarina.** *Ne moveas Camarinam* (Don't meddle with Camarina). Camarina, a lake in Sicily, was a source of malaria to the inhabitants, who, when they consulted APOLLO about draining it, received the reply, 'Do not disturb it.' Nevertheless, they drained it, and ere long the enemy marched over the bed of the lake and plundered the city. The proverb is applied to those who remove one evil, but thus give place to a greater—'leave well alone'.

**Cambalo's Ring.** Cambalo was the second son of CAMBUSCAN in Chaucer's unfinished *Squire's Tale*. He is introduced as Cambel in the *Faerie Queene*. The ring, which was given him by his sister Canace, had the virtue of healing wounds.

**Camber.** In British legend, the second son of BRUTE. Wales fell to his portion; which is one way of accounting for its name of Cambria.

**Camel.** Mohammed's favourite camel was Al Kaswa. The mosque at Koba covers the spot where it knelt when he fled from Mecca. He considered the kneeling of the camel as a sign sent by God, and remained at Koba in safety for four days. The swiftest of his camels was Al Adha, who is fabled to have performed the whole journey from Jerusalem to Mecca in four bounds, thereby gaining a place in heaven along with BORAK, Balaam's ass, Tobit's dog, and the DOG OF THE SEVEN SLEEPERS.

**Camelot** (kam'ilot). In British fable, the legendary spot where King ARTHUR held his court. It has been tentatively located at CAERLEON, the hill-fort known as Cadbury castle in Somerset, and Camelford in Cornwall, where the Duke of Cornwall resided in his castle of TINTAGEL, etc. The Cadbury site is the most probable. It is mentioned in Shakespeare's *King Lear*, II, ii, and Tennyson's *Idylls of the King* etc.

> On either side the river lie
> Long fields of barley and of rye,
> That clothe the wold and meet the sky;
> And through the field the road runs by
> To many-tower'd Camelot.
> TENNYSON: *The Lady of Shalott*.

**Camilla** (kəmil'ə). In Roman legend a virgin queen of the Volscians. She helped Turnus against AENEAS. Virgil (*Aeneid* VII, 809) says she was so swift that she could run over a field of corn without bending a single blade, or make her way over the sea without even wetting her feet.

> Not so when swift Camilla scours the plain,
> Flies o'er the unbending corn and skims along the main.
> POPE: *Essay on Criticism*, 372.

**Camlan, Battle of** (kam'lan). In Arthurian legend the battle which put an end to the KNIGHTS OF THE ROUND TABLE, and at which ARTHUR received his death wound from the hand of his nephew MODRED, who was also slain.

**Campaspe** (kampas'pi). A beautiful concubine, favourite of Alexander the Great, whom he handed over to APELLES, who it is said modelled his VENUS Anadyomene from her.

> Cupid and my Campaspe play'd
> At cards for kisses—Cupid paid.
> LYLY: Song from '*Campaspe*'.

**Campeador.** The CID.

**Cancer** (Lat. crab). One of the twelve signs of the ZODIAC, the Crab. It appears when the sun has reached its highest northern limit, and begins to go backward to the south; but like a crab the return is sideways (21 June to 23 July).

According to fable, JUNO sent Cancer against HERCULES when he combated the HYDRA of Lerna. It bit the hero's foot, but Hercules killed the creature, and Juno took it up to heaven.

**Candaules** (kandaw'lēz). King of Lydia about 710 to 668 B.C. Legend relates that he exposed the charms of his wife to GYGES, whereupon she compelled him to assassinate her husband, after which she married the murderer. Plato's version is that Gyges obtained possession of the queen by using the ring which made him invisible.

**Canephorus** (kanef'ərəs). A sculptured figure of a youth or maiden bearing a basket on the head. In ancient ATHENS the *canephori* bore the sacred things necessary at the feasts of the gods.

**Caora** (kah·aw'rə). A river described in Hakluyt's *Voyages*, on the banks of which dwelt a people whose heads grew beneath their shoulders. Their eyes were in their shoulders, and their mouths in the middle of their breasts. Ralegh, in his *Description of Guiana*, gives a similar account of a race of men. *Cp.* BLEMMYES.

**Cap. Capful of wind.** Olaus Magnus tells us that Eric, King of Sweden, was so familiar with evil spirits that whatsoever way he turned his cap the wind would blow, and for this he was called *Windy Cap*. The Laplanders drove a profitable trade in selling winds, and even so late as 1814, Bessie Millie of Pomona (Orkney), used to sell favourable winds to mariners for the small sum of sixpence.

**Capricorn** (kap'rikawn). Called by Thomson in his *Winter*, 'the centaur archer'. Anciently the winter SOLSTICE occurred on the entry of the sun into Capricorn, *i.e.* the Goat; but the stars having advanced a whole sign to the east, the winter now falls at the sun's entrance into SAGITTARIUS (the Centaur Archer), so that the poet is strictly right, though we commonly retain the classical manner of speaking. Capricorn is the tenth, or strictly, eleventh sign of the ZODIAC (21 December–20 January).

In classical mythology Capricorn was PAN, who, from fear of the great TYPHON, changed himself into a goat, and was made by JUPITER one of the signs of the Zodiac.

**Captain Moonlight.** In Ireland a mythical person to whom was attributed the performance of atrocities by night especially in the latter part of the 19th century. Arson, murder and the maiming of cattle were his specialities.

**Caradoc** (kərad'ok). A Knight of the ROUND TABLE, noted for being the husband of the only lady in the queen's train who could wear 'the mantle of matrimonial fidelity'. He appears as Craddocke in the old ballad *The Boy and the Mantle* in Percy's *Reliques. See* BRAWN.

> Craddocke called forth his ladye,
> And bade her come in;
> Saith, Winne this mantle, ladye,
> With a little dinne.

Also in history, the British king whom the Romans called Caractacus, who was taken captive to Rome in A.D. 51.

**Carpathian Wizard.** PROTEUS, who lived in the island of Carpathus (now Scarpanto), between Rhodes and Crete, and could transform himself into any shape he pleased. He is represented as carrying a sort of crook in his hand, because he was an ocean shepherd and had to manage a flock of sea-calves.

**Carpet. The magic carpet.** The apparently worthless carpet, which transported whoever sat upon it wheresoever they wished, is one of the stock properties of Eastern story-telling. It is sometimes *Prince Housain's carpet*, because of the popularity of the *Story of* PRINCE AHMED in the ARABIAN NIGHTS, when it supplies one of the main incidents; but the chief magic carpet is that of King SOLOMON which, according to the Koran, was of green silk. His throne was placed on it when he travelled, and it was large enough for all his forces to stand upon, the men and women on his right hand, and the spirits on his left. When ready, Solomon told the wind where he wished to go, and the carpet rose in the air, and landed at the place required. The birds of the air, with outspread wings, protected the party from the sun.

**Carvilia.** *See* MORGAN LE FAY.

**Casanova.** To be regarded as a 'regular Casanova' is to have a reputation for amorous escapades, in allusion to the notorious Giovanni Jacopo Casanova de Seingalt (1725–1798), who secured his own reputation as an insatiable amorist by the writing of his lengthy *Mémoires*. Expelled from a Venetian seminary for his immoral conduct, after a period in the household of Cardinal Acquaviva, he wandered the capitals of Europe mixing with aristocratic and wealthy society, posing as alchemist, preacher, gambler, diplomatist etc., and generally leading a vicious life. He was also a knight of the papal order of the Golden Spur, and was acquainted with Stanislaus Poniatowski and Frederick the Great, but he soon exhausted the goodwill of those around him and found it necessary to move on.

**Cassandra** (kəsan'drə). A prophetess. In Greek legend the daughter of PRIAM and HECUBA, gifted with the power of prophecy. She refused APOLLO's advances and he brought it to pass that no one believed in her predictions, although they were invariably correct. She appears in Shakespeare's *Troilus and Cressida*. In the figurative sense the name is usually applied to a prophet of doom.

**Cassiopeia** (kasiōpē'ə). In Greek mythology, the wife of CEPHEUS, King of Ethiopia, and mother of ANDROMEDA. In consequence of her boasting of her beauty, she was sent to the heavens as the constellation Cassiopeia, the chief stars of which form the outline of a woman sitting in a chair and holding up both arms in supplication.

**Castaly,** or **Castalia** (kas'təli, kastā'liə). A fountain of PARNASSUS sacred to the MUSES. Its waters had the power of inspiring with the gift of poetry those who drank of them.

**Castle Terabil,** or **Terrible,** in ARTHURIAN legend stood in Launceston, Cornwall. It had a steep keep environed with a triple wall. Sometimes called Dunheved Castle.

**Castor and Pollux** (kas'taw, pol'uks). In classical mythology, twin sons of JUPITER and LEDA, also known as the DIOSCURI. They had many adventures including sailing with JASON in quest of the GOLDEN FLEECE, were worshipped as gods, and finally placed among the constellations as the GEMINI.

Their names used to be given by sailors to the ST. ELMO'S FIRE, or CORPOSANT. If only one flame showed itself, the Romans called it HELEN, and said that the worst of the storm was yet to come; two or more luminous flames they called *Castor and Pollux*, and said that they boded the termination of the storm.

**Cat.** Called a 'FAMILIAR', from the mediaeval superstition that SATAN's favourite form was a black cat. Hence witches were said to have a cat as their familiar. The superstition may have arisen from the classical legend of Galenthias who was turned into a cat and became a priestess of HECATE.

In ancient Rome the cat was a symbol of liberty and the goddess of Liberty was represented with a cat at her feet. No animal is so opposed to restraint as a cat.

In Ancient Egypt the cat was held sacred. The goddess Bast (*see* BUBASTIS), representative of the life-giving solar heat, was portrayed as having the head of a cat, probably because that animal likes to bask in the sun. Diodorus tells us that in Egypt whoever killed a cat, even by accident, was punished by death. According to tradition DIANA assumed the form of a cat, and thus excited the fury of the GIANTS.

In Celtic saga there are Monster Cats to be fought by the hero, the cat taking the place of the DRAGON.

Cats draw the chariot of the Scandinavian FREYJA, goddess of love and fertility; the cat is also her attribute.

Amerindian myth has the Wild Cat as a Hunter God, younger brother of Coyote. The Wild Cat is also a totem of an Australian Aboriginal tribe.

The Hindu goddess of birth, Shosti, rides a cat as a symbol of the prolific. In China and Japan the cat is a shape-shifter and associated with powers of bewitching. The cat, with the venomous snake, is under a curse in Buddhism as they were the only two creatures who did not weep at the death of the Buddha.

Christianity connects the cat with SATAN, the Hell Cat, and with darkness and witches; the black cat is a witches' familiar.

**A cat has nine lives.** A cat is more tenacious of life than many animals, it is careful and hardy and after a fall generally lands upon its feet without injury, the foot and toes being well padded.

> Tyb: What wouldst thou have with me?
> Mer: Good king of cats, nothing but one of your nine lives.
>
> SHAKESPEARE: *Romeo and Juliet*, III, i.

A cat has nine lives, and a woman has nine cats' lives.
  FULLER: *Gnomologia*.

**Dick Whittington and his cat.** *See* WHITTINGTON.

**To fight like Kilkenny cats.** To fight till both sides have lost their all; to fight with the utmost determination and pertinacity. The story is that during the Irish rebellion of 1798 Kilkenny was garrisoned by a troop of Hessian soldiers, who amused themselves by tying two cats together by their tails and throwing them across a clothes-line to fight. When an officer approached to stop the 'sport', a trooper cut the two tails with a sword and the two cats bolted. When an explanation of the two bleeding tails was asked for, he was told that two cats had been fighting and devoured each other all but the tails.

**Catchpole, Margaret** (1773–1841). An almost legendary Suffolk character. She was the daughter of a farm labourer and eventually a servant of John Cobbold, the Ipswich brewer. According to the Revd. Richard Cobbold's *The History of Margaret Catchpole* (1845) she twice saved the lives of her employer's children but subsequently stole one of his horses and, dressed as a man, rode to London in ten hours. She intended to meet her lover, William Laud, a local sailor turned smuggler, but was captured and sentenced to death. Fortunately this was commuted to seven years imprisonment and she managed to escape to join Laud by scaling a twenty-two foot wall with the aid of a clothes line. Laud was shot dead in self defence by one of their pursuers, Margaret was caught and again sentenced to death but reprieved and transported to Botany Bay. There she duly established herself as a trusted and respectable character and by strange chance met up with John Barry, son of a Suffolk miller, now a very prosperous and influential settler, whose suit she had rejected formerly, thus causing him to emigrate. They married in 1812.

**Catherine, St.** Virgin and martyr of noble birth in Alexandria. She adroitly defended the Christian faith at a public disputation (*c.* 310) with certain heathen philosophers at the command of the Emperor Maximinus, for which she was put on a wheel like that of a chaff-cutter. Legend says that as soon as the wheel turned, her bonds were miraculously broken; so she was beheaded. Hence the name Catherine Wheel. She is the patron saint of wheel-wrights.

**Cecilia, St.** Patron SAINT of the blind and patroness of music and especially of Church music. Born in Rome, she is usually supposed to have been martyred in A.D. 230, but the date is uncertain. She was blind, and according to tradition, was inventor of the organ. An ANGEL fell in love with her for her musical skill; her husband saw the heavenly visitant, who gave to both a crown of martyrdom which he brought from PARADISE. Her day is 22 November, on which the Worshipful Company of Musicians, a livery company of the City of London, meet and go in procession for divine service in St. Paul's Cathedral. Both Dryden and Pope wrote odes in her honour.

> At length divine Cecilia came,
> Inventress of the vocal frame.
> DRYDEN: *Alexander's Feast*, 7.

**Celestial City.** HEAVEN is so called by John Bunyan in his *Pilgrim's Progress*.

**Centaur.** Mythological beast, half horse and half man. Centaurs are said to have dwelt in ancient Thessaly; a myth the origin of which is probably to be found in the expert horsemanship of the inhabitants. (*See* IXION.) The Thessalian centaurs were invited to a marriage feast and one of their number attempted to abduct the bride, whereupon conflict ensued and the centaurs were duly driven out of the country by the LAPITHAE. *See* CHIRON.

**Cephalus and Procris** (sef′ələs, prok′ris). Cephalus was husband of PROCRIS, who deserted him through jealousy. He went in search of her and rested awhile under a tree. Procris crept through some bushes to ascertain if a rival was with him and Cephalus, hearing the noise and thinking it was made by some wild beast, hurled his javelin into the bushes and slew Procris. When he discovered what he had done he slew himself with the same javelin.

> *Pyramus:* Not Shafalus to Procrus was so true.
> *Thisbe:* As Shafalus to Procrus, I to you.
>
> SHAKESPEARE: *Midsummer Night's Dream*, V, i.

**Cerberus** (sœ′bərəs). A grim, watchful keeper, house-porter, guardian etc. Cerberus according to classical mythology is the three-headed dog that keeps the entrance of the infernal regions. HERCULES dragged the monster to earth and let him go again. (*See* ACONITE.) ORPHEUS lulled Cerberus to sleep with his lyre and the SIBYL who conducted AENEAS through the INFERNO also threw the dog into a profound sleep with a cake seasoned with poppies and honey. (*See* SOP.)

The origin of the fable of Cerberus may be found in the custom of the ancient Egyptians of guarding graves with dogs.

**Cerealia** (sēriā′liə). Festivals in honour of CERES, celebrated by the Romans. First held in April, a second festival was introduced by Cicero in August.

**Ceres** (sē′rēz). The Roman name of MOTHER EARTH, the protectress of agriculture, and of all the fruits of the earth. She is the Corn Goddess and she had a daughter by JUPITER, called PROSERPINA. She is identified with the Greek DEMETER.

**Cestus** (ses′təs). The girdle of VENUS, made by her husband VULCAN; but when she wantoned with MARS it fell off, and was left on the 'Acidalian Mount'. It was of magical power to move to ardent love. By poetical fiction, all women of irresistible attraction are supposed to be wearers of Aphrodite's girdle, or the cestus.

The word is also used for the Roman boxing-glove composed of leather thongs wound round the hand and wrist, and sometimes loaded with iron.

**Chameleon.** The personification of Air in the Four Elements. Pliny says that it lived on air and that it changes to every colour except white, while Aristotle says that it varies only from black to green. Its changing colour is a symbol of inconstancy and changing fortunes. The eyes, which see independently, look into both the past and the future. In Christianity the chameleon depicts SATAN taking on different guises to deceive the faithful. In Africa it has magical properties and is a rain-bringer.

**Champak** (cham′pak). An Indian magnolia (*Michelia champaca*). The wood is sacred to BUDDHA, and the strongly scented golden flowers are worn in the black hair of Indian women.

> The Champak odours fail.
> SHELLEY: *Lines to an Indian Air*.

**Chamuel.** *See* ARCHANGEL.

**Chansons de Geste** (shã'sõ də zhest) (Fr.). Narrative poems dealing with the heroic families of French history and legend, and composed at various times between the 11th and 15th centuries. The famous *Chanson de Roland* is generally regarded as the finest. (*See under* ROLAND.) *Gestes* (Lat. *gesta*) is used to mean the deeds of a hero and the account of his deeds.

**Chanticleer.** The cock, in the tale of REYNARD THE FOX, and in Chaucer's *Nonnes Preestes Tale*; also in Rostand's play *Chantecleer*, produced in Paris in 1910 (Fr. *chanter clair*, to sing clearly).

**Chaonian Bird** (kāō'niən). This is the poetic name for a DOVE, and takes its origin from the legend that the dove bore the oracles of Chaonia.
**Chaonian food.** Acorns. So called from the acorns of Chaonia or DODONA. Some think beech-mast is meant, and tell us that the bells of the ORACLE were hung on beech-trees, not on oaks.

**Chariot.** According to Greek mythology, the chariot was invented by ERICHTHONIUS to conceal his feet, which were those of a dragon.

In mythology and legend the chariot represents the body with the driver as the directing intelligence and the team depicting the qualities, powers or intentions of the driver. Fiery chariots are driven by divinities or holy people and are involved in ascent to the heavens. The solar chariot is usually drawn by white or golden animals, such as the white horses of APOLLO, and lunar chariots are drawn by lunar animals, such as FREYJA's cats. POSEIDON/NEPTUNE has the white horses of the sea. Chariots and horses are attributes of such war gods as ARES/MARS.
**Chariot of the gods.** So the Greeks appear to have called Sierra Leone, in Africa, a ridge of mountains of great height; but some suggest the title applies to Mount Cameroon.

> Her palmy forests, mingling with the skies,
> Leona's rugged steep behind us flies.
> CAMOËNS: *Lusiad*, Bk. V.

**Chariots,** or **cars.** That of:

Admetus was drawn by lions and wild boars,
APOLLO by white horses,
CERES by winged dragons,
CYBELE by lions,
DIANA by stags, and ARTEMIS/DIANA by unicorns,
DIONYSUS/BACCHUS by panthers or goats,
EROS/CUPID by leopards or goats,
Flidass by deer,
FREYJA by cats,
HEPHAESTUS/VULCAN by dogs,
HERMES/MERCURY by cocks,
JUPITER Dolichenos by bulls,
JUNO by peacocks,
MEDUSA by winged dragons,
MITHRA by white horses,
PLUTO by black horses,
POSEIDON/NEPTUNE by white horses or Tritons,
Savitri by luminous horses,
SIVA by lunar gazelles or antelopes,
The SUN by seven horses (the days of the week),
THOR by rams or goats,
VENUS by doves,
ZEUS/JUPITER by eagles.

**Charlemagne** (shahl'mãn) (742–814). Charles the Great became sole king of the Franks in 771 and first Holy Roman Emperor in 800. He ruled over most of western Europe and was noted as a law-giver, administrator, protector of the Church and promoter of education. He was married nine times.

Charlemagne and his Paladins are the centre of a great series of chivalric romances. (*See* PALADIN.) We are told that he was eight feet tall and of enormous strength and could bend three horseshoes at once in his hands. He was buried at Aix-la-Chapelle (Aachen), but according to legend he waits, crowned and armed, in Oldenburg, Hesse, for the day when Antichrist shall appear; he will then go forth to battle and rescue Christendom. Another legend says that in years of plenty he crosses the Rhine on a BRIDGE OF GOLD, to bless the cornfields and vineyards.

**Charon** (keə'ron). In Greek mythology, the son of Erebus and Nox, the hideous old man who ferried the spirits of the dead over the rivers STYX and ACHERON for the fare of an *obolus*.
**Charon's Toll.** A coin placed in the mouth or hand of the dead by the ancient Greeks to pay Charon for ferrying the spirit across the rivers of the underworld to ELYSIUM.

**Charybdis** (kərib'dis). A whirlpool on the coast of Sicily. SCYLLA and Charybdis are employed to signify two equal dangers. Thus HORACE says an author trying to avoid

Scylla, drifts into Charybdis, *i.e.* seeking to avoid one fault, he falls into another.

The Homeric account says that Charybdis dwelt under an immense fig-tree on the rock, and that thrice every day he swallowed the waters of the sea and thrice threw them up again; but later writers have it that he stole the oxen of HERCULES, was killed by lightning, and changed into the gulf.

**Cheesewring, The Devil's.** A mass of eight stones towering to the height of thirty-two feet in the Valley of Rocks, Lynmouth, Devon, so called because it looks like a gigantic cheesepress.

**Chemosh** (kē'mosh). The national god of the Moabites; very little is known of his cult, but human beings were sacrificed to him in times of crisis.

> Next Chemos, the obscene dread of Moab's sons,
> From Aroer to Nebo and the wild
> Of southmost Abarim.
> MILTON: *Paradise Lost*, I, 406–8.

**Cheshire Cat. To grin like a Cheshire cat.** *See under* CAT.

**Chevy Chase.** There had long been a rivalry between the families of Percy and Douglas, which showed itself by incessant raids into each other's territory. Percy of Northumberland once vowed he would hunt for three days in the Scottish border, without condescending to ask leave of Earl Douglas. The Scots warden said in his anger, 'Tell this vaunter he shall find one day more than sufficient.' The ballad called *Chevy Chase* mixes up this hunt with the battle of Otterburn, which, Bishop Percy justly observes, was 'a very different event'. The ballad of *The Battle of Otterburn* is also given in Percy's *Reliques*.

**Chichevache** (chich'evash). A fabulous monster that lives only on good women, and was hence all skin and bone, because its food was so extremely scarce; the antitype to BICORN. Chaucer introduced and changed the word from the French *chichifache* (thin or ugly face) into *chichevache* (lean or meagre-looking cow).

> O noble wyves, ful of height prudence,
> Lat noon humylitee youre tonge naille,
> Ne lat no clerk have cause or diligence
> To write of yow a storie of swich mervaille
> As of Grisildis, pacient and kynde,
> Lest Chichivache yow swelwe in hire entraille.
> CHAUCER: *Lenvoy de Chaucer, Clerk's Tale*.

Lydgate wrote a poem called *Bycorne and Chichevache*.

**Chicken. Mother Carey's chickens.** *See* MOTHER.

**Children. Three hundred and sixty-five Children at a birth.** It is said that a countess of Henneberg accused a beggar of adultery because she carried twins, whereupon the beggar prayed that the countess might carry as many children as there are days in the year. According to the legend, this happened on Good Friday, 1276. All the males were named John, and all the females Elizabeth. The countess was forty-two at the time.

**The Children,** or **Babes in the Wood.** The story is that the master of Wayland Hall, Norfolk, left a little son and daughter to the care of his wife's brother; both were to have money, but if the children died first the uncle was to inherit. After twelve months the uncle hired two ruffians to murder the babes; one of them relented and killed his partner, leaving the children in a wood. They died during the night, and 'ROBIN REDBREAST' covered them over with leaves. All things now went ill with the wicked uncle; his sons died, his barns were fired, his cattle died, and he finally perished in gaol. After seven years the ruffian was taken up for highway robbery, and confessed the whole affair.

The ballad *The Children in the Wood* appears in Percy's *Reliques* and also in a crude *Melodrama*, printed in 1601 and attributed on the title-page to Rob Yarington, called *Two Lamentable Tragedies; the one of the murder of Maister Beech, a chandler in Thames-streete, etc. The other of a young child murthered in a wood by two ruffians, with the consent of his unkle*. It is uncertain which is earlier, the play or the ballad.

**Chilminar and Baalbek** (kilminah', bāl'bek). According to legend, two cities built by the Genii, acting under the orders of Jinn bin Jann, who governed the world long before ADAM. Chilminar, or the 'Forty Towers', is Persepolis. They were intended as lurking places for the Genii to hide in.

**Chimaera** (kimē'rə, kīmē'rə) (Gr. *chimaira*, a she-goat). A fabulous monster in Greek mythology. According to Homer it has a lion's head, a goat's body and a dragon's tail. It was born in Lycia and slain by BELLEROPHON. Hence the use of the name in English for an illusory fancy, a wild incongruous scheme.

**Chiromancy.** *See* PALMISTRY.

**Chiron** (kī'ron). The CENTAUR who taught ACHILLES, and many other heroes, music, medicine and hunting. JUPITER placed him in heaven among the stars as SAGITTARIUS.

Dante, in his INFERNO, gives the name to the keeper of the lake of boiling blood, in the seventh circle of HELL.

**Chloe** (klō'i). The shepherdess beloved by DAPHNIS in the Greek pastoral romance of Longus called *Daphnis and Chloe*, and hence a generic name in literature for a rustic maiden—not always of the artless variety.

In Pope's *Moral Essays* (ii) Chloe is intended for Lady Suffolk, mistress of George II, 'Content to dwell in decencies for ever'; and Prior uses the name for Mrs. Centlivre.

**Chriem-hild.** *See* KRIEMHILD.

**Christmas decorations.** The Roman festival of SATURN was held in December and the temples were decorated with greenery; holly was sacred to Saturn and was used in the SATURNALIA as a symbol of health and happiness; the DRUIDS are associated with MISTLETOE, and the Saxons used HOLLY and IVY. These customs have been transferred to the Christian festival. The holly or holy-tree is called Christ's thorn in Germany and Scandinavia, from its use in church decorations and its putting forth its berries about Christmas time. The early Christians gave an emblematic turn to the custom, referring to the 'righteous branch' and justifying it from *Isaiah* lx, 13: 'The glory of Lebanon shall come unto thee, the fir-tree, the pine-tree, and the box together, to beautify the place of my sanctuary.'

The decorated Christmas tree—the pine of ATTIS—was in use among the Romans and was introduced into England from Germany soon after Queen Victoria's marriage with Prince Albert of Saxe-Coburg-Gotha in 1840. SANTA CLAUS and his reindeer came to England at the same time.

**Christopher, St.** Legend relates that St. Christopher was a giant who one day carried a child over a brook, and said, 'Chylde, thou hast put me in gret peryll. I might bere no greater burden.' To which the child answered 'Marvel thou nothing, for thou hast borne all the world upon thee, and its sins likewise.' This is an allegory: Christopher means Christbearer; the child was Christ, and the river was the river of death.

**Cid** (sid). A corruption of *seyyid*, Arabic for lord. The title given to Roderigo or Ruy Diaz de Bivar (*c.* 1040–1099), also called El Campeador, the national hero of Spain and champion of Christianity against the MOORS. His exploits, real and legendary, form the basis of many Spanish romances and chronicles, as well as Corneille's tragedy *Le Cid* (1636).

**Cid Hamet Benengeli.** The suppositious author upon whom Cervantes fathered the *Adventures of Don Quixote*.

> If the two bad cassocks I am worth ... I would have given the latter of them freely as even as Cid Hamet offered his ... to have stood by.
> STERNE.

**Cincinnatus** (sinsinā'tus). A legendary Roman hero of about 500 to 430 B.C., who, after having been consul years before, was taken from his plough to be Dictator. After he had conquered the Aequians and delivered his country from danger, he laid down his office and returned to his plough.

**The Cincinnatus of the Americans.** George Washington (1732–1799).

**Cinderella** (sindərel'ə). Heroine of a fairy tale of very ancient, probably Eastern, origin, found in German literature in the 16th century and popularized by Perrault's *Contes de ma mère l'oye* (1697). Cinderella is drudge of the house, while her elder sisters go to fine balls. At length, a fairy enables her to go to the prince's ball; the prince falls in love with her, and she is found again by means of a glass slipper which she drops, and which will fit no foot but her own.

The glass slipper has been conjectured as a fur or sable slipper, supposedly from *pantoufle de vair* not *de verre*. Perrault's text of 1697 has '*de verre*', which is more in keeping with the story.

**Circe** (sœ'si). A sorceress in Greek mythology, who lived in the island of Aeaea. When

ULYSSES landed there, Circe turned his companions into swine, but Ulysses resisted this metamorphosis by virtue of a herb called MOLY, given him by MERCURY.

> Who knows not Circe,
> The daughter of the sun, whose charmed cup
> Whoever tasted, lost his upright shape,
> And downward fell into a grovelling swine?
> MILTON: *Comus*, 50–3.

**City. The City of Lanterns.** A supposititious city in Lucian's *Verae Historiae*, situated somewhere beyond the ZODIAC. *Cp.* LANTERN-LAND.

**The City of Legions.** Caerleon-on-Usk, where King ARTHUR held his court.

**The City of the Three Kings.** Cologne; the reputed burial place of the MAGI.

**Clavie. Burning of the Clavie** on New Year's Eve (old style) in the village of Burghead, on the southern shore of the Moray Firth. The clavie is a sort of bonfire made of casks split up. One of the casks is split into two parts of different sizes, and an important item of the ceremony is to join these parts together with a huge nail made for the purpose. Whence the name, from *clavus* (Lat.), a nail. Chambers in his *Book of Days* (vol. II, p. 789) minutely describes the ceremony and suggests that it is a relic of DRUID worship. The two unequal divisions of the cask possibly symbolize the unequal parts of the old and new year.

**Cleopatra and her pearl.** It is said that Cleopatra gave a banquet for Antony at Alexandria, the costliness of which excited his astonishment. When Antony expressed his surprise she took a pearl eardrop and dissolved it in her drink, the further to impress him.

A similar story is told of Sir Thomas Gresham when Queen Elizabeth I visited the Royal Exchange. He is said to have pledged her health in a cup of wine in which a precious stone worth £15,000 had been crushed to atoms.

Heywood refers to this in his play *If you know not me you know nobody* (1604):

> Here fifteen thousand pounds at one clap goes
> Instead of sugar; Gresham drinks the pearl
> Unto his queen and mistress.

**Clio** (klī'ō). One of the nine MUSES, the inventress of historical and heroic poetry, the Muse of history. Hence the pun, 'Can Clio do more than amuse?'

Addison adopted the name as a pseudonym, and many of his papers in the *Spectator* are signed by one of the four letters in this word, probably the initial letters of where they were written—of Chelsea, London, Islington, Office.

**Cloacina** (klōəsī'nə). (Lat. *cloaca*, a sewer). Goddess of sewers.

> Then Cloacina, goddess of the tide,
> Whose sable streams beneath the city glide,
> Indulged the modish flame: the town she roved,
> A mortal scavenger she saw, she loved.
> GAY: *Trivia, II*.

**Clootie. Auld Clootie.** OLD NICK (*see* NICK). The Scots call a cloven hoof a *cloot*, so that Auld Clootie is Old Clovenfoot.

> And maybe Tam, for a' my cants,
> My wicked rhymes an' drucken rants
> I'll gie auld Cloven Clootie's haunts
> An unco slip yet,
> An' snugly sit amang the saunts
> At Davie's hip yet!
> BURNS: *Reply to a Trimming Epistle*.

**Clotho** (klō'thō) (Gr. *klotho*, to draw thread from a distaff). One of the three FATES in classic mythology. She presided over birth and drew from her distaff the thread of life. *See* ATROPOS; LACHESIS.

**Cloven Foot. To show the cloven foot,** or **hoof.** *i.e.* to show a knavish intention; a base motive. The allusion is to SATAN, represented with the legs and feet of a goat. However disguised he could never conceal his cloven feet. *See* CLOOTIE.

**Club-bearer, The.** In Greek mythology, Periphetes, the robber of Argolis, is so called because he murdered his victims with an iron club.

**Cluricaune** (kloo'rikawn). An ELF in Irish folklore. He is of evil disposition and usually appears as a wrinkled old man. He has a knowledge of hidden treasure and is the fairies' shoemaker. Another name for him is LEPRECHAUN.

**Clym of the Clough** (klim, klŭf). A noted archer and outlaw, who, with Adam Bell and William of Cloudesley, forms the subject of a ballad in Percy's *Reliques*. The three became as famous in the north of England as ROBIN HOOD and LITTLE JOHN in the midland counties. They were presumed to have lived before Robin Hood and abode in Englewood Forest, near Carlisle. Clym of the Clough means Clement of the Cliff. He is mentioned in Ben Jonson's *Alchemist* (I, ii, 46).

**Clytemnestra** (klītimnes'trə). In Greek legend, the faithless wife of AGAMEMNON. She was a daughter of Tyndarus and LEDA. *See also* ELECTRA.

**Clytie.** In classical mythology an ocean NYMPH, in love with APOLLO. She was deserted by him and changed into the heliotrope or sunflower, which, traditionally, still turns to the sun, following him through his daily course.

**Cobalt.** From the Ger. *kobold*, a GNOME, the demon of the mines. This metal, from which a deep blue pigment is made, was so called by miners partly because it was thought to be useless and partly because the arsenic and sulphur, with which it was found in combination, had bad effects on their health and on the silver ores. Its presence was therefore attributed to the mine demon.

**Cock.** The cock was one of the chief sacrificial creatures and regarded as a guardian; it was often buried under foundations of building to ward off evil.

In Norse lore the golden cock Vithafmir, at the top of the Yggdrasil, guards against evil powers, but the underworld cock Fralar lives in VALHALLA to waken the heroes for the last battle.

Celtic myth associates the cock with underworld deities and the Mother Goddess Bride, and it was sacrificed on her day.

The cock maintains its guardian aspect in the Far East, and in China it wards off evil spirits and represents courage and fidelity, but also aggression. In Japan it is a Shinto symbol, standing on the drum which calls people to prayer in the temples. But in Buddhism it stands at the centre of the Round of Existence as pride and passion.

In Christianity the cock is associated with Christ's passion and the resurrection, and as connected with St. Peter it depicts human weakness and repentance. The Bestiaries call the cock Gallus and say that it is the only bird to be castrated. In classical mythology the cock was dedicated to APOLLO because it gives notice of the rising sun. It was also dedicated to MERCURY, because it summons men to business by its crowing; and to AESCULAPIUS, because

'early to bed and early to rise makes a man healthy'.

Muslim legend says that the Prophet found in the first HEAVEN a cock of such enormous size that its crest touched the second heaven. The crowing of this celestial bird arouses every living creature except man. When this cock ceases to crow, the Day of Judgment will be at hand.

Peter Le Neve (1661–1729), English antiquary, affirms that a cock was the warlike ensign of the GOTHS and therefore used in Gothic churches for ornament.

The weathercock is a very old symbol of vigilance. As the cock heralds the coming of day, so does the weathercock tell the wise man what the weather will likely be.

**A cock and bull story.** A long highly coloured or incredible story, a canard. It possibly derives from old fables in which cocks and bulls and other animals conversed. In Bentley's *Boyle Lecture* (1692) we find:

> That cocks and bulls might discourse, and hinds and panthers hold conferences about religion.

The 'hind and panther' allusion is an obvious reference to Dryden's poem of 1687 and 'cocks and bulls' probably had a well-known meaning at the time. The last words in Sterne's *Tristram Shandy* are:

> Lord! said my mother, what is all this story about? A Cock and a Bull, said Yorick—And one of the best of its kind, I ever heard.

The *Cock and Bull* inn sign is found in the 17th century and both *Cock* and *Bull* as separate signs were always popular. There is a story at Stony Stratford, Buckinghamshire that in the coaching days the London coach changed horses at the Bull Inn and the Birmingham coach at the Cock. From the exchange of jests and stories between the waiting passengers of both coaches the 'Cock and Bull' story is said to have originated.

The French equivalents are *faire un coq à l'âne* and *un conte de ma mère l'oie* (a mother goose tale). In Scotland a satire or rambling story was a *cockalayne* from the Fr. *coq à l'âne*.

**Nourish a cock, but offer it not in a sacrifice.** This is the eighteenth Symbolic Saying in the *Protreptics* of Iamblichus. The COCK was sacred to MINERVA, and also to the SUN and MOON, and it would be impious to offer a sacrilegious offering to the gods.

What is already consecrated to God cannot be employed in sacrifice.

**Apparitions vanish at cock-crow.** This is a Christian superstition, the cock being the watch-bird placed on church spires, and therefore sacred.

> The morning cock crew loud,
> And at the sound it [the Ghost] shrunk in haste away,
> And vanish'd from our sight.
> SHAKESPEARE: *Hamlet*, I, ii.

**Cock Lane Ghost.** A tale of terror without truth; an imaginary tale of horrors. In Cock Lane, Smithfield (1762), certain knockings were heard, which Mr. Parsons, the owner, declared proceeded from the ghost of Fanny Kent, who died suddenly. Parsons, with the hope of blackmail, wished people to suppose that she had been murdered by her husband. All London was agog with the story. Royalty and the nobility made up parties to go to Cock Lane to hear the ghost. Dr. Johnson and others of learning and repute investigated the alleged phenomena. Eventually it was found that the knockings were made by Parsons' eleven-year-old daughter rapping on a board which she took into her bed. Parsons was condemned to the pillory. *Cp.* STOCKWELL GHOST.

**Cockaigne, Land of** (kokān'). An imaginary land of idleness and luxury, famous in mediaeval story. Ellis in his *Specimens of Early English Poets* gives an early translation of a 13th-century French poem called *The Land of Cockaign* in which 'the houses were made of barley sugar cakes, the streets were paved with pastry, and the shops supplied goods for nothing'.

London has been so called, with punning reference to *cockney*. Boileau applies the name to Paris.

The name may well mean the 'land of cakes', ultimately from Lat. *coquere*, to cook. Scotland is called the 'land of cakes'.

**Cockatrice.** A fabulous and heraldic monster with the wings of a fowl, tail of a DRAGON, and head of a COCK; the same as BASILISK. Isaiah says, 'The weaned child shall put his hand on the cockatrice' den' (xi, 8), to signify that the most obnoxious animal shall not hurt the most feeble of God's creatures.

Figuratively, it means an insidious, treacherous person bent on mischief.

> They will kill one another by the look, like cockatrices.
> SHAKESPEARE: *Twelfth Night*, III, iv.

**Cocqcigrues. At the coming of the Cocqcigrues.** (kok'sēgroo). (More correctly *coquecigrues*.) Imaginary animals that have become labels for an idle story. The phrase *à la venue des cocquecigrues* used by Rabelais (*Gargantua*, Ch. V) means 'never'.

> 'That is one of the seven things', said the fairy Bedonebyasyoudid, 'I am forbidden to tell till the coming of the Cocqcigrues'.
> C. KINGSLEY: *The Water Babies*, ch. vi.

**Cocytus** (kosī'təs). One of the five rivers of HELL, which flows into the ACHERON. The word means the 'river of lamentation'. The unburied were doomed to wander about its banks for 100 years. *See* CHARON; STYX.

**Colbronde,** or **Colbrand.** The Danish giant slain by Guy of Warwick. 'By his death the land was delivered from Danish tribute.

> I am not Samson, nor Sir Guy, nor Colbrand,
> To mow 'em down before me.
> SHAKESPEARE: *Henry VIII*, V, iii.

**Colcannon Night.** HALLOWE'EN in parts of N.E. Canada, when it is traditional to eat this dish.

**Coldbrand.** *See* COLBRONDE.

**Cole, King.** A legendary British king, described in the nursery rhyme as 'a merry old soul' fond of his pipe, fond of his glass, and fond of his fiddlers three. Robert of Gloucester says he was father of St. Helena (and consequently grandfather of the Emperor Constantine). Colchester was said to have been named after him.

**Cologne** (kolōn'). **The Three Kings of Cologne.** The three Wise Men of the East, the MAGI, whose bones, according to mediaeval legend, were deposited in Cologne Cathedral.

**Colt-pixy.** A PIXY, PUCK or mischievous fairy. To *colt-pixy* is to take what belongs to the pixies, and is specially applied to the gleaning of apples after the crop has been gathered in.

**Columbine.** A stock character in old Italian comedy from about 1560 and transferred to English PANTOMIME. She was the daughter of PANTALOON and the sweetheart of HARLEQUIN, and, like him, was supposed to be invisible to mortal eyes. Columbina in Italian is a pet name for a lady-love, and means dove-like.

**Columbus's Egg.** An easy task once one knows the trick. The story is that Columbus, in reply to a suggestion that other pioneers might have discovered America had he not done so, is said to have challenged the guests at a banquet in his honour to make an egg stand on end. All having failed, he flattened one end of the egg by tapping it against the table and so standing it up, thus indicating that others might follow but he had discovered the way.

**Coma Berenices.** *See* BERENICE.

**Comazant** (kom'əzant). *See* CORPOSANT.

**Comus** (kō'məs) (Gr. *komos*, carousal). In Milton's masque of this name, the god of sensual pleasure, the son of BACCHUS and CIRCE.

In the masque, the elder brother is meant for Viscount Brackley, the younger brother is Thomas Egerton, and the lady is Lady Alice Egerton, children of the Earl of Bridgewater, at whose castle in Ludlow it was first presented in 1634. *See* SABRINA.

**Conchobar** (kong'kōə, kon'uə). In ancient Irish romance, son of Nessa, and king of ULSTER at the opening of the Christian era. He was uncle and guardian of CUCHULAIN and also responsible for the upbringing of DEIRDRE. He is said to have died of anger on the day of Christ's crucifixion.

**Consentes Dii** (konsen'tāz dē'ē). The twelve chief Roman deities, six male and six female, the same as the Athenian Twelve Gods:

JUPITER, APOLLO, NEPTUNE, MARS,
MERCURY, VULCAN, JUNO, DIANA,
MINERVA, VENUS, CERES, VESTA.

Ennius puts them into two hexameter verses:

Juno, Vesta, Minerva, Ceres, Diana, Venus, Mars,
Mercurius, Jovi', Neptunus, Vulcanus, Apollo.

Called *consentes*, says Varro.

Quia in consilium Jovis adhibebantur.
*De Lingua Latina*, vii, 28.

**Consenting Stars.** Stars forming configurations for good or evil. In *Judges* v, 20, we read that 'the stars in their courses fought against Sisera', *i.e.* formed unlucky or malignant configurations.

> ... Scourge the bad revolting stars
> That have consented unto Henry's death.
> SHAKESPEARE: *Henry VI, Pt. I*, I, i.

**Continence of a Scipio.** It is said that a beautiful princess fell into the hands of Scipio Africanus, and he refused to see her, 'lest he should be tempted to forget his principles'. Similar stories are told of many historical characters including Cyrus and Alexander.

**Cophetua** (kofet'ūə). An imaginary king of Africa who fell in love with Penelophon (Shakespeare's Zenelophon in *Love's Labour's Lost*, IV, i) and married her. They lived happily and were widely lamented at death. The story is given in the ballad *King Cophetua and the Beggar-Maid* in Percy's *Reliques* and is referred to in Shakespeare's *Romeo and Juliet* (II, i) and *Richard II* (V, iii).

**Coral.** The Romans used to hang beads of red coral on the cradles and round the necks of infants as a charm against sickness etc., and soothsayers held that it was a charm against lightning, whirlwind, shipwreck and fire. Paracelsus similarly advocated its use 'against fits, sorcery, charms and poison'. The bells on an infant's coral were a Roman Catholic addition to frighten away evil spirits.

> Coral is good to be hanged about the neck of children...to preserve them from the falling sickness. It has also some special sympathy with nature, for the best coral...will turn pale and wan if the party that wears it be sick, and it comes to its former colour again as they recover.
> SIR HUGH PLATT: *Jewel House of Art and Nature* (1594).

Sir Thomas Browne, *Pseudodoxica Epidemica*, V, xxiii, says:

> Though Coral doth properly preserve and fasten the Teeth in men, yet it is used in Children to make an easier passage for them; and for that intent is worn about their necks.

**Corineus.** A mythical hero in the suite of BRUTE, who conquered the giant GOEMAGOT, for which achievement the whole western horn of England was allotted to him. He called it Corinea, and the people Corineans from his own name. This is the legendary explanation of the name of the county of Cornwall. *See also* BELLERUS.

In meed of these great conquests by them got,
Corineus had that province utmost west
To him assyned for his worthy lot,
Which of his name and memorable gest,
He called Cornwall.
SPENSER: *Faerie Queene*, II, x.

**Cormoran.** The Cornish giant, who in the nursery tale fell into a pit dug by JACK THE GIANT-KILLER. For this doughty achievement Jack received a belt from King ARTHUR, with this inscription—

This is the valiant Cornish man
That slew the giant Cormoran.
*Jack the Giant-killer*

**Corn Dolly.** Customarily, when the last load of the corn harvest was carried home, a Corn Dolly (called in some areas a Kern Baby or Mel Doll) was made from the last sheaf and carried by one of those riding on top of the load. This female symbol of the Corn Spirit was hung in the farm kitchen until the next harvest.

**Cornucopia.** *See* AMALTHEA'S HORN.

**Coronis** (korō'nis). Mother of AESCULAPIUS by APOLLO, who slew her for her infidelity; also the daughter of Coronaeus, King of Phocis, changed by ATHENE into a crow to enable her to escape from NEPTUNE.

**Corposant.** The ball of fire which is sometimes seen playing around the masts of ships in a storm. So called from the Ital. *corpo santo*, holy body. To the Romans the phenomenon was known as CASTOR AND POLLUX, and it is also known as ST. ELMO'S FIRE, HELEN'S FIRE, and Comazant.

Upon the maintopgallant mast-head, was a ball of light, which the sailors call a corposant (*corpus sancti*), and which the mate had called out to us to look at ... for sailors have a notion that if the corposant rises in the rigging it is a sign of fair weather, but if it comes lower down there will be a storm.
R. H. DANA: *Two Years Before the Mast*, ch. XXIV.

**Corpse Candle.** The IGNIS FATUUS is so called by the Welsh because it was supposed to forbode death, and to show the road the corpse would take. The large candle used at LICH WAKES was similarly named.

When any Christian is drowned in the river Dee, there will appear over the water where the corpse is, a light, by which means they do find the body: and it is therefore called the Holy Dee.
AUBREY: *Miscellanies* (1721), p. 179.

**Corroboree.** A dance practised by Australian aborigines on festal or warlike occasions; hence any hilarious or slightly riotous assembly.

He roared, stamped, and danced corrobory, like any blackfellow.
KINGSLEY: *The Water-Babies*, ch. viii.

**Cortina** (Lat. cauldron). The tripod of APOLLO, which was in the form of a cauldron; hence any tripod used for religious purposes by the ancient Romans.

**Corybantes** (koriban'tēz). The Phrygian priests of CYBELE, whose worship was celebrated with orgiastic dances and loud, wild music. Hence a wild, unrestrained dancer is sometimes called a *corybant*. In 1890 Prof. T. H. Huxley referred to the members of the Salvation Army as being 'militant missionaries of a somewhat corybantic Christianity'.

**Corycian Cave** (koris'iən). A cave on Mount PARNASSUS named after the NYMPH Corycia. The MUSES are sometimes in poetry called Corycides or the Corycian Nymphs.

The immortal Muse
To your calm habitations, to the cave
Corycian...will guide his footsteps.
AKENSIDE: *Hymn to the Naiads*.

**Corydon** (kor'idon). A conventional name for a rustic, a shepherd; a brainless lovesick fellow; from the shepherd in Virgil's *Eclogue* vii, and in Theocritus.

**Cottus** (kot'əs). One of the hundred-handed giants, son of URANUS (HEAVEN) and GAEA (Earth). His two brothers were BRIAREUS and Gyes.

**Cotytto** (kotī'tō). The Thracian goddess of immodesty and debauchery, worshipped at Athens with licentious rites. *See* BAPTES.

Hail! goddess of nocturnal sport,
Dark-veiled Cotytto.
MILTON: *Comus*, 128, 129.

**Course.** Another course would have done it. A little more would have effected our purpose. It is said that the peasants of a Yorkshire village tried to wall in a cuckoo in order to enjoy an eternal spring. They built a wall round the bird, and the cuckoo just skimmed over it. 'Ah!' said one of the peasants, 'another carse would 'a' done it'.

**Court fools.** *See* FOOL.

Coventry. Peeping Tom of Coventry. *See* GODIVA.

**To send someone to Coventry.** To take no notice of him; to make him feel that he is in disgrace by ignoring him. It is said that the citizens of Coventry once had so great a dislike of soldiers that a woman seen speaking to one was instantly tabooed; hence when a soldier was sent to Coventry he was cut off from all social intercourse. Clarendon, in his *History of the Great Rebellion*, says that Royalist prisoners captured in Birmingham were sent to Coventry, which was a Parliamentary stronghold.

Coverley. Sir Roger de Coverley. A member of an imaginary club in the *Spectator*, 'who lived in Soho Square when he was in town'. Sir Roger is the type of an English squire in the reign of Queen Anne.

The country dance of this name (or rather the *Roger of Coverly*) was well known before Addison's time.

Cow. The cow, representing both the lunar goddesses and the nourishing Earth Mother, is equally celestial and chthonic. In Egypt it was pre-eminently the Great Mother Hathor, also Nut, the Celestial Cow, the horns being the crescent moon. The Syrian ASTARTE and the Babylonian ISHTAR were also depicted as cows with lunar horns.

Highly venerated in India, the cow is a sacred animal and the *Rig Veda* says it is 'not to be killed' (hence the phrase 'sacred cow' for something sacrosanct); it was revered from Indo-Iranian times as a source of life and nourishment. Vedic Earth Mothers were also associated with it.

Herodotus says that the Libyans and Phoenicians sacrificed and ate oxen but not the sacred cow.

The cow appears frequently in Celtic mythology as a provider of perpetual nourishment, like the magic cows of Manannan which were always in milk.

In Scandinavia the Primordial Cow, the Nourisher, sprang from the ice and licked it to produce the first man. The cow that nourished YMIR with four streams of milk was called Audhumla.

The Amerindian White Buffalo Cow brought the Sacred Pipe to the people for their rites. In Zulu myth mankind was 'belched up by a cow'.

**The whiter the cow, the surer it is to go to the altar.** The richer the prey, the more likely it is to be seized. Pagan sacrifices demanded white cattle.

**Dun Cow, The Book of the Dun Cow, The Old Dun Cow.** *See under* DUN.

Crapaud. Les anciens crapauds prendront Sara. One of the cryptic prophecies of Nostradamus (1503–1566). Sara is *Aras* reversed, and when the French under Louis XIV took Arras from the Spaniards, this verse was remembered.

Crane. In mythology cranes are frequently messengers of the gods and are credited with great intelligence and vigilance; they were reputed to post sentries while they slept, the sentry holding a stone in its claw, if it fell asleep the stone dropped and woke the bird. Pliny and Aelian state this. When flying cranes form a triangle, the old in front and the young protected in the middle. Their discipline taught men the rules of government.

The crane is of great importance in Chinese myth, it is the Patriarch of the Feathered Tribe and a messenger of the gods. White cranes are particularly sacred and live in the Isles of the Blest. In Japan it is 'Honourable Lord Crane' and in both Chinese and Japanese fable it attains the age of 1,000 years or more.

Celtic lore gives the crane both a solar and underworld significance, it is associated with the solar deities but also with Pwyll, King of the Underworld.

The crane is always at enmity with dwarfs and the serpent.

Crescent. The crescent moon is par excellence the attribute of the Great Mother, the lunar Queen of Heaven and all lunar goddesses; it is also an emblem of the Sumerian moon god Sin, of Byzantium, Islam and the Turks. The crescent can be represented by either cows' or bulls' horns.

Tradition says that, 'Philip, the father of Alexander, meeting with great difficulties in the siege of Byzantium, set the workmen to undermine the walls, but a crescent moon discovered the design, which miscarried; consequently the Byzantines erected a statue to DIANA, and the crescent became the symbol of the state.'

Another legend is that Othman, the Sultan, saw in a vision a crescent moon, which kept increasing till its horns extended from east to west, and he adopted the crescent of his dream for his standard, adding the motto, '*Donec repleat orbem*'.

The crescent as a symbol was used by the Seljuk Sultan Ala-ud-din in the mid-13th century, and it was reputedly adopted from this source by Osman, who founded the Ottoman dynasty in *c.* 1281. It is also said that the crescent was placed on the Turkish flag by Mohammed II, after the capture of Constantinople in 1453.

**Cressida, or Cressid.** Daughter of Calchas, a priest, beloved by TROILUS. They vowed eternal fidelity and as pledges Troilus gave the maiden a sleeve, and Cressid gave the Trojan prince a glove. Scarce had the vow been made when an exchange of prisoners was agreed to. Diomed gave up three Trojan princes, and was to receive Cressid in lieu thereof. Cressid vowed to remain constant, and Troilus swore to rescue her. She was led off to the Grecian's tent and soon gave all her affections to Diomed— nay, even bade him wear the sleeve that Troilus had given her in token of his love.

> As false
> As air, as water, wind, or sandy earth,
> As fox to lambs, as wolf to heifer's calf,
> Pard to the hind, or step-dame to her son;
> 'Yea,' let them say, to stick the heart of falsehood,
> 'As false as Cressid'.
> SHAKESPEARE: *Troilus and Cressida*, III, i.

**Cresswell, Madam.** A notorious bawd and procuress who flourished in London between *c.* 1670 and 1684 and was much patronized by Restoration courtiers and politicians. She wintered in CLERKENWELL and kept house in Camberwell in the summer. 'Old Mother Cresswell' was not married, although Sir Thomas Player went by the nickname of Sir Thomas Cresswell. In her old age she became religiously inclined and bequeathed £10 for a funeral sermon, in which nothing ill should be said of her. Scott attributes the sermon to the Duke of Buckingham.

> 'Why,' said the Duke, 'I had caused the little Quodling to go through his oration thus—"That whatever evil reports had passed current during the lifetime of the worthy matron whom they had restored to dust that day, malice itself could not deny that she was born well, married well, lived well, and died well; since she was born in Shadwell, married to Cresswell, lived in Camberwell, and died in Bridewell."'
> *Peveril of the Peak*, ch. xliv.

**Crete. Cretan Labyrinth.** *See* LABYRINTH.
**The infamy of Crete.** The MINOTAUR.

> At the point of the disparted ridge lay stretch'd
> The infamy of Crete, detested brood
> Of the feigned heifer.
> DANTE: *Hell*, xii (*Cary's Translation*).

**Crispin and Crispianus.** Shoemakers who became patron saints of their craft. It is said that the two brothers born at Rome, went to Soissons in France to propagate the Christian religion, and they maintained themselves wholly by making and mending shoes. They were martyred in *c.*286.
**St. Crispin's Day.** 25 October, the day of the battle of Agincourt. Shakespeare makes Crispin Crispian one person, and not two brothers. Hence Henry V says to his soldiers:

> And Crispin Crispian shall ne'er go by—
> But we in it shall be remembered.
> *Henry V*, IV, iii.

**St. Crispin's holiday.** Every Monday, with those who begin the working week on Tuesday, still a common practice with some butchers, fishmongers etc.; a no-work day with shoemakers.
**St. Crispin's lance.** A shoemaker's awl.

**Crockett, Davy** (1786–1836). American folk hero famed as a marksman, bear hunter and fighter. He served under Andrew Jackson in the Creek War (1813–1814). His popularity led him to Congress where his natural wit and homespun stories made him a noted character. He was killed at the Alamo in 1836.

**Crocodile.** A symbol of deity among the Egyptians, because, says Plutarch, it is the only aquatic animal which has its eyes covered with a thin transparent membrane, by reason of which it sees and is not seen, as God sees all, Himself not being seen. To this he adds: 'The Egyptians worship God symbolically in the crocodile, that being the only animal without a tongue, like the Divine Logos, which standeth not in need of speech.' (*De Iside et Osiride*, vol. II, p. 381). Sebek is crocodile-headed and the animal is an attribute of SET in his typhonic aspect as evil; it is also an emblem of Apep, and SERAPIS and a crocodile is portrayed at the feet of Ptah.

Achilles Tatius says, 'The number of its teeth equals the number of days in a year.' Another tradition is that, during the seven

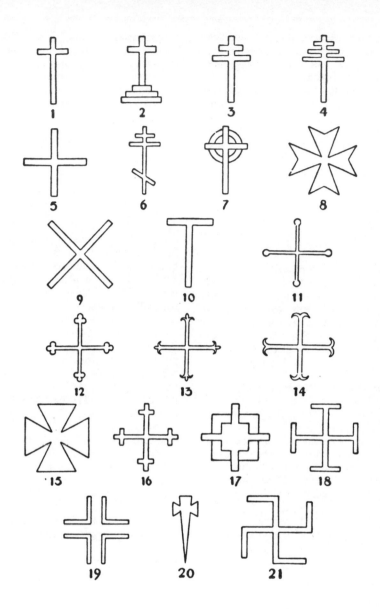

CROSSES.—1. Latin.  2. Calvary.  3. Patriarchal, Archiepiscopal, Lorraine.
4. Papal.  5. Greek.  6. Russian.  7. Celtic.  8. Maltese.  9. St. Andrew's.
10. Tau.  11. Pommé.  12. Botonné.  13. Fleury.  14. Moline.  15. Patté.
16. Crosslet.  17. Quadrate.  18. Potent.  19. Voided and couped.  20 Patté fiché.
21. Fylfot, Swastika.

days held sacred to APIS, the crocodile will harm no one. At Crocodilopolis in the Faiyum, he was worshipped under the name of Sebek or Sobek.

In Oceania the crocodile is worshipped as a god, but a dangerous one to be flattered and propitiated.

**Crocodile tears.** Hypocritical tears. The tale is that crocodiles moan and sigh like a person in deep distress, to allure travellers to the spot, and even shed tears over their prey while devouring it.

> As the mournful crocodile
> With sorrow snares relenting passengers.
> SHAKESPEARE: *Henry VI, Pt. II*, III, i.

**Cronos,** or **Cronus.** *See* KRONOS.

**Croquemitaine** (krokmētān'). A HOB-GOBLIN, an evil sprite or ugly monster, used by French nurses and parents to frighten children into good behaviour. In 1863 M. L'Epine published a romance with this title, telling the story of a god-daughter of CHARLEMAGNE whom he called 'Mitaine'. It was translated by Tom Hood (the younger).

**Cross.** The cross is not solely a Christian symbol originating with the crucifixion of the Redeemer. In Carthage it was used for ornamental purposes; runic crosses were set up by the Scandinavians as boundary marks, and were erected over the graves of kings and heroes. Cicero tells us (*De Divinatione*, ii, 27, and 80, 81) that the augur's staff with which they marked out the heaven was a cross; the Egyptians employed it as a sacred symbol, and two buns marked with a cross were discovered at Herculaneum. It was also a sacred symbol among the Aztecs; in Cozumel it was an object of worship; at Tabasco it symbolized the god of rain. It was one of the emblems of QUETZALCOATL, as lord of the four cardinal points, and the four winds that blow therefrom.

The cross of the crucifixion is said to have been made of palm, cedar, olive and cypress, to signify the four quarters of the globe.

In his *Monasteries of the Levant* (1848) Curzon gives the legend that Solomon cut down a cedar and buried it on the spot where the pool of Bethesda stood later. A few days before the crucifixion the cedar floated to the surface of the pool and was used as the upright of the Saviour's cross.

**Constantine's Cross.** It is said that Constantine on his march to Rome saw a luminous cross in the sky with the motto *In hoc vinces*, by this [sign] conquer. In the night before the battle of Saxa Rubra (312) he was commanded in a vision to inscribe the cross and motto on the shields of his soldiers. He obeyed the voice and prevailed. The LABARUM of Constantine was not really in the form of a cross but a monogram ☧ (XPI) formed of the first three letters of the word *Christ* in Greek. The legend of the Dannebrog is similar and there are others. The Scots are said to have adopted St. Andrew's cross because it appeared in the heavens the night before Achaius, King of the Scots, and Hungus, King of the Picts, defeated Athelstan.

**The Cross in heraldry.** As many as 285 varieties of cross have been recognized, but the twelve in ordinary use, from which the others are derived, are: (1) the ordinary cross; (2) the cross humetté, or couped; (3) the cross urdé, or pointed; (4) the cross potent; (5) the cross crosslet; (6) the cross botonné, or treflé; (7) the cross moline; (8) the cross potence; (9) the cross fleury; (10) the cross patté; (11) the Maltese cross (or eight-pointed cross); (12) the cross cleché and fitché.

**The tau cross** or **crux commissa.** The tau cross with a handle, or **crux ansata,** is common to several Egyptian deities as ISIS, OSIRIS etc.; and is the emblem of immortality and life generally. The circle on the top signifies the eternal preserver of the world, and the T is the monogram of THOTH, the Egyptian MERCURY, meaning wisdom.

**Crossbill.** The red plumage and curious crossing of the upper and lower bill-halves are accounted for by a mediaeval fable which says that these distinctive marks were bestowed on the bird by the Saviour at the Crucifixion, as a reward for its having attempted to pull the nails from the cross with its beak. The fable is best known to English readers through Longfellow's *Legend of the Crossbill*, a translation from the German of Julius Mosen.

**Crow.** Sacred to APOLLO who took the form of a crow when fleeing from TYPHON and to ATHENE, though she did not allow crows to alight on the Acropolis as a crow on a roof was an omen of death.

A black crow usually depicts ill-luck, but the white crow appears in Celtic myth as Branwen, sister of Bran. Fairies can take the forms of crows, usually with ill-intent.

The crow is important in Amerindian mythology where it is a totem creature, it is a keeper of the sacred law and a messenger to the spirit world, but it can also be a shape-shifter and an omen of change.

**Crown of Wild Olive.** The satisfaction of having performed a worthwhile task for its own sake rather than for gain. This crown was the only prize awarded to victors in the ancient OLYMPIC GAMES, the wild olive being held sacred from its having been first planted by HERCULES. John Ruskin has a book of this title, first published in 1866, which is a series of four essays or lectures on work, traffic, war and the future of ENGLAND.

**Cry. Crying the Mare.** *See* CRYING THE NECK.

**Crying the Neck.** Formerly, at the end of the harvest, especially in the north and west of England, the last sheaf of corn, the *Neck* (or the *Mare*) was held aloft by the leader or Harvest Lord, who shouted 'I have it! I have it! I have it!' The harvesters around him cried 'What have 'ee? What have 'ee? What have 'ee?'. The leader shouted back, 'A Neck! A Neck! A Neck!' The noise made it plain that the harvest on that particular farm was complete. There were numerous regional variants of these proceedings. *See* CORN DOLLY.

**Great cry and little wool.** A proverbial equivalent expressive of contempt for one who promises great things but never fulfils the promises—*i.e.* 'all talk and no do'. Originally the proverb ran, 'Great cry and little wool, as the Devil said when he sheared the hogs.' It appears in this form in the ancient MYSTERY of *David and Abigail*, in which Nabal is represented as shearing his sheep and the DEVIL imitates him by shearing a hog.

> Thou wilt at best but suck a bull,
> Or shear swine, all cry and no wool.
> BUTLER: *Hudibras*, I, i, 851.

**To cry wolf.** *See under* WOLF.

**Crystal Gazing,** or, as it is sometimes called, **Scrying,** is a very ancient form of DIVINATION. By gazing fixedly and deeply into a polished crystal ball, it was held that those possessing the gift could see what is about to happen or what was actually happening at some distant place etc. *To gaze into the crystal ball* is to see into the future, to seek inspiration or to answer questions. *See* CRYSTALLOMANCY.

**Crystallomancy.** DIVINATION by means of transparent bodies such as a crystal globe, polished quartz, and precious stones, especially a beryl. *See* CRYSTAL GAZING.

**Cuba.** The Roman deity who guarded infants in their cribs and sent them to sleep (Lat. *cubo*, I lie down in bed). *See* BABES, PROTECTING DEITIES OF.

**Cuchulain,** or **Cú Chulainn** (kookoo'lin). A legendary Irish hero, called the 'Hound of Culann' because, having accidentally slain the watchdog of the smith, Culann, in penance he had to take the animal's place. He was brought up in the court of King CONCHOBAR of Ulster, whose kingdom he defended single-handed against the Queen of Connaught. He is called Cuthullin by OSSIAN.

**Cuckold's Point.** A spot on the Thamesside near Deptford so called from a tradition that King John there made love successfully to a labourer's wife.

**Cuckoo.** The cuckoo was the kingly bird of the Phoenicians and was mounted on their sceptres. In Greece it was one of the transformations of ZEUS to win HERA and it figured on her sceptre.

In Hindu mythology the cuckoo represents the sun hidden by the clouds and thus the fertilizing rains. A cuckoo and bees accompany KAMA, god of love.

Cuckoo folklore and superstitions abound and are often tokens of the bird's popularity as a herald of spring. There are many old rhymes and proverbs about this bird; one says:

> In April the cuckoo shows his bill;
> In May he sings all day;
> In June he alters his tune;
> In July away he'll fly;
> In August go he must.

Also:

> Turn your money when you hear the cuckoo, and you'll have money in your purse till he come again.

And:

> The cuckoo sings from St. Tiburtius' Day (14 April) to St. John's Day (24 June).

**To wall in the cuckoo.** *See* COURSE.

**Cunning.** A Cunning Man or Woman was merely another name for a WIZARD, or WITCH. Hence the usual present meaning of sly and crafty.

**Cup. Divination by cup.** An ancient method of DIVINATION by floating certain articles on a cup of water and reading the signs. The practice survives in fortune-telling with a cup of tea. After the last of the liquid is disposed of, the arrangement of the sediment is examined for signs.
**The cup of vows.** In Scandinavia it was anciently customary at feasts to drink from cups of mead, and vow to perform some great deed worthy of the song of the skald. There were four cups: one to ODIN, for victory; one to FREYJA, for a good year; one to NIORD, for peace, and one to BRAGI, for celebration of the dead in poetry.
**There's many a slip 'twixt the cup and the lip.** Success is not always certain, things can go wrong at the last moment. *See* ANCAEUS.

**Cupid** (Lat. *cupido*, desire, love). The Roman god of love, identified with the Greek EROS. He is usually represented as a beautiful winged boy, blindfolded, and carrying a bow and arrows. There are varying legends of his parentage.
**Cupid and Psyche** (sī′ki). The story is told in the GOLDEN ASS of Apuleius. *See* PSYCHE.
**Cupid's golden arrow.** Virtuous love.
**Cupid's leaden arrow.** Sensual passion.

> Deque sagittifera promisit duo tela pharetra
> Diversorum operum; fugat hoc, facit illud amorem.
> Quod facit auratum est, et cuspide fulget acuta.—
> Quod fugat obtusum est, et habet sub arundine plumbum.
>     OVID: *Apollo and Daphne.*

> I swear to thee by Cupid's strongest bow;
> By his best arrow with the golden head...
> By that which knitteth souls and prospers love.
>     SHAKESPEARE: *Midsummer Night's Dream*, I, i.

**Curry Favour.** A corruption of the M.E. *to curry favel*, to rub down Favel: *Favel* (or *Fauvel*) being the name of the CENTAUR in the early 14th-century French satirical romance *Fauvel*. This fallow-coloured creature symbolizes cunning and bestial degradation; hence to curry, or smooth down, Favel, was to enlist the services of duplicity, and so to seek to obtain by in-sincere flattery, to ingratiate oneself by sycophantic officiousness etc.

**Curse. The curse of Tutankhamun.** A legend arising from the death of the 5th Earl of Carnarvon during the excavations at Tutankhamun's tomb. He died from pneumonia after an infection from a mosquito bite but Sir Arthur Conan Doyle, a convinced spiritualist, suggested that it might be attributed to elementals created by the priests of Tutankhamun. Coincidentally there was a power failure at Cairo when Carnarvon died and his dog in England expired at the same time. Howard Carter survived until 1939.

**Cut. Cut neither nails nor hair at sea.** Petronius says:

> Non licere cuiquam mortalium in nave neque ungues neque capillos deponere nisi cum pelago ventus irascitur.

The cuttings of the nails and hair were votive offerings to PROSERPINA, and it would excite the jealousy of NEPTUNE to make offerings to another in his own special kingdom.
**His life was cut short.** He died prematurely. The allusion is to ATROPOS, one of the three FATES, cutting the thread of life spun by her sister CLOTHO.
**To cut the knot.** To break through an obstacle. The reference is to the GORDIAN KNOT.

**Cuthbert. St. Cuthbert's Beads.** Single joints of the articulated stems of encrinites (fossil crinoids), also called *stone lilies*. They are perforated in the centre and bear a fanciful resemblance to a CROSS; hence they were once used for rosaries. Legend relates that the 7th-century St. Cuthbert sits at night on a rock in Holy Island and uses the opposite rock as an anvil while he forges the beads.

**Cutpurse. Moll Cutpurse.** The familiar name of Mary Frith (*c.* 1585–1660), a woman of masculine vigour, and who often dressed as one. In 1611 she was sentenced to do public penance by the Court of Arches for parading about FLEET STREET and the STRAND in male costume. She was a notorious thief and once attacked General Fairfax on Hounslow Heath, for which she was sent to Newgate. She escaped by bribery and finally died of dropsy. Middleton and

Dekker's *The Roaring Girle* is founded on her exploits.

**Cyanean Rocks, The** (sīān'iən). Two rocky islands at the entrance of the Euxine Sea, where the breakers make the passage very hazardous. It was anciently supposed that they floated and closed together to crush a vessel when it attempted to sail between them. *See* SYMPLEGADES.

**Cybele** (sib'ili). Mother goddess of Phrygia, also goddess of fertility and of the mountains. Commonly identified with AGDISTIS her favourite was ATYS and her priests were called CORYBANTES. She is also associated with DEMETER.

**Cyclops** (sī'klops) (Gr. circular-eye). One of a group or race of GIANTS. They had only one eye each and that in the centre of the forehead, and their work was to forge iron for VULCAN. Hesiod limits their number to three: Arges, Steropes and Brontes. *Cp.* ARIMASPIANS.

**Cygnus.** *See* PHAETON'S BIRD.

**Cylleneius** (sīlē'niəs). MERCURY. So called from Mount Cyllene, in Peloponnesus, where he was born.

**Cynthia.** The MOON; a surname of Artemis or DIANA, who represented the moon, and was called Cynthia from Mount Cynthius in Delos, where she was born.

The name was one of many applied to Elizabeth I by contemporary poets.

**Cypress.** A funeral tree; dedicated by the Romans to PLUTO, because when once cut it never grows again. It is said that its wood was once used for making coffins; hence Shakespeare's 'In sad cypress let me be laid' (*Twelfth Night*, II, iv). The Greeks and Romans put cypress twigs in the coffins of the dead and it is much associated with cemeteries. It was also traditionally the wood from which CUPID's arrows were made.

**Cyprian** (sip'riən). Cyprus was formerly famous for the worship of VENUS; hence the application of the adjective to lewd and profligate persons and prostitutes.

> A Night Charge at Bow Street Office; with other matters worth knowing, respecting the unfortunate Cyprian, the feeling Coachman, and the generous Magistrate.
> PIERCE EGAN: *Life in London*, Bk. II, ii.

**Cyrene** (sīrē'ni). A Thessalian nymph, daughter or granddaughter of the river god Peneus. She was carried off by APOLLO to the country which came to be called Cyrenaica, where she bore him a son named Aristaeus.

# D

**Dab, Din** etc.

Hab Dab and David Din
Ding the deil o'er Dabson's Linn.

'Hab Dab' (Halbert Dobson) and 'David Din' (David Dun) were Cameronians who lived in a cave near 'Dabson's Linn', a waterfall near the head of Moffat Water. Here, legend relates, they saw the DEVIL in the form of a pack of dried hides, and after fighting him for some time, they 'dinged' him into the waterfall.

**Dabbat** (Arab. *Dabbatu'l-ard*). In Muslim mythology the monster, reptile of the earth, that shall arise at the last day and cry that mankind has not believed in the Divine revelations.

By some it is identified with the Beast of the Apocalypse (*Rev.* xix, 19; xx, 10).

**Dactyls.** Mythical beings connected with the worship of CYBELE in Crete, supposed to be the discoverers of iron and copper; also called *Idoean Dactyls* (the fingers of IDA), after their mountain home. Their number is given as ten or more but was originally three—the Smelter, the Hammer, and the Anvil.

**Daedalus** (dē'dələs). A legendary Athenian, father of ICARUS, who formed the Cretan LABYRINTH and made wings, by means of which he flew from Crete across the archipelago. He is said to have invented the saw, the axe, the gimlet etc., and his name is perpetuated in our *doedal*, skilful, fertile of invention; *doedalian*, labyrinthine or ingenious.

**Daffodil.** Legend says that the daffodil, or Lent Lily was once white; but Persephone (PROSERPINA), who had wreathed her head with them and fallen asleep in the meadow, was captured by PLUTO and carried off in his chariot. She let fall some of the lilies and they turned to a golden yellow. Theophilus and Pliny tell us that they grow on the banks of ACHERON and that the spirits of the dead delight in the flower, called by them the ASPHODEL. In England it used to be called the Affodil (Fr. *asphodile*: Lat. *asphodelus*; Gr. *asphodelos*).

In the present century it has become an alternative to the LEEK as a Welsh emblem, because the leek was considered vulgar by some.

O Proserpina,
For the flowers now, that, frighted, thou lett'st fall
From Dis's waggon!—daffodils,
That come before the swallow dares, and take
The winds of March with beauty.
SHAKESPEARE: *Winter's Tale*, IV, iii.

**Dagon** (dā'gon). A Semitic god worshipped by the Philistines after their arrival in Canaan, supposed to have been symbolized as half man and half fish. Samson's vengeance on the Philistines occurred after their riotous celebrations to Dagon (*Judges* xvi, 23–30).

Dagon his name, sea-monster, upward man
And downward fish: yet had his temple high
Rear'd in Azotus, dreaded through the coast
Of Palestine, in Gath and Ascalon,
And Accaron and Gaza's frontier bounds.
MILTON: *Paradise Lost*, I, 462.

**Dagonet, Sir.** In ARTHURIAN ROMANCES, the fool of King Arthur, knighted by the king himself.

Dagonet was the name under which G. R. Sims (1847–1922) wrote his popular articles in *The Referee*.

**Daikoku** (dah·ē'kōkoo). One of the seven Japanese gods of luck. He is god of wealth and good fortune and is represented sitting on bags of rice.

**Damocles. The Sword of Damocles** (dam'əklēz). Impending evil or danger. Damocles, a sycophant of Dionysius the Elder, of Syracuse, was invited by the tyrant to try the felicity he so much envied. Accepting, he was set down to a sumptuous banquet, but overhead was a sword suspended by a hair. Damocles was afraid to stir, and the banquet was a tantalizing torment to him.

**Damon** (dā'mon). The name of a goatherd in Virgil's *Eclogues*, and hence used by pastoral poets for rustic swains. *Cp.* CORYDON.

**Damon and Pythias.** Models of devoted friendship. In the 4th century B.C. Pythias (correctly Phintias) was condemned to death by Dionysius, the tyrant of Syracuse, but obtained leave to go home to arrange his affairs after his friend Damon had agreed to take his place and be executed should Pythias not return. Pythias returned in time to save Damon, and Dionysius was so struck with this honourable friendship that he released both of them.

**Danace** (dan'ās). An ancient Persian coin, worth rather more than the Greek obolus, and sometimes placed by the Greeks in the mouth of the dead to pay CHARON'S TOLL.

**Danaë** (dan'ə̄ē). Daughter of Acrisius, King of Argos. He was told that his daughter's son would put him to death, and so resolved that Danaë should never marry. She was accordingly locked up in an inaccessible tower. ZEUS foiled the King by changing himself into a shower of gold, under which guise he readily found access to the fair prisoner, and she thus became the mother of PERSEUS.

**Danaides** (danā'idēz). The fifty daughters of Danaus, King of Argos. They married fifty sons of AEGYPTUS, and all but HYPERMNESTRA, wife of LYNCEUS, at the command of their father murdered their husbands on their wedding night. They were punished in HADES by having to draw water everlastingly in sieves from a deep well.

**Dance. Dance of Death,** or **Danse Macabre.** An allegorical representation of Death (usually a dancing skeleton or corpse) leading all sorts and conditions of men to the grave. It is first found in the 14th century, and there is a famous series of woodcuts on the subject by Hans Holbein the Younger (1497–1543). In the cloister of Old St. Paul's a 'Dance of Death' called the 'Dance of St. Paul's' was painted at the cost of John Carpenter, town clerk of London (15th century), with translations of French verses by John Lydgate. There is a copy in the Lambeth Palace library. W. H. Auden's poem *The Dance of Death* was published in 1933.

**Floral Dance,** or **Furry Dance.** *See* FURRY DANCE.

**Horn Dance.** *See* ABBOT'S BROMLEY.

**Morris Dance.** *See* MORRIS.

**Dances of the Ancient World.**

*Astronomical dances*, invented by the Egyptians, designed to represent the movements of the heavenly bodies.

*Bacchic dances* were of three sorts: grave (like the minuet), gay (like the gavotte), and a mixture of grave and gay.

*The Danse champêtre*, invented by PAN, quick and lively. The dancers (in the open air) wore wreaths of oak and garlands of flowers.

*Children's dances*, in Lacedaemonia, in honour of DIANA. The children were nude; and their movements were grave, modest and graceful.

*Corybantic dances*, in honour of BACCHUS, accompanied with timbrels, fifes, flutes and a tumultuous noise produced by the clashing of swords and spears against brazen bucklers.

*Funeral dances*, in Athens, slow, solemn dances in which the priests took part. The performers wore long white robes, and carried cypress slips in their hands.

*Hymeneal dances* were lively and joyous. The dancers were crowned with flowers.

*Jewish dances*. David danced in certain religious processions (II *Sam.* vi, 14). The people sang and danced before the golden calf (*Exod.* xxxii, 19). And in the book of *Psalms* (cl, 4) we read, 'Praise him with the timbrel and dance'. Miriam, the sister of Moses, after the passage of the Red Sea, was followed by all the women with timbrels and dances (*Exod.* xv, 20).

*Of the Lapithae*, invented by Pirithous. These were performed after some famous victory, designed to imitate the combats of the CENTAURS and LAPITHAE, and were both difficult and dangerous.

*May-day dances at Rome*. At daybreak lads and lasses went out to gather 'May' and other flowers for themselves and their elders; and the day was spent in dances and festivities.

*Military dances*. The oldest of all dances, executed with swords, javelins and bucklers. Said to be invented by MINERVA to celebrate the victory of the gods over the TITANS.

*Nuptial dances*. A Roman pantomimic performance representing the dances of our HARLEQUIN and COLUMBINE.

*Salic dances*, instituted by Numa Pompilius in honour of MARS. They were executed by twelve priests selected from the highest of the nobility, and were performed in the temple while sacrifices were being made and hymns sung to the god.

**Dancing-water.** A magic elixir, common to many fairy tales, which beautifies ladies, makes them young again and enriches them. In the Countess d'Aulnoy's *Contes des Fées* it fell in a cascade in the Burning Forest, and could only be reached by an underground passage. Prince Chery fetched a bottle of it for his beloved Fairstar, but was aided by a dove.

**Danesblood,** or **Danewort.** Dwarf elder (*Sambucus ebulus*), called Danesblood from a belief that it was supposed to flourish in places where there had been battles against the Danes; called Danewort because it is believed to have been introduced by the Danes.

**Dannebrog,** or **Danebrog.** (dan'ebrog). The national flag of Denmark (*brog* is Old Danish for cloth). The tradition is that Waldemar II of Denmark saw a fiery cross in the heavens which betokened his victory over the Estonians (1219). For similar legends of St. Andrew and Constantine *see* CONSTANTINE'S CROSS *under* CROSS.

**Daphne** (daf'ni). Daughter of the river-god Peneus in Thessaly, beloved by APOLLO. She had resolved to spend her life in perpetual virginity and fled from him, seeking the protection of the gods, who changed her into a LAUREL or BAY-tree. Apollo declared that henceforth he would wear bay-leaves instead of the oak, and that all who sought his favour should follow his example.

**Daphnis** (daf'nis). In Greek mythology, a Sicilian shepherd who invented pastoral poetry. He was a son of MERCURY and a Sicilian nymph and was protected by DIANA. He was taught by PAN and the MUSES.

Also the lover of CHLOE. Daphnis was the model of Allan Ramsay's *Gentle Shepherd* (1725), and the tale is the basis of Bernardin de St-Pierre's *Paul et Virginie* (1787).

**Dardanus.** A son of ZEUS and ELECTRA and legendary founder of the royal house of TROY. He eventually married Batea, daughter of King Teucer, who gave him land near Abydos where he established the town of Dardania or Dardanus. Hence the name *Dardanelles* for what was once called the HELLESPONT.

**Darius** (dərī'əs). A Greek form of Persian *dara*, a king, or of Sanskrit *darj*, the mountaineer. Darius the Great, son of

Hystaspes (Vishtaspa), governor of Persia, assumed the name when he became king in 521 B.C.

Legend relates that he conspired with six other Persian nobles to overthrow Smerdis, the usurper, and that they agreed that he should be king whose horse neighed first; and the horse of Darius was the first to neigh. His exploits are recorded on the rock of Behistun.

It is said that Darius III (Codomannus), the last king of the Persian empire, who was conquered by Alexander the Great (331 B.C.), sent for the tribute of golden eggs on Alexander's accession. The Macedonian replied: 'The bird which laid them is flown to the other world, where Darius must seek them.' The Persian king then sent him a bat and ball, in ridicule of his youth; but Alexander told the messengers, with the bat he would beat the ball of power from their master's hand. Lastly, Darius sent him a bitter melon as emblem of the grief in store for him; but the Macedonian declared that he would make the Persian eat his own fruit.

**Dart.** *See* ABARIS.

**David, St.,** or **Dewi Sant.** Patron SAINT of Wales, whose day is 1 March. Historical information is scanty. He lived in the 6th century and died *c.* 600, and as the chief bishop of South Wales moved the ecclesiastical centre from CAERLEON to Menevia (St. David's). Legend is far more prolific and says that he was the son of Xantus, prince of Cereticu (Cardiganshire, now in Powys), and became an ascetic in the Isle of Wight; that he visited Jerusalem, confuted Pelagius, and was preferred to the see of Caerleon. Geoffrey of Monmouth makes him the uncle of King ARTHUR.

**Davy. Davy Crockett.** *See* CROCKETT.

**Davy Jones.** An 18th-century sailor's term for the evil spirit of the sea. Of the many conjectures as to its derivation the most plausible are that Davy is a corruption of the West Indian *duppy* (devil) and that Jones is a corruption of Jonah, or that Davy Jones was a pirate.

**Davy Jones's Locker.** The sea, especially as the grave of drowned sailors.

**Davy's sow. Drunk as Davy's sow.** According to Grose (*Classical Dictionary of the Vulgar Tongue*), one David Lloyd, a

Welshman who kept an ale-house at Hereford, had a sow with six legs, which was an object of great curiosity. One day David's wife, having indulged too freely, lay down in the sty to sleep, and a company came to see the sow. David led them to the sty saying as usual, 'There is a sow for you! Did you ever see the like?' One of the visitors replied, 'Well it is the drunkenest sow I ever beheld.' Whence the woman was ever after called 'Davy's sow'.

**Dawson, Bully.** A noted London sharper, who swaggered and led a most abandoned life about Blackfriars in the reign of Charles II.

**Jemmy Dawson.** The hero of Shenstone's ballad of this name given in Percy's *Reliques*. James Dawson joined the Young Chevalier and was one of the Manchester rebels who were hanged, drawn and quartered on Kennington Common in 1746. A lady of gentle blood was in love with the gallant young rebel, and died of a broken heart after witnessing his execution.

> The dismal scene was o'er and past,
> The lover's mournful hearse retir'd;
> The maid drew back her languid head,
> And sighing forth his name expir'd.

**Dead. Book of the Dead.** *See under* BOOK.

**Dead Man's Hand.** In the western states of the USA, a combination of aces and eights in poker, so called because when Sheriff Wild Bill Hickok was shot in the back at Deadwood, S. Dakota, he held such cards in his hand.

It is said that carrying a dead man's hand will provide a dead sleep. Another superstition is that a lighted candle placed in the hand of a dead man gives no light to anyone but him who carries the hand. *See* HAND OF GLORY *under* GLORY; *Cp.* DEAD HAND.

**Dead Sea Fruit.** *See* APPLES OF SODOM.

**Deaf. Deaf as an adder.** 'Like the deaf adder that stoppeth her ear; which will not hearken to the voice of charmers: charming never so wisely' (*Ps.* lviii, 4, 5). In the East, if a viper entered the house, the charmer was sent for, who enticed the serpent and put it into a bag. According to tradition, the viper tried to stop its ears when the charmer uttered his incantation, by applying one ear to the ground and twisting its tail into the other.

**Death. Angel of Death.** *See* AZRAEL.

**Death from Strange Causes.**

*Aeschylus* was killed by a tortoise, dropped on his bald head by an eagle (Valerius Maximus, IX, xii, and Pliny, *History*, VII, vii).

*Anacreon* was choked by a grape-stone (Pliny, *History*, VII, vii).

*Bacon* died of a cold contracted when stuffing a fowl with snow as an experiment in refrigeration.

*Burton*, author of the *Anatomy of Melancholy*, died on the very day that he had himself astrologically predicted.

*Chalchas*, the soothsayer, died of laughter at the thought of having outlived the predicted hour of his death.

*Charles VIII*, of France, conducting his queen into a tennis-court, struck his head against the lintel, which caused his death.

*Fabius*, the Roman praetor, was choked by the presence of a single goat-hair in the milk which he was drinking (Pliny, *History*, VII, vii).

*Frederick Lewis, Prince of Wales*, son of George II, died from the blow of a cricketball.

*George, Duke of Clarence*, brother of Edward IV, was drowned in a butt of Malmsey.

*King John* is traditionally said to have died from a surfeit of lampreys but more probably from dysentery resulting from excessive fatigue and indulgence in food and drink.

*Lepidus* (*Quintus Aemilius*), going out of his house, struck his big toe against the threshold and died.

*Lully* (*Jean Baptiste*), the composer, when beating time by tapping the floor with his staff while directing a performance of the *Te Deum*, struck his foot and subsequently died from the abscess which set in.

*Otway*, the poet, in a starving condition, had a guinea given him, with which he bought a loaf of bread and died while swallowing the first mouthful.

*Philomenes* died of laughter at seeing an ass eating the figs provided for his own dessert (Valerius Maximus).

*Prince Philip*, eldest son of Louis VI of France, met his death when a pig ran between his horse's legs causing him to be thrown.

*William III* died from a fall from his horse which stumbled over a mole-hill.

**Death-bell.** A tinkling in the ears, supposed by the Scottish peasantry to announce the death of a friend.

O lay, 'tis dark, an' I heard the death-bell,
An' I darena gae yonder for gowd nor fee.
JAMES HOGG: *Mountain Bard.*

**Death coach.** A ghostly carriage, whose coachman is sometimes headless, which, in Irish and Breton superstition, is reputed to stop in front of a house where a death is about to occur.

**Death-watch.** Any species of *Xestobium*, a genus of wood-boring beetles, that make a clicking sound, once supposed to presage death.

**Death's head.** A skull. Bawds and procuresses used to wear a ring bearing the impression of a death's head in the time of Queen Elizabeth I.

Sell some of thy cloaths to buy thee a death's head, and put upon thy middle finger: your least considering bawd does so much.
MASSINGER: *The Old Law, IV, i.*

**Debon.** *See* DEVON.

**Dedalian.** *See* DAEDALUS.

**Deer.** In Greek mythology the deer was sacred to the moon goddesses ARTEMIS, APHRODITE, ATHENE and DIANA, but was also sacred to the solar APOLLO. Aristotle and Pliny say that if wounded by an arrow the deer finds the herb *dictanum* or *dittany* and this causes the arrow to be ejected from the body.

The Vedic god of the wind, Vayu, rides a deer. The deer is of particular significance in Buddhism as the Buddha preached his first sermon in the Deer Park at Sarnath which set the Wheel of the Law in motion.

The deer can take souls to the otherworld in Celtic myth and the chariot of Flidass, goddess of venery, is drawn by deer.

In Amerindian lore the deer plays an important part as the totem animal of several tribes, but in South America it can be a demonical animal incarnating sorcerers. It can also incarnate dead ancestors. The Aztec god of hunting, Mixcoatl, is accompanied by a two-headed deer.

**Déficit, Madame.** Marie Antoinette, because she was always in need of money. She was noted for her extravagance and popularly regarded as being responsible for the nation's bankruptcy. According to the Revolutionary song:

La Boulangère a des écus,
Qui ne lui comptent guère.
*See* BAKER.

**Deianira** (dēənī′rə). Wife of HERCULES and the unwitting cause of his death. NESSUS, the CENTAUR, having carried her across a river, attempted to assault her and was shot by Hercules with a poisoned arrow. The expiring centaur gave Deianira his tunic, steeped in blood, telling her that it would reclaim her husband from illicit loves. When she had occasion to give it to Hercules, the poisoned blood brought about his death.

**Deidamia** (dīdā′miə). Daughter of Lycomedes, King of Scyros. ACHILLES, when staying there disguised as a woman, became the father of her son Pyrrhus, or Neoptolemus.

**Deiphobus** (dīfō′bəs). Third husband of HELEN of Troy whom she married after the death of his brother PARIS. Helen betrayed Deiphobus to her first husband, MENELAUS who killed his rival.

**Deirdre** (diə′dri). In Irish romance the daughter of the king of Ulster's storyteller. At her birth it was prophesied that she would bring ruin to Ireland. King CONCHOBAR brought her up and planned to marry her, but she fell in love with Naoise, the eldest of the three sons of Usnech. She escaped to Scotland, with the three brothers but they were lured back by Conchobar with false promises. The jealous king killed the three young men. One version of the story says that Deirdre killed herself, another that she died the following year after living unhappily with Conchobar. Deirdre is the subject and title of a play by W.B. Yeats, and J.M. Synge also dramatized the legend in his *Deirdre of the Sorrows.*

**Deities.** The more important classical, Teutonic, and Scandinavian deities appear under their own names; the present list is only intended to include certain collective names and some better-known gods, sprites etc., of special localities, functions etc.

*Air.* ARIEL; *Elves* (*see* ELF).

*Caves* or *Caverns*: HILL-FOLK or Hill-people, Pixies (*see* PIXIE).
*Corn*: CERES (Gr. DEMETER).
*Domestic Life*: VESTA.
*Eloquence*: MERCURY (Gr. HERMES).
*Evening*: Vesper.
*Fairies. See* FAIRY.
*Fates*: (*q.v.*); NORNS.
*Fire*: VULCAN (Gr. Hephaistos), VESTA, MULCIBER.
*Furies*: (*q.v.*) (Gr. EUMENIDES, ERINYES).
*Gardens*: PRIAPUS; VERTUMNUS; POMONA.
*Graces: See under* GRACE (Gr. Charites).
*Hades* (*q.v.*): PLUTO with his wife PROSERPINA (Gr. Aidēs and Persephōne).
*Hills:* Pixies (*see* PIXIE), TROLLS; also Wood Trolls and Water Trolls.
*Home Spirits*: LARES AND PENATES.
*Hunting*: DIANA (Gr. Artemis).
*Justice*: THEMIS, ASTRAEA, NEMESIS.
*Love*: VENUS (Gr. APHRODITE), CUPID (Gr. EROS).
*Marriage*: HYMEN.
*Medicine*: AESCULAPIUS.
*Morning*: AURORA (Gr. EOS).
*Mountains*: OREADS, TROLLS.
*Ocean*: OCEANIDES. *See* SEA *below.*
*Poetry and Music*: APOLLO, the nine MUSES.
*Rainbow*: IRIS.
*Riches*: PLUTUS.
*Rivers and Streams*: Fluviales (Gr. Potamēides, NAIADS, Nymphs).
*Sea*: NEPTUNE (Gr. POSEIDON), TRITON, *Nixies*, MERMAIDS, NEREIDS.
*Shepherds and their flocks*: PAN, the SATYRS.
*Springs, Lakes, Brooks, etc.*: NEREIDS, NAIADS. *See* RIVERS, *above.*
*Time*: SATURN (Gr. KRONOS).
*Trees*: See WOODS, *below.*
*War*: MARS (Gr. ARES), BELLONA, THOR.
*Water-nymphs*: NAIADS, UNDINE.
*Winds*: AEŌLUS.
*Wine*: BACCHUS (Gr. DIONYSUS).
*Wisdom*: MINERVA (Gr. PALLAS, ATHENE, or PALLAS-ATHENE).
*Woods*: DRYADS (a Hamadryad presides over some particular tree), Wood Trolls.
*Youth*: HEBE.

**Delectable Mountains.** In Bunyan's *Pilgrim's Progress*, a range of mountains from which the 'CELESTIAL CITY' may be seen.

**Delos.** The smallest island of the Cyclades, sacred to APOLLO. It comes from the Greek word for a ring, as the rest of the islands encircle Delos. It was fabled to have been called out of the deep by POSEIDON, and remained a floating island until ZEUS chained it to the bottom of the sea. It was the legendary birthplace of Apollo and Artemis (DIANA).

**Delphi,** or **Delphos** (now Kastri). A town of Phocis at the foot of Mount PARNASSUS famous for a temple of APOLLO and for its celebrated oracle which was silenced only in the 4th century by the Emperor Theodosius. Delphi was regarded by the ancients as the 'navel of the earth', and in the temple there was a white stone bound with a red ribbon to represent the navel and umbilical cord.

In the *Winter's Tale* (the same play in which he gives Bohemia a sea-coast) Shakespeare makes Delphos an island.

**A Delphic utterance** is one which has the ambiguity associated with the words of the ORACLE.

> The president's broad wishes, as expressed in his periodic but carefully Delphic press conferences.
> *The Times*, 3 Jan. 1966.

**Deluge.** The Biblical story of the flood (*Gen.* vi, vii, viii) has its counterpart in a variety of mythologies. In Babylonia it appears in the 11th tablet of the GILGAMESH EPIC, but on a higher level of civilization, for Utnapishtim takes both craftsmen and treasure into his ark.

Apollodorus tells the story of DEUCALION AND PYRRHA in some versions of which Deucalion is replaced by Ogyges. (*See* OGYGIAN DELUGE.) The story is also found in Ovid's *Metamorphoses*, Bk. I, 253–415.

In India one legend tells how MANU was warned by a fish of the approaching flood and the fish subsequently towed his vessel to safety.

Kindred stories are found in China, Burma, New Guinea etc., and in both the American continents.

**Demeter** (demē'tər). The corn goddess of Greek legend, identified with the Roman CERES. She was the mother of Persephone (PROSERPINA) and the goddess of fruit, crops and vegetation.

**Demogorgon** (demōgaw'gon). A terrible deity, whose very name was capable of producing the most horrible effects. He is first mentioned by the 4th-century Christian writer, Lactantius, who in doing so broke with the superstition that the very reference to Demogorgon by name brought death and disaster.

> Must I call your master to my aid,
> At whose dread name the trembling furies quake,

Hell stands abashed, and earth's foundations shake?
ROWE: *Lucan's Pharsalia*, vi.

Milton speaks of 'the dreaded name of Demogorgon' (*Paradise Lost*, II, 966). According to Ariosto, Demogorgon was king of the elves and fays who lived on the Himalayas, and once in five years summoned all his subjects before him to give an account of their stewardship. Spenser (*Faerie Queene*, IV, ii, 47) says that he dwells 'down in the bottom of the deep abyss' with the three fatal sisters. In Dryden's *The Flower and the Leaf* (493) he appears as 'cruel Demogorgon' and in Shelley's *Prometheus Unbound* he is the eternal principle that ousts false gods.

**Demons, Prince of.** ASMODEUS, also called 'the Demon of Matrimonial Unhappiness'.

**Denmark.** According to the *Roman de la Rose*, Denmark means the country of Danaos, who settled there after the siege of TROY, as BRUTUS is said by the same sort of legend to have settled in Britain. Saxo Grammaticus (*c.* 1150–*c.* 1206) in his *Gesta Danorum*, with equal fancifulness, explains the name by making Dan, the son of Humble, the first king. His work is largely a collection of myths and oral tradition dealing with kings, heroes and national gods.

**Denys, St.** (dənē') or **St. Dionysius.** The apostle to the Gauls and a traditional patron saint of France, said to have been beheaded at Paris in 272. Legendarily, after martyrdom he carried his head in his hands for two miles and laid it on the spot where stands the cathedral bearing his name. The tale may have arisen from an ancient painting of his martyrdom in which the artist placed the head between the hands so that the martyr might be identified.

**Derrick.** A contrivance or form of crane used for hoisting heavy objects; so called from Derrick, the Tyburn hangman of the early 17th century. The name was first applied to the gibbet and, from its similarity, to the crane.

He rides circuit with the devil, and Derrick must be his host, and Tyborne the inn at which he will light.
DEKKER: *Bellman of London* (1608).

**Descent from animals.** A widespread theme in mythology, especially in tribal cultures, is that of descent from animals;

there are also numerous legends of marriage between humans and animals, such as the BEAR ancestor of the Mongols. The seal occurs as a Celtic ancestor; the WOLF in Ireland and the bear appears frequently in Irish and Welsh names. There are numerous animal tribes among the Amerindians. In India some families claim descent from the *nagas*. In Oceania various sea-creatures are progenitors and the same applies in Australian Aboriginal myth to the emu and other creatures and in Africa to the LEOPARD and HYENA, while in Madagascar cattle, sheep and even a moth can be ancestors.

**Desmas.** *See* DYSMAS.

**Despair.** Giant Despair, in Bunyan's *Pilgrim's Progress*, dwelt in DOUBTING CASTLE.

**Deucalion and Pyrrha** (dūkā'liən, pi'rə). Deucalion (the Greek counterpart of Noah) was a son of PROMETHEUS and married Pyrrha, daughter of Epimetheus. He was king of part of Thessaly. When ZEUS, angered at the evils of the Bronze Age (*see* AGE), caused the DELUGE, Deucalion built an ark to save himself and his wife, which came to rest on Mount PARNASSUS. Told by the ORACLE of THEMIS that to restore the human race they must cast the bones of their mother behind them (which they interpreted as the stones of Mother Earth), he and his wife obeyed the direction. The stones thrown by Deucalion became men and those thrown by Pyrrha became women.

And men themselves, the which at first were framed
Of earthly mould, and form'd of flesh and bone,
Are now transformed into hardest stone;
Such as behind their backs (so backward bred)
Were thrown by Pyrrha and Decucalione.
SPENSER: *Faerie Queene*, V, *Introd.*, ii.

**Devil, The.** Represented with a cloven foot, because by the Rabbinical writers he is called *seirizzim* (a goat). As the goat is a type of uncleanness, the prince of unclean spirits is aptly represented under this emblem. As the Prince of Evil he is also called SATAN.

**As the Devil loves holy water.** That is, not at all. HOLY WATER drives away the devil. The Latin proverb is, '*Sicut sus amaricinum amat*' (as swine love marjoram), which similarly means not at all, since

Lucretius, VI, 974, says, *'amaricinum fugitat sus'*.

**Between the Devil and the deep (blue) sea.** Between SCYLLA and CHARYBDIS; between two evils or alternatives, to be in a hazardous or precarious position. It is seemingly of nautical origin and means between the devil and the waterline of a ship. *See* THE DEVIL TO PAY AND NO PITCH HOT, *below*.

**Cheating the Devil.** Mincing an oath; doing evil for gain, and giving part of the profits to the Church etc. It is not unusual in monkish traditions. Thus the 'DEVIL'S BRIDGE', over the Fall of Reuss in Switzerland, is a single arch over a cataract. It is said that Satan knocked down several bridges but promised the abbot, Giraldus of Einsiedeln, to let this one stand, provided he would give him the first living thing that crossed it:

> The Abbot, standing at its head,
> Threw across it a loaf of bread,
> Which a hungry dog sprang after,
> And the rocks re-echoed with peals of laughter
> To see the Devil thus defeated!
> LONGFELLOW: *Golden Legend*, V.

Rabelais (*Pantagruel*, Bk. IV, ch. xlvi), says that a farmer once bargained with the Devil for each to have on alternate years what grew under and over the soil. The canny farmer sowed carrots and turnips when it was his turn to have the under-soil share, and wheat and barley the year following.

**The Devil and his dam.** The Devil and something worse. Dam here may mean *mother* or *wife* and numerous quotations may be adduced in support of either interpretation. Rabbinical tradition relates that LILITH was the wife of ADAM, but was such a vixen that Adam could not live with her, and she became the Devil's dam. We also read that BELPHEGOR 'came to earth to seek him out a dam'. In many mythologies the Devil is typified by an animal, and in such cases *dam* for mother is not inappropriate.

**The Devil catch the hindmost.** A phrase from late mediaeval magic. The Devil was supposed to have had a school at Toledo, or at Salamanca, where the students, after making certain progress in their mystic studies, were obliged to run through a subterranean hall, and the last man was seized by the Devil and became his imp. *See also under* SHADOW.

**The Devil dances in an empty pocket.** An old proverb. Poverty or an empty pocket leads to temptation or crime. Many coins bore a cross on the obverse and so the Devil could not gain entrance to the pocket if they were present.

**The Devil's Dandy Dogs.** A pack of fire-breathing hounds led by the Devil over the Moors of West England on stormy nights.

**The Devil's dancing-hour.** Midnight.

**The Devil's door.** A small door in the north wall of some old churches, which used to be opened at baptisms and communions to 'let the Devil out'. The north used to be known as 'the Devil's side', where SATAN and his legion lurked to catch the unwary.

**Devil's Dyke.** A ravine in the South Downs to the N.W. of Brighton. The legend is that St. Cuthman, priding himself on having christianized the area and having built a nunnery where the dyke-house was later built, was confronted by the Devil and told that all his labour was vain for he would swamp the whole country before morning. St. Cuthman went to the nunnery and told the abbess to keep the sisters in prayer till after midnight and then illuminate the windows. The Devil came at sunset with mattock and spade, and began cutting a dyke into the sea, but was seized with rheumatic pains all over his body. He flung down his tools, and the cocks, mistaking the illuminated windows for sunrise, began to crow; whereupon the Devil fled in alarm, leaving his work not half done.

**Devon.** The name is derived from the early CELTIC inhabitants, the Defnas. According to legend it is from Debon, one of the heroes who came with BRUTUS from TROY, and who was allotted this part of ALBION which was thus Debon's share.

> In meed of these great conquests by them gott,
> Corineus had that province utmost west, ...
> And Debon's shayre was that is Devonshyre.
> SPENSER: *Faerie Queene*, II, x, 12.

**Diamond. Diamond Jim.** Jim Brady, or more correctly James Buchanan Brady (1856–1917), American speculator and philanthropist, who started life as a bell-boy in a New York hotel. A well-known character in the night life of Broadway, he attracted attention and gained this nickname from the valuable and varied diamond ornaments with which he adorned his person.

**Diamond Jousts, The.** Jousts instituted by King ARTHUR 'who by that name had named them, since a diamond was the prize'. The story as embroidered by Tennyson in his *Lancelot and Elaine* (from Malory, Bk. XVIII) is that Arthur once picked nine diamonds from the crown of a slain knight and when he became king he offered them as a prize for nine successive annual jousts, all of which were won by Sir LANCELOT. The knight attempted to present them to Queen GUINEVERE but she flung them out of the casement into the river below, through jealousy of ELAINE.

**Diamond Necklace, The Affair of the.** A notorious scandal in French history (1784–1786) centring round Queen Marie Antoinette, Cardinal de Rohan, an ambitious profligate, and an adventuress, Jeanne, Countess de la Motte, who cleverly tricked Rohan by pretending to conduct for him a correspondence with the queen. Thus Rohan was induced to purchase for the queen (for 1,600,000 livres) the diamond necklace, originally intended for Madame du Barry, giving it to Jeanne de la Motte to pass to her. It was never delivered. When the jewellers, Boehmer and Bassenge of Paris, claimed payment, the queen denied all knowledge of the matter. The arrest of Rohan and Jeanne de la Motte followed. After a sensational trial, the Cardinal was acquitted and exiled to the abbey of *La Chaise-Dieu*, and the Countess was branded as a thief and consigned to the Salpêtrière, but subsequently escaped.

> That extraordinary 'Procès du Collier Necklace Trial', spinning itself through Nine other ever-memorable Months, to the astonishment of the hundred and eighty-seven assembled *parlementiers*.
> CARLYLE: *The Diamond Necklace* (1837).

**Diana.** An ancient Italian goddess identified with Artemis. Commonly regarded as a moon-goddess, on somewhat slender evidence, she was also the goddess of hunting and the woodlands. Associated with fertility, she was largely worshipped by women, and was invoked by the Romans under her three aspects. *Cp.* SELENE.

> Queen and huntress, chaste and fair,
> Now the sun is laid to sleep,
> Seated in thy silver chair,
> State in wonted manner keep.
> BEN JONSON: *Hymn to Diana.*

**Diana of Ephesus.** This statue, we are told, fell from heaven. She is represented with many breasts and with trunk and legs enclosed in an ornamental sheath. The temple of Diana of Ephesus was one of the Seven Wonders of the World (*see under* WONDER), with a roof supported by 127 columns. It was set on fire by Eratostratus for the sake of perpetuating his name.

**Diana's Worshippers.** Midnight revellers. So called because they return home by moonlight, and so, figuratively, put themselves under the protection of DIANA.

**Great is Diana of the Ephesians.** A phrase sometimes used to signify that self-interest blinds the eyes, from the story of Demetrius, the Ephesian silversmith in *Acts* xix, 24–28, who made shrines for the temple of DIANA. Demetrius stirred the people to riot, claiming that, 'this Paul hath persuaded and turned away much people, saying that they be no gods, which are made with hands: so that not only this our craft is in danger to be set at naught; but also that the great goddess Diana should be despised ...' Hence their cry 'Great is Diana of the Ephesians'.

**Diavolo, Fra.** Michele Pozza (1771–1806), an Italian brigand and enemy of the French occupation, renowned for his atrocities. He features in Auber's light opera of this name.

**Dick. Dick Turpin.** *See* TURPIN.

**Dick Whittington.** *See* WHITTINGTON.

**Dictys Cretensis** (dik'tis krēten'sis) (Dictys of Crete). A companion of Idomeneus at TROY and reputed author of an eyewitness account of the siege of Troy. The manuscript was probably written in the 2nd or 3rd century A.D. and translated into Latin in the 4th century. It is important as the chief source used by mediaeval writers on the Trojan legend.

**Dido** (dī'dō), also called Elissa, was the legendary daughter of Belus of Tyre and founder Queen of Carthage, after the murder of her husband Sichaeus by PYGMALION. According to Virgil's *Aeneid* she fell in love with Aeneas, who was driven by a storm to her shores, and committed herself to the flames through grief at his departure. Older legend says that she did it to avoid marriage with the king of Libya.

Porson said he could rhyme on any subject; and being asked to rhyme upon the
three Latin gerunds, which appeared in the
old Eton Latin grammar as *-di, -do, -dum,*
gave this couplet:

When Dido found Aeneas would not come,
She mourned in silence and was Di-do-dum(b).

**Dies nefastus** (dī'ēz nefas'təs) (Lat. *dies,*
day, *nefas,* that which is contrary to divine
law, sinful). An unlucky or inauspicious day.
For the Romans *Dies nefasti* were days on
which no judgment could be pronounced nor
any public business transacted.

**Dii Penates** (dī'i penā'tēz) (Lat.). Household gods; now colloquially used for specially prized household possessions. *See*
LARES AND PENATES.

**Dinos.** *See* FAMOUS HORSES *under* HORSE.

**Diomedes** (dīōmē'dēz), or **Diomed.** In
Greek legend, a hero of the siege of TROY,
second only to ACHILLES in bravery. With
ULYSSES he removed the PALLADIUM from
TROY. He appears as the lover of CRESSIDA
in Boccaccio's *Filostrato* and in later works.

Also the name of a king in Thrace, son of
ARES, who fed his horses on human flesh.
One of the labours of HERCULES was to
destroy Diomedes and his body was thrown
to his own horses to be devoured.

**Diomedean exchange.** One in which all
the benefit is on one side. The expression
is founded on an incident related in the
ILIAD. GLAUCUS recognizes Diomed on the
battlefield, and the friends change armour:

For Diomed's brass arms, of mean device,
For which nine oxen paid (a vulgar price),
He gave his own, of gold divinely wrought,
An hundred beeves the shining purchase bought.
POPE: *Iliad,* VI.

**Dione** (dīō'ni). Daughter of OCEANUS and
TETHYS and mother by JUPITER of VENUS.
Also applied to Venus herself; Julius
Caesar, who claimed descent from her, was
sometimes called *Dionaeus Caesar.*

So young Dione, nursed beneath the waves,
And rocked by Nereids in their coral caves, ...
Lisped her sweet tones, and tried her tender
smiles.
ERASMUS DARWIN: *Economy of Vegetation,* ii.

**Dionysius's Ear.** *See under* EAR.

**Dionysus** (dīōnī'səs). *See* BACCHUS.

**Dioscuri.** CASTOR AND POLLUX (Gr. *Dios
Kouroi,* sons of ZEUS).

**The horses of the Dioscuri.** Cyllaros and
Harpagus. *See* HORSE.

**Diphthera** (dif'thirə) (Gr.). A piece of prepared hide or leather; specifically the skin of
the goat AMALTHEA on which JOVE wrote
the destiny of man.

**Dirty Dick's.** A tavern in Bishopsgate,
London, the interior of which was festooned
with cobwebs and grimed with dirt. The
name was taken from the once famous *Dirty
Warehouse* in Leadenhall Street, owned by
Nathaniel Bentley (*c.* 1735–1809). Brought
up in easy circumstances and a frequent
visitor to Paris, he was known as the Beau
of Leadenhall Street, but suddenly his mode
of life altered completely to one of miserly
squalor and he came to be called 'Dirty
Dick'. His hardware store became famous
for its dirt and decay which increased with
the years and after his death some of its
contents were bought by the tavern keeper
to attract custom. Bentley's change from a
man of fashion to excessive slovenliness
was reputedly the consequence of a broken
engagement.

**Discord. Apple of Discord.** *See* APPLE.

**Dithyramb** (dith'iram) (Gr. *dithyrambos,* a
choric hymn). *Dithyrambic poetry* was originally a wild impetuous kind of Dorian lyric
in honour of BACCHUS, traditionally ascribed
to the invention of ARION of Lesbos who
gave it a more definite form (*c.* 600 B.C.)
and who has hence been called the father of
dithyrambic poetry.

**Divination.** There are numerous forms of
divination. The following appear in the
Bible:

ASTROLOGY (Judicial) (*Dan.* ii, 2).
CASTING LOTS (*See* LOTS) (*Josh,* xviii, 6).
HEPATOSCOPY (*Ezek.* xxi, 21–26).
ONEIROMANCY (*Gen.* xxxvii, 10).
NECROMANCY (I *Sam.* xxviii, 12–20).
RHABDOMANCY (*Hos.* iv, 12).
TERAPHIM (*Gen.* xxxi, *Zech.* x, 2).
WITCHCRAFT (I *Sam.* xxviii).

There are numerous other references in-
cluding divination by fire, air and water;
thunder, lightning, meteors etc. Consult:
*Gen.* xxxvii, 5–11; xl, xli; I *Sam.* xxviii; II
Kings xvii, 17; II *Chron.* xxxiii, 6; *Prov.*
xvi, 33; *Ezek.* xxi; *Hos.* iii, 4, etc. *See also*
ALECTRYOMANCY; AUGURY; AXINOMANCY;
BELOMANCY; BIBLIOMANCY; BOTANOMANCY;
CHIROMANCY; CRYSTALLOMANCY; DIVINATION

BY CUP *under* CUP; EMPYROMANCY; EXTISPICY; GEOMANCY; GYROMANCY; HARUSPEX; OMENS; PALMISTRY; PYROMANCY; RUNE; SIEVE AND SHEARS; SINISTER; SORTES; URIM AND THUMMIM; WITCH OF ENDOR; XYLOMANCY. *See also* ORACLE.

**Djinn.** *See* JINN.

**Djinnestan.** The realms of the jinns or genii of Oriental mythology.

**Dobby,** a silly old man, also a GOBLIN or house-elf. Like Dobbin, it is an adaptation of Robin, diminutive of Robert.

> The Dobby's walk was within the inhibited domains of the Hall.
> SCOTT: *Peveril of the Peak*, ch. x.

**Doctor Faustus.** *See* FAUST.

**Dodona** (dodō'nə). The site of a most ancient ORACLE of Epirus dedicated to ZEUS. The oracles were delivered from the tops of oak-trees, the rustling of the leaves being interpreted by the priests. The cooing of the sacred pigeons, and the clanging of brass plates suspended in the trees when the wind blew, gave further signs to the priests and priestesses. The Greek phrase *khalkos Dodones* (brass of Dodona), meaning a babbler, probably stems from this.

**The black pigeons of Dodona.** Two black pigeons, we are told, took their flight from Thebes, in Egypt; one flew to Libya, and the other to Dodona. On the spot where the former alighted, the temple of Jupiter AMMON was erected; in the place where the other settled the ORACLE of JUPITER was established, and there responses were made by the black pigeons that inhabited the surrounding groves. The fable is possibly based on a pun upon the word *peleiai* which usually meant 'old women', but in the dialect of the Epirots signified pigeons or doves.

**Dog.** Dogs were venerated in ancient times and there is evidence that they were domesticated in pre-dynastic Egypt in 7500 BC. The dog was sacred to ANUBIS who was depicted as dog- or jackal-headed; it was also sacred to the Great Mother Amenti and to HERMES, the messenger god.

The dog is the oldest animal-companion of humanity and acted as friend, guardian, hunter and herder, but in mythology it is ambivalent as being highly esteemed in some societies and despised in others. It can also be both solar and lunar in significance. Solar dogs chase away the BOAR of winter, are fire-bringers and destroy the enemies of light. Lunar dogs are associated with the moon goddesses such as ARTEMIS/DIANA, Lady of the Beasts and of the Hunt.

Sumero-Semitic myth varies: the dog was revered in Babylon; in Phoenician art it is associated with the SUN and is an emblem of Gala, the Great Physician. The Akkadian Belit-ili has her throne supported by dogs and the dog is also an attribute of ASTARTE or Ashtoreth. In some Semitic inconography it is associated with the scorpion and other baleful reptiles. This antipathy was carried over into Judaism where the dog is unclean, held in contempt and ritually taboo, except for *Tobit*, where Tobias has a dog companion. Islam also despises the dog.

Tacitus says that Heracles of the Assyrians was accompanied by a dog, as was the Tyrian HERCULES or Melcarth. Homer says that the dog is shameless and Greek myth uses the term 'cynic', or dog-like, as synonymous with flattery and impudence; but the dog is also beneficent and accompanies HERMES/MERCURY the messenger god, also the Good Shepherd, and is connected with Aesculapius or Asclepius, the great physician and healer. The dog also heals by bringing about rebirth into a new life. Its fidelity survives death.

The dog is greatly revered in Zoroastrianism where it is an integral part of Parsee life. In creation the dog ranks next to humans; it is the intermediary between this world and the next and guards the Cinvat Bridge.

The Vedic god of the dead, YAMA, is attended by two ferocious dogs who act as his messengers. INDRA has a hunting dog as companion and attribute. The hero of the Mahabharata refuses to enter heaven without his faithful dog.

The Chinese Celestial Dog is ambivalent as helping to drive off evil spirits, but is also associated with eclipses, comets and destruction and can carry off unprotected new-born children. The Buddhist Lion Dog is a guardian and defender of the Law.

In Celtic mythology the dog appears frequently with hunter gods and in Norse myth ODIN/WODEN has two dogs as messengers.

For Amerindians the dog is a guardian

and protector, represents loyalty and tolerates human failings. Dogs are essential companions of any Australian Aboriginal tribe. Among African tribes the dog is often a culture hero.

**St. Roch and his dog.** Emblematic of inseparable companions. *See* ROCH, ST.

**Aubry's Dog,** or **the Dog of Montargis.** Aubry of Montdidier was murdered in 1371 in the forest of Bondy. His dog Dragon excited suspicion of Richard of Macaire by always snarling and flying at his throat whenever he appeared. Richard, condemned to a judicial combat with the dog, was killed, and, in his dying moments, confessed the crime.

**Cuchulain's Hound.** Luath.

**Fingal's Dog.** BRAN.

**Geryon's Dogs.** Gargittios and the two-headed Orthos. Both were slain by HERCULES.

**Icarius's Dog.** Moera (the glistener). *See* ICARIUS.

**King Arthur's Favourite Hound.** Cavall.

**Llewelyn's Greyhound.** Gelert. *See* BEDDGELERT.

**Mauthe Dog.** *See* MODDEY DHOO.

**Montargis, Dog of.** AUBRY'S DOG.

**Orion's Dogs.** Arctophonos (bear-killer), and Ptoophagos (the glutton of Ptoon, in Boeotia).

**Procris's Dog.** Laelaps. *See* PROCRIS.

**Roderick the Goth's Dog.** Theron.

**Seven Sleepers, Dog of the.** Katmir who, according to Muslim tradition, was admitted to HEAVEN. He accompanied the seven noble youths (*see* SEVEN SLEEPERS) to the cavern in which they were walled up. He remained standing for the whole time, neither moving, eating, drinking nor sleeping.

**Tristran's Dog.** Hodain, or Leon.

**Ulysses's Dog.** Argos; he recognized his master after his return from TROY, and died of joy.

**Dog-whipping Day.** 18 October (St. Luke's Day). It is said that a dog once swallowed a consecrated wafer on this day.

**Dolphin.** Called the King of Fishes and the Arrow of the Sea. Pliny says the dolphin is the swiftest of all living creatures. It is a saviour and a psychopomp and in this world it saves the shipwrecked. It is regarded as kinder and more sensitive than humanity.

Telemachus and Arion were saved by dolphins.

Aelian says that dolphins are 'music-lovers'; in this aspect the dolphin is associated with APOLLO and dolphins were sculptured on his temple at DELPHI. Delphi was an omphalos and the name had a dual significance as *delphys*, the womb, and *delphis*, dolphin.

As King of the Fishes the dolphin was an emblem of POSEIDON/NEPTUNE as sea power, also of APHRODITE/VENUS, the 'woman of the sea'; it is also depicted as sea-power in Minoan art. The Nereids ride on dolphins and Thetis is depicted riding nude on a dolphin.

In Sumero-Semitic myth the dolphin can represent Ea-Oannes as god of the waters and can be connected with ASTARTE and ISHTAR. In Egypt the dolphin is an attribute of ISIS.

In Roman iconography cupids ride dolphins which also appear in funerary art as psychopomps, depicting the soul's journey over the sea of death.

Celtic lore connects the dolphin with well-worship and the power of the waters.

Early Christianity used the fish as a symbol of Christ and, in this aspect of bearing souls across the waters of death, the dolphin could be so represented.

Amerindian fable has the dolphin as a messenger between this world and the next; it can also be the essence of the Great Spirit. In South America the river dolphin can be a shape-shifter and take human form at night.

The dolphin is the totem of an Australian Aboriginal tribe.

In legend the dolphin was said to have been human in form before it took to the sea. To kill a dolphin is to bring misfortune.

**Domdaniel** (domdan'yəl). A fabled abode of evil spirits, GNOMES and enchanters 'under the roots of the ocean' off Tunis, or elsewhere. It first appears in Chaves and Gazotte's *Continuation of the Arabian Nights* (1788–1793), was introduced by Southey into his *Thalaba*, and used by Carlyle as synonymous with a den of iniquity. The word is made up from Lat. *domus*, a house, and *Danielis*, of Daniel, the latter being taken as a magician.

**Dominations.** *See* DOMINIONS.

**Dominic, St.,** de Guzman (1170–1221), the founder of the Dominican Order, or Preaching Friars, noted for his vehemence against the ALBIGENSES and called by the POPE 'Inquisitor-General'. He was canonized by Gregory IX. He is represented with a sparrow at his side and a dog carrying in its mouth a burning torch. It is said that the DEVIL appeared to him in the form of a sparrow, and the dog refers to his mother's dream, during her pregnancy, that she had given birth to a dog which lighted the world with a burning torch.

**Dominions.** The sixth of the nine orders in the mediaeval hierarchy of angels, also known as *Dominations* and symbolized in art by an ensign. *See* ANGEL.

**Donnybrook Fair.** This FAIR, held in August from the time of King John till 1855, was noted for its bacchanalian routs and light-hearted rioting. Hence it is proverbial for a disorderly gathering or regular rumpus. The village is now one of the south-eastern suburbs of Dublin.

**Doones, The.** Outlaws and desperadoes who supposedly settled in the Badgworthy area of Exmoor, Devon, about 1620. They lived by highway robbery and plundering of farmsteads. They also abducted women. Numerous murders were attributed to them. When in *c.* 1699 they killed a child and seized the mother, the people of the district stormed their stronghold and those who were not destroyed fled. Some stories claim them to be of Scottish origin but the legends vary and they were adapted and romanticized by R.D. Blackmore in *Lorna Doone* (1869).

**Dorado, El.** *See* EL DORADO.

**Doris.** *See* NEREIDS.

**Dorothea, St.** (dorōthē'ə). A martyr under Diocletian about 300. She is represented with a rose-branch in her hand, a wreath of roses on her head, and roses with fruit by her side. The legend is that Theophilus, the judge's secretary, scoffingly said to her as she was going to execution, 'Send me some fruit and roses, Dorothea, when you get to Paradise.' Immediately after her execution, a young angel brought him a basket of apples and roses, saying 'From Dorothea in Paradise', and vanished. Theophilus was a convert from that moment. The story forms

the basis of Massinger and Dekker's tragedy, *The Virgin Martir* (1622). Her day is 6 February.

**Doubting Castle.** In Bunyan's *Pilgrim's Progress*, the castle of the giant Despair and his wife Diffidence, in which Christian and Hopeful were incarcerated, but from which they escaped by means of the key called Promise.

**Douglas.** The Scottish family name is from the river Douglas in Lanarkshire, which is the Celt. *dhu glaise*, black stream, a name in use also in Ireland, the Isle of Man etc., and in Lancashire corrupted to *Diggles*. Legend explains it by the story that in 770 an unknown chief came to the assistance of a Scottish king. After the battle the king asked who was the 'Duglass' chieftain, his deliverer, and received for answer *Sholto Du-glas* which means 'Behold the dark grey man'.

> The complexion of the day is congenial with the original derivation of the name of the country, and the description of the chiefs to whom it belonged—Sholto Dhu Glass—(See yon dark grey man).
> SCOTT: *Castle Dangerous*, ch. iii.

**Black Douglas.** Sir James Douglas (1286–1330), or 'Good Sir James', champion of Robert Bruce, was called 'Black Douglas' by the English of the Border to whom he became a figure of dread. He twice took Douglas Castle from its English occupants by stratagem. The story is told in Scott's *Castle Dangerous*.

**The Douglas Larder.** On Palm Sunday 1307, Sir James Douglas regained his castle by a ruse and, knowing that he could not hold it, caused all the provisions to be heaped together in the cellar along with the bodies of the slain prisoners and dead horses. Drink was then poured over all and salt cast upon it. The castle was then fired. This cellar is known as the 'Douglas Larder'.

**Dove.** Mythologically the dove is universally associated with, and sacred to, the Great Mother goddesses and Queens of Heaven as femininity and maternity; they were sacrificial birds and connected with funerary cults. A terracotta figure of a dove was dated at 4500 B.C. in Mesopotamia and the dove was recorded at about 2500 B.C. in Egypt. Phoenicians honoured the dove as an attribute of Astarte and the Syrian ATARGATIS had a dove surmounting her sceptre. The bird was also an attribute of ZEUS who was fed by doves.

The dove frequently appears with the Tree of Life and the dove with the olive branch universally depicts peace, though the bird in Japan can be associated with war as sacred to the war god Hachiman. In China the dove represents longevity, filial piety and orderliness.

The Hebrews domesticated the turtle dove and pigeon and they were the only sacrificial birds according to the Law of Moses (*Lev.* v, 7) and were the poor man's sacrifice. In the New Testament the dove represents the Holy Spirit and is particularly connected with the Annunciation.

The dove as associated with the DELUGE appears in the mythology of the Babylonians, Hebrews, Greeks and Chaldeans.

Islam reveres the bird which flies in flocks about mosques.

The dove was called the 'Turtle' until the 17th century. *See* DODONA.

**Dovercourt.** A confused gabble, a babel. According to legend, Dovercourt church in Essex once possessed a cross that spoke; and Foxe says that the crowd in the church was so great 'that no man could shut the door'. Dovercourt also seems to have been noted for its scolds and chattering women.

And now the rood of Dovercourt did speak.
Confirming his opinions to be true.
  *Grim, the Collier of Croydon* (1600).

When bells ring round and in their order be,
They do denote how neighbours should agree;
But when they clam, the harsh sound spoils the
  sport
And 'tis like women keeping Dovercourt.
  *Lines in the Belfry of St. Peter's, Shaftesbury.*

**Drachenfels** (drahkh'ənfels) (Ger. dragon's rock). The German mountain on the right bank of the Rhine, south-east of Bonn. The legendary haunt of the DRAGON which SIEGFRIED slew. He bathed in its blood and so became invulnerable except in one spot on which a linden leaf had fallen. *See* NIBELUNGENLIED.

The castled crag of Drachenfels
Frowns o'er the wide and winding Rhine,
Whose breast of waters broadly swells
Between the banks which bear the vine.
  BYRON: *Childe Harold*, iii, 55.

**Dracula.** *See* VAMPIRE.

**Dragon.** The Greek word *drakon* comes from a verb meaning 'to see', to 'look at', and more remotely 'to watch' and 'to flash'.

In classical legend the idea of *watching* is retained in the story of the dragon who guards the golden apples in the Garden of the HESPERIDES, and in the story of CADMUS. In mediaeval romance captive ladies were often guarded by dragons.

Medusa fled from Jason in a chariot drawn by winged dragons.

In Semitic myth dragons represent malefic powers of darkness, the Adversary. In Babylonian tradition Marduk slew TIAMAT, the monster or dragon of chaos, and in Egypt the dragon of darkness, Apophis, was overcome each morning by the sun god Ra.

The Chinese dragon was originally three-clawed, later the five-clawed depicted Imperial and Celestial power and was restricted to the use of the Emperor, the four-clawed was the common dragon. The three-clawed became the Japanese dragon and remains so. In the Far East the dragon represents supreme spiritual power, wisdom and strength, it is the Celestial Stag, the sun. There are dragons of the sky, the mountains and of the deeps. The two 'contending dragons' facing each other typify all opposites and complements, the celestial and terrestrial powers of the universe, the *yin-yang*.

In Hindu mythology Vitra is the Dragon of the Waters which was slain by INDRA to release the waters.

A dragon is a fabulous winged crocodile, usually represented as of large size, with a serpent's tail; whence the words dragon and SERPENT are sometimes interchangeable. In the Middle Ages the word was the symbol of sin in general and paganism in particular, the metaphor being derived from *Rev.* xii, 9, where SATAN is termed 'the great dragon' and *Ps.* xci, 13, where it is said 'the dragon shalt thou trample under feet'. Hence, in Christian art it has the same significance.

Among the many SAINTS usually pictured as dragon-slayers are St. MICHAEL, St. GEORGE, St. Margaret, St. Samson (Archbishop of Dol), St. Clement of Metz; St. Romain of Rouen, who destroyed the huge dragon La GARGOUILLE, which ravaged the

Seine; St. Philip the Apostle; St. MARTHA, slayer of the terrible dragon Tarasque, at Aix-la-Chapelle; St. Florent, who killed a dragon which haunted the Loire; St. Cado, St. Maudet, and St. Pol, who performed similar feats in Brittany; and St. KEYNE of CORNWALL.

Among the ancient Britons and the Welsh the dragon was the national symbol on the war standard; hence the term PENDRAGON for the *dux bellorum*, or leader in war.

**A flying dragon.** A meteor.

**The Dragon of Wantley.** *See* WANTLEY.

**To sow dragon's teeth.** To foment contentions; to stir up strife or war; especially to do something which is intended to put an end to strife but which brings it about. The Philistines 'sowed dragons' teeth' when they took Samson, bound him, and put out his eyes; Ethelred II did the same when he ordered the massacre of the Danes on St. Brice's Day (1002), as did the Germans when they took Alsace-Lorraine from France in 1871.

The reference is to the classical story of CADMUS.

**Dragon's Hill.** A site in Berkshire where one legend has it that St. GEORGE killed the dragon. A bare place is shown on the hill, where nothing will grow, for there the dragon's blood was spilled.

In Saxon annals we are told that Cerdic, founder of the West Saxon kingdom, there slew Naud or Natanleod, the PENDRAGON, and five thousand men.

**Draupnir** (drawp'niə). ODIN's magic ring, from which every ninth night dropped eight rings equal in size and beauty to itself. It was made by the DWARFS.

**Dreams, The Gates of.** There are two, that of ivory and that of horn. Dreams which delude pass through the Ivory gate, those which come true pass through the Gate of Horn. This fancy depends upon two puns: ivory in Greek is *elephas*, and the verb *elephairo* means 'to cheat with empty hopes'; the Greek for horn is *keras*, and the verb *karanoo* means to accomplish.

> That children dream not the first half-year; that men dream not in some countries, with many more, are unto me sick men's dreams; dreams out of the ivory gate, and visions before midnight.
>
> SIR THOMAS BROWNE: *On Dreams.*

**Dromio** (drō'miō). **The brothers Dromio.** Two brothers who were exactly alike, who served two brothers who were exactly alike. The mistakes of masters and men form the fun of Shakespeare's *Comedy of Errors*, based on the *Menaechmi* of Plautus.

**Drows.** *See* TROWS.

**Druids.** The ancient order of priestly officials in pre-Roman Gaul, pre-Roman Britain, and Ireland. They seem to have combined priestly, judicial and political functions. The Druidic cult presents many obscurities and our main literary sources are Pliny and the *Commentaries* of Caesar. We are told that their rites were conducted in oak-groves, that human sacrifices were offered up, and that they regarded the OAK and MISTLETOE with particular veneration. It is now suggested that the name Druid is derived from some 'oak' word. They practised DIVINATION and ASTROLOGY and taught that the soul at death was transferred to another body. Their distinguishing badge was a serpent's egg. (*See* DRUID'S EGG.)

In the 18th and 19th centuries there was a revival of interest in Druidism and a new romantic and unhistorical cult grew up associated with the Welsh Eisteddfodau. This is usually termed Neo-Druidism.

**Druid's Circles.** A popular name for circles of standing stones, of which STONEHENGE is the most famous example.

**The Druid's Egg.** According to Pliny, who claimed to possess one, this wonderful egg was hatched by the joint labour of several serpents and was buoyed in the air by their hissing. The person who caught it had to escape at full speed to avoid being stung to death; but the possessor was sure to prevail in every contest, and to be courted by those in power.

**Dryad** (drī'ad). In classical mythology, a tree nymph (Gr. *drus*, an oak-tree), who was supposed to die when the tree died. Also called Hamadryads (Gr. *hama*, with). EURYDICE, the wife of ORPHEUS, was a dryad.

**Duglas,** or **Dubglas**. According to the *Historia Britonum* by Nennius, King ARTHUR fought twelve great battles against the Saxons. 'The second, third, fourth and fifth, were on another river, by the Britons called Duglas in the region Linnuis.' The topography is vague and the whereabouts of the river Duglas (or Dubglas) is open to conjecture.

**Duke Humphrey.** *See* HUMPHREY.

**Dulcinea** (dŭlsin'iə). A lady-love. Taken from the name of the lady to whom Don QUIXOTE paid his knightly homage. Her real name was Aldonza Lorenzo, but the knight dubbed her Dulcinea del Toboso.

**Dun. Squire Dun.** The hangman between Richard Brandon (executioner of Strafford, Laud and Charles) and JACK KETCH (executioner of Russell and Monmouth).

> And presently a halter got,
> Made of the best strong hempen teer;
> And, ere a cat could lick his ear,
> Had tied him up with as much art
> As Dunn himself could do for's heart
> CHARLES COTTON: *Virgil Travestied*, Bk. IV.

**Dun Cow.** The savage beast slain by GUY OF WARWICK. A huge tusk, probably that of an elephant, is still shown at Warwick Castle as one of the horns of the dun cow. The fable is that it belonged to a giant, and was kept on Mitchell Fold, Shropshire. Its milk was inexhaustible; but one day an old woman who had filled her pail wanted to fill her sieve also. This so enraged the cow that she broke loose from the fold and wandered to Dunsmore Heath, where she was slain.

> On Dunsmore heath I alsoe slewe
> A monstrous wyld and cruell beast,
> Calld the Dun-cow of Dunsmore heath;
> Which many people had opprest.
> Some of her bones in Warwicke yett
> Still for a monument doe lye.
> PERCY: *Reliques* (*The Legend of Sir Guy*).

**Dunheved Castle.** *See* CASTLE TERABIL.

**Dunmow** (dŭn'mō). **To eat Dunmow bacon.** To live in conjugal amity, without even wishing the marriage knot to be less firmly tied. The allusion is to a custom said to have been instituted by Juga, a noble lady, in 1111, and restored by Robert de Fitzwalter in 1244. It was that any person going to Dunmow, in Essex, and humbly kneeling on two sharp stones at the church door, might claim a gammon of bacon if he could swear that for twelve months and a day he had never had a household brawl or wished himself unmarried.

Between 1244 and 1772 eight claimants were awarded the flitch. Their names merit immortality:

1445 Richard Wright, labourer, Bawburgh, near Norwich.
1467 Steven Samuel, Little Ayston, Essex.
1510 Thomas Ley, fuller, Coggeshall, Essex.
1710 William (and Jane) Parsley, butcher, Much-Easton, Essex.
*Also* John (and Ann) Reynolds of Hatfield Regis
1751 Thomas Shakeshaft, woolcomber, Weathersfield, Essex.
1763 Names not recorded.
1773 John and Susan Gilder, Tarling, Essex.

Allusions to the custom are frequent in 17th- and 18th-century literature and the custom was revived again in the second half of the 19th century.

> 'Ah madam! cease to be mistaken;
> Few married folk peck Dunmow bacon'.
> PRIOR: *Turtle and Sparrow*, 233.

W. Harrison Ainsworth's *The Flitch of Bacon or The Custom of Dunmow* (1854) is dedicated to Baron and Baroness Tauchnitz 'As a record of rare conjugal attachment, this Tale may be appropriately inscribed to you, my good friends: than whom I have never known a more fondly-united couple'.

**Dunstan, St.** (*c.* 925–988). Archbishop of Canterbury (961), and patron saint of goldsmiths, being himself a noted worker in GOLD. He is represented in pontifical robes, and carrying a pair of pincers in his right hand, the latter referring to the legend that on one occasion he seized the DEVIL by the nose with a pair of red-hot tongs and refused to release him till he promised never to tempt Dunstan again. *See also* HORSESHOE.

**Durandal,** or **Duranda,** or **Durenda,** etc. *See* ROLAND'S SWORDS *under* ROLAND.

**Durden, Dame.** A generic name for a good old-fashioned housewife. In the old song she kept five serving girls to carry the milking pails, and five serving men to use the flail and spade; and of course, the five men love the five maids.

> 'Twas Moll and Bet, Doll and Kate, and Dorothy Draggletail;
> And John and Dick, and Joe and Jack, and Humphrey with his flail.
> ANON.

**Dust. To throw dust in his eyes.** To mislead, to dupe or trick. The allusion is to 'the swiftest runner in a sandy race, who to make his fellows aloofe, casteth dust with his heeles into their envious eyes' (*Cotgrave*, 1611).

The Muslims had a practice of casting dust into the air for the sake of confounding the enemies of the Faith. This was done by the Prophet on two or three occasions, as in the battle of Honein; and the Koran refers to it when it says: 'Neither didst thou, O Mahomet, cast dust into their eyes; but it was God who confounded them.'

**Dwarf.** Dwarfs have figured in the legends and mythology of nearly every people, and the success of Walt Disney's children's classic *Snow White and the Seven Dwarfs* (1938) is evidence of their enduring appeal. Pliny gives particulars of whole races of them, possibly following travellers' tales of African pygmies. They are prominent in Teutonic and Scandinavian legend and generally dwelt in rocks and caves, and recesses of the earth. They were guardians of mineral wealth and precious stones and very skilful at their work. They were not unfriendly to man, but could on occasions be intensely vindictive and mischievous.

In England, dwarfs or midgets were popular down to the 18th century as court favourites or household pets. In later times they were often exhibited as curiosities at circuses etc.

Among those recorded in legend or history (with their reputed heights) the following are, perhaps, the most famous:

ALBERICH, the dwarf of the NIBELUNGENLIED.

ANDROMEDA and CONOPAS, each 2 ft. 4 in. Dwarfs of Julia, niece of Augustus.

BEBE, or NICHOLAS FERRY, 2 ft. 9 in. A native of France (1714–1737). He had a brother and sister, both dwarfs.

BORUWLASKI (*Count Joseph*), 3 ft. 3 in. (d. 1837).

CHE-MAH (a Chinese), 2 ft. 1 in., weight 52 lb. Exhibited in London in 1880.

COLOBRI (*Prince*) of Schleswig. 2 ft. 1 in., weight 25 lb. at the age of twenty-five (1851).

CONOPAS. *See* ANDROMEDA, *above*.

COPPERNIN, the dwarf of the Princess of Wales, mother of George III. The last court dwarf in England.

CRACHAMI (*Caroline*). Born at Palermo; 1 ft. 8 in. (1814–1824). Exhibited in Bond Street, London, 1824.

DECKER or DUCKER (*John*), 2 ft. 6 in. An Englishman (1610).

FAIRY QUEEN (*The*), 1 ft. 4 in., weight 4 lb. Exhibited in Regent Street, London, 1850. Her feet were less than two inches.

GIBSON (*Richard*), a good portrait painter (1615–1690). His wife's maiden name was Anne Shepherd. Each measured 3 ft. 10 in. Waller sang their praises:

Design or chance makes others wive,
But Nature did this match contrive.

HOPKINS (*Harry*). Born at Llantrisant, Glamorgan: 2 ft. 7 in. (1737–1754).

HUDSON (*Sir Jeffrey*). Born at Oakham, Rutland; 3 ft. 9 in. at the age of thirty (1619–1682); he figures in Scott's *Peveril of the Peak*.

JACKSON (*William E.*). Born at Dunedin, New Zealand; 2 ft. 3 in. and commonly known as *Major Mite* (1864–1900).

JARVIS (*John*), 2 ft. Page of honour to Queen Mary (1508–1556).

KELLY (*Mrs. Catherine, The Irish Fairy*), 2 ft. 10 in. (1756–1785).

LOLKES (*Wybrand*), 2 ft. 3 in., weight 57 lb. Exhibited at ASTLEY's in 1790.

LUCIUS, 2 ft., weight 17 lb. The dwarf of the Emperor Augustus.

MAGRI (*Count Primo*), *see* WARREN, *below*.

MARINE (*Lizzie*), 2 ft. 9 in., weight 45 lb.

MIDGETS (*The*). Lucia Zarate, the elder sister, 1 ft. 8 in., weight 4¾ lb., at the age of eighteen. Her sister was a little taller. Exhibited in London, 1881.

NUTT, COMMODORE. *See* TOM THUMB, *below*.

PAAP (*Simon*). A Dutch dwarf, 2 ft. 4 in., weight 27 lb.

SAWYER (*A.L.*), 2 ft. 6½ in., weight 39 lb. Editor in 1833 of the *Democrat*, a paper of considerable repute in Florida.

STOBERIN (*C.H.*), of Nuremberg, 2 ft. 11 in. at the age of twenty.

STOCKER (*Nannette*), 2 ft. 9 in. Exhibited in London in 1815.

STRASSE DAVIT Family. Man 1 ft. 8 in.; woman, 1 ft. 6 in.; child at seventeen only 6 in.

TERESIA (*Madame*). A Corsican, 2 ft. 10 in., weight 27 lb. Exhibited in London, 1773.

TOM THUMB (*General*), whose name was Charles S. Stratton, born at Bridgeport in Connecticut, U.S.A. (1838–1883). Exhibited first in London in 1844. In 1863 he married Lavinia WARREN, and was then 31 in. in height, she being 32 in. and 21 years old. They visited England in the following year with their dwarf son, Commodore NUTT.

WANMER (*Lucy*), 2 ft. 6 in., weight 45 lb. Exhibited in London 1801, at the age of forty-five.

WARREN (*Lavinia*). *See* TOM THUMB *above*. In 1884 she married another dwarf, Count Primo Magri, who was 2 ft. 8 in.

WORMBERG (*John*), 2 ft. 7 in. at the age of thirtyeight (Hanoverian period).

XIT was the dwarf of Edward VI.

ZARATE. *See* MIDGETS, *above*.

*Cp.* GIANTS; HEAVIEST MEN.

**The Black Dwarf.** A GNOME of the most malignant character, once held by the dalesmen of the Border as the author of all the mischief that befell their flocks and herds. In Scott's novel of this title (1816), the name is given to Sir Edward Mauley, *alias*

Elshander, the recluse, Cannie Elshie, and the Wise Wight of Mucklestane Moor.

**Dysmas** (diz′mas). The traditional name of the Penitent Thief, who suffered with Christ at the Crucifixion. His relics are claimed by Bologna, and in some calendars he is commemorated on 25 March. In the apocryphal *Gospel of Nicodemus* he is called *Dimas* (and elsewhere *Titus*), and the Impenitent Thief *Gestas*.

In Longfellow's *The Golden Legend* (*The Miracle Play*, V), *Dumachus* (Dysmus) and *Titus* both belonged to a band of robbers who molested the Holy Family on their flight into Egypt.

# E

**Eagle.** The eagle is an attribute of all sky gods and particularly of ZEUS/JUPITER; it represents spiritual power, majesty, victory and ascension; it is also a natural attribute of war gods and of the storm gods who bring lightning and the fertilizing rain.

In mythology the solar eagle is always at enmity with the dark and chthonic powers represented by the SERPENT, while the eagle in conflict with the LION or BULL depicts the spirit or mind against the physical and material: the eagle always wins.

According to Horapollo, the Egyptian High Priest, the eagle was the royal bird of the Thebans and a symbol of the Nile.

The Amerindian eagle is of paramount importance as the greatest of birds. The eagle-feather headdress represents the Thunder Bird, the Great Spirit; it is the Master of Height and its feathers carry the prayers of the people to the Father Sun. For the shaman the bird embodies the power of the Great Spirit and represents the state of illumination attained in initiation.

In China the eagle is essentially solar and *yang* and is associated with authority and fearlessness; with the RAVEN it is also connected with war gods.

The two-headed eagle is an emblem of twin gods depicting power and omniscience. It appeared on Hittite monuments and was an attribute of Nergal, it passed from the Hittites on to Byzantium, appearing later in the Roman Empire and being retained by the Austrian Emperors as successors to the Holy Roman Empire; it was later adopted by Ivan III of Russia in 1472.

The eagle appears in the boughs of the Scandinavian YGGDRASIL as wisdom and light in conflict with the powers of darkness represented by the serpent, but the eagle can also be associated with storm and gloom.

As the eagle was believed to be able to look at the sun without blinking, so, in Christianity, did Christ gaze at the glory of God; grasping the serpent in its talons was the victory over sin; it also represents the inspiration of the Gospels, hence its use as a lectern. It is the Spirit, aspiration and endeavour, it is the emblem of St. John the Evangelist, of St. Augustine, St. Gregory the Great and SS. Prisca, Servatius and Medard. It is one of the Four Beasts of the Apocalypse.

In Heraldry it is a charge of great honour. **The Golden Eagle** and **the Spread Eagle** are commemorative of the CRUSADES and were the devices of the Eastern Roman Empire. France (under the Empires), Germany, Austria, Prussia and Russia also adopted the eagle as a royal or imperial emblem. *See* THE TWO-HEADED EAGLE.

The white-headed American eagle, *Haliaetus leucocephalus* (sometimes wrongly termed the Bald Eagle), with outspread wings or spread-eagle (the 'eagle displayed' of HERALDRY) is specifically the emblem of the U.S.A.

**Eagle stones.** *See* AETITES.

**The Eagle and Child.** The crest of the Stanley family and Earls of Derby, and a well-known PUBLIC-HOUSE SIGN. The legend is that Sir Thomas Latham, an ancestor of the house, caused his illegitimate son to be placed under the foot of a tree in which an eagle had built its nest. When out walking with his wife, they 'accidentally' found the child, which he persuaded her to adopt as their heir. Later he changed his mind and left most of his wealth to his daughter, and the family altered the eagle crest of Sir Thomas to that of an eagle preying upon a child.

**Thy youth is renewed like the eagle's** (*Ps.* ciii, 5). This refers to the ancient superstition that every ten years the eagle soars into the 'fiery region', and plunges into the sea, where, moulting its feathers, it acquires new life. *Cp.* PHOENIX.

At last she saw where he upstarted brave
Out of the well, wherein he drenched lay:

As eagle fresh out of the ocean wave,
Where he hath lefte his plumes all hory gray,
And deckt himself with fethers youthly gay.
SPENSER: *Faerie Queene*, I, xi, 34.

**Ass-eared.** *See under* ASS.

**Ear. Ear of Dionysius.** A large ear-shaped underground cave cut in a rock and so connected that Dionysius, TYRANT of Syracuse, could overhear the conversation of his prisoners from another chamber. A similar whispering gallery exists beneath Hastings Castle. It is cut from the solid rock and the listening post is shaped like an ear.

**Earthquakes.** According to Indian mythology the world rests on the head of a great elephant, 'Muhupudma', and when, for the sake of rest, the huge monster refreshes itself by moving its head, an earthquake is produced.

The lamas say that the earth is placed on the back of a gigantic frog and when it moves its limbs or head it shakes the earth. Other Eastern myths place the earth on the back of a tortoise.

Greek and Roman mythologists ascribe earthquakes to the restlessness of the giants whom JUPITER buried under high mountains. Thus VIRGIL (*Aeneid*, III, 578) ascribes the eruption of Etna to the giant ENCELADUS.

**Eat.** To eat together was, in the East, a sure pledge of protection. There is a story of a Persian grandee who gave the remainder of a peach which he was eating to a man who implored his protection, only to find that his own son had been slain by this man. The nobleman would not allow the murderer to be punished, but said, 'We have eaten together; go in peace.' *Cp.* TO EAT A MAN'S SALT *under* SALT.
**Let us eat and drink, for tomorrow we shall die.** *Is.* xxii, 13. A traditional saying of the Egyptians who, at their banquets, exhibited a skeleton to the guests to remind them of the brevity of life.
**To eat a man's salt.** *See under* SALT.

**Eblis.** A jinn of Arabian mythology, the ruler of the evil genii, or fallen angels. Before his fall he was called AZAZEL. When ADAM was created, God commanded all the angels to worship him; but Eblis replied, 'Me thou hast created of smokeless fire, and shall I reverence a creature made of dust?' God turned the disobedient ANGEL into a

Sheytan (DEVIL), and he became the father of devils.

When he said unto the angels, 'Worship Adam', all worshipped him except Eblis.
*Al Koran*, ii.

**Echidna** (ekid'nə). In classical mythology, a celebrated monster, half woman, half SERPENT and mother of the CHIMAERA, the many-headed dog ORTHOS, the hundred-headed DRAGON of the HESPERIDES, the Colchian dragon, the SPHINX, CERBERUS, SCYLLA, the GORGONS, the Lernaean HYDRA, the vulture that gnawed away the liver of PROMETHEUS and the NEMEAN LION.

Spenser makes her the mother of the BLATANT BEAST in the *Faerie Queene*, VI, vi, 10.

In zoology an echidna is a porcupine anteater found in Australia, Tasmania and New Guinea, allied to the platypus.

**Echo** (ek'ō). The Romans say that Echo was a NYMPH in love with NARCISSUS, but her love not being returned, she pined away until only her voice remained.

Sweet Echo, sweetest nymph, that liv'st unseen
Within thy airy shell,
By slow Meander's margent green—
Canst thou not tell me of a gentle pair
That likest thy Narcissus are?
MILTON: *Comus*, 230.

**To applaud to the echo.** To applaud vigorously — so loudly as to produce an echo.

**Eckhardt** (ek'haht). **A faithful Eckhardt, who warneth everyone.** Eckhardt, in German legends, appears on the evening of MAUNDY THURSDAY to warn all persons to go home, that they may not be injured by the headless bodies and two-legged horses which traverse the streets on that night. He also warned those who followed Frau Holle or Holda (VENUS) of evils to come; sometimes he appears as the companion of TANNHÄUSER.

**Eclipses** were considered by the Greeks and Romans as bad OMENS and the latter would never hold a public assembly during an eclipse. Some of their poets feign that an eclipse of the MOON is because she is on a visit to ENDYMION.

A general notion among some races was that the SUN or moon was devoured by some monster, hence the beating of drums and kettles to scare it away. The Chinese,

Lapps and Persians call the evil beast a DRAGON. The East Indians say it is a black GRIFFIN.

The ancient Mexicans thought that eclipses were caused by quarrels between sun and moon.

**Ector, Sir.** In ARTHURIAN ROMANCES the foster-father of King ARTHUR.

**Eden Hall. The Luck of Eden Hall.** An enamelled drinking-glass (probably made in Venice in the 10th century) in the possession of the Musgrave family at Eden Hall, Cumberland, and supposed to be endowed with fortune-bringing properties. The tale is told that it was taken from St. Cuthbert's Well in the garden where it was left by the fairies while they danced. The superstition is:

If that glass should break or fall,
Farewell the luck of Eden Hall.

The estate was broken up in 1920 and the glass is now in the Victoria and Albert Museum, London.

**Eel.** The ancient Greeks and Phoenicians had sacred eels. Eels were decorated and kept in the sacred fishponds at Hieropolis; they were also sacred in parts of Polynesia and were associated with DELUGE myths. The eel has a phallic significance.

**Egeria** (ejiər'iə). The NYMPH who instructed Numa Pompilius, second king of ROME (753–673 B.C.), in his wise legislation; hence a counsellor, adviser.

It is in these moments that we gaze upon the moon.
It is in these moments that Nature becomes our Egeria.
LORD BEACONSFIELD: *Vivian Grey*, III, vi.

**Egg.** Myths in which the egg is the origin of the world are widespread, being found in such diverse cultures as ancient Egypt, Phoenicia, Greece, India, China, Japan, Central America, Fiji and Finland. The Cosmic Egg is the germ of all creation, the potential, the womb, the origin of all being. In Egyptian, Greek, Hindu and Chinese myth the Cosmic Egg burst asunder. In some legends the two halves formed the sky and earth, but in Hinduism the Egg of Brahma divided into three regions—the senses, the heavens and the world. Sometimes the egg contains the Four Elements.

A large egg, sometimes hung in Coptic churches and in mosques, depicts creation and resurrection; in Christianity it can signify the Virgin Birth.

The egg is important in alchemy as representing the sealed hermetic vessel in which the Great Work is consummated.

In some mythologies a bird is represented as laying the Cosmic Egg on the primordial waters. Anciently this idea was attributed to ORPHEUS, hence it was also called the 'Orphic Egg'.

The opinion of the oval figure of the earth is ascrib'd to Orpheus and his disciples; and the doctrine of the mundane egg is so peculiarly his that 'tis called by Proclus the Orphick egg.
BURNET: *The Sacred Theory of the Earth* (1684)

The Egyptian Cosmic Egg, from which the sun god RA was hatched, was laid by the Nile Goose.

**Druid's egg.** *See under* DRUIDS.

**Egil** (ā'gil). Brother of Weland (*see* WAYLAND), the VULCAN of Northern mythology. He was a great archer and in the Saga of Thidrik there is a tale told of him exactly similar to that about William TELL and the apple.

**Egypt. Crown of Egypt.** In ancient Egypt there were many worn by kings and gods. As rulers of Upper Egypt, or the South Land, and Lower Egypt, or the Northern Land, the kings wore the double crown (*pschent*) made up of the Red Crown, the head-dress of the Delta, to which was added the White Mitre of the South. The Khepresh, called the war-helmet of the Pharaohs, was blue with round dots. Each of the many crowns had its particular significance and symbolism and the gods wore crowns which indicated their attributes.

**Egyptian Days.** Unlucky days, days on which no business should be undertaken. The Egyptian astrologers named two in each month, but the last Monday in APRIL, the second Monday of AUGUST, and the third Monday of DECEMBER seem to have been specially baneful. *Cp.* DIES NEFASTUS.

**Elagabalus,** or **Heliogabalus** (ēləgab'ələs, hēliəgab'ələs). A Syro-Phoenician sun-god. Two temples were built at Rome for this god, who was represented by a huge conical stone. Varius Avitus Bassanius (205–222), who became Roman emperor as

Marcus Aurelius Antonius (218–222), was called Elagabalus because he had been a high priest of the sun-god at Emesa. His brief reign was marked by unparalleled debaucheries, cruelties and loathsome practices. He and his mother were slain by the PRAETORIAN GUARD.

**Elaine.** The Lily Maid of ASTOLAT, whose unrequited love for Sir LANCELOT caused her death. The story is told in Tennyson's *Lancelot and Elaine* (*Idylls of the King*) based upon Malory (Bk. XVIII, ch. ix-xx). She loved him 'with that love which was her doom'. Sir Lancelot wore her favour at the ninth of the DIAMOND JOUSTS, thus arousing the jealousy of Queen GUINEVERE.

**Elden Hole. Elden Hole needs filling.** A reproof given to great braggarts. Elden Hole is a deep chasm in the Derbyshire Peak, long reputed to be bottomless. It is mentioned in Scott's *Peveril of the Peak*, ch. iii.

**Elder tree.** There are many popular traditions and superstitions associated with this tree. The Cross is supposed to have been made from its wood and, according to legend, Judas hanged himself on an elder, cup-shaped fungal excrescences on the bark still being known as Judas's (or Jew's) ears. *The Travels* of Sir John MANDEVILLE and Shakespeare in *Love's Labour's Lost*, V, ii, say that Judas was hanged on an elder.

> Judas he japed
> With Jewen silver
> And sithen on an eller
> Hanged hymselve.
> *Vision of Piers Plowman: Passus* I.

Warts are cured by being rubbed with elder and it is a protection against witchcraft.

**El Dorado** (el dərah'dō) (Sp. the gilded). Originally the name given to the supposed king of the fabulous city of MANOA believed to be on the Amazon. The king was said to be covered with oil and then periodically powdered with gold-dust so that he was permanently, and literally, gilded. Expeditions from Spain and England (two of which were led by Sir Walter Ralegh) tried to discover this territory. El Dorado and Manoa were used by the explorers as interchangeable names for the 'golden city'. Metaphorically it is applied to any place which offers

opportunities of getting rich quickly or acquiring wealth easily.

**Elecampane** (*Inula helenium*), one of the Compositae, allied to the aster. Its candied roots are used as a sweetmeat and were formerly held to confer immortality and to cure wounds. Pliny tells us that the plant sprang from HELEN's tears. It was much used in old medicines and herb remedies.

**Electra** (1) One of the PLEIADES, mother of Dardanus, the mythical ancestor of the Trojans. She is known as 'the Lost Pleiad', for she is said to have disappeared a little before the TROJAN WAR to avoid seeing the ruin of her beloved city. She showed herself occasionally to mortal eye, but always in the guise of a comet. *See Odyssey*, V, and *Iliad*, XVIII.

(2) A sister of ORESTES who features in the *Oresteia* of Aeschylus and the two other dramas entitled *Electra* by Sophocles and Euripides. The daughter of AGAMEMNON and CLYTEMNESTRA, she incited Orestes to kill their mother in revenge for the latter's murder of Agamemnon.

**Elephant.** A myth maintained by Strabo and Aelian, but denied by Aristotle and Pliny, was that the elephant had no joints in its legs and had to sleep standing up. Pliny also says that the elephant is a religious animal, worshipping the sun and stars. Aristotle called it the most intelligent of all animals, gentle and teachable.

Hinduism has the elephant as the vehicle of the god of wisdom, Ganesha, who is depicted as elephant-headed.

The elephant can personify both India and Africa.

**The Order of the Elephant.** A Danish order of knighthood said to have been instituted by Christian I in 1462, but reputedly of earlier origin. It was reconstituted by Christian V in 1693 and, besides the SOVEREIGN and his sons, consists of 30 KNIGHTS. The collar is of gold elephants and towers.

**A white elephant.** The white elephant is sacred to the Buddha as one announced his birth to his mother, Queen Maya.

In the Far East white elephants are lucky, bringing special fortune. The Chinese P'u Hsien (the Vedic god Pushan) rides on a white elephant. A white elephant also signifies some possession the expense or responsibility of which is not worth while; a burdensome possession. The allusion is to the story of a king of Siam who used to make a present of a white elephant to courtiers he wished to ruin.

**Eleusinian Mysteries.** The religious rites in honour of DEMETER or CERES, originally an agrarian cult, performed at Eleusis in Attica and later taken over by the Athenian state and partly celebrated at ATHENS. The rites included sea bathing, processions, religious dramas etc., and the initiated obtained thereby a happy life beyond the grave. Little is known about the chief rites, hence the figurative use of the phrase to mean something deeply mysterious. The Eleusinian Mysteries were abolished by the Emperor Theodosius about the end of the 4th century A.D.

**Eleven. The Eleven Thousand Virgins.** *See* URSULA.

**Elf.** Originally a dwarfish being of Teutonic mythology, possessed of magical powers which it used for the good or ill of mankind. Later the name was used for a malignant imp, and then for FAIRY creatures that dance on the grass in the full MOON, etc.

> Every elf and fairy sprite
> Hop as light as bird from brier.
> SHAKESPEARE: *A Midsummer Night's Dream*, V, ii.

The derivation of elf and GOBLIN from Guelf and Ghibelline is mentioned in Johnson (with disapproval); the word is O.E. *aelf*, from Icel. *alfr*, and Teut. *alp*, a nightmare.

**Elf-fire.** The IGNIS FATUUS.

**Elf-marked.** Those born with a natural defect, according to ancient Scottish superstition, are marked by the elves for mischief. Shakespeare makes Queen Margaret call Richard III:

> Thou elvish-mark'd, abortive, rooting hog!
> *Richard III*, I, iii.

**Elf-shot.** Afflicted with some unknown disease which was supposed to have been caused by an ELF-ARROW.

**Elidure.** A legendary king of Britain, who in some accounts was advanced to the throne in place of his brother, Arthgallo (or ARTEGAL), supposed by him to be dead. Arthgallo, after a long exile, returned to his country, and Elidure resigned the throne.

Wordsworth has a poem on the subject called *Artegal and Elidure*.

**Elissa.** DIDO, Queen of Carthage, was sometimes called Elissa.

**Elixir of Life.** The supposed potion of the alchemists that would prolong life indefinitely. It was sometimes imagined as a powder, sometimes as a fluid (Arab. a powder for sprinkling on wounds). It also meant the PHILOSOPHER'S STONE, used for transmuting base metals into GOLD. The name is now given to any sovereign remedy—especially of the 'quack' variety.

**Elizabeth. St. Elizabeth of Hungary** (1207–1231). Patron SAINT of the Third Order of St. FRANCIS of which she was a member. Her day is 19 November and she was noted for her good works and love of the poor. She is commemorated in Kingsley's poem *The Saint's Tragedy*. The story is told that her husband Louis at first forbade her abounding gifts to the poor. One day he saw her carrying away a bundle of bread and told her to open it asking what it contained. 'Only flowers, my lord,' said Elizabeth and, to save the lie, God converted the loaves into flowers and the king was confronted with a mass of red roses. This miracle converted him.

**Elysium** (iliz'iəm). In Greek mythology, the abode of the blessed; hence the **Elysian Fields**, the PARADISE or Happy Land in Greek poetry. *Elysian* means happy, delightful.

> Would take the prison'd soul,
> And lap it in Elysium.
> MILTON: *Comus*, 256, 7.

**Emerald.** According to legend, an emerald protected the chastity of the wearer. It also warded off evil spirits, and epilepsy, cured dysentery, and was anciently supposed to aid weak eyesight.

**Empyrean** (empīrē'ən). According to Ptolemy, there are five heavens, the last of which is pure elemental fire and the seat of deity; this fifth heaven is called the empyrean (Gr. *empuros*, fiery); hence in Christian angelology, the abode of God and the angels. *See* HEAVEN.

> Now had the Almighty Father from above,
> From the pure Empyrean where he sits
> High thron'd above all height, bent down his eye.
> MILTON: *Paradise Lost*, III, 56.

**Empyromancy.** An ancient method of DIVINATION by observing the behaviour of certain objects when placed on a sacrificial fire. Eggs, flour and incense were used for this purpose as well as a shoulderblade.

**Enceladus** (ensel'ədəs). The most powerful of the hundred-armed giants, sons of URANUS and GAEA, who conspired against ZEUS. The king of gods and men cast him down at Phlegra, in Macedonia, and threw Mount ETNA over him. The poets say that the flames of the volcano arise from the breath of this giant.

**End. The End of the World.** According to rabbinical legend, the world was to last six thousand years. The reasons assigned are (1) because the name *Yahweh* contains six letters; (2) because the Hebrew letter *m* occurs six times in the book of *Genesis*; (3) because the patriarch Enoch, who was taken to heaven without dying, was the sixth generation from ADAM (Seth, Enos, Cainan, Mahalaleel, Jared, Enoch); (4) because God created the world in six days; (5) because six contains three binaries—the first 2000 years were for the law of nature, the next 2000 the written law, and the last 2000 the law of grace.

**Endymion** (endim'ion). In Greek mythology, the shepherd son of Aethlius, loved by SELENE, the Moon goddess who bore him fifty daughters. Another story is that ZEUS gave him eternal life and youth by allowing him to sleep perpetually on Mount Latmus and Selene came down nightly to embrace him. The story is used by Keats in his *Endymion* (1818) and it forms the basis of Lyly's comedy, *Endimion, the Man in the Moone* (1585).

> The moon sleeps with Endymion,
> And would not be awaked.
> SHAKESPEARE: *Merchant of Venice*, V, i.

Disraeli's novel *Endymion*, was published in 1880.

**Enid.** The daughter and only child of Yniol, and wife of Prince GERAINT, one of the Knights of the ROUND TABLE. Ladies called her 'Enid the Fair', but the people named her 'Enid the Good'. Her story is told in Tennyson's *Geraint and Enid* (*Idylls of the King.*)

**Eolus.** *See* AEOLUS.

**Eon.** *See* AEON.

**Ephesians, Diana of the.** *See under* DIANA.

**Ephialtes.** A giant, son of POSEIDON and brother of Otus. When nine years old, they were nine fathoms tall and nine cubits broad. They were slain by APOLLO.

**Epigoni** (epig'ənī). *See* THE SEVEN AGAINST THEBES *under* THEBES.

**Epimenides** (epimen'idēz). A religious teacher and wonder worker of Crete (6th or 7th century B.C.). According to Pliny (*Natural History*), he fell asleep in a cave when a boy, and did not wake for 57 years. He is supposed to have lived for 299 years. *Cp.* RIP VAN WINKLE *under* WINKLE.

**Eppur si muove** (epoor' sē mwaw'vā) (Ital. and yet it [the earth] does move). The phrase said to have been uttered by Galileo immediately after his recantation of belief in the Copernican system. He appeared before the Inquisition at Rome in 1633, and record of the saying (certainly apocryphal), first occurs in 1761.

**Erato** (er'ətō). One of the nine MUSES; the Muse of erotic poetry, usually represented with a lyre.

**Erebus** (er'ibəs). In Greek mythology, the son of Chaos and brother of Night; hence darkness personified. His name was given to the gloomy underground cavern through which the Shades had to walk in their passage to HADES.

> Not Erebus itself were dim enough
> To hide thee from prevention.
> SHAKESPEARE: *Julius Caesar*, II, i.

**Erichthonius.** Fathered by VULCAN and very deformed. ATHENE put him in a box and gave its charge to the daughters of Cecrops with strict orders not to open it but they did so and out of fright at what they saw jumped off the Acropolis to their death. He became King of ATHENS and established the worship of ATHENE. He was set up as the constellation *Auriga* (Lat. charioteer). *See* CHARIOT.

**Erigone** (erig'ənē). *See* ICARIUS.

**Erinyes** (erin'yēz). In Greek mythology, avengers of wrong, the Latin FURIES. *See* EUMENIDES.

**Erlking.** In German legend, a malevolent GOBLIN who haunts forests and lures people, especially children, to destruction. Goethe has a poem on him, set to music by Schubert. He can also lead the WILD HUNT.

**Eros.** The Greek god of love, usually personified as a young boy with bow and arrows; the equivalent of the Roman CUPID. It is also the popular name for the winged archer surmounting the memorial fountain to the 7th Earl of Shaftesbury, in the centre of Piccadilly Circus, London, which is actually a symbol of Christian charity. It is the work of Sir Alfred Gilbert (1854–1934) and was unveiled in 1893.

**Esculapius.** *See* AESCULAPIUS.

**Estotiland.** An imaginary tract of land near the Arctic Circle in North America, said to have been discovered by John Scalve, a Pole. It is mentioned and shown in Peter Heylin's *Microcosmos* (1622).

> The snow
> From cold Estotiland.
> MILTON: *Paradise Lost*, x, 685.

**Eternal. The Eternal Tables.** In Muslim legend, a white pearl extending from east to west, and from HEAVEN to earth, on which God has recorded every event, past, present and to come.

**Ethon.** The EAGLE or vulture that gnawed the liver of PROMETHEUS.

**Etna,** or **Aetna** (et'nə). The highest active volcano in Europe. It stands over the Straits of Messina, *c.* 10,700 ft. high, covering an area of 460 sq. miles. In Sicily, Etna is known as Monte Gibello and many towns and villages live under its continual threat. Virgil (*Aeneid* III, 578, etc.) ascribes its eruption to the restlessness of ENCELADUS, the most powerful of all the giants who plotted against JUPITER and who lies buried under the mountain. According to the Greek and Latin poets it is the site of the smithy of CYCLOPS and the forges of VULCAN.

**Etrenne.** *See* STRENIA.

**Etzel.** In German heroic legend, Attila, King of the Huns (d. 453).

**Eulalia, St.** (ūlā'liə). Eulalon (*i.e.* the sweetly spoken) is one of the names of APOLLO, and there are two 4th-century virgin martyrs called Eulalia, both presumed to have been put to death under Diocletian in 304—St. Eulalia of Barcelona and St. Eulalia of Merida, whose ashes were scattered over a field upon which a pall of snow is said to have descended.

**Eumaeus** (ūmē'əs). The slave and swineherd of ULYSSES; hence a swineherd.

**Eumenides** (ūmen'idēz) (Gr. the goodtempered ones). The name given by the Greeks to the FURIES, as it would have been bad policy to call them ERINYES, their right name.

**Eureka** (ūrē'kə) (Gr. *heureka*, I have found it). An exclamation of delight at having made a discovery; originally that of Archimedes, the Syracusan philosopher, when he discovered how to test the purity of Hiero's crown. The tale is, that Hiero gave some gold to a smith to be made into a votive crown, but suspecting that the gold had been alloyed with an inferior metal, asked Archimedes to test it. The philosopher did not know how to proceed, but in getting into his bath, which was full, observed that some of the water ran over and immediately concluded that a body must displace its own bulk of water when immersed; silver is lighter than gold, therefore a pound weight of silver is bulkier than a pound weight of gold and would consequently displace more water. Thus he found that the crown was deficient in gold. Vitruvius says:

> When the idea flashed across his mind, the philosopher jumped out of the bath exclaiming, 'Heureka! heureka!' and, without waiting to dress himself, ran home to try the experiment.

'Eureka!' is the motto of California, in allusion to the gold discovered there.

**Euryalus.** *See* NISUS.

**Eurydice** (ūrid'isi). In Greek mythology the wife of ORPHEUS, killed by a serpent when fleeing from the attentions of Aristaeus. Orpheus sought her in HADES, charmed PLUTO by his music, and was promised her return on condition that he did not look back until Eurydice had reached the upper world. Nearing the end of his journey he turned his head to see if Eurydice was following and she was instantly caught back into Hades.

**Euterpe** (ūtœ'pi). One of the nine MUSES, daughter of JUPITER and MNEMOSYNE, inventress of the double flute, muse of Dionysiac music, patroness of joy and pleasure, and of flute-players.

**Everyman.** The central character in the most famous English MORALITY PLAY (*c.* 1529) drawn from a late 15th-century Dutch original. Everyman is summoned by Death and invites all his acquaintances (such as Kindred, Good Deeds, Goods, Knowledge, Beauty, Strength etc.) to accompany him on his journey, but only Good Deeds will go with him.

**Evil. Evil Eye.** An ancient and widespread belief that certain individuals had the power to harm or even kill with a glance. Various charms and gestures, many of an obscene kind, were employed to counteract it. Virgil speaks of an evil eye bewitching lambs.

> Nescio quis teneros oculus mihi fascinat agnos.
> *Bucolics, Ecl.* iii, 103.

**The Evil One.** The DEVIL.

**Ex pede Herculem.** From the foot (we judge) a HERCULES; from this sample we can judge the whole. Pythagoras calculated the height of Hercules by comparing the length of various stadia in Greece. A stadium was 600 feet in length but Hercules' stadium at OLYMPIA was much longer; therefore, said the philosopher, the foot of Hercules was proportionately longer than an ordinary foot; and as the foot bears a certain ratio to the height, so the height of Hercules can be easily ascertained. **Ex ungue leonem,** a lion (may be drawn) from its claw, is a similar phrase.

**Exaltation.** In ASTROLOGY, a planet was said to be in its 'exaltation' when it was in that sign of the ZODIAC in which it was supposed to exercise its strongest influence. Thus the exaltation of VENUS is in Pisces, and her 'dejection' in Virgo.

> And thus, god wot, Mercurie is desolat
> In Pisces, wher Venus is exaltat.
> CHAUCER: *Wife of Bath's Prologue.*

**Excalibur** (ekskal′ibə). The name of King Arthur's sword (O.Fr. *Escalibor*), called by Geoffrey of Monmouth *Caliburn*, and in the

MABINOGION, *Caledvwlch.* There was also a legendary Irish sword called *Caladbolg* (hard-belly), *i.e.* capable of consuming anything.

According to Sir Thomas Malory's *Le Morte d'Arthur* (1470), Arthur, being the only one who could pull the sword from a great stone in which it had been magically fixed, was acclaimed king. The name *Excalibur* does not appear until later in the book. Later still, Chapter XXV is headed 'How Arthur by the mean of MERLIN got Excalibur his sword of the LADY OF THE LAKE.' After his last battle, when he lay sore wounded, it was returned at his command, by Sir Bedivere to the water. (*See* Malory, *Le Morte d'Arthur*, Bk. XXI, ch. v, and Tennyson's *Passing of Arthur, Idylls of the King.*) There are some obvious inconsistencies in the story.

**Exorcism.** The expelling of evil spirits by prayers and incantations. An ancient practice taken over by the Christian Church, after the example of Jesus Christ and the Apostles who healed those possessed of evil spirits. The use of this rite in the Roman Catholic Church is now carefully regulated.

> And when he had called unto him his twelve disciples, he gave them power against unclean spirits, to cast them out.
> *Matt.* x, 1.

**Exter. That's Exter, as the old woman said when she saw Kerton.** A Devonshire saying, meaning, I thought my work was done, but I find much still remains before it is completed. The story is that the woman in question was going to Exeter for the first time, and seeing the fine old church of Kerton (Crediton) supposed it to be Exeter Cathedral. 'That's Exter' (a local pronunciation of Exeter), she said, 'and my journey is over'; but alas! she had still eight miles to walk.

**Extispicy** (ekstis′pisi). The ancient practice of Roman soothsayers of divination by the inspection of the entrails of sacrificed animals—*see* HARUSPEX.

# F

**Fables** (Lat. *fabula*, a narrative story or fable). Although this name is applied in a general sense to fictitious tales, legends and myths, it is more particularly applied to didactic stories of which a moral forms an integral part. In this more restricted class, human thoughts and attributes are usually portrayed by members of the animal and insect world. *See* AESOP.

**Fabulinus** (*fabulari*, to speak). The god, mentioned by Varro, who taught Roman children to utter their first word. *See* BABES, PROTECTING DEITIES OF.

**Face. The face that launched a thousand ships.** That of HELEN, the ships being the Greek fleet which sailed for Troy to avenge Menelaus. The phrase is from Marlowe's *Faustus* (*l.* 1354).

**Facilis descensus Averno.** *See* AVERNUS.

**Faerie** (fā'əri). The land of the fays or fairies, the dominions of OBERON. *See* AVALON.

> The land of faery,
> Where nobody gets old and godly and grave,
> Where nobody gets old and crafty and wise,
> Where nobody gets old and bitter of tongue.
> W. B. YEATS: *The Land of Heart's Desire.*

**Faerie Queene, The.** An allegorical romance of chivalry by Edmund Spenser (*c.* 1552–1599), originally intended to have been in twelve books, each of which was to have portrayed one of the twelve moral virtues, but only six books were completed. It details the adventures of various knights, who personify different virtues (*e.g.* ARTEGAL, justice; Sir CALIDORE, courtesy), and who belong to the court of GLORIANA, who sometimes typifies Queen Elizabeth I.

**Fair. Fair Maid of Perth.** Katie Glover, heroine of Scott's novel of this name, is supposed to have lived in the early 15th century, but is not a definite historical character, though her house is still shown at Perth. Bizet's opera, *La Jolie Fille de Perth* (1867), is based on the novel.
**Fair Maid of Ross.** *See under* ROSS.
**Fair Rosamond.** *See* ROSAMOND.

**Fairs** (O.Fr. *feire*; Lat. *feria*, a holiday). These great periodical markets of former days were often held at the time of Church festivals and came to be associated with side-shows, amusements and merry-making. Although trade fairs or exhibitions are a link with the commercial aspect of the fairs of the past, the name is now largely associated with the travelling amusement fair. *See* BARTHOLOMEW FAIR; DONNYBROOK FAIR; GOOSE FAIR.

**Fairlop Oak.** A huge tree in Hainault Forest, Essex, blown down in 1820. Prior to that, a FAIR was held annually in July beneath its spreading branches.

**Fairy,** or **Fay.** In folklore and legend, a diminutive supernatural being of human shape, with magical powers. The names of the principal fairies and sprites etc., known in fable and legend appear in this dictionary as individual entries. *See also* BROWNIE, DEITIES, DWARF, ELF, FAUNI, GNOME, GOBLIN, LEPRECHAUN, PIXIE.
**Fairy loaves,** or **stones.** Fossil sea-urchins, said to be made by the fairies.
**Fairy money.** Found money, said to be placed by some good fairy at the spot where it is picked up. Also in legend, money given by the fairies which soon turned into 'leaves' or other worthless forms.
**Fairy of the Mine.** A malevolent GNOME supposed to live in mines who busied himself cutting ore, turning the windlass etc.

> No goblin or swart fairy of the mine
> Hath hurtful power o'er true virginity.
> MILTON: *Comus*, 436.

**Fairy rings.** Circles of dark green grass often found in lawns and meadows and popularly supposed to be produced by fairies dancing on the spot. They are due to the growth of certain fungi below the surface. The spawn radiates from the centre at a similar rate annually and darker colour is due to the increased nitrogen produced by the action of the fungus.

> You demi-puppets that
> By moonshine do the green sour ringlets make,
> Whereof the ewe not bites.
> SHAKESPEARE: *Tempest*, V, i.

**Fairy sparks.** The phosphoric light from decaying wood, fish and other substances. Thought at one time to be lights prepared for the fairies at their revels.

**Falling stars.** Meteors. A wish made as a star falls is supposed to come true. Muslims believe them to be firebrands flung by good ANGELS against evil spirits when they approach too near the gates of HEAVEN.

**Familiar,** or **familiar spirit** (Lat. *famulus*, a servant). A spirit slave, sometimes in human shape, sometimes appearing as a cat, dog, raven etc., attendant upon a WITCH, WIZARD or magician, and supposed to be a demon in disguise.

> Away with him! he has a familiar under his tongue.
> SHAKESPEARE: *Henry VI, Pt. II*, IV, vii.

**Fanny Adams,** or **Sweet Fanny Adams,** or **Sweet F.A.** means 'nothing at all' or 'sweet nothing' though (especially by its initials) it has a somewhat ambiguous connotation. It is a phrase of tragic origin. In 1867 Fanny Adams, a child of eight, was murdered in a hop-garden at Alton, Hants, and her body horribly dismembered. The Royal Navy, with gruesome humour, adopted her name as a synonym for tinned mutton, which was first issued at this time. Sweet Fanny Adams became, as a consequence, a phrase for anything worthless, and then for 'nothing at all'.

**Fantom.** An old spelling of PHANTOM.

**Fata** (fah'tə) (Ital. a fairy). Female supernatural beings introduced in Italian mediaeval romance, usually under the sway of DEMOGORGON.

**Fata Morgana.** The fay, or fairy Morgana, sister of King ARTHUR; also a mirage often visible in the Straits of Messina, so named from MORGAN LE FAY who was fabled by the Norman settlers in England to dwell in Calabria.

**Fatal Gifts.** *See* CADMUS; HARMONIA; FATAL NECKLACE *under* NECKLACE; NESSUS; NIBELUNGENLIED; SEIAN HORSE.

**Fates. The Cruel Fates.** The Greeks and Romans supposed there were three Parcae or Fates, who arbitrarily controlled the birth, life and death of everyone. They were CLOTHO, LACHESIS and ATROPOS; called cruel because they paid no regard to the wishes of anyone.

**Father of Lies.** SATAN.

**Fauna** (faw'nə). The animals of a country at any given period. The term was first used by Linnaeus in the title of his *Fauna Suecica* (1746), a companion volume to his *Flora Suecica* (1745), and is the name of a rural goddess, of like attributes to FAUNUS (*see* PAN).

> Nor less the place of curious plant he knows;
> He both his Flora and his Fauna shows.
> CRABBE: *The Borough*, Letter viii.

**Fauni** or **Fauns.** Minor Roman deities of the countryside, merry and mischievous, small counterparts of FAUNUS. *Cp.* SATYR.

**Faunus.** A good spirit of forest and field, and a god of prophecy. He had the form of a SATYR and is identified with the Greek PAN. FAUNA is sometimes given as his wife, sometimes as his daughter. At his festivals, called FAUNALIA, peasants brought rustic offerings and made merry. He was also fabled to have been a king of Latium subsequently deified for his devotion to agriculture.

**Faust** (fowst). The hero of Marlowe's *Tragical History of Dr. Faustus* (*c.* 1592) and Goethe's *Faust* (1772–1831) is founded on Dr. Johann Faust, or Faustus, a magician and astrologer, who was born in Württemberg and died about 1538, and about whom many stories soon began to circulate crediting him with supernatural gifts and evil living. The suggestion that Johann Fust, or Faust, the printer and one-time partner of Gutenberg, was the original upon whom the Faust stories were built, is now completely rejected. In 1587 *The History of Dr. Faustus, the Notorious Magician and Master of the Black Art* was published by Johann Spies at Frankfurt. It immediately became popular and was soon translated into English, French and other languages. Many other accounts followed and the

Faust theme was developed by writers, artists and musicians over the years. It was Goethe who was responsible, however, for transforming the necromancer into a personification of the struggle between the higher and lower natures in man. Notable among musical compositions on the story are Spohr's opera *Faust,* 1813, Wagner's overture *Faust,* 1840; Berlioz's *Damnation de Faust,* 1846; Gounod's opera *Faust,* 1859; Boito's *Mefistofele,* 1868; and Busoni's *Doktor Faust,* 1925.

The idea of making a pact with a DEVIL for worldly reasons is of Jewish origin. The basis of the Faust story is that he sold his soul to the Devil in return for twenty-four years of further life during which he is to have every pleasure and all knowledge at his command. The climax comes when the Devil claims him for his own.

> O lente, lente currite noctis equi!
> The stars move still, time runs, the clock will strike,
> The Devil will come, and Faustus must be damned.
> O' I'll leap up to my God! Who pulls me down?
> See, see where Christ's blood streams in the firmament!
> MARLOWE: *Doctor Faustus,* V, iii.

**Favonius** (fəvō′niəs). The Latin name for the ZEPHYR or west wind. It means the wind favourable to vegetation.

> If to the torrid zone her way she bend,
> Her the cool breathing of Favonius lend,
> Thither command the birds to sing their quires,
> That zone is temp'rate.
> HABINGTON: *Castara: To the Spring* (1634).

**Fay.** *See* FAIRY.

**Morgan le Fay.** *See* FATA MORGANA *and* MORGAN.

**Feather.** The feather represents truth which must rise. In Egypt it was an emblem of Maat, goddess of truth and in Amenti Osiris weighs the soul against this feather. Wearing feathers transmits the power of the bird and puts the wearer in touch with the magic powers and instinctual knowledge. For this purpose feathered robes were worn by priests and shamans.

**A feather in your cap.** An honour to you. The allusion is to the very general custom in Asia and among the American Indians of adding a feather to the headgear for every enemy slain. The ancient Lycians and many others had a similar custom, just as the sportsman who kills the first woodcock puts a feather in his cap. In Hungary, at one time, none might wear a feather but he who had slain a Turk. When Chinese Gordon quelled the Tai-Ping rebellion he was honoured by the Chinese Government with the 'yellow jacket and peacock's feather'.

**Femynye** (fem′ini). A mediaeval name for the kingdom of the AMAZONS. John Gower (*c.* 1313–1408) terms PENTHESILEA 'queen of Feminee'.

> He [Theseus] conquered al the regne of Femynye
> That whylom was y-claped Scithia;
> And weddede the quene Ipolita.
> CHAUCER: *Knight's Tale,* 8.

**Fenrir** or **Fenris** (fen′rēr). In Scandinavian mythology, the wolf of LOKI. He was the brother of HEL and when he gaped one jaw touched earth and the other HEAVEN. At the RAGNAROK he broke his fetters and swallowed ODIN, who was avenged by VIDAR thrusting his sword into the yawning gullet and piercing the beast's heart.

**Ferdiad.** A hero of Irish legend who was persuaded to fight for Queen MAEVE against CUCHULAIN, his dearest friend. After a struggle lasting three days he was killed, to Cuchulain's bitter grief.

**Fergus mac Roich** (fœ′gəs mak roikh). The heroic tutor of CUCHULAIN, who left CONCHOBAR'S court after the treacherous murder of the sons of USNECH.

**Fern Seed. We have the receipt of fern seed, we walk invisible** (Shakespeare: *Henry IV, Pt. I,* II, i). Fern seed was popularly supposed only to be visible on St. John's Eve, and as it was thus so seldom seen it was believed to confer invisibility on those who carried it. Plants were often supposed to convey their own particular quality on their wearer. Thus the yellow celandine was said to cure jaundice; woodsorrel, which has a heart-shaped leaf, to cheer the heart; liverwort to be good for the liver etc.

> I had
> No medicine, sir, to go invisible
> No fern-seed in any pocket.
> BEN JONSON: *New Inn,* I, i.

**Ferragus.** The giant of Portugal in VALENTINE AND ORSON. The great BRAZEN HEAD, that told those who consulted it whatever they required to know, was kept in this giant's castle.

**Ferrex and Porrex.** Two sons of Gorboduc, a mythical British king, who divided his kingdom between them. Porrex drove his brother from Britain, and when Ferrex returned with an army he was slain, but Porrex was shortly after torn to pieces by his mother with the assistance of her women. The story is told in Geoffrey of Monmouth's *Historia Regum Britanniae* (ch. xvi), and it forms the basis of the first regular English tragedy, *Gorboduc, or Ferrex and Porrex*, written by Thomas Norton and Thomas Sackville, Lord Buckhurst, and acted in 1562.

**Fetch.** A WRAITH—the disembodied ghost of a living person; hence *fetch-light*, or *fetch candle*, a light appearing at night supposed to foretell someone's death. *Fetches* most commonly appear to distant friends and relations at the very moment before the death of those they represent. The word is of uncertain origin.

> The very fetch and ghost of Mrs. Gamp, bonnet and all, might be seen hanging up, any hour in the day, in at least a dozen secondhand clothes-shops about Holborn.
>
> DICKENS: *Martin Chuzzlewit*, xix.

It is also used in the sense of a stratagem, artifice or trick.

> Deny to speak with me? They are sick? they are weary?
> They have travelled all night? Mere fetches.
>
> SHAKESPEARE: *King Lear*, II, iv.

**Fetish** (Port. *fetico*, sorcery, charm; Lat. *facticius*, artificial). The name given by early Portuguese voyagers to AMULETS and other objects supposed by the natives of the Guinea Coast to possess magic powers: hence an idol, an object of devotion. Fetishism is found in all primitive nations in which the services of a spirit may be appropriated by the possession of its material emblem. In psychopathology the word is used to denote a condition or perversion in which sexual gratification is obtained from some object etc., that has become emotionally charged.

**Field of the Forty Footsteps,** or **The Brothers' Steps.** The land at the back of the British Museum, once called Southampton Fields, near the extreme north-east of the present Montague Street. The tradition is that at the time of the Duke of Monmouth's Rebellion (1685) two brothers fought each other here until both were killed, and for many years forty impressions of their feet remained on the field. No grass would grow there, nor upon the bank where the young woman sat who was the object of their contest. The site was built upon about 1800.

**Fierabras, Sir** (fī'ərəbras). The son of BALAN, King of Spain. For height of stature, breadth of shoulder and hardness of muscle, he knew no equal, but his pride was laid low by OLIVER. He became a Christian, was accepted by CHARLEMAGNE as a PALADIN and ended his days in an odour of sanctity.

**Fiery Cross, The.** An ancient signal in the Scottish Highlands when a chieftain wished to summon his clan in an emergency. It was symbolical of fire and sword and consisted of a light wooden cross the ends of which were dipped in the blood of a goat slain for the purpose. It was carried from settlement to settlement by swift runners. Disobedience to the summons implied infamy, hence the alternative name of *Cross of Shame*.

Scott's *Lady of the Lake* (canto iii) contains a graphic account of the custom.

When the Ku Klux Klan arose after the American Civil War, it adopted this symbol.

**Fig. Mercury fig.** *See under* MERCURY.

**Figaro.** A type of daring, cunning and witty roguery and intrigue. The character is in *Le Barbier de Séville* (1775), and *Le Mariage de Figaro* (1784) by Beaumarchais. There are several operas based on these dramas, as Mozart's *Nozze di Figaro*, and Paisiello's and Rossini's *Il Barbiere di Siviglia*.

Hence the name of the famous Parisian periodical which appeared from 1826 to 1833 and its successor which began life in 1854. *Le Figaro* is one of the foremost French dailies to survive World War II.

**Fight. To fight like Kilkenny cats.** *See under* CAT.

**Fimbul-Winter.** In Norse legend, such a severe winter of horrors as never before known which lasted three years without any summer to lessen its onslaught; trees, plants and men died of hunger. It was the forerunner of RAGNAROK.

**Findabair.** In Irish legend, the wondrously beautiful daughter of Queen MAEVE of Connacht. She was promised in marriage to the man who would challenge CUCHULAIN in the

War of the Brown Bull and died after her lover, Fraech, was slain in battle by Cuchulain.

**Fingal.** The great Gaelic legendary hero, father of OSSIAN, who was purported by Macpherson to have been the original author of the long epic poem *Fingal* (1762), which narrates the hero's adventures.
**Fingal's Cave.** The basaltic cavern on Staffa, said to have been a home of FINGAL. It is the name given to Mendelssohn's *Hebridean Overture* (1830).

**Finger** (O.E. *finger*). The old names for the fingers are:
*Thuma* (O.E.), the thumb.
*Towcher* (M.E. the finger that touches), *foreman* or pointer. This was called the *scite-finger* (shooting finger) by the Anglo-Saxons, now usually known as the first or fore-finger and *index finger* because it is used for pointing.
*Long-man*, or *long-finger*.
*Lech-man*, or *ring-finger*. The former means the 'medical finger' and the latter is the Roman *digitus annularis*, called by the Anglo-Saxons the *gold-finger*. This finger was used as the ring finger (also *annular finger*) in the belief that a nerve ran through it to the heart. Hence the Greeks and Romans called it the *medical finger*, and used it for stirring mixtures under the notion that it would give instant warning to the heart if in contact with anything noxious. It is still a popular superstition that it is bad to rub salve or scratch the skin with any other finger, also being the least used it is the cleanest.

> At last he put on her medical finger a pretty, handsome gold ring, whereinto was enchased a precious toadstone of Beausse.
> RABELAIS: *Pantagruel*, III, xviii.

*Little man*, or *little finger*. Called by the Anglo-Saxons the ear-finger. It is also known as the *auricular finger*.
The fingers each had their special significance in ALCHEMY, and Ben Jonson says:
> The thumb, in chiromancy, we give to Venus,
> The fore-finger to Jove; the midst to Saturn;
> The ring to Sol; the least to Mercury.
> *Alchemist*, I, ii.

**To keep one's fingers crossed.** To hope for success, to try to ensure against disaster. From the superstition that making the sign of the CROSS will avert bad luck.

**Fionnuala** (finoo′ələ) In Irish legend, the daughter of LIR, who was transformed into a swan and condemned to wander over the lakes and rivers until Christianity came to IRELAND. Moore has a poem on the subject in his *Irish Melodies*.

**Firbolgs.** *See* MILESIANS.

**Fire. St. Anthony's Fire.** *See under* ANTHONY.
**St. Elmo's Fire; St. Helen's Fire.** *See* CORPOSANT.
**Men stand with their backs to the fire.** An old explanation is that when the dog's nose proved too small to stop a leak in the Ark, Noah sat on the hole to keep the water out. Ever since men have felt the need to warm their backs, and the dogs have had cold noses.
**Fire-cross.** *See* FIERY CROSS.
**Fire-drake,** or **fire-dragon.** A fiery serpent, an IGNIS FATUUS of large proportions, superstitiously believed to be a flying DRAGON keeping guard over hidden treasures.

> There is a fellow somewhat near the door, he should be a brazier by his face, for, o' my conscience, twenty of the dog-days now reign in 's nose … that fire-drake did I hit three times on the head.
> SHAKESPEARE: *King Henry VIII*, V, iii.

**Fire-worship** is said to have been introduced into Persia by Phoedima, widow of Smerdis, and wife of Hystaspes. It is not the SUN that is worshipped, but the god who is supposed to reside in it; at the same time the fire worshippers reverence the sun as the throne of the deity.

**Fish. A pretty kettle of fish.** *See under* KETTLE.
**Fisher King.** In the legends of the Holy GRAIL, the uncle of PERCEVAL.

**Five. The Five Alls.** *See* PUBLIC-HOUSE SIGNS.

**Flatter. When flatterers meet, the devil goes to dinner.** Flattery is so pernicious, so fills the heart with pride and conceit, so perverts the judgment and disturbs the balance of mind, that SATAN himself could do no greater mischief, so he may go to dinner and leave the leaven of wickedness to work its own mischief.

**Fleet, The.** A famous London prison of mediaeval origin which stood on the east side of Farringdon Street, until its demolition (1845–1846), on the site now partly occupied by the Memorial Hall. It took its name from the river Fleet which (now piped) enters the Thames at Blackfriars Bridge. As a royal prison it housed some distinguished prisoners in Tudor and Stuart times, including those committed by Star Chamber, but mainly owes its notoriety to its subsequent use as a debtor's prison. It was destroyed in the Great Fire of London, rebuilt, and again burned during the Gordon Riots. The Warden farmed out the prison to the highest bidder which encouraged the shameful treatment of its occupants. *Cp.* FLEET MARRIAGES.

> Most of our readers will remember that, until within a very few years past, there was a kind of iron cage in the wall of the Fleet Prison, within which was posted some man of hungry looks, who, from time to time, rattled a money-box, and explained, in a mournful voice 'Pray, remember the poor debtors; pray, remember the poor debtors'.
>
> DICKENS: *Pickwick Papers*, ch. xlii.

**Fleet Book Evidence.** No evidence at all. The books of the Old Fleet prison are not admissible as evidence of a marriage. *See* FLEET MARRIAGES *below*.

**Fleet Marriages.** Clandestine marriages, especially of minors, at one time performed without banns or licence in the chapel of the FLEET, but from the latter part of Queen Anne's reign performed by the Fleet clergy in rooms of nearby taverns and houses.

> Before the door of the Fleet prison, men plied in behalf of a clergyman, literally insisting people to walk in and be married. They performed the ceremony inside the prison, to sailors and others for what they could get.
>
> LEIGH HUNT: *The Town*, ch. ii.

James Malcolm, the topographer, tells us that as many as 'thirty couple were joined in one day' and that 2954 marriages were registered in the four months ending 12 February 1705. The practice was destroyed by Lord Hardwicke's Marriage Act of 1753 which declared such marriages void.

**The Liberties of the Fleet.** The district immediately surrounding the FLEET, in which prisoners were sometimes allowed to reside, and beyond which they were not permitted to go. They included the north side of Ludgate Hill and the Old Bailey to Fleet Lane, down the lane to the market, and on the east side along by the prison wall to the foot of Ludgate Hill.

**Flibbertigibbet.** One of the five fiends that possessed 'poor Tom' in *King Lear* (IV, i). Shakespeare got the name from Harsnet's *Declaration of Egregious Popish Impostures* (1603), where we are told of forty fiends which the JESUITS cast out, and among the number was 'Fliberdigibet', a name which had been previously used by Latimer and others for a mischievous GOSSIP. Elsewhere the name is apparently a synonym for PUCK.

**Flood, The.** *See* DELUGE.

**Flora.** The Roman goddess of flowers especially associated with Spring. Her festivals, the *Floralia*, were from 28 April to 3 May. The term *Flora* also denotes the native or indigenous plants of a country or region. *Cp.* FAUNA.

**Flora's Dial.** A fanciful dial formed of flowers which open or close at the various hours.

## Flowers and Trees, etc.

(1) Dedicated to heathen gods:

| | |
|---|---|
| The Cornel cherry-tree | to APOLLO |
| ,, CYPRESS | ,, PLUTO |
| ,, DITTANY | ,, DIANA |
| ,, LAUREL | ,, APOLLO |
| ,, LILY | ,, JUNO |
| ,, Maidenhair | ,, PLUTO |
| ,, MYRTLE | ,, VENUS |
| ,, Narcissus | ,, CERES |
| ,, OAK | ,, JUPITER |
| ,, OLIVE | ,, MINERVA |
| ,, POPPY | ,, CERES |
| ,, VINE | ,, BACCHUS |

(2) Dedicated to saints:

| | |
|---|---|
| Canterbury Bells | to St. AUGUSTINE of CANTERBURY |
| Crocus | ,, St. VALENTINE |
| Crown Imperial | ,, Edward the Confessor |
| DAISY | ,, St. Margaret |
| Herb Christopher | ,, St. Christopher |
| LADY'S-SMOCK | ,, the Virgin MARY |
| ROSE | ,, Mary Magdalene |
| St. John's-wort | ,, St. John |
| St. Barnaby's Thistle | ,, St. Barnabas |

(3) National emblems:

| | | |
|---|---|---|
| LEEK, Daffodil | emblem of | Wales |
| LILY (FLEUR-DE-LYS) | ,, | BOURBON France |
| ,, (Giglio bianco) | ,, | Florence |
| ,, white | ,, | Ghibellines |
| ,, red | ,, | Guelphs |
| Linden | ,, | Prussia |
| Mignonette | ,, | Saxony |
| Pomegranate | ,, | Spain |

| ROSE | ,, | England |
|------|-----|---------|
| ,, red, Lancastrians: white, Yorkists | | |
| SHAMROCK | emblem of | Ireland |
| Thistle | ,, | Scotland |
| Violet | ,, | Athens |
| Sugar Maple | ,, | Canada |

(4) In Christian Symbolism:

| Box | a symbol of | the Resurrection |
|-----|-------------|------------------|
| Cedars | ,, | the faithful |
| Corn-ears | ,, | the Holy Communion |
| Dates | ,, | the faithful |
| Grapes | ,, | this is my blood |
| HOLLY | ,, | the Resurrection |
| IVY | ,, | the Resurrection |
| Lily | ,, | purity |
| OLIVE | ,, | peace |
| Orange-blossom | ,, | virginity |
| Palm | ,, | victory |
| Rose | ,, | incorruption |
| Vine | ,, | Christ our Life |
| Yew | ,, | death |

N.B.—The laurel, oak, olive, myrtle, rosemary, cypress and amaranth are all funereal plants.

**The Flower of Kings** (Lat. *flos regum*). King ARTHUR was so called by John of Exeter, Bishop of Winchester (d. 1268).

**Flute. The Magic Flute.** In Mozart's opera of this name (*Die Zauberflöte*, 1791) the magic flute was bestowed by the powers of darkness, and had the power of inspiring love. By it Tamino and Pamina are guided through all worldly dangers to knowledge of Divine Truth.

**Fly.** An insect (*plural* **flies**). It is said that no fly was ever seen in Solomon's temple, and according to Muslim legend, all flies shall perish except one, the bee-fly.

**The God,** or **Lord of Flies.** Every year, in the temple of Actium, the Greeks used to sacrifice an ox to ZEUS, who in this capacity was surnamed Apomyios, the averter of flies. Pliny tells us that at Rome sacrifice was offered to flies in the temple of HERCULES Victor, and the Syrians also offered sacrifice to these insects. *See* ACHOR; BEELZEBUB.

**The fly on the coach-wheel.** One who fancies himself of great importance, one who is in reality of none at all. The allusion is to AESOP's fable of a fly sitting on a chariot-wheel and saying, 'See what dust I make.'

**Flying-the-garter.** *See under* GARTER.

**The Flying Dutchman.** In maritime legend, a spectral ship that is supposed to haunt the seas around the Cape of Good Hope and to lure other vessels to their destruction or to cause other misfortune. According to Jal's *Scènes de la Vie Maritime*, he is said to be a Dutch captain, who persisted in trying to round the Cape, in spite of the violence of the storm, and the protests of passengers and crew. Eventually a form, said to be the Almighty, appeared on the deck, but the Captain did not even touch his cap but fired upon the form and cursed and blasphemed. For punishment, the Dutchman was condemned to sail and to be a torment to sailors until the Day of Judgment. A skeleton ship appears in Coleridge's *Ancient Mariner*, and Washington Irving tells of 'the Flying Dutchman of the Tappan Sea' in his *Chronicles of Woolfert's Roost*. Wagner has an opera *Der Fliegende Holländer* (1843) and Captain Marryat's novel *The Phantom Ship* (1839) tells of Philip Vanderdecken's successful but disastrous search for his father, the captain of the Flying Dutchman. Similar legends are found in many other countries.

> The Demon Frigate braves the gale;
> And well the doom'd spectators know
> The harbinger of wreck and woe.
> SCOTT: *Rokeby*, canto II, xi.

**Folk-lore.** The traditional beliefs, customs, popular superstitions and legends of a people. The word was coined in 1846 by W. J. Thomas (1803–1885), editor of the *Athenaeum* and founder of *Notes and Queries*.

**Fontarabia** (fontərä′biə). Now called Fuenterrabia (Lat. *fons rapidus*), near the Gulf of Gascony. Here, according to legend, CHARLEMAGNE and all his chivalry fell by the swords of the Saracens. The French romancers say that, the rear of the king's army being cut to pieces, Charlemagne returned to life and avenged them by a complete victory.

> When Charlemain with all his peerage fell
> By Fontarabia.
> MILTON: *Paradise Lost*, I, 587.

**Food. The food of the gods.** *See* AMBROSIA; NECTAR.

**Fool. All Fools' Day.** The first day of April. *See* APRIL FOOL.

**April Fool.** *See* APRIL.

**Court Fools.** From mediaeval times until the 17th century licensed fools or jesters were commonly kept at court; and frequently in the retinue of wealthy nobles. Holbein painted Sir Thomas More's jester, Patison, in his picture of the chancellor; the Earl of Morton, Scottish Regent (executed 1581), had a fool called Patrick Bonny; and as late as 1728 Swift wrote an epitaph on Dickie Pierce, the Earl of Suffolk's fool, who is buried in Berkeley Churchyard, Gloucestershire. *See also* DAGONET.

Among the most celebrated court fools are:

Rahère (founder of St. Bartholomew's Hospital), of Henry I (according to a tradition); John Scogan (*see* SCOGAN'S JESTS), of Edward IV; Patch, of Elizabeth, wife of Henry VII; Will Somers, of Henry VIII; Jenny Colquhoun and James Geddes, of Mary Queen of Scots; Robert Grene, of Queen Elizabeth I; Archie Armstrong and Thomas Derrie, of James I; Muckle John, of Charles I, who was probably also the last court fool in England.

In France, Miton and Thévenin de St. Léger were fools of Charles V; Haincelin Coq belonged to Charles VI, and Guillaume Louel to Charles VII, Triboulet was the jester of Louis XII and Francis I; Brusquet, of Henri II; Sibilot and Chicot, of Henri III and IV; and l'Angély, of Louis XIII and Louis XIV.

In chess the French name for the 'bishop' is *fou* (a fool) and they used to represent it in a fool's dress.

**The Feast of Fools.** A kind of clerical SATURNALIA, popular in the Middle Ages and not successfully suppressed until the REFORMATION, and even later in France. The feast was usually centred on a cathedral and most commonly held on the Feasts of St. STEPHEN (26 December), St. JOHN (27 December), Holy Innocents (28 December). The mass was burlesqued and braying often took the place of the customary responses. Obscene jests and dances were common as well as the singing of indecent songs. The ass was a central feature and the **Feast of Asses** was sometimes a separate festival.

**Foot. To show the cloven foot,** or **hoof.** To betray an evil intention. An allusion to the DEVIL who is represented with a cloven hoof.

**Forbidden. Forbidden City.** Lhasa (the seat of the gods), the ancient religious and political capital of Tibet, some 12,000 ft. above sea level. The palace of the Dalai-Lama or Grand Lama stands on the neighbouring Potala hill. This sacred city of Lamaist Buddhism containing fifteen monasteries fell under Chinese control (*c.* 1720) and when, in 1959, the Tibetans unsuccessfully tried to cast off the Chinese yoke, the Dalai-Lama fled to India. Its first European mention was by Friar Odoric, the famous traveller (*c.* 1330). Long closed to Europeans, hence the epithet, it is still largely a forbidden city.

**Forbidden Fruit.** Forbidden or unlawful pleasure of any kind, especially illicit love. The reference is to *Gen.* ii, 17, 'But of the tree of knowledge of good and evil, thou shalt not eat of it.' According to Muslim tradition the forbidden fruit partaken of by ADAM and Eve was the banyan or Indian fig.

**Forgery. The Poems of Ossian.** *See* OSSIAN.

**Psalmanazar, George.** *See* PSALMANAZAR.

**The Turin Shroud.** The shroud of twill linen kept in Turin Cathedral and claimed to be that which wrapped the body of Christ after His crucifixion. The Pope agreed to radio-carbon dating in 1987 and in 1988 the Archbishop of Turin appointed the Oxford Research Laboratory for Archaeology, the Department of Physics of Arizona University and the Swiss Federal Institute of Technology at Zurich, to date the shroud, pieces of which were given to these institutes in April 1988. The results were announced on 13 October and the cloth was dated between 1260 and 1390. There is no historical evidence that it was known before the 14th century. Although not accepted by all the general conclusion is that the shroud is a mediaeval forgery.

**The Vinland Map.** Norse exploration from the end of the 10th century led to the discovery of part of North America. According to the Norse Saga, *Flateyjarbók*, 'When spring came they made ready and left, and Leif named the land after its fruits, and called it *Vinland*'. In 1957 the discovery of a map of the NE American coast was announced and said to be the most exciting cartographic find of the century. Supposedly drawn about 1440, it substantially preceded the voyages of Columbus (1492) and of John Cabot (1497), thus conclusively establishing the extent of the Viking explorations. It was presented to Yale University by an anonymous giver in 1965. In 1974 Yale announced that it was a fake. The pigment of the ink with which it was drawn was found to contain titanium dioxide, first used in the 1920s.

**Forget-me-not.** According to German legend this flower takes its name from the last words of a knight, who was drowned while trying to pick some from the riverside for his lady. The botanical name *myosotis* (mouse-ear) refers to the shape of the leaves.

**Fortunate Islands.** An ancient name for the Canary Islands; also for any imaginary lands set in distant seas, like the 'Islands of the Blest'.

> Their place of birth alone is mute
> To sounds that echo farther west
> Than your sire's Islands of the Blest.
> BYRON: *Don Juan*, canto III, lxxxvi, 2.

**Fortunatus** (fawtūnā′təs). A hero of mediaeval legend (derived from Eastern sources) who possessed an inexhaustible purse, a wishing cap etc. He appears in a German *Volksbuch* of 1509. Hans Sachs dramatized the story in 1553, and Dekker's *Pleasant Comedy of Old Fortunatus* was first performed in December 1599.
**You have found Fortunatus's purse.** You are in luck's way.

**Forty. Field of the Forty Footsteps.** See *under* FIELD.

**Fountain of Arethusa.** See ALPHEUS AND ARETHUSA.
**Fountain of Youth.** In popular legend, a fountain with the power of restoring youth. Much sought after, at one time it was supposed to be in one of the Bahama Islands. Ponce de León, discoverer of Florida, set out in search of BIMINI.

**Four. Four Horsemen of the Apocalypse.** In *The Revelation of St. John the Divine* (ch. vi), four agents of destruction, two being agents of war and two of famine and pestilence. The first appeared on a white horse, the second on a red horse, the third on a black horse, and the fourth on a pale horse.

Vicente Blasco Ibáñez (1867–1928), the Spanish writer, published a novel of this title in 1916 which appeared in English in 1918.
**Four Sons of Aymon.** See AYMON.

**Fox.** Credited with more guile and cunning than any other animal, the fox appears extensively in myth and fable; it is one of the great tricksters and shape-shifters, its history as such going back to Sumerian times, being associated with the trickster god Enki. DIONYSUS/BACCHUS was associated with the fox as protecting the vines from the 'little foxes' who spoiled them. In Thrace the fox was the counterpart of the Dionysian bull. The 'spoiling of the vines' theme is repeated in the Old Testament. Christianity equates the deceitful fox with the Devil.

The fox is the subject of innumerable legends in China and Japan where it is represented as the archetypal illusionist, taking human form to deceive and bring disaster. Its most usual guise is that of a beautiful maiden, but in Japan it is a 'Spirit of Rain' and an attribute of the rice deity Inari. Fox spirits can compound the elixir of life and spirits of the dead can be embodied in foxes.

Amerindian myth also has the fox as a trickster and shape-shifter and there are fox tribes. As Br'er Fox the animal has passed into modern legend and literature. See REYNARD.
**Reynard the Fox.** See REYNARD.
**A case of the fox and the grapes.** Said of one who wants something badly, but cannot obtain it, and so tries to pretend that he does not really want it at all. See GRAPE.
**Foxglove** (*Digitalis purpurea*). The flower is named from the animal and the glove. It is not known how the fox came to be associated with it, but one suggestion is that it is a corruption of 'folk's glove', folks being the fairies or little people. In Welsh it is called *menygellyllon* (elves' gloves) or *menyg y llwynog* (fox's gloves) and in Ireland it is called a *fairy thimble*.

**Fra Diavolo.** See DIAVOLO.

**Frankenstein.** The young student in Mary Wollstonecraft Shelley's romance of that name (1818), a classic horror story. Frankenstein made a soulless monster out of corpses from churchyards and dissecting-rooms and endued it with life by galvanism. The tale shows the creature longed for sympathy, but was shunned by everyone and became the instrument of dreadful retribution on the student who usurped the prerogative of the Creator. *Cp.* VAMPIRE.

**Fraternity, The.** A term highwaymen used to apply to themselves as a body but the 'Gentlemen of the road' were by no means always on friendly terms with one another.

**Freemasonry.** As a secret society it has existed for many centuries and professes to trace its origins to the building of Solomon's Temple. In mediaeval times stonemasons banded together with their secret signs, passwords and tests. Freemasonry in its modern form, as a body with no trade connexions, began to flourish in the 17th century and it is likely that Sir Christopher Wren was a member. Ashmole was initiated in 1646. The mother Grand Lodge of England was founded in London in 1717 and took under its aegis the many small lodges in the provinces. Even the ancient York Lodge, which has given its name to the rites of the Continent and the USA, acknowledged its authority. From this Grand Lodge of England derive all Masonic lodges throughout the world.

In Britain, Masonry has three degrees, the first is called Entered Apprentice; the second Fellow Craft, the third, Master Mason. Royal Arch Masonry is an adjunct to these, and is peculiar to Britain. In the USA the first regular lodge was founded at Boston in 1733, though there are minutes extant of a lodge in Philadelphia in 1730. The ritual side of Freemasonry has appealed to American more than it has to British Masons, and many degrees are worked in the USA with elaborate ritual and mysteries. In addition to the three degrees of British Masonry there are the Cryptic Degrees of Royal and Select Masters; the Chivalric Rite, with three degrees of Knights Red Cross, Temple and of Malta; and the 33 degrees of the Ancient and Accepted Scottish Rite. The various Grand Orients of the Continent (all disowned by the Grand Lodge of England on account of their political activities) were founded at different times and work modifications of the Scottish Rite. The part played by

Masonic lodges in the French Revolution is still obscure; Philippe Égalité was head of the Grand Orient, but repudiated it during the Terror. Napoleon was reported to have been initiated at Malta in 1798; he certainly favoured Masonry and during the Empire Cambacérès, Murat and Joseph Bonaparte were successive Grand Masters. Freemasonry has been condemned by the Holy See, not only for being a secret society, but for its alleged subversive aims which, if supported by Continental Masons, were quite unknown to their British and American brethren. Charity and 'brotherly love' are characteristics of the fraternity and much is done to help members and their dependants with the provision of hospitals, schools etc., and relief for widows and orphans. It is, however, commonly held that Masonry is responsible for a good deal of favouritism in appointments and promotions.

**The Lady Freemason.** Women were not admitted into FREEMASONRY, but the story goes that a lady was initiated in the early 18th century. She was the Hon. Elizabeth St. Leger, daughter of Lord Doneraile, who hid herself in an empty clock-case when the lodge was held in her father's house, and witnessed the proceedings. She was discovered, and compelled to submit to initiation as a member of the craft.

**Freischütz** (frī'shutz) (the freeshooter). A legendary German marksman in league with the DEVIL, who gave him seven balls, six of which were to hit infallibly whatever the marksman aimed at, and the seventh was to be directed as the devil wished. Weber's opera, *Der Freischütz*, based on the legend (libretto by F. Kind) was first produced in Berlin in 1821.

**Freyja** (frā'yǝ). In Scandinavian mythology the sister of FREYR, goddess of love, marriage and of the dead. She was the wife of ODIN and always wore the shining necklace called *Brisingamen* and was consequently called 'ornament loving'. Her husband is also given in some legends as *Odhr*, and she shed golden tears when he left her. The counterpart of VENUS, she is also commonly identified with Frigg, wife of Odin, who in Scandinavian myth ranked highest among the goddesses.

**Freyr.** In Norse mythology, god of fruitfulness and crops, and of the sun and rain. His horse was called Bloodyhoof and his ship SKIDBLADNIR.

**Friar. Curtal Friar.** *See* BRAZEN HEAD.

**Friar Bungay.** Thomas de Bungay of Suffolk, a Franciscan who lectured at Oxford and Cambridge in the 13th century, whose story is much overlaid with legend. He came to be portrayed as a magician and necromancer. In the old prose romance, *The Famous History of Friar Bacon*, and in Greene's *Honourable History of Friar Bacon and Friar Bungay* (1587), he appears as the assistant to Roger Bacon (d. 1292). He also features anachronistically in Lytton's *Last of the Barons*.

**Friar Rush.** A legendary house-spirit who originated as a kind of ultramischievous ROBIN GOODFELLOW in German folklore. He later acquired more devilish attributes and appeared in the habit of a Friar to lead astray those under religious vows. Dekker's play, *If it be not Good, the Divel is in it* (printed 1612), was based upon *The Pleasant History of Friar Rush* (1567).

**Friar Tuck.** Chaplain and steward of ROBIN HOOD.

> In this our spacious isle I think there is not one
> But he hath heard some talk of Hood and Little John;
> Of Tuck the merry friar, which many a sermon made
> In praise of Robin Hood, his outlaws, and their trade.
> DRAYTON: *Poly-Olbion*, xxvi, 311–16.

**Friar's Lanthorn.** One of the many names given to the Will o' the Wisp. *See* IGNIS FATUUS.

**Friday. Friday the Thirteenth.** A particularly unlucky Friday.

**Man Friday.** The young savage found by ROBINSON CRUSOE on a Friday and kept as his servant and companion on the desert island. Hence a faithful and willing attendant, ready to turn his hand to anything.

**Friendship.** The classical examples of lasting friendship between man and man are ACHILLES and PATROCLUS, PYLADES and ORESTES, NISUS and EURYALUS, DAMON and PYTHIAS. To these should be added David and Jonathan.

**Frigg.** *See* FREYJA.

**Frithiof** (frit'yof). A hero of Icelandic myth who married Ingeborg, daughter of a minor king of Norway, and widow of Sigurd Ring, to whose dominions he succeeded. His name signifies 'the peacemaker' and his adventures are recorded in the saga which bears his name. It was paraphrased by Esaias Tegner in his famous poem (1825) of the same name.

**Frog.** In mythology the frog is widely represented as lunar, as a rain-bringer and a fertility symbol; its skin, being moist, as opposed to the dryness of death, also represents renewal of life and the fecundity of the waters.

The ancient Egyptian frog goddess Hekt or Hequat was the embryonic powers of the waters and protector of the new-born. The Green Frog of the Nile typified the new life and abundance with the coming of the inundations. Amulets of frogs were found in tombs in Egypt as symbols of resurrection.

In the *Rig Veda* (VII, 103) frogs are invoked as deities and the Great Frog supports the universe; a theme which occurs in various traditions.

Graeco-Roman myth has the frog as an attribute of APHRODITE/VENUS as fertility. Plato calls the frog a rain-bringer and a devotee of the nymphs. Juvenal says that the entrails of the frog were used as charms in ancient times. Frogs croak in the swamps of the underworld.

Celtic tradition calls the frog the Lord of the Earth and associates it with the healing waters.

Amerindians have the Great Frog as the power of the waters, it is a rain-bringer and represents initiation by water, and for the shaman it is a cleansing power. It is also a totem creature.

In Christian fable the frog is ambivalent as representing new life and resurrection but also as the repulsive aspect of sin and heresy and of greed.

A frog and a mouse agreed to settle by a single combat their claims to a marsh; but, while they fought, a kite carried them both off (AESOP: *Fables*, clxviii).

> Old Aesop's fable, where he told
> What fate unto the mouse and frog befel.
> CARY: *Dante*, xxiii.

In Ovid's *Metamorphoses* (vi, 4) we are told that the Lycian shepherds were changed into frogs for mocking LATONA.

As when those hinds that were transformed to
frogs
Railed at Latona's twin-born progeny.
MILTON: *Sonnets*, xi.

Frenchmen, properly *Parisians*, have
been nicknamed Frogs or Froggies, from
their ancient heraldic device which was
three frogs or toads. (*See* FLEUR-DE-LIS.)
*Qu'en disent les grenouilles?* What do the
frogs (people of Paris) say?—was in 1791 a
common court phrase at VERSAILLES. There
was point in the pleasantry, Paris having
once been a quagmire, called *Lutetia* (mud-
land). Further point is given to the
nickname by the fact that the back legs of
the edible frog (*Rana esculenta*) form a
delicacy in French cuisine that aroused
much disparaging humour from the English.

**Frozen Words.** A conceit used by the
ancient Greeks. Antiphanes applies it to
the discourses of PLATO: 'As the cold of
certain cities is so intense that it freezes
the very words we utter, which remain con-
gealed till the heat of summer thaws them,
so the mind of youth is so thoughtless that
the wisdom of Plato lies there frozen, as it
were, till it is thawed by the ripened judgment of mature age.' Münchhausen relates
an incident of the 'frozen horn' and Rabelais
(Bk. IV, ch. lvi) tells how PANTAGRUEL and
his friends, on the confines of the Frozen
Sea, heard the uproar of a battle, which had
been frozen the preceding winter, released
by a thaw.

Where truth in person doth appear.
Like words congeal'd in northern air.
BUTLER: *Hudibras*, canto I, 147–8.

**Fum-hwang.** *See* FUNG-HWANG.

**Funeral** (Late Lat. *funeralis*, adj. from
*funus*, a burial). *Funus* is connected with
*fumus*, smoke, and the word seems to refer
to the ancient practice of disposing of the
dead by cremation. Roman funerals were
conducted by torchlight at night, that
magistrates and priests might not be made
ceremonially unclean by seeing the corpse.

Most of our funeral customs derive from
the Romans; as dressing in BLACK, walking
in procession, carrying insignia on the bier,
raising a mound on the grave (called
*tumulus*, whence *tomb*) etc. The Greeks
crowned the dead body with flowers, and
also placed flowers on the tomb; the
Romans had similar customs. In England
the Passing Bell or the *Soul Bell* used to be

tolled from the church when a parishioner
was dying and the funeral bell would be
tolled as many times as the dead person's
years of age.

Public games were held in Greece and
Rome in honour of departed heroes; as the
games instituted by HERCULES at the death
of Pelops, those held by ACHILLES in honour
of PATROCLUS (*Iliad*, Bk. xxiii), those held
by AENEAS in honour of his father Anchises
(Aeneid, Bk. V) etc. The custom of giving a
feast at funerals came to us from the
Romans, who not only feasted the friends of
the deceased, but also distributed meat to
the persons employed. *See* NEMEAN GAMES.

**Fung-hwang,** or **Fum-.** The PHOENIX of
Chinese legend, one of the four symbolical
creatures presiding over the destinies of
China. It originated from fire, was born in
the Hill of the Sun's Halo, and has its body
inscribed with the five cardinal virtues.
The phoenix represented the Empress
when portrayed with the Dragon as Emper-
or, together depicting the masculine (fung)
and the feminine (kwang) powers. *See*
PHOENIX.

**Furies, The.** The Roman name (*Furiae*) for
the Greek ERINYES, said by Hesiod to have
been the daughters of GAEA (the Earth) and
to have sprung from the blood of URANUS,
and by other accounts to be daughters of
Night or of Earth and Darkness. They were
three in number, Tisiphone (the Avenger of
blood), ALECTO (the Implacable), and Me-
gaera (the Jealous one).

They were merciless goddesses of
vengeance and punished all transgressors,
especially those who neglected filial duty or
claims of kinship etc. Their punishments
continued after death. *See* EUMENIDES.

**Furry Dance.** Part of the spring festival held
at Helston, Cornwall, on 8 May (now the
nearest Saturday). Furry Day, which is derived from the Lat. *Feriae* (festivals, holi-
days), was incorrectly changed to *Flora* in
the 18th century and in the 19th century
the dance was called the *Floral Dance*, as in
the well-known song. It is derived from a
pre-Christian festivity and is copied in some
other towns. In its present form prominent
townsfolk dance through the town. There is
a similar spring festival at Padstow beginning at midnight on 30 April.

**Fylfot** (fil'fət). A mystic sign or emblem known also as the swastika and gammadion, and in heraldry as the *cross cramponnée*, used (especially in Byzantine architecture and among the North American Indians) as an ornament of religious import. It has been found at Hissarlik, on ancient Etruscan tombs, Celtic monuments, Buddhist inscriptions, Greek coins, etc. It has been thought to have represented the power of the SUN, of the four winds, of lightning, and so on. It is used nowadays in jewellery as an emblem of luck and was also adopted as the Nazi badge.

The name *fylfot* was adopted by antiquaries from a MS. of the 15th century, and is possibly *fill foot*, signifying a device to fill the foot of a stained-glass window.

# G

**Gabbara.** The giant who, according to Rabelais, was 'the first inventor of the drinking of healths'.

**Gabble Ratchet.** *See* GABRIEL'S HOUNDS.

**Gabriel** (*i.e.* man of God). One of the ARCHANGELS, sometimes regarded as the ANGEL of death, the prince of fire and thunder, but more frequently as one of God's chief messengers, and traditionally said to be the only angel that can speak Syriac and Chaldee. Muslims call him the chief of the four favoured angels and the spirit of truth. Milton makes him chief of the angelic guards placed over PARADISE (*Paradise Lost*, IV, 549).

In the Talmud Gabriel appears as the destroyer of the hosts of Sennacherib, as the man who showed Joseph the way, and as one of the angels who buried Moses.

According to the KORAN it was Gabriel who took Mohammed to heaven on Al BORAK and revealed to him his 'prophetic love'. In the Old Testament Gabriel is said to have explained to Daniel certain visions (*Dan.* viii. 16–26); in the New Testament he announced to Zacharias the future birth of John The Baptist (*Luke* i, 13 etc.) and appeared to Mary the mother of Jesus (*Luke* i, 26 etc.).

**Gabriel's horse.** Haizum.

**Gabriel's hounds,** called also *Gabble Ratchet.* Wild geese. The noise of geese in flight is like that of a pack of hounds in full cry. The legend is that they are the souls of unbaptized children wandering through the air till the Day of Judgment.

**Gaea** (jē'ə, gī'ə) or **Ge** (jē, gā). The Greek goddess of the Earth who gave birth to sky, mountains and sea. By URANUS she brought forth the TITANS, the CYCLOPS and other GIANTS and according to some legends she was the mother of the EUMENIDES.

**Galahad, Sir.** In Arthurian legend the purest and noblest knight of the ROUND TABLE. He is a late addition and was invented by Walter Map in his *Quest of the San Graal*. He was the son of LANCELOT and ELAINE. At the institution of the Round Table one seat (the Siege Perilous) was left unoccupied for the knight who could succeed in the Quest. When Sir Galahad sat there it was discovered that it had been left for him. The story is found in Malory's *Morte d'Arthur*, Tennyson's *The Holy Grail* etc.

**Galatea** (galətē'ə). A sea NYMPH, beloved by the monster POLYPHEMUS, but herself in love with the beautiful ACIS, who was killed by the jealous CYCLOPS. Galatea threw herself into the sea where she joined her sister nymphs. Handel has an opera entitled *Acis and Galatea* (1720). The Galatea beloved by PYGMALION was a different person.

**Galaxy, The** (Gr. *gala, galaktos*, milk). The 'Milky Way'. A long white luminous track of stars which seems to encompass the heavens like a girdle. It is composed of a vast collection of stars so distant that they are indistinguishable as separate stars, and they appear as a combined light. According to classic fable, it is the path to the palace of ZEUS.

**Ganelon** (gan'əlon). A type of black-hearted treachery, figuring in Dante's *Inferno* and grouped by Chaucer (*Nun's Priest's Tale*, 407) with Judas Iscariot and—

> Greek Sinon,
> That broghtest Troye al outrely to sorwe.

He was Count of Mayence, and PALADIN of CHARLEMAGNE. Jealousy of ROLAND made him a traitor; and in order to destroy his rival, he planned with Marsillus, the Moorish king, the attack of RONCESVALLES.

**Ganesha** (ganē'shə). In Hindu mythology, the god of wisdom and good luck, lord of the Ganas, or lesser deities. He was the son of SIVA and is invoked at the beginning of a journey, or when commencing important work, and on the first pages of books, especially ledgers and text books. He is depicted as elephant-headed and rides on, or is accompanied by, a rat; both the elephant and rat are symbols of wisdom.

**Ganymede** (gan'iméd), or **Ganymedes.** In Greek mythology, the cup-bearer of ZEUS, successor to HEBE, and the type of youthful male beauty. This Trojan youth was taken up to OLYMPUS and made immortal. Hence a cup-bearer generally.

> Nature waits upon thee still,
> And thy verdant cup does fill;
> 'Tis fill'd wherever thou dost tread,
> Nature's self's thy Ganimede.
> COWLEY: *The Grasshopper (Anacreontics).*

**Garden of the Hesperides.** *See* HESPERIDES.

**Gargantua.** A giant of mediaeval or possibly CELTIC legend famous for his enormous appetite (Sp. *garganta*, gullet), adopted by Rabelais in his great satire (1535), and made the father of PANTAGRUEL. One of his exploits was to swallow five pilgrims, complete with their staves, in a salad. He is the subject of a number of chap-books, and became proverbial as a voracious and insatiable guzzler.

> You must borrow me Gargantua's mouth first before I can utter so long a word; 'tis a word too great for any mouth of this age's size.
> SHAKESPEARE: *As You Like It,* III, ii.

**Gargouille** (gahgooél'). The great DRAGON that lived in the Seine, ravaged Rouen, and was slain by St. Romanus, Archbishop of Rouen, in the 7th century.

**Garlic.** The old superstition that garlic can destroy the magnetic power of the LODESTONE has the sanction of Pliny, Solinus, Ptolemy, Plutarch, Albertus, Mathiolus, Rueus, Rulandus, Renodaeus, Langius and others. Sir Thomas Browne places it among *Vulgar Errors* (Bk. II, ch. iii).

> Martin Rulandus saith that Onions and Garlick ... hinder the attractive power of the magnet and rob it of its virtue of drawing iron, to which Renodaeus agrees; but this is all lies.
> W. SALMON: *The Complete English Physician,* ch. xxv (1693).

**Garratt. The Mayor of Garratt.** The 'mayor' of Garratt, Wandsworth, was really the chairman of an association of villagers formed to resist encroachments on the common in the latter part of the 18th century. It became the practice to choose a new 'mayor' at the same time as the occurrence of a General Election. These events became popular public occasions and at one such there were more than 80,000 people present—the candidates usually being lively characters. During one election a dead cat was thrown at the hustings and a bystander remarked that it stank 'worse than a fox.' 'That's no wonder', replied Sir John Harper (one of the mayors), 'For you see, it's a poll-cat.'

The election addresses were written by Garrick, Wilkes and others, and were satires on electoral corruption and contemporary political life. The first recorded mayor was 'Squire Blowmedown'; the last (1796) was 'Sir' Harry Dimsdale, a muffin-seller and dealer in tinware.

Foote has a farce called *The Mayor of Garratt* (1764). The place-name still survives in Garratt Lane.

**Garter. Magic garters.** In the old romances etc., garters made of the strips of a young hare's skin saturated with motherwort. Those who wore them excelled in speed.

**Flying-the-garter.** Springing or jumping lightly over something. Flying-the-garter was a one-time children's game, in which the players jumped over the *garter* or line (usually of stones), and the back of another player. In circuses, the tapes held up for performers to jump over were called *garters.*

> 'Who do you suppose will ever employ a professional man, when they see his boy playing at marbles, or flying the garter in the horse road?'
> DICKENS: *The Pickwick Papers,* ch. xxxviii.

**Garuda.** As the Hindu Bird of Life the Garuda is possibly the oldest of the great sky birds such as the Arabian ROC, the Persian SIMURGH and the Chinese Fei Lien, so large that they could blot out the sun. The Garuda is the vehicle of VISHNU and is depicted as half-man, half-eagle; it emerges fully grown from the egg and nests in the Wish-fulfilling Tree of Life. It is the traditional enemy of the Nagas.

**Gautama** (gow'təmə). The family name of BUDDHA. His personal name was Siddhartha, his father's name Suddhodana, and his mother's name Maya. He assumed the title Buddha at about the age of 36, when, after seven years of seclusion and spiritual struggle, he attained enlightenment.

**Gauvaine.** GAWAIN.

**Gawain** (gah'wān). One of the most famous of the Arthurian knights, nephew of King ARTHUR and probably the original hero of the GRAIL quest. He appears in the Welsh Triads and in the MABINOGION as Gwalchmei, and in the Arthurian cycle is the centre of many episodes and poems. The Middle English poem *Sir Gawain and the Green Knight* (*c.* 1360) is a romance telling how Gawain beheads the Green Knight in single combat.

**Gazelle boy, The.** In 1961, Jean-Claude Armen, travelling by camel through the Spanish Sahara in W. Africa, was told by nomad tribesmen of the whereabouts of a young boy living with a herd of gazelles. In due time he sighted the boy and eventually attracted him to close quarters by playing a Berber flute. The boy fed on the same plants as the animals, sometimes eating worms and lizards. On a subsequent expedition in 1963, this time in a jeep, the speed of the boy when galloping with the herd was established at over 30 m.p.h.

**Ge.** *See* GAEA.

**Gelert** (gel'ət). Llewelyn's dog. *See* BEDD-GELERT.

**Gemini** (Lat. the Twins). A constellation and one of the signs of the ZODIAC (21 May to 21 June); representing CASTOR AND POLLUX, the 'great twin brethren' of classical mythology.

**Genius** (pl. *Genii*). In Roman mythology the tutelary spirit that attended a man from cradle to grave, governed his fortunes, determined his character. The *Genius* wished a man to enjoy pleasure in life, thus to *indulge one's Genius* was to enjoy pleasure. The *Genius* only existed for man, the woman had her JUNO. Another belief was that a man had two *genii*, one good and one evil, and bad luck was due to his *evil genius*. The Roman *genii* were somewhat similar to the guardian angels spoken of in *Matt.* xviii, 10. The word is from the Lat. *gignere*, to beget (Gr. *gignesthai*, to be born), from the notion that birth and life were due to these *dii genitales*. Thus it is used for birth-wit or innate talent; hence propensity, nature, inner man.

The Eastern *genii* (sing. *genie*) were JINNS, who were not attendant spirits but fallen angels under the dominion of EBLIS.

**Genius loci.** The tutelary deity of a place.

In the midst of this wreck of ancient books and utensils, with a gravity equal to Marius among the ruins of Carthage, sat a large black cat, which to a superstitious eye, might have presented the *genius loci*, the tutelar demon of the apartment.
SCOTT: *The Antiquary*, ch. iii.

**Gentleman. The Old Gentleman.** The DEVIL; Old Nick (*see under* NICHOLAS). Also a special card in a prepared pack, used for tricks or cheating.

**Geomancy** (jē'ōmansi) (Gr. *ge*, the earth; *manteia*, prophecy). DIVINATION by means of the observation of points on the earth or by the patterns made by throwing some earth into the air and allowing it to fall on a flat surface.

**George. St. George.** The patron SAINT of England since his 'adoption' by Edward III. His day is 23 April. The popularity of St. George in England stems from the time of the early crusades, for he was said to have come to the assistance of the Crusaders at Antioch in 1098. Many of the Normans under Robert Curthose, son of William The Conqueror, took him as their patron.

Gibbon and others argued that George of Cappadocia, the Arian bishop of Alexandria, became the English patron saint but it is more generally accepted that he was a Roman officer martyred (*c.* 300) near Lydda during the Diocletian persecution. He is also the patron saint of Aragon and Portugal.

The legend of St. George and the DRAGON is simply an allegorical expression of the triumph of the Christian hero over evil, which St. John the Divine beheld under the image of a dragon. Similarly, St. MICHAEL, St. Margaret, St. Sylvester, and St. MARTHA are all depicted as slaying dragons; the Saviour and the Virgin as treading them under their feet; St. John the Evangelist as charming a winged dragon from a poisoned chalice given him to drink; and Bunyan avails himself of the same figure when he makes Christian prevail upon Apollyon.

The legend forms the subject of the ballad *St. George for England* in Percy's *Reliques*.

**Geraint** (ger'int). In Arthurian legend, a tributary prince of Devon, and one of the Knights of the ROUND TABLE. In the MABINOGION, he is the son of Erbin, as he is in the French original *Erec et Enide*, from which Tennyson drew his *Geraint and Enid* in the *Idylls of the King*.

**Geranium.** The Turks say this was a common mallow changed by the touch of Mohammed's garment.

The word is Gr. *geranos*, a crane; and the wild plant is called 'crane's bill', from the resemblance of the fruit to the bill of a crane.

**Gerda,** or **Gerdhr** (gœ'də). In Scandinavian mythology (the *Skirnismal*) daughter of the Frost-giant Gymir and wife of Freyr. She was so beautiful that the brightness of her naked arms illumined both air and sea.

**Geryon** (giə'riən). In Greek mythology, a monster with three bodies and three heads, whose oxen ate human flesh, and were guarded by Orthrus, a two-headed dog. HERCULES slew both Geryon and the dog.

**Gestas** (ges'tas). The traditional name of the impenitent thief. *See* DYSMAS.

**Giants,** *i.e.* persons well above normal height and size, are found as 'sports' or 'freaks of nature'; but the widespread belief in pre-existing races of giants among primitive peoples is due partly to the ingrained idea that mankind has degenerated—'There were giants in the earth in those days' (*Gen.* vi, 4)—and partly to the existence from remote antiquity of cyclopaean buildings, gigantic sarcophagi etc., and to the discovery from time to time in pre-scientific days of the bones of extinct monsters which were taken to be those of men. Among instances of the latter may be mentioned:

A 19 ft. skeleton was discovered at Lucerne in 1577. Dr. Plater is our authority for this measurement.

'Teutobochus', whose remains were discovered near the Rhône in 1613. They occupied a tomb 30 ft. long. The bones of another gigantic skeleton were exposed by the action of the Rhône in 1456. If this was a human skeleton, the height of living man must have been 30 ft.

Pliny records that an earthquake in Crete exposed the bones of a giant 46 cubits (*i.e.* roughly 75 ft.) in height; he called this the skeleton of ORION, others held it to be that of Otus.

Antaeus is said by Plutarch to have been 60 cubits (about 90 ft.) in height. He furthermore adds that the grave of the giant was opened by Serbonius.

The 'monster Polypheme'. It is said that his skeleton was discovered at Trapani, in Sicily, in the 14th century. If this skeleton was that of a man, he must have been 300 ft. in height.

### Giants of the Bible.

Anak. The eponymous progenitor of the Anakim (*see below*). The Hebrew spies said they were mere grasshoppers in comparison with these giants (*Josh.* xv, 14; *Judges* i, 20; and *Numb.* xiii, 33).

Goliath of Gath (I *Sam.* xvii etc.). His height is given as 6 cubits and a span: the cubit varied and might be anything from about 18 in. to 22 in., and a span was about 9 in.; this would give Goliath a height of between 9 ft. 9 in. and 11 ft. 3 in.

OG, King of Bashan (*Josh.* xii, 4; *Deut.* iii, 10, iv, 47 etc.), was 'of the remnant of the Rephaim'. According to tradition, he lived 3000 years and walked beside the Ark during the Flood. One of his bones formed a bridge over a river. His bed (*Deut.* iii, II) was 9 cubits by 4 cubits.

Anakim and Rephaim were tribes of reputed giants inhabiting the territory on both sides of the Jordan before the coming of the Israelites. The Nephilim, the offspring of the sons of God and the daughters of men (*Gen.* vi, 4), a mythological race of semi-divine heroes, were also giants.

### Giants of Legend and Literature.
The giants of Greek mythology were, for the most part, sons of URANUS and GAEA. When they attempted to storm heaven, they were hurled to earth by the aid of HERCULES, and buried under Mount ETNA (*see* TITANS). Those of Scandinavian mythology dwelt in JOTUNHEIM and these 'voracious ones' personified the unbridled forces of nature with superhuman powers against which man strove with the help of the gods. Giants feature prominently in nursery tales such as JACK THE GIANT-KILLER and Swift peopled BROBDINGNAG with giants. *See* ALIFANFARON; ANTAEUS; ATLAS; BALAN; BELLERUS; BLUNDERBORE; BRIAREUS; BRONTES; CACUS; COLBRONDE; CORMORAN; COTTUS; CYCLOPS; DESPAIR; ENCELADUS; EPHIALTES; FERRAGUS; FIERABRAS; GARGANTUA; GOG AND MAGOG; IRUS; MORGANTE MAGGIORE; ORION; PALLAS; PANTAGRUEL; POLYPHEMUS; TYPHOEUS; YMIR.

### Giants of Other Note.

Anak. *See* BRICE *below*.

Andronicus II, grandson of Alexius Comnenus, was 10 ft. in height. Nicetas asserts that he had seen him.

Bamford (Edward) was 7 ft. 4 in. He died in 1768 and was buried in St. Dunstan's churchyard, London.

Bates (Captain) was 7 ft. 11½ in. A native of Kentucky, he was exhibited in London in 1871. His wife, Anne Hannen Swan, a native of Nova Scotia, was the same height.

Blacker (Henry) was 7ft. 4 in. and most symmetrical. A native of Cuckfield, Sussex, he was called 'the British Giant'.

Bradley (William) was 7 ft. 9 in. Born in 1787 at Market Weight, Yorkshire, he died in 1820. His right hand is preserved in the museum of the Royal College of Surgeons.

Brice (M. J.), exhibited under the name of Anak, was 7 ft. 8 in. at the age of 26. He was born in 1840 at Ramonchamp in the Vosges and visited England 1862–1865. His arms had a stretch of 95½ in.

Brusted (Von) of Norway was 8 ft. He was exhibited at London in 1880.

Byrne. *See* O'BRIEN *below.*

Chang, the Chinese giant, was 8 ft. 2 in. He was exhibited in London in 1865–1866 and in 1880.

CHARLEMAGNE, according to tradition, was nearly 8 ft. and was so strong that he could squeeze together three horseshoes with his hands.

Cotter (Patrick), an Irish bricklayer, who exhibited as O'Brien, was 8 ft. 1 in. Born in 1761, he died at Clifton, Bristol, in 1806. A cast of his hand is preserved in the museum of the Royal College of Surgeons.

Daniel, the porter of Oliver Cromwell, was a man of gigantic stature.

Eleazer was 7 cubits (nearly 11 ft.). Vitellius sent this giant to Rome. He is mentioned by Josephus who also speaks of a Jew of 10 ft. 2 in.

Eleizegue (Joachim) was 7 ft. 10 in. A Spaniard, he was exhibited in the Cosmorama, Regent Street, London, in the mid-19th century.

Evans (William) was 8 ft. He was a porter of Charles I, and died in 1632.

Frank (Big) was 7 ft. 8 in. He was Francis Sheridan, an Irishman, and died in 1870.

Gabara, the Arabian giant, was 9 ft. 9 in. Pliny says he was the tallest man seen in the days of Claudius.

Gilly was 8 ft. This Swedish giant was exhibited at London in the early part of the 19th century.

Gordon (Alice) was 7 ft. She was a native of Essex, and died in 1737, at the age of 19.

Hale (Robert) was 7 ft. 6 in. and was born at Somerton, Norfolk in 1802. He died in 1862 and was called 'the Norfolk Giant'.

Hardrada (Harald) was nearly 7 ft. and was called 'the Norway Giant'. He was slain at Stamford Bridge in 1066.

Holmes (Benjamin) of Northumberland was 7 ft. 7 in. He became sword-bearer to the Corporation of Worcester and died in 1892.

McDonald (James) of Cork, Ireland, was 7 ft. 6 in. He died in 1760.

McDonald (Samuel) was 6 ft. 10 in. This Scot was usually called 'Big Sam'. He was the Prince of

Wales's footman, and died in 1802.

Macgrath (Cornelius) was 7 ft. 10 in. at the age of 16. He was an orphan reared by Bishop Berkeley and died in 1760 at the age of 20.

Maximus I, Roman Emperor (235–238) was 8 ft. 6 in.

Middleton (John) was 9 ft. 3 in. He was born at Hale, Lancashire, in the reign of James I. 'His hand was 17 in. long and 8½ in. broad' (Dr. Plot: *Natural History of Staffordshire*).

Miller (Maximilian Christopher) was 8 ft. His hand measured 12 in., and his forefinger 9 in. He died at London in 1734 at the age of 60.

Murphy, an Irish giant of the late 18th century, was 8 ft. 10 in. He died at Marseilles.

O'Brien, or Charles Byrne (1761–1783), was 8 ft. 4 in. He died in Cockspur Street, London and the skeleton of this Irish giant is preserved in the Royal College of Surgeons.

O'Brien (Patrick). *See* COTTER *above.*

Porus was 5 cubits in height (about 7½ ft.). He was an Indian king who fought against ALEXANDER the Great near the Hydaspes. (Quintus Curtius: *De rebus gestis Alexandri Magni.*)

Sam (Big). *See* MACDONALD *above.*

Sheridan. *See* FRANK *above.*

Swan (Anne Hannen). *See* BATES *above.*

Toller (James) was 8 ft. at the age of 24. He died in 1819.

Wadlow (Robert P.) of Illinois, USA, was 8 ft. 11.1 in. (1918–1940), the tallest man of whose measurements there is complete certainty.

Winkelmaier (Josef), an Austrian, was 8 ft. 9 in. (1865–1887).

In addition to the above:

Del Rio tells us that he saw a Piedmontese in 1572 more than 9 ft. high.

M. Thevet published (1575) an account of a South American giant, the skeleton of which he measured. It was 11 ft. 5 in.

Gaspard Bauhin (1560–1624), the anatomist and botanist, speaks of a Swiss 8 ft. high.

A Mr. Warren (in *Notes and Queries*, 14 August 1875) said that his father knew a woman 9 ft. in height, and adds 'her head touched the ceiling of a good-sized room'.

There is a human skeleton 8 ft. 6 in. in height in the museum of Trinity College, Dublin.

There were over 100 applicants in response to an advertisement in *The Times* (25 July 1966) for 'giants' of minimum height 6 ft. 7 in. for the premiere of *Cast a Giant Shadow* at the London Pavilion. The tallest was 7 ft. 3 in. *Cp.* DWARF.

**Giants' Cauldrons.** *See* GIANTS' KETTLES.

**Giant's Causeway.** A formation of some 40,000 basaltic columns, projecting into the sea about 8 miles ENE of Portrush, Co. Antrim, on the north coast of Ireland. It is fabled to be the beginning of a road to be constructed by the giants across the channel from Ireland to Scotland. Here are to be found the *Giants' Loom*, the *Giants' Well* and the *Giants' Chair*. Other formations in the district are called the *Giants' Organ*, the *Giants' Peep-hole*, and the *Giants' Granny*, also reefs called the *Giants' Eye-glass*.

**Giants' Dance, The.** STONEHENGE, which Geoffrey of Monmouth says was removed from Killaurus, a mountain in Ireland, by Uther Pendragon and his men under the direction of MERLIN.

**Giants' Kettles,** or **Giants' Cauldrons.** A name given to glacial pot-shaped cylindrical holes worn in rocks by the rotary currents of sub-glacial streams, often containing water-worn stones, boulders etc. They are found in Norway, Germany, the USA etc.

**Giants' Leap, The.** A popular name in many mountainous districts given to two prominent rocks separated from each other by a wide chasm or stretch of open country across which some giant is fabled to have leapt and so baffled his pursuers.

**Giants' Ring.** A prehistoric circular mound near Milltown, Co. Down, IRELAND. It is 580 ft. in diameter and has a CROMLECH in the centre.

**Giants' Staircase.** The staircase which rises from the courtyard of the Doge's Palace, Venice. So named from the figures of two giants at its head.

**Giants' War with Zeus.** The War of the Giants and the War of the TITANS should be kept distinct. The latter was before ZEUS became god of HEAVEN and earth, the former was after that time. The Giants' War was a revolt by the giants against Zeus, which was readily put down by the help of the other gods and the aid of HERCULES.

**Gilderoy.** A noted robber and cattle-stealer of Perthshire who was hanged with five of his gang in July 1638, at Gallowlee near Edinburgh. He was noted for his handsome person and his real name was said to be Patrick Macgregor. He is credited with having picked the pocket of Cardinal Richelieu, robbed Oliver Cromwell, and hanged a judge. There are ballads on him in Percy's *Reliques*, Ritson's *Collection* etc., and a modern one by Campbell.

> Oh! sike twa charming een he had,
> A breath as sweet as rose,
> He never ware a Highland plaid,
> But costly silken clothes.
> PERCY: *Reliques: Gilderoy*.

**To be hung higher than Gilderoy's kite** is to be punished more severely than the very worst criminal. The greater the crime, the higher the gallows, was at one time a legal axiom. The gallows of Montrose was 30 ft. high. The ballad in Percy's *Reliques* says:

> Of Gilderoy sae fraid they were,
> They bound him mickle strong,
> Tull Edenburrow they led him thair,
> And on a gallows hung;
> They hung him high aboon the rest,
> He was sae trim a boy ...

**Gilgamesh Epic** (gil′gǝmesh). A collection of ancient Babylonian stories and myths, older than HOMER, seemingly brought together around Gilgamesh, king of Erech, as the central hero. He was two-thirds a god, one-third a man. It appears to have covered 12 tablets (*c.* 3000 lines), portions of which were found among the relics of the library of Assur-bani-pal, King of Assyria (668–626 B.C.). Some of the tablets date back to *c.* 2000 B.C.

**Ginnunga gap** (gin′ung·gǝ). In Scandinavian mythology, the great abyss between NIFLHEIM, the region of fogs and MUSPELHEIM, the region of intense heat. It was without beginning and without end, there was neither day or night, and it existed before either land or sea, HEAVEN or earth.

**Giotto's O.** The old story goes that the POPE, wishing to employ artists from all over Italy, sent a messenger to collect specimens of their work. When the man visited Giotto (*c.* 1267–1337) the artist paused for a moment from the picture he was working on and with his brush drew a perfect circle on a piece of paper. In some surprise the man returned to the Pope, who, appreciating the perfection of Giotto's artistry and skill by his unerring circle, employed Giotto forthwith.

> I saw ... that the practical teaching of the masters of Art was summed up by the O of Giotto.
> RUSKIN: *Queen of the Air*, iii.

**Giovanni, Don.** *See* DON JUAN.

**Girdle. The Girdle of Venus.** *See* CESTUS.

**Glass slipper** (of Cinderella). *See* CINDERELLA.

**Glastonbury.** An ancient town in Somerset, almost twelve miles from Cadbury Castle, 'the many-towered CAMELOT'. It is fabled to be the place where Joseph of Arimathea brought the Christian faith to Britain, and the Holy GRAIL in the year 63. It was here Joseph's staff took root and budded—the famous Glastonbury Thorn, which flowers every Christmas in honour of Christ's birth. The name is now given to a variety of *Crataegus* or hawthorn, which flowers about old Christmas Day. It is the isle of AVALON, the burial place of King ARTHUR.

**Glaucus** (glaw'kəs). The name of a number of heroes in classical legend, including:

(1) A fisherman of Boeotia, who became a sea-god endowed with the gift of prophecy by APOLLO. Milton alludes to him in *Comus* (1. 895), and Spenser mentions him in *The Faerie Queene* (IV, xi, 13):

And Glaucus, that wise soothsayer understood,

and Keats gives his name to the old magician whom ENDYMION met in NEPTUNE'S hall beneath the sea (*Endymion*, Bk. III). *See also* SCYLLA.

(2) A son of SISYPHUS who would not allow his horses to breed; VENUS so infuriated them that they tore him to pieces. Hence the name is given to one who is so overfond of horses that he is ruined by them.

(3) A commander of the Lycians in the TROJAN WAR (*Iliad*, Bk. VI) who was connected by ties of ancient family friendship with his enemy, DIOMED. When they met in battle they not only refrained from fighting but exchanged arms in token of amity. As the armour of the Lycian was of GOLD, and that of the Greek of bronze, it was like bartering precious stones for French paste. Hence the phrase **A Glaucus swap**.

**Gleipnir** (glīp'nər) (Old Norse, the fetter). In Scandinavian legend the fetter by which the dwarfs bound the wolf FENRIR. It was extremely light and made of the noise of a cat moving, the roots of a mountain, the sinews of a bear, the breath of a fish, the beard of a woman, and the spittle of a bird.

**Gloriana.** Spenser's name in *The Faerie Queene* for the typification of Queen Elizabeth I. Gloriana held an annual feast for twelve days, during which time adventurers appeared before her to undertake whatever task she chose to impose upon them. On one occasion twelve knights presented themselves before her, and their exploits form the scheme of Spenser's allegory of which only six and a half books remain.

**Glory. Hand of Glory.** In folklore, a dead man's hand, preferably one cut from the body of a man who has been hanged, soaked in oil, and used as a magic torch by thieves. Robert Graves points out that the *Hand of Glory* is a translation of the French *main de gloire*, a corruption of *mandragore*, the plant *mandragora* (mandrake), whose roots had a similar magic value to thieves. *Cp.* DEAD MAN'S HAND.

**Glubbdubdrib.** The land of sorcerers and magicians visited by Gulliver in Swift's *Gulliver's Travels*.

**Glumdalclitch.** A girl, nine years old, and forty feet high, who, in Swift's *Gulliver's Travels*, had charge of Gulliver in BROBDINGNAG.

**Gnome.** According to the ROSICRUCIAN system, a misshapen elemental spirit, dwelling in the bowels of the earth, and guarding mines and quarries. Gnomes of various sorts appear in many FAIRY tales and legends. The word seems to have been first used (and perhaps invented) by Paracelsus and is probably the Gr. *ge-nomos*, earth-dweller. *Cp.* SALAMANDER.

**Goat.** The goat is possibly the oldest domesticated animal after the dog. It is a sacrificial animal and was sacred to the Sumerian god MARDUK, who is accompanied by a goat, and to the Babylonian Ningirsu, also to ARTEMIS and other hunting goddesses. In Greece the goat was an attribute of Silvanus and DIONYSUS who took the form of a goat when fleeing from TYPHON. Goats were sacrificed to FAUNUS. Satyrs were half goats with goats' horns and beards; Pan also appears in this form. The goat was also sacred to ZEUS Dictynnos who was suckled by a goat AMALTHEA, whose skin became the Aegis and her horn the cornucopia; she thus represented both protection and abundance.

The Teutonic Thor had a chariot drawn by goats which were sacred to him; his goat Heidrum supplied the mead, the drink of the gods.

The Vedic Agni, god of fire and creative heat, rides a goat. The Chinese Goat Spirit, Yang Ching, the Transcendent Goat, is the god of the star Fan-yin; he is also a Mongolian god.

There were strange legends concerning goats. Oppian says they breathe through their horns, but Varro maintains that they breathe through their ears. There was a general belief, expressed by Pliny, that they were perpetually feverish.

**The Goat and Compasses.** The origin of this PUBLIC-HOUSE SIGN is uncertain. A once popular suggestion was that it is a corruption of 'God encompasseth us'. Other suggestions are that it was derived from the arms of the Wine Cooper's Company of Cologne, or merely the addition of the masonic emblem of the compasses to an original sign of a goat.

**Goblin.** A familiar demon, dwelling, according to popular legend, in private houses, chinks of trees etc. In many parts miners attributed to them the strange noises they heard in the mine. The word is Fr. *gobelin*, probably a diminutive of the surname *Gobel*, but perhaps connected with Gr. *kobalos*, an impudent rogue, a mischievous sprite, or with the Ger. *Kobold. Cp.* GNOME.

**God.** A word common, in slightly varying forms, to all Teutonic languages, probably from an Aryan root, *gheu*—to invoke; it is in no way connected with *good*.

It was Voltaire who said, '*Si Dieu n'existait pas, il faudrait l'inventer.*' For the various gods listed in this Dictionary see under their individual names.

Greek and Roman gods were divided into *Dii Majores* and *Dii Minores*, the greater and the lesser. The *Dii Majores* were twelve in number:

| Greek | Latin |
|---|---|
| ZEUS | JUPITER (King) |
| APOLLON | APOLLO (the sun) |
| ARES | MARS (war) |
| HERMES | MERCURY (messenger) |
| POSEIDON | NEPTUNE (ocean) |
| HEPHAESTUS | VULCAN (smith) |
| HERA | JUNO (Queen) |
| DEMETER | CERES (tillage) |
| ARTEMIS | DIANA (moon, hunting) |
| ATHENE | MINERVA (wisdom) |
| APHRODITE | VENUS (love and beauty) |
| Hestia | VESTA (home-life) |

Their blood was ICHOR, their food was AMBROSIA, their drink NECTAR.

Four other deities are often referred to:

| | |
|---|---|
| DIONYSUS | BACCHUS (wine) |
| EROS | CUPID (love) |
| PLUTON | PLUTO (the underworld) |
| KRONOS | SATURN (time). |

PERSEPHONE (Greek) or PROSERPINA (Latin), was the wife of Pluto, CYBELE was the wife of Saturn, and RHEA of Kronos.

Hesiod says (i, 250):

Some thirty thousand gods on earth we find
Subjects of Zeus, and guardians of mankind.

The Greeks observed a *Feast of the Unknown Gods* that none might be neglected.

**Godiva, Lady** (godī'və). Patroness of Coventry. In 1040 Leofric, Earl of Mercia and Lord of Coventry, imposed certain exactions on his tenants, which his lady besought him to remove. He said he would do so if she would ride naked through the town. Lady Godiva did so and the Earl faithfully kept his promise.

The legend is recorded by Roger of Wendover (d. 1236), in his *Flores Historiarum*, and this was adapted by Rapin in his *History of England* (1723–1727) into the story commonly known. An addition of the time of Charles II asserts that everyone kept indoors at the time, but a certain tailor peeped through his window to see the lady pass and was struck blind as a consequence. He has ever since been called 'Peeping Tom of Coventry'. Since 1768 the ride has been annually commemorated at Coventry by a procession in which 'Lady Godiva' features centrally.

**Gog and Magog.** In British legend, the sole survivors of a monstrous brood, the offspring of demons and the thirty-three infamous daughters of the Emperor Diocletian, who murdered their husbands. Gog and Magog were taken as prisoners to London after their fellow giants had been killed by BRUTE and his companions, where they were made to do duty as porters at the royal palace, on the site of the Guildhall, where their effigies have stood at least from the reign of Henry V. The old giants were destroyed in the Great Fire, and were replaced by figures 14 ft. high, carved in 1708 by Richard Saunders. These were subsequently demolished in an air raid in 1940 and new figures were set up in 1953. Formerly wickerwork models were carried in the LORD MAYOR'S SHOWS.

In the Bible Magog is spoken of as a son of Japhet (*Gen.* x, 2), in the *Revelation* Gog and Magog symbolize all future enemies of the Kingdom of God, and in *Ezekiel* Gog is prince of Magog, a ruler of hordes to the north of Israel.

**Gogmagog Hill.** The higher of two hills some 3 miles south-east of Cambridge. The legend is that Gogmagog fell in love with the nymph Granta, but she would have nothing to say to the giant, and he was metamorphosed into the hill (Drayton, *Poly-Olbion*, xxi).

**Golconda** (golkon'də). An ancient kingdom and city in India, west of Hyderabad, which was conquered by Aurangzeb in 1687. The name is emblematic of great wealth and proverbially famous for its diamonds, but the gems were only cut and polished there.

**Gold. The gold of Nibelungen.** *See* NIBELUNGENLIED.

**Golden Apples.** *See* APPLE OF DISCORD; ATALANTA'S RACE; HESPERIDES.

**The Golden Fleece.** The old Greek story is that Ino persuaded her husband Athamus that his son Phrixus was the cause of a famine which desolated the land. Phryxus was thereupon ordered to be sacrificed but, being apprised of this, he made his escape over the sea on the winged ram, Chrysomallus, which had a golden fleece (*see* HELLESPONT). When he arrived at Colchis, he sacrificed the ram to ZEUS, and gave the fleece to king Aeetes, who hung it on a sacred OAK. JASON subsequently set out to recover it.

Australia has been called 'The Land of the Golden Fleece' from its abundant wool production.

**The Golden Legend** (*Aurea Legenda*). A collection of so-called lives of the SAINTS made by the Dominican, Jacobus de Voragine, in the 13th century; valuable for the picture it gives of mediaeval manners, customs and thought. It was translated from the Latin into most of the languages of western Europe and an English edition was published by Caxton in 1483.

Longfellow's *The Golden Legend* is based on a story by Hartmann von Aue, a German Minnesinger of the 12th century.

**Golden Shower,** or **Shower of Gold.** A bribe, money. The allusion is to the classical tale of ZEUS and DANAË.

**Goose.** In Egyptian mythology the Nile Goose, the Great Chatterer, was the creator of the world, it laid the Cosmic Egg from which Ra, the sun god, was hatched. The goose is also an attribute of Isis, Osiris, Horus and Seb. In Sumeria it was sacred to Bau, goddess of the farmyard.

Tame geese were kept in temples by the Greeks and Romans as guardians and were said to have saved Rome by their warning cries when the Gauls attacked. The goose was an attribute of Hera/Juno, signifying love, guardianship and the good housewife; it was also associated with Apollo as solar, with Ares/Mars as war, with Hermes/Mercury as messenger and with Peitho, goddess of eloquence and Priapus, a fertility god.

The goose and swan are interchangeable in mythology, particularly in India where the Ham-sa can be depicted as either as a form or vehicle of Brahman, representing the creative principle.

In China and Japan the goose is the Bird of Heaven, bringing good tidings. As seasonal change it is frequently portrayed with the autumn moon in art.

Celtic, Teutonic and Gallic myth associate the goose with war gods. Epona, the Divine Horse, is depicted riding on a horned goose. Caesar, in the *Gallic Wars*, said the goose was sacred to the Britons and therefore not used as food. The Norse also did not eat the goose.

**Goose and Gridiron, The.** A PUBLIC-HOUSE SIGN, probably in ridicule of the Swan and Harp, a popular sign for the early music-houses (*see* MUSIC HALL), but properly the coat-of-arms of the Company of Musicians—*viz.* azure, a *swan* with wings expanded argent, within *double tressure* [the gridiron] flory counterflory.

In the United States the name is humorously applied to the national coat-of-arms—the American EAGLE with a gridiron-like shield on its breast.

**Goose Fair.** A fair formerly held in many English towns about the time of MICHAELMAS, when geese were plentiful. That still held at Nottingham was the most important. Tavistock Goosey Fair is still held, though geese are seldom sold, but goose lunches etc., are available.

Tes jist a month cum Vriday nex'
Bill Champernown an' me
Us druv a-crost ole Dartymoor

Th' Goozey Vair to zee.
*Tavistock Goozey Vair Song.*

The goose is associated with St. Martin who ordered a particularly annoying goose to be killed and eaten. This gave rise to the Goose Fair in France, held on his day, November 11.

**Michaelmas Goose.** *See* MICHAELMAS DAY.

**He killed the goose that laid the golden eggs.** He grasped at what was more than his due and lost what was a regular source of supply; he has sacrificed future reward for present gain. The Greek fable says a countryman had a goose that laid golden eggs; thinking to make himself rich, he killed the goose to get the whole stock of eggs at once, thus ending the supply.

**Gorboduc.** *See* FERREX AND PORREX.

**Gordian Knot.** A great difficulty. Gordius, a peasant, being chosen king of Phrygia, dedicated his wagon to JUPITER, and fastened the yoke to a beam with a rope of bark so ingeniously that no one could untie it. Alexander was told that 'whoever undid the knot would reign over the whole East'. 'Well then,' said the conqueror, 'it is thus I perform the task,' and, so saying, he cut the knot in two with his sword; thus **To cut the Gordian Knot** is to get out of a difficult position by one decisive step; to resolve a situation by force or by evasive action.

If then such praise the Macedonian got
For having rudely cut the Gordian Knot.
    WALLER: *To the King.*

Turn him to any cause of policy,
The Gordian Knot of it he will unloose,
Familiar as his garter.
    SHAKESPEARE: *Henry V,* I, i.

**Gorgon.** Anything unusually hideous, especially such a woman. In classical mythology there were three Gorgons, with serpents on their heads instead of hair. MEDUSA was their chief, the others, Stheno and Euryale, were immortal. They also had brazen claws and monstrous teeth. Their glance turned their victims to stone. *Cp.* PERSEUS.

**Gotham. Wise men of Gotham**—fools, wiseacres. The village of Gotham in Nottinghamshire was proverbial for the folly of its inhabitants and many tales have been fathered on them, one of which is their joining hands round a thorn-bush to shut in a cuckoo.

It is said that King John intended to make a progress through the town with the view of establishing a hunting lodge but the townsmen had no wish to be saddled with the cost of supporting the court. Wherever the royal messengers went they saw the people engaged in some idiotic pursuit and the king, when told, abandoned his intention and the 'wise men' cunningly remarked, 'We ween there are more fools pass through Gotham than remain in it.' The nursery rhyme says:

Three wise men of Gotham
Went to sea in a bowl,
If the bowl had been stronger,
My story would have been longer.

A collection of popular tales of stupidity was published in the reign of Henry VIII as *Merie tales of the Mad Men of Gotam, gathered together by A. B. Phisike, Doctour.* This 'A. B.' is assumed to be Andrew Boorde (*c.* 1490–1549), physician and traveller, but the use of his initials was probably to promote sales.

Most nations have some locality renowned for fools; thus we have Phrygia as the fools' home of Asia Minor, ABDERA of the Thracians, BOEOTIA of the Greeks, Nazareth of the ancient Jews, Swabia of the Germans, etc.

**Govan. St. Govan's Bell.** *See* INCHCAPE ROCK.

**Graal** (grāl). *See* GRAIL.

**Grace. The Three Graces.** In classical mythology, the goddesses who bestowed beauty and charm and were themselves the embodiment of both. They were the sisters AGLAIA, THALIA and Euphrosyne. *Cp.* MUSES.

They are the daughters of sky-ruling Jove,
By him begot of faire Eurynome, ...
The first of them hight mylde Euphrosyne,
Next faire Aglaia, last Thalia merry;
Sweete Goddesses all three, which me in mirth do cherry.
    SPENSER: *Faerie Queene,* VI, x, 22.

Andrea Appiani (1754–1817), the Italian fresco artist, was known as *the Painter of the Graces.*

**Grail, The Holy.** The cup or chalice traditionally used by Christ at the Last

Supper, the subject of a great amount of mediaeval legend, romance and allegory.

According to one account, JOSEPH OF ARI-MATHEA preserved the Grail and received into it some of the blood of the Saviour at the Crucifixion. He brought it to England, but it disappeared. According to others it was brought by angels from HEAVEN and entrusted to a body of knights who guarded it on top of a mountain. When approached by anyone not of perfect purity it vanished, and its quest became the source of most of the adventures of the knights of the ROUND TABLE. *See also* PERCEFOREST.

There is a great mass of literature concerning the Grail Cycle, and it appears to be a fusion of Christian legend and pre-Christian ritual origins. Part of the subject matter appears in the MABINOGION in the story of *Peredur son of Efrawg*. The first Christian Grail romance was that of the French trouvère Robert de Borron who wrote his *Joseph d'Arimathie* at the end of the 12th century, and it next became attached to the Arthurian legend. In Robert de Borron's work the Grail took the form of a dish on which the Last Supper was served.

Malory's *Le Morte d'Arthur* (printed by Caxton in 1485) is an abridgment from French sources. The framework of Tennyson's *Holy Grail* (*Idylls of the King*) in which the poet expressed his 'strong feeling as to the Reality of the Unseen' is based upon Malory.

**Granby, The Marquis of.** At one time this was a popular PUBLIC-HOUSE SIGN, and such signs are still numerous. John Manners, Marquis of Granby (1721–1770), commanded the Leicester Blues against the Pretender in the Forty-five; was a Lieutenant-General at Minden (1759), and commander-in-chief of the British army in 1766. He was a very bald man and this was exaggerated on most of the inn-signs.

**Grape. Sour grapes.** Something disparaged because it is beyond one's reach. The allusion is to AESOP's well-known fable of the FOX who tried in vain to get at some grapes, but when he found they were beyond his reach went away saying, 'I see they are sour.'

**Great Spirit.** *See* MANITOU.

**Greegrees.** The name given in Africa to AMULETS, CHARMS, FETISHES etc.

**A greegree man.** One who sells these.

**Green Man.** The Green Man, representing the spirit of vegetation, is seen widely in spring festivals and can be traced back to ancient times. He appeared as the Green Thing of the Indus region, as TAMMUZ and ISHTAR in Babylonian myth, as Al-Khidr or Ilyas (Elijah) in Islam and in European legend and festivals as Jack-in-the-Green, King of the May, and associated with St. GEORGE AND THE DRAGON in plays. He is also ROBIN HOOD, the Garland, the Wild Man of Germany, the *pfingstl* of Sweden and the Green George of the Gypsies. He appears dressed from head to foot in green boughs or leaves in festivals, dances, mummers' plays and processions, symbolizing the ancient initiatory emergence from the death of winter to the birth of new life in spring.

As a PUBLIC-HOUSE SIGN, it probably represents either a JACK-IN-THE-GREEN or a forester, who, like ROBIN HOOD, was once clad in green.

But the 'Green Man' shall I pass by unsung,
Which mine own James upon his sign-post hung?
His sign, his image—for he once was seen
A squire's attendant, clad in keeper's green.
  CRABBE: *The Borough.*

The public-house sign, *The Green Man and Still*, is probably a modification of the arms of the Distiller's Company, the supporters of which were two Indians, for which the sign painters usually substituted foresters or green men drinking out of a glass barrel.

**Gremlin.** One of a tribe of imaginary GNOMES or GOBLINS humorously blamed by the RAF in World War II for everything that went wrong in an aircraft or an operation. The name was probably coined at the end of World War I or in the 1920s and was apparently in use on RAF stations in India and the Middle East in the 1930s. The name is first traced in print in *The Aeroplane* (10 April 1929). A common explanation is that a gremlin was the goblin which came out of Fremlin's beer bottles (Fremlin being a brewer in Kent), although there are numerous other stories.

**Grendel.** The mythical half-human monster

killed by BEOWULF. Grendel nightly raided the king's hall and killed the sleepers.

**Griffin.** A mythical monster; also called *Griffon, Gryphon* etc., fabled to be the offspring of the LION and the EAGLE. Its legs and all from the shoulders to the head are like an eagle, the rest of the body is that of a lion. This creature was sacred to the sun and kept guard over hidden treasures. *See* ARIMASPIANS.

> [The Griffin is] an Emblem of valour and magnanimity, as being compounded of the Eagle and the Lion, the noblest Animals in their kinds; and so is it appliable unto Princes, Presidents, Generals, and all heroik Commanders; and so is it also born in the Coat-arms of many noble Families of Europe.
>
> SIR THOMAS BROWNE: *Pseudodoxia Epidemica*, III, xi.

The griffin appeared in Assyria and the East as the 'cloud cleaving eagle' and the 'king of beasts' and shares the symbolism of the DRAGON as wisdom. In Greece the griffin was sacred to APOLLO as solar, to ATHENE as wisdom and NEMESIS as retribution. In Roman art griffins draw the chariot of Nemesis.

Dante says the griffin is 'the mystic shape that joins the two natures in one form' and Christianity uses this to represent the dual human and divine natures of Christ.

The Londoner's familiar name for the figure on the site of Temple Bar is *The Griffin*.

Among Anglo-Indians a newcomer, a greenhorn, was called a *griffin*; and the residue of a contract feast, taken away by the contractor, half the buyer's and half the seller's, is known in the trade as *griffins*.

**Gryphon.** *See* GRIFFIN.

**Guadiana.** According to the old legend the Spanish river was so called from Durandarte's Squire of this name. Mourning the fall of his master at RONCESVALLES, he was turned into a river (*see Don Quixote*, ii, 23). Actually, it is Arab. *wadi*, a river, and *Anas*, its classical name.

**Gubbins.** The wild and savage inhabitants of the neighbourhood of Brentor, Devon, who according to Fuller in his *Worthies* (1661)—

> lived in cots (rather holes than houses) ..., having all in common, multiplying without marriage into many hundreds ... Their language is the dross of the dregs of the vulgar Devonian ... They held together like burrs.

As explanation of the name he says, 'We call the shavings of fish (which are of little worth) *gubbins*'.

William Browne in a poem on Lydford Law (1644) says:

> And near hereto's the Gubbins Cave;
> A people that no knowledge have
> Of law, of God, or men;
> Whom Caesar never yet subdued;
> Who've lawless lived; of manners rude
> All savage in their den.

**Gudrun** (gud'run), or **Kudrun**. The heroine of the great 13th-century German epic poem of this name founded on a passage in the *Prose* Edda. The third part describes how Gudrun, daughter of King Hettel, was carried off by Hochmut of Normandy and made to work like a menial in his mother's house, because she would not break her troth to Herwig, King of Zealand. She was eventually rescued by her brother. This poem is sometimes known as the German ODYSSEY.

**Guenever.** *See* GUINEVERE.

**Guinea Fowl.** In Greek myth the sisters of Meleager were metamorphosed into guinea fowl and the birds were kept at the Acropolis. Stratus says they were among the presents thrown to the populace at the SATURNALIA and Sophocles says that guinea fowl wept tears of amber and were associated with amber in Greek literature. The birds were also sacred to ISIS in Egypt.

**Guinevere, Guinever,** or **Guenever** (gwin'əviə). The wife of King ARTHUR. The name is a corruption of *Guanhumara* (from Welsh *Gwenhwyfar*) as she appears in Geoffrey of Monmouth's *Historia Regum Britanniae*, a principal source of ARTHURIAN ROMANCES.

**Gunnar.** The Norse form of GUNTHER.

**Gunther** (gun'tə), or **Gunnar**. In the Nibelungen saga, a Burgundian king, brother of KRIEMHILD, the wife of SIEGFRIED. He resolved to wed the martial BRUNHILD (or Brynhild) who had made a vow to marry only the man who could ride through the flames that encircled her castle. Gunther failed, but Siegfried did so in the shape of Gunther, and remained with her three nights, his sword between them all the time. Gunther then married Brunhild, but later Kriemhild told Brunhild that it was

Siegfried who had ridden through the fire, thus arousing her jealousy. Siegfried was slain at Brunhild's instigation, and she then killed herself, her dying wish being to be burnt at Siegfried's side. Gunther was slain by ATLI because he refused to reveal where he had hidden the hoard of the Nibelungs. Gundaharius, a Burgundian king, who, with his men, perished by the sword of the Huns in 436, is supposed to be the historical character around which these legends collected. *See also* NIBELUNGENLIED.

**Guy of Warwick.** An English hero of legend and romance, whose exploits were first written down by an Anglo-Norman poet of the 12th century and were accepted as history by the 14th century.

To obtain the hand of the fair Félice or Phelis, daughter of the Earl of Warwick, he performed many doughty deeds abroad. Returning to England he married Phelis, but after forty days set off on pilgrimage to the Holy Land, again performing deeds of prowess. Back in England he slew COL-BRONDE, and then the DUN COW. After these achievements he became a hermit near Warwick and daily begged bread of his wife at his own castle gate. On his death-bed he sent her a ring, by which she recognized her lord, and she went to close his dying eyes. The story is told in the *Legend of Sir Guy* in Percy's *Reliques*.

**Gyges** (gī′jēz). A king of Lydia of the 7th century B.C., who founded a new dynasty, warred against Asurbanipal of Assyria, and is memorable in legend for his ring and for his prodigious wealth.

According to Plato, Gyges went down into a chasm in the earth, where he found a brazen horse; opening the sides of the animal, he found the carcass of a man, from whose finger he drew a brazen ring which rendered him invisible.

Why, did you think that you had Gyges ring
Or the herb that gives invisibility [FERN-SEED]?
BEAUMONT and FLETCHER:
*Fair Maid of the Inn*, I, i.

It was by the aid of the ring that Gyges obtained possession of the wife of CANDAULES and through her, of his kingdom.

**Gyromancy.** A kind of DIVINATION performed by walking round in a circle or ring until one fell from dizziness, the direction of the fall being of significance. (Gr. *guros*, ring; *manteia*, divination.)

**Gytrash** (gīt′rash). A north of England spirit, which in the form of horse, mule or large dog, haunts solitary ways, and sometimes comes upon belated travellers.

I remember certain of Bessie's tales, wherein figured a … spirit called a Gytrash.
CHARLOTTE BRONTË: *Jane Eyre*, ch, xii.

# H

**Hackell's Coit.** A huge stone said to weigh about 30 tons, near Stanton Drew, Somerset; so called from a tradition that it was a quoit or coit thrown by Sir John Hautville (13th century). In Wiltshire three huge stones near Kennet are called the *Devil's Coits* and there is a DOLMEN at St. Breock, Wadebridge, Cornwall, called the *Giant's Quoit.*

**Hades** (hā′dēz). In Homer, the name of the god (PLUTO) who reigns over the dead; but in later classical mythology the abode of the departed spirits, a place of gloom but not necessarily a place of punishment and torture. As the state or abode of the dead it corresponds to the Heb. *Sheol*, a word which, in the Authorized Version of the BIBLE, has frequently been translated by the misleading HELL. Hence *Hades* is often used as a euphemism for Hell. *Cp.* INFERNO.

**Hag.** A witch or sorceress, an ugly old woman.

> How now, you secret, black, and midnight hags?
> SHAKESPEARE: *Macbeth*, IV, i.

**Hag-knots.** Tangles in the manes of horses and ponies, supposed to be used by witches for stirrups.

**Hag's teeth.** A seaman's term to express those parts of a matting etc., which spoil its general uniformity.

**Hair.** The serpent hair of Medusa and the Erinyes represented the baleful aspect of the feminine power.

Egyptian royal children were portrayed with a heavy tress of hair on the right hand side.

The matted hair of SIVA depicts the ascetic; the black hair of Kali is Time and the symmetrically arranged hair of the Buddha represents control and serenity. Dishevelled or torn hair is grief or mourning.

To cut off or steal hair is to deprive the masculine solar power of its rays and is thus also a castration symbol, as in the case of Samson and Delilah.

Hair, like finger nails, must not fall into the hands of witches as they give power over the person.

One single tuft is left on the shaven crown of a Muslim for Mohammed to grasp hold of when drawing the deceased to PARADISE.

The scalp-lock on the otherwise bald head of North American Indians is for a conquering enemy to seize when he tears off the scalp.

The ancients believed that till a lock of hair was devoted to PROSERPINA, she refused to release the SOUL from the dying body. When DIDO mounted the funeral pile, she lingered in suffering till JUNO sent IRIS to cut off a lock of her hair; THANATOS did the same for Alcestis when she gave her life for her husband; and in all sacrifices a forelock was first cut off from the head of the victim as an offering to the black queen.

It was an old idea that a person with red hair could not be trusted, from the tradition that Judas had red hair. Shakespeare says:

> *Rosalind:* His very hair is of the dissembling colour.
> *Celia:* Something browner than Judas's.
> *As You Like It*, III, iv.

A man with black hair but a red beard was the worst of all. The old rhyme says:

> A red beard and a black head,
> Catch him with a good trick and take him dead.

Byron says in *The Prisoner of Chillon:*

> My hair is grey, but not with years,
> Nor grew it white
> In a single night,
> As men's have grown from sudden fears.

It is a well-authenticated fact that this can happen, and has happened. It is said that Ludovico Sforza became grey in a single night; Charles I, also, while he was undergoing trial, and Marie Antoinette grew grey from grief during her imprisonment.

**Hal-an-tow** (hal-ən-tō). The song and procession at Helston which preceded the FURRY DANCE on Furry Day. Men and maids went into the country in early morning, returning with green boughs and flowers, with twigs in their hats and caps. Led by an elderly person riding a donkey they entered the decorated streets singing the *Morning Song,* the chorus being:

Hal-an-Tow, jolly rumble-O
And for to fetch the Summer home, the Summer and the May-O,
For Summer is acome-O and Winter is agone-O.

Of considerable antiquity, the Hal-an-Tow eventually lapsed but was revived in 1930. The name is possibly from Cornish *hayl* and *tyow*, which freely rendered would mean 'in the moorland and in the town'.

**Halgaver.** Summoned before the mayor of Halgaver. The mayor of Halgaver is an imaginary worthy, and the threat for those whose offence is slovenliness and untidiness. Halgaver or Goat's Moor near Bodmin, Cornwall, was famous for an annual carnival held there in the middle of July. Charles II was so pleased with the diversions when he passed through on his way to Scilly that he became a member of the 'self-constituted' corporation. *Cp.* MAYOR OF GARRATT *under* GARRATT.

**Hallowe'en** (halōēn'). 31 October, which in the old CELTIC calendar was the last day of the year, its night being the time when all the witches and warlocks were abroad. On the introduction of Christianity it was taken over as the Eve of ALL HALLOWS or All Saints.

**Hamadryads.** *See* DRYAD.

**Hamet.** *See* CID HAMET.

**Hand.** A symbol of fortitude in Egypt, of fidelity in Rome. Two hands symbolize concord; by a closed hand Zeno represented dialectics and by an open hand eloquence.

In early art, the Deity was frequently represented by a hand extended from the clouds, with rays issuing from the fingers, but generally it was in the act of benediction, *i.e.* two fingers raised.

The Great Hand depicts supreme divine power, protection and justice. The hand is also an attribute of the Great Mother in Sumero-Semitic tradition as the bounteous giver and protector.

The right hand is the 'hand of power' and used in blessing and pledges. The left hand is the passive aspect of power and is associated with theft and cheating.

The votive hand of Sabazios, with its various symbols, was a talisman and apotropaic.

In Islam the Hand of Fatima represents divine power, the hand of God; the thumb is the Prophet and the fingers his four companions.

**Hand of Glory.** *See* GLORY.

**Hang. To hang by a thread.** To be in a very precarious situation. The allusion is to the sword of DAMOCLES.

**Hanging Gardens of Babylon.** A square garden (according to Diodorus Siculus), 400 ft. each way, rising in a series of terraces, and provided with earth to a sufficient depth to accommodate trees of a great size. Water was lifted from the Euphrates by a screw and the gardens were irrigated from a reservoir at the top.

These famous gardens were one of the SEVEN WONDERS OF THE WORLD (*see under* WONDERS) and were said to have been built by Queen SEMIRAMIS and by Nebuchadnezzar, to gratify his wife Amyitis, who felt weary of the flat plains of Babylon, and longed for something to remind her of her native Median Hills. They may have been associated with the great ziggurat of Babylon.

**Hangmen and Executioners.** Some practitioners have achieved a particular notice, *e.g.*:

BULL (*c.* 1593), the earliest hangman whose name survives.

DERRICK (*q.v.*), who cut off the head of Essex in 1601.

GREGORY BRANDON and his son RICHARD (1640), who executed Charles I, known as 'the two Gregories'.

SQUIRE DUN, mentioned in *Hudibras* (Pt. III, ii).

JACK KETCH (1663) executed Lord Russell and the Duke of Monmouth. His name later became a generic word for a hangman.

ROSE, the butcher (1686).

EDWARD DENNIS (1780), introduced in Dickens's *Barnaby Rudge.*

THOMAS CHESHIRE, nicknamed 'Old Cheese'.

WILLIAM CALCRAFT (1800–1879) was

appointed hangman in 1829 and was pensioned off in 1874.

WILLIAM MARWOOD (1820–1883), who invented the 'long drop'.

Of French executioners, the most celebrated are Capeluche, headsman of Paris during the days of the Burgundians and Armagnacs; and the two brothers Sanson who worked the GUILLOTINE during the French Revolution.

The fee given to the hangman at Tyburn used to be 13½d., with 1½d. for the rope.

> For half of thirteen-pence ha'penny wages
> I would have cleared all the town cages,
> And you should have been rid of all the stages
> I and my gallows groan.
> *The Hangman's Last Will and Testament*
> (*Rump Songe*).

Noblemen who were to be beheaded were expected to give the executioner from £7 to £10 for cutting off their head; any peer who came to the halter could claim the privilege of being suspended by a silken rope.

**Hänsel and Gretel.** The inseparables of the famous fairy story found among the tales of the brothers Grimm. Hänsel was a woodcutter's son and the little girl Gretel was found in the forest. When starvation threatened the household the woodcutter, at his wife's behest, abandoned the children in the forest. Hänsel laid a trail by which they found their way home, but they were subsequently again cast adrift. After several escapes from the machinations of a wicked fairy, Hänsel was at last transformed into a fawn and taken with Gretel to the king's castle, where Hänsel was restored to human form and enabled to marry Gretel. The story forms the basis of Humperdinck's opera (1893) of this name.

**Happy hunting ground.** The North American Indians' HEAVEN. Figuratively, where one finds happy leisure occupation.

**Hare.** *See* BURKE.

**Hare.** The mythology of the hare goes back to ancient times when it was depicted on Assyrian reliefs and Egyptian wall-paintings. It was one of the chief animals of the hunt.

The hare-in-the-moon is an almost universal myth, occurring in the Far East, India, South Africa, Mexico and other places. The hare is always an attribute of lunar deities and with them depicts the periodic death and rebirth of the moon. The hare also symbolizes fertility and as such is depicted with CUPIDS and APHRODITE/VENUS; it is also a messenger animal and an attribute of HERMES/MERCURY.

Pliny expresses the belief that every hare is androgynous and in Egypt this was depicted as the moon being masculine while waxing and feminine when waning; this myth was carried over into mediaeval literature.

Caesar says that the hare was important to the early Britons and that BOADICEA released one at the start of a campaign. For the Celts the hare was an attribute of all moon deities who were often depicted holding a hare. The animal was also of great importance in Teutonic myth; the lunar goddess Oestra or Eostre was hare-headed, representing fertility, new life in spring, resurrection. It was she who gave her name to the Easter festival. Her hare (incorrectly called the Easter Bunny) laid the Easter Egg of new life. The Teutonic Holda, Herke or Harfer was followed by a train of hares carrying torches. The Norse FREYJA also had attendant hares.

Hinduism and Buddhism both have the hare-in-the-moon and the hare appears also with the crescent moon; the Hindu god Chandras carries a hare. The Buddha put the hare in the moon to commemorate its sacrificing itself to him when he was hungry. In Chinese myth the hare represents the *yin* lunar power and the animal can be seen in the moon mixing the elixir of immortality. Figures of hares were made at the Moon Festival.

The Great Hare Manabazho is an Amerindian culture hero, a saviour, creator and transformer, also a trickster figure. The Great MANITOU, who lives in the moon with his grandmother, is a 'provider of all waters', master of winds and brother of the snow. The trickster-hero also appears in West African lore; together with the rabbit he was the origin of the Caribbean-American legends of Br'er Rabbit.

It is unlucky for a hare to cross your path, because witches were said to transform themselves into hares.

Geo.:  A witch is a kind of hare.
Scath.:  And marks the weather
       As the hare doth.

BEN JONSON: *Sad Shepherd*, II, iii.

The superstitious is fond in observation, servile in feare...This man does not stirre forth till his breast be crossed, and his face sprinkled: if but an hare crosse him the way, he returnes.

BP. HALL: *Characters of Virtues and Vices* (1608).

According to mediaeval 'science', the hare was a melancholy animal, and ate wild succory in the hope of curing itself; its flesh was supposed to generate melancholy in any who partook of it.

*Fal.*: 'Sblood, I am so melancholy as a gib cat, or a lugged bear.
*Prince:* Or an old lion, or a lover's lute.
*Fal.*: Yea, or the drone of a Lincolnshire bagpipe.
*Prince:* What sayest thou to a hare, or the melancholy of Moor-ditch?

SHAKESPEARE: *Henry IV, Pt. I*, I, ii.

Another superstition was that hares are sexless, or that they change their sex annually.

Snakes that cast your coats for new,
Camelions, that alter hue,
Hares that yearly sexes change.

FLETCHER: *Faithful Shepherdess*, III, i.

**The Hare and the Tortoise.** An allusion to the well-known fable of the race between them, which was won by the tortoise; the moral being, 'Slow and steady wins the race.'

**Hare-lip.** A cleft lip; so called from its resemblance to the upper lip of a hare. It was fabled to be caused at birth by an ELF or malicious FAIRY.

This is the foul fiend Flibbertigibbit. He begins at curfew, and walks till the first cock. He ... squints the eye and makes the hare-lip.

SHAKESPEARE: *King Lear*, III, iv.

**Harlequin** (hah'ləkwin). In British PANTOMIME, a mischievous fellow supposed to be invisible to all eyes but those of his faithful COLUMBINE. His function is to dance through the world and frustrate all the knavish tricks of the clown, who is supposed to be in love with Columbine. He wears a tight-fitting spangled or parti-coloured dress and is usually masked. He derives from Arlecchino, a stock character of Italian comedy (like PANTALOON and SCARAMOUCH), whose name was in origin probably that of a sprite or HOBGOBLIN. One of the demons in Dante is named 'Alichino', and another DEVIL of mediaeval demonology was 'Hennequin'.

What Momus was of old to Jove
The same a Harlequin is now.
The former was buffoon above,

The latter is a Punch below.

SWIFT: *The Puppet Show*.

The prince of Harlequins was John Rich (1682–1761).

**Harlequin.** So the Emperor Charles V or Charles Quint (1550–1558) was called by Francis I of France.

**Harmonia. Harmonia's Necklace.** An unlucky possession, something that brings evil to all who possess it. Harmonia was the daughter of MARS and VENUS and she received such a necklace on her marriage to King CADMUS. VULCAN, to avenge the infidelity of her mother, also made the bride a present of a robe dyed in all sorts of crimes which infused wickedness and impiety into all her offspring. *Cp.* NESSUS. Both Harmonia and Cadmus, having suffered many misfortunes, were changed into serpents.

MEDEA, in a fit of jealousy, likewise sent Creusa a wedding robe, which burnt her to death. *Cp.* FATAL GIFTS.

**Harpocrates** (hahpok'rətēz). The Greek form of the Egyptian Harpa-Khruti (HORUS the child). Represented as a naked boy sucking his finger, the Greeks made him the god of silence and secrecy.

I assured my mistress she might make herself perfectly easy on that score for I was the Harpocrates of trusty valets.

A.R. LESAGE: *Gil Blas*, IV, ii.

**Harpy.** In classical mythology, a winged monster with the head and breasts of a woman, very fierce, starved-looking and loathsome, living in an atmosphere of filth and stench and contaminating everything it came near. HOMER mentions but one harpy, Hesiod gives two, and later writers three. Their names, *Aello* (storm), *Celeno* (blackness), and *Ocypete* (rapid), indicate their early association with whirlwinds and storms.

**A regular harpy.** A merciless sponger; one who wants to appropriate everything.

I will ... do you any embassage ... rather than hold three words conference with this harpy.

SHAKESPEARE: *Much Ado about Nothing*, II, i.

**Harry. Old Harry.** A familiar name for the DEVIL; probably from the personal name (*cp.* OLD NICK *under* NICHOLAS), but perhaps with some allusion to the word *harry*, meaning to plunder, harass, lay waste, from which comes the old *harrow*, as in the title as in the title of the 13th-century MIRACLE PLAY, *The Harrowing of Hell*.

> Pitch Greek to Old Harry, and stick to conundrums!!
>
> R.H. BARHAM: *Ingoldsby Legends*, II (*The Merchant of Venice*).

**By the Lord Harry.** A mild imprecation, *Lord Harry* here being the equivalent of the DEVIL.

> By the Lord Harry, he says true.
>
> CONGREVE: *Old Bachelor*, II, ii.

**To play Old Harry.** To play the DEVIL; to ruin, or seriously damage.

**Haruspex** (hərŭs'peks) (pl. *haruspices*). A Roman official of Etruscan origins who interpreted the will of the gods by inspecting the entrails of animals offered in sacrifice (O. Lat. *haruga*, a victim; *specio*, I inspect). Cato said, 'I wonder how one haruspex can keep from laughing when he sees another.' *Cp.* AUSPICES. *See* DIVINATION.

**Hatchet. To bury the hatchet.** *See* BURY.

**Hatto.** A 10th-century archbishop of Mainz, a noted statesman and counsellor of Otto the Great, who, according to some, was noted for his oppression of the poor. In time of famine, that there might be more for the rich, he was supposed to have assembled the poor in a barn and burnt them to death, saying: 'They are like mice, only good to devour the corn.' Presently an army of mice came against the archbishop, who removed to a tower on the Rhine to escape the plague, but the mice followed in their thousands and devoured him. The tower is still called the MOUSE TOWER. Southey has a ballad on Bishop Hatto.

Many similar legends, or versions of the same legend, are told of the mediaeval Rhineland:

Count Graaf raised a tower in the midst of the Rhine, and if any boat attempted to avoid payment of toll, the warders shot the crew with crossbows. In a famine year the count profiteered greatly by cornering wheat, but the tower was invaded by hungry rats who worried the old baron to death and then devoured him.

Widerolf, bishop of Strasbourg (in 997), was devoured by mice because he suppressed the convent of Seltzen, on the Rhine.

Bishop Adolf of Cologne was devoured by mice or rats in 1112.

Freiherr von Güttingen collected the poor in a great barn and burnt them to death. He was pursued to his castle of Güttingen by rats and mice who ate him clean to the bones. His castle then sank to the bottom of the lake 'where it may still be seen'. *Cp.* PIED PIPER OF HAMELIN.

**Hautville Coit.** *See* HACKELL'S COIT.

**Havelock the Dane.** A hero of mediaeval romance, the orphan son of Birkabegn, King of Denmark. He was cast adrift on the sea through the treachery of his guardians and the raft bore him to the Lincolnshire coast. He was rescued by a fisherman called Grim and brought up as his son. He eventually became King of Denmark and of part of England; Grim was suitably rewarded and with the money built Grim's town or Grimsby.

**Hawk.** Having the same connotations as the EAGLE, the hawk is a solar bird and an attribute of all sun gods. Both birds have similar legends, such as that of flying up to the sun and gazing at it without flinching. The hawk, or falcon, was the Egyptian royal bird, the Bird of Khensu and of RA, the sun, who were represented as hawk- or falcon-headed. Other hawk-headed gods, or those accompanied by hawks, were Ptah, HORUS, Mentu, Rehu, Sokar and Kebhsenuf; the hawk is also an attribute of the Great Mother Amenti. The sphinx is sometimes hawk-headed.

In Greek myth the hawk is 'the swift messenger of Apollo' according to Homer; it was also an attribute of Circe.

The Hindu Gayatri, the hawk, brought *soma* from the heavens and the bird is a vehicle of the Vedic INDRA; it is also an attribute of ORMUZD in Iranian myth and of MITHRA as a sun god.

The hawk, in Amerindian lore, was one of the creatures which helped create the world after the Flood. Polynesia has the hawk as a prophetic bird with healing powers and among the Australian Aboriginals the eagle-hawk is a totem deity.

**Hawthorn.** The symbol of 'Good Hope' in the language of FLOWERS because it shows winter is over and spring is at hand. The Athenian girls used to crown themselves with hawthorn flowers at weddings, and the marriage-torch was made of hawthorn. The Romans considered it a charm against sorcery, and placed leaves of it on the cradles of new-born infants.

The hawthorn was chosen by Henry VII, as his device, because Richard III's crown was recovered from a hawthorn bush at Bosworth. *Haw* here is the O.E. *haga*, hedge.

**Hazazel.** The scapegoat. *See* AZAZEL.

**Heart of Oak.** This famous sea song and naval march is from Garrick's pantomime, *Harlequin's Invasion*, with music by Dr. Boyce. It was written in 1759, 'the year of victories' (Quiberon Bay, Quebec, Minden), hence the allusion to 'this wonderful year' in the opening lines. 'Heart of Oak' refers, of course, to the timber from which the ships were built.

> Come, cheer up my lads! 'tis to glory we steer,
> To add something more to this wonderful year.

**Heaven** (O.E. *heofon*). The word properly denotes the abode of the Deity and His ANGELS—'heaven is my throne' (*Is.* lxvi, 1, and *Matt.* v, 34)—but it is also used in the BIBLE and elsewhere for the air, the upper heights, as 'the fowls of heaven', 'the dew of heaven', 'the clouds of heaven'; 'the cities are walled up to heaven' (*Deut.* i, 28); and a tower whose top should 'reach unto heaven' (*Gen.* xi, 4); the starry firmament, as 'Let there be lights in the firmament of the heaven' (*Gen.* i, 14).

In the Ptolemaic system, the heavens were the successive spheres surrounding the central earth. *See also* EMPYREAN; PARADISE.

**The Seven Heavens** (of Muslims).

*The first heaven* is of pure SILVER, and here the stars, each with its ANGEL warder, are hung out like lamps on golden chains. It is the abode of ADAM and Eve.

*The second heaven* is of pure GOLD and is the domain of John The Baptist and Jesus.

*The third heaven* is of PEARL, and is allotted to JOSEPH. Here AZRAEL is stationed, and is forever writing in a large book (the names of the new-born) or blotting names out (those of the newly dead).

*The fourth heaven* is of white gold, and is Enoch's. Here dwells the angel of Tears, whose height is '500 days' journey', and who sheds ceaseless tears for the sins of man.

*The fifth heaven* is of silver and is Aar-

on's. Here dwells the Avenging Angel, who presides over elemental fire.

*The sixth heaven* is composed of ruby and garnet, and is presided over by Moses. Here dwells the Guardian Angel of heaven and earth, half-snow and half-fire.

*The seventh heaven* is formed of divine light beyond the power of tongue to describe, and is ruled by ABRAHAM. Each inhabitant is bigger than the whole earth, and has 70,000 heads, each head 70,000 faces and each face 70,000 mouths, each mouth 70,000 tongues and each tongue speaks 70,000 languages, all for ever employed in chanting the praises of the Most High.

**To be in the seventh heaven.** Supremely happy. The CABBALISTS maintained that there are seven heavens, each rising above the other, the seventh being the abode of God and the highest class of ANGELS.

**Hebe** (hē′bi). In Greek mythology, daughter of ZEUS and HERA, goddess of youth, and cup-bearer to the gods. She had the power of restoring youth and vigour to gods and men.

**Hecate** (hek′əti). In Greek mythology, daughter of the TITAN Perses and of Asteria, and high in favour with ZEUS. Her powers extended over HEAVEN and HELL, the earth and the sea. She came to combine the attributes of SELENE, ARTEMIS and PERSEPHONE and to be identified with them. She was represented as a triple goddess sometimes with three heads, one of a horse, one of a dog and one of a boar; sometimes with three bodies standing back to back. As goddess of the lower world she became the goddess of magic, ghosts and WITCHCRAFT. Her offerings consisted of dogs, honey and black lambs, which were sacrificed to her at crossroads. Shakespeare refers to the triple character of this goddess:

> And we fairies that do run
> By the triple Hecate's team.
> *Midsummer Night's Dream*, V, ii.

**Hector.** Eldest son of PRIAM, the noblest and most magnanimous of all the Trojan chieftains in Homer's ILIAD. After holding out for ten years, he was slain by ACHILLES, who lashed him to his chariot, and dragged the dead body in triumph thrice round the walls of TROY.

Somewhat curiously his name has come to be applied to a swaggering bully, and 'to hector' means to browbeat, bully, bluster.

**The Hector of Germany.** Joachim II, Elector of Brandenburg (1505, 1535–1571).

**You wear Hector's cloak.** You are paid in your own coin for trying to deceive another. When Thomas Percy, Earl of Northumberland, was routed in 1569, he hid in the house of Hector Graham of Harlaw, who betrayed him for the reward offered. Fortune never favoured this traitor thereafter, and he eventually died a beggar on the roadside.

**Hecuba** (hek'ūbə). Second wife of PRIAM and mother of nineteen children, including HECTOR. When TROY was taken she fell to the lot of ULYSSES. She was afterwards metamorphosed into a bitch and finding she could only bark, threw herself into the sea. Her sorrows and misfortunes are featured in numerous Greek tragedies.

**Hedgehog.** In early times the hedgehog was associated with the Great Mother, particularly ISHTAR.

There was a widespread legend that the hedgehog collected fruit, particularly grapes, by rolling on them and taking them home on its spines; Plutarch said he had seen this done. Aristotle, Pliny and Aelian say that the hedgehog foretells a change of wind and accordingly 'shifts the outlook of its earth holes'. Another belief was that the animal, if it falls from a height, takes the shock on its spines. Country traditions, particularly in Ireland, connect the hedgehog with witches who take its form to suck cows dry.

**Heel. The heel of Achilles.** *See under* ACHILLES.

**Heimdall** (hīm'dahl). In Scandinavian mythology, a god of light who guards the rainbow bridge, BIFROST. He was the son of the nine daughters of AEGIR, and in many attributes identical with TIW.

**Heimskringla** (hīmzkring'lə) (Orb of the world). An important collection of sixteen sagas on the lives of the early kings of Norway to 1184, the work of Snorri Sturluson (1179–1241).

**Hel.** In early Scandinavian mythology the name of the abode of the dead and of its goddess; later, the home of those not slain in battle; slain warriors entered VALHALLA. Hel and her realm eventually acquired more sinister attributes after the advent of Christianity.

**Heldenbuch** (hel'dənbuk) (Ger. Book of Heroes). The name given to a collection of 13th-century German epic poetry. The stories are based upon national sagas, Dietrich of Bern being a central figure.

**Helen.** The type of female beauty. In Greek legend, she was the daughter of ZEUS and LEDA, and wife of MENELAUS, King of Sparta. She eloped with PARIS and thus brought about the siege and destruction of TROY.

> For which men all the life they here enjoy
> Still fight, as for the Helens of their Troy.
> FULKE GREVILLE, LORD BROOKE:
> *Treatise of Humane Learning.*

**Helen's fire.** *See* CORPOSANT.

**Helicon.** The home of the MUSES, a part of PARNASSUS. It contained the fountains of AGANIPPE and HIPPOCRENE, connected by 'Helicon's harmonious stream'. The name is used allusively of poetic inspiration.

> From Helicon's harmonious springs
> A thousand rills their mazy progress take.
> The laughing flowers, that round them blow,
> Drink life and fragrance as they flow.
> GRAY: *The Progress of Poesy.*

**Heliogabalus.** *See* ELAGABALUS.

**Helios** (hē'lios). The Greek sun-god, who climbed the vault of HEAVEN in a chariot drawn by snow-white horses to give light, and in the evening descended into the Ocean. He is called HYPERION by Homer, and in later times, APOLLO.

**Heliotrope** (Gr. turn-to-sun). For the story of the flower, *see* CLYTIE.

The bloodstone, a greenish quartz with veins and spots of red, used to be called 'heliotrope', the story being that if thrown into water it turned the rays of the sun to blood-colours. This stone also had the power of rendering its bearer invisible.

> Nor hope had they of crevice where to hide,
> Or heliotrope to charm them out of view.
> DANTE: *Vision, Hell,* xxiv (*Cary's Translation*).

**Hell.** The abode of the dead, then traditionally the place of torment or punishment after death (O.E. *hel*, hell, from root *hel-*, hide).

According to the Koran, Hell has seven portals leading into seven divisions (*Surah* XV, 44).

True Buddhism admits of no Hell properly so called, but certain of the more superstitious Buddhists acknowledge as many as 136 places of punishment after death, where the dead are sent according to their deserts.

Classic authors tell us that the INFERNO is encompassed by five rivers: ACHERON, COCYTUS, STYX, PHLEGETHON, and LETHE. *See also* AVERNUS, HADES, HEAVEN, TARTARUS.

**The road to hell is easy.** *Facilis descensus Averno. See* AVERNUS.

**Hellespont** (hel'ispont). The 'sea of Helle'; so called because Helle, the sister of Phrixus, was drowned there. She was fleeing with her brother through the air to Colchis on the golden ram to escape from INO, her mother-in-law, who most cruelly oppressed her, but, turning giddy, she fell into the sea. It is the ancient name of the Dardanelles and is celebrated in the legend of HERO AND LEANDER. *See also* GOLDEN FLEECE.

**Helmet.** The helmets of Saragossa were in most repute in the days of chivalry.

*Bever*, or *drinking-piece*. One of the movable parts, which was lifted up when the wearer ate or drank. It comes from the old Italian verb *bevere*, to drink.

*Close helmet*. The complete headpiece, having in front two movable parts, which could be lifted up or down at pleasure.

*Morion*. A low iron cap, worn only by infantry.

*Visor*. One of the movable parts; it was to look through.

**The helmet of Perseus** rendered the wearer invisible. This was the 'helmet of HADES', which, with winged sandals and magic wallet, he took from certain NYMPHS; but after he had slain MEDUSA he restored them again, and presented the GORGON's head to ATHENE, who placed it in the middle of her AEGIS.

**Hen.** Known in Egypt in the 14th century B.C., the hen was domesticated about 3000 B.C., becoming common in Greece and Rome in the 6th century. Hens were kept in the temple of Hebe in Rome, with cocks at the temple of Hercules. Domestic hens were used in divination from the manner in which they approached their food.

In the Bible the hen is used to depict maternal care (*Matt.* xxiii, 37) and the hen with chicks was likened to Christ and his flock.

A crowing hen typifies a domineering woman. A Greek legend said that if a hen defeats a cock in battle it crows and takes on a cock's plumage.

**Hengist and Horsa.** The semi-legendary leaders who led the first Saxon war-band to settle in England. They are said to have arrived in Kent in 449 at the invitation of Vortigern, who offered them land on the understanding that they would help against the PICTS. Horsa is said to have been slain at the battle of Aylesford (*c.* 455), and Hengist to have ruled in Kent till his death in 488. The name Horsa is connected with our word *horse* and Hengist is the Ger. *hengst*, a stallion. The traditional badge of Kent is a white horse.

**Hepatoscopy.** A very ancient form of DIVINATION based upon inspection of the liver from the animal sacrificed (Gr. *hepar, hepatos*, liver). It rested on the belief that the liver was the seat of vitality and of the soul.

> For the king of Babylon stood at the parting of the way ... to use divination: he made his arrows bright, he consulted with images, he looked in the liver.
> *Ezek.* xxi, 21.

**Hephaestus** (hife'stəs). The Greek VULCAN.

**Heptameron, The** (heptam'ərən). A collection of Italian and other mediaeval stories written by, or ascribed to, Marguerite of Angoulême, Queen of Navarre (1492–1549), and published posthumously in 1558. They were supposed to have been related in seven days (Gr. *hepta*, seven; *hemera*, day).

**Hera** (hē'rə) (Gr. *haireo*, chosen one). The Greek JUNO, the wife of ZEUS.

**Herba sacra.** The 'divine weed', vervain, said by the Romans to cure the bites of all rabid animals, to arrest the progress of venom, to cure the plague, to avert sorcery and WITCHCRAFT, to reconcile enemies etc. So highly esteemed was it that feasts called *Verbenalia* were annually held in its honour. Heralds wore a wreath of vervain when they declared war; and the DRUIDS are supposed to have held it in veneration.

Lift your boughs of vervain blue.
Dipt in cold September dew;
And dash the moisture, chaste and clear,
O'er the ground, and through the air.
Now the place is purged and pure.

W. MASON: *Caractacus* (1759).

**Hercules** (hœ'kūlēz). In Greek mythology, a hero of superhuman physical strength, son of ZEUS and ALCMENA. He is represented as brawny, muscular, short-necked, often holding a club and a lion's skin. In a fit of madness inflicted on him by JUNO, he slew his wife and children, and as penance was ordered by APOLLO to serve for 12 years the Argive king, Eurystheus, who imposed upon him twelve tasks of great difficulty and danger:

(1) To slay the NEMEAN LION.
(2) To kill the Lernean HYDRA.
(3) To catch and retain the Arcadian stag.
(4) To destroy the Erymanthian boar.
(5) To cleanse the AUGEAN STABLES.
(6) To destroy the cannibal birds of the Lake Stymphalis.
(7) To take captive the Cretan bull.
(8) To catch the horses of the Thracian Diomedes.
(9) To get possession of the girdle of HIPPOLYTA, Queen of the Amazons.
(10) To capture the oxen of the monster GERYON.
(11) To obtain the apples of the HESPER-IDES.
(12) To bring CERBERUS from the infernal regions.

After these labours and many other adventures he was rewarded with immortality.

**The Attic Hercules.** THESEUS, who went about like Hercules, destroying robbers and achieving wondrous exploits.

**Hercules and his load.** The sign of the Globe Theatre showing Hercules carrying the globe upon his shoulders. Shakespeare alludes to it in *Hamlet*, II, ii:

*Ham.:* Do the boys carry it away?
*Ros.:* Ay, that they do, my lord; Hercules and his load too.

**Hercules' choice.** Immortality, the reward of toil in preference to pleasure. Xenophon tells us that when Hercules was a youth he was accosted by Virtue and Pleasure, and asked to choose between them. Pleasure promised him all carnal delights, but Virtue promised immortality. Hercules gave his hand to the latter, and, after a life of toil, was received amongst the gods.

**Hercules' horse.** *See* FAMOUS HORSES *under* HORSE.

**Hercules' Pillars.** *See under* PILLAR.

**Hercules Secundus.** Commodus, the Roman Emperor (A.D. 161, 180–192), gave himself this title. Dissipated and inordinately cruel, he claimed divine honours and caused himself to be worshipped as Hercules. It is said that he killed 100 lions in the amphitheatre, and that he slew over 1000 defenceless gladiators.

**Herculean knot** (hœkūlē'ən). A snaky complication on the rod or CADUCEUS of MERCURY, adopted by Grecian brides as the fastening of their woollen girdles, which only the bridegroom was allowed to untie. As he did so he invoked JUNO to render his marriage as those of Hercules, whose numerous wives all had families, among them being the 50 daughters of Thestius, all of whom conceived in one night.

**Ex pede Herculem.** *See under* EX.

**Hermae.** *See* HERMES.

**Hermaphrodite** (hœmaf'rōdīt). A person or animal with indeterminate sexual organs, or those of both sexes; a flower containing both male and female reproductive organs. The word is derived from Hermaphroditus, son of HERMES and APHRODITE. The nymph Salmacis became enamoured of him, and prayed that she might be so closely united that 'the twain might become one flesh'. Her prayer being heard, the NYMPH and boy became one body (Ovid: *Metamorphoses*, IV, 347–88).

According to fable, all persons who bathed in the fountain Salmacis, in Caria, became hermaphrodites.

**Hermes** (hœ'mēz). The Greek MERCURY, whose busts, known as *Hermae*, were affixed to pillars and set up as boundary marks at street corners etc. The Romans also used them for garden ornaments.

Among alchemists, Hermes was the usual name for quicksilver or mercury (*see* Milton: *Paradise Lost*, III, 603).

**Hermetic Art,** or **Philosophy.** The art or science of ALCHEMY; so called from Hermes Trismegistus (the Thrice Greatest Hermes) the name given by the Neoplatonists to the Egyptian god THOTH, its hypothetical founder.

**Hermetic books.** Forty-two books fabled to have been written from the dictation of Hermes Trismegistus, dealing with the life and thought of ancient Egypt. They state that the world was made out of fluid; that the SOUL is the union of light and life; that nothing is destructible; that the soul transmigrates, and that suffering is the result of motion.

**Hermetic powder.** A sympathetic powder, supposed to possess a healing influence from a distance; so called by mediaeval philosophers out of compliment to Hermes Trismegistus (Sir Kenelm Digby: *Discourse Touching the Cure of Wounds by the Powder of Sympathy*, 1658).

> For by his side a pouch he wore
> Replete with strange hermetic powder,
> That wounds nine miles point-black would solder.
> BUTLER: *Hudibras*, I, ii.

**Hermetically sealed.** Closed securely; from sealing a vessel hermetically, *i.e.* as a chemist, a disciple of Hermes Trismegistus, would, by heating the neck of the vessel till it is soft, and then twisting it till the aperture is closed up.

**Herne the Hunter.** *See* WILD HUNTSMAN.

**Hero and Leander.** The old Greek tale is that Hero, a priestess of VENUS, fell in love with Leander, who swam across the HELLESPONT every night to visit her. One night he was drowned, and heart-broken Hero drowned herself in the same sea. The story is told in one of the poems of Musaeus, and in Marlowe and Chapman's *Hero and Leander*.

Lord Byron and Lieutenant Ekenhead repeated the experiment of Leander in 1810 and accomplished it in 1 hour 10 minutes. The distance, allowing for drifting, would be about four miles. In *Don Juan* (Canto II, cv), Byron says of his hero:

> A better swimmer you could scarce see ever,
> He could, perhaps, have pass'd the Hellespont,
> As once (a feat on which ourselves we prided)
> Leander, Mr. Ekenhead, and I did.

**Hertha.** *See* NERTHUS.

**Hesperides** (hesper'idēz). Three sisters who guarded the golden apples which HERA received as a marriage gift. They were assisted by the dragon LADON. HERCULES, as the eleventh of his 'twelve labours', slew the DRAGON and carried some of the apples to Eurystheus.

Many poets call the place where these golden apples grew the 'Garden of the Hesperides'. Shakespeare (*Love's Labour's Lost*, IV, iii) speaks of 'climbing trees in the Hesperides'. (*Cp.* Milton's *Comus*, lines 393–7.)

**Hesperus** (hes'pərəs). The name given by the Greeks to the planet VENUS as an evening star. As a morning star it was called LUCIFER or *Phosphorus*.

> Ere twice in murk and occidental damp
> Moist Hesperus hath quenched his sleepy lamp.
> SHAKESPEARE: *All's Well that Ends Well*, II, i.

**Hiawatha.** The Iroquois name of a hero of miraculous birth who came (under a variety of names) among the North American Indian tribes to bring peace and goodwill to man.

In Longfellow's poem (1855) he is an Ojibway, son of Mudjekeewis (the west wind) and Wenonah, and married Minnehaha, 'Laughing Water'. He represents the progress of civilization among his people. When the white man landed and taught the Indians the faith of Jesus, Hiawatha exhorted them to receive the words of wisdom, to reverence the missionaries who had come so far to see them.

**Hickathrift, Tom.** A hero of nursery rhyme and mythical strong man, fabled to have been a labourer at the time of the Conquest. Armed with an axle-tree and cartwheel he killed a GIANT who dwelt in a marsh at Tilney, Norfolk. He was knighted and made a governor of Thanet. *Cp.* JACK THE GIANT-KILLER.

**Hildebrand** (hil'dibrand). A celebrated character of German romance whose story is told in *Das Hildebrandslied*, an old German alliterative poem (written *c.* 800), and he also appears in the NIBELUNGENLIED, Dietrich von Bern etc. He is an old man, who returns home after many years among the Huns through following his master Theodoric, only to be challenged to single combat by his own son Hadubrand.

The name is better known as that of the great reforming pope St. Gregory VII (*c.* 1020, 1073–1085) whose attempts to prohibit lay investiture brought Henry IV to Canossa and made him many enemies. He did much to remove abuses and to regenerate the Church.

**Hildesheim** (hil'dəshīm). Legend relates that a monk of Hildesheim, an old city of Hanover, doubting how with God a thousand years could be as one day, listened to the singing of a bird in a wood, as he thought for three minutes, but found the time had been three hundred years. Longfellow makes use of the story in his *Golden Legend* (II), calling the monk Felix.

**Hill folk.** So Scott calls the Cameronian Scottish Covenanters, who met clandestinely among the hills. Sometimes the Covenanters generally are so called.

In Scandinavian tradition they are a type of being between elves and human beings. The 'hill people' were supposed to dwell in caves and small hills.

**Hind. The Hind of Sertorius.** Sertorius (*c.* 122–72 B.C.), Marian governor of Hispania Citerior was proscribed by Sulla and forced to flee. Later he was invited to return by the Lusitani and held Spain against the Senatorial party until his death through treachery. He had a tame white hind, which he taught to follow him, and from which he pretended to receive the instructions of DIANA. By this artifice, says Plutarch, he imposed on the superstition of the people.

**Hippocampus** (hip'ōkam'pəs) (Gr. *hippos*, horse; *kampos*, sea monster). A sea-horse, having the head and forequarters resembling those of a horse, with the tail and hindquarters of a fish or dolphin. It was the steed of NEPTUNE.

**Hippocrene** (hip'ōkrēn) (Gr. *hippos*, horse; *krene*, fountain). The fountain of the MUSES on Mount HELICON, produced by a stroke of the hoof of PEGASUS; hence, poetic inspiration.

O for a beaker full of the warm South,
Full of the true, the blushful Hippocrene.
KEATS: *Ode to a Nightingale.*

**Hippodamia.** *See* BRISEIS.

**Hippogriff** (Gr. *hippos*, a horse; *gryphos*, a griffin). The winged horse, whose father was a GRIFFIN and mother a filly. A symbol of love (Ariosto: *Orlando Furioso*, iv, 18, 19).

It appeared largely in mediaeval legends.

It was the uncontrollable mount of ATLANTIS.

So saying, he caught him up, and without wing
Of hippogriff, bore through the air sublime,
Over the wilderness and o'er the plain.
MILTON: *Paradise Regained*, IV, 541–3.

**Hippolyta** (hipol'itə). Queen of the AMAZONS, and daughter of MARS. SHAKESPEARE introduced the character in his *A Midsummer Night's Dream*, where he betroths her to THESEUS, Duke of Athens. In classic fable it is her sister Antiope who married Theseus, although some writers justify Shakespeare's account. Hippolyta was famous for a girdle given by her father, and it was one of the 'twelve labours' of HERCULES to possess himself of this prize.

**Hippolytus** (hipol'itəs). Son of THESEUS, King of Athens; when he repulsed his stepmother PHAEDRA'S advances she accused him of attempting her seduction. In anger his father sought NEPTUNE'S aid, who sent a sea monster which so terrified Hippolytus' horses that they dragged him to death. He was restored to life by AESCULAPIUS.

**Hippomenes** (hipom'enēz). In Boeotian legend, the Greek prince who won the race with Atalanta. *See* ATALANTA'S RACE.

**Hippopotamus.** Associated with Egypt, the Greeks and Romans called the hippopotamus the 'Beast of the Nile' and the Nile god either rides on, or is accompanied by, a hippopotamus; it is also the attribute of the Great Mother Amenti, the 'bringer forth of the waters, and of the goddess Rerat who was one of the keepers of the gates passed by the soul on its journey after death; she is depicted as a hippopotamus standing upright on its hind legs. Ta-urt or Taueret, wife of Set, takes the form of a hippopotamus and the thigh of the animal is the 'phallic leg of Set', representing virility. Egyptian myth tells the story of Horus overcoming Set who takes the form of a red hippopotamus.

It is suggested that the Behemoth of the Bible was the hippopotamus as being the largest animal known to the Jews.

**Hiram Abif** (hī'rəm abif') is a central figure in the legend and ritual of FREEMASONRY, the craftsman builder of King Solomon's Temple who died rather than yield up the secrets of masonry. He appears as Huram, the alternative form of the name, in II

*Chron.* ii and iv. He must not be confused with Hiram or Huram, King of Tyre, who supplied much of the material.

**Hobbit.** A benevolent hospitable burrow people, two to four feet high, and fond of bright colours, the creation of Professor J.R.R. Tolkien. They are featured in his two works, *The Hobbit* (1937) and *The Lord of the Rings* (1954–1955).

**Hobgoblin.** An impish, ugly and mischievous sprite, particularly PUCK or ROBIN GOOD-FELLOW. The word is a variant of Rob-goblin—*i.e.* the goblin Robin (*cp.* HODGE).

> Those that Hobgoblin call you, and sweet Puck,
> You do their work, and they shall have good luck.
> SHAKESPEARE: *A Midsummer Night's Dream*,
> II, i.

**Hock-day,** or **Hock Tuesday.** The second Tuesday after Easter Day, long held as a festival in England and observed until the 16th century. According to custom, on Hock Monday, the women of the village seized and bound men, demanding a small payment for their release. On the Tuesday of Hocktide the men similarly waylaid the women. The takings were paid to the churchwardens for parish work. This was later modified, as shown below:

> Hock Monday was for the men and Hock Tuesday for the women. On both days the men and women, alternately, with great merriment, intercepted the public roads with ropes, and pulled passengers to them, from whom they exacted money, to be laid out in pious uses.
> BRAND: *Antiquities,* vol. I.

**Hogmanay.** In Scotland, the last day of the year, the day when children demanded gifts or *hogmanay* of oat-cake or oaten bread etc.

> Hogmanay, Trollolay,
> Give us your white bread and none of your gray.

In olden times it was a kind of annual SATURNALIA. The word is of uncertain origin and of the numerous suggestions made, the most likely is that it is from the North French dialect word *hoginane*, O.Fr. *aguillaneuf* (to the mistletoe go this New Year).

**Holger Danske.** The national hero of Denmark. *See* OGIER THE DANE.

**Holly.** The custom of decorating churches and houses with holly at CHRISTMAS-time is of great antiquity and may derive from its earlier use by the Romans in the festival of the SATURNALIA, which occurred at the

same season, or from the old Teutonic custom. It is held to be unlucky by some to bring it into the house before Christmas Eve. Holly was sacred to Saturn and is apotropaic. In Christianity it was sometimes depicted as the tree of the cross; its spiked leaves representing the crown of thorns and the red berries the blood of Christ. It is an emblem of SS. John the Baptist and Jerome. *See also* IVY; MISTLETOE.

**Homer, a cure for the ague.** Among the old cures it was held that if the fourth book of the ILIAD was laid under the head of a patient, it would provide instant remedy. This book contains the cure of MENELAUS (when wounded by Pandarus) by Machaon, 'a son of AESCULAPIUS'.

**Honour. Crushed by one's honours.** The allusion is to the legend of the Roman damsel, Tarpeia, who agreed to open the gates of Rome to King Tatius, provided his soldiers would give her the ornaments which they wore on their arms (meaning their bracelets). As they entered, they threw their shields on her and crushed her, saying as they did so, 'These are the ornaments worn by Sabines on their arms.'

Draco, the Athenian legislator, was crushed to death in the theatre of Aegina, by the number of caps and cloaks showered on him by the audience, as a mark of their high appreciation of his merits. A similar story is told of the mad Emperor, ELAGABALUS, who smothered the leading citizens of Rome with roses.

**Hood, Robin.** *See* ROBIN HOOD.

**Hoopoe.** The bird features prominently in Arabic and Sufi mythology. It is the 'Doctor Bird' finding wells and springs and, according to *The Conference of the Birds*, it is a messenger of the world invisible. Solomon gave it its crest as a reward of shading him in the desert. The bird brings food to its parents in old age and so typifies filial devotion.

In Egypt it was held in great reverence and it occurs repeatedly in African and South European legend; and in one version of the Greek Tereus myth the gods changed him into a hoopoe or hawk.

In the *Bestiaries,* on the other hand, the hoopoe is called the Upupa and it is 'a filthy creature, feeding on stinking excrement' and its blood causes nightmares about suffocating devils, but in another version, as Epopus, it depicts devotion as caring for its parents.

**Hop-o'-my-thumb.** A pygmy or dwarf. *Cp.* TOM THUMB.

> Plaine friend, Hop-o'-my-Thumb, know you who we are?
> *Taming of a Shrew* (Anon., 1594).

**Hope.** *See* PANDORA'S BOX.

**Horae** (haw'rī) (Lat. hours, seasons). In classical mythology, the three sisters Eunomia (Good order), Dice (Justice) and Irene (Peace), who presided over spring, summer and winter. According to Hesiod they were the daughters of JUPITER and THEMIS.

**Horn. Astolpho's horn.** Logistilla gave Astolpho at parting a horn that had the virtue of being able to appal and put to flight the boldest knight or most savage beast (Ariosto: *Orlando Furioso*, Bk. VIII).

**The Horn Gate.** *See* DREAMS, THE GATES OF.

**Horn of Fidelity.** MORGAN LE FAY sent a horn to King ARTHUR, which had the following 'virtue': No lady could drink out of it who was not 'to her husband true'; all others who attempted to drink were sure to spill what it contained. This horn was carried to King MARK, and 'his queene with a hundred ladies more' tried the experiment, but only four managed to 'drink cleane'. Ariosto's *enchanted cup* possessed a similar spell.

**Horn of Plenty** or **Cornucopia.** AMALTHEA'S HORN, an emblem of plenty. CERES is drawn with a ram's horn in her left arm, filled with fruits and flowers; sometimes they are being poured on the earth, and sometimes they are piled high in the horn as in a basket.

**Horn Childe.** An early 14th-century metrical romance with a story closely related to that of KING HORN.

**Horner, Little Jack.** *See under* JACK.

**Horoscope** (Gr. *horoskopos, hora,* an hour; *skopos,* observer). The observation of the heavens at the hour of a person's birth, used by astrologers for predicting the future events of his life. Also the figure or diagram of the twelve houses of HEAVEN, showing the positions of the planets at a given time as used by astrologers for calculating nativities and working out answers to horary questions. *See* HOUSES, ASTROLOGICAL.

**Horsa.** *See* HENGIST.

**Horse.** There are records of the domestication of the horse from about 1750 B.C. It was a sign of wealth to own horses and next to the dog the animal was always the closest associate of humans. It represented fleetness, power and the intellect but was also credited with psychic and magical qualities.

The colour of the horse determined its significance in mythology. The white horse is solar power on land and in the air, drawing the chariot of sun gods, but the white horse of the sea is associated with the watery and lunar element. The golden horse has the same significance as the white and solar. The black horse is connected with the Devil, the Wild Huntsman, witches, destruction and death, also with rain gods.

Egyptian horses were famous and Solomon imported them and resold them to Hittite and Armenian kings. They were sacred to the sun god. (II *Kings,* xxiii, 11).

The horse was one of the great sacrificial animals, the Vedic Horse Sacrifice being possibly the oldest and most famous. The animal was greatly venerated by the Aryans and the sacrifice was attended by the King and Queen with four hundred attendants; the occasion was an erotic spring fertility rite. There is also Varuna, god of the waters, as the Cosmic Horse and when Vishnu appears for the tenth and last time at the end of this era it will be as Kalki, a white horse. Another famous sacrifice was that of the Roman October Horse, the festival was dedicated to Mars, the near horse of the winning team being sacrificed to him.

In China the Cosmic Horse is white and is an avatar of Kwan-yin and of Kwannon in Japan. The Horse King, Ma-wang, the Celestial Charger, is the ancestor of all horses.

Norse and Teutonic myth has the horse as sacred to ODIN/WODEN who had the eight-legged mare Sleipnir, and the horse is associated with the VANIR as gods of sun and rain. The horse is also highly important in Celtic lore and is frequently an attribute of deities. The Gaulish Epona, the Divine

Horse, was introduced into Britain and later adopted by the Romans; she is sometimes horse-headed. Horses were magical animals and could carry people to the otherworld. There were also monster horses capable of carrying fifteen people at a time and there were magical water-horses which, if mounted, carried the rider below the waters.

Islam says the horse is 'God sent' and the Prophet was carried to heaven by the steed BORAK. The horse prays for its owner; it has prognostic and psychic powers, foreseeing danger and seeing the dead.

According to classical mythology, POSEIDON created the horse; and according to Virgil, the first person that drove a four-in-hand was ERICHTHONIUS. In Christian art, the horse is held to represent courage and generosity. It is an attribute of St. MARTIN, St. Maurice, St. GEORGE and St. Victor, all of whom are represented on horseback.

It is a not uncommon emblem in the catacombs and probably typifies the swiftness of life.

The use of *horse* attributively usually denotes something that is coarse, inferior, unrefined, as in *horse-parsley, horseradish, horse mushroom. See* HAND.

**The brazen horse.** A magic horse given to Cambuscan by the king of Arabia and India. By giving it instructions and turning a pin in its ear it would carry its rider anywhere.

Or, if you list to bid him thennes gon,
Trill this pin, and he will vanish anon.
CHAUCER: *The Squire's Tale* (Pars Prima).

**Flesh-eating horses.** The horses of Diomedes, tyrant of Thrace, who fed his horses on the strangers who visited his kingdom. HERCULES vanquished the tyrant and gave the carcass to the horses to eat.

**The Pale Horse.** Death. 'I looked and behold a pale horse; and his name that sat on him was Death' (*Rev.* vi, 8). *See also* FOUR HORSEMEN OF THE APOCALYPSE *under* FOUR.

**O'Donohue's white horses.** Waves which come on a windy day, crested with foam. The hero reappears every seventh year on MAY-DAY, and is seen gliding, to sweet but unearthly music, over the lakes of Killarney, on his favourite white horse. He is preceded by fairies who strew spring flowers in his path. Moore has a poem on the subject in his *Irish Melodies*.

**Winged horse.** *See* PEGASUS.

**The Wooden Horse,** called *Clavileno el Aligero*, in DON QUIXOTE, is governed by a peg in its forehead and has the same magical qualities as the Brazen Horse given to Cambuscan. The similar *Magic Horse* in the ARABIAN NIGHTS was of ivory and ebony.

A former instrument of military punishment was called a *wooden horse*. The victim was seated on the horse's back, a beam of ridged oak, with a firelock tied to both feet to keep him in this painful position. This was known as **riding the wooden horse.**

Before the days of iron and steel construction, a ship was sometimes called a *wooden horse*.

**The Wooden Horse of Troy.** Virgil tells us that, after the death of HECTOR, ULYSSES had a monster wooden horse made by Epios and gave out that it was an offering to the gods to secure a prosperous voyage back to Greece. The Trojans dragged the horse within their city, but it was full of Grecian soldiers, including MENELAUS, who stole out at night, slew the guards, opened the city gates, and set fire to TROY.

**Famous Horses of Myth and Legend.**

In classical mythology the names given to the horses of HELIOS, the Sun, are:

*Actaeon* (effulgence); *Aethon* (fiery red); *Amethea* (no loiterèr); *Bronte* (thunderer); *Erythreos* (red producer); *Lampos* (shining like a lamp); *Phlegon* (the burning one); and *Purocis* (fiery hot).

AURORA'S horses were:

*Abraxa, Eoos* (dawn) and *Phaethon* (the shining one).

PLUTO'S horses were:

*Abaster* (away from the stars); *Abatos* (inaccessible); *Aeton* (swift as an eagle); and *Nonios*.

The ensuing list is arranged alphabetically:

*Aarvak* or *Arvak* (early-waker). In Norse mythology, the horse that draws the sun's chariot driven by the maiden Sol.
*Alborak. See* BORAK.
*Alfana* (mare). Gradasso's horse, in Orlando Furioso.
*Alsvid* or *Alswider* (All-swift). The horse that draws the chariot of the moon (Norse mythology).
*Aquiline* (like an eagle). Raymond's steed, bred on the banks of the Tagus (Tasso: *Jerusalem Delivered*).

131

*Arion* (martial). HERCULES' horse, given to ADRASTUS. Formerly the horse of NEPTUNE, brought out of the earth by striking it with his trident; its right feet were those of a man, it spoke with a human voice and ran with incredible swiftness.

*Arundel.* The horse of BEVIS OF HAMPTON. The word means 'swift as a swallow' (Fr. *hirondelle*).

*Balios* (Gr., swift). One of the horses given by NEPTUNE to Peleus. It afterwards belonged to ACHILLES. Like Xanthos (*see below*), its sire was the west wind, and its dam Swift-foot the HARPY.

*Bavieca.* The CID's horse. He survived his master two years and a half, during which time no one was allowed to mount him; he was buried before the gates of the monastery at Valencia and two elms were planted to mark the grave.

*Bayard. See* BAYARD.

*Bayardo. See* BAYARDO.

*Black Bess.* The mythical mare, created for Dick TURPIN by Harrison Ainsworth in his *Rookwood*, which carried Dick from London to York.

*Black Saladin.* Warwick's famous coal-black horse. Its sire was Malech, and according to tradition, when the race of Malech failed, the race of Warwick would fail also. And thus it was.

*Brigadore*, or *Brigliadore* (Golden bridle). Sir Guyon's horse in Spenser's *Faerie Queene* (V, iii etc.). It had a distinguishing black spot on its mouth, like a horseshoe.

ORLANDO's famous charger, second only to BAYARDO in swiftness and wonderful powers, was called *Brigiliadoro.*

*Bucephalus* (ox-head). The famous charger of Alexander The Great, who was the only person who could mount him, and he always knelt down to take up his master. He was 30 years old at death and Alexander built the city of Bucephala for a mausoleum.

*Carman.* The Chevalier BAYARD's horse, given to him by the Duke of Lorraine. It was a Persian horse from Kerman or Carmen (Laristan).

*Celer* (swift). The horse of the Roman Emperor Lucius Versus. It was fed on almonds and raisins, covered with royal purple, and stalled in the imperial palace.

*Cerus* (fit). The horse of ADRASTUS, swifter than the wind.

*Clavileno. See* WOODEN HORSE *under* HORSE.

*Cyllaros.* Named from Cylla in Troas, a celebrated horse of CASTOR AND POLLUX.

*Dinos* (the marvel). DIOMEDES' horse.

*Ethon* (fiery). One of the horses of HECTOR.

*Fadda.* Mohammed's white mule.

*Ferrant d'Espagne* (The Spanish traveller). The horse of OLIVER.

*Galathe* (cream-coloured). One of the horses of HECTOR.

*Grani* (grey-coloured). SIEGFRIED's horse, of marvellous swiftness.

*Haizum.* The horse of the archangel GABRIEL (Koran).

*Harpagus* (one that carried off rapidly). One of the horses of CASTOR AND POLLUX.

*Hippocampus.* One of NEPTUNE's horses. It had only two legs, the hind quarter being that of a dragon or fish.

*Hrimfaxi* (frost-mane). The horse of Night, from whose bit fall the 'rime-drops' which nightly bedew the earth (Scandinavian legend).

*Incitatus* (spurred-on). The Roman Emperor Caligula's horse, made priest and consul. It had an ivory manger and drank wine from a golden pail.

*Kantaka.* The white horse of Prince GAUTAMA, the Buddha.

*Lampon* (the bright one). One of DIOMEDES' horses.

*Lamri* (the curvetter). King ARTHUR's mare.

*Malech. See* BLACK SALADIN, *above.*

*Pegasus. See* PEGASUS.

*Phallus* (stallion). The horse of Heraclius.

*Phrenicos* (intelligent). The horse of Hiero of Syracuse, that won the prize for single horses in the 73rd OLYMPIAD.

*Podarge* (swift-foot). One of the horses of HECTOR.

*Shibdiz.* The Persian BUCEPHALUS, fleeter than the wind; charger of Chosroes II.

*Skinfaxi* (shining-mane). The horse of day (Norse legend). *Cp.* HRIMFAXI, *above.*

*Sleipnir.* ODIN's eight-footed grey horse which could traverse both land and sea. The horse typifies the wind which blows from the eight principal points.

*Strymon.* The horse immolated by XERXES before he invaded Greece. It came from the vicinity of the river Strymon in Thrace.

*Tachebrune.* The horse of OGIER THE DANE.

*Trebizond.* The grey horse of Guarinos, one of the French Knights taken at RONCESVALLES.

*Vegliantino* (the little vigilant one). ORLANDO's famous steed, called in Fr. romance *Veillantif*, Orlando there appearing as ROLAND.

*Xanthos. See* XANTHUS.

**Horseshoes.** The belief that it is lucky to pick up a horseshoe is from the idea that it was a protection against WITCHES and evil generally. According to Aubrey, the reason is 'since MARS (iron) is the enemy of SATURN (God of the Witches)'. Consequently they were nailed to the house door with two ends uppermost, so that the luck did not 'run out'. Nelson had one nailed to the mast of the *Victory*.

One legend is that the DEVIL one day asked St. DUNSTAN, who was noted for his skill as a farrier, to shoe his 'single hoof'. Dunstan, knowing who his customer was, tied him tightly to the wall, and proceeded with the job, but purposely put the devil to such pain that he roared for mercy. Dunstan at last agreed to release his captive on condition that he would never again enter a place where he saw a horseshoe displayed.

**Horus.** One of the major gods of the ancient Egyptians, originally a great sky-god and sun-god, who became merged with Horus the son of OSIRIS and ISIS, and Horus the Child (*see* HARPOCRATES). He was also identified with the King himself and the Horus-name was the first of the five names of the Egyptian King. He was the most famous of the Falcon-gods and was represented in hieroglyphics by the winged sun-disc.

**Hour. In an evil hour.** Acting under an unfortunate impulse. In ASTROLOGY there are lucky and unlucky hours.

**Houri** (hoo'ri). One of the black-eyed damsels of the Muslim PARADISE, possessed of perpetual youth and beauty, whose virginity is renewable at pleasure, and who are the reward of every believer; hence, in English use, any dark-eyed attractive beauty.

**House-leek.** Grown formerly on house-roofs from the notion that it warded off lightning, fever and evil spirits; also called *Jove's Beard*. An edict of CHARLEMAGNE ordered that every one of his subjects should have a house-leek on his roof (*Et habet quisque supra domum suum Jovis barbam*).

> If the herb house-leek or syngren do grow on the housetop, the same house is never stricken with lightning or thunder.
> THOMAS HILL: *Naturall and Artificiall Conclusions* (1586).

**Houses, Astrological.** In judicial ASTROLOGY, the whole HEAVEN is divided into twelve portions by means of great circles crossing the north and south points of the horizon, through which the heavenly bodies pass every twenty-four hours. Each of these divisions is called a *house*; and in casting a HOROSCOPE the whole is divided into two parts (beginning from the east), six above and six below the horizon. The eastern ones are called the *ascendant*, because they are about to rise; the other six are the *descendant*, because they have already passed the zenith. The twelve houses each have their special functions—(1) the house of life; (2) fortune and riches; (3) brethren; (4) parents and relatives; (5) children; (6) health; (7) marriage; (8) death; (9) religion; (10) dignities; (11) friends and benefactors; (12) mystery and uncertainty.

Three houses were assigned to each of the four ages of the person whose horoscope was to be cast, and his lot in life was governed by the ascendancy of these at the various periods, and by the stars which ruled in the particular 'houses'.

**Houses of Life.** In ancient Egypt, centres of priestly learning attached to the large temples where scribes copied religious texts, the art of medicine was furthered etc.

**Household gods.** The LARES AND PENATES who presided over the dwellings and domestic concerns of the ancient Romans; hence, in modern use, the valued possessions of home, all those things that go to endear it to one.

**Houssain,** or **Housain** etc. In the ARABIAN NIGHTS, brother of Prince AHMED and owner of the MAGIC CARPET (*see under* CARPET).

**Houyhnhnms** (hwin'imz). In *Gulliver's Travels*, a race of horses endowed with reason and all the finer qualities of man. Swift coined the word in imitation of 'whinny'.

**Hrimfaxi** (rēm'faksi). *See* FAMOUS HORSES *under* HORSE.

**Hubert, St.** Patron saint of huntsmen (d. 727), reputedly son of Bertrand, Duke of Guienne. He so neglected his religious duties for the chase that one day a stag bearing a crucifix menaced him with eternal perdition unless he reformed. Upon this he entered the cloister and duly became Bishop of Liège, and the apostle of Ardennes and Brabant. Those who were descended of his race were supposed to possess the power of curing the bite of a mad dog.

In art he is represented as a bishop with a miniature stag resting on the book in his hand, or as a huntsman kneeling to the miraculous crucifix borne by the stag. His day is 3 November.

**Hugh of Lincoln, St.** There are two saints so designated.

(1) St. Hugh (*c.* 1140–1200), a Burgundian by birth, and founder of the first Carthusian house in England. He became bishop of Lincoln in 1186. He was noted for his charitable works and kindness to the Jews. His day is 17 November.

(2) St. Hugh (13th century), the boy of about ten years of age allegedly tortured and crucified in mockery of Christ. The story goes that the affair arose from his having driven a ball through a Jew's window while at play with his friends. The boy was finally thrown into a well from which he spoke miraculously. Eighteen Jews were purported to have been hanged. The story is paralleled at a number of other places in England and on the Continent (*cp.* WILLIAM OF NORWICH), and forms the subject of Chaucer's *The Prioress's Tale*. It is also found in Matthew Paris and elsewhere.

**Huitzilopochtli.** *See* MEXITL.

**Hulda** (hul′də). The old German goddess of marriage and fecundity. The name means 'the Benignant'.
**Hulda is making her bed.** It snows.

**Humber.** The legendary king of the Huns, fabled by Geoffrey of Monmouth to have invaded Britain about 1000 B.C. He was defeated in a great battle by LOCRIN near the river which bears his name. 'Humber made towards the river in his flight, and was drowned in it, on account of which it has since borne his name.'

**Hummingbird.** Being able to hover and fly backwards, the hummingbird was credited with magical powers and its feathers were used as charms. It is also the Bird of the Gods and represents harmony and the vibration of pure joy. It was said to live on dew and to hibernate until April, so was called the Revival Bird. In Mayan and Aztec myth it was associated with the Black Sun, with Quetzalcoatl and the Aztec war god. The Feathered Serpent wears the bird's plumage. The blue hummingbird is a messenger, a helpful animal and a psychopomp. In both Amerindian and Basque lore the hummingbird always tells the truth.

**Humphrey. To dine with Duke Humphrey.** To have no dinner to go to. The Good Duke Humphrey was renowned for his hospitality. At death it was reported that a monument would be erected to him in St. Paul's, but he was buried at St. Alban's. The tomb of Sir John Beauchamp (d. 1358), on the south side of the nave of old St. Paul's was popularly supposed to be that of the Duke, and when the promenaders left for dinner, the poor stay-behinds who had no dinner to go to, or who feared arrest for debt if they left the precincts, used to say, when asked by the gay sparks if they were going, that they would 'dine with Duke Humphrey' that day.

The expression was once very common, as was the similar one *To sup with Sir Thomas Gresham*, the Exchange built by Sir Thomas being a common lounge.

Though little coin thy purseless pocket line,
Yet with great company thou art taken up;
For often with Duke Humphrey thou dost dine,
And often with Sir Thomas Gresham sup.
    HAYMAN: *Quodlibets* (*Epigram on a Loafer*), 1628.

**Hundred. Hero of the hundred fights.** Conn, a semi-legendary Irish king, of the 2nd century.
**The hundred-eyed.** ARGUS in Greek and Latin fable. JUNO appointed him guardian of IO (the cow), but JUPITER caused him to be put to death; whereupon Juno transplanted his eyes into the tail of her peacock.
**The Hundred-handed.** Three of the sons of URANUS, namely, Aegaeon or BRIAREUS, Cottys or COTTUS, and Gyges or Gyes. After the TITANS were overcome during the war with ZEUS and hurled into TARTARUS, the Hundred-handed ones were set to keep watch and ward over them.

CERBERUS is sometimes so called because from its three necks sprang writhing snakes instead of hair.

**Hunt.** Like Hunt's dog, he would neither go to church nor stay at home. A Shropshire saying. The story is that one Hunt, a labouring man, kept a mastiff, which, on being shut up while his master went to church, howled and barked so as to disturb the whole congregation. Hunt thought he would take him to church the next Sunday, but the dog positively refused to enter. The proverb is applied to a self-willed person, who will neither be led nor driven.
**Hunters and Runners of classic renown:**

ACASTUS who took part in the famous Calydonian hunt (*see under* BOAR).
ACTAEON, the famous huntsman who was transformed by DIANA into a stag, because he chanced to see her bathing.
ADONIS, beloved by VENUS, slain by a wild boar while hunting.
ADRASTUS, who was saved at the siege of Thebes by the speed of his horse Arion, given him by HERCULES.

ATALANTA, who promised to marry the man who could outstrip her in running.

CAMILLA, the swiftest-footed of all the companions of DIANA.

LADAS, the swiftest-footed of all the runners of Alexander The Great.

MELEAGER, who took part in the great Calydonian boar-hunt (*see under* BOAR).

ORION, the great and famous hunter, changed into the constellation so conspicuous in November.

PHEIDIPPIDES, who ran 150 miles in two days.

**Hyacinth** (hī'əsinth). According to Greek fable, the son of Amyclas, a Spartan king. The lad was beloved by APOLLO and ZEPHYR and as he preferred the sun-god, Zephyr drove Apollo's quoit at his head, and killed him. The blood became a flower, and the petals are inscribed with the signature AI, meaning woe (Virgil: *Eclogues*, iii, 106).

> The hyacinth bewrays the doleful 'A I',
> And culls the tribute of Apollo's sigh.
> Still on its bloom the mournful flower retains
> The lovely blue that dyed the stripling's veins.
> CAMŌENS: *Lusiad*, ix.

**Hyades** (hī'ədēz) (Gr. *huein*, to rain). Seven NYMPHS, daughters of ATLAS and Pleione, placed among the stars, in the constellation TAURUS, which threaten rain when they rise with the sun. The fable is that they wept at the death of their brother Hyas so bitterly that ZEUS out of compassion took them to HEAVEN. *Cp.* PLEIADES.

> The seaman sees the Hyades
> Gather an army of Cimmerian clouds ...
> All-fearful folds his sails, and sounds the main,
> Lifting his prayers to the heavens for aid
> Against the terror of the winds and waves
> MARLOWE: *Tamburlaine*, Pt I, III, ii.

**Hydra.** A many-headed water-snake of the Lernaean marshes in Argolis. It was the off-spring of TYPHON and ECHIDNA and was variously reputed to have one hundred heads, or fifty, or nine. It was one of the 'twelve labours' of HERCULES to kill it, and, as soon as he struck off one of its heads, two shot up in its place. Hence **Hydra-headed** applied to a difficulty which goes on increasing as it is combated. The monster was eventually destroyed by Hercules with the assistance of his charioteer, who applied burning brands to its wounds as soon as each head was severed by his master.

**Hyena** (hīē'nə). Held in veneration by the ancient Egyptians, because it is fabled that a certain stone, called the 'hyaenia', is found in the eye of the creature, and Pliny asserts (*Nat. Hist.*, xxxvii, 60), that when placed under the tongue it imparts the gift of prophecy.

> The skilful Lapidarists of Germany affirm that this beast hath a stone in his eye (or rather his head) called Hyaena or Hyaenius.
> TOPSELL: *Historie of foure-footed Beasts* (1607).

The hyena, like the HARE, was believed to change its sex. Aelian and Oppian state this, but it is denied by Aristotle, though again asserted in the *Epistle of Barnabas*, included in the *Codex Sinaiticus*, where it says 'That creature every year changes its kind and is sometimes male and sometimes female' (ix, 8). Diodorus Siculus says that the hyena is a cross between a dog and a wolf from Ethiopia, but later Sir Walter Ralegh called it a cross between a dog and a cat. Aristotle, Pliny and Aelian say that the animal imitates the human voice to lure men to their deaths and that it imitated vomiting to entice dogs to kill them.

Arabic tradition quotes numerous instances of wizards taking the form of hyenas and in the East the animal can be the incarnation of a sorcerer.

In Africa the hyena is dreaded for its magical powers and souls of men can enter hyenas to attack those who have wronged them. There are various hyena gods associated with the elements and spirits. The hyena can also be an animal-ancestor in East Africa where it is the sacred animal of a secret society.

The hyena is generally regarded as one of the most unclean of animals, a scavenger, feeder on corpses and haunter of graveyards; it also represents treachery and the desolation of the wilderness.

**Hygeia** (hījē'ə). Goddess of health in Greek mythology, and the daughter of AESCULAPIUS. Her symbol was a serpent drinking from a cup in her hand.

**Hylas** (hī'ləs). A boy beloved by HERCULES, carried off by the NYMPHS while drawing water from a fountain in Mysia.

**Hymen** (hī'men). Properly, a marriage song of the ancient Greeks; later personified as the god of marriage, represented as a youth carrying a torch and veil—a more mature EROS or CUPID.

**Hyperboreans.** In Greek legend, a happy people dwelling beyond the North Wind, BOREAS, from which their name was supposedly derived. They were said to live for a thousand years under a cloudless sky, knowing no strife or violence. The word is applied in general to those living in the extreme north.

**Hyperion** (hīpiə'riən). In Greek mythology, one of the TITANS, son of URANUS and GAEA, and father of HELIOS, SELENE and Eos (the Sun, Moon and Dawn). The name is some-times given by poets to the sun itself, but not by Keats in his 'Fragment' of this name.

**Hypermnestra** (hīpəmnes'trə). Wife of LYNCEUS and the only one of the fifty daughters of Danaus who did not murder her husband on their bridal night. *See* DANAIDES.

# I

**Ianthe** (īan'thi). A Cretan girl who, as told in Ovid's *Metamorphoses*, ix, 714–797, married Iphis, who had been transformed for the purpose from a girl into a young man. The Ianthe to whom Lord Byron dedicated his *Childe Harold* was Lady Charlotte Harley, born 1801, and only eleven years old at the time. Shelley gave the name to his eldest daughter.

**Iapetus** (īap'itəs). Son of URANUS and GAEA, father of ATLAS, PROMETHEUS, Epimetheus and Menoetius, and, for the Greeks, father of the human race, hence called *genus Iapeti*, the progeny of Iapetus.

**Ibex.** The horns of the ibex frequently appear in the art of Mesopotamia and the northern steppes of Asia. Pliny says that the ibex can hurl itself from great heights and land on its horns which are elastic and take the shock. The Nubian ibex is the Wild Goat of the Bible and in Arabic tradition it represents beauty.

**Ibis** (ī'bis). A sacred bird of the ancient Egyptians, with white body and black head and tail. It was the incarnation of THOTH. It is still found in the Nile marshes of the upper Sudan. The sacred ibis was often mummified after death. The bird was lunar and sacred to Isis, and the moon god Aah was sometimes ibis-headed. Pliny says the ibis was the Egyptian bird par excellence. Being heart-shaped it represented the heart under the protection of THOTH/HERMES as god of wisdom, learning and writing. Thoth was ibis-headed. Hermes took the form of an ibis when fleeing from Typhon.

**Iblis.** *See* EBLIS.

**Icarius** (īkeə'riəs). In Greek legend an Athenian who was taught the cultivation of the vine by DIONYSUS. He was slain by some peasants who had become intoxicated with wine he had given them, and who thought they had been poisoned. They bur-ied him under a tree; his daughter Erigone, searching for her father, was directed to the spot by the howling of his dog Moera, and when she discovered the body she hanged herself for grief. Icarius, according to this legend, became the constellation Boötes, Erigone the constellation VIRGO, and Moera the star PROCYON, which rises in July, a little before the dog-star.

**Icarus** (ik'ərəs). Son of DAEDALUS. He flew with his father from Crete; but the sun melted the wax with which his wings were fastened on, and he fell into the sea. Those waters of the Aegean were thenceforward called the Icarian Sea.

**Ichneumon.** A species of mongoose venerated by the ancient Egyptians and called 'Pharaoh's rat' because it fed on vermin, crocodiles' eggs etc. The word is Gr. and means 'the tracker'. The ichneumon, in Egyptian hieroglyphics, represents strength in unity as it was said to combine in numbers to attack the asp. Aristotle says it fights only with the asp but Pliny, Strabo, Aelian, Oppian and Solinus say it is the enemy of both the asp and crocodile. Strabo says it was worshipped in Herakleopolis as the destroyer of the crocodile. It was said to kill the crocodile by entering its mouth when open and devouring the entrails, emerging when the crocodile was dead. Ancient traditions attribute the same feat to the otter and to the water-snake or hydrus and the animals are confused in legends. Martial says the ichneumon was kept as a pet in Rome and it is depicted in Pompeii destroying a snake. The ichneumon appeared frequently in classical literature, but less often by the Middle Ages.

**Ichor** (ī'kaw). In classical mythology, the colourless blood of the gods (Gr. juice).

[St. Peter] patter'd with his keys at a great rate,
And sweated through his apostolic skin:

137

Of course his perspiration was but ichor,
Or some such other spiritual liquor.
 BYRON: *Vision of Judgment*, xxv.

**Ida. Mount Ida.** A mountain or ridge of mountains in the vicinity of TROY; the scene of the Judgment of PARIS. *See* APPLE OF DISCORD.

**Idomeneus** (īdom'inūs). King of Crete and ally of the Greeks at TROY. After the city was burnt he made a vow to sacrifice whatever he first encountered if the gods granted him a safe return to his kingdom. He met his own son and duly sacrificed him, but a plague followed, and the king was banished from Crete as a murderer. *Cp.* IPHIGENIA.

**Idris** (id'ris). Traditionally a Welsh giant, prince and astronomer. His rock-hewn seat is on the summit of *Cader Idris* (the chair of Idris) in Gwynedd. According to legend, any person passing a night upon this will be either dead in the morning, in a state of frenzy, or endowed with the highest poetical inspiration.

And, as from the grave, I awoke to inherit
A flame all immortal, a voice, and a power!
Day burst on that rock with the purple cloud
 crested,
And high Cader Idris rejoiced in the sun;
 MRS HEMANS: *The Rock of Cader Idris*, iv.

**Iduna** (ē'dunə). In Scandinavian mythology, daughter of the dwarf Svald and wife of BRAGI. She was guardian of the golden apples which the gods tasted whenever they wished to renew their youth. Iduna was lured away from ASGARD by LOKI, but eventually restored, and the gods were once more able to grow youthful again and Spring came back to the earth.

**Ifreet.** *See* AFREET.

**Igerna.** *See* IGRAINE.

**Ignis Fatuus.** The 'Will o' the wisp' or 'Friar's lanthorn', a flame-like phosphorescence flitting over marshy ground (due to the spontaneous combustion of gases from decaying vegetable matter), and deluding people who attempt to follow it; hence any delusive aim or object, or some Utopian scheme that is utterly impracticable. The name means 'a foolish fire' and is also called 'Elf-fire', 'Jack o'lantern', 'Peg-a-lantern', 'Kit o' the canstick', 'Spunkie', 'Walking

Fire', 'Fair Maid of Ireland', 'John in the Wad'.

When thou rannest up Gadshill in the night to catch my horse, if I did not think thou hadst been an *ignis fatuus* or a ball of wildfire, there's no purchase in money.
 SHAKESPEARE: *Henry IV, Pt. I*, III, iii.

According to Russian folklore, these wandering fires are the spirits of stillborn children which flit between HEAVEN and the INFERNO.

**Igraine, Igerna** (ēgrān', ēgœ'nə). In ARTHURIAN ROMANCE, the wife of Gerlois (Gorlois), Duke of Tintagel, in Cornwall, and mother of King ARTHUR. His father, UTHER Pendragon, married Igraine the day after her husband was slain.

**Iliad** (Gr. *Iliados*, of Ilium or Troy). The epic poem of twenty-four books attributed to HOMER, recounting the siege of TROY. PARIS, son of King PRIAM of Troy, when guest of MENELAUS, King of Sparta, ran away with his host's wife, HELEN. Menelaus induced the Greeks to lay siege to Troy to avenge the perfidy, and the siege lasted ten years. The poem begins in the tenth year with a quarrel between AGAMEMNON, King of Mycenae and commander-in-chief of the allied Greeks, and ACHILLES, the hero who had retired from the army in ill temper. The Trojans now prevail and Achilles sends his friend PATROCLUS to oppose them, but Patroclus is slain. Achilles in a desperate rage rushes into the battle and slays HECTOR, the commander of the Trojan army. The poem ends with the funeral rites of Hector.

**An Iliad of woes.** A number of evils falling one after another; virtually the whole catalogue of human ills finds mention in the *Iliad*.

Demosthenes used the phrase (*Ilias kakon*) and it was adopted by Cicero (*Ilias malorum*) in his *Ad Atticum*, viii, II,

It opens another Iliad of woes to Europe.
 BURKE: *On a Regicide Peace*, ii.

**The French Iliad.** The *Romance of the Rose* (*see under* ROSE) has been so called. Similarly the NIBELUNGENLIED has been called **the German Iliad,** and the *Lusiad,* the **Portuguese Iliad.**

**Imp. Lincoln Imp.** *See* LINCOLN.

**Inchcape Rock.** A dangerous rocky reef (also called the Bell Rock) about 12 miles from Arbroath in the North Sea (Inch or Innis means *island*). The abbot of Arbroath or 'Aberbrothok' fixed a bell on a timber float as a warning to mariners. Southey's ballad of this name tells how the pirate Ralph the Rover cut the bell adrift and was himself wrecked on the very rock as a consequence.

A similar tale is told of St. Govan's bell in Pembrokeshire (Dyfed). In the chapel was a silver bell, which was stolen one summer evening by pirates, but no sooner had their boat put to sea than it was wrecked.

**Incubus.** A nightmare, anything that weighs heavily on the mind. In mediaeval times it denoted an evil demon who was supposed to have sexual intercourse with women during their sleep (L.Lat. *incubus*, a nightmare). *Cp.* SUCCUBUS.

Wommen may now go saufly up and doun;
In every bussh or under every tree,
Ther is noon oother incubus but he,
And he ne wol doon hem but dishonour.
CHAUCER: *Wife of Bath's Tale*, 1.24.

**Indra.** An ancient Hindu god of the sky, originally the greatest, who was the hurler of thunderbolts and giver of rain, a god of warriors and of nature. He is represented as four-armed and his steed is an elephant. He is the son of HEAVEN and Earth and lives on the fabulous Mount MERU, the centre of the earth, north of the Himalayas. With Agni and Sarya he forms the Vedic trinity.

**Inferno.** We have Dante's notion of the infernal regions in his *Inferno*: Homer's in the *Odyssey*, Bk. XI; Virgil's in the AENEID, Bk. VI; Spenser's in THE FAERIE QUEENE, Bk. II, canto vii; Ariosto's in *Orlando Furioso*, Bk. XVII; Tasso's in *Jerusalem Delivered*, Bk. IV; Milton's in PARADISE LOST; Fénelon's in *Télémaque*, Bk. XVIII; and Beckford's in his romance of *Vathek*. *See* HADES; HELL.

**Ino.** *See* LEUCOTHEA.

**Insane Root, The.** A plant, probably henbane or hemlock, supposed to deprive of his senses anyone who partook of it. Banquo says of the witches:

Were such things here as we do speak about?
Or have we eaten of the insane root
That takes the reason prisoner?
SHAKESPEARE: *Macbeth*, I, iii.

Similar properties were attributed to

MANDRAKE, BELLADONNA, poppy, etc. *Cp.* MOLY.

**Inscription** (on coins). *See* LEGEND.

**Invisibility,** according to fable, was obtainable in many ways. For example:

*Alberich's cap*, 'Tarnkappe', which SIEGFRIED obtained, rendered him invisible (NIBELUNGENLIED).

*The helmet of* PERSEUS, loaned by PLUTO and made by the CYCLOPS for the god of the underworld, rendered its wearer invisible.

JACK THE GIANT-KILLER had a cloak of invisibility as well as a cap of knowledge.

*Otnit's ring.* The ring of Otnit, King of Lombardy, according to the HELDENBUCH, rendered its wearer invisible.

*Reynard's wonderful ring*, according to REYNARD THE FOX, had three colours, one of which (green), made the wearer invisible.

*See also* FERN SEED; GYGES; HELIOTROPE; DEAD MAN'S HAND.

**Invulnerability.** There are many fabulous instances of this having been acquired. According to Greek legend, a dip in the river STYX rendered ACHILLES invulnerable, and MEDEA rendered JASON, with whom she had fallen in love, proof against wounds and fire by anointing him with the PROMETHEAN UNGUENT.

SIEGFRIED was rendered invulnerable by anointing his body with dragon's blood.

**Io.** The priestess of JUNO of whom JUPITER became enamoured. When Juno discovered his liaison, Jupiter transformed Io into a heifer and she wandered over the earth, finally settling in Egypt, when she was restored to human form.

**Iphigenia** (ifijinī'ə). In classical legend, the daughter of AGAMEMNON and CLYTEMNESTRA. One account says that her father, having offended ARTEMIS by killing her favourite stag, vowed to sacrifice the most beautiful thing the year brought forth; this was his infant daughter. He deferred the sacrifice till the Greek fleet that was proceeding to TROY reached AULIS and Iphigenia had grown to womanhood. Then CALCHAS told him that the fleet would be wind-bound till he had fulfilled his vow; accordingly the king prepared to sacrifice his daughter, but Artemis at the last moment snatched her from the altar and carried her to HEAVEN, substituting a hind in her place. Euripides wrote a tragedy *Iphigenia in Tauris* and Gluck has an opera *Iphigénie en Tauride* (1779); the former's *Iphigenia in Aulis* was incomplete at his death. *Cp.* IDOMENEUS.

**Ireland. The fair maid of Ireland.** Another name for the IGNIS FATUUS.

**Irene** (īrē'nē). The Greek goddess of peace and wealth (Gr. *Eirene*). She is represented as a young woman carrying PLUTUS in her arms. Among her attributes are the OLIVE branch and CORNUCOPIA.

**Iris.** Goddess of the rainbow, or the rainbow itself. In classical mythology she was the messenger of the gods, and of JUNO in particular, and the RAINBOW is the bridge or road let down from heaven for her accommodation.

Besides being poetically applied to the rainbow, the name, in English, is given to the coloured membrane surrounding the pupil of the eye, and to a family of plants (Iridaceae) having large, bright-coloured flowers and tuberous roots.

**Iron. Iron Mask, The Man in the.** In the reign of Louis XIV, a mysterious state prisoner held for over forty years in various gaols until he finally died in the Bastille on 19 November 1703. When travelling from prison to prison he always wore a mask of black velvet, not iron. His name was never revealed but he was buried under the name of 'M. de Marchiel'. Many conjectures have been made about his identity, one of them being that he was the Duc de Vermandois, an illegitimate son of Louis XIV. Dumas, in his romantic novel on the subject, adopted Voltaire's suggestion that he was an illegitimate elder brother of Louis XIV with Cardinal Mazarin for his father. The most plausible suggestion is that of the historians Lord Acton and Funck-Brentano, who suggested a minister of the Duke of Mantua (Count Mattiolo, b. 1640), who, in his negotiations with Louis XIV, was found to be treacherous, and imprisoned at Pignerol.

**Iron-hand,** or **The iron-handed.** Götz von Berlichingen (1480–1562), a German knight who lost his right hand at the siege of Landshut (1505) and contrived one of steel to replace it. He was brave and chivalrous but something of a brigand. His autobiography was used by Goethe for his drama *Götz von Berlichingen* (1773).

**Irresistible.** Alexander The Great, before starting on his expedition against Persia, went to consult the Delphic ORACLE on a day when no responses were made. Nothing daunted, he sought out PYTHIA and when she refused to attend took her to the temple by force. 'Son,' said the priestess, 'thou art irresistible.' 'Enough,' cried Alexander, 'I accept your words as an answer.'

**Irus** (ī'rəs). The gigantic beggar who carried out the commissions of the suitors of PENELOPE. When he sought to hinder the returning ULYSSES, he was felled to the ground by a single blow. 'Poorer than Irus' was a classical proverb.

**Isenbras,** or **Isumbras, Sir** (ī'zənbrahs). A hero of mediaeval romance who made visits to the Holy Land and slaughtered thousands of Saracens. At first proud and presumptuous, when he was visited by all sorts of punishments; afterwards penitent and humble when his afflictions were turned into blessings. It was in this latter stage that he one day carried on his horse two children of a poor woodman across a ford.

**Iseult** (ēsoolt'). *See* YSOLDE.

**Ishtar.** The Babylonian goddess of love and war (Gr. *Astarte*), corresponding to the Phoenician ASHTORETH, except that, while the latter was identified with the moon, Ishtar was more frequently identified with the planet VENUS. She was also identified with the Sumerian Inanna.

**Isis** (ī'sis). The principal goddess of ancient Egypt, sister and wife of OSIRIS, and mother of HORUS, she typified the faithful wife and devoted mother. The cow was sacred to her, and she is represented as a queen, her head being surmounted by horns and the solar disc or by the double crown (*see* EGYPT). Her chief shrines were at Abydos and Busiris; later a splendid temple was built at Philae. Proclus mentions a statue of her which bore the inscription 'I am that which is, has been, and shall be. My veil no one has lifted. The fruit I bore was the Sun', hence **to lift the veil of Isis** is to pierce the heart of a great mystery.

She was worshipped as a nature goddess throughout the Roman world and was identified with JUNO, IO, APHRODITE, ASTARTE and others, and in due course she became an embodiment of the universal goddess. Milton, in *Paradise Lost* (I, 478), places her among the fallen ANGELS.

**Islands of the blest.** *See* FORTUNATE ISLANDS.

**Ismene** (ismē'nē). In Greek legend, daughter of OEDIPUS and Jocasta. ANTIGONE was to be buried alive by order of King Creon for burying her brother Polynices (slain in combat with his brother Eteocles) against the tyrant's express command. Ismene declared that she had aided her sister and asked to share the same fate.

**Israfel** (iz'rəfel). The angel of music for Muslims. He possesses the most melodious voice of all God's creatures, and is to sound the Resurrection Trump which will ravish the ears of the saints in PARADISE. Israfel, GABRIEL and MICHAEL were the three ANGELS that, according to legend, warned ABRAHAM of Sodom's destruction.

> In Heaven a spirit doth dwell
> Whose heart-strings are a lute;
> None sing so wildly well
> As the angel Israfel,
> And the giddy stars (so legends tell),
> Ceasing their hymns, attend the spell
> Of his voice, all mute.
>   E. A. POE: *Israfel.*

**Istar.** ISHTAR.

**Isumbras.** *See* ISENBRAS.

**Ivory, Ivory Gate.** *See* DREAMS, GATES OF.
**Ivory shoulder.** *See under* PELOPS.

**Ivy** (O.E. *ifig*). Ivy was dedicated to DIONYSUS/BACCHUS from the belief that it is a preventive of drunkenness. The god wears a crown of ivy, his cup is an 'ivy cup' and his thyrsus is encircled with ivy. The plant is also sacred to the Phrygian Attis and is also 'the plant of OSIRIS' in Egypt. The ivy leaf is phallic, depicting the male trinity; it also represents revelry.

In Christian symbolism ivy typifies everlasting life and immortality as an evergreen.

**Ixion.** In Greek legend, a treacherous king of the LAPITHAE who was bound to a revolving wheel of fire in the Infernal regions for boasting of having won the favours of HERA, ZEUS having sent a cloud to him in the form of Hera, and the cloud having become by him the mother of the CENTAURS.

**Izanagi** and **Izanami.** The Japanese deities, husband and wife, sometimes said to be brother and sister, were the first couple. The Japanese islands and numerous gods were the result of their union. There is a myth of the descent to the underworld type associated with Izanagi's attempt to rescue Izanami from the lower kingdom after she had died in giving birth to the god of fire.

# J

**Jabberwocky.** The eponymous central figure of a strange, almost gibberish poem in Lewis Carroll's *Through the Looking-glass*. It contains many significant portmanteau words, as subsequently explained to Alice by Humpty Dumpty.

**Jack. Jack and the Beanstalk.** A nursery tale found among many peoples in varying forms. In the English version Jack exchanges his poor mother's cow for a handful of beans which miraculously produce stalks reaching the sky. Jack climbs up them and steals treasures from the ogre's castle—a bag of gold, a wonderful lamp and the hen that lays the golden eggs, thus redeeming their poverty.

**Jack and Jill.** In the familiar nursery rhyme Jack and Jill who went up the hill 'to fetch a pail of water' are probably generic names for lad and lass. Somewhat unconvincingly, attempts have been made to link them with Norse legend.

**Jack Frost.** The personification of frost or frosty weather.

**Jack the Giant-killer.** The hero of the old nursery tale owed much of his success to his four marvellous possessions. When he put on his coat no eye could see him; when he had his shoes on no one could overtake him; when he put on his cap he knew everything he required to know and his sword cut through everything. The story is given by Walter Map (d. *c.* 1209), who obtained it from a French source.

**Jack Horner.** A very fanciful explanation of the old nursery rhyme 'Little Jack Horner' is that Jack was steward to the Abbot of Glastonbury at the time of the Dissolution of the Monasteries, and that by a subterfuge he gained the deeds of the Manor of Mells. It is said that these deeds, with others, were sent to Henry VIII concealed, for safety, in a pasty; that 'Jack Horner' was the bearer and that on the way, he lifted the crust and extracted this 'plum'.

**Jack-in-the-green.** A youth or boy who moves about concealed in a wooden framework covered with leaves and boughs as part of the chimney-sweeps' revels on MAY DAY. An obsolete English custom.

**Jack Ketch.** A notorious hangman and executioner, who was appointed about 1663 and died in 1686. He was the executioner of William, Lord Russell, for his share in the Rye House Plot (1683), and of Monmouth (1685). In 1686 he was removed from office for insulting a sheriff and succeeded by a butcher named Rose, who was himself hanged within four months, when Ketch was reinstated. As early as 1678 his name had appeared in a ballad, and by 1702 was associated with the PUNCH AND JUDY puppet-play, which had recently been introduced from Italy.

**Jack o' the bowl.** The BROWNIE or house spirit of Switzerland; so called from the nightly custom of placing for him a bowl of fresh cream on the cowhouse roof. The contents are sure to disappear before morning.

**Jack-o'-lantern.** The IGNIS FATUUS; in the USA, the hollowed pumpkin of HALLOWE'EN games.

**Jack of Newbury.** John Winchcombe alias Smallwood (d. 1520), a wealthy clothier in the reign of Henry VIII. He was the hero of many chap-books, and is said to have kept 100 looms in his own house at Newbury, and equipped at his own expense 100–200 of his men to aid the king against the Scots at Flodden Field.

**Jack the Ripper.** The name adopted by an unknown killer who murdered at least five prostitutes in Whitechapel in 1888 and mutilated their bodies.

I'm not a butcher,
I'm not a Yid,
Nor yet a foreign skipper,
But I'm your own light-hearted friend,

Yours truly, Jack the Ripper.

Among suspects at the time were Michael Ostrog, a Russian doctor; Kosminski, a Polish Jew; and M.J. Druitt, unsuccessful son of a Dorsetshire surgeon. One recent fanciful theory was that the murders were planned by a group of high-ranking freemasons, among them being Sir William Gull, the royal physician, their motive being to suppress scandals involving Prince Albert Victor, Duke of Clarence (1846–1892), elder son of the then Prince of Wales (later King Edward VII). Another theory was that it was the Duke of Clarence himself but a more likely candidate is J.K. Stephen, the Duke's lover.

**Jack Sprat.** A DWARF; as if sprats were dwarf herrings. Children, by a similar METAPHOR, are called SMALL FRY.

> Jack Sprat could eat no fat,
> His wife could eat no lean,
> And so, betwixt them both you see,
> They licked the platter clean.
> *Nursery Rhyme.*

**To play the Jack.** To play the rogue, the knave. To deceive or lead astray like Jack-o'-lantern, or IGNIS FATUUS.

> Your fairy which you say, is a harmless fairy, has done little better than played the Jack with us.
> SHAKESPEARE: *The Tempest*, IV, i.

**Jackal.** The Egyptian god ANUBIS is represented as jackal-headed, a black jackal, or sometimes dog-headed. The jackal, associated with the dead and burial grounds, is a psychopomp and in this respect is connected with ANUBIS as the Opener of the Way or the Pathfinder, receiving the dead and conducting them to the Judgment of OSIRIS. ANUBIS was one of the oldest of the deities; Ap-uat or Upuat was a jackal-headed variant of Anubis.

In the Bible the jackal is an unclean animal and represents desolation. The jackal in Buddhism depicts the evil person incapable of understanding the Dharma, while in Hinduism jackals are associated with ravens as scavengers following KALI, the destroyer.

**Jackdaw.** A prating nuisance.

**The Jackdaw of Rheims.** One of the best known of the Ingoldsby *Legends* in which the cardinal's ring mysteriously vanished and he solemnly cursed the thief by Bell, Book and Candle. The jackdaw's bedraggled

appearance brought on by the curse revealed him as the culprit.

**Jacob's stone.** The Coronation stone of Scone is sometimes so called, from the legend that Jacob's head had rested on this stone when he had the vision of the ANGELS ascending and descending the ladder (*Gen.* xxviii, 11).

**Jagganath.** *See* JUGGERNAUT.

**Jaguar.** The largest spotted cat, the jaguar is the pre-eminent animal of Central American mythology, the Master of Animals, it was the chief figure in Mayan rites and sacrifices were made to the Jaguar God who could also take human form. Jaguars were founders of the Mayan Quiche lineage. The Aztec warrior god Tezcatlipoca is depicted as a jaguar, he was knocked from the sky by the Feathered Serpent and became a jaguar on falling into the sea. In Toltec tradition the Jaguar and Eagle symbolize Night and Day; the jaguar is also identified with thunder and rain and his yellow skin is the sun. There were also military orders of jaguars. Sometimes called the Dog of the Shaman, the jaguar is a cult figure in shamanism and the shaman can take jaguar shape to travel through time and space. It is also a were-animal. Shamans may turn into jaguars after death. In Amazonian myth the Jaguar woman marries the masculine Anaconda; in another legend the Jaguar married a human wife in order to steal the secret of fire. Black jaguars become demons after death.

**James. St. James.** The apostle **St. James the Great** is the patron saint of Spain. One legend states that after his death in Palestine his body was placed in a boat with sails set, and that next day it reached the Spanish coast. At Padron, near Compostela, they used to show a huge stone as the veritable boat. Another legend says that it was the relics of St. James that were miraculously conveyed from Jerusalem, where he was Bishop, to Spain, in a marble ship. A KNIGHT saw the ship entering port and his horse took fright and plunged into the sea but the knight saved himself by boarding the vessel and found his clothes entirely covered with scallop shells.

The saint's body was discovered in 840 by Bishop Theudemirus of Iria through divine revelation, and a church was built at Compostela for its shrine.

St. James is commemorated on 25 July and is represented in art sometimes with the sword by which he was beheaded, and sometimes attired as a pilgrim, with his cloak covered with shells.

**Jesse James** (1837–1882). A notorious American bandit. In 1867 he organized a band of bank and train robbers who perpetrated a number of infamous murders and daring crimes. A reward of $10,000 was put on his head. He retired to St. Joseph, Missouri, under the name of Howard and was shot by a reward-seeker while hanging a picture in his house. He undeservedly passed into legend as another ROBIN HOOD.

Poor Jesse left a wife to mourn all her life,
His children three were brave
But the dirty little coward that shot Mr. Howard,
He laid Jesse James in his grave.

**Jamshid.** In Persian legend, the fourth king of the Pishdadian, or earliest, dynasty who reigned for 700 years and had Devs or demons as his slaves. He was credited with 300 years of beneficent rule, but when he forgot God, was driven out and remained hidden for 100 years. He was eventually sawn apart. Among his magical possessions was a cup containing the ELIXIR OF LIFE which is mentioned in Fitzgerald's *Omar Khayyám* and Moore's *Lalla Rookh*.

**Janissaries,** or **Janizaries** (Turk, *yenitscheri*, new corps). Celebrated troops of the Ottoman Empire, raised by Orchan in 1330; originally, and for some centuries, compulsorily recruited from Christian subjects of the Sultan. They were blessed by Hadji Becktash, a saint, who cut off the sleeve of his fur mantle and gave it to the captain, who put in on his head. Hence the fur cap worn by these footguards. In 1826 the Janissaries, long a tyrannical military caste, rebelled when their privileges were threatened, and they were abolished by total massacre.
**Janissary music.** Military music of the Turkish kind. Also called Turkish music.

**Janus** (jā'nəs). The ancient Roman deity who kept the gate of HEAVEN; hence the guardian of gates and doors. He was represented with two faces, one in front and one behind, and the doors of his temple in ROME were thrown open in times of war and closed in times of peace. The name

continues as January, the door of the New Year, but the backward-facing head looks back to the past year. The name is also used allusively both with reference to the double-facedness and to war. Thus Milton says of the Cherubim:

Four faces each
Had, like a double-Janus.
*Paradise Lost*, XI, 129.

And Tennyson:

State-policy and church-policy are conjoint,
But Janus-faces looking diverse ways.
*Queen Mary*, III, ii.

While Dante says of the Roman eagle that it:

composed the world to such a peace,
That of his temple Janus barr'd the door.
*Paradiso*, vi, 83 (*Cary's tr.*).

**Jason.** The hero of Greek legend who led the ARGONAUTS in the quest of the GOLDEN FLEECE, the son of Aeson, King of Iolcus, brought up by the centaur CHIRON. When he demanded his kingdom from his uncle Pelias who had deprived him of it, and was told he could have it in return for the Golden Fleece, Jason gathered around him the chief heroes of Greece and set sail in the ARGO. After many tests and trials, including sowing the remaining dragon's teeth left unsown by CADMUS, he was successful through the help of MEDEA, whom he married. He later deserted her and subsequently killed himself through melancholy. Another account says he was crushed to death by the stern of his old ship Argo, while resting beneath it. *See* AESON'S BATH.

**Jay.** Like the Magpie and Jackdaw the Jay is a chatterer and imitator. Blue Jay is a character in Amerindian myth, he is both a creator, being one of the creatures which brought up the first mud after the Deluge, and a trickster-hero; he is also a guardian spirit. Shamans can take the form of the bird and in that form perch on rafters at ceremonies. The Jay-bird occurs frequently in legends of the Southern States, there it is the Devil's messenger and is not seen on Fridays as it takes sticks to the Devil in hell on that day.

**Jekyll** (jek'il). **Dr. Jekyll and Mr. Hyde.** Two aspects of one man. Jekyll is the 'would do good,' Hyde is 'the evil that is present'. The phrase comes from R. L.

Stevenson's *The Strange Case of Dr. Jekyll and Mr. Hyde*, first published in 1886.

**Jemmy Twitcher.** *See* TWITCHER.

**Jesse James.** *See under* JAMES.

**Jettatura** (Ital.). The evil eye, a superstition that certain persons have the power, by looking at one, of casting a malevolent spell.

**Jew. Wandering Jew.** *See* WANDERING.
**Jews born with tails.** *See* TAILED MEN.

**Jinn.** Demons of Arabian mythology fabled to dwell in the mountains of Kâf, which encompass the earth; they were created two thousand years before ADAM and assume the forms of serpents, dogs, cats, monsters and even human shape. The evil *jinn* are hideously ugly, but the good are singularly beautiful. The word is plural; its singular is *jinnee; genii* is a variant form.

**Joan of Arc, St.** (1412–1431), the Maid of Orleans (*La Pucelle d'Orléans*). Born at Domrémy in Lorraine, the daughter of a peasant, she was directed by heavenly voices to undertake her mission to deliver France, then undergoing the ravages of the Hundred Years War. She convinced the DAUPHIN of her sincerity, donned male dress, and inspired the French army in the relief of Orléans (1429) and then the advance to Rheims. She was captured by the Burgundians at Compiègne (May 1430) and sold to the English by the Count of Luxembourg for 10,000 livres. She was condemned to death by the Bishop of Beauvais for WITCHCRAFT and heresy and burned at the stake at Rouen (30 May 1431). Her last words were the name of Jesus repeated thrice. She was canonized in 1920 as the second patron of France but as such is not recognised by the State. There has been no official patron saint of France since the separation of Church and State in 1905.

**Jocasta.** *See* OEDIPUS.

**John. John Bull.** The nickname for an Englishman or Englishmen collectively. The name was used in Dr. John Arbuthnot's satire, *Law is a bottomless Pit* (1712), republished as *The History of John Bull*. Arbuthnot did not invent the name but established it.
**John o' Groats.** The site of a legendary house 1¾ miles west of Duncansby Head,

Caithness, Scotland. The story is that Malcolm, Gavin and John o'Groat (or Jan de Groot), three Dutch brothers, came to this part of Scotland in the reign of James IV. There came to be eight families of the name and they met annually to celebrate. On one occasion a question of precedency arose, consequently John o'Groat built an eight-sided room with a door to each side and placed an octagonal table therein so that all were 'head of the table'. This building went ever after with the name of *John o'Groat's House*.
**From Land's End to John o'Groats.** From one end of Great Britain to the other; from Dan to Beersheba.
**John Roberts.** Obsolete slang for a very large tankard, supposed to hold enough for any ordinary drinker to last through Saturday and Sunday. It was introduced in Wales in 1886 to compensate topers for Sunday closing of public houses, and derived its name from John Roberts, M.P., author of the Sunday Closing Act.
**John in the Wad.** The IGNIS FATUUS.
**Little John.** *See* ROBIN HOOD.
**Prester John.** In mediaeval legend a fabulous Christian emperor of Asia who occurs in documents from the 12th century onwards. In Marco Polo's *Travels* he is lord of the Tartars. From the 14th century he becomes the Emperor of Ethiopia or Abyssinia where he was apparently still reigning in the time of Vasco da Gama.

**Johnstone. St. Johnstone's Tippet.** A halter; so called from Johnstone the HANGMAN.

**Jolly. The jolly god.** BACCHUS. The BIBLE speaks of wine 'that maketh glad the heart of man' (*Ps.* civ, 15).

**Jones, Davy.** *See* DAVY JONES.

**Jophiel.** *See* ARCHANGEL.

**Joseph of Arimathea, St.** The rich Jew, probably a member of the Sanhedrin, who believed in Christ, but feared to confess it, and, after the Crucifixion, begged the body of the Saviour and deposited it in his own tomb (*see Matt.* xxvii, 57–60; *Mark* xv, 43–46). His day is 17 March.

Legend relates that he was imprisoned for 12 years and was kept alive miraculously by the holy GRAIL, and that on his release by Vespasian, about the year 63, he brought the Grail and the spear with which Longinus wounded the crucified Saviour to Britain, and founded the abbey of GLASTONBURY whence he commenced the conversion of Britain.

The origin of these legends is to be found in a group of Apocryphal writings of which the *Evangelium Nicodemi* is the chief; these were worked upon at Glastonbury and further established by Robert de Borron in the 13th century, the latter version (by way of Walter Map) being woven by Malory into his *Morte d'Arthur*.

**Joss.** A Chinese god or idol. The word is probably a Pidgin English corruption of Port. *deos*, Lat. *deus*, god. A temple is called a *joss-house*, and a *joss-stick* is a stick made from clay mixed with the powder of various scented woods burnt as incense.

**Jotunheim** (yō′tənhīm). The land of the Scandinavian *Jotuns* or GIANTS.

**Jove.** Another name of JUPITER, being *Jovis pater*, father Jove. Milton, in *Paradise Lost*, makes Jove one of the fallen angels (I, 512).

**Jovial.** Merry and sociable, like those born under the planet JUPITER, which astrologers considered the happiest of the natal stars. *Cp.* SATURNINE.

> Our Jovial star reign'd at his birth.
> SHAKESPEARE: *Cymbeline*, V, iv.

**Joyeuse** (zhwaycez′). A name given to more than one famous sword in romance, especially to CHARLEMAGNE'S, which bore the inscription *Decem praeceptorum custos Carolus*, and was buried with him.

**Joyeuse Garde,** or **Garde-Joyeuse.** The estate given by King ARTHUR to Sir LANCELOT of the Lake for defending the Queen's honour against Sir Mador. It is supposed to have been at Berwick-on-Tweed.

**Juan. Don Juan.** Don Juan Tenorio, the legendary hero of many plays, poems, stories and operas, was the son of a notable family in 14th-century Seville. The story is that he killed the commandant of Ulloa after seducing his daughter. He then invited the statue of the murdered man (erected in the Franciscan convent) to a feast, at the end of which the sculptured figure delivered him over to HELL. He is presented as the complete profligate.

His name is synonymous with rake, roué and aristocratic libertine, and in Mozart's opera *Don Giovanni* (1787) the valet says that his master had 'in Italy 700 mistresses, in Germany 800, in Turkey and France 91, in Spain 1,003'. Don Juan's dissolute life was dramatized by the monk Gabriel Tellez in the 17th century, followed by Molière, Corneille, Shadwell and others. BYRON, the elder Dumas, Balzac, de Musset and Shaw (*Man and Superman*) all utilized the story and helped to maintain its popularity.

**Juan Fernandez.** *See* ROBINSON CRUSOE.

**Judgment of Paris.** *See* PARIS.

**Judicial Astrology.** *See* ASTROLOGY.

**Judy.** *See* PUNCH, MR.

**Juggernaut,** or **Jagganath.** A Hindu god, 'Lord of the World', having his temple at Puri in Orissa. It is a cult-title of VISHNU, and the pyramidal temple was erected in the 12th century and held the Golden Tooth of BUDDHA. The chief festival is the car festival when Jagganath is dragged in his car (35 feet square and 45 feet high) over the sand to another temple. The car has sixteen wheels, each seven feet in diameter. The belief that fanatical pilgrims cast themselves under the wheels of the car to be crushed to death on the last day of the festival is largely without foundation. However, it has led to the phrase the **car of the juggernaut,** used to denote customs institutions etc. beneath which people are ruthlessly and unnecessarily crushed. The word *juggernaut* is also applied humorously to any wheeled 'monster'. More recently, juggernaut is the name given to the giant articulated lorries increasingly prevalent since Britain's entry into the Common Market, which pose another threat to the environment.

**Julian, St.** A patron SAINT of travellers and of hospitality, looked upon in the Middle Ages as the epicure of saints. Thus Chaucer says that the Franklin was 'Epicurus owne sone', and:

> An house holdere, and that a greet was he;
> Seint Julian in his contree.
> *Canterbury Tales: Prologue*, 339.

He seems to be essentially a mythical saint. He is supposed to have unwittingly slain his parents and devoted his life to helping strangers by way of atonement.

**Junius. Junius Brutus.** Son of M. Junius and Tarquinia and nephew of Tarquin. When his father and elder brother were murdered by Tarquin the Proud, he feigned insanity, thereby saving his life, and was called *Brutus* for his apparent stupidity. He later inspired the Romans to get rid of the Tarquins and became a consul. *Cp.* AMYRIS PLAYS THE FOOL.

**Juno.** In Roman mythology 'the venerable ox-eyed' wife and sister of JUPITER, and queen of HEAVEN. She is identified with the Greek HERA, was the special protectress of marriage and of women, and was represented as a war goddess. *Cp.* GENIUS.

**Junonian Bird.** The peacock, dedicated to the goddess-queen.

**Jupiter.** Also called JOVE, the supreme god of Roman mythology, corresponding to the Greek ZEUS, son of SATURN or Kronos (whom he dethroned) and Ops or Rhea. He was the special protector of Rome, and as Jupiter Capitolinus (his temple being on the Capitoline Hill) presided over the Roman games. He determined the course of human affairs and made known the future through signs in the heavens, the flight of birds etc. *See* AUGURY.

As Jupiter was lord of HEAVEN and bringer of light, white was the colour sacred to him; hence among the alchemists Jupiter designated tin. In heraldry Jupiter stands for azure, the blue of the heavens.

His statue by Phidias at OLYMPIA was one of the Seven Wonders of the World (*see under* WONDER). It was removed to Constantinople by Theodosius I and destroyed by fire in 475. *See* THEMIS.

**Jupiter** is also the name of the largest of the planets.

**Jupiter Ammon.** A name under which JUPITER was worshipped in Libya where his temple was famous for its ORACLE which was consulted by HERCULES. *Cp.* AMMON.

**Jupiter Scapin.** A nickname of NAPOLEON, given him by the Abbé de Pradt. Scapin is a valet famous for his knavish tricks, in Molière's comedy *Les Fourberies de Scapin.*

**Jupiter tonans** (the thundering Jupiter). A complimentary nickname given to *The Times* in the mid-19th century.

**Jupiter's beard.** HOUSE LEEK.

# K

**Kaaba** (kah'bə) (Arab. *kabah*, a cube). The ancient stone building said to have been first built by Ishmael and ABRAHAM and incorporated in the centre of the Great Mosque at Mecca. It forms a rough square and is about 40 feet high, containing the BLACK STONE in the east corner. The present Kaaba was built in 1626 and is covered with a cloth of black brocade that is replaced with annual ceremony.

**Kaf, Mount.** *See* JINN.

**Kalevala** (kah'livahlə). The national epic of the Finns, compiled from popular songs and oral tradition by the Finnish philologist, Elias Lönnroth (1802–1884), who published his first edition of 12,000 verses in 1835, and a second, of some 22,900 verses, in 1849. Its name is taken from the three sons of Kalewa (Finland), who are the heroes of the poem—Väinämöinen, Ilmarinen, and Lemminkäinen. Prominent in the action is the magical mill, the Sampo, an object that grants all one's wishes. The epic is influenced by Teutonic and Scandinavian mythology, and to a lesser extent by Christianity. It is written in unrhymed alliterative trochaic verse, and is the prototype both in form and content of Longfellow's *Hiawatha*.

**Kali** (kah'lē). The cult name of the Hindu goddess Durga, wife of SIVA goddess of death and destruction. Calcutta receives its name from her, Kali-ghat, the steps of Kali, by which her worshippers descended from the bank to the waters of the Ganges. It was to her that the THUGS sacrificed their victims. Her idol is black, besmeared with blood; she has red eyes, four arms, matted hair, huge fang-like teeth, and a protruding tongue that drips with blood. She wears a necklace of skulls, earrings of corpses, and is girdled with serpents.

**Kalki.** *See* AVATAR.

**Kalyb** (kal'ib). The 'Lady of the Woods', who stole St. GEORGE from his nurse, and endowed him with gifts. St. George enclosed her in a rock where she was torn to pieces by spirits. The story occurs in the *Famous History of the Seven Champions of Christendom*, Pt. I. *See* SEVEN CHAMPIONS.

**Kama.** In Hindu mythology Kama, god of love and desire, is the son of VISHNU and LAKSHMI and husband of Rati, goddess of voluptuousness who is the Hindu VENUS; she is also known as Kami. Kama is represented as riding on a SPARROW, he holds either a bow of flowers or a bow with a string of bees, depicting the 'sweet pain' of love and he is followed by a train of BEES. He has five arrows as the five senses.

**Kami** (kah'mē). A god or divinity in Shintoism, the native religion of Japan; also the title given to daimios and governors, comparable to our 'lord'. Their respective ideographs are different.

**Kamikaze** (kamikah'zi). A Japanese word meaning 'divine wind', in reference to the providential typhoon which once balked a Mongol invasion. In World War II it was applied to the 'suicide' aircraft attacks organized under Vice-Admiral Onishi in the Philippines between October 1944 and January 1945. Some 5000 young pilots gave their lives when their bomb-loaded fighters crashed into their objectives.

**Kamsa.** *See* KRISHNA.

**Karttikeya** (kahtikā'ə). The Hindu god of war. He is shown riding on a peacock, with a bow in one hand and an arrow in the other, and is known also as *Skanda* and *Kumara*.

**Kaswa, Al.** Mohammed's favourite camel, which fell on its knees when the prophet delivered the last clause of the KORAN to the assembled multitude at MECCA.

**Kay, Sir.** In ARTHURIAN ROMANCE, son of Sir Ector and foster-brother of King ARTHUR who made him his seneschal.

**Kelpie,** or **kelpy.** A spirit of the waters in the form of a horse, in Scottish fairy-lore. It was supposed to delight in the drowning of travellers, but also occasionally helped millers by keeping the mill-wheel going at night.

> Every lake has its Kelpie or Water-horse, often seen by the shepherd sitting upon the brow of a rock, dashing along the surface of the deep, or browsing upon the pasture on its verge.
>
> GRAHAM: *Sketches of Perthshire.*

**Kenelm, St.** An English SAINT, son of Kenwulf, King of Mercia in the early 9th century. He was only seven years old when, by his sister's order, he was murdered at Clent, Worcestershire. The murder, says Roger of Wendover, was miraculously notified at Rome by a white dove, which alighted on the altar at St. Peter's, bearing in its beak a scroll with

> In Clent cow pasture, under a thorn,
> Of head bereft, lies Kenelm, King-born.

His day is 17 July.

**Kenne.** A stone, fabled by mediaeval naturalists to be formed in the eye of a stag. It was used as an antidote to poison. *Cp.* HYENA.

**Kentish. Kentish Fire.** Rapturous applause, or three times three and one more. The expression probably originated with the protracted cheers given in Kent to the No-Popery orators in 1828–1829. Lord Winchelsea, proposing the health of the Earl of Roden on 15 August 1834, said: 'Let it be given with the Kentish Fire.'
**Kentishman's Tails.** *See* TAILED MEN.

**Kern Baby.** *See* CORN DOLLY.

**Kerton.** *See* EXTER.

**Ketch.** *See* JACK KETCH *under* JACK.

**Kettle. A kettle of fish.** An old Border name for a kind of *fête champêtre* or riverside picnic where a newly caught salmon is boiled and eaten. The discomfort of this sort of party may have led to the phrase, 'A pretty kettle of fish', meaning an awkward state of affairs, a mess, a muddle.

> As the whole company go to the water-side today to eat a kettle of fish, there will be no risk of interruption.
>
> SCOTT: *St. Ronan's Well*, ch. XII.

**Kevin, St.** An Irish saint of the 6th century, of whom legend relates that he retired to a cave on the steep shore of a lake where he vowed no woman should ever land. A girl named Kathleen followed him, but the saint flogged her with a bunch of nettles or, according to the more romantic story, hurled her from a rock and her ghost never left the place where he lived. A cave at Glendalough, Wicklow, is shown as the bed of St. Kevin. Moore has a poem on this tradition (*Irish Melodies*, IV).

**Key. The Cross Keys.** The emblem of St. PETER and also St. Servatius, St. Hippolytus, St. Geneviève, St. Petronilla, St. Osyth, St. MARTHA and St. Germanus of Paris. They also form the arms of the Archbishop of York. The Bishop of Winchester bears two keys and a sword in saltire and the bishops of St. Asaph, Gloucester, Exeter and Peterborough bear two keys in saltire. The Cross Keys are also used as a PUBLIC-HOUSE SIGN.

**Keyne, St.** A CELTIC saint of the 5th century, daughter of Brychan, King of Brecknock. St. Keyne's Well, near Liskeard, Cornwall, is reputed to give the upper hand to the first of the marriage partners to drink from it.

**Kid.** In Dionysian rites the sacrificial kid represented the god dying preliminary to rebirth. It was sacrificed by the Maenads and was also sacrificed to Silvanus and Faunus. The ritual of sacrificing a kid was one of the early customs of pastoral peoples. The Phrygian Mysteries used it in initiation ceremonies. In the Old Testament the Mosaic Law forbade the seething of a kid in its mother's milk.

**Kildare's Holy Fane.** Famous for the 'Fire of St. Bridget' which the nuns never allowed to go out. Every twentieth night St. Bridget was fabled to return to tend the fire. St. Bridget founded a nunnery at Kildare in the 5th century. Part of the chapel still remains and is called 'The Firehouse'.

**King. King Cole.** *See* COLE.

**King Horn.** The hero of a late 13th-century English metrical romance. His father, King of Sudenne, was killed by Saracen pirates who set young Horn adrift in a boat with twelve other children. After many adventures he reconquers his father's kingdom and marries Rymenhild, daughter of King Aylmer of Westernesse. *Cp.* HORN CHILDE *under* HORN.

**King Log and King Stork.** *See under* LOG.

**The King of Men.** A title given to both ZEUS and AGAMEMNON.

**King of Misrule.** In mediaeval and Tudor times the director of the Christmas-time horseplay and festivities, called also the Abbot, or Lord, of Misrule, and in Scotland the Abbot of Unreason. A King of Misrule was appointed at the royal court, and at Oxford and Cambridge one of the Masters of Arts superintended the revelries. Stow tells us that the Lord Mayor of London, the sheriffs and the noblemen each had their Lord of Misrule. Philip Stubbs (*Anatomie of Abuses*, 1595) says that these mock dignitaries had from twenty to a hundred officers under them, furnished with HOBBY-HORSES, dragons and musicians. They first paraded in church with such a babble of noise that no one could hear his own voice. Polydore Vergil says that the Feast of Misrule was derived from the Roman SATURNALIA. According to Stow, 'this pageant potentate began his rule at ALL-HALLOWS' EVE, and continued the same till the morrow after the Feast of the Purification.'

**The Three Kings of Cologne.** THE MAGI.

**The King's Cave.** On the west coast of the Isle of Arran; so called because it was here that King Robert Bruce and his retinue are said to have lodged before they landed in Carrick (1307).

**The King's Oak.** The OAK under which Henry VIII sat in Epping Forest, while Queen Anne (Boleyn) was being executed.

**Days fatal to kings.** Certain days were superstitiously held to be fatal to the sovereigns of Great Britain, but with little resemblance to the facts. Of those who have died since 1066 *Sunday* has been the last day of the reign of seven, *Monday, Tuesday* and *Thursday* that of six each, *Friday* and *Wednesday* of five, and *Saturday* of four.

*Sunday:* Henry I, Edward III, Henry VI, James I, William III, Anne, George 1.
*Monday:* Stephen, Richard II, Henry IV, Henry V, Richard III, George V.
*Tuesday:* Richard I, Edward II, Charles I, James II, William IV, Victoria.
*Wednesday:* John, Henry III, Edward IV, Edward V, George VI.
*Thursday:* William I, William II, Henry II, Edward VI, Mary I, Elizabeth I.
*Friday:* Edward I, Henry VIII, Charles II, Mary II, Edward VII.
*Saturday:* Henry VII, George II, George III, George IV.

**Kingfisher.** Also known as the Halcyon, the kingfisher is the origin of the term 'Halcyon Days' as it was believed that the bird made its nest either on the edge of the sea-shore or on the sea itself and that, during the time between the laying of the eggs and when the young birds flew, the sea was stilled and remained calm. These days were the seven before and the seven after the winter solstice, although accounts vary from seven to nine to eleven days, but seven is the most usual number. Oppian says the nest is 'along side the waves which may wet the breasts but the tails are dry' and the Bestiaries continue this legend, calling the bird the Halcyon or Altion, but classical and eastern myth says that the nest actually floats on the sea.

In Greek myth Alcyone, daughter of Aeolus, king of the winds, found her husband drowned and cast herself into the sea; the gods, rewarding her devotion, turned her into a kingfisher and Aeolus forbade the winds to blow during the Halcyon Days. Kingfishers are beloved by sea-nymphs and are associated with Pallas, HERA and THETIS.

A dead kingfisher's body can turn aside thunderbolts and its beak points in the direction of the wind, hence a mummified kingfisher with extended wings could be used as a weather-vane.

Mediaeval myth said that the kingfisher, originally grey, got its colouring after the flood when it flew up to the heavens to survey the waters, taking on the colour of the sky, but, flying too near the sun, scorched its breast.

In the Far East the feathers of the kingfisher are highly prized and used as talismans or in fine decoration. In Madagascar the bird is venerated and regarded as a helper and messenger.

**Kit's Coty House.** A great cromlech, $3\frac{1}{2}$ m. north-west of Maidstone on the Rochester road, consisting of a 12-feet long block of sandstone resting on three standing blocks. The name may be British for 'the tomb in the wood' (Wel. *coed*, a wood). It is near the ancient battlefield where Vortigern is supposed to have fought HENGIST AND HORSA.

**Knight. Knights of the Round Table.** *See* ROUND TABLE.
**The Knight of the Rueful Countenance.** Don QUIXOTE.
**The Knight of the Swan.** LOHENGRIN.

**Knockers.** GOBLINS or KOBOLDS who dwell in mines and indicate rich veins of ore by their presence. In Cardiganshire (Powys) and elsewhere miners attributed the strange noises so frequently heard in mines to these spirits.

**Knot. Gordian knot.** *See* GORDIAN.

**Know. Do you know the Bishop of Norwich?** A reminder to those who forget to pass the port wine to their neighbour because they are too busy conversing. The hint stems from a certain Bishop of Norwich who was said to be such a persistent talker that he often forgot to pass the port.

**Kowtow** (Chin. knocking the head). A Chinese custom of kneeling down and knocking the head on the ground as a sign of reverence, homage, respect etc. Hence in popular usage to behave obsequiously to someone, to fawn or grovel.

**Kraken** (krah'kən). A fabulous sea-monster supposed to have been seen off the coast of Norway and probably founded on an observation of a gigantic cuttle-fish. It was first described by Pontoppidan in his *History of Norway* (1752). It was supposed to be capable of dragging down the largest ships and when submerging could suck down a vessel by the whirlpool it created. *Cp.* LOCH NESS MONSTER.

**Kratim.** The dog of the SEVEN SLEEPERS, more correctly called Katmir or Ketmir, which according to Mohammed sleeps with them and is one of the ten animals to be admitted into his PARADISE.

**Kriemhild** (krēm'hild). The legendary heroine of the NIBELUNGENLIED, a woman of unrivalled beauty, daughter of King Dankrat, and sister of GUNTHER, Gernot and Giselher. She first married SIEGFRIED and next Etzel (Attila), King of the Huns.

**Krishna** (the black one). A popular Hindu deity and an avatar of VISHNU. One myth says he was the son of Vasudeva and Devaki and was born at Mathura between Delhi and Agra. His uncle King Kamsa, who had been warned that one of his nephews would kill him, murdered Devaki's children on birth; accordingly Krishna was smuggled away and brought up among cow-herds and lived to kill his uncle. He was the APOLLO of India and the idol of women. He features in the MAHABHARATA, the BHAGAVAD-GITA and the *Bhagavata-Purana*. Another story is that Vishnu plucked out two of his own hairs, one white and one black, and the black one became Krishna.

**Kronos,** or **Cronos.** One of the TITANS of Greek mythology, son of URANUS and GE, father (by RHEA) of Hestia, DEMETER, HERA, HADES, POSEIDON and ZEUS. He dethroned his father as ruler of the world, and was in turn dethroned by his son Zeus. By the Romans he was identified with SATURN.

**Kurma.** *See* AVATAR.

**Kwan-yin.** The Chinese goddess of mercy, the female form of Avalokitesvara of Mahayana Buddhism, she is frequently depicted as holding a child in her arms. In Japan she appears as Kwannon.

**Ky-lin.** Like the PHOENIX or FENG-HUANG in China, the Ky-lin is a fabulous creature of dual nature, embodying the *yin-yang* balance, the Ky being the masculine and the Lin the feminine. The animal also embodies the five elements, the five virtues and the five symbolic colours. It is sometimes called the UNICORN as it is one-horned and as such represents unity under a great ruler. It appears to herald the advent of virtuous monarchs and such famous people as Confucius. Being of exceptional gentleness the Ky-lin never strikes with its horn and so symbolizes goodwill and benevolence.
    The Japanese Ki-rin is adopted from the Chinese Ky-lin. *See* FUNG-HWANG.

# L

**La Belle Sauvage** (lah bel sōvahzh'). The site on the north side of LUDGATE Hill occupied by the House of Cassell from 1852 until 11 May 1941, when the whole area was demolished in an air raid. The name is a corruption of 'Savage's Bell Inn' and the French form appears to have been first used by Addison in *The Spectator* (No. 82). There seems to have been an inn on the site from about the 14th century, originally called 'The Bell on the Hope', the *Hope* or *hoop* being the garlanded ivy-bush (*see* IVY). From its position just outside LUDGATE its yard became a rendezvous for bear-baiting, play-acting etc., and, from the 17th century until the mid-19th, it was a starting place for coach traffic. The inn licence was not renewed after 1857.

> Tom had never been in London, and would have liked to have stopped at the Belle Savage. Where they had been put down by the Star, just at dusk, that he might have gone roving about those endless, mysterious gas-lit streets....
>
> T. HUGHES: *Tom Brown's Schooldays*, ch, iv.

**La Mancha, The Knight of** (laman'chə). Don QUIXOTE de la Mancha, the hero of Cervantes' romance *Don Quixote*. La Mancha was a province of Spain now the main part of Ciudad Real, an arid land with much heath and waste, and the most thinly populated part of Spain.

**Labyrinth** (lab'irinth). A Greek word of unknown (but probably Egyptian) origin, denoting a structure with complicated passages through which it is baffling to find one's way. The labyrinth used as a design on houses and other buildings protects against evil spirits and hostile powers. On graves and funereal monuments the labyrinth both protects the dead and prevents them from returning. The maze at Hampton Court, formed of high hedges, is a labyrinth on a small scale. The chief labyrinths of antiquity were:

(1) The Egyptian, by Petesuchis or Tithoes, near the Lake Moeris. It had 3000 apartments, half of which were underground (1800 B.C.).—*Pliny*, xxxvi, 13; and *Pomponius Mela*, I, ix.

(2) The Cretan, by DAEDALUS, for imprisoning the MINOTAUR. The only means of finding a way out was by help of a skein of thread. (*See* Virgil: *Aeneid*, V.)

(3) The Cretan conduit, which had 1000 branches or turnings.

(4) The Lemnian, by the architects Smilis, Rholus and Theodorus. It had 150 columns, so nicely adjusted that a child could turn them. Vestiges of this labyrinth were still in existence in the time of Pliny.

(5) The labyrinth of Clusium, made by Lars Porsena, King of Etruria, for his tomb.

(6) The Samian, by Theodorus (540 B.C.). Referred to by Pliny; by Herodotus, II, 145; by Strabo, X; and by Diodorus Siculus, I.

(7) The labyrinth at Woodstock, built by Henry II to protect Fair ROSAMOND.

**Lachesis** (lak'esis). The Fate who spins life's thread and determines its length. *See* FATES.

**Ladon** (lā'don). The name of the DRAGON which guarded the apples of the HESPERIDES, also one of the dogs of ACTAEON.

**Lady. Lady Bountiful.** The original character comes from Farquhar's *Beaux' Stratagem* (1706), and about a century later the term acquired the generic application of a village benefactress now in use.

**The Lady of the Lake.** In Arthurian legend, Vivien, the mistress of MERLIN. She lived in the midst of a lake surrounded by knights and damsels. *See* LANCELOT OF THE LAKE.

In Scott's poem of this name (1810), the lady is Ellen Douglas, who lived with her father near Loch Katrine.

**The Lady of Shalott.** *See* SHALOTT.

**Laestrygones.** *See* LESTRIGONS.

**Lagado.** In Swift's *Gulliver's Travels*, the capital of Balnibarbi, celebrated for its grand academy of projectors, where the scholars spend their time in such projects as making pincushions from softened rocks, extracting sunbeams from cucumbers, and converting ice into gunpowder.

**Lais** (lā'is). The name of three celebrated Greek courtesans. One flourished in Corinth in the 5th century B.C. and was visited by Aristippus the philosopher, but the best known was the daughter of Timandra, the mistress of Alcibiades. She was born *c.* 420 B.C. and came to Corinth as a child. She was patronized by princes, philosophers and plebeians alike. Her charges were sufficiently exorbitant to deter Demosthenes. Her later success in Thessaly so enraged the women that they pricked her to death with their bodkins. There was a third Lais, contemporary with ALEXANDER THE GREAT, who sat for Apelles.

**Lake. Lady of the Lake.** *See* LADY.
**Lancelot of the Lake.** *See* LANCELOT.

**Laksmi,** or **Lakshmi.** One of the consorts of VISHNU, and mother of Kama. She is the goddess of beauty, wealth and pleasure, and the *Ramayana* describes her as springing from the foam of the sea. *Cp.* APHRODITE.

**Lamb.** Used widely as a sacrificial animal, the lamb represented innocence and the unblemished, and evil was held to be powerless against this innocence. The unblemished paschal lamb was sacrificed at the Hebrew Passover and its blood sprinkled on the lintels as warding off evil. Christianity adopted this sacrifice as that of Christ dying for the sins of the world and the lamb is frequently depicted with the cross in Christian art. The lamb also represents the good shepherd. The lamb with the lion depicts the paradisial state. The Apocalyptic Lamb with seven horns signifies the seven gifts of the Spirit.
**The Vegetable, Tartarian** or **Scythian Lamb.** The woolly rootstalk of a fern (*Cibotium barometz*), found in Asia, and supposed in mediaeval times to be a kind of hybrid animal and vegetable. The down is used in India for staunching wounds.

**Lamia** (lā'miə). Among the Greeks and Romans a female demon who devoured children and whose name was used to frighten them. She was a Libyan queen beloved by JUPITER, but, robbed of her offspring by the jealous JUNO, she became insane and vowed vengeance on all children, whom she delighted to entice and devour. The race of *Lamiae*, in Africa, were said to have the head and breasts of a woman and the body of a serpent and they enticed strangers into their embraces to devour them.

Witches in the Middle Ages were called *Lamiae*, and Keats' poem *Lamia* (1820) relates the story of how a bride, when recognized by APOLLONIUS as a serpent or lamia, vanished in an instant. Keats took the substance of his poem from Burton's *Anatomy of Melancholy* (Pt. III, sect. ii, memb. i, subsect. i) whose source was Philostratus (*De Vita Apollonii*, Bk. IV). *Cp.* LILITH.

**Lamp. The Lamp of Phoebus.** The sun. PHOEBUS is the mythological personification of the sun.

**Lampos.** One of the steeds of AURORA, also the name of one of the horses of DIOMEDES, and of HECTOR.

**Lancelot du lac,** or **of the Lake.** One of the Knights of the ROUND TABLE, son of King BAN of Brittany, and stolen in infancy by the LADY OF THE LAKE. She plunged with the baby into the lake (whence the cognomen *du Lac*), and when her protégé was grown to manhood, presented him to King ARTHUR. Sir Lancelot went in search of the GRAIL and twice caught sight of it. Though always represented in ARTHURIAN ROMANCE as the model of chivalry, bravery and fidelity, Sir Lancelot was the adulterous lover of Queen GUINEVERE, and it was through this liaison that war resulted which led to the disruption of the Round Table and the death of King Arthur.

**Land. The Land of Beulah** (*Is.* lxii, 4). In Bunyan's *Pilgrim's Progress* it is that land of heavenly joy where the pilgrims tarry till they are summoned to enter the CELESTIAL CITY.
**The Land o' the Leal.** The land of the faithful or blessed; a Scotticism for a Happy Land or HEAVEN, as in Lady Nairn's song of this title:

I'm wearin' awa'
To the land o' the leal.

**Land of the White Eagle.** Poland. The White Eagle, with a crown on its head, formed part of the Polish coat-of-arms. An old legend tells us that Prince Lech, when out hunting, came to a great oak-tree, where he saw a pair of huge white eagles over their nest. The prince regarded this as a prophetic sign and decided to establish his capital there. He called it *Gniezno* ('Nest-town'), saying, 'Here shall be our nest.'

**Lang. Auld Lang Syne.** This song, commonly sung at the conclusion of dances and revelries and usually attributed to Robert Burns, is really a new version by him of a very much older song. In Watson's Collection (1711), it is attributed to Francis Sempill (d. 1682), but is probably older. Burns says in a letter to Thomson 'It is the old song of the olden times, which has never been in print.... I took it down from an old man's singing.' And in another letter, 'Light be on the turf of the heaven-inspired poet who composed this glorious fragment.'

**Language. The three primitive languages.** The Persians say that Arabic, Persian and Turkish are the three primitive languages. Legend has it that the serpent that seduced Eve spoke Arabic, the most suasive language in the world; that ADAM and Eve spoke Persian, the most poetic of all languages; and that the angel GABRIEL spoke Turkish, the most menacing.

**Lantern. The Feast of Lanterns.** A popular Chinese New Year festival, celebrated annually at the first full moon. Tradition says that the daughter of a famous mandarin one evening fell into a lake. Her father and his neighbour took lanterns to look for her, and happily she was rescued. A festival was ordained to commemorate the rescue, which in time developed into the 'Feast of Lanterns'.

**Lantern Land.** The land of literary charlatans, pedantic graduates in arts, doctors, professors, prelates etc., ridiculed as 'Lanterns' by Rabelais (with a side allusion to the divines assembled in conference at the Council of Trent) in his *Pantagruel*, v, 33. *Cp.* CITY OF LANTERNS.

**Laocoön** (lāok'ōon). A son of PRIAM and priest of APOLLO, famous for the tragic fate of himself and his two sons, who were squeezed to death by serpents while he was sacrificing to POSEIDON. Their death was said to be in consequence of his having offended Apollo, or for having sought to prevent the entry of the WOODEN HORSE into TROY. The group representing these three in their death agony, now in the Vatican, was discovered in 1506 at Rome. It is a single block of marble, and is attributed to Agesandrus, Athenodorus and Polydorus of the School of Rhodes in the 2nd century B.C.

Lessing called his treatise on the limits of poetry and the plastic arts (1766) *Laocoön*, because he uses the famous group as the peg on which to hang his dissertation.

> Since I have, as it were, set out from the Laocoön, and several times return to it, I have wished to give it a share also in the title.
> *Preface.*

**Laodamia** (lāōdəmī'ə). The wife of Protesilaus, who was slain before TROY by HECTOR. According to one account, she begged to be allowed to converse with her dead husband for only three hours, and her request was granted; she afterwards voluntarily accompanied the dead hero to the shades. Wordsworth had a poem on the subject (1814).

**Lapithae** (lap'ithē). A people of Thessaly, noted in Greek legend for their defeat of the CENTAURS at the marriage-feast of HIPPODAMIA, when the latter were driven out of PELION. The contest was represented on the Parthenon, the Theseum at ATHENS, the Temple of APOLLO at Bassae, and on numberless vases.

**Laputa** (ləpū'tə). The flying island inhabited by scientific quacks, and visited by Gulliver on his 'travels'. These dreamy philosophers were so absorbed in their speculations that they employed attendants called 'flappers', to flap them on the mouth and ears with a blown bladder when their attention was to be called off from 'high things' to vulgar mundane matters.

**Lapwing.** Solomon was said to have chosen the lapwing, or peewit, with the COCK and HOOPOE, as his favourite birds since they were able to detect water under the earth. According to the Koran the lapwing was the means of introducing Solomon to the Queen of Sheba. In the Old Testament, in

Leviticus and Deuteronomy, the same bird is called the lapwing in the Authorized Version and the hoopoe in the Revised Version. Being crested, both birds are solar.

In Greek mythology the same association occurs as the cruel King Tereus of Thrace, pursuing PHILOMEL and PROCNE, was turned into either a lapwing or hoopoe, giving the bird the significance of treachery.

**Lar.** *See* LARES.

**Larder. Robin Hood's Larder.** *See* SOME FAMOUS OAKS *under* OAK.

**Lares and Penates** (leə'rēz, penā'tēz). Used as a collective expression for home, and for those personal belongings that make it homely and individual. In ancient ROME the *lares* (sing. *lar*) were the household gods, usually deified ancestors or heroes, and the *lar familiaris* was the spirit of the founder of the house which never left it. The *penates* were the gods of the store-room and guardian deities of the household and the state, whose duty was to protect and ward off dangers. Their images stood in a special shrine in each house and offerings were made to them of wine, incense, cakes and honey on special family occasions.

**Larvae** (lah'vē). Among the ancient Romans, a name for malignant spirits and ghosts. The larva or ghost of Caligula was often seen (according to Suetonius) in his palace.

[Fear] sometimes representeth strange apparitions, as their fathers and grandfathers ghosts, risen out of their graves, and in their winding sheets: and to others it sometimes sheweth Larves, Hobgoblins, Robbin-good-fellows, and such other Bug-beares and Chimeraes.
*Florio's Montaigne*, I, xvii.

**Last. The Last of the Mohicans.** The Indian chief Uncas is so called by Fenimore Cooper in his novel of this title (1826).

**Lateran.** The ancient palace of the Laterani family which was appropriated by NERO (A.D. 66) and later given to Pope (St.) Sylvester by the Emperor Constantine. It remained the official residence of the Popes until the departure to AVIGNON in 1309. The present palace is now a museum. Fable derives the name from *lateo*, to hide, and *rana*, a frog, and accounts for it by saying that Nero once vomited a frog covered with blood, which he believed to be his own progeny, and had it hidden in a vault. The palace built on its site was called the 'Lateran', or the palace of the hidden frog.

**Latin.** The language of the ancient inhabitants of Latium in Italy and spoken by the ancient Romans (Alba Longa was head of the Latin League and ROME was a colony of Alba Longa). According to one story Latium is from *lateo*, I lie hid, and was so called because SATURN lay hid there, when he was driven out of HEAVEN by the gods. According to Roman tradition the Latini were the aborigines. *See* LATINUS.

The earliest specimen of the Latin language is an inscription on the Praeneste fibula (a gold brooch) found in 1886; it dates from the 6th century B.C.

**Latinus.** Legendary king of the Latini, the ancient inhabitants of Latium (*see* LATIN). According to Virgil, he opposed AENEAS on his first landing, but later formed an alliance with him, and gave him his daughter, Lavinia, in marriage. Turnus, King of the Rutuli, declared that Lavinia had been betrothed to him and the issue was decided by single combat. Aeneas, being the victor, became the husband of Lavinia and ancestor of ROMULUS and Remus (Virgil, *Aeneid*, VII).

**Latium.** *See* LATIN.

**Latona.** The Roman name of the Gr. Leto, mother by JUPITER of APOLLO and DIANA. Milton (*Sonnet XII*) refers to the legend that when she knelt with her infants in arms by a fountain at Delos to quench her thirst, some Lycian clowns insulted her and were turned into frogs.

As when those hinds that were transformed to frogs
Railed at Latona's twin-born progeny,
Which after held the sun and moon in fee.

**Launcelot.** *See* LANCELOT.

**Launfal, Sir.** One of the Knights of the ROUND TABLE. His story is told in a metrical romance written by Thomas Chestre in the reign of Henry VI. James Russell Lowell has a poem entitled *The Vision of Sir Launfal* (1845).

**Laurel.** The Greeks gave a wreath of laurels to the victor in the PYTHIAN GAMES, but the victor in the OLYMPIC GAMES had a wreath of wild olives, in the NEMEAN GAMES, a wreath of green parsley, and in the

ISTHMIAN GAMES, a wreath of dry parsley or green pine leaves.

The ancients held that laurel communicated the spirit of prophecy and poetry, hence the custom of crowning the Pythoness (the PYTHIA) and poets, and of putting laurel leaves under one's pillow to acquire inspiration. Another superstition was that the bay laurel (*see* DAPHNE) was antagonistic to the stroke of lightning; but Sir Thomas Browne, in his *Vulgar Errors*, tells us that Vicomereatus proves from personal knowledge that this is untrue.

The Laurel in modern times is a symbol of victory and peace, and of excellence in literature and the arts. St. Gudule (patron saint of Brussels), in Christian art, carries a laurel crown. *See also* APOLLO.

**To look to one's laurels.** To have to try to maintain the lead in any field in which one has already excelled.

**To rest on one's laurels.** To be satisfied with the degree of success one has already achieved and to refrain from further effort.

**Laurin.** The dwarf-king in the German folk-legend *Laurin*, or *Der Kleine Rosengarten*. He possesses a magic ring, girdle and cap, and is attacked by Dietrich of Bern in his rose-garden, which no one may enter on pain of death. The poem belongs to the late 13th century and is attributed to Heinrich von Ofterdingen.

**Lavinia.** *See* LATINUS.

**Lavolta** (Ital. the turn). A lively dance, in which was a good deal of jumping or capering, whence its name. Troilus says: 'I cannot sing, nor heel the high lavolt' (Shakespeare, *Troilus and Cressida*, IV, iv). It originated in 16th-century Provence or Italy, and is thus described:

A lofty jumping or a leaping round,
Where arm in arm two dancers are entwined,
And whirl themselves with strict embracements bound.
And still their feet an anapest do sound.
SIR JOHN DAVIES: *The Orchestra* (1594).

**Lawnmarket.** The higher end of High Street, Edinburgh, once a place for executions; hence, **to go up the Lawnmarket** is to go to be hanged.

They [the stolen clothes] may serve him to gang up the Lawn-market in, the scoundrel.
SCOTT: *Guy Mannering*, ch. xxxii.

**Lawrence, St.** (of Rome). The patron saint of curriers, who was roasted on a grid-iron. He was archdeacon to Pope (St.) Sixtus II and was charged with the care of the poor, the orphans and the widows. When summoned by the praetor to deliver up the treasures of the church, he produced the poor etc., under his charge, and said, 'These are the church's treasures.' His day is 10 August. Fragments of his relics were taken to the Escorial.

The phrase **Lazy as Lawrence** is said to originate from the story that when being roasted over a slow fire he asked to be turned. 'For', said he, 'that side is quite done.' This expression of Christian fortitude was interpreted by his torturers as evidence of the height of laziness, the martyr being too indolent to wriggle.

'Flo and I have got a new name for you; it's "Lazy Laurence." How do you like it?'
LOUISA M. ALCOTT: *Good Wives*, ch. xxxix.

**St. Laurence's tears** or **The fiery tears of St. Laurence.** *See* SHOOTING STARS.

**Lazy. Lazy as Ludlam's dog,** which leaned his head against the wall to bark. Ludlam was reputed to be a sorceress who lived in a cave near Farnham, Surrey. Her dog was so lazy that when the rustics came to consult her it would hardly condescend to announce their approach, even with the ghost of a bark (Ray: *Proverbs*).

**Lead. The Leads.** The famous prison in Venice in which CASANOVA was incarcerated and from which he escaped.

**Leader. Bear-leader.** *See under* BEAR.

**Leal. Land o' the leal.** *See* LAND.

**Leander.** *See* HERO AND LEANDER.

**Lear, King.** A legendary king of Britain whose story is told by Shakespeare. His immediate source was Holinshed, who in turn derived it from Geoffrey of Monmouth's *Historia Regum Britanniae*. It is also given in the *Gesta Romanorum* and in PERCEFOREST. Spenser uses it in his *Faerie Queene* (ii, x) and Camden tells a similar story of Ina, King of the West Saxons. According to Shakespeare's version, King Lear in his old age divided his kingdom between his daughters Goneril and Regan, who professed great love for him but then harassed him into madness. Cordelia, left portionless, succoured him and came with an army to dethrone her sisters, but was captured and slain. King Lear died over her body. *See* LIR.

**Leather. Nothing like leather.** The story is that a town in danger of a siege called together a council of the chief inhabitants to know what defence they recommended. A mason suggested a strong wall, a shipbuilder advised 'wooden walls', and when others had spoken, a currier arose and said, 'There's nothing like leather.'

Another version is, 'Nothing like leather to administer a thrashing.'

**Leda** (lē'də). In Greek mythology, the wife of Tyndarus. JUPITER came to her in the guise of a swan when she was bathing, and in due time she brought forth two eggs, from one of which came CASTOR and CLYTEMNESTRA, and from the other POLLUX and HELEN. The two former are usually held to be the children of Tyndarus.

**Leek.** The national emblem of Wales. (*Cp.* DAFFODIL.) The story is that St. DAVID, on one occasion, caused his countrymen under King Cadwaladr to distinguish themselves from their Saxon foes by wearing a leek in their caps.

Shakespeare makes out that the Welsh wore leeks at the battle of Poitiers, for Fluellen says:

> If your majesties is remembered of it, the Welshmen did goot service in a garden where leeks did grow, wearing leeks in their Monmouth caps; which, your majesty knows, to this hour is an honourable padge of the service; and I do believe your majesty takes no scorn to wear the leek upon Saint Tavy's Day.
> *Henry V*, IV, vii.

**To eat the leek.** To be forced to eat your own words, or retract what you have said. Fluellen (in Shakespeare's *Henry V*, V, i) is taunted by Pistol for wearing a leek in his hat. 'Hence,' says Pistol, 'I am qualmish at the smell of leek.' Fluellen replies 'I peseech you...at my desires...to eat...this leek.' The ancient answers, 'Not for Cadwallader and all his goats.' Then the peppery Welshman beats him, nor desists till Pistol has swallowed the entire abhorrence.

**Legend** (Lat. *legenda*; from *legere*, to read). Literally and originally 'something to be read'; hence the narratives of saints and martyrs were so termed from their being read, especially at Matins, and after dinner in monastic refectories. Exaggeration and a love for the wonderful so predominated in these readings, that the word came to signify a traditional story, a fable, a myth.

In numismatics the legend is the inscription impressed in letters on the edge or rim of a coin or medal and often used synonymously with *inscription*, which is strictly the words in the *field* of a coin. The *field* is the whole part of a coin not occupied by the device. Legend is also applied to the title on a map or under a picture.

**Legenda Aurea.** *See* GOLDEN LEGEND.

**Lemnos.** The island were VULCAN fell, when JUPITER flung him out of HEAVEN. Lemnos was mythically celebrated for two massacres. The men were said to have killed all the children of their abducted Athenian consorts, and the Lemnian women to have murdered their husbands; hence **Lemnian actions** signifies barbarous and inhuman actions. The ARGONAUTS were received with great favour by the women of Lemnos and as a result of their short stay the island was repopulated; the queen Hypsipyle became the mother of twins by JASON.

**Lemnian earth.** A kind of bole or clayey earth of reddish colour found in the island of Lemnos, said to cure festering wounds and snake bites. This medical earth was made into blocks and anciently stamped with the head of DIANA and hence called *terra sigillata* ('sealed earth'). It is still used locally, and a ceremonial digging of this earth took place on a particular day under the supervision of a priestess. The ceremony eventually became fixed on 6 August, the feast of Christ the Saviour in the Greek Church.

**Lemures** (lem'ūrēz). The name given by the Romans to evil spirits of the dead, especially spectres which wandered about at night-time to terrify the living. *Cp.* LARVAE.

> The lars and lemures moan with midnight plaint.
> MILTON: *On the Morning of the Christ's Nativity* (*The Hymn* xxi).

**Lemuria** (limū'riə). The lost land that is supposed to have connected Madagascar with India and Sumatra in prehistoric times. The German biologist E. H. Haeckel (1834–1919) thought that it was the original habitat of the lemur. *See* W. Scott Elliott's *The Lost Lemuria* (1904). *Cp.* ATLANTIS; LYONESSE.

**Leo.** A constellation, and fifth sign of the ZODIAC.

**Leopard.** So called because it was thought in mediaeval times to be a cross between the lion (*leo*) and the *pard*, which was the name given to a panther that had no white specks on it.

In Egypt the leopard was an attribute of OSIRIS and priests were often depicted wearing leopard skins. In Greek mythology the animal is the traditional mount of Dionysus and leopards draw his chariot and act as playmates.

The Old Testament uses the leopard as representing extreme ferocity, in contrast to the gentle kid, when 'the leopard shall lie down with the kid', symbolizing the coming millenium (*Isaiah* xi, 6). The well-known saying 'can the leopard change his spots?' occurs in *Jeremiah* xiii, 23.

The leopard's fierceness appears also in Chinese myth where it represents all that is warlike and fearless.

In Africa the leopard is a widely-distributed cult and totem animal. It is an attribute of the storm god and, as in Egypt, priests are seen wearing leopard skins. The animal is sacred to the royal family in Dahomey and among the Ibo it is particularly revered and is associated with fertility. In many tribes it can embody spirits of the dead and be the vehicle of a chief. If sighted, the animal must not be named and the flesh must never be eaten as the leopard helped the ancestors.

The leopard is also the Lybbard of heraldry and represents warriors, bravery or some bold achievement.

In Christian art, the leopard represents that beast spoken of in *Revelation* xiii, 1–8, with seven heads and ten horns; six of the heads bear a nimbus, but the seventh, being 'wounded to death', lost its power, and consequently is bare.

> And the beast which I saw was like unto a leopard, and his feet were as the feet of a bear, and his mouth as the mouth of a lion.
> *Rev.* xiii, 2.

The leopard's head, or King's Mark, on silver is really a lion's head. It is called a leopard, because the O.Fr. heraldic term *leopard* means a lion passant gardant. *See also* THE LION IN HERALDRY *under* LION.

**Leprechaun** (lep'rəkawn). The fairy shoemaker of Ireland, so called because he is always seen working at a single shoe (*leith*, half; *brog*, a shoe or brogue). Another of his peculiarities is that he has a purse that never contains more than a single shilling.

> Do you not catch the tiny clamour,
> Busy click of an elfin hammer,
> Voice of the Leprecaun singing shrill,
> As he merrily plies his trade.
> WM. ALLINGHAM: *The Leprecaun; or Fairy Shoemaker.*

He is also called lubrican, CLURICAUNE etc. In Dekker and Middleton's *Honest Whore* (Pt. II, III, i), Hippolito speaks of Bryan, the Irish footman, as 'your Irish lubrican'.

**Lernaean Hydra** (lœnē'ən). *See* HYDRA.

**Lesbian.** Pertaining to Lesbos, one of the islands of the Greek Archipelago, or to SAPPHO, the famous poetess of Lesbos, and the homosexual practices attributed to her.
**The Lesbian Poets.** Terpander, Alcaeus, Arion and SAPPHO, all of whom came from Lesbos.

**Lestrigons,** or **Laestrygones.** A fabulous race of cannibal giants who lived in Sicily. ULYSSES (*Odyss.*, X) sent two sailors and a messenger to request that he might land, but the king of the place ate one for dinner and the other fled. The Lestrigons gathered on the coast and threw stones at Ulysses and his crew; they departed with all speed, but many men were lost. *Cp.* POLYPHEMUS.

**Lethe** (lē'thi). In Greek mythology, one of the rivers of HADES, which the souls of all the dead are obliged to taste, that they may forget everything said and done when alive. The word means 'forgetfulness'.

> Here, in a dusky vale where Lethe rolls
> Old Bavius sits, to dip poetic souls,
> And blunt the sense.
> POPE: *Dunciad*, III, 23.

**Letter. Letter of Bellerophon.** *See* BELLEROPHON.
**Letters of Junius.** *See* JUNIUS.

**Leucothea** (lūkōthē'ə) (The White Goddess). So Ino, the mortal daughter of CADMUS and wife of Athamas, was called after she became a sea goddess. Athamas in a fit of madness slew one of her sons;

she threw herself into the sea with the other, imploring assistance of the gods, who deified both of them. Her son, then re-named PALAEMON, was called by the Romans Portunus or Portumnus, and became the protecting genius of harbours.

**Leviathan** (livī'əthən). The Hebrew name for a monster of the waters. In *Job* xli, 1, and *Ps.* lxxiv, 14, it appears to refer to the crocodile; in *Ps.* civ, 26, it is probably the whale; and in *Is.* xxvii, 1, it is a sea-serpent.

> This great and wide sea, wherein are things creep-ing innumerable, both small and great beasts. There go the ships: there is that leviathan, whom thou hast made to play therein.
> *Ps.* civ, 25–26.

Hence the name is applied to any huge sea-animal or ship of great size.

> Like leviathans afloat,
> Lay their bulwarks on the brine.
> T. CAMPBELL: *The Battle of the Baltic.*

It also appears as the Islamic Nun.

Hobbes took the name as the title for his famous treatise on 'the Matter, Forme and Power of a Commonwealth Ecclesiastical and Civil' (1651) from the Scriptures as he also did for his BEHEMOTH. His *Leviathan* is the absolute state.

> I have set forth the nature of man (whose Pride and other Passions have compelled him to sub-mit himselfe to Government;) together with the great power of his Governour, whom I compared to Leviathan, taking that comparison out of the two last verses of the one and fortieth of Job; where God having set forth the great power of Leviathan, called him King of the Proud.
> *Leviathan*: Pt. II, ch. xxviii.

**Levitation** is a term applied to the phenomenon of heavy bodies rising and floating in the air. It is frequently mentioned in Hindu and other writings, and is a not un-common attribute of Roman Catholic saints. Joseph of Cupertino (1603–1663) was the subject of such frequent levitation that he was forbidden by his superiors to attend choir, and performed his devotions privately where he would not distract others. D. D. Home was alleged by Sir W. Crookes to have this power. Science has not yet found an explanation.

**Libitina** (libitī'nə). In ancient Italy, the goddess who presided over funerals, her name often being a synonym for death

itself. The Romans identified her with PROSERPINA.

**Libra** (Lat., the balance). The seventh sign of the ZODIAC and the name of one of the ancient constellations, which the SUN enters about 22 September and leaves about 22 October. At this time the day and night being 'weighed' would be found equal.

**Lich-wake,** or **Lyke-wake.** The funeral feast or the *waking* of a corpse, *i.e.* watch-ing it all night.

In a pastoral written by Aelfric in 998 for Wilfsige, Bishop of Sherborne, the attendance of the clergy at lyke-wakes is forbidden.
**Lich-way.** The path by which a funeral is conveyed to church, which not infrequently deviates from the ordinary road. It was long supposed that wherever a dead body passed became a public thoroughfare.

**Lick. To lick into shape.** To make present-able; to bring children up well etc. Derived from the widespread mediaeval belief that bear cubs are born shapeless and have to be licked into shape by their mothers. The story gained currency apparently from the Arab physician Avicenna (979–1037) who tells it in his encyclopaedia.

**Lie. The greatest lie.** In Heywood's *Four P's*, an interlude (*c.* 1544), a Palmer, a Pardoner, a Poticary and a Pedlar disputed as to which could tell the greatest lie. The Palmer said he had never seen a woman out of patience; whereupon the other three threw up the sponge, saying such falsehood could not possibly be outdone.

**Lie** (O.E. *licgan*, to bide or rest).
**To lie at the catch.** In Bunyan's *Pilgrim's Progress* (ch. xii), Talkative says to Faithful, 'You lie at the catch, I perceive.' To which Faithful replies, 'No, not I; I am only for setting things right.' To lie at or on the catch is to lie in wait or to lay a trap to catch one.

**Lightning preservers.** The EAGLE, the sea-calf and the LAUREL were the most approved classical preservatives against lightning. JUPITER chose the first, Augustus Caesar the second, and Tiberius the third (Columella, x; Suetonius in *Vit. Aug.*, xc; ditto in *Vit. Tib.*, lxix). *Cp.* HOUSE-LEEK.

**Lilith.** A night monster and VAMPIRE, probably of Babylonian origin, supposed to haunt wildernesses in stormy weather, and to be especially dangerous to children. The name is from a Semitic root meaning 'night' which was the special time of this demon's activities. In Rabbinical writings, she is supposed to have been the first wife of ADAM. *See* THE DEVIL AND HIS DAM *under* DEVIL. She is referred to in *Is.* xxxiv, 14, as the 'screech-owl' in the Authorized Version; in the Revised Version as the 'night-monster', and in the Vulgate as LAMIA. A superstitious cult of Lilith persisted among certain Jews until the 7th century. Goethe introduced her in his *Faust,* and Rossetti in his *Eden Bower* made the serpent the instrument of Lilith's vengeance—

'Help, sweet snake, sweet lover of Lilith!
(Alas the hour!)
And let God learn how I loved and hated
Men in the image of God created.'

**Lilliput.** The land of pygmies or Lilliputians (Swift: *Gulliver's Travels*).

**Lily. Lily of France.** The device of Clovis was three black toads, but the story goes that an aged hermit of Joye-en-valle saw a miraculous light stream into his cell one night and an ANGEL appeared to him holding an azure shield of wonderful beauty, emblazoned with three gold lilies that shone like stars. This he was commanded to give to Queen Clothilde, who gave it to her husband, and his arms were everywhere victorious. The device thereupon became the emblem of France (*see Les Petits Bollandistes,* Vol. VI).
**Lily-livered.** *See* LIVER.

**Limbo** (Lat. *limbus,* border, fringe, edge). The borders of HELL; that portion assigned by the schoolmen to those departed spirits to whom the benefits of redemption did not apply through no fault of their own.
**The Limbo of Children** (Lat. *limbus infantium*). The limbo for children who die before baptism or before they are responsible for their actions.
**Limbo of the Fathers** (Lat. *limbus patrum*). The half-way house between earth and HEAVEN, where the Patriarchs and prophets who died before Christ's crucifixion await the last day, when they will be received into HEAVEN. Some hold that this is the 'HELL' into which Christ

descended after He gave up the ghost on the cross.

Shakespeare (*Henry VIII,* V, iv) uses *limbo patrum* for 'QUOD', jail, confinement.

I have some of 'em in Limbo Patrum, and there they are like to dance these three days.

**The Limbus of Fools,** or **Limbus Fatuorum,** or **Paradise of Fools.** As fools or idiots are not responsible for their works, the schoolmen held that they were not punished in Purgatory and could not be received into HEAVEN, so they were destined to go to a special 'Paradise of Fools' (*cp.* FOOL'S PARADISE *under* FOOL).

Then might you see
Cowls, hoods, habits, with their wearers tossed
And fluttered into rags; then relics, beads,
Indulgences, dispenses, pardons, bulls,
The sport of winds. All these, upwhirled aloft,
Fly o'er the backside of the world far-off,
Into a Limbo large and broad, since called
The Paradise of Fools
MILTON: *Paradise Lost,* III, 498.

**Lincoln Imp.** A grotesque carving having weird and prominent ears and nursing the right leg crossed over the left, in the ANGEL choir of Lincoln Cathedral. He is said to have been turned to stone by the angels for misbehaving in the Angel Choir. The Imp is now the county emblem.

**Lindabrides** (lindəbrī'dēz). A heroine in *The Mirror of Knighthood,* whose name at one time was a synonym for a kept mistress or courtesan.

'Well—I have my Master Tressilian's head under my belt by this lucky discovery, that is one thing certain; and I will try to get a sight of this Lindabrides of his, that is another.'
SCOTT: *Kenilworth,* ch. xxviii.

**Line. Crossing the line.** Sailing across the Equator; advantage is usually taken of this for ceremonial practical joking aboard ship. Those who have not previously crossed the line are summoned to the court of NEPTUNE for trial, and are usually ducked by 'bears', sometimes lathered and roughly shaved, given 'soap pills' to swallow etc. As at present practised the whole affair constitutes a good-humoured and amusing interlude, but in former days some of the buffoonery and horse-play was decidedly rough. Such performances have a long history and may have begun as propitiatory rites to the deities of the ocean. At one time similar ceremonies were performed when a ship crossed the thirty-ninth parallel (about the latitude of Lisbon) and also when passing through the Straits of Gibraltar and rounding the Cape of Good Hope.

**Line of life.** In palmistry, the crease in the left hand beginning above the web of the thumb, and running towards or up to the wrist. The nearer it approaches the wrist, the longer will be the life, according to palmists. If long and deeply marked, it indicates long life with very little trouble; if crossed or cut with other marks, it indicates sickness.

**Linne, The Heir of.** The hero of an old ballad given in Percy's *Reliques,* which tells how he wasted his substance in riotous living, and, having spent all, sold his estates to his steward, keeping only a poor lodge. When no one would lend him more money he tried to hang himself but fell to the ground instead. When he came to he espied two chests full of beaten gold, and a third full of white money, over which was written:

Once more, my sonne, I sette thee clere;
Amend thy life and follies past;
For but thou amend thee of thy life,
That rope must be thy end at last.

He now returned to his old hall, where he was refused the loan of forty pence by his quondam steward; one of the guests remarked to the steward that he ought to have lent it, as he had bought the estate cheap enough. 'Cheap call you it?' said the steward, 'why, he shall have it back for 100 marks less.' 'Done,' said the heir of Linne, and recovered his estates.

**Lion. The Lion in Story and Legend.**

CYBELE is represented as riding in a chariot drawn by two lions.

Hippomenes and ATALANTA (fond lovers) were metamorphosed into lions by Cybele.

HERCULES is sometimes represented clad in the skin of the NEMEAN LION.

In Roman funerary art the lion depicts the devouring power of death but also its conquest. Lions drew the chariots of JUNO and Cybele. In Mithraism the lion was the fourth grade of initiation.

In western cultures the lion is the King of Beasts and represents the solar power and the fiery principle and sun gods, but the lioness is associated with the lunar Great Mother goddesses, drawing their chariots and supporting their thrones or being the mount of the goddess. These goddesses were worshipped in widespread regions from the Mediterranean to Africa, the Middle East, Sumeria, India and on to Tibet where the lioness was an attribute of TARA.

Lions were both hunted and used in hunting; they were also pre-eminently guardians. Plutarch says 'the lion was worshipped by the Egyptians who ornamented their doors with the gaping mouth of that animal because the Nile began to rise when the sun was in LEO', while Aelian says that lions were kept at temples at Heliopolis and that temples were dedicated to them. Horapollo says that the lion figures both protected the temples and represented the inundation. In the 3rd century B.C. lions appeared in a procession in honour of Dionysus. A lion guarded the tunnel through which the sun god RA passed at night.

Hinduism has the lion as the fourth avatar of VISHNU and it represents Durga as destroyer of demons and is an attribute of Devi. The lion and lioness together depict the *shakta-shakti.* In Buddhism the lion is the Defender of the Law; and the Buddha, who was called the Lion of the Shakya clan, is sometimes seated on the lion throne. The lion's roar is his fearless teaching of the Dharma.

The Chinese Immortal Chiu-shou was a lion which took human shape and fought in wars; when ordered to resume his lion form he became the mount of the Buddha Wen Shu. Stone lions guarded the courts of justice; they came to life at night and roamed about.

The lion figures prominently in the Old Testament, as in the myths of David and Goliath and Samson. The winged lion represents the Lion of Judah. The lion died out in Palestine at the time of the Crusades.

Christianity uses the lion as both Christ and the Devil. The Devil is 'a roaring lion ... seeking whom he may devour' and Christ rescues the faithful from its mouth, but the animal also depicts Christ's kingly nature and power; this aspect is represented by the lion of St. Mark who stresses the royalty and majesty of Christ.

There were strange myths associated with the lion. It was said that the cubs were born dead and that after three days the sire breathed life into them, or that the dam howled over them and they came to life. It was also stated that the animal slept with its eyes open and that when moving it destroyed its tracks with its tail. The Bestiaries used these legends in moralizing and associating them with Christ as reviver of the dead; the watchfulness over the faithful and Christ yielding his godhead when he came to earth.

The story of ANDROCLES and the lion has many parallels, the most famous of which are those related of St. JEROME and St. Gerasimus:

While St. Jerome was lecturing one day, a lion entered the schoolroom, and lifted up one of its paws. All his disciples fled; but Jerome, seeing that the paw was wounded, drew a thorn out if it and dressed the wound. The lion, out of gratitude, showed a wish to stay with its benefactor, hence the SAINT is represented as accompanied by a lion.

St. Gerasimus, says the story, saw on the banks of the Jordan a lion coming to him limping on three feet. When it reached the saint it held up to him the right paw, from which St. Gerasimus extracted a large thorn. The grateful beast attached itself to the saint, and followed him about as a dog.

Similar tales are told by the Bollandists in the *Acta Sanctorum*; and in more recent times a story was told of Sir George Davis, an English consul at Florence at the beginning of the 19th century, when he went to see the Duke of Tuscany's lions. There was one that the keepers could not tame; but no sooner did Sir George appear than it showed every symptom of joy. He entered its cage, and the lion licked his face and wagged its tail. Sir George told the duke that he had brought up the creature, but had sold it when it became older and more dangerous.

Sir Iwain de Galles, a hero of romance, was attended by a lion which he had delivered from the attacks of a serpent.

Sir Geoffrey de Latour was aided by a lion against the Saracens, but it was drowned on attempting to board the vessel which was carrying Sir Geoffrey away from the Holy Land.

**Lions in Public-house Signs.** *See* PUBLIC-HOUSE SIGNS.

**Lion's share.** The larger part: all or nearly all. In *Aesop's Fables*, several beasts joined the lion in a hunt; but, when the spoil was divided, the lion claimed one quarter in right of his prerogative, one for his superior courage, one for his dam and cubs, 'and as

for the fourth, let who will dispute it with me'. Awed by his frown, the other beasts silently withdrew.

**Lir, King.** The earliest known original of the king in Shakespeare's *King Lear*, an ocean god of early Irish and British legend. He figures in the romance *The Fate of the Children of Lir* as the father of FIONNUALA. On the death of Fingula, the mother of his daughter, he married the wicked Aoife, who, through spite, transformed the children of Lir into swans.

Lir appears in the MABINOGION as *Llyr* and Geoffrey of Monmouth's *Historia Regum Britanniae* as *Leir*, the founder of Leicester, from which later source Shakespeare derived his plot. *See* LEAR, KING.

**Little. Little-endians.** *See* BIG-ENDIANS *under* BIG.
**Little Jack Horner.** *See* JACK HORNER *under* JACK.
**Little John.** A character in the ROBIN HOOD cycle, a big stalwart man whose surname was also said to be Nailor. On his first encounter with Robin Hood he 'tumbl'd him into the brook' and the outlaws changed the victor's name from John Little to 'Little John'.

> He was, I must tell you, but seven foot high,
> And, maybe, an ell in the waste;
> A sweet pretty lad; much feasting they had;
> Bold Robin the christ'ning grac'd.
>> *Robin Hood and Little John* (given in RITSON'S *Robin Hood*).

**Little People.** Fairies (*see* FAIRY).
**Little Red Ridinghood.** This nursery story is also common to Sweden, Germany and France. It comes from the French *Le Petit Chaperon Rouge*, in Charles Perrault's *Contes des Temps*, and was probably derived from Italy. The finale, which tells of the arrival of a huntsman who slits open the wolf and restores Little Red Ridinghood and her grandmother to life, is a German addition.

**Liver.** In the AUSPICES taken by the Greeks and Romans before battle, if the liver of the animals sacrificed was healthy and blood-red, the OMEN was favourable; but if pale it augured defeat.

The liver was anciently supposed to be the seat of love; hence in Shakespeare's *Love's Labour's Lost* (IV, iii), when Longaville reads the verses, Biron says in an aside. 'This is the liver-vein, which makes flesh a deity.' In the *Merry Wives of Windsor* (II, i) Pistol speaks of Falstaff as loving Ford's wife 'with liver burning hot'.

Another superstition was that the liver of a coward contained no blood; hence such expressions as **white-livered, lily-livered, pigeon-livered,** and Sir Toby's remark in Shakespeare's *Twelfth Night* (III, ii):

> For Andrew, if he were opened, and you find so much blood in his liver as will clog the foot of a flea, I'll eat the rest of the anatomy.

**Lizard.** Ancient legend said that the lizard was tongueless and so depicted silence and the Romans believed that it slept all winter and reappeared in spring, thus typifying death and rebirth, and as such was portrayed with sleeping cupids in Roman art and in funerary art. It also appears with other apotropaic creatures on the Votive Hand of Sabazius. Egyptian and Greek myth represented the lizard as wisdom and good fortune; it was an emblem of HERMES and Serapis.

In Amerindian lore the lizard is one of the manifestations of the Amazonian tribe's Master of Animals and Fish and is a messenger of the god who told men they were mortal. Among the desert tribes the lizard can be a form of the Spirit, or Master, of the species and is a totem creature. It appears also as a totem in Africa but can also have a sinister aspect as used in 'evil medicine' and can transform itself into a HYENA, LEOPARD or LION.

The lizard is important in Polynesian mythology where its cult is widespread. Moko, the King of Lizards, is generally held as a god in his own right and protects fishing. Hawaii has lizard gods who are revered as animal ancestors and tutelary deities and in Tahiti a temple was dedicated to such a divinity who was represented by a stone figure of a lizard. Lizards can be guardians of the soul in the body. In Maori myth it was the lizard who drew the first of the race from the waters of creation. There is also a lizard culture hero among the Australian Aboriginals; he first separated the sexes and taught the people arts.

European myth generally holds the lizard as sinister. It was supposed at one time, to be venomous, hence a 'lizard's leg' was an ingredient of the witches' cauldron in Shakespeare's *Macbeth*.

> Poison be their drink!...
> Their chiefest prospect murd'ring basilisks!
> Their softest touch as smart as lizard's stings!
> SHAKESPEARE: *Henry VI, Pt. II,* III, ii

**Lliannan-She** (lēan'ən-shē). In the Isle of Man, a spirit friend, a female FAIRY who waited to encounter men. If one spoke to her she followed him always, but remained invisible to everyone else.

**Loamshire.** An imaginary county of southern England used as a setting by writers of fiction to avoid identification with actual towns and villages. Hence the *Loamshires* as an equally fictitious regiment of the line. **Loamshire dialect.** Said of a rustic dialogue used by a writer with no real knowledge of the forms of speech peculiar to a given district.

**Loathly Lady.** A stock character of old romance who is so hideous that everyone is deterred from marrying her. When, however, she at last finds a husband her ugliness, the effect of enchantment, disappears, and she becomes a model of beauty. Her story is the feminine counterpart of BEAUTY AND THE BEAST.

**Lobster. Died for want of lobster sauce.** Sometimes said of one who dies or suffers severely because of some trifling disappointment, pique or wounded vanity. At a grand feast given by the great Condé to Louis XIV at Chantilly, Vatel, the chef, was told that the lobsters intended for sauce had not arrived, whereupon he retired to his room and ran his sword through his body, unable to survive the disgrace thus brought upon him.

**Loch Ness Monster.** In April 1933, a motorist driving along the shore of Loch Ness, Scotland, saw a strange object at some distance out, subsequently described as being 30 ft. long with two humps, a snake-like head at the end of a long neck, and two flippers about the middle of the body. It was 'seen' by others and much featured by the newspapers. Investigations showed no substantial evidence of the existence of the supposed prehistoric monster but more recent observations have increased the belief in its presence.

**Lockhart.** Legend has it that the good Lord James, on his way to the Holy Land with the heart of the King Robert Bruce, was killed in Spain fighting against the Moors. Sir Simon Locard of Lee was commissioned to carry the heart back to Scotland and it was interred in Melrose Abbey. In consequence he changed his name to *Lockheart*, and adopted the device of *a heart within a fetterlock*, with the motto *Corda serrata pando* (Locked hearts I open).

**Locrin** (lō'krin). Father of SABRINA, and eldest son of the mythical BRUTUS, King of Britain. On the death of his father he became King of Loegria (Geoffrey of Monmouth: *Historia Regum Britanniae*, ch. I-V).

An anonymous tragedy, based on Holinshed and Geoffrey of Monmouth, called *Locrine* was published in 1595 bearing Shakespeare's initials (W.S.). This tragedy contains borrowings from Spenser, and Marlowe has also been suggested as its author. It is almost certainly not by Shakespeare.

**Locusta.** A woman who murders those she professes to nurse, or those whom it is her duty to take care of. Locusta lived in the early days of the Roman Empire, poisoned Claudius and Britannicus, and attempted to destroy Nero. Being found out, she was put to death.

**Lodona.** The Loddon, a tributary entering the Thames at Shiplake. Pope, in *Windsor Forest*, says it was a NYMPH, fond of the chase, like DIANA. It chanced one day that PAN saw her, and tried to catch her; but Lodona fled from him, imploring CYNTHIA to save her. No sooner had she spoken that she became 'a silver stream' which 'virgin coldness keeps'.

**Log. A King Log.** A king who rules in peace and quietness, but never makes his power felt. In allusion to the FABLE of *The Frogs desiring a King*: JUPITER first threw them down a log of wood, but they grumbled at so spiritless a King. He then sent them a stork, which devoured them eagerly. *See* KING STORK *under* STORK.

**Logan Stones** (lō'gən). Rocking stones; large masses of stone so delicately poised by nature that they will rock to and fro at a touch. There are many such, especially in Cornwall, Derbyshire, Yorkshire and Wales; also in Scotland and Ireland.

The famous Logan Rock (about 70 tons) at Land's End was displaced by Lieutenant Goldsmith, R.N. (nephew of the poet Oliver Goldsmith) and his boat's crew in 1824. It cost him over £2000 to get it replaced.

Pliny tells of a rock near Harpasa which might be moved with a finger.

Ptolemy says the Gygonian rock might be stirred with a stalk of ASPHODEL.

Half a mile from St. David's is a Logan stone, mounted on divers other stones, which may be shaken with one finger.

**Logris** (lō'gris). Same as LOCRIN.

**Lohengrin** (lō'əngrin). A son of PERCIVAL in the German legend of the Knight of the Swan and attached to the GRAIL cycle. In France it was used to enhance the family of Godfrey of Bouillon. He appears at the close of Wolfram von Eschenbach's *Parzival* (*c.* 1210), and in other German romances, where he is the deliverer of Elsa, Princess of Brabant, who has been dispossessed by Tetramund and Ortrud. He arrives at Antwerp in a skiff drawn by a swan, champions Elsa, and becomes her husband on the sole condition that she shall not ask him his name or lineage. She is prevailed upon to do so on the marriage night, and he, by his vows to the Grail, is obliged to disclose his identity, but at the same time disappears. The swan returns for him, and he goes; but not before retransforming the swan into Elsa's brother Gottfried, who, by the wiles of the sorceress Ortrud, had been obliged to assume that form. Wagner's opera of this name was first produced in 1850.

**Loki** (lō'ki). The god of strife and spirit of evil in Norse mythology, son of the GIANT Farbauti and Laufey, and father of the MIDGARD snake, HEL, and FENRIR. It was he who artfully contrived the death of BALDER. He was finally chained to a rock and, according to one legend, there to remain until the Twilight of the Gods, when he will break his bonds; the heavens will disappear, the earth be swallowed up by the sea, fire shall consume the elements, and even ODIN, with all his kindred deities, shall perish. Another story has it that he was freed at RAGNAROK, and that he and HEIMDALL fought till both were slain.

**Long. Long Meg and her daughters.** In the neighbourhood of Penrith, Cumbria is a prehistoric circle of 64 stones, some of them 10 ft. high. Some 17 paces off, on the south side, is a single stone, 15 ft. high, called *Long Meg*, the shorter ones being called *her daughters*.

**Longchamps** (longshā). The racecourse at the end of the Bois de Boulogne, Paris. An abbey formerly stood there, and it was long celebrated for the parade of smartly dressed Parisians which took place on the Wednesday, Thursday and Friday of Holy Week.

The custom dates from the time when all who could do so went to the abbey to hear the Tenebrae sung in Holy Week; and it survives as an excellent opportunity to display the latest spring fashions.

**Longtail, Cut and Longtail.** One and another, all of every description. The phrase had its origin in the practice of cutting the tails of certain dogs and horses, and leaving others in their natural state, so that the cut and long-tail horses or dogs included all the species. Master Slender in Shakespeare's *Merry Wives of Windsor* (III, iv) says he will maintain Anne Page like a gentlewoman. 'Ay!' says he. 'That I will, come cut and long tail under the degree of a squire' [*i.e.* as well as anyone below the rank of squire].

**How about the long-tailed beggar?** A reproof to one who is drawing the longbow too freely. The tale is that a boy on returning from a short voyage pretended to have forgotten everything belonging to his home and asked his mother what she called that 'long-tailed beggar', meaning the cat.

**Longevity.** Among the traditional stock cases of longevity are Harry Jenkins, who is reputed to have lived 169 years; Thomas Parr, who died at the age of 152; Catherine, Countess of Desmond, who died at the age of 140; and Thomas Carn of Shoreditch, listed by Dr. Brewer as living 207 years and in the reign of ten sovereigns. Carn's actual dates were 1471 to 1578 (107 years), a figure '2' having been superimposed over a '1' on his tombstone.

It must be noted that all these cases belong to the days before the Registration Act of 1836 ensured a really efficient system of recording births, marriages and deaths.

The longest authenticated life in the United Kingdom is that of Ada Roe (née Giddings, 1858–1970), who lived 111 years 339 days. The French Canadian, Pierre Joubert (1701–1814), has been proved to have lived 113 years 124 days.

**Longinus,** or **Longius** (lonjī'nəs). The traditional name of the Roman soldier who smote Our Lord with his spear at the Crucifixion. The only authority for this is the apocryphal *Acts of Pilate*, dating from the 6th century. According to Arthurian Legend, this spear was brought by JOSEPH OF ARIMATHEA to Listenise, when he visited King Pellam, 'who was nigh of Joseph's kin'. Sir Balim the Savage seized this spear, with which he wounded King Pellam and destroyed three whole countries with that one stroke. William of Malmesbury says the spear was used by CHARLEMAGNE against the Saracens.

**Look. It is unlucky to break a looking-glass.** The nature of the ill-luck varies; thus, if a maiden, she will never marry; if a married woman, it betokens death etc. This superstition arose from the use made of mirrors in former times by magicians etc. If in their operations the mirror used was broken, the unlucky inquirer could receive no answer.

**Loose. To play fast and loose.** *See under* FAST.

**Lord. The Lord Mayor's Show.** The annual procession which accompanies the Lord Mayor through the City of London to the Royal Courts of Justice on the second Saturday in November. It has developed in scale over the years, and from 1453 until 1856 a river pageant was part of the proceedings. A few days later the **Lord Mayor's Banquet** is held in the Guildhall where it is now customary for the Prime Minister to make a political speech. The bill for the Procession and Banquet is settled by the Lord Mayor and the Sheriffs.

**Lord of the Ascendant.** *See under* ASCENDANT.

**Lord of Misrule.** *See* KING OF MISRULE.

**Lorelei** (law'rəlī). The name of a steep rock, some 430 ft. high, on the right bank of the Rhine opposite St. Goar, noted for its remarkable echo. It is the traditional haunt of a SIREN who lures boatmen to their death. Heine and others have poems on it, and Max Bruch made it the subject of an opera, *Die Lorelei*, produced in 1864. Mendelssohn has an incomplete opera of the same title.

**Lothario. A gay Lothario.** A gay libertine, a seducer of women, a debauchee. The character is from Rowe's tragedy *The Fair Penitent* (1703). He probably got the name from Davenant's *Cruel Brother* (1630) in which there is a similar character with this name.

> Is this that haughty, gallant, gay Lothario?
> *Fair Penitent*, V, i.

**Lothian,** in Scotland, traditionally takes its name from King Lot, or Lothus Llew, the brother-in-law of ARTHUR, and father of MODRED.

**Lots. Casting Lots.** To obtain a decision by casting (or drawing from) a set of objects selected for the purpose was a very old form of DIVINATION and an established practice in WITCHCRAFT. Lots were used in ancient Israel in deciding the division of property, appointing to office, the discovering of culprits etc. (*see Lev.* xvi, 7–10) with the presupposition of divine influence affecting the result.

> The lot is cast into the lap; but the whole disposing thereof is of the Lord.
> *Prov.* xvi, 33.

**Lotus.** A name given to many plants, *e.g.* by the Egyptians to various species of water-lily, by the Hindus and Chinese to the Nelumbo (a water-bean), their 'sacred lotus', and by the Greeks to *Zizyphus lotus*, a North African shrub of the order *Rhamnaceae*, the fruit of which was used for food.

The lotus appears with Egyptian and Hindu sun gods, but also with Semitic moon gods and with lunar Great Mother goddesses. It was the flower of the waters 'wherein existence comes to be and passes away'. In Phoenician, Hittite and Assyrian cultures it also had a funerary significance as death and rebirth and hence resurrection.

The lotus is particularly significant in Buddhism where it is sacred to the Buddha who is manifest as a flame rising from the lotus, the 'Jewel in the Lotus'; he is depicted enthroned on a lotus and the full bloom also represents the Round of

Existence and is an attribute of KWAN-YIN, Amitabha and the Matreya Buddha, also of the White TARA.

In Egypt the lotus was an emblem of the Upper Nile with the papyrus as the Lower Nile. HORUS was 'he of the lotus ... a pure lotus, issue of the field of the sun' (*Book of the Dead*). The flower was also an attribute of the lunar ISIS, the Maiden Mother.

The Hindu BRAHMA was born of the lotus and Agni also rises from it; Surya and VISHNU as sun gods have the lotus as an emblem and it also represents the lunar LAKSHMI or Padma. The *chakras* are depicted as lotuses.

The lotus is the Golden Flower of Taoism, representing the heart and spiritual unfolding. It is an emblem of the Immortal Ho Hsien-ku.

According to Mohammed, a lotus-tree stands in the seventh HEAVEN, on the right hand of the throne of God, and the Egyptians pictured the creator springing from the heart of a lotus flower. Iamblichus says the leaves and fruit of the lotus-tree, being round, represent 'the motion of intellect', its towering up through mud symbolizes the eminency of divine intellect over matter; and the Deity sitting on it implies His intellectual sovereignty (*On the Egyptian Mysteries*, sec. vii, cap. ii). It also signifies the world rising from the watery element, with the lotus as the sun emerging from the waters of chaos.

The classic myth is that *Lotis*, a daughter of NEPTUNE fleeing from PRIAPUS was changed into a tree, called *Lotus* after her. Another story is that Dryope of Oechalia and her infant son Amphisus were each changed into a lotus.

**Lotus-eaters,** or **Lotophagi,** in Homeric legend, are a people who ate of the lotus-tree, the effect of which was to make them forget their friends and homes, and to lose all desire of returning to their native country, their only wish being to live in idleness in Lotus-land (*Odyssey*, XI). Hence a *lotus-eater* is one living in ease and luxury. One of Tennyson's greatest poems is *The Lotos-Eaters*.

**Love. The God of Love.** Generally implies either EROS or CUPID. Among the Scandinavians FREYJA was the goddess of sexual love, and among the Hindus Kama is the approximate equivalent of Eros.

**Love's Girdle.** The CESTUS.

**Love Feast.** *See* AGAPE.

**Love-in-idleness.** The heartsease, *Viola tricolor*. Fable has it that it was originally white, but was changed to purple by Cupid.

> Yet marked I where the bolt of Cupid fell.
> It fell upon a little western flower.
> Before, milk-white, now purple with love's wound;
> And maidens call it Love-in-idleness.
>
> SHAKESPEARE: *A Midsummer Night's Dream*, II, i.

**Loving,** or **Grace Cup.** A large cup, tankard or goblet passed round from guest to guest at formal banquets. Agnes Strickland (1786–1874) says that Margaret Atheling, wife of Malcolm Canmore, in order to induce the Scots to remain for grace, devised the grace cup, which was filled with the choicest wine, and of which each guest was allowed to drink *ad libitum*, after grace had been said.

The monks took over the WASSAIL bowl of their heathen predecessors and called it *poculum caritatis*, or the loving-cup. At the Lord Mayor's or City Companies' banquets the loving-cup is a silver bowl with two handles, a napkin being tied to one of them. Two persons stand up, one to drink and the other to defend the drinker. Having taken his draught, the first wipes the cup with the napkin and passes it to his 'defender', when the next person rises up to defend the new drinker, and so on.

At the universities of Oxford and Cambridge, the term Grace Cup is more general. The name is also applied to a strong brew of beer flavoured with lemon-peel, nutmeg and sugar, and very brown toast.

**Loyal. The Loyal Toast.** This time-honoured toast to the King (or the Queen) is normally drunk while standing, but it is the Royal Navy's privilege to drink it sitting. The story is that this custom arose when George IV (or William IV), when acknowledging the toast in a ship, bumped his head on a beam as he stood up. However apocryphal such stories may be, it is probably due to the difficulty of standing upright between decks in the old wooden warships.

**Lubber's Hole.** In sailing ships the open space in the top near the head of a lower mast through which seamen ascend to the top, to avoid the danger and difficulties of climbing over the rim by the futtock shrouds. It was once held only a fit method for timid greenhorns or lubbers. Hence, some way of evading or wriggling through one's difficulties.

**Lubberkin,** or **Lubrican.** *See* LEPRECHAUN.

**Lucian.** The personification of the follies and vices of the age. Such was Lucian, the chief character in the *Golden Ass* of Apuleius (2nd century A.D.).

**Lucifer** (Lat. lightbringer). VENUS, as the morning star. When she follows the SUN, and is an evening star, she is called HESPERUS.

Isaiah applied the epithet 'Daystar' to the King of Babylon who proudly boasted he would ascend to the heavens and make himself equal to God, but who was fated to be cast down to the uttermost recesses of the pit. This epithet was translated into 'Lucifer'—

> Take up this proverb against the king of Babylon and say, ... How art thou fallen from heaven, O Lucifer, son of the morning!
> *Is.* xiv, 4, 12.

By St. Jerome and other Fathers the name was applied to SATAN. Hence poets feign that Satan, before he was driven out of heaven for his pride, was called Lucifer. Milton, in *Paradise Lost* (X, 425), gives this name to the demon of 'Sinful Pride', hence the phrase *Proud as Lucifer*.

**Lucius.** One of the mythical kings of Britain, the son of Coillus, and fabled as the first Christian British King according to Geoffrey of Monmouth.

**Luck. The luck of Eden Hall.** *See* EDEN HALL.

**Lucullus sups with Lucullus** (lookŭl′əs). Said of a glutton who gourmandizes alone. Lucius Lucullus (*c.* 117–56 B.C.) was a successful Roman military leader and administrator whose latter years were given over to rich and elegant living. On one occasion a superb supper was prepared, and when asked who were to be his guests he replied, 'Lucullus will sup tonight with Lucullus.'

He was essentially a man of cultural tastes and more likely a *gourmet* than a gourmand.

**Lucy, St.** Patron SAINT for those afflicted in the eyes. She is supposed to have lived in

Syracuse and to have suffered martyrdom there about 304. One legend relates that a nobleman wanted to marry her for the beauty of her eyes; so she tore them out and gave them to him, saying, 'Now let me live to God.' Hence she is represented in art carrying a palm branch and a platter with two eyes on it.

**Lud.** A mythical king of Britain. According to Geoffrey of Monmouth, the beautifier of London who was buried by the gate which bears his name. It is also suggested that the name is that of a Celtic river god.

**Ludlam.** *See* LAZY.

**Luke. As light as St. Luke's bird.** Not light at all. In art St. Luke is represented with an ox lying near him.

**Lunatics.** Literally, moon-struck persons. The Romans believed that the mind was affected by the moon, and that lunatics grew more and more frenzied as the moon increased to its full (Lat. *luna*, moon).

**Lundi, St.** *See* ST. MONDAY *under* MONDAY.

**Lupercal, The** (loo'pəkal). In ancient Rome the spot where ROMULUS and Remus were suckled by the wolf (*lupus*). An annual festival, the *Lupercalia* was held there on 15 February, in honour of Lupercus the Lycaean PAN (so called because he protected the flocks from wolves). The name *Lupercal* is sometimes, inaccurately, used for the Lupercalia. It was on one of these occasions that Antony thrice offered Julius Caesar the crown, but he refused, saying, 'JUPITER alone is king of Rome.'

> You all did see that on the Lupercal,
> I thrice presented him a kingly crown,
> Which he did thrice refuse.
> SHAKESPEARE: *Julius Caesar*, III, ii

**Lusiads, The.** The Portuguese national epic, written by Camoëns, and published in 1572. It relates the stories of illustrious actions of the *Lusians* or Portuguese, and primarily the exploits of Vasco da Gama and his comrades in their 'discovery of India' (1497–1499). The intervention of VENUS and BACCHUS and other classical deities makes it far more than the narrative of a voyage. It has been said that Camoëns did for the Portuguese language what Dante did for Italian, and Chaucer for English.

**Lustral.** Properly, pertaining to the LUSTRUM; hence purificatory, as *lustral water*, the water used in Christian as well as many pagan rites for aspersing worshippers. In Rome the priest used a small OLIVE or LAUREL branch for sprinkling infants and the people.

**Lustrum.** In ancient Rome the purificatory sacrifice made by the censors for the people once in five years, after the census had been taken (from *luere*, to wash, to purify); hence a period of five years.

**Lutin.** A GOBLIN in the folklore of Normandy; similar to the house-spirits of Germany. The name was formerly *netun*, and is said to be derived from NEPTUNE. When the *lutin* assumes the form of a horse ready equipped, it is called *Le Cheval Bayard. See* BAYARD.
**To lutin.** To twist hair into ELF-LOCKS. These mischievous urchins are said to tangle the mane of a horse or the locks of a child so that the hair must be cut off.

**Luz** (lŭz). The indestructible bone of the human body according to Rabbinical legend; the nucleus of the resurrection body. A bone in the spine and the sacrum (sacred bone) may have been so called in allusion to it.

**Lycanthropy** (līkan'thrəpi). The insanity afflicting one who imagines himself to be some kind of animal and exhibits the tastes, voices etc., of that animal. Formerly, the name given by the ancients to those who imagined themselves to be wolves (Gr. *lukos*, wolf; *anthropos*, man). The WERE-WOLF has sometimes been called a *lycanthrope*; and *lycanthropy* was sometimes applied to the form of witchcraft by which WITCHES transformed themselves into wolves.

**Lycaon** (līkā'on). In classical mythology, a king of ARCADIA, who, desirous of testing the divine knowledge of JOVE, served up human flesh on his table; for which the god changed him into a wolf. His daughter, CALLISTO, was changed into the constellation the Bear, which is sometimes called *Lycaonis Arctos*.

**Lying for the whetstone.** *See* WHETSTONE.

**Lyke-wake.** *See* LICH-WAKE.

**Lynceus** (lin'sūs). One of the ARGONAUTS. He was so sharp-sighted that he could see through the earth, and distinguish objects that were miles off.

> Non possis oculo quantum contendere Lynceus.
> HORACE: I *Epistles*, i, 28.

Also the name of the husband of HYPERMNESTRA. *See* DANAIDES.

**Lynx** (lingks). The animal proverbial for its piercing eyesight is a fabulous beast, half dog and half panther, but not like either in character. The cat-like animal now called a lynx is not remarkable for keen-sightedness. The word is probably related to Gr. *lussein*, to see. *Cp.* LYNCEUS.

**Lyonesse** (līənes'). A rich tract of land fabled to stretch between Land's End and the Scilly Isles on which stood the *City of Lions* and some 140 churches. King ARTHUR came from this mythical country. 'That sweet land of Lyonesse' was, according to Spenser (*Faerie Queene*), the birthplace of TRISTRAM, and, according to Tennyson, the scene of King Arthur's death.

> Of Faery damsels met in forest wide
> By knights of Logres, or of Lyones,

Lancelot, or Pelleas, or Pellenore.
MILTON: *Paradise Regained*, II, 359.

**Lyre.** The most ancient of all stringed instruments. That of Terpander and Olympus had only three strings; the Scythian lyre had five; that of Simonides had eight, and that of Timotheus had twelve. It was played either with the fingers or with a plectrum. The lyre is called by poets a 'shell', because the cords of the lyre used by ORPHEUS, AMPHION and APOLLO were stretched on the shell of a tortoise. HERCULES used box-wood.

*Amphion* built Thebes with the music of his lyre.

*Arion* charmed the dolphins by the music of his lyre, and when the bard threw himself into the sea one of them carried him safely to Taenarus.

*Hercules* was taught music by Linus. One day, being reproved, the strong man broke the head of his master with his own lyre.

*Orpheus* charmed savage beasts, and even the infernal gods, with the music of his lyre. Mountains moved to hear his song and rivers ceased to flow.

# M

**Mab** (perhaps the Welsh *maban*, a baby). The 'fairies' midwife'—*i.e.* employed by the fairies as midwife to deliver man's brain of dreams. Thus when Romeo says, 'I dreamed a dream tonight,' Mercutio replies, 'Oh, then, I see Queen Mab hath been with you.' When Mab is called 'queen' it does not mean sovereign, for TITANIA as wife of King OBERON was Queen of Faery, but simply 'female' (O.E. *quēn* or *cwēn*, modern *quean*).

Excellent descriptions of Mab are given by Shakespeare (*Romeo and Juliet*, I, iv), by Ben Jonson, by Herrick, and by Drayton in *Nymphidea*.

**Mabinogion** (mabinog'iən). A collection of eleven mediaeval Celtic stories of which the Four Branches of the Mabinogi are the most outstanding. Originally they were probably essentially concerned with the life and death of Pryderi, but a considerable amount of additional material has complicated the structure. The tales are basically Welsh mythology and folklore together with ARTHURIAN ROMANCE. The title 'Mabinogion' was given by Lady Charlotte Guest to her translations of these stories (1838–1849); but this only properly applies to the Four Branches (*Pwyll, Branwen, Manawydan* and *Math*) and not the remainder. The last three stories, *The Lady of the Fountain, Peredur* and *Gereint son of Erbin*, show marked Norman-French influence, often attributed to Chrétien de Troyes, but it is now thought that his material may have derived from Welsh sources.

Mabinogi is derived from *mab* (youth) and was applied to a 'tale of youth', then to any 'tale'. Lady Guest's translation long held the field, but the best and most complete English translation is now that of Gwyn Jones and Thomas Jones (1948).

**Macabre,** or **Macaber, The Danse**. *See* DANCE OF DEATH.

**Macaire.** A French CHANSON DE GESTE of the 12th century. Macaire was the name of the murderer of Aubry de Montdidier and he was brought to justice by the sagacity of AUBRY'S DOG (*see under* DOG). The story was transferred to the 14th century in another version and a 15th-century mural painting of the legend in the chateau of Montargis gave rise to Aubry's dog being called the 'dog of Montargis'.

**Robert Macaire.** A typical villain of French comedy; from the play of this name (a sequel to *L'Auberge des Adrets* (1834), by Frédéric Lemaître and Benjamin Antier. Macaire is—

> le type de la perversité, de l'impudence, de la friponnerie audacieuse, le héros fanfaron du vol et de l'assassinat.

**Macdonald. Lord Macdonald's breed.** Parasites. It is said that Lord Macdonald (son of the Lord of the Isles) once made a raid on the mainland. He and his followers replaced their own rags with the smarter clothes stripped off their enemies, with the result of being overrun with parasites.

**Macfarlane's Geese.** The proverb is that, 'MacFarlane's geese like their play better than their meat.' The wild geese of Inch-Tavoe (Loch Lomond) used to be called *Macfarlane's Geese* because the MacFarlanes had a house on the island, and it is said that the geese never returned after the destruction of the house. One day James VI visited the chieftain and was highly amused by the gambols of the geese, but one served at table was so tough that the king exclaimed, 'Macfarlane's geese like their play better than their meat.'

**MacGregor.** The motto of the MacGregors is, 'E'en do and spair nocht,' said to have been given them in the 12th century by a king of Scotland. While the king was hunting, he was attacked by a wild boar and Sir Malcolm asked permission to encounter the creature. 'E'en do,' said the king, 'and spair nocht.' Whereupon the baronet tore up an oak sapling and dispatched the enraged animal. For this the king gave Sir Malcolm permission to use the said motto, and, in place of a Scots fir, to adopt for crest *an oak tree eradicate, proper.*

Another motto of the MacGregors is *Srioghal mo dhream, i.e.* 'Royal is my tribe.'

The MacGregors furnish the only instance of a clan being deprived of its family name. In 1603, as a result of their ruthless ferocity at the battle of Glenfruin against the Colquhouns of Luss, it was proscribed by James VI and the clan assumed the names of neighbouring families such as the Campbells, Buchanans, Grahams, Murrays etc. The laws against them were annulled by Charles II in 1661 but in 1693, under William and Mary, similar measures were enacted against them. These penalties were finally abolished by the British Parliament and John Murray of Lanrick resumed the name MacGregor as chief of the clan in 1822. *See* ROB ROY.

**MacPherson.** Fable has it that during the reign of David I of Scotland (1084, 1124–1153) a younger brother of the chief of the powerful clan Chattan became abbot of Kingussic. His elder brother died childless, and the chieftainship devolved on the abbot. He is supposed to have obtained a papal dispensation (a most improbable story) to marry the daughter of the thane of Calder. A swarm of little 'Kingussies' was the result. The people of Inverness-shire called them the Mac-phersons, *i.e.* the sons of the parson.

**Mad. Mad as a hatter.** A phrase popularized by Lewis Carroll in *Alice in Wonderland* (1865). It is found in Thackeray's *Pendennis* (1850) and is recorded in America in 1836. Mercurous nitrate was used in the making of felt hats and its effects can produce St. VITUS'S DANCE or lesser tremulous manifestations, hence the likely origin of the phrase. It has also been suggested that the original 'mad hatter' was Robert Crab, a 17th-century eccentric living at Chesham, who gave all his goods to the poor and lived on dock leaves and grass.

**Madoc,** or **Madog.** A Welsh prince, son of Owain Gwynedd, and legendary discoverer of America in 1170. He is supposed to have sailed from Aber-Cerrig-Gwynion near Rhos-on-Sea with two ships and reached Mobile Bay, Alabama. The Mandan Indians (extinct since the mid-19th century) have been held as the descendants of Madoc's voyagers, and there are fortifications north of Mobile Bay resembling Welsh pre-Norman castles. Madoc is also supposed to have made a second voyage to establish a colony, supposedly setting out from Lundy.

Southey has a poem called *Madoc* (1805) which also embodies the foundation of the Mexican Empire by the Aztecs from Aztlan. The story is first found in a 15th-century Welsh poem.

**Maeander.** *See* MEANDER.

**Maelduin,** or **Maeldune** (māl'doon). **The Voyage of.** In early Irish romance, Maeldune was the son of Ailill, who had been killed by a robber from Leix. As a young man, he set sail to seek the murderer and voyaged for three years and seven months visiting many islands and seeing marvels hitherto unknown. He eventually found the culprit, but took no vengeance, out of gratitude to God for his deliverance from such a variety of great dangers. The story has much in common with the voyage of St. BRANDAN.

**Maenads** (mē'nadz) (frenzied women). The Bacchae or Bacchantes, female attendants of BACCHUS. The name arises from their extravagant gestures and frenzied rites.

**Maera.** *See* MOERA.

**Maeve,** or **Medb** (māv). In Irish legend, a mythical queen of Connacht, wife of Ailill and mother of FINDABAIR who sought the downfall of CUCHULAIN and trained sorcerers to help bring this about. She instigated the Cattle Raid of Cuailnge, thus initiating the War of the Brown Bull.

**Magi** (mā'jī) (Lat. pl. of *magus*). Literally 'wise men'; specifically, the Three Wise Men of the East who brought gifts to the infant Saviour. Tradition calls them Melchior, Gaspar (or Caspar) and Balthazar, three kings of the East. The first offered gold, the emblem of royalty; the second, frankincense in token of divinity; and the third, myrrh, in prophetic allusion to the persecution unto death which awaited the 'Man of Sorrows'.

Melchior means 'king of light'

Gaspar or Caspar means 'the white one'.
Balthazar means 'the lord of treasures'.

Mediaeval legend calls them the *Three Kings of* COLOGNE, and the cathedral there claimed their relics. They are commemorated on 2, 3 and 4 January, and particularly at the Feast of the EPIPHANY.

Among the ancient Medes and Persians, the Magi were members of a priestly caste credited with great occult powers, and in Camoëns' LUSIAD (pub. 1572) the term denotes Indian BRAHMINS. Ammianus Marcellinus says the Persian magi derived their knowledge from the Brahmins of India (i, 23), and Arianus expressly calls the Brahmins 'magi' (i, 7).

**Magnetic Mountain.** A mountain of mediaeval legend which drew out the nails of any ship that approached within its influence. It is referred to in Mandeville's *Travels* and in other stories.

**Magog.** *See* GOG.

**Magpie.** Formerly 'maggot-pie', *maggot* representing *Margaret* (cp. *Robin* redbreast, *Tom*-tit, and the old *Phyllyp*-sparrow, and *pie* being *pied*, in allusion to its white and black plumage.

Augurs and understood relations have
(By maggot pies, and choughs, and rooks) brought forth
The secret'st man of blood.
SHAKESPEARE: *Macbeth*, III, iv.

The magpie has generally been regarded as an uncanny bird; in Sweden it is connected with WITCHCRAFT; in Devonshire it was a custom to spit three times to avert ill luck when the bird was sighted; in Scotland magpies flying near the windows of a house foretold death. The old rhyme about magpies seen in the course of a walk says:

One's sorrow, two's mirth,
Three's a wedding, four's a birth,
Five's a christening, six a dearth,
Seven's heaven, eight is hell,
And nine's the devil his ane sel'.

A legend said that the magpie was not allowed into the Ark but had to perch on the roof as its incessant chattering was unbearable.

In target-shooting the score made by a shot striking the outermost division but one is called a *magpie* because it was customarily signalled by a black and white flag; and formerly bishops were humorously or derisively called *magpies* because of their black and white vestments.

Lawyers as Vultures, had soared up and down;
Prelates, like Magpies, in the Air had flown.
Howell's Letters: *Lines to the Knowing Reader* (1645).

In the East the magpie is the Bird of Joy and good fortune. Its chattering signifies good news and the arrival of guests. The bird was an imperial emblem under the Manchu dynasty in China.

**Magus.** *See* MAGI; SIMON MAGUS.

**Mahabharata** (məhahbah'rətə). One of the two great epic poems of ancient India, the other being the *Ramayana*. It is about eight times the combined length of the ILIAD and ODYSSEY. Its main story is the war between the Kauravas (descendants of Dhritarashtra) and the Pandavas (descendants of Pandu), but there are innumerable episodes. Dhritarashtra and Pandu were sons of Kuru, a descendant of Bharata from whom the poem gets its name. It contains the BHAGAVAD GITA.

**Maha-pudma.** *See* TORTOISE.

**Mahogany.** An old Cornish drink used by fishermen on account of its warming quality; so called from its colour. The name has also been given to a strong concoction of brandy and water. Boswell at a dinner party at Sir Joshua Reynolds's says:

Mr Eliot mentioned a curious liquor peculiar to his country, which the Cornish fishermen drink. They call it Mahogany; and it is made of two parts gin, and one part treacle, well beaten together...I thought it very good liquor and said it was a counterpart of what is called Athol Porridge in the Highlands of Scotland, which is a mixture of whisky and honey. Johnson...observed, 'Mahogany must be a modern name; for it is not long since the wood called mahogany was known in this country'.
BOSWELL: *The Life of Dr. Johnson*, March 30, 1781.

**Maia** (mī'ə). The eldest and most lovely of the PLEIADES and mother, by JUPITER, of MERCURY. *See* MAY.

**Maid. Maid Marian.** A female character in the old May games and MORRIS DANCES, usually as Queen of the May. In the later ROBIN HOOD ballads she became attached to the cycle as the outlaw's sweetheart, probably through the performance of Robin Hood plays at MAY-DAY festivities. The part of Maid Marian, both in the games and the dance, was frequently played by a man in female costume.

> [The Courier] must, if the least spot of morphew come on his face, have his oil of tartar, his *lac virginis*, his camphor dissolved in verjuice, to make the foole as faire, for sooth, as if he were to play Maid Marian in a May-game or moris-dance.
>
> GREENE: *Quip for an Upstart Courtier* (1592).

**Maid of Buttermere.** Mary Robinson, the beautiful and innocent daughter of an inn-keeper in the valley of Buttermere, who married an unscrupulous impostor posing as the younger brother of the Earl of Hope-town in 1802. He proved to be a much-married confidence trickster and had served numerous prison sentences. Publicized and exposed by Coleridge, Hope was eventually hanged for forgery. The story was the sub-ject of numerous songs, ballads and poems at the time. Wordsworth called Mary *The Maid of Buttermere* 'unspoiled by commendation and the excess of public notice'

> I mean, O distant friend a story drawn
> From our own ground,—The Maid of
> Buttermere,—
> And how, unfaithful to a virtuous wife
> Deserted and deceived, the spoiler came
> And wooed the artless daughter of the hills
> And wedded her in cruel mockery....
>
> WORDSWORTH: *The Prelude*, Bk. vii.

**Maid of Orleans.** JOAN OF ARC.
**Old Maid.** A spinster who remains un-married, and also the name of a card game. The lapwing is so called, from the fancy that old maids are changed into lapwings after death.

**Maize.** American superstition had it that if a damsel found a blood-red ear of maize, she would have a suitor before the year was out.

> Even the blood-red ear to Evangeline brought not her lover.
>
> LONGFELLOW. *Evangeline*, II, iv.

**Makara.** In Hindu mythology the Makara is a vehicle of VARUNA, god of the deeps, who rides one; it is depicted in various composite forms as sea-elephant, SHARK, DOLPHIN, NAGA, CROCODILE, half-antelope, half-fish, and represents the dual nature of good and evil. It is the sign of CAPRICORN in the Hindu Zodiac. *See* VARUNA.

**Malaprop, Mrs.** The famous character in Sheridan's *The Rivals*. Noted for her blunders in the use of words (Fr. *mal à propos*). 'As headstrong as an *allegory* [alligator] on the banks of the Nile' (III, iii), is one of her grotesque misapplications. Hence the words *malaprop* and *malaprop-ism* to denote such mistakes.

**Malebolge** (mahləbol'jā). The eighth circle of Dante's *Inferno* (Canto xviii), containing ten *bolge* or pits. The name is used figurat-ively of any cesspool of filth or iniquity.

**Malley's Cow** (Austr.). Someone who dis-appears leaving no clue to his whereabouts. The story is that a certain Malley, who could not explain the disappearance of a cow he had been told to hold at a cattle muster, said, 'She's a goner.'

**Mambrino.** A pagan king of old romance, in-troduced by Ariosto into *Orlando Furioso*. He had a helmet of pure gold which made the wearer invulnerable, and was taken possession of by RINALDO. This is frequently referred to in DON QUIXOTE, and we read that when the barber was caught in a shower, and clapped his brazen basin on his head, Don Quixote insisted that this was the enchanted helmet of the Moorish king.

**Mammon.** The god of this world. The word in Syriac means riches, and it occurs in the Bible (*Matt.* vi, 24; *Luke* xvi, 13): 'Ye cannot serve God and mammon.' Spenser (*Faerie Queene*, II, vii), and Milton, who identifies him with VULCAN or MULCIBER (*Paradise Lost*, I, 738–51), both make Mammon the personification of the evils of wealth and miserliness.

> Mammon led them on—
> Mammon the least erected spirit that fell
> From Heaven; for even in Heaven his looks and
> thoughts
> Were always downward bent; admiring more
> The riches of Heaven's pavement, trodden gold,
> Than aught divine or holy.
>
> MILTON: *Paradise Lost*, I, 678.

**Man. Man Friday.** *See under* FRIDAY.
**Man in the Iron Mask.** *See* IRON MASK.
**Man of Ross.** *See* ROSS.
**The man who broke the bank at Monte Carlo.** Joseph Hobson Jagger, who, in 1886, won over 2,000,000 francs in 8 days. An expert on spindles, he suspected one of the roulette wheels of a faulty spindle and had it watched for a week.

Thereafter he staked on the numbers which were turning up with much more than mathematical probability and won a fortune. He died in 1892, probably mainly from boredom. His exploit became the subject of the famous Victorian Music Hall ballad in the repertoire of the inimitable Charles Coborn, written and composed by Fred Gilbert.

As I walk along the Bois Boolong, with an independent air,
You can hear the girls declare—'He must be a millionaire';
You can hear them sigh and wish to die,
You can see them wink the other eye
At the man who broke the bank at Monte Carlo.

**The New Man.** The regenerated man. In scripture phrase the unregenerated state is called *the old man.*

**The Threefold Man.** According to Diogenes Laertius, the body was composed of (1) a mortal part; (2) a divine and ethereal part called the *phren*; (3) an ethereal and vaporous part, called the *thumos*.

According to the Romans, man has a threefold soul, which at the dissolution of the body resolves itself into (1) the MANES; (2) the *Anima* or *Spirit*; (3) the *Umbra*. The Manes went either to ELYSIUM or TARTARUS; the Anima returned to the gods; but the umbra hovered about the body as unwilling to quit it.

According to the Jews, man consists of body, SOUL and spirit.

**Man, Isle of.** One explanation of the name is that given by Richard of Cirencester— 'Midway between the two countries [Britain and Ireland] is the island called Monoeda, but now Monavia', *i.e.* that it is from *menagh* or *meanagh* meaning *middle*. Another is that it is from *Mannanan*, a wizard who kept the Land of *Mann* under mists when marauders threatened it. Mannanan was one of the TUATHA DE DANANN and god of the sea which covers the underworld. He had magic pigs which provided perpetual food; eaten one day, they came to life again to be eaten next day.

**Mancha, La.** *See* LA MANCHA.

**Mandeville, Sir John** (or **Jehan De**). The name assumed by the compiler of a famous and influential 14th-century book of travels, originally written in French. The author claimed to have been born at St. Albans and

from 1322 to have travelled through Turkey, Armenia, Tartary, Persia, Syria, Arabia, Egypt, Libya, Ethiopia, Amazonia and India, to have visited Prester John and served under the Emperor of China. The work contains many stories of fabulous monsters and legends, but was essentially derived from the writings of others, especially such noted mediaeval travellers as Friar Odoric and John de Plano Carpini. The book was probably the work of a Liège physician, Jean de Bourgogne or Jehan à la Barbe. An English version had appeared by the beginning of the 15th century.

**Mandrake.** The root of the mandrake, or mandragora, often divides in two, presenting a rough appearance of a man. In ancient times human figures were cut out of the root and wonderful virtues ascribed to them, such as the production of fecundity in women (*Gen.* xxx, 14–16). They could not be uprooted without supposedly producing fatal effects, so a cord used to be fixed to the root and round a dog's neck, and the dog when chased drew out the mandrake and died. A small dose was held to produce vanity in one's appearance, and a large dose, idiocy. The mandrake screamed when uprooted.

Of this latter property Thomas Newton, in his *Herball to the Bible*, says, 'It is supposed to be a creature having life, engendered under the earth of the seed of some dead person put to death for murder.'

Shrieks like mandrakes, torn out of the earth.
SHAKESPEARE: *Romeo and Juliet*, IV, iii.

**Mandrakes called love-apples.** From the old notion that they were aphrodisiacs. Hence VENUS is called *Mandragoritis*, and the Emperor Julian, in his epistles, tells Calixenes that he drank its juice nightly as a love-potion.

**Manes** (mā'nēz). **To appease his Manes.** To do when a person is dead what would have pleased him or was due to him when alive. The spirit or ghost of the dead was called by the Romans his *Manes*, which never slept quietly in the grave while survivors left its wishes unfulfilled. 19 February was the day when all the living sacrificed to the shades of dead relations and friends—a kind of pagan ALL SOULS' DAY. *See* THE THREEFOLD MAN *under* MAN.

**Mani** (mah'ni). The MOON. In Scandinavian mythology, the beautiful boy driver of the moon-car, the son of Mundilfoeri. He is followed by a wolf, which, when time shall be no more, will devour both Mani and his sister SOL.

**Manitou** (man'itoo). The Great Spirit of certain American Indians, either the Great Good Spirit or the Great Evil Spirit. The word is Algonkian, meaning mystery, supernatural.

**Manna.** The miraculous food provided for the children of Israel on their journey from Egypt to the Holy Land.

> And when the children of Israel saw it, they said to one another, It is manna: for they wist not what it was. And Moses said unto them, This is the bread which the Lord hath given you to eat.
> *Exod.* xvi. 15.

The word is popularly said to be a corrupt form of *man-hu* (What is this?) but is probably Heb. *man*, a gift, and ultimately the Arab. *mann*, an exudation of the tamarisk.

> And the house of Israel called the name thereof Manna: and it was like coriander seed, white; and the taste of it was like wafers made with honey.
> *Exod.* xvi, 31.

**Manna of St. Nicholas of Bari.** AQUA TOFANA.

**Manoa.** The fabulous capital of EL DORADO, the houses of which city were said to be roofed with gold. There were numerous attempts by Sir Thomas Roe, Ralegh and others to locate it during the reigns of Elizabeth I and James I.

**Mansfield. The King and the Miller of Mansfield.** This old ballad, given in Percy's *Reliques*, tells how Henry II, having lost his way, met a miller, who took him home to his cottage. Next morning the courtiers tracked the king, and the miller discovered the rank of his guest, who in merry mood knighted his host as 'Sir John Cockle'. On St. GEORGE's Day, Henry II invited the miller, his wife and son to a royal banquet, and after being amused with their rustic ways, made Sir John overseer of Sherwood Forest, with a salary of £300 a year.

**Manticore** (man'tikaw). (Pers. *mardkhora*, man-eater). A fabulous beast usually given as having the head of a man, the body of a lion, a porcupine's quills and the tail of a scorpion. It is mentioned by Ctesias, a Greek living in the late 5th and early 4th centuries B.C., who wrote a history of Persia. It features in mediaeval BESTIARIES and also in heraldry where it generally has horns and the tail and feet of a DRAGON. Martinus Scriblerus says that it was 'the most noxious animal that ever infested the earth'.

**Mantle of Fidelity.** The old ballad *The Boy and the Mantle* in Percy's *Reliques* tells how a little boy showed King ARTHUR a curious mantle which should become no wife 'that hath once done amisse'. Queen GUINEVERE tried it, but it changed from green to red, and red to black, and seemed rent into shreds. Sir KAY's lady tried it, but fared no better; others followed, but only Sir Cradock's wife could wear it. The theme is a very common one in old story and was used by Spenser in the incident of Florimell's girdle. *Cp.* BRAWN.

**Manu.** In Hindu philosophy, one of a class of DEMIURGES of whom the first is identified with BRAHMA. Brahma divided himself into male and female, these produced *Viraj*, from whom sprang the first *Manu*, a kind of secondary creator. He gave rise to ten *Prajapatis* ('lords of all living'); from these came seven *Manus*, each of these presiding over a certain period, the seventh of these being *Manu Vaivasvata* ('the sun-born') who is now reigning and who is looked upon as the creator of the living races of beings. To him are ascribed the *Laws of Manu*, now called *Manavadharmashastra*, a section of the Vedas containing a code of civil and religious law compiled by the Manavans. *See* DELUGE.

**Manure** (O.Fr. *manoverer*). Literally 'handwork', hence tillage by manual labour, hence the dressing applied to land. Milton uses the word in its original sense in *Paradise Lost*, IV, 628:

> You flowery arbours...with branches overgrown
> That mock our scant manuring.

And in XI, 28, says that the repentant tears of ADAM brought forth better fruits than all the trees of PARADISE that his hands 'manured' in the days of innocence.

**Marathon Race.** A long-distance race, named after the battle of Marathon (490 B.C.), the result of which was announced at Athens by an unnamed courier who fell dead on his arrival, having run nearly 23 miles. This runner is sometimes cited as Pheidippides (or Philippides), who actually ran from Athens to Sparta to seek help against the Persians before the battle. In the modern OLYMPIC GAMES, the Marathon race was instituted in 1896, the distance being standardized at 26 miles 385 yards in 1924.

**Marcley Hill.** Legend states that this hill in Herefordshire, at six o'clock in the evening on 7 February 1571, 'roused itself with a roar, and by seven next morning had moved 40 paces'. It kept on the move for three days, carrying all with it. It overthrew Kinnaston chapel and diverted two high roads at least 200 yards from their former route. Twenty-six acres of land are said to have been moved 400 yards (Speed: *Herefordshire*).

**Marduk** (mah'duk). The Babylonian god of HEAVEN and earth, light and life, and god of battle. He was identified with numerous other Babylonian deities. *See* BEL.

**Mare. Away with the mare.** Off with the blue devils, goodbye to care. This mare is the INCUBUS, called the *nightmare*.

**Marforio.** *See* PASQUINADE.

**Mari Lwyd** (mah'ri loo'id). *Singing with Mari Lwyd* (Holy Mary) is an old Welsh Christmastide custom still surviving at Llangynwyd, Glamorgan, and may have derived from the old miracle plays (*see* MYSTERIES). The chief character wears a white cowl and a horse's skull bedecked with ribbons and is accompanied by two or three fantastically dressed followers. They sing outside houses, demanding an entrance. This is, at first, refused until the callers give evidence of their worth in song and repartee. They are then made welcome and suitably refreshed or recompensed.

**Maria Marten.** *See* RED BARN.

**Marie Celeste.** Properly MARY CELESTE.

**Marigold.** The plant *Calendula officinalis* with its bright yellow or orange flowers is so called in honour of the Virgin Mary.

This riddle, Cuddy, if thou can'st, explain...

What flower is that which bears the Virgin's name,
The richest metal joined with the same?
JOHN GAY: *The Shepherd's Week* (Monday).

In 17th-century slang a marigold (or 'marygold') meant a sovereign.

**Marine. The female Marine.** Hannah Snell of Worcester (1723–1792) who, passing herself off as a Marine, took part in the attack on Pondicherry. It is said that she ultimately opened a public-house in Wapping, but retained her male attire.

**Tell that to the Marines.** Said of a far-fetched yarn. The story is that Pepys, when re-telling stories gathered from the Navy to Charles II, mentioned flying fish. The courtiers were sceptical, but an officer of the Maritime Regiment of Foot said that he too had seen such. The king accepted this evidence and said, 'From the very nature of their calling no class of our subjects can have so wide a knowledge of seas and lands as the officer and men of Our Loyal Maritime Regiment. Henceforward ere ever we cast doubts upon a table that lacks likelihood we will first "Tell it to the Marines".'

**Mark. King Mark.** In ARTHURIAN ROMANCE, a king of Cornwall, Sir TRISTRAM'S uncle. He lived at TINTAGEL, and is principally remembered for his treachery and cowardice, and as the husband of YSOLDE the Fair, who was passionately enamoured of Tristram.

**St. Mark's Eve.** An old custom in North-country villages was for people to sit in the church porch on this day (24 April) from 11 p.m. till 1 a.m. for three years running, in order to see on the third year the ghosts of those who were to die that year, pass into the church. In other parts this custom was observed on MIDSUMMER-eve.

*Poor Robin's Almanack* for 1770 refers to another superstition:

On St. Mark's Eve, at twelve o'clock,
The fair maid will watch her smock,
To find her husband in the dark,
By praying unto good St. Mark.

Keats has an unfinished poem on the subject, and he also refers to it in *Cap and Bells* (lvi).

**Marocco,** or **Morocco.** The name of BANKS'S HORSE.

**Marriage. The Marriage knot.** The bond of marriage effected by the legal marriage ceremony. The Latin phrase is *nodus*

*Herculeus*, and part of the marriage service was for the bridegroom to loosen (*solvere*) the bride's girdle, not to tie it. In the Hindu marriage ceremony the bridegroom knots a ribbon round the bride's neck. Before the knot is tied the bride's father may refuse consent, but immediately it is tied the marriage is indissoluble. The PARSEES bind the hands of the bridegroom with a seven-fold cord, seven being a sacred number. The ancient Carthaginians tied the thumbs of the betrothed with a leather lace.

**Close seasons for marriage.** These were of old, from Advent to St. Hilary's Day (13 January); Septuagesima to Low Sunday; Rogation Sunday to Trinity Sunday. They continued to be upheld in the English Church after the Reformation, but lapsed during the Commonwealth.

> Advent marriage doth thee deny,
> But Hilary gives thee liberty.
> Septuagesima says thee nay,
> Eight days from Easter says you may.
> Rogation bids thee to contain,
> But Trinity sets thee free again.

The Roman Catholic Church does not allow nuptial mass during what is left of the 'close season', *i.e.* between the first Sunday of Advent and the Octave of the Epiphany, and from Ash Wednesday to Low Sunday.

**Mars.** The Roman god of war; identified in certain aspects with the Greek ARES. He was also the patron of husbandmen.

The planet of this name was early so called because of its reddish tinge, and under it, says the *Compost of Ptholomeus*, 'is borne theves and robbers...nyght walkers and quarell pykers, bosters, mockers, and skoffers; and these men of Mars causeth warre, and murther, and batayle. They wyll be gladly smythes or workers of yron...lyers, gret swerers.'

Among the alchemists *Mars* designated iron, and in Camoëns' LUSIADS typified divine fortitude. *See also* MARTIANS.

**Marsyas** (mah'sias). The Phrygian flute-player who challenged APOLLO to a contest of skill, and, being beaten by the god, was flayed alive for his presumption. From his blood arose the river so called. The flute on which Marsyas played had been discarded by MINERVA, and, being filled with the breath of the goddess, discoursed most

beautiful music. The interpretation of this fable is as follows:

The Dorian mode, employed in the worship of Apollo, was performed on lutes; and the Phrygian mode, employed in the rites of CYBELE, was executed by flutes, the reeds of which grew on the river Marsyas. As the Dorian mode was preferred by the Greeks, they said that Apollo beat the flute-player.

**Martha, St.** Sister of St. Lazarus and St. Mary Magdalene; patron saint of good housewives. She is represented in art in homely costume, bearing at her girdle a bunch of keys, and holding a ladle or pot of water in her hand. Like St. Margaret she is accompanied by a DRAGON bound, for she is said to have destroyed one that ravaged the neighbourhood of Marseilles. She is commemorated on 29 July and is patron of Tarascon.

**Martians.** The hypothetical inhabitants of the planet MARS, which has a much less dense atmosphere than the Earth. In 1898 H. G. Wells wrote *The War of the Worlds*, in which he recounted the adventures and horrors of a war between the men of Mars and the dwellers on Earth.

**Martin. St. Martin** (of Tours). The patron SAINT of innkeepers and reformed drunkards, usually shown in art as a young mounted soldier dividing his cloak with a beggar; in allusion to the legend that in midwinter, when a military tribune at Amiens, he divided his cloak with a naked beggar who sought alms and that at night Christ appeared to him arrayed in this very garment. This effected his conversion.

He was born of heathen parents in Pannonia but was converted at Rome and became Bishop of Tours in 371, dying at Candes *c.* 400. His day is 11 November, the day of the Feast of Bacchus; hence his purely accidental patronage and also the phrase *martin drunk*.

**St. Martin's goose.** St. Martin's day (11 November) was at one time the great goose feast in France. The legend is that St. MARTIN was annoyed by a goose which he ordered to be killed and served up for dinner. Hence, the goose was 'sacrificed' to him on each anniversary. *Cp.* GOOSE FAIR; MICHAELMAS DAY.

**St. Martin of Bullions.** The St. SWITHIN of Scotland. His day is 4 July, and the saying is that if it rains then, rain may be expected for forty days.

**St. Martin's running footman.** The DEVIL, traditionally assigned to St. Martin for such duties on a certain occasion.

> How do we know whether St. Martin's running footman is not brewing another storm?
>
> RABELAIS: *The Fourth Book: Pantagruel,* ch. xxiii.

**Mary. Highland Mary.** *See under* HIGHLANDS.

**Mary Celeste.** A brigantine found abandoned, with sails set, between the Azores and Portugal on 5th December 1872. The ship's one boat, sextant, chronometer, register and crew were missing and no trace of them was ever found. It remains one of the unsolved mysteries of the sea.

**Marygold.** *See* MARIGOLD.

**Masada** (məsah'də). The great rock on the edge of the Judaean desert, the site of Herod the Great's palace, where the Zealots made their last heroic stand against the Romans. When defeat was certain their leader Eleazar ben Ya'ir persuaded them to draw lots to select 10 men to kill the remaining 960 defenders. One of these finally slew his nine fellows and then pushed his sword through his own body. The story is told by Josephus. Among the relics revealed by Professor Yigael Yadin's excavation exhibited at London in 1966 were eleven small potsherds inscribed with names, on one of which was the name 'ben Ya'ir'. They are probably the lots in question. *See* LOT.

**Masaniello** (masənyel'ō). A corruption of *Tommaso Aniello,* a fisherman's son who led the Neapolitan revolt of July 1647 and ruled Naples for nine days. He was finally betrayed and shot. His body was flung into a ditch but was reclaimed and interred with great pomp and ceremony. The discontent was caused by excessive taxation and Masaniello's immediate grievance was the seizure of his property because his wife had smuggled flour.

Auber's opera *La Muette de Portici* (1828) is based on these events.

**Mascot.** A person or thing that is supposed to bring good luck (*cp.* JETTATURA). The word is French slang (perhaps connected with Provençal *masco,* a sorcerer), and was popularized in England by Audran's opera, *La Mascotte* (1880).

> Ces envoyés du paradis
> Sont des Mascottes, mes amis,
> Heureux celui que le ciel dote d'une Mascotte.

**Mask, The Man in the Iron.** *See under* IRON.

**Matsya.** *See* AVATAR.

**Maundy Thursday.** The day before GOOD FRIDAY is so called from the first words of the antiphon for that day being *Mandatum novum do vobis,* a new commandment I give unto you (*St. John* xiii, 34), with which the ceremony of the washing of the feet begins. This is still carried out in Roman Catholic cathedrals and monasteries. It became the custom of popes, Catholic sovereigns, prelates and priests to wash the feet of poor people. In England the sovereign did the same as late as the reign of James II. The word has been incorrectly derived from *maund* (a basket), because on the day before the great fast it was an ancient church custom to bring out food in maunds to distribute to the poor.

**Mauthe Dog.** *See* MODDEY DHOO.

**Mawworm.** A hypocritical pretender to sanctity, a pious humbug. From the character of this name in Isaac Bickerstaffe's *The Hypocrite* (1769).

**May. Cast not a clout till May is out.** An old warning not to shed winter clothing too early in the year. *Clout* here is a rag or patch, hence a piece of clothing. *May* is also another name for hawthorn, which blossoms in May. Thus some hold that the proverb means 'do not discard clothing until the hawthorn blossoms' but more likely it means 'wait until the end of May'. F.K. Robinson's *Whitby Glossary* (1855) has:

> The wind at North and East
> was never good for man nor beast,
> so never think to cast a clout
> until the month of May be out.

**Here we go gathering nuts in May.** *See under* NUT.

**May unlucky for weddings.** This is a Roman superstition, and is referred to by Ovid. In this month were held the festivals of *Bona Dea* (the goddess of chastity), and the feasts of the dead called *Lemuralia.*

> Nec viduae taedis eadem, nec virginis apta
> Tempora; quae nupsit, non diuturna fuit;

Haec quoque de causa, si te proverbia tangunt,
Mente malum Maio nubere vulgus ait.
    OVID: *Fasti*, v, 487, etc.

**Unlucky to wash blankets in May.** This superstition still survives in parts of Britain, especially in the S.W. The old rhyme says:

Wash a blanket in May
Wash a dear one away.

**May-day.** Polydore Vergil says that the Roman youths used to go into the fields and spend the Calends of May in dancing and singing in honour of FLORA, goddess of fruits and flowers. The English celebrated May-day with games and sports, particularly archery and MORRIS dancing and the setting up of the MAYPOLE. In due time ROBIN HOOD and MAID MARIAN came to preside as Lord and Lady of the May, and by the 16th century May-day was Robin Hood's day and Robin Hood plays became an integral part of the festivities.

May-day was also formerly the day of the London chimney-sweepers' festival.

**Evil May Day.** *See* DEVIL.

**Maypole, May Queen.** etc. Dancing round the Maypole on MAY-DAY, 'going-a-Maying', electing a May Queen, and lighting bonfires, are all ancient relics of nature-worship. In Cornhill, London, before the Church of St. Andrew, a great shaft or maypole was set up, round which the people danced, whence the church came to be called St. Andrew Undershaft. In the first May morning people went 'a-maying' to fetch fresh flowers and branches of hawthorn (hence its name *may*) to decorate their houses, and the fairest maid of the locality was crowned 'Queen of the May'.

A very tall ungainly woman is sometimes called a 'Maypole', a term which was bestowed as a nickname on the Duchess of Kendal, one of George I's German mistresses.

**Maya.** The mother of GAUTAMA who saw in a dream the future BUDDHA enter her womb in the shape of a little white elephant. Seven days after his birth she died from joy.

**Mayonnaise.** A sauce made with pepper, salt, oil, vinegar, the yolk of egg etc. beaten up together. When the Duc de Richelieu captured Port Mahon, Minorca, in 1756, he demanded food on landing; in the absence of a prepared meal, his chef took whatever he could find and beat it up together—hence the original form *mahonnaise*.

**Mayor. Mayor of the Bull-ring.** In the Dublin of former times, this official and his sheriffs were elected on MAY-DAY and St. Peter Eve 'to be captaine and guardian of the batchelers, and the unwedded youth of the civitie'. For the year the 'Mayor' had authority to punish those who frequented houses of ill-fame. He was termed 'Mayor of the Bull-ring' because he conducted any bachelor who married during his term of office to an iron ring in the market place to which bulls were tied for baiting, and made him kiss it.

**Mayor of Garratt.** *See* GARRATT.

**Mazikeen,** or **Shedeem.** A species of being in Jewish mythology resembling the Arabian JINN said to be agents of magic and enchantment. When ADAM fell, says the Talmud, he was excommunicated for 130 years, during which time he begat demons and spectres.

**Swells out like the Mazikeen ass.** The allusion is to a Jewish tradition that a servant, whose task it was to rouse the neighbourhood to midnight prayer, one night mounted a stray ASS and neglected his duty. As he rode along the ass grew bigger and bigger, till at last it towered as high as the tallest edifice, where it left the man, and there next morning he was found.

**Meander.** To wind, to saunter about at random; so called from the Maeander, a winding river of Phrygia. It is said to have given DAEDALUS his idea for a LABYRINTH. The term is also applied to an ornamental pattern of winding lines, used as a border on pottery, wall decorations etc.

**Meat. To carry off meat from the graves.** To be as poor as a church mouse; to be so poor as to descend to robbing the graves of offerings. The Greeks and Romans used to make feasts at certain seasons, when spirits were supposed to return to their graves, and the fragments were left on the tombs for them. Hence the Latin proverb *Eleemosynam sepulcri patris tui* (Alms on your father's grave).

**Médard, St.** (mā′dah). The French St. SWITHIN; his day is 8 June.

Quand il pleut à la Saint-Médard
Il pleut quarante jours plus tard.

He was bishop of Noyon and Tournai in the 6th century and founded the Festival of the Rose at Salency, in which the most virtuous girl in the parish receives a crown of roses and a purse of money. Legend says that a sudden shower once fell which soaked everyone except St. Médard who remained dry as toast, for an EAGLE had spread its wings over him, and ever after he was termed *maître de la pluie*.

**Medb.** *See* MAEVE.

**Medea** (medē'ə). In Greek legend, a sorceress, daughter of Aeetes, king of Colchis. She married JASON, the leader of the ARGONAUTS, whom she aided to obtain the GOLDEN FLEECE, and was the mother of Medus, regarded by the Greeks as the ancestor of the Medes.

**Medea's kettle**, or **cauldron.** A means of restoring lost youth. MEDEA cut an old ram into pieces, threw the bits into her cauldron, and a young lamb came forth. The daughters of Pelias accordingly killed and cut up their father thinking to restore him to youth in the same way, but Medea refused to save the situation.

> Get thee Medea's kettle and be boiled anew.
> CONGREVE: *Love for Love*, IV, vii.

**Medicine.** From Lat. *medicina*, which meant both the physician's art and his laboratory, and also a medicament. The alchemists applied the word to the PHILOSOPHER'S STONE and the ELIXIR OF LIFE; hence Shakespeare's.

> How much unlike art thou, Mark Antony!
> Yet, coming from him, the great medicine hath
> With his tinct gilded thee.
> *Antony and Cleopatra*, I, v.

The word was, and is, frequently used in a figurative sense, as

> The miserable have no other medicine
> But only hope.
> SHAKESPEARE: *Measure for Measure*, III, i.

Among North American Indians *medicine* is generally mistranslated; while it can refer to spells, charms or fetishes, it is more accurately spiritual power and though the **Medicine-man** may also have the powers of a magician, he is primarily the custodian and exponent of the ancient wisdom of the race.

**Medusa.** In classical mythology, the chief of the GORGONS. Her face was so terrible that all who looked on it were turned to stone.

Her head was struck off by PERSEUS. Medusa was the mother, by POSEIDON of Chrysaor and PEGASUS.

**Meg. Long Meg** etc. *See under* LONG.

**Megarians.** The inhabitants of Megara and its territory, Megaris, Greece, were proverbial for their stupidity; hence the proverb 'Wise as a Megarian', *i.e.* not wise at all; yet *see below*. *Cp.* ABDERA.

**Melampode** (melam'pōd). Black Hellebore; so called from Melampus, a famous soothsayer and physician of Greek legend, who with it cured the daughters of Proetus of their madness (Virgil: *Georgics*, iii, 550).

> My seely sheep, like well below,
> They need not melampode;
> For they been hale enough I trow,
> And liken their abode.
> SPENSER: *Shepheard's Calendar* (July).

**Meleager** (melēā'gə). A hero of Greek legend, son of Oeneus of Calydon and Althaea, distinguished for throwing the javelin, for slaying the Calydonian BOAR, and as one of the ARGONAUTS. *See* ALTHAEA'S BRAND.

**Melicertes** (melisœ'tēz). Son of Ino, a sea deity of Greek legend. Athamas imagined his wife Ino to be a lioness, and her two sons to be lion's cubs. In his frenzy he slew one of the boys and drove Melicertes and his mother into the sea. *See* LEUCOTHEA.

**Mélisande.** *See* MELUSINA.

**Melon.** Muslims say that the eating of a melon produces a thousand good works.

**Melpomene** (melpom'ini). The muse of *Tragedy*.

> Up then, Melpomene, thou mournfullest Muse of nine,
> Such cause of mourning never hadst afore.
> SPENSER: *Shepheard's Calendar* (*November*).

**Melusina**, or **Mélisande.** The most famous of all the fées of French romance, looked upon by the houses of Lusignan, Rohan, Luxembourg and Sassenaye as their ancestor and founder. Having enclosed her father in a high mountain for offending her mother, she was condemned to become every Saturday a serpent from her waist downward. She married Raymond, count of Lusignan, and made her husband vow never to visit her on a Saturday; but the count hid himself on one of the forbidden days, and saw his wife's transformation. Melusina was now obliged to quit her husband, and was destined to wander about as a spectre till the day of doom, though some say that the count immured her in the dungeon of his castle.

A sudden scream is called *un cri de Mélusine*, in allusion to the scream of despair uttered by Melusina when she was discovered by her husband; and in Poitou certain gingerbread cakes bearing the impress of a beautiful woman '*bien coiffée*', with a serpent's tail, made by confectioners for the MAY fair in the neighbourhood of Lusignan, are still called *Mélusines*.

**Memnon.** The Oriental or Ethiopian prince who, in the TROJAN WAR, went to the assistance of his uncle PRIAM and was slain by ACHILLES. His mother Eos (the Dawn) was inconsolable for his death, and wept for him every morning. The Greeks called the statue of Amenophis III at Thebes that of Memnon. When first struck by the rays of the rising sun it is said to have produced a sound like the snapping asunder of a cord. Poetically, when Eos kissed her son at daybreak, the hero acknowledged the salutation with a musical murmur.

**Menelaus** (menəlā'əs), son of Atreus, brother of AGAMEMNON, and husband of HELEN whose desertion of him brought about the TROJAN WAR. He was the king of Sparta or Lacadaemon.

**Menthu.** *See* BAKHA.

**Mentor.** A guide, a wise and faithful counsellor; so called from Mentor, a friend of ULYSSES, whose form MINERVA assumed when she accompanied TELEMACHUS in his search for his father.

**Menu.** *See* MANU.

**Mephistopheles** (mefistof'əlēz). A manu-factured name (possibly from three Greek words meaning 'not loving the light') of a DEVIL or familiar spirit which first appeared in the late mediaeval FAUST legend; he is well known as the sneering, jeering, leering tempter in Goethe's *Faust*.

**Mercury.** The Roman counterpart of the Greek HERMES, son of MAIA and JUPITER, to whom he acted as messenger. He was the god of science and commerce, the patron of travellers and also of rogues, vagabonds and thieves. Hence, the name of the god is used to denote both a messenger and a thief.

> My father named me Autolycus; who being, as I am, littered under Mercury, was likewise a snapper-up of unconsidered trifles.
> SHAKESPEARE: *The Winter's Tale*, IV, iii.

Mercury is represented as a young man with winged hat and winged sandals (*talaria*), bearing the CADUCEUS, and sometimes a purse.

Posts with a marble head of Mercury used to be erected where two or more roads met, to point out the way (*Juvenal*, viii, 53).

In astrology, Mercury 'signifieth subtill men, ingenious, inconstant: rymers, poets, advocates, orators, phylosophers, arithmeticians, and busie fellowes'. The alchemists credited mercury with great powers and used it for many purposes, for which see Ben Jonson's masque, *Mercury Vindicated*.

**Mercury fig** (Lat. *Ficus ad Mercurium*). The Romans devoted the first fig gathered off a fig-tree to MERCURY. The proverbial saying was applied generally to all first fruits or first works.

**You cannot make a Mercury of every log.** Pythagoras said: *Non ex quovis ligno Mercurius fit.* That is, 'Not every mind will answer equally well to be trained into a scholar.' The proper wood for a statue of Mercury was box—*Vel quod hominis pultorem prae se ferat, vel quod materies sit omnium maxime aeterna* (Erasmus).

**Mercurial.** Light-hearted, gay, volatile; such were supposed by the astrologers to be born under the planet Mercury.

**Mercurial finger.** The little finger, which, if pointed, denotes eloquence; if square, sound judgment.

> The thumb in Chiromancy, we give Venus,
> The forefinger to Jove, the midst to Saturn,
> The ring to Sol, the least to Mercury.
> BEN JONSON: *Alchemist*, I, i.

**Merlin.** The historical Merlin was a Welsh or British BARD, born towards the close of the 5th century, to whom a number of poems have been very doubtfully attributed. He is said to have become a bard of king ARTHUR and to have perished after a terrible battle about 570 between the Britons and their Romanized compatriots.

His story has been mingled with that of the enchanter Merlin of the ARTHURIAN ROMANCE. This Prince of Enchanters was the son of a damsel seduced by a friend, but was baptized by Blaise, and so rescued from the power of SATAN. He became an adept in NECROMANCY, but was beguiled by the enchantress Nimue who shut him up in a rock; and later Vivien, the LADY OF THE LAKE, entangled him in a thornbush by means of spells, and there he still sleeps, though his voice may be sometimes heard.

He first appears in Nennius as the boy Ambrosius and in Geoffrey of Monmouth's *Historia Regum Britanniae* and the *Vita Merlini*. These were developed by Robert Wace and Robert de Borron and later writers. See also Spenser's *Faerie Queene* (III, iii) and Tennyson's *Idylls*.

> Now, though a Mechanist, whose skill
> Shames the degenerate grasp of modern science,
> Grave Merlin (and belike the more
> For practising occult and perilous lore)
> Was subject to a freakish will
> That sapped good thoughts, or scared them with defiance.
> WORDSWORTH: *The Egyptian Maid*, iv.

**Mermaid.** The popular stories of this fabulous marine creature, half woman and half fish, allied to the SIREN of classical mythology, probably arose from sailors' accounts of the dugong, a cetacean whose head has a rude approach to the human outline. The mother while suckling her young holds it to her breast with one flipper, as a woman holds her infant in her arm. If disturbed, she suddenly dives under water, and tosses up her fish-like tail. *Cp.* MERROW.

Ovid mentions a legend that mermaids rose from the burning galleys of the Trojans when the timbers turned into flesh and blood and 'the green daughters of the sea'.

Legend says that a mermaid was caught in Holland in 1404 and taken to Haarlem where she was taught to spin and was converted to the Catholic faith.

There were also mermen and both they and mermaids were said to have been seen off coasts.

The Japanese mermaid Ningyo is represented as a fish with a human head. Polynesian myth has a creator-god, Vatea, depicted as half-human, half porpoise.

In later 16th-century plays the term is often used for a courtesan. *See* Massinger's *Old Law*, IV, i, and Shakespeare's *Comedy of Errors*, III, ii etc.

**The Mermaid Tavern.** The famous meeting place (in Bread Street, Cheapside) of the wits, literary men and men about town in the early 17th century. Among those who met there at a sort of early club were Ben Jonson, Sir Walter Ralegh, Beaumont, Fletcher, John Selden and in all probability Shakespeare.

> What things have we seen
> Done at the Mermaid! Heard words that have been
> So nimble, and so full of subtile flame,
> As if that everyone from whence they came
> Had meant to put his whole wit in a jest.
> BEAUMONT: *Lines to Ben Jonson*.

**Mermaid's glove.** The largest of the British sponges (*Halichondria palmata*), so called because its branches resemble fingers.

**Mermaid's purses.** The horny egg cases of the ray, skate or shark, frequently cast up by the waves on the sea-beach.

**Merope** (mer'ōpi). One of the PLEIADES; dimmer than the rest, because, according to Greek legend, she married SISYPHUS, a mortal. She was the mother of GLAUCUS.

**Merops' Son.** One who thinks he can set the world to rights, but can't. Agitators, demagogues etc. are sons of Merops. The allusion is to PHAETON, a reputed son of Merops (king of Ethiopia), who thought himself able to drive the car of PHOEBUS, but, in the attempt, nearly set the world on fire.

**Merrow** (Irish, *muirrúhgach*). A MERMAID, believed by Irish fishermen to forebode a coming storm.

> It was rather annoying to Jack that, though living in a place where the merrows were as plenty as lobsters, he never could get a right view of one.
> W.B. YEATS: *Irish Folk Stories and Fairy Tales*.

**Merry. Merry Andrew.** A buffoon, jester or attendant on a quack doctor at fairs. Said by Thomas Hearne (1678–1735)—with no evidence—to derive from Andrew Boorde (*c.* 1490–1549), physician to Henry VIII, who to his vast learning added great eccentricity. Prior has a poem on 'Merry Andrew'.

**Merry Dancers.** The Northern Lights, so called from their undulatory motion. The French call them *chèvres dansantes* (dancing goats).

**Merry Monday.** An old name for the day before SHROVE TUESDAY.

**Meru.** The 'OLYMPUS' of the Hindus; a fabulous mountain in the centre of the world, 80,000 leagues high, the abode of VISHNU, and a perfect PARADISE.

**Mesopotamia. The true 'Mesopotamia' ring.** Something high-sounding and pleasing, but wholly past comprehension. The allusion is to the story of the old woman who told her pastor that she 'found great support in the blessed word *Mesopotamia*'.

**Messalina.** Wife of the Emperor Claudius of Rome, executed by order of her husband in A.D. 48. Her name has become a byword for lasciviousness and incontinency. Catherine II of Russia (1729–1796) has been called *The Modern Messalina*.

**Metal. The seven metals in alchemy:**
  Gold, APOLLO or the sun.
  Silver, DIANA or the moon.
  Quicksilver, MERCURY.
  Copper, VENUS.
  Iron, MARS.
  Tin, JUPITER.
  Lead, SATURN.

**Methuselah** (mithoo′zələ). **Old as Methuselah.** Very old indeed, almost incredibly old. He is the oldest man mentioned in the Bible, where we are told (*Gen.* v, 27) that he died at the age of 969.

**Meum est propositum in taberna mori.** A famous drinking song usually accredited to Walter Map (*fl.* 1200), but by the anonymous German 'Archpoet' (*fl.* 1160).

  Meum est propositum in taberna mori;
  Ubi vinum proximum morientis ori
  Tunc cantabit laetius angelorum chori;
  Deus sit propitius huic potatori (etc.).
  'It is my intention to die in a tavern. May wine be placed to my dying lips, that when the choirs of angels shall come they may say, God be merciful to this drinker'.

**Mexitl,** or **Mextli.** The principal god of the ancient Mexicans (hence the name of their country), to whom hundreds of human beings were offered annually as sacrifices. More usually called *Huitzilopochtli* (Humming-bird of the South, or He of the South), he was the god of war and storms and was born fully armed.

**Micah Rood's Apples.** Apples with a spot of red in the heart. The story is that Micah Rood was a prosperous farmer at Franklin, Pennsylvania. In 1693 a pedlar with jewellery called at his house, and next day was found murdered under an apple-tree in Rood's orchard. The crime was never brought home to the farmer, but next autumn all the apples of the fatal tree bore inside a red blood-spot, called 'Micah Rood's Curse', and the farmer died soon afterwards.

**Michael, St.** The ARCHANGEL. The great prince of all the ANGELS and leader of the celestial armies.

  Go, Michael, of celestial armies prince,
  And thou, in military prowess next,
  Gabriel; lead forth to battle these my sons
  Invincible; lead forth my armed saints
  By thousands and by millions ranged for fight.
    MILTON: *Paradise Lost*, VI, 44.

His day (St. Michael and All Angels) is 29 September (*see* MICHAELMAS DAY). He appears in the Bible in *Dan.* x, 13, and xii, 1; *Jude*, verse 9; and *Rev.* xii, 7–9, where he and his angels fight the DRAGON. His cult was popular in the Middle Ages and he was also looked on as the presiding spirit of the planet MERCURY, and bringer to man of the gift of prudence.

In art St. Michael is depicted as a beautiful young man with severe countenance, winged, and clad in either white or armour, bearing a lance and shield, with which he combats a dragon. In the final judgment he is represented with scales, in which he weighs the souls of the risen dead.

**St. Michael's Chair.** An old beacon turret at the top of the chapel tower at St. Michael's Mount, Cornwall. It is said that whichever of a newly-married couple first sits there will gain marital supremacy. There is also a rock on the island called St. Michael's Chair.

**Michaelmas Day.** 29 September, the Festival of St. MICHAEL and all Angels, one of the quarter days when rents are due and the day when magistrates are chosen.

The custom of eating goose at Michaelmas (*see also* St. MARTIN'S GOOSE) is very old and is probably due to geese being plentiful and in good condition at this season. We are told that tenants formerly presented their landlords with one to keep in their good graces. The popular story is that Queen Elizabeth I, on her way to Tilbury Fort on 29 September 1588, dined with Sir Neville Umfreyville, and partook of geese, afterwards calling for a bumper of

Burgundy, and giving as a toast 'Death to the Spanish Armada!' Scarcely had she spoken when a messenger announced the destruction of the fleet by a storm. The Queen demanded a second bumper, and said, 'Henceforth shall a goose commemorate this great victory.' The tale is marred by the fact that the Armada was dispersed by winds in July and the thanksgiving sermon for victory was preached at St. Paul's on 20 August.

George Gascoigne, the poet, who died in 1577, refers to the custom of goose-eating at Michaelmas:

At Christmas a capon, at Michaelmas, a goose.
And somewhat else at New Yere's tide for feare
the lease flies loose.

**Mickey Finn.** A draught or powder slipped into liquor to render the drinker unconscious. The term comes from a notorious figure in 19th-century Chicago.

**Midas** (mī'dəs). A legendary king of Phrygia who requested of the gods that everything that he touched might be turned to GOLD. His request was granted, but as his food became gold the moment he touched it, he prayed the gods to take their favour back. He was then ordered to bathe in the Pactolus, and the river ever after rolled over golden sands.

Another story told of him is, that when appointed to judge a musical contest between APOLLO and PAN, he gave judgment in favour of the SATYR; whereupon Apollo in contempt gave the king a pair of ass's ears. Midas hid them under his Phrygian cap; but his barber discovered them, and, not daring to mention the matter, dug a hole and relieved his mind by whispering in it 'Midas has ass's ears', then covering it up again. Budaeus gives a different version. He says that Midas kept spies to tell him everything that transpired throughout his kingdom, and the proverb 'kings have long arms' was changed to 'Midas has long ears'.

A parallel of this tale is told of Portzmach, king of a part of Brittany. He had all the barbers of his kingdom put to death, lest they should announce to the public that he had the ears of a horse. An intimate friend was found willing to shave him, after swearing profound secrecy; but not able to contain himself he confided his secret to a river bank. The reeds of this river were used for pan-pipes and hautbois, which repeated the words, 'Portzmach—King Portzmach has horse's ears'.

**Midgard.** In Scandinavian mythology, the abode of the first pair, from whom sprang the human race. It was midway between NIFLHEIM and MUSPELHEIM, formed from the flesh and blood of YMIR and joined to ASGARD by the rainbow bridge BIFROST. *Cp.* UTGARD.

**Mid-Lent Sunday.** The fourth Sunday in Lent. It is called *dominica refectionis* (Refreshment Sunday) because the first lesson is the banquet given by Joseph to his brethren, and the Gospel of the day is the miraculous feeding of the five thousand. It is the day on which simnel cakes are eaten and it is also called Mothering Sunday.

**Midsummer. Midsummer madness.** The height of madness. Olivia says to Malvolio in Shakespeare's *Twelfth Night* (III,iv), 'Why, this is very midsummer madness'. The reference is to the heat of the sun or the wild celebrations on midsummer eve or possibly the midsummer moon when lunacy was held to be widespread. People who were inclined to be mad used to be said *to have but a mile to midsummer.*

**Midsummer men.** Orpine or Live-long, a plant of the *Sedum* genus; so called because it used to be set in pots or shells on midsummer eve, and hung up in the house to tell damsels whether their sweethearts were true or not. If the leaves bent to the right, it was a sign of fidelity; if to the left, the 'true-love's heart was cold and faithless'.

**Midsummer moon** *'Tis midsummer moon with you'*; you are stark mad. Madness was supposed to be affected by the MOON, and to be aggravated by summer heat; so it naturally follows that the full moon at midsummer is the time when madness would be most pronounced.

What's this, Midsummer moon?
Is all the world gone a-madding?
DRYDEN: *Amphitryon*, IV, i.

**Milanion.** See ATALANTA'S RACE.

**Milesians** (mīlē'zyənz). Properly, the inhabitants of *Miletus*; but the name has been given to the ancient Irish because of the legend that two sons of Milesius, a fabulous king of Spain, conquered the country, and repeopled it after exterminating the Firbolgs (the aborigines).

**Milesian Fables.** A Greek collection of witty but obscene short stories by Antonius Diogenes, no longer extant, and compiled by Aristides of *Miletus* (2nd cent. B.C.), whence the name. They were translated into Latin by Sidenna about the time of the civil wars of Marius and Sulla, and were greedily read by luxurious Sybarites. Similar stories are still sometimes called *Milesian Tales*.

**Milky Way.** *See* GALAXY.

**Millstone. The millstones of Montisci.** The stones produce flour of themselves, whence the proverb, 'Grace comes from God, but millstones from Montisci' (Boccaccio: *Decameron*, day viii, novel iii).

**Milo** (mī'lō). A celebrated Greek athlete of Crotona in the late 6th century B.C. It is said that he carried through the stadium at OLYMPIA a heifer four years old, and ate the whole of it afterwards. When old, he attempted to tear in two an oak-tree, but the parts closed upon his hands, and while held fast hc was devoured by wolves.

**Mince Pies** at Christmas time are said to have been emblematical of the manger in which our Saviour was laid. The paste over the 'offering' was made in the form of a cratch or hay-rack. Southey speaks of—

> Old bridges dangerously narrow and angles in them like the corners of an English mince-pie, for the foot-passengers to take shelter in.
> *Esprinella's Letters*, III, 384 (1807).

*Mince pies* is also rhyming slang for 'the eyes'.

**Minerva.** The Roman goddess of wisdom and patroness of the arts and trades, fabled to have sprung, with a tremendous battle-cry, fully armed from the brain of JUPITER. She was subsequently identified by the Romans with the Greek ATHENE (Athena), and was one of the three chief deities, the others being Jupiter and JUNO. She is represented as being grave and majestic, clad in a helmet and with drapery over a coat of mail, and bearing the AEGIS on her breast. Phidias made a statue of her of ivory and gold 39 ft. high which was placed in the Parthenon.

**Minoan.** *See* MINOS.

**Minos** (mī'nos). A legendary king and law-giver of Crete, made at death supreme judge of the lower world, before whom all the dead appeared to give an account of their stewardship, and to receive the reward of their deeds. He was the husband of PASIPHAE and the owner of the LABYRINTH constructed by DAEDALUS. From his name we have the adjective *Minoan*, pertaining to Crete; the Minoan period is the Cretan bronze age, roughly about 2500–1200 B.C.

**Minotaur** (mīn'ōtaw). A mythical monster with the head of a bull and the body of a man, fabled to have been the offspring of PASIPHAE and a bull that was sent to her by POSEIDON. MINOS kept it in his LABYRINTH and fed it on human flesh, seven youths and seven maidens being sent as tribute from Athens every year for the purpose. THESEUS slew this monster.

**Mint.** The name of the herb is from Lat. *mentha* (Gr. *minthe*), so called from *Minthe*, a NYMPH of the COCYTUS, and beloved by PLUTO. This nymph was metamorphosed by PROSERPINA (Pluto's wife) out of jealousy, into the herb called after her.

**Miracle plays.** *See* MYSTERIES.

**Mirror. Alasnam's mirror** *See under* ALASNAM.

**Cambuscan's mirror.** Sent to Cambuscan by the King of Araby and Ind; it warned of the approach of ill fortune, and told if love was returned (Chaucer: *Canterbury Tales*, 'The Squire's Tale').

**Merlin's magic mirror**, given by MERLIN to King Ryence. It informed the king of treason, secret plots and projected invasions (Spenser: *The Faerie Queene*, III, ii).

**Reynard's wonderful mirror.** This mirror existed only in the brain of Master Fox. He told the queen lion that whoever looked in it could see what was done a mile off. The wood of the frame was not subject to decay, being made of the same block as King Crampart's magic horse (REYNARD THE FOX, ch. xii).

**Vulcan's mirror** showed the past, the present and the future. Sir John Davies tells us that CUPID gave it to Antinous and Antinous gave it to PENELOPE, who saw therein 'the court of Queen Elizabeth'.

**The Mirror of Diana.** A lake in the Alban hills in the territory of ancient Aricia, in

Italy, on the shores of which stood the earliest known temple of DIANA. The priest of this temple, called *Rex Nemorensis,* was either a gladiator or runaway slave who retained office until slain by a successor. The cult is described in the first chapter of Sir James Frazer's *Golden Bough.* The lake, *Nemorensis Lacus* (modern Nemi), is 110 ft. deep and some 3½ miles in diameter.

**Misers.** Among the most renowned are:

Baron Aguilar, or Ephraim Lopes Pereira d'Aguilar (1740–1802), born at Vienna and died at Islington, worth £200,000.

Daniel Dancer (1716–1794). His sister lived with him, and was a similar character, but died before him, and he left his wealth to the widow of Sir Henry Tempest, who nursed him in his last illness.

Sir Hervey Elwes, who died in 1763 worth £250,000, but never spent more than £110 a year. His sister-in-law inherited £100,000, but actually starved herself to death, and her son John (1714–1789), M.P., an eminent brewer in Southwark, never bought any clothes, never suffered his shoes to be cleaned, and grudged every penny spent on food.

Thomas Guy (*c.* 1645–1724), founder of Guy's Hospital.

William Jennings (1701–1797), a neighbour and friend of Elwes, died worth £200,000.

**Misrule, Feast of.** *See* KING OF MISRULE *under* KING.

**Mistletoe** (O.E. *mistiltan*; *mist* being both basil and mistletoe, and *tan*, a twig). The plant grows on various trees as a parasite, especially the apple-tree, and was held in great veneration by the DRUIDS when found on the OAK. Shakespeare calls it 'the baleful mistletoe' (*Titus Andronicus*, II, iii), perhaps in allusion to the Scandinavian legend that it was with an arrow made of mistletoe that BALDER was slain, or to the tradition that it was once a tree from which the wood of Christ's CROSS was formed; or possibly with reference to the popular belief that mistletoe berries are poisonous, or to the connection of the plant with the human sacrifices of the Druids. It is for this reason and for its connections with pagan Norse mythology that it is excluded from church decorations except at York Minster which has Norse associations. Culpeper says

'some, for the virtues thereof, have called it *lignum sanctae crucis,* wood of the holy cross, as it cures falling sickness, apoplexy and palsy very speedily, not only to be inwardly taken, but to be hung at their neck'. Mistletoe is said to have certain toxic qualities when taken in large doses.

Mistletoe is the Golden Bough of AENEAS and of the Druids, it represents the sacred feminine principle with the OAK, on which it grows, as the masculine. It was thought to grow as a result of lightning striking the oak; this gave it a special quality and made it a magical plant. In Celtic rites it had to be cut left-handed by a Druid who was fasting and wearing a white tunic, using a golden sickle. The mistletoe was caught in a white cloth as it must never touch the ground or be touched by iron.

In Norse myth it is the plant of peace, and meeting under it forms a truce. It is also apotropaic and so wards off trolls and lightning and for this purpose is hung from roofs and over cribs.

**Kissing under the mistletoe.** As being neither tree nor shrub, neither one thing nor the other, mistletoe represents freedom from limitations and thus freedom from protection, hence anyone under the mistletoe is in the realm of chaos and must accept responsibility for being there. No boon asked there can be refused. It is a Yuletide and Christmas custom. The correct procedure, now seldom observed, is that a man should pluck a berry when he kisses a girl under the mistletoe, and when the last berry is gone there should be no more kissing.

**Mistpoeffers.** *See* BARISAL GUNS.

**Mithra,** or **Mithras.** The god of light of the ancient Persians, one of their chief deities, and the ruler of the universe, sometimes used as a synonym for the SUN. The word means *friend,* and this deity is so called because he befriends man in this life, and protects him against evil spirits after death. He is represented as a young man with a Phrygian cap and plunging daggers into the neck of a bull that lies upon the ground.

Sir Thomas More called the Supreme Being of his *Utopia*, 'Mithra' and the cult of Mithraism had certain affinities with Christianity.

**Mithridate** (mith'ridāt). A concoction named from Mithridates VI, King of Pontus and Bithynia (d. *c.* 63 B.C.), who is said to have made himself immune from poisons by the constant use of antidotes. It was supposed to be an antidote against poisons and contained 46 or more ingredients.

> What brave spirit could be content to sit in his shop ... selling Mithridatum and dragon's water to infected houses?
>> BEAUMONT and FLETCHER: *Knight of the Burning Pestle*, I (1608).

**Mnemosyne** (nemoz'ini). Goddess of memory and mother by ZEUS of the nine MUSES of Greek mythology. She was the daughter of heaven and earth (URANUS and GAEA).

> To the Immortals every one
> A portion was assigned of all that is;
> But chief Mnemosyne did Maia's son
> Clothe in the light of his loud melodies.
>> SHELLEY: *Homer's Hymn to Mercury*, lxxiii.

**Moddey Dhoo** (maw'dhə doo). (Manx, Black Dog). A ghostly black spaniel that for many years haunted Peel Castle in the Isle of MAN. It used to enter the guard room as soon as candles were lighted, and leave it at daybreak. While this spectre dog was present, the soldiers forebore all oaths and profane talk, but they always carried out their nightly duties of locking up and conveying the keys to the captain accompanied by one of their fellows. One night a drunken trooper, from bravado, performed the rounds alone but lost his speech and died in three days. The dog never appeared again.

During excavations in 1871 the bones of Simon, Bishop of Sodor and Man (died 1247) were uncovered, with the bones of a dog at his feet.

**Modred**, or **Mordred** (mō'drid, maw'drid). In ARTHURIAN ROMANCE, one of the Knights of the ROUND TABLE, nephew and betrayer of King ARTHUR. He is represented as the treacherous knight. He revolted against the king, whose wife he seduced, was mortally wounded in the battle of CAMLAN and was buried in AVALON. The story is told, with a variation, in Tennyson's *Guinevere* (*Idylls of the King*).

**Moera**, or **Maera**. The dog of ICARIUS.

**Mohocks**. A class of ruffians who in the 18th century infested the streets of London. So called from the Mohawk Indians. One of

their 'new inventions' was to roll people down Snow Hill in a tub; another was to overturn coaches on rubbish-heaps. (*See* Gay: *Trivia*, III.)

A vivid picture of the misdoings of these and other brawlers is given in the *Spectator*, No. 324.

**Moira**. Fate or Necessity, supreme even over the gods of OLYMPUS.

**Moll, Molly. Moll Cutpurse.** *See* CUTPURSE.

**Molly Mog.** This celebrated beauty was an innkeeper's daughter, at Oakingham, Berks. She was the toast of the gay sparks of the first half of the 18th century, and died unmarried in 1766, at the age of sixty-seven. Gay has a ballad on this *Fair Maid of the Inn*, in which the 'swain' alluded to is Mr. Standen, of Arborfield, who died in 1730. It is said that Molly's sister Sally was the greater beauty. A portrait of Gay still stands in the inn.

**Molloch, May** (mol'ək), or **The Maid of the Hairy Arms.** An ELF of folklore who mingles in ordinary sports, and will even direct the master of the house how to play dominoes or draughts. Like the WHITE LADY of Avenel, May Molloch is a sort of BANSHEE.

> Meg Mullack and Brownie mentioned in the end of it [this letter], are two Ghosts, which (as it is constantly reported) of old, haunted a Family in Strathspey of the Name of Grant. They appeared at first in the likeliness of a young Lass; the second of a young Lad.
>> JOHN AUBREY: *Miscellanies*.

**Molmutine Laws.** According to Geoffrey of Monmouth, the laws of Dunwallo Molmutius, legendary king of Britain, son of Cloten, king of Cornwall.

> He enacted that the temples of the gods, as also cities, should have the privilege of giving sanctuary and protection to any fugitive or criminal, that should flee to them from his enemy.
>> *Historia Regum Britanniae*, II, xvii.

**Moly** (mō'li). According to HOMER, the mythical herb given by HERMES to ULYSSES as an antidote against the sorceries of CIRCE.

> Black was the root, but milky white the flower,
> Moly the name, to mortals hard to find.
>> POPE: *Odyssey*, X, 365.

The name is given to a number of plants, especially of the *Allium* (garlic) family, as the wild garlic, the Indian moly, the moly of Hungary, serpent's moly, the yellow moly, Spanish purple moly, Spanish silver-capped moly, and Dioscorides' moly. They all flower in May except 'the sweet moly of Montpelier', which blossoms in September.

**Momus** (mō′məs). One who carps at everything. Momus was the god of ridicule and the son of Nox (Night), who was driven out of HEAVEN for his criticisms of the gods. VENUS herself was censured for the noise made by her feet, although he could find no fault with her naked body.

**Monday. St. Monday,** or **St. Lundi.** A facetious name given to Monday (also called *Cobblers' Monday*) because it was observed by shoemakers and others as a holiday (*holy day!*).

There is a story in the *Journal of the Folk-lore Society* (Vol. I), that, while Cromwell lay encamped at Perth, one of his zealous partisans, named Monday, died and Cromwell offered a reward for the best lines on his death. A shoemaker of Perth brought the following:

Blessed be the Sabbath Day,
And cursed by worldly pelf,
Tuesday will begin the week,
Since Monday's hanged himself.

This so pleased Cromwell that he not only gave the promised reward but decreed that shoemakers should be allowed to make Monday a standing holiday.

**Monday's child.** The traditional rhyme says:

Monday's child is fair of face,
Tuesday's child is full of grace,
Wednesday's child is full of woe.

**Monkey.** The Hindu god Hanuman, son of Vayu, a wind god, has the monkey as his attribute and can be portrayed as monkeyheaded. He is noted for bravery, speed and strength and is the epitome of the useful companion. He features largely in the *Ramayana*; he helped RAMA in the rescue of Sita when she was abducted by the demon Ravana. At the Ram Lila festival little boys dress as monkeys, the occasion being particularly enjoyed by children.

One of the early incarnations of the Buddha was as a monkey, but the animal is also one of the Three Senseless Creatures. It is also one of the animals of the Twelve Terrestrial Branches, the Chinese ZODIAC.

Monkey is the hero of the Chinese classic of the *Journey to the Western Paradise*, in which he depicts unregenerate human nature.

The monkey is revered in Japan and the Three Mystic Monkeys of mythology represent 'See no evil; Hear no evil; Speak no evil'.

Monkeys and monsters guard shrines and temples in Cambodia.

The Mayan god of the north is portrayed with a monkey's head and monkey deities occur in Peruvian art.

African tribes have monkey servant-guardians and certain monkeys can embody the souls of the dead.

**To pay in monkey's money** (Fr. *en monnaie de singe*). In goods, in personal work, in mumbling and grimace. In Paris when a monkey passed the Petit Pont, if it was for sale four deniers' toll had to be paid; but if it belonged to a showman and was not for sale, it sufficed if the monkey went through his tricks.

... being an original by Master Charles Charmois, principal painter to King Megistus, paid for in court fashion with monkey's money.
RABELAIS, IV, iii.

**Mont** (Fr., hill). The technical term in PALMISTRY for the eminences at the roots of the fingers.

That at the root of the
*thumb* is the Mont de Mars.
*index finger* is the Mont de Jupiter.
*long finger* is the Mont de Saturne.
*ring finger* is the Mont du Soleil.
*little finger* is the Mont de Vénus.

The one between the thumb and the index finger is called the Mont de Mercure and the one opposite the Mont de la Lune.

**Montjoie St. Denis,** or **Denys.** The war cry of mediaeval France. *Montjoie* is a corruption of *Mons Jovis*, as the little mounds were called which served as direction-posts in ancient times; hence it was applied to whatever showed or indicated the way, as the banner of St. DENYS, called the Oriflamme. The Burgundians had for their war-cry, 'Montjoie St. André'; the Dukes of Bourbon, 'Montjoie Notre Dame'; and the Kings of England used to have 'Montjoie St. George'.

*Montjoie* was also the cry of the French heralds in the Tournaments, and the title of the French King of Arms.

Where is Mountjoy the herald? speed him hence:
Let him greet England with our sharp defiance.
SHAKESPEARE: *Henry V*, III, v.

**Montserrat** (Lat. *mons serratus*, the mountain jagged like a saw). The Catalonians aver that this mountain was riven and shattered at the Crucifixion. Every rift is filled with evergreens. The monastery of Montserrat is famous for its printing-press and for its Black Virgin.

**Moon.** The word is probably connected with the Sanskrit root *me-*, to measure, because time was measured by it. It is common to all Teutonic languages (Goth. *mena*; O.Frisian *mona*; O.Norse. *mani*; O.E. *mona* etc.) and is almost invariably masculine. In the Edda the son of Mundilfoeri is MANI (moon), and daughter SOL (sun); so it is still with the Lithuanians and Arabians, and so it was with the ancient Slavs, Mexicans, Hindus etc., and the Germans still have *Frau Sonne* (Mrs. Sun) and *Herr Mond* (Mr. Moon).

The moon is represented in five different phases: (1) new; (2) full; (3) crescent or decrescent; (4) half; and (5) gibbous, or more than half. In pictures of the Assumption it is shown as a crescent under Our Lady's feet; in the Crucifixion it is eclipsed, and placed on one side of the CROSS, the SUN being on the other; in the Creation and Last Judgment it is also depicted.

In classical mythology the moon was known as HECATE before she had risen and after she had set; as ASTARTE when crescent; as DIANA or CYNTHIA (she who 'hunts the clouds') when in the open vault of heaven; as PHOEBE when looked upon as the sister of the sun (*i.e.* PHOEBUS); and was personified as SELENE or Luna, the lover of the sleeping ENDYMION, *i.e.* moonlight on the fields.

The moon is called *triform*, because it presents itself to us either round, or waxing with horns towards the east, or waning with horns towards the west.

One legend connected with the moon was that there was treasured everything wasted on earth, such as misspent time and wealth, broken vows, unanswered prayers, fruitless tears, unfulfilled desires and intentions etc. In Ariosto's *Orlando Furioso*, Astolpho found on his visit to the moon (Bk. XXXIV, lxx) that bribes were hung on gold and silver hooks; princes' favours were kept in bellows; wasted talent was kept in vases, each marked with the proper name etc.; and in *The Rape of the Lock* (canto V) Pope tells us that when the Lock disappeared—

Some thought it mounted to the lunar sphere,
Since all things lost on earth are treasured there,
There heroes' wits are kept in pondr'ous vases,
And beaux' in snuff-boxes and tweezer-cases.
There broken vows and death-bed alms are found
And lovers' hearts with ends of riband bound,
The courtier's promises, and sick man's prayers,
The smiles of harlots, and the tears of heirs,
Cages for gnats, and chains to yoke a flea,
Dried butterflies, and tomes of casuistry.

Hence the phrase, the **limbus of the moon.** *Cp.* LIMBO.

**The man in the moon.** Some say it is a man leaning on a fork, on which he is carrying a bundle of sticks picked up on a Sunday. The origin of this fable is from *Numb.* xv, 32–36. Some add a dog also; thus SHAKESPEARE'S *Midsummer Night's Dream* (V, i) says:

This man with lantern, dog, and bush of thorn,
Presenteth moonshine.

Another tradition says that the man is Cain, with his dog and thorn bush; the thorn bush being emblematical of the thorns and briars of the fall, and the dog being the 'foul fiend'. Some poets make out the 'man' to be ENDYMION, taken to the moon by DIANA.

The FROG and TOAD also live in the moon as do, almost universally, the HARE and rabbit. Often, as in China, the creature is three-legged, representing the three lunar phases. The hare in the moon, with pestle and mortar, mixes the ELIXIR OF IMMORTALITY in Chinese and Japanese mythology. In Hinduism the crescent moon is the cup of the elixir and is associated with the sacred SOMA.

**You have found an elephant in the moon.** You have found a mare's nest. Sir Paul Neale, a conceited virtuoso of the 17th century, gave out that he had discovered 'an elephant in the moon'. It turned out that a mouse had crept into his telescope, and had been mistaken for an elephant in the moon. Samuel Butler has a satirical poem on the subject called *The Elephant in the Moon.*

**Moon-drop.** In Latin, *virus lunare*, a vaporous foam supposed anciently to be shed by the moon on certain herbs and objects, when influenced by incantations.

Upon the corner of the moon

There hangs a vaporous drop profound;
I'll catch it ere it come to ground.
SHAKESPEARE: *Macbeth*, III, v.

*Cp.* Lucan's *Pharsalia*, vi, 699, where Erichtho is introduced using it:
Et virus large lunare ministrat.

**Moonrakers.** A nickname of Wiltshire folk; also of simpletons. From the story that Wiltshire yokels, with typical country guile, when raking a pond for kegs of smuggled brandy, feigned stupidity when surprised by the excise men, and said that they were trying to rake out the moon, which was reflected in the water.

**Moor-slayer,** or **Mata-moros.** A name given to St. JAMES, the patron saint of Spain, because, as the legends say, in encounters with the Moors he came on his white horse to the aid of the Christians.

**Mop,** or **Mop Fair.** A statute or hiring fair. So called from the 'mop' (a turf or tassel) worn as a badge by those seeking hire. Carters fastened a piece of whipcord to their hats; shepherds, a lock of wool; grooms, a piece of sponge etc.

**Moran's Collar.** In Irish folk-tale, the collar of Moran, the wise councillor of King Feredach the Just, which strangled the wearer if he deviated from the strict rules of equity.

**Mordred.** *See* MODRED.

**More of More Hall.** *See* WANTLEY, DRAGON OF.

**Morgan Le Fay.** The fairy sister of King ARTHUR, a principal figure in Celtic legend and ARTHURIAN ROMANCE, also known as *Morgane, Morganetta, Morgaine, Morgue la Faye* and (especially in *Orlando Furioso*) as *Morgana. See* FATA MORGANA.

It was Morgan le Fay who revealed to King Arthur the intrigues of LANCELOT and GUINEVERE. She gave him a cup containing a magic draught and he had no sooner drunk it than his eyes were opened to the perfidy of his wife and friend.

In *Orlando Furioso*, she is represented as living at the bottom of a lake, and dispensing her treasures to whom she liked. In *Orlando Innamorato*, she first appears as 'Lady Fortune', but subsequently assumes her witch-like attributes. In *Tasso*, her three daughters, Morganetta, Nivetta and Carvilia, are introduced.

In the romance of OGIER THE DANE she receives Ogier in the Isle of AVALON when he is over 100 years old, restores him to youth, and becomes his bride.

**Morgane, Morganetta.** *See* MORGAN LE FAY.

**Morgante Maggiore** (mawgan'ti məjaw'rā). A serio-comic romance in verse by Pulci of Florence (1482). The characters had appeared previously in many old romances; Morgante is a ferocious giant, converted by ORLANDO (the real hero) to Christianity. After performing the most wonderful feats, he dies at last from the bite of a crab.

Pulci was practically the inventor of this burlesque form of poetry, called by the French *Bernesque*, from the Italian, Berni (1497–1535), who excelled in it.

**Morgiana** (mawjian'ə). In the ARABIAN NIGHTS (*Ali Baba and the Forty Thieves*), the clever, faithful slave of ALI BABA, who pries into the forty jars and discovers every jar but one contains a man. She takes the oil from the only jar containing it, and having made it boiling hot, pours enough into each jar to kill the thief therein. Finally she kills the captain of the gang and marries her master's son.

**Morgue la Faye.** The form of the name MORGAN LE FAY in OGIER THE DANE.

**Morpheus.** Ovid's name for the son of Sleep, and god of dreams; so called from Gr. *morphe*, form, because he gives these airy nothings their form and fashion. Hence the name of the narcotic, *morphine*, or *morphia*.

**Morrice, Gil,** or **Childe.** The hero of an old Scottish ballad, a natural son of an earl and the wife of Lord Barnard, and brought up 'in gude grene wode'. Lord Barnard, thinking the Childe to be his wife's lover, slew him with a broadsword, and setting his head on a spear gave it to 'the meanest man in a' his train' to carry to the lady. When she saw it she said to the baron, 'Wi' that saim speir, O pierce my heart, and put me out o' pain'; but the baron replied, 'Enouch of blood by me's bin spilt ... sair, sair I rew the deid,' adding:

I'll ay lament for Gill Morice,
As gin he were mine ain;
I'll neir forget the dreiry day
On which the youth was slain.
PERCY: *Reliques* (*Gil Morrice*), xxvi.

Percy says this pathetic tale suggested to Home the plot of his tragedy, *Douglas*.

**Morris Dance.** A dance, popular in England in the 15th century and later, in which the dancers often represented characters from the ROBIN HOOD stories (*see* MAID MARIAN). Other stock characters were Bavian the fool, Malkin the clown, the hobby-horse, or a DRAGON, and foreigners, probably Moors or Moriscos. It was commonly part of the MAY-games and other pageants and festivals and the dancers were adorned with bells. It was brought from Spain in the reign of Edward III, and was originally a military dance of the Moors or Moriscos, hence its name.

**Nine Men's Morris.** An ancient game (similar to draughts) once popular with shepherds, still found in East Anglia, and either played on a board or on flat greensward. Two persons have each nine pieces or 'men' which they place down alternately on the spots (*see* diagram), and the aim of

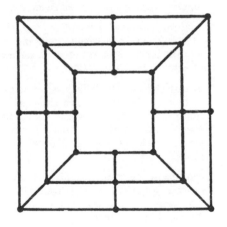

either player is to secure a row of three men on any line on the board, and to prevent his opponent achieving this by putting one of his own men on a line which looks like being completed, etc. Strutt says, 'The rustics, when they have not materials at hand to make a table, cut the lines in the same form upon the ground, and make a small hole for every dot.'

> The fold stands, empty in the drowned field,
> And crows are fatted with the murrain flock;
> The nine men's morris is fill'd up with mud.
>> SHAKESPEARE: *A Midsummer Night's Dream*, II, ii.

It is also called *Merelles*.

**Morte d'Arthur, Le.** *See* ARTHURIAN ROMANCES.

**Mother. Mother Carey's Chickens.** Sailor's name for stormy petrels, probably derived from *mater cara* or *madre cara* ('mother dear', with reference to the Virgin Mary). Sailors also call falling snow *Mother Carey's Chickens*. See Marryat's *Poor Jack* for an account of sailors' superstitions on such matters.

**Mother Carey is plucking her goose.** It is snowing. *Cp.* HULDA.

**Mother Earth.** When Junius BRUTUS (after the death of Lucretia) formed one of the deputation to DELPHI to ask the ORACLE which of the three would succeed TARQUIN, the response was, 'He who should first kiss his mother.' Junius instantly threw himself on the ground, exclaiming, 'Thus, then, I kiss thee, Mother Earth', and he was elected consul.

**Mouse. The Mouse Tower.** A mediaeval watch-tower on the Rhine, near Bingen, so called from the tradition that Archbishop HATTO was there devoured by mice. Actually it was built by Bishop Siegfried 200 years after Hatto's death, as a toll-house. The German *Maut* means 'toll' (mouse is *Maus*), and the similarity of these words together with the unpopularity of the toll on corn gave rise to the legend.

**Moutons. Revenons à nos moutons** (Fr., 'Let us come back to our sheep'). A phrase used to express 'Let us return to the subject'. It is taken from the 14th century French comedy *La Farce de Maître Pathelin*, or *l'Avocat Pathelin* (line 1282), in which a woollen-draper charges a shepherd with ill-treating his sheep. In telling his story he continually ran away from the subject; and to throw discredit on the defendant's attorney (Pathelin), accused him of stealing a piece of cloth. The judge had to pull him up every moment, with '*Mais, mon ami, revenons à nos moutons*'. The phrase is frequently quoted by Rabelais.

**Much.** The miller's son in the ROBIN HOOD stories. In the MORRIS-DANCE he played the part of the Fool, and his great feat was to bang the head of the gaping spectators with a bladder of peas.

**Mulberry.** Fable has it that the fruit was originally white and became blood-red from the blood of PYRAMUS and Thisbe. In the *Language of Flowers*, Black Mulberry (*Morus nigra*) means 'I shall not survive you' and White Mulberry (*Morus alba*) signifies 'widsom'. Culpeper says that the tree is ruled by MERCURY and it is noted as a vermifuge. The old Gloucestershire proverb says, 'After the mulberry-tree has shown green leaf, there will be no more frost'. Silkworms are fed on the leaves of the mulberry, especially the white mulberry. The Paper Mulberry (*Broussonetia papyrifera*) is so called from its use in Japan and the Far East for making paper with the pulped shoots.

In the SEVEN CHAMPIONS (Pt. I, ch. iv), Eglantine, daughter of the King of Thessaly, was transformed into a mulberry-tree. *See* PYRAMUS.

**Here we go round the mulberry bush.** An old game in which children join hands and dance round in a ring, singing the song of which this is the refrain.

**Mulciber** (mŭl′sibə). Among the Romans, a name of VULCAN; it means the softener, because he softened metals.

> And round about him [Mammon] lay on every side
> Great heaps of gold that never could be spent;
> Of which some were rude ore, not purified
> Of Mulciber's devouring element.
> SPENSER: *The Faerie Queene*, II, vii, 5.

**Mulmutine Laws.** *See* MOLMUTINE.

**Mumbo Jumbo.** The name given by Europeans (possibly from some lost native word) to a BOGY or grotesque idol venerated by certain African tribes; hence any object of blind unreasoning worship.

Mungo Park, in his *Travels in the Interior of Africa* (1795–1797), says (ch. iii) that Mumbo Jumbo 'is a strange bugbear, common to all Mandingo towns, and much employed by the Pagan natives in keeping their wives in subjection'. When the ladies of the household become too quarrelsome, Mumbo Jumbo is called in. He may be the husband or his agent suitably disguised, who comes at nightfall making hideous noises. When the women have been assembled and songs and dances performed. 'Mumbo fixes on the offender', she is 'stripped naked, tied to a post, and severely scourged with Mumbo's rod,

amidst the shouts and derision of the whole assembly.'

**Mumping Day.** St. THOMAS's Day, 21 December, is so called in some parts of the country, because on this day the poor used to go about begging, or, as it was called, 'a-gooding', that is, getting gifts to procure good things for Christmas, or begging corn. In Lincolnshire the name used to be applied to Boxing Day; in Warwickshire the term used was 'going a-corning'.

**Mundane Egg.** *See* EGG.

**Muses.** In Greek mythology the nine daughters of ZEUS and MNEMOSYNE; originally goddesses of memory only, but later identified with individual arts and sciences. The paintings of Herculaneum show all nine in their respective attributes. Their names are: CALLIOPE, CLIO, EUTERPE, THALIA, MELPOMENE, TERPSICHORE, ERATO, POLYHYMNIA, URANIA. Three earlier Muses are sometimes given, *i.e.* Melete (Meditation), Mneme (Remembrance) and Aoide (Song).

**Museum.** Literally, a home or seat of the MUSES. The first building to have this name was the university erected at Alexandria by Ptolemy Soter about 300 B.C.

**Muspelheim** (mŭs′pəlhīm). In Scandinavian mythology, the 'Home of Brightness' to the south of NIFLHEIM, where Surt (black smoke) ruled with his flaming sword and where dwelt the sons of Muspel the fire giant.

**Myrmidons** (lit. ant people, from Gk. *myrmix*) gained their name from the legend that when Aegina was depopulated by a plague, its king, Aeacus, prayed to JUPITER that the ants running out of an OAK tree should be turned to men. According to one account they emigrated with Peleus to Thessaly, whence they followed ACHILLES to the siege of TROY. They were noted for their fierceness, diligence and devotion to their leader, hence their name is applied to a servant who carries out his orders remorselessly.

**Myrmidons of the Law.** Bailiffs, sheriffs' officers, policemen and other servants of the law. Any rough fellow employed to annoy another is the employer's myrmidon.

**Myron** (mī′ron). A famous Greek sculptor noted for his realistic statues of gods, heroes, athletes and animals. It is said that he made a cow so lifelike that even bulls were deceived and made their approaches. He was an older contemporary of Phidias.

**Myrrha** (mi'rə). The mother of ADONIS, in Greek legend. She is fabled to have had an un-natural love for her own father, and to have been changed into a MYRTLE. The resinous juice called *myrrh* is obtained from the Arabian myrtle (*Balsamodendron myrrha*).

**Myrtle.** A leaf of myrtle, viewed in a strong light, is seen to be pierced with innumerable little punctures. According to fable, PHAEDRA, wife of THESEUS, fell in love with HIPPOLYTUS, her stepson. When Hippolytus went to the arena to exercise his horses, Phaedra repaired to a myrtle-tree in Troezen to await his return, and beguiled the time by piercing the leaves with a hairpin.

In *Orlando Furioso* Astolpho is changed into a myrtle-tree by Acrisia. *Cp*. MYRRHA.

The ancient Jews believed that the eating of myrtle leaves conferred the power of detecting witches; and it was a superstition that if the leaves crackled in the hands the person beloved would prove faithful.

Myrtle is also the flower of the Tabernacle.

In Mandaean rites myrtle is a sacred plant and is part of a priest's ritual headdress; it is also placed on the heads of the new-born, the baptized, at marriage and in dying.

In Egypt myrtle was sacred to HATHOR and in Graeco-Roman myth to ADONIS, APHRODITE/VENUS, ARTEMIS and Europa, also to POSEIDON/NEPTUNE as the power of the waters.

Myrtle is a 'flower of the gods', a magic herb, having a vital essence which transmits the breath of life.

**The myrtle which dropped blood.** AENEAS (Virgil's *Aeneid*, Bk. III) tells the story of how he tore up a myrtle to decorate a sacrificial altar, but was terrified to find it dripped blood, while a voice came from the ground saying, 'Spare me, now that I am in my grave.' It was that of Polydorus, the youngest son of PRIAM and HECUBA, who had been murdered with darts and arrows for the gold he possessed. The deed was perpetrated by Polymnestor, King of Thrace, to whose care Polydorus had been entrusted.

**Mystery.** In English two distinct words are represented: *mystery*, the archaic term for a handicraft, as in *the art and mystery of printing*, is the same as the Fr. *métier* (trade, craft, profession), and is the M.E. *mistere*, from Med. Lat. *misterium*, *ministerium*, ministry. *Mystery*, meaning something hidden, inexplicable or beyond human comprehension, is from Lat. *mysterium* (through French) and Gr. *mustēs*, from *muen*, to close the eyes or lips.

It is from this latter sense that the old miracle plays, mediaeval dramas in which the characters and story were drawn from sacred history, came to be called **Mysteries,** though they were frequently presented by members of a guild or *mystery*. *Miracle plays* (as they were called at the time) developed from liturgical pageantry, especially in the Corpus Christi processions, and were taken over by the laity. They were performed in the streets on a wheeled stage or on stages erected along a processional route, and non-Biblical subjects were also introduced. They flourished in England from the 13th to the 15th century but morality plays continued into the 16th century.

# N

**Naevius** (nē'viəs). *See* ACCIUS NAEVIUS.

**Nagas.** Depicted as either human-headed snakes, monsters, or more usually, serpents, nagas appear extensively in Hindu myth and legend. They sprung from Kadru, wife of Kasyapa, and peopled the underworld and the watery deeps where they reign as semi-divine creatures in magnificent palaces. The Naga and Nagina are serpent kings and queens or genii. Naga women can marry humans and some Indian families claim descent from nagas. VISHNU, Lord of the Deeps, sleeps on the coiled serpent of the primordial waters and his two nagas, with intertwined bodies, represent the already fertilized waters. Representing the underworld, watery element, nagas are at perpetual enmity with the solar GARUDA BIRD. They are guardians of treasures, both material and of esoteric knowledge.

**Naiad** (nī'ad). In classical mythology, a NYMPH of lake, fountain, river or stream.

> You nymphs, call'd Naiads, of the wand'ring brooks,
> With your sedg'd crowns, and ever-harmless looks,
> Leave your crisp channels, and on this green land
> Answer your summons: Juno does command.
> SHAKESPEARE: *The Tempest*, IV, i.

**Nail-paring.** Superstitious people are particular as to the day on which they cut their nails. The old ryhme is:

> Cut them on Monday, you cut them for health;
> Cut them on Tuesday, you cut them for wealth;
> Cut them on Wednesday, you cut them for news;
> Cut them on Thursday, a new pair of shoes;
> Cut them on Friday, you cut them for sorrow;
> Cut them on Saturday, you see your true love tomorrow
> Cut them on Sunday, your safety seek,
> The devil will have you the rest of the week.

Another rhyme conveys an even stronger warning on the danger of nail-cutting on a Sunday:

> A man had better ne'er be born
> As have his nails on a Sunday shorn.

**Nain Rouge** (nān roozh) (Fr., red dwarf). A LUTIN or house spirit of Normandy, kind to fishermen. There is another called *Le petit homme rouge* (the little red man).

**Naked. The naked truth.** The plain, unvarnished truth; truth without trimmings. The fable says that Truth and Falsehood went bathing; Falsehood came first out of the water, and dressed herself in Truth's garments. Truth, unwilling to take those of Falsehood, went naked.

**Naphtha** (naf'thə). The Greek name for an inflammable, bituminous substance coming from the ground in certain districts; in the MEDEA legend it is the name of the drug used by the witch for anointing the wedding robe of Glauce, daughter of King Creon, whereby she was burnt to death on the morning of her marriage with JASON.

**Naraka** (nah'rəkə). In Hindu mythology and Buddhism, the place of torture for departed evil-doers. It consists of many kinds of hells, hot and cold.

**Narcissus.** In Greek mythology, the son of Cephisus; a beautiful youth who saw his reflection in a fountain, and thought it the presiding nymph of the place. He jumped in the fountain to reach it, where he died. The NYMPHS came to take up the body to pay it FUNERAL honours but found only a flower, which they called by his name (Ovid: *Metamorphoses*, iii, 346, etc.).

Plutarch says the plant is called Narcissus from the Gr. *narkē*, numbness, and that it is properly *narcosis*, meaning the plant which produces numbness or palsy. ECHO fell in love with Narcissus.

> Sweet Echo, sweetest nymph that liv'st unseen...
> Canst thou not tell me of a gentle pair,
> That likest thy Narcissus are?
> MILTON: *Comus*, 230.

**Narcissism** is the psychoanalytical term for excessive love and admiration of one-self.

**Naseby.** Fable has it that this town in Northamptonshire is so called because it was considered the *navel* (O.E. *nafela*) or centre of England, just as DELPHI was considered 'the navel of the earth'. In fact the town's name appears in Domesday Book as *Navesberi*, showing that it was a burgh or dwelling of Hnaef, a Dane.

**Nativity. To cast a man's nativity.** The astrologers' term for constructing a plan or map of the position of the twelve 'houses' which belong to him and explaining its significance. *See* HOUSES, ASTROLOGICAL.

**Nausicaa** (nawsik'iə). The Greek heroine whose story is told in the ODYSSEY. She was the daughter of Alcinous, king of the Phaeacians, and the shipwrecked Odysseus found her playing ball with her maidens on the shore. Pitying his plight she conducted him to her father, by whom he was entertained.

**Necklace. The Fatal Necklace.** The necklace which CADMUS gave to HARMONIA; some say that VULCAN, and others that Europa, gave it to him. It possessed the property of stirring up strife and bloodshed. It is said to have eventually become the property of Phaÿllus, who gave it to his mistress. Her youngest son set fire to the house and mother, son and the necklace were destroyed.

**Necromancy** (nek'rōmansi) (Gr. *nekros*, the dead; *manteia*, prophecy). Prophesying by calling up the dead, as the WITCH OF ENDOR called up Samuel (I *Sam.* xxviii, 7 ff.). Also the art of magic generally, the BLACK ART. *See* DIVINATION.

**Nectar** (Gr.). In classical mythology, the drink of the gods. Like their food AMBROSIA, it conferred immortality, hence the name of the *nectarine*, so called because it is as 'sweet as nectar'.

**Need. Needfire.** Fire obtained by friction; a beacon. It was formerly supposed to defeat sorcery, and cure diseases ascribed to WITCHCRAFT, especially cattle diseases. We are told in Henderson's *Agricultural Survey of Caithness* (1812), that as late as 1785 it

was so used as a charm when stock were seized with the murrain.

> The ready page, with hurried hand,
> Awaked the need-fire's slumbering brand.
> SCOTT: *The Lay of the Last Minstrel*, Canto Third, xxix.

**Nelly.** A popular name in Australia for MOTHER CAREY'S GOOSE.

**Nemean** (nimē'ən). **Nemean Games.** One of the four great festivals of ancient Greece, held in the valley of Nemea in Argolis every alternate year, the first and third of each OLYMPIAD. Legend states that they were instituted in memory of Archemorus who died from the bite of a serpent as the expedition of the SEVEN AGAINST THEBES was passing through the valley. It was customary for the games to open with a funeral oration in his honour. After HERCULES had slain the NEMEAN LION the games were held in honour of ZEUS. Athletic contests were added after the model of the OLYMPIC GAMES. The victor's reward was at first a crown of OLIVES, later of green parsley. PINDAR has eleven odes in honour of victors.

**The Nemean Lion.** A terrible lion which kept the people of the valley of Nemea in constant alarm. The first of the Twelve Labours of HERCULES was to slay it; he could make no impression on the beast with his club, so he caught it in his arms and squeezed it to death. Hercules ever after wore the skin as a mantle.

> My fate cries out,
> And makes each petty artery in this body
> As hardy as the Nemean lion's nerve.
> SHAKESPEARE: *Hamlet*, I, iv.

**Nemesis.** The Greek goddess, daughter of Nox; a divinity of vengeance who rewarded virtue and punished the wicked and all kinds of impiety; the personification of divine retribution. Hence, retributive justice generally, as *the Nemesis of Nations*, the fate which, sooner or later, overtakes every great nation.

> And though circuitous and obscure
> The feet of Nemesis how sure!
> SIR WILLIAM WATSON: *Europe at the Play*.

**Nepenthe,** or **Nepenthes** (nipen'thi, nipen'thēz) (Gr. *ne*, not; *penthos*, grief). An Egyptian drug mentioned in the ODYSSEY (IV, 228) that was fabled to drive away care and make people forget their woes. Polydamna, wife of Thonis, King of Egypt, gave it to HELEN.

> That nepenthes which the wife of Thone
> In Egypt gave to Jove-born Helena.
> MILTON: *Comus*, 675–6.

**Neptune.** The Roman god of the sea corresponding to the Greek POSEIDON, hence, allusively, the sea itself. Neptune is represented as an elderly man of stately mien, bearded, carrying a trident, and sometimes astride a dolphin or horse. *See* HIPPOCAMPUS.

**Neptunian,** or **Neptunist.** The name given to certain 18th-century geologists, who held the opinion of Abraham Gottlob Werner (1750–1817), that all the great rocks of the earth were once held in solution in water and were deposited as sediment. *Cp.* VULCANIST.

**Nereus** (niə'rūs). 'THE OLD MAN OF THE SEA', a sea-god of Greek mythology represented as a very old man. He was the father of the NEREIDS and his special dominion was the Aegean Sea.

**Nereids** (niə'ri·idz). The sea-nymphs of Greek mythology, the fifty daughters of NEREUS and 'grey-eyed' Doris. The best known are AMPHITRITE, THETIS and GALATEA. Milton refers to another, Panope, in his *Lycidas* (line 99):

> The air was calm and on the level brine
> Sleek Panope with all her sisters played.

And the names of all will be found in Spenser's *The Faerie Queene*, Bk. IV, c. xi, verses 48–51.

**Nerthus,** or **Hertha** (nœ'thəs, hœ'thə). The name given by Tacitus to a German or Scandinavian goddess of fertility, or 'Mother Earth', who was worshipped on the island of Rügen. She roughly corresponds with the classical CYBELE; and is probably confused with the Scandinavian god *Njorthr* or NIORDHR, the protector of sailors and fishermen. *Nerthus* and *Njorthr* alike mean 'benefactor'.

**Nessus. Shirt of Nessus.** A source of misfortune from which there is no escape. The shirt of Nessus killed HERCULES. *See* DEIANIRA; *cp.* HARMONIA.

**Nibelungenlied, The** (nēbəlung'ənlēd). A great mediaeval German epic poem founded on old Scandinavian legends contained in the *Volsunga Saga* and the Edda.

Nibelung was a mythical king of a race of Scandinavian dwarfs dwelling in *Nibelheim* (*i.e.* 'the home of darkness, or mist'). These *Nibelungs* or *Nibelungers* were the possessors of the wonderful 'Hoard' of gold and precious stones guarded by the dwarf ALBERICH, and their name passed to later holders of the Hoard, SIEGFRIED's following and the Burgundians being in turn called 'the Nibelungs'.

Siegfried, the hero of the first part of the poem, became possessed of the Hoard and married KRIEMHILD, sister of GUNTHER, King of Worms, whom he helped to secure the hand of BRUNHILD of Iceland. After Siegfried's murder by Hagen at Brunhild's instigation, Kriemhild carried the treasure to Worms where it was seized by Gunther and his retainer Hagen. They buried it in the Rhine, intending later to enjoy it; but they were both slain for refusing to reveal its whereabouts, and the Hoard remains for ever in the keeping of the Rhine Maidens. The second part of the Nibelungenlied tells of the marriage of the widow Kriemhild with King Atli or ETZEL (Attila), her invitation of the Burgundians to the court of the Hunnish King, and the slaughter of all the principal characters, including Gunther, Hagen and Kriemhild.

**Nicholas, St.** One of the most popular saints in Christendom, especially in the East. He is the patron SAINT of Russia, of Aberdeen, of parish clerks, of scholars (who used to be called clerks), of pawnbrokers (because of the three bags of gold—transformed to the three gold balls—that he gave to the daughters of a poor man to save them from earning their dowers in a disreputable way), of little boys (because he once restored to life three little boys who had been cut up and pickled in a salting-tub to serve for bacon), and is invoked by sailors (because he allayed a storm during a voyage to the Holy Land) and against fire. Finally he is the original of SANTA CLAUS.

Little is known of his life but he is said to have been Bishop of Myra (Lycia) in the early 4th century, and one story relates that he was present at the Council of Nicaea (325) and buffeted Arius on the jaw. His day is 6 December, and he is represented in episcopal robes with either three purses of gold, three gold balls or three small boys, in allusion to one or other of the above legends.

**Old Nick.** The DEVIL. The term was in use in the 17th century, and is perhaps connected with the German *Nickel*, a GOBLIN, or in some forgotten way with St. NICHOLAS. Butler's derivation from Niccolò Machiavelli is, of course, poetical licence:

Nick Machiavel had ne'er a trick
(Though he gave name to our old Nick).
*Hudibras*, III, i.

**Nicka-Nan Night.** The night preceding Shrove Tuesday was so called in Cornwall because boys played tricks and practical jokes on that night. The following night they went from house to house singing—

Nicka, nicka nan,
Give me some pancake and then I'll be gone;
But if you give me none
I'll throw a great stone
And down your doors shall come.

**Nicker,** or **Nix.** In Scandinavian folklore, a water-wraith or KELPIE, inhabiting sea, lake, river and waterfall. They are sometimes represented as half-child, half-horse, the hoofs being reversed, and sometimes as old men sitting on rocks wringing the water from their hair. The female nicker is a *nixy*.

**Niflheim** (niv'lhīm) (*i.e.* mist-home). In Scandinavian mythology, the region of endless cold and everlasting night, ruled over by the goddess HEL. It consisted of nine worlds, to which were consigned those who die of disease or old age; it existed in the north and out of its spring Hvergelmir flowed twelve ice-cold streams. *Cp.* MUSPELHEIM.

**Nightingale.** The Greek legend is that Tereus, King of Thrace, fetched Philomela to visit his wife, Procne, who was her sister; but when he reached the 'solitudes of Heleas' he dishonoured her, and cut out her tongue that she might not reveal his conduct. Tereus told his wife that Philomela was dead, but Philomela made her story known by weaving it into a robe, which she sent to Procne. Procne, in revenge, cut up her own son and served him to Tereus, and as soon as the king discovered it he pursued his wife, who fled to Philomela; whereupon the gods changed all three into birds; Tereus became the HAWK, his wife the swallow, and Philomela, the nightingale, which is still called Philomel (lit., lover of song) by the poets.

Youths and maidens most poetical...
Full of meek sympathy must heave their sighs
O'er Philomela's pity-pleading strains.
COLERIDGE: *The Nightingale.*

Eastern myth says the nightingale is in love with the ROSE, it presses its heart against the thorn to kill the love pain; it appears in Persian literature as the 'Bulbul'. Pliny says that the bird often dies with its singing, having a special 'variety of song of long continuance' until it dies of the love of the music. Aristotle and Plutarch maintain that the nightingale teaches its young to sing and if reared in captivity they do not sing so well.

**Nightmare.** A sensation in sleep as if something heavy were sitting on one's breast, formerly supposed to be caused by a monster who actually did this. It was not infrequently called the *night-hag*, or the *riding of the witch*. The second syllable is the O.E. *mare* (Old Norse *mara*), an INCUBUS, and it appears in the Fr. *cauchemar*, 'the fiend that tramples'. The word now usually denotes a frightening dream, a night terror.

**Nike** (nī'kē). The Greek winged goddess of victory, according to Hesiod, the daughter of PALLAS and STYX, she helped Zeus and other Olympian gods in the fight against the TITANS. She was an attribute of both Zeus and ATHENE and can be depicted as a small figure carried by them. The Athena Nike is always wingless and as such is called Nike Apteros.

**Nile.** The Egyptians used to say that the rising of the Nile was caused by the tears of ISIS. The feast of Isis was celebrated at the anniversary of the death of OSIRIS, when Isis was supposed to mourn for her husband.

**Nimrod.** Any daring or outstanding hunter; from the 'mighty hunter before the Lord' (*Gen.* x, 9), which the Targum says means a 'sinful hunting of the sons of men'. Pope says of him, he was 'a mighty hunter, and his prey was man' (*Windsor Forest*, 62); so also Milton interprets the phrase (*Paradise Lost*, XII, 24 etc.).

The legend is that the tomb of Nimrod still exists in Damascus, and that no dew ever falls upon it, even though all its surroundings are saturated.

## Nine

*Nimrod* was the pseudonym of Major Charles Apperley (1779–1843), a devotee of hunting and contributor to the *Sporting Magazine*. His best-known works are *The Life of John Mytton Esq.*, *The Chase, the Turf, and the Road*, and the *Life of a Sportsman*.

**Nine.** Nine, Five, Three are mystical numbers—the *diapason*, *diapente*, and *diatrion* of the Greeks. Nine consists of a trinity of trinities. According to the Pythagoreans man is a full chord, or eight notes, and deity comes next. Three, being the trinity, represents a perfect *unity*; twice three is the perfect *dual*; and thrice three is the perfect *plural*. This explains why nine is a mystical number.

From ancient times the number nine has been held of particular significance. DEUCALION'S ark was tossed about for *nine* days before it ran aground on the top of Mount PARNASSUS. There were *nine* MUSES, *nine* Gallicenae or virgin priestesses of the ancient Gallic ORACLE; and Lars Porsena swore by *nine* gods.

NIOBE'S children lay *nine* days in their blood before they were buried; the HYDRA had *nine* heads; at the *Lemuria*, held by the Romans on 9, 11 and 13 May, persons haunted threw black beans over their heads, pronouncing *nine* times the words: 'Avaunt, ye spectres, from this house!' and the EXORCISM was complete (*see* Ovid's *Fasti*).

There were *nine* rivers of HELL, or, according to some accounts, the STYX encompassed the infernal regions in *nine* circles; and Milton makes the gates of HELL 'thrice three-fold', 'three folds were brass, three iron, three of adamantine rock'. They had *nine* folds, *nine* plates and *nine* linings (*Paradise Lost*, II, 645).

VULCAN, when kicked from OLYMPUS, was *nine* days falling to the island of LEMNOS; and when the fallen ANGELS were cast out of HEAVEN Milton says '*Nine* days they fell' (*Paradise Lost*, VI, 871).

In the early Ptolemaic system of astronomy, before the primum mobile was added, there were *nine* spheres; hence Milton, in his *Arcades*, speaks of

The celestial siren's harmony,
That sat upon the nine enfolded spheres.

In Scandinavian mythology there were *nine* earths, HEL being the goddess of the ninth; there were *nine* worlds in NIFLHEIM, and ODIN'S ring dropped eight other rings every *ninth* night.

In folklore *nine* appears frequently. The ABRACADABRA was worn *nine* days, and then flung into a river; in order to see the FAIRIES one is directed to put '*nine* grains of wheat on a four-leaved clover'; *nine* knots are made on black wool as a charm for a sprained ankle; if a servant finds *nine* green peas in a peascod, she lays it on the lintel of the kitchen door, and the first man that enters is to be her cavalier; to see *nine* magpies is most unlucky; a cat has *nine* lives; and the *nine* of Diamonds is known as the Curse of Scotland.

The weird sisters in Shakespeare's *Macbeth* (I, iii) sang, as they danced round the cauldron, 'Thrice to thine, and thrice to mine, and thrice again to make up nine'; and then declared 'the charm wound up'; and we drink a *Three-times-three* to those most highly honoured.

Leases are sometimes granted for 999 years, that is *three* times *three-three-three*. Many run for 99 years, the dual of a trinity of trinities.

There are *nine* orders of angels; in heraldry there are *nine* marks of cadency and *nine* different crowns recognized.

**Nine Men's Morris.** *See under* MORRIS.

**Ninus** (nī'nəs). Son of Belus, husband of SEMIRAMIS, and the reputed builder of Nineveh. It is at his tomb that the lovers meet in the PYRAMUS and Thisbe travesty:

> *Pyr.:* Wilt thou at Ninny's tomb meet me straightway?
> *This.:* 'Tide life, 'tide death, I come without delay.
> SHAKESPEARE: *Midsummer Night's Dream*, V, i.

**Niobe** (nī'əbē). The personification of maternal sorrow. According to Greek legend, Niobe, the daughter of TANTALUS and wife of AMPHION, King of THEBES, was the mother of fourteen children, and taunted LATONA because she had but two—APOLLO and DIANA. Latona commanded her children to avenge the insult and they consequently destroyed Niobe's sons and daughters. Niobe, inconsolable, wept herself to death, and was changed into a stone, from which ran water, 'Like Niobe, all tears' (SHAKESPEARE: *Hamlet*, I, ii).

**Niord, Niordhr,** or **Njorthr** (nyawd, nyawd'ər). A Scandinavian god, protector of wealth and ships, who dwelt at Noatun by the sea-shore. His wife Skadi lived in the mountains, for the gulls disturbed her sleep! *See* CUP OF VOWS; NERTHUS.

**Nip. Number Nip.** Another name for RÜBEZAHL.

**Nisus and Euryalus** (nī'səs, ūrī'ələs). An example of proverbial friendship comparable to that of PYLADES and Orestes. Nisus with a Trojan friend raided the camp of the Rutulians and slaughtered many of the enemy in their drunken sleep, but the youthful Euryalus was killed by Volscens. Nisus rushed to avenge his death and in slaying Volscens was himself killed (*Aeneid*, IX).

**Nivetta.** *See* MORGAN LE FAY.

**Njorthr.** *See* NIORD.

**Noah. Noah's Ark.** A name given by sailors to a white band of cloud spanning the sky like a rainbow and in shape something like the hull of a ship. If east and west, expect dry weather, if north and south, expect wet. Noah's Ark is also used as a PUBLIC-HOUSE SIGN.
**Noah's wife.** According to legend she was unwilling to go into the ark, and the quarrel between the patriarch and his wife forms a prominent feature of *Noah's Flood*, in the Chester and Townley MYSTERIES.

> Hastow not herd, quod Nicholas, also
> The sorwe of Noe with his felawshipe
> Er that he mighte gete his wyf to shipe?
> CHAUCER: *Miller's Tale*, 352.

**Norns, The.** The fates, dispensers of destiny in Norse mythology. They lived at the foot of the ash-tree YGGDRASIL which they watered daily from the fountain called Urd. These sisters eventually became three in number in imitation of the three FATES of classical legend.

**North.** There was an old belief that only evil-doers should be buried on the north side of a churchyard, which probably arose from the lack of sun on this side. The east was *God*'s side, where his throne is set; the west, *man*'s side, the Galilee of the Gentiles; the south, the side of the '*spirits made just*', where the sun shines in his strength; and the north, the *devil*'s side. *Cp.* THE DEVIL'S DOOR *under* DEVIL.

> As men die, so shall they arise; if in faith in the Lord, towards the south...and shall arise in glory; if in unbelief...towards the north, then they are past all hope.
> COVERDALE: *Praying for the Dead.*

**Norwich. Do you know the Bishop of Norwich?** *See under* KNOW.

**Number. There's luck in odd numbers.** This is an ancient fancy. According to the Pythagorean system nine represents Deity. A major chord consists of a fundamental or tonic, its major third, and its just fifth. As the odd numbers are the fundamental notes of nature, the last being the Deity, it is understandable how they came to be considered the great or lucky numbers.

> Good luck lies in odd numbers...They say, there is divinity in odd numbers, either in nativity, chance or death.
> SHAKESPEARE: *The Merry Wives of Windsor*, V, i.

The odd numbers 1, 3, 5, 7, 9 (which *see*), seem to play a far more important part than the even numbers. Virgil (*Eclogues*, viii, 75) says *Numero Deus impare gaudet* (the god delights in odd numbers). THREE indicates the 'beginning, middle and the end'. The Godhead has three persons; so in classical mythology HECATE had threefold power; JOVE's symbol was a triple thunderbolt, NEPTUNE's a sea-trident, PLUTO's a three-headed dog; the Horae three. There are SEVEN notes, NINE planets, nine orders of ANGELS, seven days a week, thirteen lunar months, or 365 days a year etc.; FIVE senses, five fingers, five toes, five continents etc.

In Chinese lore the even numbers are *yin* and inauspicious, with the *yang* odd numbers as auspicious.

**Nut. Here we go gathering nuts in May.** This burden of the old children's game is a corruption of 'Here we go gathering *knots of may*', referring to the old custom of gathering knots of flowers on MAY-DAY *i.e.* 'to go a-maying'. There are no nuts to be gathered in May.
**The Nut-brown Maid.** An English ballad probably dating from the late 15th century, first printed (*c.* 1520) in Arnold's *Chronicle* at Antwerp. It tells how the 'Not-browne Mayd' was wooed and won by a knight who gave out that he was a banished man. After describing the hardships she would have to undergo if she married him, and finding her love true to the test, he revealed himself to

be an earl's son, with large estates in Westmorland.

The ballad is given in Percy's *Reliques*, and forms the basis of Matthew Prior's *Henry and Emma*.

**Nutcrack Night.** ALL HALLOWS' EVE from the customary cracking of nuts.

**Nutter's Dance.** A dance still performed at Bacup, Lancashire, on Easter Saturday. The 'nutters' are eight men clad in black, with white skirts and stockings, with wooden 'nuts' fastened to their hands, waist and knees. The dance is performed to music and time is kept by clapping the nuts.

**Nymphs** (nimfs) (Gr. young maidens). In classical mythology, minor female divinities of nature, of woods, groves, springs, streams, rivers etc. They were young and beautiful maidens and well disposed towards mortals. They were not immortal, but their life span was several thousand years. Particular kinds of nymphs were associated with the various provinces of nature. *See* DRYADS; HAMADRYADS; NAIADS; NEREIDS; OREADS.

# O

**Oak.** The oak was in ancient times sacred to the god of thunder because these trees are said to be more likely to be struck by lightning than any other. The DRUIDS held the oak in greatest veneration and the Wooden Walls of England depended upon it. About 3500 full-grown oaks or 900 acres of oak forest were used in selecting the timber for a large three-decker line-of-battle ship. (*See* HEART OF OAK.) The strength, hardness and durability of the timber, as well as the longevity of the tree, have given the oak a special significance to Englishmen, hence its name the *Monarch of the Forest. See* MISTLETOE.

> I sit beneath your leaves, old oak,
> You mighty one of all the trees;
> Within whose hollow trunk a man
> Could stable his big horse with ease.
>
> W. H. DAVIES: *The Old Oak Tree.*

The oak was sacred to ZEUS/JUPITER in Graeco-Roman myth and there was a yearly ceremony of the marriage of JUPITER to JUNO in an oak grove when the devotees wore oak crowns. The crown of oak leaves was awarded for victory at the PYTHIAN GAMES. DRYADS were oak nymphs and the oak was an emblem of CYBELE and SYLVANUS.

Oak groves were places of worship in Teutonic rites and the tree was sacred to Donas and was THOR's Tree of Life.

Among Amerindians the oak is sacred to the Earth Mother.

Among the famous oaks of Britain are:

The *Abbot's Oak*, near Woburn Abbey, was so called because the abbot of Woburn was hanged on one of its branches, in 1537, by order of Henry VIII.

The *Bull Oak*, Wedgenock Park, was growing at the time of the Conquest.

Cowthorpe Oak, near Wetherby, Yorkshire, will hold 70 persons in its hollow. It is said to be over 1600 years old.

The *Ellerslie Oak*, near Paisley, is reported to have sheltered Sir William Wallace and 300 of his men.

FAIRLOP OAK. *See* FAIRLOP.

*Herne's Oak.* An oak in Windsor Great Park, reputed to be haunted by the ghost of Herne the Hunter (*see* WILD HUNTSMAN). It was supposed to be 650 years old when blown down in 1863. Queen Victoria planted a young oak on the site.

*Honour Oak.* This boundary oak still standing at Whitchurch, Tavistock, marked the Tavistock limit for French prisoners on parole from Princetown prison during the years 1803–1814, when England was at war with France. It was also the place where money was left in exchange for food during the cholera epidemic of 1832.

*King Oak. See William the Conqueror's Oak, below.*

The *Major Oak*, Sherwood Forest, Edwinstowe, is supposed to have been a full-grown tree in the reign of King John. The hollow of the trunk will hold 15 persons, but new bark has considerably diminished the opening. Its girth is 37 or 38 ft., and the head covers a circumference of 240 ft. ROBIN HOOD is supposed to have hidden in it. Originally called the *Queen Oak*, its present name may be a tribute to Major Rooke, an 18th century antiquarian, who was particularly fond of this tree in the Dukeries.

*Meavy Oak.* A venerable oak in front of the lych-gate of Meavy Church, near Yelverton, Devon, some 25 ft. in circumference, in the hollow of which nine persons are once reputed to have dined. According to tradition it dates back to Saxon times.

*Owen Glendower's Oak*, at Shelton, near Shrewsbury, was in full growth in 1403, for in this tree Owen Glendower witnessed the great battle between Henry IV and Henry Percy. Six or eight persons can stand in the hollow of its trunk. Its girth is 40¼ ft.

The *Parliament Oak*, Clipston, in Sherwood Forest, was the tree under which

Edward I held a Parliament in 1282. He was hunting when a messenger announced the Welsh were in revolt under Llewelyn ap Gruffydd. He hastily convened his nobles under the oak and it was resolved to march against the Welsh at once. The tree no longer exists.

*Queen's Oak*, Huntingfield, Suffolk, is so named because near this tree Queen Elizabeth I shot a buck.

The *Reformation Oak*, on Mousehold Heath, near Norwich, is where the rebel Ket held his court in 1549, and when the rebellion was stamped out nine of the ringleaders were hanged on this tree.

*Robin Hood's Larder* was an oak in Sherwood Forest. The tradition is that ROBIN HOOD used its hollow trunk as a hiding-place for the deer he had slain. Late in the last century some schoolgirls boiled their kettle in it, and burnt down a large part of the tree, which was reputed to be 1000 years old. It was blown down in 1966, and the Duke of Portland gave a suitably inscribed remnant to the Mayor of Toronto.

*Sir Philip Sidney's Oak*, near Penshurst, Kent, was planted at his birth in 1554, and was commemorated by Ben Jonson and Waller.

The *Swilcar Oak*, in Needwood Forest, Staffordshire, is between 600 and 700 years old.

The *Watch Oak*, in Windsor Great Park, said to be 800 years old. So called because the Duke of Cumberland (3rd son of George II, who defeated the Jacobites at Culloden in 1745) was said to have stationed a lookout in its branches during target practices to signal the accuracy of the cannon shots.

*William the Conqueror's Oak*, or the King Oak, in Windsor Great Park, which is supposed to have afforded him shelter, is 38 ft. in girth.

**Oakley, Annie.** An expert American markswoman (1860–1926), who in Buffalo Bill's Wild West Show, using a playing card as a target, centred a shot in each of the pips. From this performance of hers, and the resemblance of the card to a punched ticket, springs the American use of the name 'Annie Oakley' to mean a complimentary ticket to a show, a meal ticket, or a pass on a railway.

**Oannes** (ōan'ēz). A Babylonian god having a fish's body and a human head and feet. In the daytime he lived with men to instruct them in the arts and sciences, but at night returned to the depths of the Persian Gulf.

**Obeah, Obi** (ō'biə, ō'bi). The belief in and practice of *obeah*, *i.e.* a kind of sorcery or witchcraft prevalent in West Africa and formerly in the West Indies. *Obeah* is a native word and signifies something put into the ground, to bring about sickness, death, or other disaster. *Cp.* VOODOO.

**Oberon.** King of the FAIRIES, husband of TITANIA. Shakespeare introduced them in his *Midsummer Night's Dream*. The name is probably connected with ALBERICH, the king of the elves.

He first appeared in the mediaeval French romance, *Huon de Bordeaux*, where he is the son of Julius Caesar and MORGAN LE FAY. He was only three feet high, but of angelic face, and was the lord and king of Mommur. At his birth, the fairies bestowed their gifts—one was insight into men's thoughts, and another was the power of transporting himself to any place instantaneously; and in the fullness of time legions of ANGELS conveyed his soul to PARADISE.

**Obi.** *See* OBEAH.

**Occult Sciences** (Lat. *occultus*; related to *celare*, to hide). Magic, ALCHEMY, ASTROLOGY, PALMISTRY, DIVINATION etc.; so called because they were hidden mysteries.

**Oceanus** (ōsē'ənəs). A Greek sea-god; also the river of the world which circles the earth and as such is represented as a snake with its tail in its mouth. As a sea-god, he is an old man with a long beard and with bull's horns on his head.

**Od.** *See* ODYLE.

**Odin** (ō'din). The Scandinavian name of the GOD called by the Anglo-Saxons WODEN. He was god of wisdom, poetry, war and agriculture. As god of the dead, he presided over banquets of those slain in battle. (*See* VALHALLA.) He became the All-wise by drinking of Mimir's fountain, but purchased the distinction at the pledge of one eye, and is often represented as a one-eyed man wearing a hat and carrying a staff. His remaining eye is the SUN, his horse Sleipnir. He was master of magic and discovered the RUNES.

**The promise of Odin.** The most binding of all oaths to a Norseman. In making it the hand was passed through a massive silver ring kept for the purpose; or through a sacrificial stone, like that called the 'Circle of Stennis'. *Cp.* THE STANDING STONES OF STENNESS *under* STONE.

**The vow of Odin.** A matrimonial or other vow made before the 'Stone of Odin' in the Orkneys. This was an oval stone, with a hole in it large enough to admit a man's hand. Anyone who violated a vow made before this stone was held infamous.

**Odyle** (od'il). The name formerly given to the hypothetical force which emanates from a medium to produce the phenomena connected with mesmerism, spirit-rapping, table-turning and so on. Baron von Reichenbach (1788–1869) called it *Od force*, and taught that it pervaded all nature, especially heat, light, crystals, magnets etc., and was developed in chemical action; and also that it streamed from the fingers of specially sensitive persons.

> That od-force of German Reichenbach
> Which still from female finger-tips burns blue.
> BROWNING: *Aurora Leigh*, vii, 566.

**Odyssey** (od'isi). The epic poem of HOMER which records the adventures of Odysseus (ULYSSES) on his homeward voyage from TROY. The word implies the things or adventures of ULYSSES.

**Oedipus** (ē'dipəs) was the son of Laius, King of Thebes, and of Jocasta the Queen. To avert the fulfilment of the prophecy that he would murder his father and marry his mother, Oedipus was exposed on the mountains as an infant and taken in and reared by the shepherds. When grown to manhood he unwittingly killed his father; then, having solved the riddle of the SPHINX, he became King of THEBES, thereby gaining the hand in marriage of Jocasta, his mother, of whose relationship to himself they were both ignorant. When the facts came to light Jocasta hanged herself and Oedipus tore out his own eyes.

**Oenone** (ēnō'nē). A NYMPH of Mount IDA, the wife of PARIS before he abducted HELEN. She prophesied the disastrous consequences of his voyage to Greece and, on the death of Paris, killed herself.

**Og,** King of Bashan, according to Rabbinical legend, was an antediluvian GIANT, saved from the Flood by climbing on the roof of the ark. After the passage of the Red Sea, MOSES first conquered Sihon, and then advanced against the giant Og whose bedstead, made of iron, was 9 cubits long and 4 cubits broad (*Deut.* iii, 11). The legend says that Og plucked up a mountain to hurl at the Israelites, but he got so entangled with his burden that Moses was able to kill him without much difficulty.

In Dryden's *Absalom and Achitophel*, Og is used for Thomas Shadwell, who was very large and fat.

**Ogier the Dane** (ō'jiə). One of the great heroes of mediaeval romance whose exploits are chronicled in the CHANSONS DE GESTE; son of Geoffrey, King of Denmark, of which country (as Holger Danske) he is still the national hero. In one account his son was slain by CHARLEMAGNE'S son Charlot and in revenge Ogier killed the king's nephew and was only prevented from slaying Charlemagne himself. He eventually returned from exile to defend France against the Saracen chief Brehus. In another romance, it is said, FAIRIES attended his birth, among them MORGAN LE FAY, who eventually took him to AVALON where he dwelt for 200 years. She then sent him to defend France against invasion, after which she took him back to Avalon. William Morris gives a rendering of this romance in his *Earthly Paradise* (*August*).

**Ogres** of nursery story are GIANTS of very malignant disposition, who live on human flesh. The word was first used (and probably invented) by Perrault in his *Histoires ou Contes du temps passé* (1697), and is thought to be made up from *Orcus*, a name of PLUTO.

**Ogygia** (ōjij'iə). *See* CALYPSO.

**Ogygian Deluge.** In Greek legend, a flood said to have occurred when Ogyges was King of Boeotia, some 200 years before DEUCALION'S flood. Varro says that the planet VENUS underwent a great change in the reign of Ogyges. It changed its diameter, its colour, its figure and its course.

**Old. Old Man of the Sea.** In the story of *Sinbad the Sailor* (ARABIAN NIGHTS), the Old Man of the Sea hoisted himself on Sinbad's shoulders and clung there for many days and nights, much to the discomfort of Sinbad, who finally got rid of the Old Man by making him drunk. Hence, any burden, figurative or actual, of which it is impossible to free oneself without the greatest exertions is called an Old Man of the Sea. *Cp.* NEREUS.

**Old Mother Hubbard.** This lastingly popular nursery rhyme is one of definitely known origin and was first published in 1805. It was written by Sarah Catherine Martin (1768–1821) while staying with her brother-in-law, J. P. Bastard of Kitley, Yealmpton, South Devon. It is traditionally said that Mother Hubbard was the housekeeper at Kitley and there is a cottage at Yealmpton purporting to be her one-time residence.

> Old Mother Hubbard
> Went to the cupboard
> To fetch her poor dog a bone;
> But when she came there
> The cupboard was bare
> And so the poor dog had none.

**Old Nick.** *See under* NICHOLAS.

**Olive.** In ancient Greece the olive was sacred to PALLAS, in allusion to the story that at the naming of ATHENS she presented it with an olive branch. It was the symbol of peace and fecundity, brides wearing or carrying an olive garland as ours do a wreath of orange blossom. A crown of olive was the highest distinction of a citizen who deserved well of his country, and was the highest prize in the OLYMPIC GAMES.

In the Old Testament, the subsiding of the FLOOD was demonstrated to Noah by the return of a DOVE bearing an olive leaf in her beak (*Gen.* viii, 11).

**Oliver.** CHARLEMAGNE's favourite PALADIN, who, with ROLAND, rode by his side. He was the son of Regnier, Duke of Genoa (another of the paladins), and brother of the beautiful Aude. His sword was called *Hauteclaire*, and his horse *Ferrant d'Espagne*.

**A Roland for an Oliver.** *See under* ROLAND.

**Olympia.** The ancient name of a valley in Elis, Peloponnesus, so called from the famous games held there in honour of the OLYMPIAN ZEUS. The ALTIS, an enclosure of about 500 ft. by 600 ft., was built in the valley, containing the temple of Zeus, the Heroeum, the Metroum etc., the STADIUM, with gymnasia, baths etc. Hence the name is applied to large buildings for sporting events, exhibitions etc., such as the Olympia at Kensington, London.

**Olympiad.** Among the ancient Greeks, a period of four years, being the interval between the celebrations of the OLYMPIC GAMES. The first Olympiad began in 776 B.C., and the last (the 293rd) in A.D. 392.

**Olympian Zeus,** or **Jove.** A statue by Phidias, one of the 'Seven Wonders of the World' (*see under* WONDER). Pausanias (vii, 2) says when the sculptor placed it in the temple at OLYMPIA (433 B.C.), he prayed to the god to indicate whether he was satisfied with it, and immediately a thunderbolt fell on the floor of the temple without doing the slightest harm.

It was a chryselephantine statue, *i.e.* made of ivory and gold; and, though seated on a throne, was 60 ft. in height. The left hand rested on a sceptre, and the right palm held a statue of Victory in solid gold. The robes were of gold and so were the four lions which supported the footstool. The throne was of cedar, embellished with ebony, ivory, gold and precious stones.

It was removed to Constantinople in the 5th century A.D., and perished in the great fire of 475.

**Olympic Games.** The greatest of the four sacred festivals of the ancient Greeks, held every fourth year at OLYMPIA in July. After suitable sacrifices, racing, wrestling and other contests followed, ending on the fifth day with processions, sacrifices and banquets and OLIVE garlands for the victors.

The games were revived in 1896 as international sporting contests, the first being held at Athens, and subsequently at Paris (1900), St. Louis (1904), London (1908), Stockholm (1912), Antwerp (1920), Paris (1924), Amsterdam (1928), Los Angeles (1932), Berlin (1936), London (1948), Helsinki (1952), Melbourne (1956), Rome (1960), Tokyo (1964), Mexico City (1968), Munich (1972), Montreal (1976), Moscow (1980), Los Angeles (1984), Seoul (1988), Barcelona (1992).

Winter Olympic Games were inaugurated in 1924.

**Olympus.** The home of the gods of ancient Greece, where ZEUS held his court, a mountain about 9800 ft. high on the confines of Macedonia and Thessaly. The name is used for any PANTHEON, as, 'ODIN, THOR, BALDER, and the rest of the Northern Olympus.'

**Om.** Among the BRAHMINS, the mystic equivalent for the name of the Deity; it has been adopted by modern occultists to denote absolute goodness and truth or the spiritual essence.

**Om mani padme hum** ('Omm, the jewel, is in the lotus: Amen'). The mystic formula of the Tibetans and northern Buddhists used as a charm and for many religious purposes. They are the first words taught to a child and the last uttered on the death-bed of the pious. The LOTUS symbolizes universal being, and the jewel the individuality of the utterer.

**Omens.** Phenomena or unusual events taken as a prognostication of either good or evil; prophetic signs or auguries. *Omen* is a Latin word adopted in the 16th century. Some traditional examples of accepting what appeared to be evil omens, as of good AUGURY, are:

Leotychides II, of Sparta, was told by his augurs that his projected expedition would fail because a viper had got entangled in the handle of the city key 'Not so,' he replied, 'the key caught the viper.'

When Julius Caesar landed at Adrumetum he tripped and fell on his face. This would have been considered a fatal omen by his army, but, with admirable presence of mind, he explained, 'Thus I take possession of thee, O Africa!' A similar story is told of Scipio.

When William the Conqueror leaped upon the English shore he fell on his face and a great cry went forth that it was an ill-omen; but the duke exclaimed, 'I have taken seisin of this land with both my hands.'

**Omphale** (om'fəlē). In Greek legend, the Queen of Lydia of masculine inclinations to whom HERCULES was bound a slave for three years. He fell in love with her and led a submissive life spinning wool. Omphale wore the lion's skin while Hercules wore a female garment.

**Oneiromancy** (ōnī'rōmansi) (Gr. *oneiros*, a dream; *manteia*, prophecy). DIVINATION from dreams.

**Open Sesame.** *See* SESAME.

**Ops.** The old SABINE fertility goddess and wife of SATURN. She was later identified with RHEA.

**Oracle** (Lat. *oraculum*; from *orare*, to speak, to pray). The answer of a god or inspired priest to an inquiry respecting the future; the deity giving responses; the place where the deity could be consulted etc.; hence, a person whose utterances are regarded as profoundly wise and authoritative.

> I am Sir Oracle,
> And when I ope my lips let no dog bark.
> SHAKESPEARE: *The Merchant of Venice*, I, i.

The most famous of the very numerous oracles of ancient Greece were those of:

APOLLO, at DELPHI, the priestess of which was called the Pythoness; at DELOS, and at Claros.

DIANA, at Colchis.

AESCULAPIUS, at Epidaurus, and at Rome.

HERCULES, at ATHENS and Gades.

JUPITER, at DODONA (the most noted), AMMON in Libya, and in Crete.

MARS, in Thrace.

MINERVA, at Mycenae.

PAN, in ARCADIA.

TROPHONIUS, in BOEOTIA, where only men made the responses.

VENUS, at Paphos, another at Aphaea etc.

In most of the temples, women, sitting on a tripod, made the responses, many of which were ambiguous and so obscure as to be misleading; to this day, our word *oracular* is still used of obscure as well as of authoritative pronouncements. Examples are:

When CROESUS consulted the Delphic oracle respecting a projected war, he received for answer, *'Croesus Halyn penetrans magnum pervertet opum vim'* (When Croesus crosses over the river Halys, he will overthrow the strength of an empire). Croesus supposed the oracle meant he would overthrow the enemy's empire, but it was his own that he destroyed when defeated by Cyrus.

Pyrrhus, being about to make war against Rome, was told by the oracle: *'Credo te, Aeacide, Romanos vincere posse'* (I believe, Pyrrhus, that you the Romans can conquer), which may mean either 'You, Pyrrhus, can overthrow the Romans', or 'Pyrrhus, the Romans can overthrow you'.

Another prince, consulting the oracle on a similar occasion, received for answer. *'Ibis redibis nunquam per bella peribis'* (You shall go you shall return never you shall perish by the war), the interpretation of which depends on the position of the comma; it may be 'You shall return, you shall never perish in the war', or 'You shall return never, you shall perish in the war', which latter was the fact.

Philip of Macedon sent to ask the oracle of Delphi if his Persian expedition would prove successful, and received for answer—

The ready victim crowned for death
Before the altar stands

Philip took it for granted that the 'ready victim' was the King of Persia, but it was Philip himself.

When the Greeks sent to Delphi to know if they would succeed against the Persians, they were told

Seed-time and harvest, weeping sires shall tell
How thousands fought at Salamis and fell.

But whether the Greeks or the Persians were to be the 'weeping sires', no indication was given, nor whether the thousands 'about to fall' were to be Greeks or Persians.

When Maxentius was about to encounter Constantine, he consulted the guardians of the SIBYLLINE BOOKS as to the fate of the battle, and the prophetess told him, *'Illo die hostem Romanorum esse periturum'*, but whether Maxentius or Constantine was the 'enemy of the Roman people' the oracle left undecided.

In the Bible (I *Kings* xxii, 15, 35) we are told that when Ahab, King of Israel, was about to wage war on the King of Syria, and asked Micaiah if Ramoth-Gilead would fall into his hands, the prophet replied, 'Go, for the Lord will deliver the city into the hand of the king.' In the event, the city fell into the hands of the King of Syria.

**The Oracle of the Holy Bottle.** The oracle to which Rabelais (Bks. IV and V) sent PANURGE and a large party to obtain an answer to a question which had been put to SIBYL and poet, monk and fool, philosopher and witch, judge and fortune-teller: 'whether Panurge should marry or not?' The oracle was situated at BACBUC 'near Catay in Upper India', and the story has been interpreted as a satire on the Church. The celibacy of the clergy was for long a moot point, and the 'Holy Bottle' or cup to the laity was one of the moving causes of the schisms from the Church. The crew setting sail for the Bottle refers to Anthony, Duke of Vendôme, afterwards King of Navarre, setting out in search of religious truth.

**Orc.** A sea-monster fabled by Ariosto, Drayton, Sylvester etc. to devour men and women. According to Pliny, it was a huge creature 'armed with teeth'. The name was sometimes used for a whale.

> An island salt and bare,
> The haunt of seals and orcs, and sea-mews clang.
> MILTON: *Paradise Lost*, XI, 829.

**Orcus.** A Latin name for HADES. Spenser speaks of a DRAGON whose mouth was:

> All set with iron teeth in ranges twain,
> That terrified his foes, and armed him,
> Appearing like the mouth of Orcus grisely grim.
> *The Faerie Queene*, VI, xii, 26.

**Oreads** (aw'riadz) or **Oreades.** NYMPHS of the mountains (Gr. *oros*, mountain).

> The Ocean-nymphs and Hamadryades,
> Oreads and Naiads, with long weedy locks,
> Offered to do her bidding through the seas,
> Under the earth, and in the hollow rocks.
> SHELLEY: *Witch of Atlas*, xxii.

**Orestes.** *See* PYLADES.

**Orgies.** Drunken revels, riotous feasts, wild or licentious extravagance. So called from the Gr. *orgia*, the secret nocturnal festivals in honour of BACCHUS.

**Orion** (orī'ən). A giant hunter of Greek mythology, noted for his beauty. He was blinded by Oenopion, but VULCAN sent Cedalion to be his guide, and his sight was restored by exposing his eyeballs to the sun. Being slain by DIANA, he was made one of the constellations and is supposed to be attended with stormy weather. His wife was named Side and his dogs Arctophonus and Ptoophagus.

The constellation Orion is pictured as a giant hunter with belt and sword surrounded by his dogs and animals. Betelgeuse and Bellatrix are the 'shoulder' stars and three bright stars in a line form the belt, below which is the sword-handle containing a remarkable nebula.

**Orlando.** The Italian form of ROLAND, one of the great heroes of mediaeval romance, and the most celebrated of CHARLEMAGNE's PALADINS.

**Ormuzd** (aw'məzd), or **Ahura Mazda** (əhoo'rə maz'də). In Zoroastrianism, the principle or ANGEL of light and good, and creator of all things and judge of the world. He is in perpetual conflict with AHRIMAN but in the end will triumph.

And Oromaze, Joshua, and Mahomet,
Moses and Buddha, Zerdusht, and Brahm, and Foh,
A tumult of strange names, which never met
Before, as watchwords of a single woe, Arose.
SHELLEY: *Revolt of Islam*, X, xxxi.

**Orpheus** (aw'fiəs). In Greek legend, a Thracian poet, son of Oeagrus and CALL-IOPE (held by some to be a son of APOLLO), who could move even inanimate things by his music—a power that was also claimed for the Scandinavian ODIN. When his wife EURYDICE died he went into the infernal regions and so charmed PLUTO that she was released on the condition that he would not look back till they reached the earth. When about to place his foot on the earth he turned round and Eurydice vanished instantly.

That Orpheus' self may ... hear
Such strains as would have won the ear
Of Pluto, to have quite set free
His half regain'd Eurydice.
MILTON: *L'Allegro*, 145–50.

The prolonged grief of Orpheus at his second loss so enraged the Thracian women that in one of their Bacchanalian ORGIES they tore him to pieces. The fragments of his body were collected by the MUSES and buried at the foot of Mount OLYMPUS, but his head, thrown into the river Hebrus, was carried into the sea, and so to Lesbos, where it was buried.

What could the Muse herself that Orpheus bore,
The Muse herself, for her enchanting son,
Whom universal nature did lament,
When by the rout that made the hideous roar
His gory visage down the stream was sent,
Down the swift Hebrus to the Lesbian shore?
MILTON: *Lycidas*, 58.

**Orpheus of Highwaymen.** So John Gay (1685–1732) has been called on account of his *Beggar's Opera* (1728).
**The Orphic Egg.** *See* MUNDANE EGG *under* EGG.

**Orthos,** or **Orthrus.** The dog of GERYON, destroyed by HERCULES. *See* ECHIDNA.

**Osiris** (ōsī'ris). One of the chief gods of ancient Egypt; son of Nut, brother of SET, his jealous and constant foe, and husband of ISIS. Set encompassed his death, but Osiris underwent resurrection with the aid of THOTH. His son HORUS became his avenger. He was the god of the dead and of the after-life and resurrection.

The name means *Many-eyed* and Osiris is usually depicted as a man wearing the White Crown and holding a sceptre and flail, as a mummy.

**Osmand.** A necromancer in *The Seven Champions of Christendom*, I, xix, who by enchantment raised an army to resist the Christians. Six of the Champions fell, whereupon St. GEORGE restored them; Osmand tore out his own hair, in which lay his magic power, bit his tongue in two, disembowelled himself, cut off his arms and then died. *See* SEVEN CHAMPIONS.

**Ossa.** *See* PELION.

**Ossian,** or **Oisin.** The legendary Gaelic bard and celebrated warrior hero of the 3rd century, the son of Fionn Mac Cumhail (FINGAL). He is best known from the publications (1760–1763) of James Macpherson born at Ruthven, Inverness (1736–1796), purporting to be translations of poems by Ossian, the son of Fingal, from original MSS. Macpherson became famous and his works were widely translated, but their authenticity was challenged by Dr. Johnson in his *Journey to the Western Islands of Scotland*, and others. They seem to have been essentially made up by Macpherson himself with some use of ancient sources.

'I [Johnson] look upon M'Pherson's Fingal to be as gross an imposition as ever the world was troubled with.'
BOSWELL: *The Journal of a Tour to the Hebrides* (Wed., 22 Sept.).

**Ostrich.** The mythology of the ostrich varies greatly in significance, on the one hand it can be demonic; on the other it can have divine qualities. The demonic aspect appears in Semitic myth where the bird can represent a dragon, as in the Babylonian MARDUK versus TIAMAT conflict; Marduk could be represented by an EAGLE and Tiamat by an ostrich, but in Egyptian myth the ostrich feather is an attribute of Maat, goddess of truth and justice, and it is this feather against which the heart of the deceased is weighed in the Judgment Hall of OSIRIS. The feather is also worn on the heads of divinities as Masters of Truth and the bird is an emblem of Amenti, goddess of the west and the dead.

In Zoroastrianism the ostrich is a divine storm bird.

Both the ostrich and its eggs are the subject of many strange myths. The best known is probably that of hiding its head in the sand if danger approaches; the belief is maintained by Pliny and Oppian and Pliny adds that it also hides its head in a bush, but Diodorus says that the hiding of the head is not stupidity, as is usually assumed, but that it hides it to protect 'the tenderest part of the body'.

As for its legendary digestive powers, Pliny says it can eat anything; Aelian and Albertus say it eats stones, while one version of the Physiologus asserts that it swallows iron and fiery coals which are good for its cold stomach. These fables found their way into heraldry where the ostrich usually holds a horseshoe, key or piece of iron in its beak. Ostrich feathers play a large part in heraldry.

Mythology is equally ambivalent over the eggs, their care and symbolism. The Old Testament says the ostrich 'leaveth her eggs on the earth and warmeth them in the dust and forgetteth that the foot may crush them ... she is hardened against her young ones'. (*Job* xxxix, 14–16). Aelian, on the contrary, says she shows solicitude for her eggs. As to their hatching, the Physiologus says that, like the TORTOISE, the ostrich hatches the eggs by the heat of the parents' gaze and if this is removed the eggs become addled and break, but the Bestiaries (which also call the bird the Assida) say the eggs are left to hatch by the warmth of heaven and that they are laid when the PLEIADES appear.

In Arabian legend the ostrich is a cross between a camel and a bird and can adopt the form of a JINN, but it is regarded as stupid.

The ostrich is an African cult bird and there are ritual ostrich dances. It typifies both light and water, the latter from its undulating movement, and its eggs are a vehicle of supernatural power among the Kung Bushmen and the Dogons. The eggs may also be seen suspended in Coptic churches, temples and mosques as signifying creation, life and resurrection.

South American Indian myth associates the bird, or its counterpart, with the dead; it is the male incarnation coupled with the female armadillo and dances are performed at festivals of the dead.

**Otus.** *See* EPHIALTES.

**Ouzelum Bird** (oo'zələm). This fanciful bird is reputed to fly backwards and thus does not know where it is going but likes to know where it has been.

**Owain.** The hero of a 12th-century legend, *The Descent of Owain*, written by Henry of Saltrey, an English Cistercian. Owain was an Irish knight of Stephen's court who, by way of penance for a wicked life, entered and passed through St. Patrick's Purgatory.

**Owl.** The emblem of Athens, where owls abounded. Hence MINERVA (ATHENE) was given the owl for her symbol. The Greeks had a proverb, **To send owls to Athens,** which meant the same as our *To carry coals to Newcastle.*

The owl was also sacred to DEMETER and was regarded as prophetic; the death of DIDO and several Roman emperors was foretold by an owl alighting on the house, the hoot was also a death warning.

In Hebrew lore the bird represents blindness and desolation and is unclean.

The magical, sacred aspect of the owl is prominent in Celtic myth where, in early times, it was depicted in La Tène figures and where it preceded the cult of Athene and her owl. It was a bird of darkness and the underworld, the 'night hag', the 'corpse bird' and was an attribute of Gwyan or Gwynn, god of the underworld who ruled the souls of warriors.

The Vedic god of the dead, YAMA, has the owl as an attribute and could employ it as one of his messengers instead of his two DOGS.

The owl as a bird of ill omen occurs in the Middle East where it can be the embodiment of evil spirits and can carry off children at night, while in China and Japan it also signifies crime and ungrateful children, though among the Ainu of Japan the Eagle Owl is beneficent and revered as a messenger between gods and humanity; the Screech Owl warns against danger and helps the hunter, but the Horned Owl and Barn Owl are demonic and ill-omened.

The death-warning legends also obtain among Amerindians where the owl is called the Night Eagle and is a bird of sorcerers, and can be a ghost of the dead and a messenger to the otherworld. An exception occurs among the South East Woodland people who hold the owl and cougar sacred for their ability to see in the dark; the owl is the Chief of the Night and gives protection.

The owl can be used by WIZARDS and is their messenger among West African tribes and the head is used for evil spells; again, its cry presages evil. Australian Aboriginals also say the owl is a messenger of the evil deity Muurup who eats children and kills people. The bird is also unlucky among the Maoris, but is sacred in Samoa.

**I live too near a wood to be scared by an owl.** I am too old to be frightened by a BOGY.

**Like an owl in an ivy-bush.** Having a sapient, vacant look, as some persons have when in their cups; having a stupid vacant stare. Owls are proverbial for their judge-like solemnity; IVY is the favourite plant of BACCHUS, and was supposed to be the favourite haunt of owls.

> Good ivy, say to us, what birds hast thou?
> None but the owlet that cries 'How How!'
> *Carol* (15th century).

Gray, in his *Elegy*, and numerous other poets bracket the two:

> From yonder ivy-mantled tower
> The moping owl doth to the moon complain.

**The owl was a baker's daughter.** According to a Gloucestershire legend, our Saviour went into a baker's shop for something to eat. The mistress put a cake into the oven for Him, but her daughter said it was too large, and reduced it by half. The dough, however, swelled to an enormous size, and the daughter cried out, 'Heugh! heugh! heugh!' and was transformed into an OWL. Ophelia alludes to the tradition:

> Well, God 'ield you! They say the owl was a baker's daughter.
> SHAKESPEARE: *Hamlet*, IV, v.

**Ox.** The ox is one of the chief sacrificial animals and according to Varro it was a capital offence to kill one in Attica and Peleponnesus except in sacrifice; even then a scapegoat had to be found to bear the blame for the murder, this could be either a person or it could be the knife used which was cursed and thrown away.

At Pompeii BACCHUS and ARIADNE are depicted in their triumphal car drawn by oxen and a catacomb painting shows Jacob and his sons travelling to Egypt in carts drawn by oxen. There was a Hebrew ban on oxen and asses being yoked together (*Deut.* xxii, 10).

In the Far East the ox and the water-buffalo are interchangeable in legend, as is the yak of Tibet. In China there was a god of oxen, Niu-Wang, and the Golden Haired Buffalo protected against epidemics affecting oxen; his image was placed on stables for protection and he was also the spirit of the star T'ien-wen.

**The black ox hath trod on your foot,** or **hath trampled on you.** Misfortune has come to you or your house; sometimes, you are henpecked. A black ox was sacrificed to PLUTO, the infernal god, as a white one was to JUPITER.

> Venus waxeth old; and then she was a pretie wench, when Juno was a young wife; now crowes foote is on her eye, and the blacke oxe hath trod on her foot.
> LYLY: *Sapho and Phao*, IV, ii.

# P

**Pactolus. The golden sands of the Pactolus.** The Pactolus is a small river in Lydia, Asia Minor, once famous for the particles of gold in its sands, which legendarily were due to MIDAS having bathed there. Its gold was exhausted by the time of Augustus.

**Padua** was long supposed in Scotland to be the chief school of NECROMANCY, hence Scott says of the Earl of Gowrie:

> He learned the art that none may name
> In Padua, far beyond the sea.
> *Lay of the Last Minstrel*, I, xi.

**Paean** (pē'ən). According to HOMER, the name of the physician to the gods. It was used in the phrase *Io Paean* as the invocation in the hymn to APOLLO, and later in hymns of thanksgiving to other deities, hence *paean* has come to mean any song of praise or thanksgiving, any shout of triumph or exultation.

**Painter.** It is said that Apelles, being at a loss to delineate the foam of ALEXANDER's horse, dashed his brush at the picture in despair, and did by accident what he could not accomplish by art. Similar stories are told of many other artists and also of the living quality of their paintings. It is reputed that Apelles painted Alexander's horse so realistically that a living horse mistook it and began to neigh. Velasquez painted a Spanish Admiral so true to life that Philip IV mistook the painting for the man and reproved the portrait for not being with the fleet. Birds flew at grapes painted by Zeuxis; and Mandyn tried to brush off a fly from a man's leg, both having been painted by Matsys. Parrhasios of Ephesus painted a curtain so well that Zeuxis told him to draw it aside to reveal the picture behind it; and Myron, the Greek sculptor, is said to have fashioned a cow so well that a bull mistook it for a living creature.

Similar legends occur in Chinese art where horses gallop off the canvas and a dragon took flight as soon as its eyes had been painted in.

**Palaemon** (palē'mən). In Roman legend, a son of Ino (*see* LEUCOTHEA), and originally called MELICERTES. Palaemon is the name given to him after he was made a sea-god, and as Portumnus he was the protecting god of harbours. The story is given in Spenser's *Faerie Queene* (IX, xi); in the same poet's *Colin Clout* his name is used for Thomas Churchyard (*c.* 1520–1604), the poet.

**Palamedes** (paləmē'dēz). In Greek legend, one of the heroes who fought against TROY. He was the son of Nauplius and Clymene, and was the reputed inventor of lighthouses, scales and measures, the discus, dice etc., and was said to have added four letters to the original alphabet of CADMUS. It was he who detected the assumed madness of ULYSSES, in revenge for which the latter encompassed his death. The phrase, *he is quite a Palamedes*, meaning 'an ingenious person' is an allusion to this hero.

In ARTHURIAN ROMANCE, Sir Palamedes is a Saracen knight who was overcome in single combat by TRISTRAM. Both loved YSOLDE, the wife of King Mark; and after the lady was given up by the Saracen, Tristram converted him to the Christian faith, and stood his godfather at the font.

**Palamon and Arcite.** *See* ARCITE.

**Pales** (pā'lēz). The Roman god (later a goddess) of shepherds and their flocks whose festivals, *Palilias*, were celebrated on 21 April, the 'birthday of Rome', to commemorate the day when ROMULUS, the wolf-child, drew the first furrow at the foot of the hill, and thus laid the foundations of the 'Rome Quadrata', the most ancient part of the city.

**Palinurus** (palinū'rəs), or **Palinure.** Any pilot, especially a careless one; from the steersman in Virgil's AENEID who went to sleep at the helm, fell overboard and was swept ashore three days later, only to be murdered on landing.

Lost was the nation's sense, nor could be found,
While the long solemn unison went round;
Wide and more wide, it spread o'er all the realm;
Even Palinurus nodded at the helm.
POPE: *The Dunciad*, IV, 611.

**Palladium.** In classical legend, the colossal wooden statue of PALLAS in the citadel of TROY, which was said to have fallen from HEAVEN, and on the preservation of which the safety of the city was held to depend. It was said to have been taken by the Greeks and the city burned down; and later said to have been removed to Rome by AENEAS.

Hence the word is now figuratively applied to anything on which the safety of a people etc. is supposed to depend.

The liberty of the press is the palladium of all the civil, political, and religious rights of an English man.
*Letters of Junius: Dedication.*

*See also* ANCILE; EDEN HALL.

The rare metallic element, found associated with platinum and gold, was named palladium by its discoverer, Wollaston (1803), from the newly discovered asteroid, Pallas. The London theatre called *The Palladium* appears to derive its name from the mistaken notion that the ancient Palladium, like the Colosseum, was something akin to a circus.

**Pallas,** or **Pallas Athene.** A name of MINERVA, sometimes called *Pallas Minerva* daughter of JUPITER, perhaps so called from the spear which she brandished. Another suggestion is that she was named after Pallas, one of the TITANS, whom she flayed, using his skin as a covering.

**Palmistry,** or **Chiromancy** (Gr. *cheir*, the hand, *manteia*, DIVINATION). The art of reading the palm (of the hand) and deducing the character, temperament, fortune etc. of the owner from the lines upon it. The art is ancient and was practised by the Greeks, Chaldean astrologers, gypsies etc.

**Pan** (Gr. all, everything). In Greek mythology, the god of pastures, forests, flocks and herds; also the universal deity. Another more probable etymology is that the name is derived from the same root as Lat. *pascere*, to graze. His parentage is variously given as born of JUPITER and CALLISTO, HERMES and PENELOPE etc., and he is represented with the upper part of a man and the body and legs of a goat. His lustful nature was a characteristic and he was the symbol of fecundity.

Universal Pan,
Knit with the Graces and the Hours in dance,
Led on the eternal spring.
MILTON: *Paradise Lost*, IV, 266.

Legend has it that at the time of the Crucifixion, just when the veil of the temple was rent in twain, a cry swept across the ocean in the hearing of a pilot, 'Great Pan is Dead', and at the same time the responses of the ORACLES ceased for ever. (See E.B. Browning's poem of this name.) It has been suggested that what the mariner heard was a ritual lamentation in honour of ADONIS. *See also* PANIC.

**Pan-pipes.** A wind instrument of great antiquity, consisting of a series of pipes of graduated length, across the upper ends of which the player blows, obtaining a scale of thin, reedy notes. The story is that it was first formed by PAN from a reed into which the nymph SYRINX was transformed when fleeing from his amorous intentions.

**Panacea** (panəsē′ə) (Gr. all-healing). A universal remedy. Panacea was the daughter of AESCULAPIUS, and the medicine that cures is the daughter or child of the healing art.

In the Middle Ages the search for the panacea was one of the self-imposed tasks of the alchemists. Fable tells of many panaceas, such as the PROMETHEAN UN-GUENT which rendered the body invulnerable, ALADDIN'S ring, the balsam of FIERA-BRAS, and PRINCE AHMED'S APPLE (*see under* APPLE). *Cp.* ACHILLES'S SPEAR; MEDEA'S KETTLE etc.

**Panchaea** (pankē′ə). A fabulous land, possibly belonging to Arabia Felix, renowned among the ancients for the quality of its perfumes, such as myrrh and incense.

**Pandarus** (pan′dərəs). In Greek legend, a Lycian leader and ally of the Trojans. Owing to his later connection with the story of TROILUS and CRESSIDA, he was taken over by the romance-writers of the Middle Ages as a procurer.

**Pandemonium** (Gr. all the demons). A wild, unrestrained uproar, a tumultuous assembly, the word was first used by

Milton as the name of the principal city in HELL. It was formed on the analogy of PANTHEON.

> The rest were all
> Far to the inland retired, about the walls
> Of Pandemonium city and proud seat
> Of Lucifer.
> *Paradise Lost*, X, 424 (*see also* I, 756).

**Pandora's Box.** A present which seems valuable, but which in reality is a curse; like that of MIDAS, who found his very food became gold, and so uneatable.

To punish PROMETHEUS, ZEUS ordered HEPHAESTUS to fashion a beautiful woman who was named Pandora (*i.e.* the All-gifted), because each of the gods gave her some power which was to bring about the ruin of man. According to Hesiod, she was the first mortal female and was sent by Zeus as a gift to Epimetheus who married her, against the advice of his brother, Prometheus. She brought with her a large jar or vase (Pandora's box) which she opened and all the evils flew forth, and they have ever since continued to afflict the world. Hope alone remained in the box.

**Pangloss, Dr.** (Gr. all tongues). The pedantic old tutor to the hero in Voltaire's *Candide, ou l'optimisme* (1759). His great point was his incurable and misleading optimism; it did him no good and brought him all sorts of misfortune, but to the end he reiterated 'all is for the best in this best of all possible worlds'. This was an attack upon the current theories of Leibnitz.

**Panic.** The word comes from the god PAN because the sounds heard by night in the mountains and valleys, which give rise to sudden and unwarranted fear, were attributed to him. There are various legends accounting for the name; one is that BACCHUS, in his eastern expeditions, was opposed by an army far superior to his own, and Pan advised him to command all his men at dead of night to raise a simultaneous shout. The innumerable echoes made the enemy think they were surrounded on all sides, and they took to sudden flight. Another belief is that he could make men, cattle etc. bolt in 'Panic' terror. *Cp. Judges* vii, 18–21.

**Panope.** *See* NEREIDS.

**Pantagruel** (pantəgruel'). The principal character in Rabelais' great satire *The History of Gargantua and Pantagruel* (the first part published in 1532, the last posthumously in 1564). He was King of Dipsodes and son of GARGANTUA and by some identified with Henri II of France. He was the last of the giants, and Rabelais says he got his name from the Gr. *panta*, all, and Arab. *gruel*, thirsty, because he was born during the drought which lasted thirty and six months, three weeks, four days, thirteen hours, and a little more, in that year of grace noted for having 'three Thursdays in one week'. Though he was chained in his cradle with four great iron chains, like those used in ships, he stamped out the bottom, which was made of weavers' beams. When he grew to manhood he knew all languages, all sciences, and all knowledge of every sort, out-Solomoning Solomon in wisdom. His immortal achievement was his voyage to UTOPIA in quest of the ORACLE of The Holy Bottle. *See* PANURGE.

> Wouldst thou not issue forth …
> To see the third part of this earthy cell
> Of the brave acts of good Pantagruel.
> RABELAIS: *To the Spirit of the Queen of Navarre.*

**Pantagruelism.** Coarse and boisterous buffoonery and humour, especially with a serious purpose—like that for which PANTAGRUEL was famous.

**Pantaloon.** Breeches, trousers, underdrawers or *pants*, get their name from *Pantaloon*, a lean and foolish old Venetian of 16th-century Italian comedy, who was dressed in loose trousers and slippers. His name is said to come from San Pantaleone (a patron SAINT of physicians and very popular in Venice), and he was adopted in later harlequinades and PANTOMIMES as the butt of the clown's jokes.

**Pantheon** (Gr. *pan*, all; *theos*, god). A temple dedicated to all the gods; especially that at Rome built by Hadrian (*c.* 120 A.D.), its predecessor (begun by Agrippa in 27 B.C.) having been largely destroyed by fire. It is circular and over 140 ft. in diameter and of similar height. Since the early 7th century, as Santa Maria Rotunda, it has been used as a Christian Church. Among the national heroes buried there are Raphael, Victor Emmanuel II, and Humbert I. Hadrian also built the Pantheon at Athens.

The Panthéon at Paris was originally the church of Ste. Geneviève, started by Louis

XV in 1764 and completed in 1812. In 1791 the Constituent Assembly renamed it the Panthéon and decreed that men who had deserved well of their country should be buried there. Among them are Rousseau, Voltaire and Victor Hugo. Hence, a building to commemorate national heroes, or a mausoleum for such. Thus Westminster Abbey is sometimes called 'The British Pantheon'.

The Pantheon opened in Oxford Street in 1772 was built by Wyatt for musical promenades, and was much patronized by those of rank and fashion. It was converted into a theatre for Italian opera in 1791 and the orchestra included Cramer, La Motte and Cervetto. It was burned down in 1792, rebuilt in 1795 as a theatre etc., eventually becoming a bazaar in 1835 and subsequently being used for business premises. The original building was ornamented with Grecian reliefs, and statues of classical deities, Britannia, George III and Queen Charlotte.

**Panther** (earlier **Panthera**). In mediaeval times this animal was supposed to be friendly to all beasts except the DRAGON, and to attract them by a peculiarly sweet odour it exhaled. Swinburne, in *Laus Veneris*, gives this characteristic a more sinister significance:

As one who hidden in deep sedge and reeds
Smells the rare scent made when the panther feeds,
And tracking ever slotwise the warm smell
Is snapped upon by the warm mouth and bleeds,
His head far down the hot sweet throat of her—
So one tracks love, whose breath is deadlier.

In the old *Physiologus*, the panther was the type of Christ, but later, when the savage nature of the beast became more widely known, it became symbolical of evil and hypocritical flattery; hence Lyly's comparison (in *Euphues, The Anatomy of Wit*) of the beauty of women to 'a delicate bait with a deadly hook, a sweet panther with a devouring paunch, a sour poison in a silver pot'.

The mediaeval idea perhaps arose from the name which is taken from Gr. *panther*, all beasts.

Among the Algonquins and Ojibwas of North America the panther lives in the evil underworld, but for the Cherokees it is a sacred animal credited with special powers,

like the cougar and OWL, as being able to see in the dark.

Polynesia has a sacred panther which is depicted with flames coming from its head, back and legs.

**Pantomime.** According to etymology this should be all dumb show, but the word was commonly applied to an adaptation of the old Commedia dell'Arte that lasted down to the 19th century. The principal characters are HARLEQUIN and COLUMBINE, who never speak, and Clown and PANTALOON, who keep up a constant fire of joke and repartee. The old Christmas pantomime or harlequinade as an essentially British entertainment was first introduced by John Weaver (1673–1760), a dancing-master of Shrewsbury, in 1702. It is now usually based on a nursery tale such as CINDERELLA, Mother Goose, JACK AND THE BEANSTALK, PUSS IN BOOTS etc., enlivened by catchy songs, pretty chorus girls and considerable buffoonery.

**Panurge** (Gr. *pan*, all; *ergos*, worker); the 'all-doer', *i.e.* the rogue, he who will 'do anything or anyone'. The roguish companion of PANTAGRUEL, and one of the principal characters in Rabelais's satire. A desperate rake, always in debt, he had a dodge for every scheme, knew everything and something more, and was a boon companion of the mirthfullest temper and most licentious bias; but was timid of danger and a desperate coward. He consulted LOTS, dreams etc., and finally the ORACLE of The Holy Bottle; and found insuperable objections to every one of its obscure answers.

Some commentators on Rabelais have identified Panurge with Calvin, others with the Cardinal of Lorraine; and this part of the satire seems to be an echo of the great Reformation controversy on the celibacy of the clergy.

**Paphian** (pā'fiən). Relating to VENUS, or rather to Paphos, a city of Cyprus, where Venus was worshipped; a Cyprian; a prostitute.

**Paradise.** The Greeks borrowed this word from the Persians, among whom it denoted the enclosed and extensive parks and pleasure grounds of the Persian kings. The Septuagint translators adopted it for the garden of EDEN, and in the New Testament and by early Christian writers it was applied to HEAVEN, the abode of the blessed dead.

**The Paradise of Fools.** *See* LIMBUS OF FOOLS *under* LIMBO.

**Paradise and the Peri.** *See under* PERI.

**Paradise Lost.** Milton's epic poem was first published in 1667. It tells the story:

Of Man's first disobedience and the fruit
Of that forbidden tree whose mortal taste
Brought death into the World, and all our woe
With loss of Eden.

SATAN rouses the panic-stricken host of fallen angels with tidings of a rumour current in HEAVEN of a new world about to be created. He calls a council to discuss what should be done, and they agree to send him to search for this new world. Seating himself on the Tree of Life, Satan overhears ADAM and Eve talking about the prohibition made by GOD, and at once resolves upon the nature of his attack. He takes the form of a mist, and, entering the serpent, induces Eve to eat of the FORBIDDEN FRUIT. Adam eats 'that he may perish with the woman whom he loved'. Satan returns to HELL to tell his triumph, and MICHAEL is sent to lead the guilty pair out of the Garden.

Milton borrowed largely from the epic of Du Bartas (1544–1590), entitled *The First Week of Creation* which was translated into almost every European language; and he was indebted to St. Avitus (d. 523), who wrote in Latin hexameters *The Creation, The Fall,* and *The Expulsion from Paradise*, for his description of Paradise (Bk. I), of Satan (Bk. II), and other parts.

In 1671 *Paradise Regained* (in four books) was published. The subject is the Temptation. Eve, being tempted, fell, and lost Paradise; Jesus, being tempted, resisted, and regained Paradise.

**Paradise shoots.** The lign aloe; said to be the only plant descended to us from the Garden of EDEN. When ADAM left Paradise he took a shoot of this tree, and from it the lign aloes have been propagated.

**The Earthly Paradise.** It was a popular mediaeval belief that paradise, a land or island where everything was beautiful and restful, and where death and decay were unknown, still existed somewhere on earth. It was usually located far away to the east and in 9th-century maps it is shown in China, and the fictitious letter of PRESTER JOHN to the Emperor Emmanuel Comnenus

states that it was within three days' journey of his own territory—a 'fact' that is corroborated by MANDEVILLE. The Hereford map (13th century) shows it as a circular island near India. *Cp.* BRANDAN, ST.

William Morris's poem of this title (1868–1870) tells how a band of Norsemen seek vainly for this paradise, and return in old age to a nameless city where the gods of ancient Greece are still worshipped.

**Parcae** (pah'sē). *See* FATES.

**Paris.** In Greek legend, the son of PRIAM, King of TROY, and HECUBA; and through his abduction of HELEN the cause of the siege of Troy. Hecuba dreamed that she was to bring forth a firebrand, and as this was interpreted to mean that the unborn child would bring destruction to his house, the infant Paris was exposed on Mount IDA. He was, however, brought up by a shepherd and grew to perfection of beautiful manhood. At the judgment on the APPLE OF DISCORD, HERA, APHRODITE and ATHENE had each offered him a bribe—the first power, the second the most beautiful of women, and the third martial glory. In return for her victory, Aphrodite assisted him in the abduction of Helen, for whom he deserted his wife OENONE, daughter of the river-god, Cebren. At Troy, Paris, having killed ACHILLES, was fatally wounded with a poisoned arrow by PHILOCTETES at the taking of the city.

**Parnassus.** A mountain near DELPHI, Greece, with two summits, one of which was consecrated to APOLLO and the MUSES, the other to BACCHUS. It is supposedly named from Parnassus, a son of NEPTUNE, and DEUCALION's ark came to rest there after the flood. Owing to its connection with the Muses it came to be regarded as the seat of poetry and music, hence **To climb Parnassus** is 'to write poetry'.

**Parsifal, Parsival.** *See* PERCIVAL, SIR.

**Parsley. He has need now of nothing but a little parsley,** *i.e.* he is dead. A Greek saying; the Greeks decked tombs with parsley, because it keeps green a long time.

**Parthenope** (pahthen'ōpi). Naples; so called from Parthenope, the SIREN, who threw herself into the sea out of love for ULYSSES, and was cast up in the Bay of Naples. Parthenope was an early Greek settlement, later called *Palaeopolis* (the old city), after subsequent settlers had established *Neapolis* (the new city), from which Naples derives its name.

**Parthenopean Republic.** The transitory Republic of Naples, established with the aid of the French in 1799, and overthrown by the Allies in the following June, when the Bourbons were restored.

**Parthian shot,** or **shaft.** A parting shot; a telling or wounding remark made on departure, giving one's adversary no time to reply. An allusion to the ancient practice of Parthian horsemen turning in flight, to discharge arrows and missiles at their pursuers.

**Pasiphae** (pas'ifē). In Greek legend, a daughter of the SUN and wife of MINOS, King of Crete. She was the mother of ARIADNE, and also through intercourse with a white bull (given by POSEIDON to Minos) of the MINOTAUR.

**Pasquinade** (paskwinād'). A lampoon or political squib, having ridicule for its object; so called from Pasquino, an Italian tailor or barber of the 15th century, noted for his caustic wit. After his death, a mutilated statue was dug up and placed near the Piazza Navona. As it was not clear whom the statue represented, and as it stood opposite Pasquin's house, it came to be called 'Pasquin'. The people of Rome affixed their political, religious and personal satires to it, hence the name. At the other end of the city was an ancient statue of MARS, called *Marforio*, to which were affixed replies to the Pasquinades.

**Patrick, St.** The apostle and patron SAINT of Ireland (commemorated on 17 March) was not an Irishman but was born at Bannavem (*c.* 389). Its location is unknown but it may have been in Glamorgan and his father, Calpurnius, was a Roman official and deacon. As a boy he was captured in a Pictish raid and sold as a slave in Ireland. He escaped to Gaul where he probably studied in the monastery of Lérins before returning to Britain. After receiving a supernatural call to preach to the heathen of Ireland, he returned to Gaul and was ordained deacon. He landed in Wicklow (432) and going north converted the people of Ulster and later those of other parts of Ireland. He established many communities and churches including the cathedral church of Armagh. He is said to have died in 461 and to have been buried at Down in Ulster.

St. Patrick left his name to many places and numerous legends are told of his miraculous powers. Perhaps the best known tradition is that he cleared Ireland of its vermin. The story goes that one old SERPENT resisted him, so he made a box and invited the serpent to enter it. The serpent objected, saying it was too small; but St. Patrick insisted it was quite large enough to be comfortable. Eventually the serpent got in to prove it was too small, whereupon St. Patrick slammed down the lid and cast the box into the sea.

In commemoration of this he is usually represented banishing the serpents, and with a SHAMROCK leaf.

**Patroclus** (pətrok'ləs). The gentle and amiable friend of ACHILLES. When the latter refused to fight in order to annoy AGAMEMNON, Patroclus appeared in the armour of Achilles at the head of the MYRMIDONS and was slain by HECTOR.

**Paul. St. Paul the Hermit.** The first of the Egyptian hermits. When 113 years old, he was visited by St. ANTONY, himself over 90, and when he died in 341, St. Antony wrapped his body in the cloak given to him by St. Athanasius, and his grave was dug by two lions. He lived in a cave, and he is represented as an old man, clothed with palm-leaves, and seated under a palm-tree, near which are a river and loaf of bread.

**Pay. Here's the devil to pay, and no pitch hot.** *See under* DEVIL.

**Peacock.** The grandeur of the peacock associates it naturally with royalty and there was a peacock throne in ancient Babylon and Persia. In Egyptian art the bird can accompany ISIS and in Greece it was an emblem of the bird-god Phaon, the 'Shiverer'. Originally associated with PAN, he was said to have yielded it to HERA as representing the starry firmament; the Argus Eyes were scattered over the tail by Hera while the circular form of the tail depicts the vault of heaven. Hera's mythology passed on to the Roman JUNO and Ovid calls the peacock Juno's Bird. It was her emblem with the EAGLE as that of JUPITER. There was a belief that the flesh of the peacock was immune from decay and this legend, coupled with the bird's celestial symbolism, made it an appropriate representation of immortality and apotheosis and as such was adopted by the Romans as the apotheosis of the Emperor and Empress, and its image was carved on tombs and funeral lamps.

Hindu mythology says that the peacock has angels' feathers, a devil's voice and the walk of a thief. It is so ashamed of its ugly feet and black legs that it screams when it sees them. The bird is the mount of the Vedic Sarasvati, goddess of wisdom, learning and music; it can also be a vehicle of LAKSHMI and of BRAHMA. When ridden by KAMA, god of love, it represents impatient desire.

In Buddhism the peacock's feather is an attribute of Avalokitesvara who becomes the Chinese goddess KWAN-YIN, the Kwannon of Japan, and the Amitabha Buddha; it represents compassion but also fidelity as it was fabled to die of grief, or remain single, if its mate died. In China the peacock has been held as a sacred bird and depicted in art from ancient times. The peacock feather was a badge of high rank and awarded for special service; it was also an emblem of the Ming Dynasty.

The Physiologus says that the cry of the peacock at night rises from its fear of losing its beauty. In the Bestiaries the bird is called the Parvo and the legend of its incorruptibility is perpetuated. It has showy plumage but ugly feet and the devil's cry.

The peacock is referred to in the Old Testament in connection with Solomon's treasures and freight (1 *Kings* x, 22). Christianity uses the bird as a symbol of resurrection and its 'hundred eyes' depict the all-seeing church.

Islamic myth associates the peacock-eye with the Eye of the Heart and with light. It is depicted in Moorish art.

Legend says the peacock hates gold and will not go near it; it was also said to be a weather prophet, dancing to foretell rain.

The qualities of vanity and pride attached to the peacock are relatively modern attributes.

**Peeping Tom of Coventry.** *See* GODIVA, LADY.

**Pegasus.** The winged horse on which BELLEROPHON rode against the CHIMAERA. When the MUSES contended with the daughters of Pieros, HELICON rose heavenward with delight; but Pegasus gave it a kick, stopped its ascent, and brought out of the mountain the soul-inspiring waters of HIPPOCRENE; hence, the name is used for the inspiration of poetry.

> Then who so will with vertuous deeds assay
> To mount to heaven, on Pegasus must ride,
> And with sweete Poets verse be glorified.
> SPENSER: *Ruines of Time*, 425.

**Pelican.** Martial says the pelican is a gluttonous bird and in Greek legend it is hostile to the QUAIL, while for the Hebrews it is a bird of ill-omen and represents desolation and the wilderness (*Psalms* cii, 6), but later myth, following the Physiologus, tells of the pelican's maternal devotion and self-sacrifice. The young were said to be smothered by the excessive devotion of the mother but she revived them with her blood which she drew from her breast. Another version said that when the young flapped their wings she struck back and killed them; she mourned for three days then revived them with her blood. Dante uses this myth as depicting Christ's sacrifice and calls him *nostro Pelicano*. The Bestiaries continue this legend of the killing of the young and their revival by the mother and call the bird the Pelicanus; they use both the pelican and the PHOENIX to illustrate the power of celestial and also earthly love.

**Pelion** (pē'lion). **Heaping Pelion upon Ossa.** Adding difficulty to difficulty, embarrassment to embarrassment etc. When the giants tried to scale HEAVEN, they placed Mount Pelion upon Mount Ossa, two peaks in Thessaly, for a scaling ladder (*Odyssey*, XI, 315).

**Pelleas, Sir** (pel'ias). One of the Knights of the ROUND TABLE, famed for his great strength. He is introduced in Spenser's *The Faerie Queene* (VI, xii) as going after the BLATANT BEAST. *See also* Tennyson's *Pelleas and Ettare*.

**Pelops** (pē'lops). Son of TANTALUS, and father of Atreus and Thyestes. He was king of Pisa in Elis, and was cut to pieces and served as food to the gods. The Morea was called *Peloponnesus*, 'the island of Pelops', from this mythical king.

**The ivory shoulder of Pelops.** The distinguishing or distinctive mark of anyone. The tale is that DEMETER ate the shoulder of Pelops when it was served by TANTALUS; when the gods put the body back into the cauldron to restore it to life, this portion was lacking, whereupon Demeter supplied one of ivory.

**Penates.** *See* DII PENATES; LARES AND PENATES.

**Penelope** (pinel'əpi). The wife of ULYSSES and mother of TELEMACHUS in Homeric legend. She was a model of all the domestic virtues.
**The Web of Penelope.** A work 'never ending, still beginning'; never done, but ever in hand. Penelope, according to HOMER, was pestered with suitors at Ithaca while ULYSSES was absent at the siege of TROY. To relieve herself of their importunities, she promised to make a choice of one as soon as she had finished a shroud for her father-in-law. Every night she unravelled what she had done in the day, and so deferred making any choice until Ulysses returned and slew the suitors.

**Pentacle.** A five-pointed star, or five-sided figure, used in sorcery as a TALISMAN against WITCHES etc., and sometimes worn as a folded headdress of fine linen, as a defence against demons in the act of conjuration. It is also called the *Wizard's Foot*, and is supposed to typify the five senses. Its five points are also symbolic of spirit, air, fire, water, earth. In Christianity they signify the five wounds of Christ and as such GAWAIN had the pentacle on his shield. Being without beginning or end the pentacle shares the significance of the perfection and power of the circle. It also represents the figure of man with outstretched arms and legs.
It is also a candlestick with five branches. *Cp.* SOLOMON'S SEAL.

And on her head, lest spirits should invade,
A pentacle, for more assurance, laid.
ROSE: *Orlando Furioso*, III, xxi.

The Holy Pentacles numbered forty-four, of which seven were consecrated to each of the planets SATURN, JUPITER, MARS and the SUN; five to both VENUS and MERCURY; and six to the MOON. The divers figures were enclosed in a double circle, containing the name of God in Hebrew, and other mystical words.

**Penthesilea** (penthəsilā'ə). Queen of the AMAZONS who, in the post-Homeric legends, fought for TROY; she was slain by ACHILLES. Hence any strong, commanding woman. Sir Toby Belch in Shakespeare's *Twelfth Night* (II, iii) calls Maria by this name.

**Peony.** According to fable, so called from Paeon, the physician who cured the wounds received by the gods in the Trojan war. The seeds were, at one time, worn round the neck as a charm against the powers of darkness.
In China the peony was an imperial flower fabled to be untouched by any insect other than the bee. It is one of the few *yang* flowers, representing masculinity, light, good fortune, spring and happiness. It is often associated with the PEACOCK in art.

About an Infant's neck hang Peonie,
It cures Alcydes cruell maladie.
SYLVESTER: *Du Bartas*, I, iii, 712.

**People. The good,** or **little people.** FAIRIES, ELVES etc.

**Perceforest** (pœs'forist). An early 14th-century French prose romance (said to be the longest in existence), belonging to the Arthurian cycle, but mingling with it the ALEXANDER romance. After Alexander's war in India, he comes to England, of which he makes Perceforest, one of his knights, king. The romance tells how Perceforest establishes the Knights of the Franc Palais, how his grandson brings the GRAIL to England, and includes many popular tales, such as that of the SLEEPING BEAUTY.

**Percival, Sir.** The Knight of the ROUND TABLE who, according to Malory's *Morte d'Arthur* (and Tennyson's *Idylls of the King*) finally won a sight of the Holy GRAIL. He was the son of Sir Pellinore and brother of Sir Lamerocke. In the earlier French romances (based probably on the MABINOGION and other Celtic originals) he has no connection with the Grail, but here (as in the English also) he sees the lance dripping with blood, and the severed head surrounded with blood in a dish. The French version of the romance is by Chrétien de Troyes (12th century), which formed the basis of Sebastian Evans's *The High History of the Holy Graal* (1893). The German version, *Parsifal* or *Parzival*, was written some 50 years later by Wolfram von

Eschenbach and it is principally on this version that Wagner drew for his opera, *Parsifal* (1882).

**Percy.** When Malcolm III of Scotland invaded England and reduced the castle of Alnwick, Robert de Mowbray brought to him the keys of the castle suspended on his lance; and handing them from the wall, thrust his lance into the king's eye; from which circumstance, the tradition says, he received the name of 'Pierce-eye', which has ever since been borne by the Dukes of Northumberland.

> This is all a fable. The Percies are descended from a great Norman baron, who came over with William, and who took his name from his castle and estate in Normandy.
> SCOTT: *Tales of a Grandfather*, iv.

**Peri** (pē'ri). Originally, a beautiful but malevolent sprite of Persian myth, one of a class which was responsible for comets, eclipses, failure of crops etc.; in later times applied to delicate, gentle, fairy-like beings, begotten by fallen spirits who direct with a wand the pure in mind the way to HEAVEN. These lovely creatures, according to the Koran, are under the sovereignty of EBLIS; and Mohammed was sent for their conversion, as well as for that of man.

The name used sometimes to be applied to any beautiful girl.

**Paradise and the Peri.** The second tale in Moore's *Lalla Rookh*. The Peri laments her expulsion from HEAVEN, and is told she will be readmitted if she will bring to the gate of heaven the 'gift most dear to the Almighty'. After a number of unavailing offerings she brought a guilty old man, who wept with repentance, and knelt to pray. The Peri offered the Repentant Tear, and the gates flew open.

**Persephone** (pœsef'əni). *See* PROSERPINA.

**Perseus** (pœ'siəs). In Greek legend, the son of ZEUS and DANAË. He and his mother were set adrift in a chest but rescued by the intervention of Zeus. He was brought up by King Polydectes, who, wishing to secure DANAË, got rid of him by encouraging him in the almost hopeless task of obtaining the head of the MEDUSA. With the help of the gods, he was successful, and with the head (which turned all that looked on it into stone) he rescued ANDROMEDA,

and later metamorphosed Polydectes and his guests to stone.

Before his birth, an ORACLE had foretold that Acrisius, father of Danaë, would be slain by Danaë's son (hence Perseus being originally cast adrift to perish). This came to pass, for while taking part in the games at Larissa, Perseus accidentally slew his grandfather with a discus.

**Phaedra** (fē'drə). Daughter of MINOS and PASIPHAE, who became enamoured of her stepson HIPPOLYTUS. On her rejection by him she brought about his death by slandering him to her husband THESEUS. She subsequently killed herself in remorse. *See* MYRTLE.

**Phaeton** (fā'tən). In classical myth, the son of PHOEBUS (the Sun); he undertook to drive his father's chariot, and was upset. He thereby caused Libya to be parched into barren sands, and all Africa to be more or less injured, the inhabitants blackened, and vegetation nearly destroyed; he would have set the world on fire had not ZEUS transfixed him with a thunderbolt.

> Gallop apace, you fiery-footed steeds,
> Towards Phoebus' lodging; such a waggoner
> As Phaeton would whip you to the west,
> And bring in cloudy night immediately.
> SHAKESPEARE: *Romeo and Juliet*, III, ii.

**Phaeton's Bird.** The swan. Cygnus, son of NEPTUNE, was the friend of PHAETON and lamented his fate so grievously that APOLLO changed him into a swan, and placed him among the constellations.

**Phantom fellow.** One who is under the ban of some HOBGOBLIN; a half-witted person.

**Pharamond** (far'əmond). In the ARTHURIAN ROMANCES, a knight of the ROUND TABLE, said to have been the first king of France and to have reigned in the early 5th century. He was the son of Marcomir and father of Clodion.

La Calprenède's novel *Pharamond, ou l'Histoire de France* was published in 1661.

**Pharaoh's rat.** *See* ICHNEUMON.

**Phasian Bird.** The pheasant (*Phasianus colchicus*); so called from Phasis, a river of Colchis, whence the bird is said to have been introduced elsewhere in Europe by the ARGONAUTS.

**Pheidippides** (fīdip'idēz). *See* MARATHON.

**Philemon and Baucis** (fīlē'mon, baw'sis). Poor cottagers of Phrygia (husband and wife), who, in Ovid's story (*Metamorphoses*, viii, 631), entertained JUPITER and MERCURY, in the guise of travellers, so hospitably that Jupiter transformed their cottage into a temple, making them its priest and priestess. They asked that they might die together, and it was so. Philemon became an OAK, Baucis a linden tree, and their branches intertwined at the top.

**Philoctetes** (filoktē'tēz). The most famous archer in the TROJAN WAR, to whom HERCULES, at death, gave his arrows. In the tenth year of the siege Odysseus (ULYSSES) commanded that he should be sent for, as an ORACLE had declared that TROY could not be taken without the arrows of Hercules. Philoctetes accordingly went to Troy, slew PARIS and Troy fell.

The *Philoctetes* of Sophocles is one of the most famous Greek tragedies.

**Philomel.** *See* NIGHTINGALE.

**Philosophers' Stone.** The hypothetical substance which, according to the alchemists, would convert all baser metals into gold; by many it was thought to be compounded of the purest sulphur and mercury. Mediaeval experimenters toiled endlessly in the search, thus laying the foundations of the science of chemistry, among other inventions. It was in this quest that Bötticher stumbled on the manufacture of Dresden porcelain, Roger Bacon on the composition of gunpowder, Geber on the properties of acids, Van Helmont on the nature of gas, and Dr. Glauber on the 'salts' which bear his name.

In Ripley's treatise, *The Compound of Alchemie* (*c*. 1471), we are told the 12 stages or 'gates' in the transmutation of metals are: (1) Calcination; (2) Dissolution; (3) Separation; (4) Conjunction; (5) Putrefaction; (6) Congelation; (7) Cibation; (8) Sublimation; (9) Fermentation; (10) Exaltation; (11) Multiplication; and (12) Projection. Of these the last two were much the most important; the former consisting of the ELIXIR, the latter in the penetration and transfiguration of metals in fusion by casting the powder of the philosophers' stone upon them, which is then called the 'powder of projection'. According to one legend, Noah was commanded to hang up the true philosophers' stone in the ark, to give light to every living creature therein; while another related that DEUCALION had it in a bag over his shoulder, but threw it away and lost it.

**Phlegethon** (fleg'ithon) (Gr. *phlego*, to burn). A river of liquid fire in HADES, flowing into the ACHERON.

> Fierce Phlegethon,
> Whose waves of torrent fire inflame with rage.
> MILTON: *Paradise Lost*, II, 580.

**Phoebe** (fē'bi). A female TITAN of classical myth, daughter of URANUS and GAEA; also a name of DIANA, as goddess of the MOON.

**Phoebus** (Gr. the Shining One). An epithet of APOLLO, god of the SUN. In poetry the name is sometimes used of the sun itself, sometimes of Apollo as leader of the MUSES.

> The Rosy Morne long since left Tithones bed,
> All ready to her silver coche to clyme;
> And Phoebus gins to shew his glorious hed.
> SPENSER: *Epithalamion*.

**Phoenix** (fē'niks). The phoenix was first mentioned in the West by Hesiod in the eighth century B.C. Ovid, Pliny and Tacitus all refer to it but Aristotle does not. Herodotus and Pliny call it the Arabian Bird, but in the classics it appears as of Egyptian origin and in that tradition it is equated with the Bennu, the Sun Bird, emblem of the sun god RA and, as a symbol of resurrection, associated with both Ra and OSIRIS.

The phoenix is of great importance in Chinese myth as the Feng-huang, it is one of the Four Spiritually Endowed, or Sacred, creatures. Like the DRAGON and KY-LIN it is a fabulous creature which combines the *yin-yang* powers, it is also, like them, a composite, composed of various elements symbolizing the entire cosmos, it has the head of the COCK as solar, the curved back of the SWALLOW as the crescent moon, the wings represent the wind, its tail trees and flowers and its feet the earth. It has the Five Colours and the Five Virtues. An ancient manual of rites says: 'Its colour delights the eye, its comb expresses righteousness, its tongue utters sincerity, its voice chants melody, its ear enjoys music, its heart conforms to regulations, its breast contains the treasures of literature and its spurs are powerful against transgressors.' Like the Ky-lin, its appearance was highly auspicious and heralded the coming of a great Emperor or Sage.

In Japanese mythology the bird appears as the Ho-ho and its appearance announces the coming of a new era; as in China, it is associated with the Empress.

The Physiologus says that the phoenix comes from India and Arabia and, when it is five hundred years old, flies to Lebanon, fills its wings with fragrant gum and then hastens to Egypt where it immolates itself on the altar of the sun at Heliopolis. The Bestiaries call the bird the Fenix but follow the Physiologus in legend; they adapt it to Christianity as a symbol of the resurrection; as such the bird appeared on both Roman and early Christian tombs and in funerary art. Christianity said that the phoenix alone of all birds did not share the sin of Eve in eating the forbidden fruit.

The phoenix is of great size but is the acme of gentleness as it kills nothing, feeding only on dew and crushing nothing it touches. The mythology of the phoenix is used extensively in literature. It is to this bird that Shakespeare refers in *Cymbeline* (I, vi):

> If she be furnished with a mind so rare,
> She is alone the Arabian bird.

*The Phoenix and Turtle* (attributed to Shakespeare) is based on the legendary love and death of this bird and the turtledove.

The phoenix was adopted as a sign over chemists' shops through the association of this fabulous bird with ALCHEMY. Paracelsus wrote about it, and several of the alchemists employed it to symbolize their vocation.

The phoenix is also a symbol of the Resurrection.

*Phoenix*, the son of Amyntor king of Argos, was tutor to ACHILLES.

*See* FUNG-HWANG.

**Phoenix dactylifera.** The date-palm; so called from the ancient idea that this tree, if burnt down or if it falls through old age, will rejuvenate itself and spring up fairer than ever.

**Phoenix period,** or **cycle,** generally supposed to be 500 years; Tacitus tells us it was 500 years; R. Stuart Poole that it was 1460 Julian years, like the Sothic period; and Lipsius that it was 1500 years. Opinions vary between 250 and 7000 years. Tacitus

(*Annales*, vi, 28) mentions four appearances of the bird in Egypt.

**Phoenix Park** (Dublin). A corruption of the Gaelic *Fionn-uisge*, the clear water, so called from a spring at one time resorted to as a chalybeate spa.

**Phryne** (frī'ni). A famous Athenian courtesan of the 4th century B.C., who acquired so much wealth by her beauty that she offered to rebuild the walls of Thebes if she might put on them the inscription: 'Alexander destroyed them, but Phryne the hetaera rebuilt them.' It is recorded of her that, when she was being tried on a capital charge, her defender, who failed to move the judges by his eloquence, asked her to uncover her bosom. She did so, and the judges, struck by her beauty, acquitted her on the spot.

She is said to have been the model for Praxiteles' Cnidian VENUS, and also for APELLES' picture of Venus Rising from the Sea.

**Phynnodderee** (finod'ərē). A Manx HOBGOBLIN combining the properties of the Scandinavian TROLL, the Scottish BROWNIE and the Irish LEPRECHAUN. He drives home straying sheep and helps in the harvesting if a storm is brewing, and is possessed of great strength for his size.

**Pied Piper of Hamelin.** The legend is that the town of Hamelin (Westphalia) was infested with rats in 1284, that a mysterious piper in a parti-coloured suit appeared in the town and offered to rid it of vermin for a certain sum, which offer was accepted by the townspeople. The Pied Piper fulfilled his contract but payment was not forthcoming. On the following St. John's Day he reappeared, and again played his pipe. This time all the children followed him and he led them to a mountain cave where all disappeared save two—one blind, the other dumb, or lame. Another version is that they were led to Transylvania where they formed a German colony. The story, familiar in England from Robert Browning's poem, appeared earlier in James Howell's *Familiar Letters* (1645–1655). The legend has its roots in the story of the *Children's Crusade*.

**Pierrot** (pē'rō) (*i.e.* 'Little Peter'). A traditional character in French PANTOMIME, a kind of idealized clown. He is generally tall and thin, has his face covered with white powder or flour, and wears a white costume with very long sleeves and a row of big buttons down the front. *Cp.* HARLEQUIN.

**Pig.** The pig was held sacred by the ancient Cretans because JUPITER was suckled by a sow; it was immolated in the ELEUSINIAN MYSTERIES; was sacrificed to HERCULES, to VENUS and to the LARES by all who sought relief from bodily ailments. The sow was sacrificed to CERES 'because it taught men to turn up the earth'. The pig is unclean to Jews and Muslims.

The five dark marks on the inner side of each of a pig's forelegs are supposed to be the marks of the DEVIL's claws when they entered the swine (*Mark* v, 11–15). *See also* HOG; SOW.

The pig played an important part in Celtic lore. Its flesh was food for the gods at feasts in the otherworld and Manannan, god of the sea, had magic pigs which, eaten one day, returned the next to be eaten once more. There was a Celtic sow-goddess Keridwin, the Old White Sow, who was a Mother Goddess, while Phaea, the Shining One, represented the moon and fertility. The worship of the pig was widespread. It was eaten in Ireland, but not among the Galatian Celts and little in the highlands of Scotland, but in Scandinavian myth the Black Sow typified coldness, death and evil.

The pig was ambivalent in Egypt; although sacred to ISIS as a great mother, the black pig was a form taken by SET in his typhonic aspect. The pig was unclean for the Egyptians and Phoenicians and forbidden as food.

Hinduism has Vajravarahi, Queen of Heaven as the Adamantine Sow, she represents the feminine counterpart of the BOAR as VISHNU's third incarnation. She also appears in Tibetan Buddhism. The pig, as ignorance and greed, is depicted at the centre of the Round of Existence in Buddhism. In Chinese legend the pig is used to represent untamed nature.

The pig is a lunar animal for the Amerindians and is a rain-bearer.

**The Pig and the Tinderbox.** An old colloquial name for the Elephant and Castle public-house; in allusion to its sign of a pig-like elephant surmounted by the representation of a castle which might pass as a tinderbox.

**Pigeon. The Black Pigeons of Dodona.** *See under* DODONA.

**Pigmies.** *See* PYGMIES.

**Pigwidgin,** or **Pigwiggen.** A FAIRY or DWARF; anything very small.

> Pigwiggen, was this Fairy Knight,
> One wond'rous gracious in the sight
> Of fair Queen Mab, which day and night
> He amorously observed.
> DRAYTON: *Nymphidia*, I, 89.

**Pilatus, Mount** (pilah'tus). In Switzerland, between the cantons of Lucerne and Unterwalden. So called because during westerly winds it is covered with a white 'cap' of cloud (Lat. *pileatus*, covered with the *pileus*, or felt cap). The similarity of the name gave rise to a fabled connection with PILATE. One tradition is that Pilate was banished to Gaul by Tiberius and threw himself into the lake near the summit of this mountain, where he appears annually. Whoever sees the ghost will die before the year is out. In the 16th century a law was passed forbidding anyone to throw stones into the lake for fear of bringing a tempest on the country.

**Pilgrim. The Pilgrim's Progress.** The allegorical masterpiece of John Bunyan, the first part of which appeared in 1678 and the second in 1684. It tells of Christian's pilgrimage, beset with trials and temptations, but with incidental encouragement, until he reached the Celestial City where he was later joined by his wife and children. The rustic simplicity and directness of its story gave it lasting appeal and many expressions have become part of the language. 'The Slough of Despond', 'Vanity Fair', 'Mr. Worldly Wiseman' and 'Mr. Facing-both-ways' are notable examples.

**Pillar. The Pillars of Hercules.** The opposite rocks at the entrance to the Mediterranean, one in Spain and the other in Africa, anciently called Calpe and Abyla, now Gibraltar and Mount Hacho (on which stands the fortress of Ceuta). The tale is that they were bound together till HERCULES tore them asunder in order to get to Gades (Cadiz). Macrobius ascribes the feat of making the division to Sesostris (the Egyptian Hercules), Lucan follows the same tradition; and the Phoenicians are said to have set on the opposing rocks two large pyramidal columns to serve as seamarks, one dedicated to Hercules and the other to ASTARTE.

**I will follow you even to the Pillars of Hercules.** To the end of the world. The ancients supposed that these rocks marked the utmost limits of the habitable globe.

**Pinocchio** (pinō′kiō). The mischievous hero of the famous puppet story *Le Avventure di Pinocchio* (1883) by G. Lorenzini, who wrote under the name of 'Collodi', which was taken from his birthplace.

The story tells how a carpenter found a piece of wood that laughed and cried like a child and gave it to his friend Geppetto who fashioned from it the puppet Pinocchio. His creation proved unusually mischievous and had many bizarre adventures including having his feet burned off, his nose elongated, and being transformed into a donkey. Eventually he learned to show sympathy and goodness and 'the fairy' changed him to a real boy back at home with Geppetto.

**Piper. The Pied Piper.** *See* PIED.

**Pisces** (pis′kēz, pī′sēz) (Lat. the fishes). A constellation and the twelfth sign of the ZODIAC.

**Pixie**, or **Pixy.** A sprite or FAIRY of folklore, especially in Cornwall and Devon, where some held pixies to be the spirits of infants who died before baptism. In Cornwall and West Devon figures of 'piskeys' or pixies are still very much in evidence at 'beauty spots' as souvenirs and lucky charms for tourists.

**Pleiades** (plī′ədēz). In classical myth, the seven daughters of ATLAS and Pleione, sisters of the HYADES. They were transformed into stars, one of which, MEROPE, is invisible, out of shame, because she married a mortal man; while others say it is ELECTRA who hides herself from grief for the destruction of TROY and its royal race. Electra is known as 'the lost Pleiad'.

> One of these forms which flit by us, when we
> Are young, and fix our eyes on every face …
> Whose course and home we know not, nor shall
>   know,
> Like the lost Pleiad seen no more below.
> BYRON: *Beppo*, xiv.

The great cluster of stars in the constellation TAURUS, especially the seven larger ones, were called **the Pleiades** by the Greeks from the word *plein*, to sail, because they considered navigation safe at the rising of the constellation, and their setting marked the close of the sailing season.

**The Pleiad.** A name frequently given to groups of seven particularly illustrious persons.

**The Philosophical Pleiad.** The Seven WISE MEN OF GREECE are sometimes so called.

**The Pleiad of Alexandria.** A group of seven contemporary poets in the 3rd century B.C., *viz.* Callimachus, Apollonius of Rhodes, Aratus, Philiscus (called HOMER the Younger), Lycophron, Nicander and Theocritus.

**Charlemagne's Pleiad,** the group of scholars with which the Emperor surrounded himself, *viz.* CHARLEMAGNE (who, in this circle, was known as 'David'), Alcuin ('Albinus'), Adelard ('Augustine'), Angilbert ('Homer'), Riculfe ('Damaetas'), Varnefrid and Eginhard.

**The French Pleiad** of the 16th century, who wrote poetry in the metres, style etc. of the ancient Greeks and Romans. Ronsard was their leader, the others being Daurat, Du Bellay, Belleau, Baïf, Jodelle and Pontus de Tyard. Scévole de Sainte-Marthe and Muretus are sometimes given instead of Jodelle and Pontus de Tyard.

**The second French Pleiad.** Some contemporary poets in the reign of Louis XIII (1610–1643), very inferior to the 'First Pleiad'. They are Rapin, Commire, Larue, Santeuil, Ménage, Dupérier and Petit.

**Pluto.** In Roman mythology, the ruler of the infernal regions, son of SATURN, brother of JUPITER and NEPTUNE, and husband of PROSERPINA; hence, the grave, the place where the dead go before they are admitted into ELYSIUM or sent to TARTARUS.

**Plutonian** or **Plutonist.** *See* VULCANIST.

**Plutonic Rocks.** Granites, certain porphyries and other igneous unstratified crystalline rocks, supposed to have been formed at a great depth and pressure, as distinguished from the volcanic rocks which were formed near the surface. So called from PLUTO, as the lord of elemental fire. Richard Kirwan used the term in his *Elements of Mineralogy*, 1796.

**Plutus.** In Greek mythology, the god of riches. Hence, *rich as Plutus*, and *plutocrat*, one who exercises influence or possesses power through his wealth. The legend is that he was blinded by ZEUS so that his gifts should be equally distributed and not go only to those who merited them.

**Poison.** *See* MITHRIDATE.

**Pollux.** In classical mythology the twin brother of CASTOR.

**Polycrates** (polik'rətēz). *See* AMASIS.

**Polyhymnia**, or **Polymnia** (polihim'niə, polim'niə). The Muse of lyric poetry and the inventor of the lyre. She invented harmony and presided over singing. *See* MUSES.

**Polyphemus** (polifē'məs). One of the CYC-LOPS, who ruled over Sicily. When ULYSSES landed on the island the monster made him and twelve of his crew captives; six of them he ate, and then Ulysses contrived to blind him and escape with the rest of the crew (*cp.* LESTRIGONS). *See also* ACIS; GALATEA.

**Pomona** (pomō'nə). The Roman goddess of fruits and fruit-trees (Lat. *pomum*), hence fruit generally.

**Pongo.** In the old romance of THE SEVEN CHAMPIONS of Christendom he was an amphibious monster of Sicily who preyed on the inhabitants of the island for many years. He was slain by the three sons of St. GEORGE.

*Pongo* was also a nickname for a monkey, an Australian aboriginal name for flying squirrel, and one-time sailors' slang for a marine (now a *bootneck*), and then for a soldier.

Then an old 'possum would sing out, or a black-furred flying squirrel — pongoes, the blacks call 'em — would come sailing down from the top of an ironbark tree ...
BOLDREWOOD: *Robbery Under Arms*, ch xx.

**Poplar.** The poplar was consecrated to HERCULES, because he destroyed Kakos in a cavern of Mount Aventine, which was covered with poplars. In the moment of triumph, the hero plucked a branch from one of the trees and bound it round his head. When he descended to the infernal regions, the heat caused a profuse perspiration which blanched the under surface of the leaves, while the smoke of the eternal flames blackened the upper surface. Hence

the leaves of the poplar are dark on one side and white on the other.

**The white poplar** is fabled to have originally been the NYMPH Leuce, beloved by PLUTO. He changed her into this at death.

**Portumnus** (pawtŭm'nəs). *See* PALAEMON.

**Poseidon** (pəsī'don). In Greek mythology, the god of the sea, the counterpart of the Roman NEPTUNE. He was the son of KRONOS and RHEA, brother of ZEUS and HADES, and husband of AMPHITRITE. It was he who, with APOLLO, built the walls of TROY, and as the Trojans refused to give him his reward he hated them and took part against them in the TROJAN WAR. Earthquakes were attributed to him, and he was said to have created the first HORSE.

**Prajapatis** (prəjah'pətēz). *See* MANU.

**Precious Stones.** The ancients divided precious stones into male and female, the darker being the males and the light ones the females. Male sapphires approach indigo in colour, but the females are sky-blue. Theophrastus mentions the distinction.

And the tent shook, for mighty Saul shuddered—
and sparkles 'gan dart
From the jewels that woke in his turban, at once
with a start—
All its lordly male-sapphires, and rubies courageous at heart.
BROWNING: *Saul*, viii.

According to the Poles, each month is under the influence of a precious stone:

| | | |
|---|---|---|
| January | Garnet | *Constancy* |
| February | Amethyst | *Sincerity* |
| March | Bloodstone | *Courage* |
| April | DIAMOND | *Innocence* |
| May | Emerald | *Success in love* |
| June | Agate | *Health and long life* |
| July | Cornelian | *Content* |
| August | Sardonyx | *Conjugal felicity* |
| September | Chrysolite | *Antidote to madness* |
| October | Opal | *Hope* |
| November | Topaz | *Fidelity* |
| December | Turquoise | *Prosperity* |

*In relation to the signs of the* ZODIAC:

| | | | |
|---|---|---|---|
| Aries | Ruby | Libra | Jacinth |
| Taurus | Topaz | Scorpio | Agate |
| Gemini | Carbuncle | Sagittarius | Amethyst |
| Cancer | Emerald | Capricornus | Beryl |
| Leo | Sapphire | Aquarius | Onyx |
| Virgo | Diamond | Pisces | Jasper |

*In relation to the planets*:

| | | |
|---|---|---|
| Saturn | Turquoise | *Lead* |

| Jupiter | Cornelian | *Tin* |
|---------|-----------|-------|
| Mars | Emerald | *Iron* |
| Sun | Diamond | *Gold* |
| Venus | Amethyst | *Copper* |
| Moon | Crystal | *Silver* |
| Mercury | Loadstone | *Quicksilver* |

*In heraldry*:

The topaz represents 'or' (*gold*), or Sol, the Sun.

The pearl or crystal represents 'argent' (*silver*), or Luna, the Moon.

The ruby represents 'gules' (*red*), or the planet Mars.

The sapphire represents 'azure' (*blue*), or the planet Jupiter.

The diamond represents 'sable' (*black*), or the planet Saturn.

The emerald represents 'vert' (*green*), or the planet Venus.

The amethyst represents 'purpure' (*purple*), or the planet Mercury.

Many precious stones were held to have curative and magical properties, e.g. *loadstone* prevented quarrels between brothers; *jasper* worn by the ploughman ensured the fertility of a field; *turquoise* protected the wearer from injury if he fell; *jade* for the Chinese was the most pure and divine of natural materials and had many properties, including stimulating the flow of milk in nursing mothers when powdered and mixed with milk and honey.

**Priam** (prī'əm). King of TROY when that city was sacked by the Greeks, husband of HECUBA, and father of 50 children, the eldest of whom was HECTOR. When the gates of Troy were thrown open by the Greeks who had been concealed in the wooden horse, Pyrrhus, the son of ACHILLES, slew the aged Priam.

**Priapus** (prīā'pəs). In Greek mythology, the son of DIONYSUS and APHRODITE, the god of reproductive power and fertility (hence of gardens), the protector of shepherds, fishermen and farmers. He was later regarded as the chief deity of lasciviousness and obscenity and the phallus was his attribute.

**Principalities.** Members of one of the nine orders of angels in mediaeval angelology. *See* ANGEL.

In the assembly next upstood
Nisroch, of Principalities the prime.
MILTON: *Paradise Lost*, VI, 447.

**Procne** (prok'ni). *See* NIGHTINGALE.

**Procris** (prok'ris). **Unerring as the dart of Procris.** When Procris fled from CEPHALUS out of shame, DIANA gave her a dog (Laelaps) that never failed to secure its prey, and a dart which not only never missed aim, but which always returned of its own accord to the shooter.

**Procrustes' Bed** (prōkrŭs'tēz). Procrustes, in Greek legend, was a robber of Attica, who placed all who fell into his hands upon an iron bed. If they were longer than the bed he cut off the overhanging parts, if shorter he stretched them till they fitted it. He was slain by THESEUS. Hence, any attempt to reduce men to one standard, one way of thinking, or one way of acting, is called *placing them on Procrustes' bed*.

Tyrants more cruel than Procrustes old,
Who to his iron-bed by torture fits
Their nobler parts, the souls of suffering wits.
MALLET: *Verbal Criticism* (1733).

**Projection. Powder of projection.** A form of the PHILOSOPHERS' STONE, which was supposed to have the virtue of changing baser metals into gold. A little of this powder, being cast into the molten metal, was to *project* from it pure gold.

**Prometheus** (prōmē'thiəs) (Gr. Forethought). One of the TITANS of Greek myth, son of IAPETOS and the ocean-nymph Clymene, and famous as a benefactor to man. It is said that ZEUS, having been tricked by Prometheus over his share of a sacrificial ox, denied mankind the use of fire. Prometheus then stole fire from HEPHAESTUS to save the human race. For this he was chained by Zeus to Mount Caucasus, where an EAGLE preyed on his liver all day, the liver being renewed at night. He was eventually released by HERCULES, who slew the eagle. It was to counterbalance the gift of fire to mankind that Zeus sent PANDORA to earth with her box of evils.

**Promethean.** Capable of producing fire; pertaining to PROMETHEUS.

**Promethean fire.** The vital principle; the fire with which PROMETHEUS quickened into life his clay images.

I know not where is that Promethean heat
That can thy light relume.
SHAKESPEARE: *Othello*, V, ii.

**Promethean unguent.** Made from a herb on which some of the blood of PROMETHEUS had fallen. MEDEA gave JASON some of it, and thus rendered his body proof against fire and warlike instruments.

**Proserpina,** or **Proserpine** (prōsœ'pinə, pros'əpīn). The Roman counterpart of the Greek goddess Persephone, queen of the infernal regions and wife of PLUTO (*see* DAFFODIL), and sometimes identified with HECATE.

**Protean.** *See* PROTEUS.

**Proteus** (prō'tiəs). In Greek legend, NEPTUNE'S herdsman, an old man and a prophet, famous for his power of assuming different shapes at will. Hence the phrase, *As many shapes as Proteus, i.e.* full of shifts, aliases, disguises etc., and the adjective **protean,** readily taking on different aspects, ever-changing, versatile.

Proteus lived in a vast cave, and his custom was to tell over his herds of sea-calves at noon, and then to sleep. There was no way of catching him but by stealing upon him at this time and binding him; otherwise he would elude anyone by a rapid change of shape.

**Psalmanazar, George** (salmənaz'ər). A classical example of the impostor. A Frenchman whose real name is unknown to this day, he appeared in London in 1703 claiming to be a native of Formosa, at that time an almost unknown island. In 1704 he published an account of Formosa with a grammar of the language, which from beginning to end was a fabrication of his own. The literary and critical world of London was taken in, but his imposture was soon exposed by Roman Catholic missionaries who had laboured in Formosa, and after a time Psalmanazar publicly confessed his fraud. He turned over a new leaf and applied himself to the study of Hebrew and other genuine labours, ending his days in 1763 as a man of some repute and the friend of Dr. Johnson. *See* OSSIAN.

**Psyche** (sī'ki) (Gr. breath; hence, life, or soul itself). In 'the latest-born of the myths', *Cupid and Psyche*, an episode in the *Golden Ass*, Psyche is a beautiful maiden beloved by CUPID, who visited her every night but departed at sunrise. Cupid bade her never seek to know who he was, but one night curiosity got the better of her; she lit the lamp to look at him, a drop of hot oil fell on his shoulder and he awoke and fled. The abandoned Psyche then wandered far and wide in search of her lover; she became the slave of VENUS, who imposed on her heartless tasks and treated her most cruelly. Ultimately she was united to Cupid and became immortal. The tale appears in Walter Pater's *Marius the Epicurean*.

**Public-house signs** are in themselves a fascinating study and much of Britain's history may be gleaned from them, as well as folklore, heraldry, social customs etc. Many are a compliment to the lord of the manor or a nobleman or his cognizance, as the *Warwick Arms*, the BEAR AND RAGGED STAFF. Others pay tribute to distinguished warriors or their battles, as *The Marquis of Granby*, the *Duke of Wellington*, the *Waterloo*, the *Keppel's Head*, the *Trafalgar*. Royalty is conspicuously represented by the *Crown*, the *King's Arms*, the *Prince Regent*, the *Prince of Wales*, the *Victoria*, the *Albert*, the *George* etc. Literary names are less conspicuous, but there is a *Shakespeare*, *Milton Arms*, *Macaulay Arms*, *Sir Richard Steele*, and *Sir Walter Scott*, as well as *The Miller of Mansfield*, *Pindar of Wakefield*, *Sir John Falstaff*, *Robinson Crusoe*, and *Valentine and Orson*. *Simon the Tanner*, *The Good Samaritan*, *Noah's Ark*, the *Gospel Oak*, the *Angel* have a Biblical flavour, and myth and legend are represented by *The Apollo*, *Hercules*, *Phoenix*, *King Lud*, *Merlin's Cave*, *The Man in the Moon*, *Punch*, *Robin Hood*, the *Moonrakers*, *Cat and the Fiddle* etc.

Some signs indicate sporting associations, such as the *Cricketers*, the *Bat and Ball*, the *Bowling Green*, the *Angler's Rest*, the *Huntsman*; or trades associations as *Coopers'*, *Bricklayers'*, *Plumbers'*, *Carpenters'*, *Masons'* Arms etc. Others show a whimsical turn as *The Who'd a Thought It*, *The Five Alls*, *The World Turned Upside Down*, *The Good Woman*.

The following list will serve to exemplify the subject:

*The Bag o'Nails.* From a tradesman's sign — that of an ironmonger. Said by some 19th-century writers to be a corruption of 'Bacchanals'.

*The Bear.* From the popular sport of bear-baiting.

*The Bell.* Mostly derived from the national addiction to bell-ringing.

*The Bell Savage. See* LA BELLE SAUVAGE.

*The Blue Boar. See under* BLUE.

*The Blue Lion.* Denmark (possibly a compliment to James I's queen, Anne of Denmark), also the badge of the Earl of Mortimer.

*Bolt in Tun.* The punning heraldic badge of Prior Bolton, last of the clerical rulers of St. Bartholomew's before the Reformation.

*The Bull and Dog.* From the sport of bull-baiting.

*The Bull and Gate, Bull and Mouth.* A corruption of Boulogne Gate or Mouth, adopted out of compliment to Henry VIII, who took Boulogne in 1544. Fielding's Tom Jones stayed at the 'Bull and Gate' in Holborn.

*The Case is Altered.* Apart from the explanation that the circumstances of a particular inn have altered substantially, there are various supposed origins of the sign. One is (as at Ravensden, Bedfordshire) that it is from Plowden's use of the expression. Another (as in Middlesex) is that it is a corruption of *Casa Alta* (Sp. High House), which was said to be used as a public-house name when soldiers of the 57th Foot returned to Middlesex after the Peninsular War.

*The Cat and Wheel.* A corruption of St. 'CATHERINE'S Wheel'.

*The Coach and Horses.* A favourite sign of a posting-house or stage-coach inn.

*The Cock and Bull. See under* COCK.

*The Cross Keys. See under* KEY.

*The Dog and Duck,* or *The Duck in the Pond,* indicating that the sport so called could be seen there. A duck was put into the water, and a dog set to hunt it; the fun was to see the duck diving and the dog following it under water.

*The Five Alls* consists of a king (I rule all), a priest (I pray for all), a soldier (I fight for all), a JOHN BULL or a farmer (I pay for all), and a lawyer (I plead for all).

*The Four Alls.* The first four of the FIVE ALLS, above.

*The Fox and Goose.* Sometimes signifying that there were arrangements within for playing the game of Fox and Goose.

*The Golden Fleece.* An allusion to the fable of the GOLDEN FLEECE and to the woollen trade.

*The Golden Lion.* The badge of Henry I and the PERCYS of Northumberland.

*The Goat and Compasses. See under* GOAT.

*The Golden Cross.* A reference to the emblems carried by the crusaders.

*The Goose and Gridiron. See under* GOOSE.

*The Green Man, The Green Man and Still. See under* GREEN.

*Hearts of Oak.* A compliment to the British naval tradition. *See under* HEART.

*The Hole in the Wall.* Perhaps an allusion to the hole in the wall of a prison through which the inmates received donations, or a reference to the narrow alley or passage by which the tavern was approached.

*The Horse and Jockey.* An obvious allusion to the Turf.

*The Man with a Load of Mischief.* A sign in Oxford Street, London, nearly opposite Hanway Yard, said to have been painted by Hogarth, showing a man carrying a woman with a glass of gin in her hand, a magpie, and a monkey etc.

*The Marquis of Granby.* In compliment to John Manners (*see* GRANBY), eldest son of John, third Duke of Rutland—a bluff, brave soldier, generous and greatly beloved by his men.

What conquest now will Britain boast
Or where display her banners?
Alas! in Granby she has lost
True courage and good Manners.

*The Pig and Tinderbox. See under* PIG.

*The Pig and Whistle.* Said by some to be a corruption of *pig and wassail, pig* being an abbreviation of *piggin,* an earthen vessel; or a facetious form of the BEAR AND RAGGED STAFF etc.; but possibly a sign-painter's whimsy.

*The Plum and Feathers.* A corruption of *The Plume and Feathers,* the *Prince of Wales's Feathers.*

*The Queen of Bohemia.* In honour of James I's daughter Elizabeth who married Frederick, Elector of the Palatinate, who was chosen King of Bohemia in 1619.

*The Red Cow.* Possibly because at one time red cows were more esteemed in England than the more common 'black'.

*The Red Lion.* Rampant, Scotland; also the badge of John of Gaunt, Duke of Lancaster.

*The Rising Sun.* A badge of Edward III.

*The Rose.* A symbol of England.

*The Rose and Crown.* One of the 'loyal' public-house signs.

*The Running Footman.* From the liveried servant who used to run before the nobleman's carriage.

*St. George and the Dragon.* In compliment to the patron saint of England.

*The Salutation.* Refers to the angel saluting the Virgin Mary.

*The Saracen's Head.* Reminiscent of the crusades.

*The Seven Stars.* An astrological sign.

*The Ship and Shovel.* Said to be a corruption of Sir Cloudesley Shovel, the admiral of Queen Anne's reign, but probably refers to the shovels used for unloading coal etc.

*The Star and Garter.* The insignia of the Order of the Garter.

*The Swan and Antelope.* Supporters of the arms of Henry IV.

*The Swan and Harp.* See GOOSE AND GRIDIRON *under* GOOSE.

*The Swan with Two Necks.* See under SWAN.

*The Tabard.* A sleeveless coat, worn by noblemen and heralds, upon which a coat of arms was embroidered. The tavern with this sign at Southwark was where Chaucer's pilgrims 'assembled'.

*The Talbot* (a hound). The arms of the Talbot family.

*The Three Kings.* An allusion to the three kings of Cologne, the MAGI.

*The Turk's Head.* Like the Saracen's Head, an allusion to the crusades.

*The Two Chairmen.* Found in the neighbourhood of fashionable quarters when sedan chairs were in vogue.

*The Unicorn.* The Scottish supporter in the royal arms of Great Britain.

*The White Hart.* The cognizance of Richard II.

*The White Lion.* The cognizance of Edward IV as Earl of March. Also the device of the Dukes of Norfolk, the Earls of Surrey etc.

See also A COCK AND BULL STORY *under* COCK; MERMAID TAVERN.

**Pucelle, La** (pūsel') (Fr. 'The Maid'), *i.e.* of Orléans, JOAN OF ARC. Chapelain and Voltaire wrote a poem with this title.

**Puck.** A mischievous sprite of popular folklore, also called ROBIN GOODFELLOW. In Spenser's *Epithalamion* he is an evil goblin:

Ne let the Pouke, nor other evill sprights,

but Shakespeare's *Midsummer Night's Dream* (II,i) shows him as:

that shrewd and knavish sprite
Call'd Robin Goodfellow; are not you he
That frights the maidens of the villagery;
Skim milk, and sometimes labour in the quern
And bootless make the breathless housewife
churn;
And sometime make the drink to bear no barm;
Mislead night wanderers, laughing at their harm?
Those that Hobgoblin call you, and sweet Puck,
You do their work, and they should have good
luck.

**Punch and Judy.** The name of Mr. Punch, the hero of the puppet play, probably comes from Ital. *pulcinello*, a diminutive of *pulcino*, a young chicken. His identification with Pontius Pilate and of Judy with Judas is imaginary. The story roughly in its present form is attributed to an Italian comedian, Silvio Fiorillo (about 1600), and it appeared in England about the time of the Restoration. Punch, in a fit of jealousy, strangles his infant child, whereupon his wife Judy belabours him with a bludgeon until he retaliates and beats her to death. He flings both bodies into the street, but is arrested and shut in prison whence he escapes by means of a golden key. The rest is an allegory showing how the light-hearted Punch triumphs over (1) Ennui, in the shape of a dog; (2) Disease, in the disguise of a doctor; (3) Death, who is beaten to death; and (4) the DEVIL himself, who is outwitted. In subsequent English versions JACK KETCH, instead of hanging Punch, gets hanged himself.

The satirical humorous weekly paper, *Punch*, or *The London Charivari*, is, of course, named after Mr. Punch, who naturally featured prominently on the cover design for very many issues. It first appeared in July 1841 under the editorship of Mark Lemon and Henry Mayhew.

**Pleased as Punch.** Greatly delighted. Punch is always singing with self-satisfaction at the success of his evil actions.

**Punctual.** No bigger than a point, exact to a point or moment (Lat. *ad punctum*). Hence the ANGEL, describing this earth to ADAM calls it, 'This spacious earth, this punctual spot'—*i.e.* a spot not bigger than a point (Milton: *Paradise Lost*, VIII, 23).

**Puss in Boots.** This nursery tale, *Le Chat Botté*, is from Straparola's *Nights* (1530),

No. xi, where Constantine's cat procures his master a fine castle and the king's heiress. It was translated from the Italian into French in 1585, and appeared in Perrault's *Les contes de ma Mère l'Oye* (1697), through which medium it reached England. In the story the clever cat secures a fortune and a royal partner for his master, who passes off as the Marquis of Carabas, but is in reality a young miller without a penny in the world.

**Pygmalion** (pigmā'liən). In Greek legend, a sculptor and king of Cyprus. According to Ovid's *Metamorphoses*, he fell in love with his own ivory statue of his own ideal woman. At his earnest prayer the goddess APHRODITE gave life to the statue and he married it. The story is found in Marston's *Metamorphosis of Pygmalion's Image* (1598). Morris retold it in *The Earthly Paradise* (*August*), and W. S. Gilbert adapted it in his comedy of *Pygmalion and Galatea* (1871), in which the sculptor is a married man. His wife, Cynisca, was jealous of the animated statue (Galatea), which, after considerable trouble, voluntarily returned to its original state. The name was used figuratively by G. B. Shaw for a play produced in 1912 from which the popular musical *My Fair Lady* was derived.

**Pygmy.** The name used by Homer and other classical writers for a supposed race of DWARFS said to dwell in Ethiopia, Africa or India; from Gr. *pugme*, the length of the arm from elbow to the knuckles. They cut down corn with hatchets and made war against cranes which came annually to plunder them. When HERCULES visited their country they climbed up his goblet by ladders to drink from it, and while he was asleep two whole armies of pygmies fell upon his right hand and two on his left and were rolled up by Hercules in the skin of the NEMEAN LION. Swift's debt to this legend is apparent in his *Gulliver's Travels*.

The term is now applied to certain under-sized races of central Africa (whose existence was established late in the 19th century), Malaysia etc.; also to small members of a species, as the *pygmy hippopotamus*.

**Pylades and Orestes** (pī'lədēz, ores'tēz). Two friends in Homeric legend, whose names have become proverbial for friend-ship, like those of DAMON AND PYTHIAS, David and Jonathan. Orestes was the son, and Pylades the nephew, of AGAMEMNON, after whose murder Orestes was put in the care of Pylades' father (Strophius), and the two became fast friends. Pylades assisted Orestes in obtaining vengeance on Aegisthus and CLYTEMNESTRA, and afterwards married ELECTRA, his friend's sister.

**Pyramus** (pi'rəməs). A Babylonian youth in classic story (*see* Ovid's *Metamorphoses*, iv), the lover of Thisbe. Thisbe was to meet him at the white MULBERRY-tree near the tomb of Ninus, but she, scared by a lion, fled and left her veil, which the lion besmeared with blood. Pyramus, thinking his lady-love had been devoured, slew himself, and Thisbe, coming up soon after-wards, stabbed herself also. The blood of the lovers stained the white fruit of the mulberry-tree into its present colour. The 'tedious brief scene' and 'very tragical mirth' presented by the rustics in Shakespeare's *Midsummer Night's Dream* is a travesty of this legend.

**Pyromancy** (Gr. *pur*, fire; *manteia*, divination). DIVINATION by fire or the shapes observed in fire.

**Pyrrha** (pi'rə). The wife of DEUCALION.

**Pythia** (pith'iə). The priestess of APOLLO at DELPHI who delivered ORACLES. Inspiration was obtained by inhaling sulphureous vapours which issued from the ground from a hole over which she sat on a three-legged stool or tripod. Oracles were only available in the spring and were originally spoken in hexameter verses.
**Pythian Games.** The Greek games held in honour of APOLLO at Pytho in Phocis, subsequently called DELPHI. They took place every fourth year, in the third year of each OLYMPIAD, and were next in importance to the OLYMPIC GAMES.

**Pythias** (pith'ias). *See* DAMON.
**The Knights of Pythias.** A benevolent fraternity in the USA and Canada, founded at Washington, DC, in 1864. The *Pythian Sisters*, founded in 1888, are recruited from female relatives of the Knights.

**Python** (pī'thon). The monster serpent hatched from the mud of DEUCALION's deluge, and slain by APOLLO at DELPHI (Pytho).

# Q

**Quail.** In mythology and legend the quail is widespread and appears in many different cultures and has an ambivalent symbolism for, though it is a night bird, its reputation as hot-blooded and amorous associates it with fire and so with the solar PHOENIX. It represents the coming of Spring in some parts and Summer in others. It was also a fighting bird and so depicted courage and victory in battle for the Romans, though they also kept the birds as pets and playthings for children. The term 'quail' was one of endearment; the bird was also a lover's gift.

In Greek legend the jealous HERA turned Leto into a quail; she was the mother of APOLLO and ARTEMIS in DELOS, so the bird was associated with them also. Asteria changed into a quail to escape ZEUS. The bird is connected with HERACLES/HERCULES and featured at the Phoenician spring festival which commemorated his resurrection. The Phoenicians also sacrificed the quail to Melkarth when he defeated TYPHON, or Sephon, as darkness. It was sacrificed to the Tyrian Baal.

There are various myths associated with the quail. Pliny says that, like the CRANE, it posts sentries when the birds sleep; also that they carry stones on migration and drop them to hear if they are over the sea. In migration they were said to land in such numbers on ships that they sank them. Quails were believed to be immune from poisons and could eat hemlock with impunity. Aristotle says: 'Henbane and hellebore are harmful to men but food for quails,' and Lucretius maintains that these poisonous plants fatten quails and GOATS. The brain of a quail was a specific against epilepsy.

Hinduism associates the quail with the coming of Spring; the WOLF of darkness swallows the quail and it disappears for the Winter, but the Asvins, as day and night, light and darkness, revive the quail and it returns in Spring.

Chinese myth associates the quail closely with the phoenix, both being birds of fire. Shen Kua, 11th century A.D., says: 'The Scarlet Bird of the astronomers is a symbol based on the quail. Therefore they are called the seven 'mansions' of the Scarlet Bird in the Southern Quadrant by the names of 'head', 'fire' (*i.e.* heart) and tail of the quail.' The Taoist Ho-kuan Tzu, in the 4th century B.C., says: 'The phoenix is the bird of the quail's heart, it is the essence of the principle of *yang*.' Shen Kua also says that the Red Quail 'alighting on a tree is as fire lighting on wood, wood being the element of Spring, fire of Summer'.

In Russian legend the quail appears as solar, coupled with the HARE as lunar; they were the sun and moon found by the Dawn Maiden. In imperial times the quail was an emblem of the Czar.

The Bestiaries call the quail the Coturnix and say that it is 'the only animal which suffers from the falling sickness like man'. This bird was formerly supposed to be of an inordinately amorous disposition, hence its name was given to a courtesan.

> Here's Agamemnon, an honest fellow enough, and one that loves quails.
> SHAKESPEARE: *Troilus and Cressida*, V, i.

**Queen of Heaven.** The Virgin Mary. In ancient times, among the Phoenicians, ASTARTE; Greeks, HERA; Romans, JUNO; HECATE; the Egyptian ISIS etc. were also so called; but as a general title it applied to DIANA, or the MOON, also called *Queen of the Night*, and *Queen of the Tides*. In *Jer.* vii, 18, we read: 'The children gather wood...and the women knead dough, to make cakes to the queen of heaven', *i.e.* the Moon.

**Queen of Love.** APHRODITE or VENUS.

> Poor queen of love in thine own law forlorn
> To love a cheek that smiles at thee in scorn!
> SHAKESPEARE: *Venus and Adonis*, 251.

**Queen of the May.** *See under* MAY.

**Querno** (kwœ'nō). Camillo Querno, of Apulia, hearing that Pope Leo X (1475, 1513–1522) was a great patron of poets, went to Rome with a harp in his hand and sang a poem called *Alexias* containing 20,000 verses. He was introduced to the Pope as a buffoon, but was promoted to the LAUREL and became a constant frequenter of the Pope's table.

> Rome in her Capitol saw Querno sit,
> Thron'd on seven hills the Antichrist of wit.
> POPE: *Dunciad*, II, i, 15.

**Quetzalcoatl** (ketsəlkōat'l). An Aztec deity whose name means 'feathered serpent', a god of the air or a sun-god and a benefactor of their race who instructed them in the use of agriculture, metals etc. According to one account, he was driven from the country by a superior god and on reaching the shores of the Mexican Gulf promised his followers that he would return. He then embarked on his magic skiff for the land of Tlapallan. Prescott (*Conquest of Mexico*, ch. III) tells us that 'He was said to have been tall in stature, with a white skin, long, dark hair, and a flowing beard. The Mexicans looked confidently to the return of the benevolent deity; and this remarkable tradition, deeply cherished in their hearts, prepared...for the future success of the Spaniards.'

**Quixote, Don** (kwik'zət). The hero of the famous romance of this name by Miguel de Cervantes Saavedra (1547–1616). It was published at Madrid in 1605 with the continuation or second part in 1615. It ridicules the more tedious chivalric romances. Don Quixote is a gaunt country gentleman of La Mancha, gentle and dignified, affectionate and simple-minded, but so crazed by reading books of knight-errantry that he believes himself called upon to redress the wrong of the whole world. Hence a **quixotic** man is a romantic idealist, one with impractical ideas of honour or schemes for the general good. *See also* SANCHO PANZA.

**The Quixote of the North.** Charles XII of Sweden (1682, 1697–1718) also called *The Madman*.

**Quos ego** (kwōs eg'ō). A threat of punishment for disobedience. The words, from Virgil's *Aeneid* (I, 135), were uttered by NEPTUNE to the disobedient and rebellious winds, and are sometimes given as an example of aposiopesis, *i.e.* a stopping short for rhetorical effect. 'Whom I—,' said Neptune, the 'will punish' being left to the imagination.

# R

**Ra,** or **Re** (rah, rā). The sun-god of ancient Egypt, and from the time of Chephren (IVth Dynasty) the supposed ancestor of all the Pharaohs. His chief centre was at Heliopolis where he was also known as Aton. His great enemy was the serpent Apep with whom he fought continually, but always eventually defeated. According to one legend, Ra was born as a child every morning and died at night as an old man. His name and cult was assimilated with that of Amon (AMEN-RA) and many others and he was commonly represented with the head of a falcon surmounted by a solar disc surrounded with the Uraeus, the sacred flame-spitting asp which destroyed his enemies.

**Raboin.** *See* TAILED MEN.

**Ragnarok** (rag′nərok). The *Götterdämmerung* or Twilight of the Gods in Scandinavian mythology. The day of doom, when the old world and all its inhabitants were annihilated. Out of the destruction a new world was born, a world at peace. Of the old gods BALDER returned, and ODIN′S two sons VIDAR and Vail, Vili and Ve (Odin's brother's sons), Magni and Modi, sons of THOR, and Hoenir (Odin's companion).

**Rahu** (rah′hū). The demon that, according to Hindu legend, causes eclipses. One day he quaffed some of the NECTAR of immortality, but was discovered by the SUN and MOON, who informed against him, and VISHNU cut off his head. As he had already taken some of the nectar into his mouth, the head was immortal, and he ever afterwards hunted the sun and moon, which he sometimes caught, thus causing eclipses.

**Rain. To rain cats and dogs.** In northern mythology the CAT is supposed to have great influence on the weather and 'The cat has a gale of wind in her tail' is a seafarer's expression for when a cat is unusually frisky. Witches that rode on storms were said to assume the form of cats. The DOG is a signal of wind, like the WOLF, both of which were attendants of ODIN, the storm god.

Thus cat may be taken as a symbol of the down-pouring rain, and dog of the strong gusts of wind accompanying a rainstorm.

Both are also rain-makers as witches' familiars.

**Raining-tree,** or **Rain-tree.** Old travellers to the Canaries told of a linden tree from which sufficient water to supply all the men and beasts of the island of Hierro was said to fall. In certain weather conditions moisture condenses and collects on the broad leaves of many trees. The genisaro or guango, *Pithecolobium saman*, or ornamental tropical tree, one of the Leguminosae, is known as the rain-tree. In this case ejections of juice by the cicadas are responsible for the 'rain' under its branches. Another is the *Andira inermis*, found in tropical Africa and America.

**Rainbow.** The old legend is that if one reaches the spot where a rainbow touches the earth and digs there one will be sure to find a pot of gold. Hence visionaries, wool-gatherers, day-dreamers etc. are sometimes called *rainbow chasers*, because of their habit of hoping for impossible things.

**Ram.** Pre-eminently representing male virility, the ram is naturally associated with sun gods, but its spiral horns introduce a thunder and lunar symbolism and so connect it with storm and lunar deities. As solar the ram is creative heat and the Egyptian sun god RA is addressed as 'Ra...thou ram, mightiest of created things'. There were various ram-headed gods such as Khnemu, an ancient cosmic deity, who later became Knemu-Ra and was associated with other Nilotic ram-headed gods, he had long, wavy horns while those of Amon-Ra were curved. The Sacred Ram of Mendes embodied the souls of Ra, OSIRIS, Kephera and Shu. A ram was sacrificed to Amon at Thebes and at the Feast of Optet his boat was decorated with rams' heads fore and aft.

The Phoenician sun god Baal/Hamon is portrayed with rams' horns and the Babylonian Ea/OANNES, god of the deeps, represented as part man, part fish; or as goat-fish as CAPRICORN in the ZODIAC, has either goats' or rams' horns representing renewed solar power.

The ram was sacred to ZEUS/Sabazios as fertility; it was also sacred to Dionysus as generative power. The Ram of Mendes was also an attribute of PAN. Devotees of ATTIS were bathed in the blood of the ram at initiation. Phrixus and Helle were carried away across the sea by a ram with the GOLDEN FLEECE. In Rome the ram was often associated with the hearth and a ram was sacrificed to the domestic LAR in a rite of purification.

The *shofar*, the Hebrew ritual horn, blown at festivals or on special occasions, is a ram's horn representing the substitute sacrifice of Isaac. Rams' skins, dyed red, were the inner covering of the Tabernacle (*Exodus* xxvi, 14). Christianity used the ram-substitute as depicting the sacrifice of Christ and the Bestiaries said that the ram portrayed him as the leader of the flock. The ram is the chief sacrificial animal of Islam.

The Vedic Agni, god of fire, has the ram as his attribute, representing the sacred fire in Hinduism.

In Celtic myth the ram is important but is largely chthonic and associated with the hearth which is the entrance to the underworld. The ram is naturally connected with the Horned Gods as fertility but, again, has death connotations; it was also an attribute of war gods. Andirons decorated with rams' horns were found by Celtic hearths and in Gaul fire-dogs were made in ram effigy and rams' heads appeared on Gaulish tombs and monuments to gods of the underworld. The great god of the Gauls was Belin, the ram, and his consort Belishma was his earthly manifestation. The ram was a Celtic and Gaulish sacrificial animal. There are supernatural rams and sheep in Celtic lore, much of which was taken over by Christianity in legends of the saints.

**The Ram Feast.** Formerly held on MAY morning at Holne, Dartmoor, when a ram was run down in the 'Ploy Field' and roasted, complete with fleece, close by a granite pillar. At midday, a scramble took place for a slice, which was supposed to bring luck to those who got it. At Kingsteignton, Devon, a decorated carcase is still escorted through the town on Whit Monday and afterwards roasted in the open.

**Rama.** The seventh incarnation of VISHNU (*see* AVATAR). His beautiful wife, Sita, was abducted by Ravana, the demon-king of Ceylon. With the aid of HANUMAN and his monkeys who collected trees and rocks, a bridge, Adam's bridge, was built across the straits. Rama and his invading army gradually overcame the enemy and Rama's arrow slew the demon-monster. The story is told in the *Ramayana*.

**Ramachandra.** *See* AVATAR.

**Ramora.** One of the most strange of mythological creatures, the Ramora is called the Echeneis in Greek, the Delaya in Latin and the Essinus in the Bestiaries. This small fish which Pliny said was 'not above a foot long' was capable of keeping a ship anchored in the strongest wind or fiercest storm. Pliny also said that it was this little fish which decided the result of the battle of Actium by holding Antony's ship and keeping it from going into action. Aelian corroborates this. A number of these fish saved three hundred children from the murderous Periander by anchoring his ship. The fish was said to live in the Indian Ocean and stopped ships by fastening on to the keels. It is sometimes confused with the Serra, but the latter is generally represented as a fire-breathing, griffin-like monster.

**Ran.** *See* AEGIR.

**Raphael** (raf'āel). One of the principal ANGELS of Jewish angelology. In the book of *Tobit* we are told how he travelled with Tobias into Media and back again, instructing him on the way how to marry Sara and to drive away the wicked spirit. Milton calls him the 'sociable spirit' and the 'affable archangel' (*Paradise Lost*, VII, 40), and it was he who was sent by God to warn ADAM of his danger.

Raphael, the sociable spirit that deigned
To travel with Tobias, and secured
His marriage with the seven-times-wedded maid.
 *Paradise Lost*, V, 221.

Raphael is usually distinguished in art by a pilgrim's staff or carrying a fish, in allusion to his aiding Tobias to capture the fish which performed the miraculous cure of his father's eyesight.

**Rat.** The Egyptians and Phrygians deified rats. In Egypt the rat symbolized utter destruction, and also wise judgment, the latter because rats always choose the best bread.

Pliny tells us (VIII, lvii) that the Romans drew presages from rats and to see a white rat foreboded good fortune. Clothing or equipment gnawed by rats presaged ill fortune.

In Hinduism the rat is the most powerful of the demons and represents foresight and prudence and as such is the vehicle of GANESHA, the elephant-headed god of wisdom, prosperity and successful endeavour, and is a object of veneration.

The rat is the first of the animals of the Twelve Terrestrial Branches of the Chinese ZODIAC. In Japan a white rat accompanies the god of happiness and is also an attribute of the god of wealth; it can be depicted as emerging from a bale of rice or wielding the mallet. Among the Ainu of Japan a legend says that God created the rat to punish the Devil, the rat bit off the Devil's tongue and he was so enraged that he caused rats to increase until they became a plague and God had to create cats.

Among the Australian Aboriginals the rat is a totem animal.

It was an old superstition among sailors that rats deserted a ship before she set out on a voyage that was to end in her loss. Similarly rats were said to leave a falling house.

In few, they hurried us aboard a bark,
Bore us some leagues to sea; where they prepared
A rotten carcass of a butt, not rigg'd,
Nor tackle, sail, nor mast; the very rats
Instinctively have quit it.
 SHAKESPEARE: *The Tempest*, I, ii.

**Irish rats rhymed to death.** It was once a common belief that rats in pasturages could be destroyed by anathematizing them in rhyming verse or by metrical charms. Thus Ben Jonson (*Poetaster, Apologetical Dialogue*) says: 'Rhime them to death, as they do Irish rats.' Sir Philip Sidney says (*Defence of Poesie*): 'I will not wish unto you … to be rimed to death, as is said to be done in Ireland'; and Shakespeare makes Rosalind say (*As You Like It*, III, ii): 'I was never so be-rhymed since Pythagoras' time, that I was an Irish rat.'

**Pharaoh's rat.** *See* ICHNEUMON.

**Rat-killer.** APOLLO received this derogatory title from the following incident: Apollo sent a swarm of rats against Crinis, one of his priests, for neglect of his office; but the priest seeing the invaders coming, repented and obtained pardon and the god annihilated the rats with his far-darting arrows.

**Raven.** A bird of ill omen; fabled to forbode death, and to bring infection and bad luck.

The raven himself is hoarse
That croaks the fatal entrance of Duncan
Under my battlements.
 SHAKESPEARE: *Macbeth*, I, v.

The boding raven on her cottage sat,
And with hoarse croakings warned us of our fate.
 GAY: *Pastorals; The Dirge*.

Cicero was forewarned of his death by the fluttering of ravens, and Macaulay relates the legend that a raven entered the chamber of the great orator the very day of his murder and pulled the clothes off his bed. Like many other birds, ravens indicate the approach of foul weather. When ravens forsake their normal abode we may look for famine and mortality, because ravens bear the characters of SATURN, the author of these calamities, and have a very early knowledge of the bad disposition of that planet.

According to Roman legend, ravens were once as white as swans and not inferior in size; but one day a raven told APOLLO that CORONIS, a Thessalian NYMPH whom he passionately loved, was faithless. The god shot the nymph with his dart; but hating the tell-tale bird:

He blacked the raven o'er,
And bid him prate in his white plumes no more.
 ADDISON: *Translation of Ovid*, Bk. II.

Ovid said it was formerly silver but became black from its chattering tongue and its desire to be first with evil news. As a prophet it foretells death but can also be helpful in finding lost property: this was known as Ravens' Knowledge. The bird is also solar in Greek myth as a messenger of the sun god APOLLO and is an attribute of ATHENE, KRONOS and AESCULAPIUS; it was also a symbol of fertility and as such was invoked at weddings, but in Orphic art it represents death.

In Zoroastrianism the raven is a 'pure' bird as it removes pollution and in Mithraism it represents the first grade of initiation.

Chinese myth has the three-legged raven in the sun, depicting its rising, noontide and setting. In Hinduism BRAHMA appeared as a raven in one incarnation.

The raven-crow goddess, the Blessed Raven, is important in Celtic lore and has a three-fold function as war, fertility and prophecy. The Raven of Battle, the goddess Badb, represents war and bloodshed and is ill-omened. Morrigan, Bran and Lugh or Lugos are associated with the raven and the last had two magic ravens similar to those of ODIN.

Among Amerindians Raven is one of the chief and most widespread of the trickster-heroes and shape-shifters; he is not only the archetypal trickster but also a creator and appears as Raven Man, the Big Grandfather. He was one of the creatures which recreated the land after the Flood and stole the sun. Raven is also a messenger of the Great Spirit.

In Christian art, the raven is an emblem of God's Providence, in allusion to the ravens which fed ELIJAH. St. Oswald holds in his hand a raven with a ring in its mouth; St. Benedict has a raven at his feet; ST. PAUL THE HERMIT is drawn with a raven bringing him a loaf of bread.

**The fatal raven,** consecrated to ODIN, the Danish war-god, was the emblem of the Danish Standard, *Landeyda* (the desolation of the country), and was said to have been woven and embroidered in one noontide by the daughters of Ragnar Lodbrok, son of SIGURD. If the Danish arms were destined to defeat, the raven hung his wings; if victory was to attend them, he stood erect and soaring, as if inviting the warriors to follow.

The Danish raven, lured by annual prey,
Hung o'er the land incessant.
JAMES THOMSON: *Liberty*, Pt. IV.

The two ravens that sit on the shoulders of Odin are called Huginn and Muninn (Mind and Memory).

**Red. Red Barn, The murder in the.** A sensational murder at Polstead, near Ipswich, that achieved lasting notoriety in melodrama and story. *The Red Barn* or *The Gypsy's Curse* was first performed at Weymouth in 1828 and gained immediate and widespread popularity. The theme, essentially that of the innocent village maiden, seduced, and later murdered, by a local man of property, next appeared in book form as *The Awful Adventure of Maria Monk*, and in other titles. They are all founded on the murder of Maria Marten, a mole-catcher's daughter of loose morals who first bore a child to Thomas Corder, the son of a prosperous farmer. Later William Corder, younger brother of Thomas, became enamoured of her with the inevitable consequences, but avoided marriage. In May 1827 it seems that arrangements were made for Maria to meet him at the Red Barn on his farm with the intention of going to Ipswich to be married. Maria was not seen alive again, but Corder decamped to London and married one Mary Moore, who kept a school. Eventually Maria's body was discovered in the Red Barn and William Corder was hanged for her murder at Bury St. Edmunds in August 1828.

**The Red Cross Knight** in Spenser's *Faerie Queene* (Bk. I) is a personification of St. GEORGE, the patron saint of England. He typifies Christian holiness and his adventures are an allegory of the Church of England. The knight is sent by the Queen to destroy a DRAGON which was ravaging the kingdom of Una's father. After many adventures and trials Una and the knight are united in marriage.

**Re'em** (rēm). The name Re'em is used in the Old Testament for the UNICORN, but is usually applied to a huge wild ox of which there are only two in the world, one lives in the Far East and the other in the West. They meet and mate every seventy years and die after the female gives birth to male-female twins. Being too big to get into the Ark, Noah tied them to the stern and they swam in the waters and so were saved from the flood.

**Remus.** *See* ROMULUS.

**Renard** (ren'ahd). **Une queue de renard** (Fr. a fox's tail). A mockery. At one time it was a common practical joke to fasten a fox's tail behind a person against whom a laugh was designed. PANURGE never lost a chance of attaching a fox's tail, or the ears of a leveret, behind a Master of Arts or Doctor of Divinity (*Gargantua*, II, xvi). *See also* REYNARD.

> C'est une petite vipère
> Qui n'épargneroit pas son père
> Et qui par nature ou par art
> Sçait couper la queue au renard.
> BEAUCAIRE: *L'Embarras de la Foire.*

**Revenant** (rev'inənt) (Fr., present participle of *revenir*, to come back). One who returns after long exile; an apparition, a ghost, one who returns from the dead.

**Revenons à nos moutons.** *See* MOUTONS.

**Reynard the Fox.** A mediaeval beast-epic satirizing contemporary life and events, found in French, Dutch and German literature. Chaucer's *Nun's Priest's Tale* is part of the Reynard tradition. Most of the names in the Reynard cycle are German but it found its greatest vogue in France as the *Roman de Renart*. Caxton's *Hystorie of Reynart the Foxe* (1481) was based on a Dutch version published at Gouda in 1479. The oldest version (12th century) is in Latin.

**Reynard's Globe of Glass.** Reynard, in REYNARD THE FOX, said he had sent this invaluable treasure to her majesty the Queen as a present; but it never came to hand as it had no existence except in the imagination of the fox. It was supposed to reveal what was being done—no matter how far off— and also to afford information on any subject that the person consulting it wished to know. **Your gift was like the globe of glass of Master Reynard.** A great promise but no performance.

**Reynard's Wonderful ring.** *See* RINGS NOTED IN FABLE.

**Rhabdomancy.** A form of DIVINATION by means of a rod or wand, dowsing (Gr. *rhabdomanteia; rhabdos*, rod; *manteia*, prophecy).

**Rhadamanthus** (radəman'thəs). In Greek mythology, one of the three judges of HELL; MINOS and Aeacus being the other two.

**Rhea** (rē'ə). In Greek mythology, Mother of the gods, daughter of URANUS and GAEA, and sister of KRONOS by whom she bore ZEUS, HADES, POSEIDON, HERA, Hestia and DEMETER. She is identified with CYBELE and also known as AGDISTIS.

**Rhea Sylvia.** The mother of ROMULUS and Remus.

**Rhyming to death.** *See* IRISH RATS *under* RAT.

**Rick Mould. Fetching the rick mould.** An old catch played during the hay harvest. The greenhorn was sent to borrow a rickmould with strict injunctions not to drop it. Something very heavy was put in a sack and hoisted on to his back; when he had carried it carefully in the hot sun to the hayfield he was laughed at for his pains.

**Riding.** In Cornwall a 'riding' was a practice similar to the SKIMMINGTON, designed to shame and publicize those guilty of marital infidelity. Two people, representing the offenders, were driven through the streets in a cart pulled by a donkey with a suitable accompanying din.

The three historic divisions of Yorkshire called **ridings**, because each formed a third part of the county, derive from the Danish occupation. Originally *thriding*; the initial *th-* of the word being lost through the amalgamation with *east, west,* or *north*. The divisions of Tipperary are (and those of Lincolnshire formerly were) also called ridings.

**Rimmon.** The Babylonian god who presided over storms. Milton identifies him with one of the fallen angels:

> Him followed Rimmon, whose delightful seat
> Was fair Damascus, on the fertile bank
> Of Abbana and Pharphar, lucid streams.
> *Paradise Lost*, Bk. I, 467.

**To bow down in the house of Rimmon.** To palter with one's conscience; to do that which one knows to be wrong so as to save one's face. The allusion is to Naaman obtaining Elisha's permission to worship the god when with his master (II *Kings* v, 18).

**Rinaldo.** One of the great heroes of mediaeval romance (also called Renault of Montauban, Regnault etc.), a PALADIN of CHARLEMAGNE, cousin of ORLANDO, and one of the four sons of AYMON. He was the owner of the famous horse BAYARDO, and is always painted with the characteristics of a borderer—valiant, ingenious, rapacious and unscrupulous.

Tasso's romantic epic *Rinaldo* appeared in 1562 and his masterpiece *Jerusalem Delivered*, in which Rinaldo was the ACHILLES of the Christian army, despising GOLD and power but craving renown, was published (without permission) in 1581.

In Ariosto's *Orlando Furioso* (1516), Rinaldo appears as the son of the fourth Marquis d'Este, Lord of Mount Auban or Albano, eldest son of Amon or Aymon, nephew of Charlemagne. He was the rival of his cousin Orlando.

## Rings noted in Fable and Legend

*Agramant's Ring.* This enchanted ring was given by Agramant to the dwarf Brunello from whom it was stolen by Bradamant and given to Melissa. It passed successively into the hands of ROGERO and ANGELICA, who carried it in her mouth (*Orlando Furioso*).

*The Ring of Amasis. See* AMASIS.

*Cambalo's Ring. See* CAMBALO.

*The Doge's Ring. See* BRIDE OF THE SEA.

*The Ring of Edward the Confessor.* It is said that Edward the Confessor was once asked for alms by an old man, and gave him his ring. In time some English pilgrims went to the Holy Land and happened to meet the same old man, who told them he was John the Evangelist, and gave them the identical ring to take to 'Saint' Edward. It was preserved in Westminster Abbey.

*The Ring of Gyges. See* GYGES.

*The Ring of Innocent.* On 29 May 1205, Innocent III sent John, King of England, four gold rings set with precious stones, and explained that the *rotundity* signifies *eternity*—'remember we are passing through time into eternity'; the *number* signifies the *four* virtues which make up constancy of mind—*viz.* justice, fortitude, prudence and temperance; the *material* signifies 'the wisdom from on high', which is as gold purified in the fire; the *green* emerald is emblem of 'faith', the *blue* sapphire of 'hope', the *red* garnet of 'charity', and the *bright* topaz of 'good works' (Rymer: *Foedera*, vol. I, 139).

*Luned's Ring* rendered the wearer invisible. Luned gave it to Owain, one of King ARTHUR'S knights.

> Take this ring and put it on thy finger, and put this stone in thy hand, and close thy fist over the stone; and so long as thou conceal it, it will conceal thee too.
> MABINOGION (*Lady of the Fountain*).

*The Ring of Ogier* was given him by MORGAN LE FAY. It removed all infirmities, and restored the aged to youth again.

*Otnit's Ring of Invisibility* belonged to Otnit, King of Lombardy, and was given to him by the queen-mother when he went to gain the soldan's daughter in marriage. The stone had the virtue of directing the wearer the right road to take in travelling (the HELDENBUCH).

*Polycrates' Ring. See* AMASIS.

*Reynard's Wonderful Ring.* This ring, which existed only in the brain of REYNARD, had a stone of three colours—red, white and green. The red made the night as clear as day; the white cured all manner of diseases; and the green rendered the wearer invisible (*Reynard the Fox*, ch. xii).

*Solomon's Ring* enabled the monarch to overcome all opponents, to transport himself to the celestial spheres where he learned the secrets of the universe. It also sealed up the refractory JINN in jars and cast them into the Red Sea, and conferred upon the wearer the ability to understand and converse with the animal world.

*The talking ring* in Basque legend was given by Tartaro, the Basque CYCLOPS, to a girl whom he wished to marry. Immediately she put it on, it kept incessantly saying, 'You there, and I here.' In order to get rid of the nuisance, the girl cut off her finger and threw it and the ring into a pond. The story is given in Campbell's *Popular Tales of the West Highlands*, and in Grimm's *Tales* (*The Robber and His Sons*).

**Rip Van Winkle.** The famous character whose fabled adventures are recounted in Washington Irving's *Sketch Book* (1819). The tale is represented as being found among the papers of one Diedrich Knickerbocker, a Dutch antiquary of New York. Rip Van Winkle was a happy-go-lucky, henpecked husband of a 'well-oiled' disposition. During a ramble on the Kaatskill Mountains he met some quaint personages dressed in the old Flemish style playing at ninepins. Unobserved he took a draught of their Hollands and soon fell asleep. He awoke to find himself alone, even his dog had disappeared and his firearm was heavy with rust. He made his way homewards in trepidation only to find his house deserted and none of his former companions about. He had apparently slept for 20 years and after establishing his identity became a village patriarch. He had set out as a subject of George III and returned as a free citizen of the United States!

**Rob. To rob Peter to pay Paul.** To take away from one person in order to give to another; or merely to shift a debt—to pay it off by incurring another one. Fable has it that the phrase alludes to the fact that on 17 December 1540 the abbey church of St. Peter, Westminster, was advanced to the dignity of a cathedral by letters patent; but ten years later was joined to the diocese of London, and many of its estates appropriated to the repairs of St. Paul's Cathedral. But it was a common saying long before and was used by Wyclif about 1380:

> How should God approve that you rob Peter, and give this robbery to Paul in the name of Christ.
> *Select Works*, III, 174.

The hint of the President Viglius to the Duke of Alva when he was seeking to impose ruinous taxation in the Netherlands (1569) was that:

> It was not desirable to rob Saint Peter's altar in order to build one to St. Paul.
> MOTLEY: *The Rise of the Dutch Republic*, Pt. III, ch. V.

**Rob Roy** (Robert the Red). Nickname of Robert MacGregor (1671–1734), Scottish outlaw and freebooter, on account of his red hair. He assumed the name of Campbell about 1716, and was protected by the Duke of Argyll. He may be termed the ROBIN HOOD of Scotland.

> Rather beneath the middle size than above it, his limbs were formed upon the very strongest model that is consistent with agility ... Two points in his person interfered with the rules of symmetry:—his shoulders were so broad ... as ... gave him something the air of being too square in respect to his stature; and his arms, tough, round, sinewy, and strong, were so very long as to be rather a deformity.
> SCOTT: *Rob Roy*, ch. xxiii.

**Robert the Devil**, or **Le Diable**. Robert, sixth Duke of Normandy (1028–1035), father of William the Conqueror. He supported the English athelings against Canute, and made the pilgrimage to Jerusalem. He got his name for his daring and cruelty. He is also called *Robert the Magnificent*. A Norman tradition is that his wandering ghost will not be allowed to rest till the Day of Judgment, and he became a subject of legend and romance.

Meyerbeer's opera *Roberto il Diavolo* (1831) portrays the struggle between the virtue inherited from his mother and the vice imparted by his father.

Robert François Damiens (1715–1757), who attempted to assassinate Louis XV, was also called 'Robert le Diable'.

**Robin. Robin Goodfellow.** Another name for PUCK. His character and activities are given fully in the ballad of this name in Percy's *Reliques*, as exemplified in the following verse:

> When house or harth doth sluttish lye,
> I pinch the maidens black and blue;
> The bed-clothes from the bedd pull I,
> And lay them naked all to view.
> 'Twixt sleepe and wake,
> I do them take,
> And on the key-cold floor them throw.
> If out they cry
> Then forth I fly,
> And loudly laugh out, ho, ho, ho!

**Robin Hood.** This traditional outlaw and hero of English ballads is mentioned by Langland in the *Vision of Piers Plowman*, Bk. V, 402 (1377), and there are several mid-15th-century poems about him. The first published collection of ballads about him, *A Lytell Geste of Robyn Hode* was printed by Wynkyn de Worde (*c.* 1489). The earliest tales were set in Barnsdale, Yorkshire, or in Sherwood Forest, Nottinghamshire, and his adventures have been variously assigned from the reign of Richard I (1189–1199) to that of Edward II (1307–1327). One popular legend was that he was the outlawed Earl of Huntingdon, Robert Fitzooth, in disguise. The name may have been that of an actual outlaw around whose name the legends accumulated. He suffered no woman to be molested and he is credited with robbing the rich and helping the poor.

Robin's earlier companions included LITTLE JOHN, Will Scarlet, MUCH, the miller's son, ALLAN-A-DALE, George-a-Green and later FRIAR TUCK and MAID MARIAN.

The stories formed the basis of early dramatic representations and were later amalgamated with the MORRIS dancers' MAY-DAY revels. *Cp.* TWM SHON CATTI.

> Robyn was a proude outlawe,
> Whyles he walked on grounde,
> So curteyse an outlawe as he was one
> Was never none yfounde.
> *A Lytell Geste of Robyn Hode*, I.

**Bow and arrow of Robin Hood.** The traditional bow and arrow of Robin Hood are religiously preserved at Kirklees Hall, Yorkshire, the seat of the Armytage family; and the site of his grave is pointed out in the park.

**Death of Robin Hood.** He was reputedly bled to death treacherously by a nun, instigated to the foul deed by his kinswoman, the prioress of Kirklees, near Halifax (1247).

**Many talk of Robin Hood who never shot with his bow.** Many brag of deeds in which they took no part.

**Robin Hood and Guy of Gisborne.** A ballad given in Percy's *Reliques*. ROBIN HOOD and LITTLE JOHN, having had a tiff, part company, when Little John falls into the hands of the Sheriff of Nottingham, who binds him to a tree. Meanwhile Robin Hood meets with Guy of Gisborne, sworn to slay the 'bold forrester'. The two bowmen struggle together, but Guy is slain and Robin Hood rides till he comes to the tree where Little John is bound. The sheriff mistakes him for Guy of Gisborne, and gives him charge of the prisoner. Robin cuts the cord, hands Guy's bow to Little John, and the two soon put to flight the sheriff and his men.

**A Robin Hood wind.** A thaw-wind which is particularly raw and piercing being saturated with moisture scarcely above freezing-point. Tradition runs that ROBIN HOOD used to say he could bear any cold except that which a thaw-wind brought with it.

**Robin Hood's Bay,** between Whitby and Scarborough, Yorkshire, is mentioned by Leland. Robin Hood is supposed to have kept fishing boats there to put to sea when pursued by the soldiery. He also went fishing in them in the summer.

**Robin Hood's Larder.** *See under* OAK.

**To go round Robin Hood's barn.** To arrive at the right conclusion by circuitous methods.

**To sell Robin Hood's pennyworth** is to sell things at half their value. As Robin Hood stole his wares he sold them under their intrinsic value, for what he could get.

**Robin Redbreast.** The tradition is that when Our Lord was on His way to Calvary, a robin picked a thorn out of his crown, and the blood which issued from the wound falling on the bird dyed its breast red.

Another fable is that the robin covers the dead with leaves; this is referred to in Webster's *White Devil*, V, i (1612):

Call for the robin-red-breast and the wren,
Since o'er shady groves they hover,
And with leaves and flowers do cover
The friendless bodies of unburied men.

When so covering Christ's body, their white breasts touched his blood and they have ever since been red.

And in the ballad of the *Children in the Wood* Percy's *Reliques*:

No burial this pretty pair
Of any man receives,
Till Robin-red-breast piously
Did cover them with leaves.

Yet another fable says that the red breast came from being scorched when the bird took drops of water to souls in hell.

Soaked toast was offered to robins at Christmas wassailing. There was a saying that 'The robin and the WREN are God's COCK and hen'.

In early mythology the robin was associated with a Promethean legend of fire which it brought from the underworld; this associated it with death and it is unlucky for a robin to enter a house; otherwise it is a lucky bird and a weather prophet.

Scandinavian myth also connects the robin with fire as sacred to THOR, god of thunder and fire; it is a storm-cloud bird.

Amerindian lore says that the culture-hero RAVEN created Robin to give pleasure with his song. *Cp.* RUDDOCK.

**Robin and Makyne.** An ancient Scottish pastoral given in Percy's *Reliques*. Robin is a shepherd for whom Makyne sighs. She goes to him and tells her love, but Robin turns a deaf ear, and the damsel goes home to weep. After a time the tables are turned, and Robin goes to Makyne to plead for her heart and hand; but the damsel replies:

The man that will not when he may,
Sall have nocht when he wald.

**Robinson Crusoe.** The ever-popular castaway of Defoe's novel of this name (1719) was suggested by the adventures of Alexander Selkirk. Crusoe's Island was not Juan Fernandez in the South Pacific where Selkirk was put ashore, but an imaginary island near Trinidad; Defoe's description most nearly fits Tobago.

**Roc.** In Arabian legend, a fabulous white bird of enormous size and such strength that it can 'truss elephants in its talons', and carry them to its mountain nest, where it devours them. It is described in the ARABIAN NIGHTS (SINBAD THE SAILOR).

It is a storm bird, associating the wind with its wings and lightning with its flight. Tradition says it never alights on the earth except on Mount Qaf, the *axis mundi*. Its huge egg is luminous and represents the sun. The roc is the rook of the game of chess.

**Roch,** or **Roque, St.** (rōsh, rōk). Patron of those afflicted with the plague, because 'he worked miracles on the plague-stricken, while he was himself smitten with the same judgment'. He is depicted in a pilgrim's habit, lifting his dress, to display a plague-spot on his thigh, which an ANGEL is touching that he may cure it. Sometimes he is accompanied by a DOG bringing bread in his mouth, in allusion to the legend that a hound brought him bread daily while he was perishing of pestilence in a forest.

His feast day, 16 August, was formerly celebrated in England as a general harvest-home, and styled 'the great August festival'.

**Rocking Stones.** *See* LOGAN STONES.

**Roderick,** or **Rodrigo.** A Spanish hero round whom many legends have collected. He was the last of the Visigothic kings. He came to the throne in 710, and was routed, and probably slain, by the Moors under Tarik in 711. Southey took him as the hero of his *Roderick, the last of the Goths* (1814), where he appears as the son of Theodofred.

According to legend he violated Florinda, daughter of Count Julian of Ceuta, who called in the Saracens by way of revenge. It is related that he survived to spend the rest of his life in penance and was eventually devoured by snakes until his sin was atoned for. It was also held that he would return in triumph to save his country.

**Rodrigo.** *See* RODERICK.

**Rogero, Ruggiero,** or **Rizieri** (rojəə'rō, roojəə'rō, ritsiəə'ri) of Risa (in Ariosto's *Orlando Furioso*), was brother of Marphisa, and son of Rogero and Galacella. His mother was slain by Agolant and his sons, and he was nursed by a lioness. He deserted from the Moorish army to CHARLEMAGNE, and was baptized. His

marriage with BRADAMANTE, Charlemagne's niece, and election to the crown of Bulgaria conclude the poem.

**Roland,** or (in Ital.) **Orlando.** The most famous of Charlemagne's PALADINS, called 'the Christian THESEUS' and 'the ACHILLES of the West'. He was Count of Mans and knight of Blaives, and son of Duke Milo of Aiglant, his mother being Bertha, the sister of CHARLEMAGNE. Fable has it that he was eight feet high, and had an open countenance which invited confidence, but inspired respect. When Charlemagne was returning from his expedition against Pamplona and Saragossa the army fell into a natural trap at Roncesvalles, in the Pyrenees, and Roland, who commanded the rearguard, was slain with all the flower of the Frankish chivalry (778).

His achievements are recorded in the Chronicle attributed to Turpin (d. 794), Archbishop of Rheims, which was not written till the 11th or 12th century. He is the hero of the SONG OF ROLAND (*see below*), Boiardo's *Orlando Innamorato*, and Ariosto's *Orlando Furioso*. He is also a principal character in Pulci's MORGANTE MAGGIORE and converts the giant Morgante to Christianity.

**A Roland for an Oliver.** A blow for a blow, *tit for tat*. The exploits of these two PALADINS are so similar that it is difficult to keep them distinct. What Roland did Oliver did, and what Oliver did Roland did. At length the two met in single combat, and fought for five consecutive days, but neither gained the least advantage. Shakespeare alludes to the phrase: 'England all Olivers and Rolands bred' (*Henry VI, Pt. I,* I, ii) and Edward Hall, the historian, almost a century before Shakespeare, writes:

> But to have a Roland to resist an Oliver, he sent solempne ambassadors to the King of Englande, offeryng hym hys doughter in mariage.
> *Henry VI.*

**Childe Roland.** Youngest brother of the 'fair burd Helen' in the old Scottish ballad. Guided by MERLIN, he successfully undertook to bring his sister from Elfland, whither the fairies had carried her.

> Childe Roland to the dark tower came;
> His word was still 'Fie, foh, fum,
> I smell the blood of a British man.'
> SHAKESPEARE: *King Lear,* III, iv.

Browning's poem, *Child Roland to the Dark Tower Came*, is not connected, other than by the first line, with the old ballad.

**Like the blast of Roland's horn.** Roland had a wonderful ivory horn, named 'Olivant', that he won from the giant Jutmundus. When he was attacked by the Saracens at Roncesvalles (Roncesvaux) he sounded it to give CHARLEMAGNE notice of his danger. At the third blast it cracked in two, but it was so loud that birds fell dead and the whole Saracen army was panic-struck. Charlemagne heard the sound at St.-Jean-Pied-de-Port, and rushed to the rescue, but arrived too late.

Oh, for a blast of that dread horn
On Fontarabian echoes borne,
That to King Charles did come.
SCOTT: *Marmion*, vi, xxxiii.

**Roland's sword.** Duranda, Durindana or Durandal etc., which was fabled to have once belonged to HECTOR, and which, like the horn, ROLAND won from the giant Jutmundus. It had in its hilt a thread from the Virgin Mary's cloak, a tooth of St. Peter, one of ST. DENYS'S hairs, and a drop of St. Basil's blood. Legend relates that Roland, after he had received his death wound, strove to break Durandal on a rock to prevent it falling to the Saracens; but it was unbreakable so he hurled it into a poisoned stream, where it remains for ever.

**The Song (Chanson) of Roland.** The 11th-century CHANSON DE GESTE ascribed to the Norman Trouvère Théroulde or Turoldus, which tells the story of the death of ROLAND and all the PALADINS at Roncesvalles, and of CHARLEMAGNE'S vengeance. When Charlemagne had been six years in Spain he sent GANELON on an embassy to Marsillus, the pagan king of Saragossa. Ganelon, out of jealousy, betrayed to Marsillus the route which the Christian army designed to take on its way home, and the pagan king arrived at Roncesvalles just as Roland was conducting through the pass a rearguard of 20,000 men. He fought till 100,000 Saracens lay slain, and only 50 of his own men survived, when another army of 50,000 men poured from the mountains. Roland now blew his enchanted horn. Charlemagne heard the blast but Ganelon persuaded him that Roland was but hunting deer. Thus Roland was left to his fate.

The *Chanson* runs to 4000 lines, the oldest manuscript being preserved in the Bodleian library, and Wace (*Roman de Rou*) tells us that the Norman minstrel sang parts of this to encourage William's soldiers at the Battle of Hastings.

Taillefer, the minstrel-knight, bestrode
A gallant steed, and swiftly rode
Before the Duke, and sang the song
Of Charlemagne, of Roland strong,
Of Oliver, and those beside
Brave knights at Roncesvaux that died.
*A. S. Way's rendering.*

**To die like Roland.** To die of starvation or thirst. One legend has it that ROLAND escaped the general slaughter in the defile of Roncesvalles, and died of hunger and thirst in seeking to cross the Pyrenees. He was buried at Blayes, in the church of St. Raymond; but his body was removed afterwards to Roncesvalles.

**Rolandseck Tower,** opposite the Drachenfels on the Rhine, 22 miles above Cologne. The legend is that when ROLAND went to the wars, a false report of his death was brought to his betrothed, who retired to a convent in the isle of Nonnenwerth. When he returned flushed with glory and found she had taken the veil, he built the castle to overlook the nunnery, that he might gain a glimpse of his lost love.

**Rollright Stones.** An ancient stone circle between the villages of Great and Little Rollright on the Oxfordshire-Warwickshire border. The structure consists of the King Stone, a circle of about 70 stones called the King's Men, and a few others called the Whispering Knights. 'The King' at this point could look over Oxfordshire and said:

When Long Compton I shall see,
King of England I shall be.

But he and his men were petrified by a witch.

**Roman de la Rose.** *See* ROSE, ROMANCE OF THE.

**Romance.** Applied in linguistics to the languages, especially Old French, sprung from the Latin spoken in the European provinces of the Roman Empire; hence, as a noun, the word came to mean a mediaeval tale in Old French or Provençal describing usually in mixed prose and verse the marvellous adventures of a hero of chivalry. The modern application to a work of fiction containing incidents more or less removed from ordinary life, or to a love story or love affair, followed from this.

The mediaeval romances fall into three main groups or cycles, *viz.* the Arthurian (*see under* ARTHUR), the CHARLEMAGNE cycle, and the cycle of Alexander The Great.

**Romulus** (rom'ūləs). With his twin brother Remus, the legendary and eponymous founder of Rome. They were sons of MARS and Rhea Sylvia (Ilia), who, because she was a VESTAL virgin, was condemned to death, while the sons were exposed. They were, however, suckled by a she-wolf, and eventually set about founding a city, but quarrelled over the plans and Remus was slain by his brother in anger. Romulus was later taken to the heavens by his father, MARS, in a fiery chariot, and was worshipped by the Romans under the name of Quirinus.

**The Second Romulus.** Camillus was so called because he saved ROME from the Gauls, 365 B.C.

**The Third Romulus.** Caius Marius, who saved Rome from the Teutons and Cimbri in 101 B.C.

**We need no Romulus to account for Rome.** We require no hypothetical person to account for a plain fact.

**Roncesvalles** (ron'səvalz). *See* THE SONG OF ROLAND, *under* ROLAND.

**Rosamond, The Fair.** Higden, monk of Chester, writing about 1350, says: 'she was the fayre daughter of Walter, Lord Clifford, concubine of Henry II, and poisoned by Queen Eleanor, A.D. 1177. Henry made for her a house of wonderful working, so that no man or woman might come to her. This house was named Labyrinthus, and was wrought like unto a knot in a garden called a maze. But the queen came to her by a clue of thredde, and so dealt with her that she lived not long after. She was buried at Godstow, in an house of nunnes, with these verses upon her tombe:

Hic jacet in tumba Rosa mundi, non Rosa munda;
Non redolet, sed olet, quae redolere solet.'

Here Rose the graced, not Rose the chaste, reposes;
The smell that rises is no smell of roses.
E.C.B.

The legend of her murder by Queen Eleanor first appears in the 14th century and the story of the LABYRINTH even later. There is no evidence to support the stories that Fair Rosamond was the mother of William Longsword and Geoffrey, Archbishop of York. A subterranean labyrinth in Blenheim Park, near Woodstock, is still pointed out as 'Rosamond's Bower'.

Jane Clifford was her name, as books aver:
Fair Rosamond was but her *nom de guerre*.
DRYDEN: *Epilogue to Henry II.*

**Rose.** Mediaeval legend asserts that the first roses appeared miraculously at Bethlehem as the result of the prayers of a 'fayre Mayden' who had been falsely accused and sentenced to death by burning. As Sir John MANDEVILLE tells the tale (*Travels*, ch. vi), after her prayer:

sche entered into the Fuyer; and anon was the Fuyr quenched and oute; and the Brondes that weren brennynge, becomen red Roseres; and the Brondes that weren not kyndled, becomen white Roseres, fulle of Roses. And these weren the first Roseres and Roses, both white and rede, that evere any Man saughe. And was this Mayden saved be the Grace of God.

In Christian symbolism the *Rose*, as being emblematic of a paragon or one without peer, is peculiarly appropriated to the Virgin MARY, one of whose titles is 'The Mystical Rose'. It is also the attribute of St. DOROTHEA, who carries roses in a basket; of St. Casilda, St. Elizabeth of Portugal, and St. Rose of Viterbo, who carry roses in either their hands or caps; of St. Thérèse of Lisieux, who scatters red roses; and of St. Rosalie, St. Angelus, St. Rose of Lima and St. Victoria, who wear crowns of roses.

The Rose is an emblem of England and in heraldry is used as the mark of cadency for a seventh son.

In the language of FLOWERS, different roses have a different signification as:

The Burgundy Rose signifies simplicity and beauty.

The China Rose, grace or beauty ever fresh.

The Daily Rose, a smile.

The Dog Rose, pleasure mixed with pain.

A Faded Rose, beauty is fleeting.

The Japan Rose, beauty your sole attraction.

The Moss Rose, voluptuous love.

The Musk Rose, capricious beauty.

The Provence Rose, my heart is in flames.

The White Rose Bud, too young to love.

The White Rose full of buds, secrecy.

A Wreath of Roses, beauty and virtue rewarded.

The Yellow Rose, infidelity. *See* ST. ANTHONY'S FIRE *under* ANTHONY.

**Rose, The Romance of the.** An early French poem of over 20,000 lines; an elaborate allegory on the Art of Love beneath which can be seen a faithful picture of contemporary life. It was begun by Guillaume de Lorris in the latter half of the 13th century, and continued by Jean de Meung in the early part of the 14th. The poet is accosted by Dame Idleness, who conducts him to the Palace of Pleasure, where he meets Love, accompanied by Sweet-looks, Riches, Jollity, Courtesy, Liberality and Youth, who spend their time in dancing, singing and other amusements. By this retinue the poet is conducted to a bed of roses, where he singles out one and attempts to pluck it, when an arrow from CUPID'S bow stretches him fainting on the ground, and he is carried far from the flower of his choice. As soon as he recovers, he finds himself alone, and resolves to return to his rose. Welcome goes with him; but Danger, Shame-face, Fear and Slander obstruct him at every turn. Reason advises him to abandon the pursuit, but this he will not do; whereupon Pity and Liberality aid him in reaching the rose of his choice, and VENUS permits him to touch it with his lips. Meanwhile Slander rouses up Jealousy, who seizes Welcome, and casts him into a strong castle, giving the key of the castle door to an old hag. Here the poet is left to mourn over his fate, and the original poem ends.

In the second part—which is much the longer—the same characters appear, but the spirit of the poem is altogether different, the author being interested in life as a whole instead of solely love; and directing his satire especially against women.

An English version, *The Romaunt of the Rose*, was translated by Chaucer, but in the extant version (first printed in 1532) it is generally held that only the first 1700 lines or so are his.

**Sub rosa** (Lat.), or **Under the rose.** In strict confidence. The origin of the phrase is obscure but the story is that CUPID gave HARPOCRATES (the god of silence) a rose, to bribe him not to betray the amours of VENUS. Hence the flower became the emblem of silence and was sculptured on the ceilings of banquet-rooms, to remind the guests that what was spoken *sub vino* was not to be repeated *sub divo*. In the 16th century it was placed over confessionals.

**Rosemary** (Lat. *Ros marinus*, sea-dew). The shrub (*Rosmarinus officinalis*) is said to be useful in love-making. As VENUS, the love goddess, was sprung from the foam of the sea, rosemary or sea-dew would have amatory qualities.

> The sea his mother Venus came on;
> And hence some rev'rend men approve
> Of rosemary in making love.
> BUTLER: *Hudibras*, Pt. II, Canto i, l. 843.

**Rosicrusians** (rōzikroo'shənz). A secret society of CABBALISTS, occultists and alchemists that is first heard of in 1614 when the anonymous *Fama fraternitatis des löblichen Ordens des Rosenkreuzes* was published at Cassel, duly followed by the *Confessio* and *The Chemical Wedding of Christian Rosenkreutz*. The Rosicrucian Order was reputedly founded by the mythical Rosenkreutz (the cross of roses) in 1459. In FREEMASONRY there is still a degree known as the *Rose Croix*. Rosicrucian philosophy played a part in the early struggle for intellectual progress by clothing its progressive ideas in mystical guise. It seems to have influenced the Elizabethan, Dr. John Dee, and Sir Francis Bacon among others, and to have some links with the work of Paracelsus.

> As for the Rosicross philosophers,
> Whom you will have to be but sorcerers,
> What they pretend to is no more
> Than Trismegistus did before,
> Pythagoras, old Zoroaster,
> And Apollonius their master.
> BUTLER: *Hudibras*, Pt. II, iii, l. 651.

Rosicrucian societies still exist.

**Rosinante** (rozinan'ti). *See* ROZINANTE.

**Ross, Betsy** (1752–1836). She is said to have made the first Stars and Stripes in 1776. The story is that George Washington, with Robert Morris and General George Ross, visited Betsy's upholstery shop in Philadelphia and asked her to make a flag from their design. The stars had six points but Betsy said they would look better with five. This was agreed and in due course she produced the flag.

**Ross. The Fair Maid of Ross.** Amy, the daughter of Captain Browne, the warden of Ross Castle, Killarney, was known as 'The Fair Maid of Ross' and attracted the attention of most of the young officers, especially Raymond Villiers whom her father wanted her to marry, but she was already in love with Donough McCarthy whose estates had been seized by the enemy. When the castle was besieged by the Cromwellians in 1652, Villiers, having been refused by Amy, resolved to betray Ross Castle to Ludlow, Cromwell's general, but when engaged on this mission Amy followed him and learned of his treason. When Villiers finally left the castle Amy again followed him but was wounded by his pistol shot. In a subsequent skirmish McCarthy killed Villiers and Captain Browne surrendered the castle on honourable terms. In due course McCarthy recovered his land and married Amy.

**The Man of Ross.** John Kyrle (1637–1724) who spent most of his life at Ross, Herefordshire. He was famous for his benevolence and for supplying needy parishes with churches. The Kyrle Society was named in his honour.

> Who taught the heaven-directed spire to rise?
> 'The Man of Ross', each lisping babe replies.
> Behold the market-place with poor o'erspread!
> He feeds yon alms-house, neat, but void of state,
> Where Age and Want sit smiling at the gate;
> Him portioned maids, apprenticed orphans blest,
> The young who labour, and the old who rest.
> POPE: *Moral Essays*, Epistle III, l. 261.

**Rosse.** A famous sword which the dwarf ALBERICH gave to Otwit, King of Lombardy. It struck so fine a cut that it left no 'gap', shone like glass, and was adorned with gold.

> This sword to thee I give: it is all bright of hue;
> Whatever it may cleave, no gap will there ensue,
> From Almari I brought it, and Rosse is its name;
> Wherever swords are drawn, 'twill put them all to shame.
> *The Heldenbuch.*

**Rouncival,** or **Rounceval** (rown'sivəl). Very large or strong; of gigantic size. Certain large bones said to have been dug up at Roncesvalles (*see* THE SONG OF ROLAND *under* ROLAND) were believed to have belonged to the heroes who fell with Roland, hence the usage. 'Rouncival peas' are the large marrowfat peas and a very big woman is called a *rouncival*.

**Round. The Round Table.** The Table fabled to have been made by MERLIN at Carduel for Uther Pendragon. Uther gave it to King Leodegraunce of Cameliard, who gave it to King ARTHUR when the latter married GUINEVERE, his daughter. It was circular to prevent any jealousy on the score of precedency; it seated 150 knights, and a place was left in it for the SANGRAIL. The first reference to it is in Wace's *Roman de Brut* (1155); these legendary details are from Malory's *Morte d'Arthur*, III, i and ii.

The table shown at Winchester was recognized as ancient in the time of Henry III, but its anterior history is unknown. It is of wedge-shaped oak planks, and is 17 ft. in diameter and $2\frac{3}{4}$ in. thick. At the back are 12 mortice holes in which 12 legs probably used to fit. It was for the accommodation of 12 favourite knights. Henry VIII showed it to Francis I, telling him that it was the one used by the British king. The Round Table was not peculiar to the reign of Arthur. Thus the king of Ireland, father of the fair Cristabelle, says in the ballad given in Percy's *Reliques*:

> Is there never a Knighte of my round table
> This matter will undergo?
> *Sir Cauline* (Part the Second).

In the eighth year of Edward I, Roger de Mortimer established a Round Table at Kenilworth for 'the encouragement of military pastimes'. At this foundation, 100 knights and as many ladies were entertained at the founder's expense. About 70 years later, Edward III erected a splendid table at Windsor. It was 200 ft. in diameter, and the expense of entertaining the knights thereof amounted to £100 a week. *Cp.* JOHN O'GROATS.

**Knights of the Round Table.** According to Malory (*Morte d'Arthur*, III, i and ii) there were 150 knights who had 'sieges' at the table. King Leodegraunce brought 100 when he gave the table to King ARTHUR; MERLIN filled up 28 of the vacant seats, and the king elected GAWAIN and Tor; the remaining 20 were left for those who might prove worthy.

A list of the knights (151) and a description of their armour is given in the *Theatre of Honour* (1622) by Andrew Fairne. These knights went forth in quest of adventures, but their chief exploits were concerned with the quest of the Holy GRAIL.

Sir LANCELOT is meant for a model of fidelity, bravery, frailty in love and repentance; Sir GALAHAD of chastity; Sir GAWAIN of courtesy; Sir KAY of a rude, boastful knight, and Sir MODRED of treachery.

There is still a 'Knights of the Round Table' Club which claims to be the oldest social club in the world, having been founded in 1721. Garrick, Dickens, Toole, Sir Henry Irving and Tenniel are among those who have been members.

**Sellinger's round.** *See* SELLINGER'S.

**Rowan,** or **Mountain Ash** (row′ən, rō′ən). Called in Westmorland the 'Wiggentree'. It was greatly venerated by the DRUIDS and was formerly known as the 'Witchen' because it was supposed to ward off WITCHES.

> Rowan-tree or reed
> Put the witches to speed.

Many mountain-ash berries are said to denote a deficient harvest. In Aberdeenshire it was customary to make crosses of rowan twigs on the eve of the Invention of the Cross and to put them over doors and windows to ward off witches and evil spirits.

**Rozinante, Rosinante** (rozinan′ti). The wretched jade of a riding-horse belonging to Don QUIXOTE. Although it was nothing but skin and bone—and worn out at that— he regarded it as a priceless charger surpassing 'the BUCEPHALUS of ALEXANDER and the Babieca of the CID'. The name, which is applied to similar hacks, is from Span. *rocin*, a jade, the *ante* (before) implying that once upon a time, perhaps, it had been a horse.

**Rübezahl** (rüb′ətsahl). A mountain spirit of German folklore, ruler of the weather, also called Herr Johannes, whose home is in the Riesengebirge (Giant Mountains), the mountain range which separates Prussian Silesia (now in Poland) and Bohemia (Czechoslovakia).

**Ruby.** The ancients considered the ruby to be an antidote to poison, to preserve persons from plague, to banish grief, to repress the ill effects of luxuries, and to divert the mind from evil thoughts.

It has always been a valuable stone, and even today a fine Burma ruby will cost more than a diamond of the same size.

> Who can find a virtuous woman? for her price is far above rubies.
> *Prov.* xxxi, 10; *cp.* also *Job* xxviii, 18, and *Prov.* viii, 11.

Marco Polo said that the king of Ceylon had the finest ruby he had ever seen. 'It is a span long, as thick as a man's arm, and without a flaw.' Kublai Khan offered the value of a city for it, but the king would not part with it, though all the treasures of the world were to be laid at his feet.

**The perfect ruby.** An alchemist's term for the ELIXIR, or PHILOSOPHER'S STONE.

> He that has once the flower of the sun,
> The perfect ruby which we call elixir, ...
> Can confer honour, love, respect, long life,
> Give safety, valour, yea, and victory,
> To whom he will.
> BEN JONSON: *The Alchemist*, II, i.

**Ruddock.** The redbreast 'sacred to the household gods'; *see* ROBIN REDBREAST. The word is ultimately from O.E. *rudu*, redness, whence *ruddy*. Shakespeare makes Arviragus say over Imogen:

> Thou shalt not lack
> The flower that's like thy face, pale primrose; nor
> The azur'd hare-bell...the ruddock would,
> With charitable bill...bring thee all this.
> *Cymbeline*, IV, ii.

**Ruggiero.** *See* ROGERO.

**Rumpelstiltskin,** or **Rumpelstilzchen** (rŭmpəlstilt′skin). A passionate little deformed DWARF of German folk-tale. A miller's daughter was enjoined by a king to spin straw into gold, and the dwarf did it for her, on condition that she would give him her first child. The maiden married the king, and grieved so bitterly when the child was born that the dwarf promised to relent if within three days she could find out his name. Two days were spent in vain guesses, but the third day one of the queen's servants heard a strange voice singing:

> Little dreams my dainty dame
> Rumpelstilzchen is my name.

The child was saved, and the dwarf killed himself with rage.

**Run. Runners of Classic Renown.** *See* HUNTERS AND RUNNERS *under* HUNT.

**Runcible Hat, Spoon.** In Edward Lear's *How Pleasant to know Mr. Lear* there is mention of a runcible hat and in the *Owl and the Pussycat* a runcible spoon. What *runcible* denotes is not apparent. Some who profess to know describe the spoon as a kind of fork having three broad prongs, one of which has a sharp cutting edge.

> They dined on mince and slices of quince
> Which they ate with a runcible spoon.
> *The Owl and the Pussycat.*

**Rune** (roon). A letter or character of the earliest alphabet in use among the Gothic tribes of northern Europe. Runic inscriptions most commonly occur in Scandinavia and parts of the British Isles. Runes were employed for purposes of secrecy, charms or DIVINATION; and the word is also applied to ancient lore or poetry expressed in runes. *Rune* is related to O.E. *rūn*, secret. The deeds of warriors were recorded on runic staves and knowledge of rune writing was supposed to have been introduced by ODIN.

**Running the Hood,** or **the Hood Game.** It is said that (in the 13th century) Lady Mowbray was passing over Haxey Hill (Lincolnshire) when the wind blew away her hood. It was recovered by 12 rustics who tossed it from one to the other. The event is celebrated annually on 6 January, when the participants called *boggans* play a curious kind of rugby with rolled canvas hoods.

**Ruritania** (rooritā'nyə). An imaginary kingdom in pre-World War I Europe where Anthony Hope placed the adventures of his hero in the novels *The Prisoner of Zenda* (1894) and *Rupert of Hentzau* (1898). The name is frequently applied to any small state where politics and intrigues of a melodramatic and romantic interest are the natural order of the day.

**Rush. Friar Rush.** *See under* FRIAR.

**Rush-bearing Sunday.** A Sunday, generally near the festival of the SAINT to whom the church is dedicated, when anciently it was customary to renew the rushes with which the church floor was strewn. The custom is still observed at St. Mary Redcliffe, Bristol, on Whit Sunday and at Ambleside, Grasmere, and elsewhere in Cumbria. At Ambleside, a rush-bearing procession is held on the Saturday nearest St. Anne's Day (26 July), the church being dedicated to St. Anne.

**Rustam,** or **Rustem** (rŭst'əm). The Persian HERCULES, the son of Zal, prince of Sedjistan, famous for his victory over the white DRAGON Asdeev. His combat for two days with Prince Isfendiar is a favourite subject with the Persian poets. Matthew Arnold's poem *Sohrab and Rustam* gives an account of Rustam fighting with and killing his son Sohrab.

> Let Zal and Rustrum bluster as they will,
> Or Hatim call to Supper—heed not you.
> FITZGERALD: *Omar Khayyám*, x.

**Rymenhild.** *See* KING HORN.

# S

**Sabine. The Rape of the Sabine Women.**
The legend, connected with the foundation of Rome, is that, as ROMULUS had difficulty in providing his followers with wives, he invited the men of the neighbouring tribes to a festival. In the absence of the menfolk, the Roman youths raided the Sabine territory and carried off all the women they could find. The incident has frequently been depicted in art; Rubens's canvas in the National Gallery, London, is one of the best known examples.

**Sabrina** (sabrī'nə). The Roman name of the river Severn, but according to Geoffrey of Monmouth (*Historia Regum Britanniae*) it is from Sabre, daughter of Locrin and his concubine Estrildis, whom he married after divorcing Guendoloena. The ex-Queen gathered an army and Locrin was slain. Estrildis and Sabre were consigned to the waters of the Severn. NEREUS took pity on Sabre, or Sabrina, and made her the river goddess.

> There is a gentle nymph not far from hence,
> That with moist curb sways the smooth Severn stream,
> Sabrina is her name, a virgin pure.
> MILTON: *Comus*, 824.

**Saga** (pl. *sagas*) (sah'gə). In Icelandic the word is applied to any kind of narrative, but in English it particularly denotes heroic biographies written in Iceland and Norway mainly during the 12th, 13th and 14th centuries. From this comes its English application to a story of heroic adventure.

The sagas are a compound of history and myth in varying proportions, the *King's Sagas* being the oldest, the *First Saga of King Olaf* dating from 1180. Other notable examples are the *Saga of Hallfred*, the *Saga of Björn*, the *Grettis Saga*, the *Saga of Burnt Njáll*, the *Egils Saga* the *Islendinga Saga*, the *Ynglinga Saga*, the *Volsunga Saga*, *Tristram's Saga*, and the *Karlomagnus Saga*. Snorri Sturluson's

*Heimskringla* (Orb of the World) is a collection of biographies of Norwegian kings from the 9th to the 12th century.

**Sagittarius** (sajiteə'riəs) (Lat. the archer). One of the old constellations, the ninth sign of the ZODIAC, which the sun enters about 22 November. *See* CHIRON.

**Sagittary** (saj'itəri). The name given in mediaeval romances to the CENTAUR, whose eyes sparkled like fire and struck dead like lightning, fabled to have been introduced into the TROJAN armies.

> The dreadful Sagittary
> Appals our numbers.
> SHAKESPEARE: *Troilus and Cressida*, V, v.

The 'sagittary' referred to in *Othello* I, i:

> Lead to the Sagittary the raised search,
> and there will I be with him,

was probably an inn, but may have been the arsenal.

**Saint.** Individual saints are entered under their respective names.

The title of saint was from early Christian times applied to apostles, evangelists, martyrs and confessors of remarkable virtue, especially martyrs. In due course the need arose for bishops to intervene against local recognition of the undeserving and eventually Pope Alexander III (1159–1181) asserted the exclusive right of the Papacy to add to the roll of saints. Nowadays canonization is dependent upon a lengthy legal process where the case for the canonization of a particular person is thoroughly explored and contested. JOAN OF ARC was canonized in 1920; Sir Thomas More (1478–1535) and John Fisher (1459–1535), Bishop of Rochester, in 1935.

In Christian art, saints are often depicted with a nimbus, aureole or glory and individual symbols by which they can be recognized. *See* SYMBOLS OF SAINTS, *below*.

**Popes numbered among the saints.**
From the time of St. Peter to the end of the 4th century all the Popes (with a few minor and doubtful exceptions) are popularly entitled 'Saint'; since then the following are the chief of those given the honour:

Innocent I (402–417).
Leo the Great (440–461).
John I (523–526).
Gregory the Great (590–604).
Deusdedit I (615–619).
Martin I (649–654).
Leo II (682–683).
Sergius I (687–701).
Zacharias (741–752).
Paul I (757–767).
Leo III (795–816).
Paschal I (817–824).
Nicholas the Great (858–867).
Leo IX (1049–1054).
Gregory VII, HILDEBRAND (1073–1085).
Celestine V (1294).
Pius V (1566–1572).
Pius X (1903–1914).

**Kings and Queens honoured as Saints.**
Among them are:

Edward the Martyr (961, 975–978).
Edward the Confessor (1004, 1042–1066).
Eric VIII of Sweden (1150–1160).
Ethelred I, King of Wessex (866–871).
Ferdinand III of Castile and Leon (1200, 1217–1252).
Louis IX of France (1215, 1226–1270).
Margaret, Queen of Scotland (d. 1093), wife of Malcolm III.
Olaf II of Norway (1015–1030).
Stephen I of Hungary (979, 997–1038).

**Patron Saints.** (1) a selected list of trades and professions with their patron saints:

| | |
|---|---|
| Accountants, bankers, book-keepers | St. MATTHEW |
| Actors | St. Genesius |
| Advertising | St. Bernadine of Siena |
| Airmen | Our Lady of Loreto, SS. Thérèse of Lisieux, Joseph Cupertino |
| Architects | SS. Thomas Ap., Barbara |
| Artists | St. Luke |
| Athletes (and Archers) | St. Sebastian |
| Authors and Journalists | St. Francis de Sales |
| Bakers | SS. ELIZABETH OF HUNGARY. NICHOLAS |
| Barbers | SS. Cosmas and Damian, Louis |
| Blacksmiths | St. DUNSTAN |
| Booksellers | St. John of God |
| Brewers | SS. Augustine of Hippo, Luke, NICHOLAS of Myra |
| Bricklayers | St. Stephen |
| Builders | St. Vincent Ferrer |
| Cab-drivers | St. Fiacre |
| Carpenters | St. JOSEPH |
| Children | St. Nicholas |
| Comedians | St. VITUS |
| Cooks | SS. LAWRENCE, Martha |
| Dentists | St. Apollonia |
| Dieticians (Medical) | St. MARTHA |
| Domestic Servants | St. Zita |
| Editors | St. John Bosco |
| Engineers | St. Ferdinand III |
| Farmers | SS. GEORGE, Isidore |
| Firemen | St. Florian |
| Florists | SS DOROTHEA, Thérèse |
| Funeral Directors | SS. JOSEPH OF ARIMATHEA, DYSMAS |
| Gardeners | SS. Dorothea, Adelard, Tryphon, Fiacre, Phocas |
| Goldsmiths and Metalworkers | SS. Dunstan, Anastasius |
| Gravediggers | St. ANTHONY (Ab.) |
| Grocers | St. MICHAEL |
| Gunners | St. Barbara |
| Housewives | St. Anne |
| Hunters | St. HUBERT |
| Infantrymen | St. Maurice |
| Innkeepers and Wine merchants | St Amand |
| Jewellers | St. Eloi |
| Lawyers | SS. Ivo, Genesius, Thomas More |
| Librarians | St. Jerome |
| Lighthousekeepers | St. Venerius |
| Miners | St. Barbara |
| Motorcyclists | Our Lady of Grace |
| Motorists | SS. Frances of Rome, CHRISTOPHER |
| Musicians and Singers | SS. Gregory the Great, CECILIA, Dunstan |
| Nurses | SS. Camillus of Lellis, John of God, Agatha, Alexius, RAPHAEL |
| Paratroopers | St. Michael |
| Pawnbrokers | St. Nicholas |
| Physicians | SS. Pantaleon, Cosmas and Damian, Luke, Raphael |
| Poets | SS. DAVID, Cecilia |
| Policemen | St. Michael |
| Postal, Radio, Telecommunications and Telephone, Telegraph and Television Workers | St. Gabriel |
| Printers | SS John of God, AUGUSTINE of Hippo |
| Sailors | SS. CUTHBERT, Brendan, Eulalia, Christopher, Peter Gonzales, Erasmus |

| | |
|---|---|
| Scholars | St. Bridget |
| Scientists | St. Albert |
| Scouts | St. GEORGE |
| Sculptors | St. Claude |
| Secretaries | SS. Genesius, Cassian |
| Shoemakers | SS. CRISPIN and Crispinianus |
| Soldiers | SS. Adrian, GEORGE, Ignatius, SEBASTIAN, MARTIN, JOAN OF ARC |
| Speleologists | St. Benedict |
| Students | SS. Thomas Aquinas, Catherine |
| Surgeons | SS. Cosmas and Damian |
| Tailors | St. Homobonus |
| Tax-collectors | St. Matthew |
| Teachers | SS. Gregory the Great, CATHERINE, John Baptist de la Salle |
| Television | St. Clare |
| Travellers | SS. Anthony of Padua, NICHOLAS, CHRISTOPHER, RAPHAEL |
| Wine-growers | St. Vincent |
| Workers | St. JOSEPH |
| Yachtsmen | St. Adjutor |

(2) Some European and Commonwealth countries with their patron saints:

| | |
|---|---|
| Australia | Our Lady Help of Christians |
| Belgium | St. JOSEPH |
| Canada | SS. Joseph, Anne |
| Czechoslovakia | SS. Wenceslas, John of Nepomuk, Procopius |
| Denmark | SS. Asgar, Canute |
| England | St. GEORGE |
| France | Our Lady of the ASSUMPTION, SS. JOAN OF ARC, DENYS, Louis, Thérèse. There is no official patron saint of France, those listed are recognized as patron saints by the Church. |
| Germany | SS. Boniface, Michael |
| Greece | SS. NICHOLAS, Andrew |
| Holland | St. Willibrord |
| Hungary | Our Lady, St. Stephen |
| India | Our Lady of the Assumption |
| Ireland | St. PATRICK |
| Italy | SS. FRANCIS of Assisi, Catherine of Siena |
| New Zealand | Our Lady Help of Christians |
| Norway | St. Olaf |
| Poland | Our Lady of Czestochowa, SS. Casimir, Stanislaus |
| Portugal | Immaculate Conception, SS. Francis Borgia, Anthony of Padua, George, Vincent |
| Russia | SS. Andrew, NICHOLAS, Thérèse of Lisieux |
| Scotland | SS. Andrew, Columba |
| South Africa | Our Lady of the Assumption |
| Spain | SS. JAMES, Teresa |
| Sweden | SS. Bridget, Eric |
| Wales | St. DAVID |
| West Indies | St. Gertrude |

**Symbols of Saints.** The symbol common to all saints is the nimbus which encircles the head. Martyrs alone have the common symbols of the crown of eternal life won by their heroism and the palm of triumph. With these is generally associated some symbol peculiar to the individual saint, often the instrument of his or her martyrdom, such as the Gridiron of St. LAWRENCE or the windlass on which the bowels were drawn from St. Erasmus' body.

Saints not martyrs will be depicted with an object symbolizing their particular virtue (St. Ambrose has the beehive emblematic of eloquence) or relating to some incident in their lives (as St. DUNSTAN pinching the DEVIL's nose). All saints are depicted in their proper dress, as soldiers in armour, bishops or priests in appropriate vestments, kings robed and crowned, religious in the habits of their order.

Below is a selection of some of the many symbols of saints with some of the saints to which they are applied. (*See also entries for individual saints.*)

Alms-box: *hung round his neck:* St. John of God
Anchor: SS. Clement, Felix, NICHOLAS
Angel(s): Singly or in their host, angels have constantly appeared to aid and protect the saints and are their companions in sacred iconography. For example: *Angel holding plough:* St. Isidore of Madrid;—*fish on a plate:* St. Bertold;—*crosier:* St. Bernard;—*basket of flowers:* St. DOROTHEA;—*bottle:* St. Leontius; *Angel playing violin:* St. FRANCIS of Assisi;—*organ:* St. CECILIA; *Angel bringing monastic rule:* SS. Pachomius, Paphnutius;—*fish:* SS. Bertold, Boniface, Congal; *Angel defending from lightning:* St. HUGH OF LINCOLN
Anvil: SS. Adrian, Eloi
Apple: Malachy; *three golden:* St. Nicholas
Arrow(s): *as instruments of martyrdom:* SS. Anastasius, Canute, Christina, Edmund, Faustus, SEBASTIAN, URSULA MM.; *two, piercing heart:* St. Augustine; *bunch held:* St. Otto;—*and bent bow:* St. Mackessog
Ass: SS. Gerlach, Germanus, Philibert;—*kneeling to Blessed Sacrament:* St. Anthony of Padua
Axe: *as instrument of martyrdom:* SS. Anastasius, Josophat, Malchus, Martian, Matthew, Matthias, Proculus, Rufus

Barge: St. Bertulphus

Barn: SS. Ansovinus, Bridget of Kildare

Barrel: Ss. Antonia, Bercher; *cross in—*: St. Willibrord

Basket: SS. Frances, Joanna, JOHN DAMASCENE;—*of bread: SS. Philip, Romanus;—of flowers:* St. DOROTHEA;—*of fruit:* SS. Ann, Dorothea, Sitha;—*of roses:* St. ELIZABETH OF HUNGARY

Bear: SS. Columba, Edmund, Gallus, Humbert, Maximinus;—*keeping sheep:* St. Florentius;—*laden with baggage:* SS. Corbinian, Maximinus;—*ploughing:* St. James

Beard: *obtained by prayers of* SS. Galla, Paula Barbata, Wilgefortis

Bed of Iron: St. Faith

Beehive: SS. Ambrose, Bernard, John Chrysostom

Bell: SS. ANTHONY THE GREAT, Gildas, Kenan;—*and fishes:* St. Winwaloc;—*in fish's mouth:* St. Paul de Leon

Bellows: *held by devil:* St. Genevieve

Boar: St. Emilion

Boat: SS. Bertin, Jude, Mary Magdalene

Boathook: St. Jude

Bodkin: SS. Leger, Simon of Trent

Book: Common attribute of Apostles, Abbots, Abbesses, Bishops etc.; specifically:—*with child Jesus standing on it:* St. Anthony of Padua;—*with hunting horn or stag with crucifix between horns:* St. HUBERT;—*with wine vessel on it:* St. Urban;—*in bag:* SS. Antoninus, Sitha

Broom: SS. Gisella, Martin of Siguenza, Petronilla

Bull: SS. Adolphus, Regnier, Sylvester; *tossed or gored by—:* SS. Blandina, Marciana, Saturninus

Calves: *two at feet:* St. Walstan

Camel: SS. Aphrodicius, Hormisdas; *bound to:* St. Julian of Cilicia

Candle: St. Beatrix

Cauldron: *as an instrument of martyrdom by boiling in lead, oil, pitch, water etc.:* SS. Boniface, CECILIA, Emilian, Erasmus, Felicity, LUCY, VITUS MM.; John the Evangelist

Chafing dish: St. Agatha

Church: A common symbol of Abbots, Abbesses, Bishops etc. as builders of churches and monasteries

City: The attribute of a saint as protector of a particular city

Club(s): *as instrument of martyrdom:* Boniface, Ewald the White, Eusebius, Fabian, Lambert, Magnus, Nicomedes, Pantaleon, VALENTINE, Vitalis MM.

Colt: St. MEDARD

Cow: SS. Berlinda, Bridget, Modwena, Perpetua

Crocodile: SS. Helenus, Theodore

Crow: St. Vincent

Cup and Serpent: *symbolizing poison detected by:* SS. Benedict, James of Marchia, John the Evangelist, John a Facundo

Dagger: *as instrument of martyrdom:* SS. Agnes, Canute, Edward, Irene, Kilian, Olave, Solange MM.

Deer: St. Henry

Devil(s): In Christian art the Devil is shown both tormenting the saints (throwing St. Euphrasia

down a well, disturbing the prayers of SS. CUTHBERT or Madalberte, for example), and worsted by their virtue (holding a candle for St. DOMINIC or seized by the nose in St. DUNSTAN's pincers). The incidents are too various for separate mention.

Distaff: SS. Genevieve, Rosalie

Doe: SS. Fructuosus, Mammas, Maximus of Turin

Dog: SS. Benignus, BERNARD;—*with loaf:* St. ROCH;—*with torch:* St. Dominic

Dolphin: St. Martianus;—*bearing corpse:* St. Adrian;—*supporting:* St. Calistratus

Dove: *on or over:* SS. Ambrose, Basile, Bridget of Sweden, CATHERINE, Catherine of Siena, Cunibert, DAVID, DUNSTAN, Gregory the Great, Hilary of Arles, John Columbini, Lo, Louis, MEDARD, Oswald, Peter of Alcantara, Peter Celestin, Sampson, Thomas Aquinas

Eagle: SS. Augustine, Gregory the Great, John the Evangelist, Prisca

Ear(s) of Corn: SS. Bridget, Fara, Walburge

Falcon or Hawk: SS. Bavo, Edward, JULIAN Hospitator:—*on cottage:* St. Otto

Feather: St. Barbara

Firebrand: St. ANTHONY THE GREAT

Fish(es): SS. Andrew, Eanswide, Gregory of Tours, John of Burlington, RAPHAEL, SIMON. *See also* Angel, Bell, Key

Fish hooks: St. Zeno

Flail: St. Varus

Flower(s): SS. Dorothea, Hugh of Lincoln, Louis of Toulouse;—*in apron:* St. Zita

Fountain: *obtained by prayer:* SS. Alton, Antoninus of Toulouse, Apollinaris, Augustine of Canterbury, Clement, Egwin, Guntilda, Humbert, Isidore of Madrid, Julian of Mans, Leonard, Nicholas of Tolentino, Omer, Philip Beniti, Riquier, Servatius, Trond, Venantius, Wolfgan;— *springing from their blood:* SS. Boniface, Eric MM.

Frog(s): SS. Huvas, Rieul, Sinorina, Ulphia

Goose: St. MARTIN

Gosling: St Pharaildis

Gridiron: *as instrument of martyrdom:* SS. Cyprian, Donatilla, Erasmus, Faith, LAWRENCE, Vincent MM.

Hammer: SS. Adrian, Reinoldus;—*and chalice:* SS. Bernward, Eloi

Hare: St. Albert of Siena

Harp: SS. Cecilia, Dunstan

Hatchet: SS. Adjutus, Matthew, Matthias

Heart: SS. Augustine, Catherine of Siena, Francis de Sales, Jane Frances;—*with sacred monogram:* SS. Ignatius, Teresa

Hen: St. Pharaildis

Hind: SS. Catherine of Sweden, Genevieve of Brabant, Lupus of Sens;—*with two fawns:* St. Bassian

Hoe: St. Isidore of Madrid

Hook: *as instrument of martyrdom:* SS. Agatha, EULALIA, Felician, Vincent MM.

Hops: St. Arnold of Soissons

Horse: SS. Barochus, Irene, Severus of Avranches

Hourglass: SS. Hilarion, Theodosius

Ink-bottle: St. Jerome

Jug or Pitcher: SS. Agatha, Bede, Benedict, Elizabeth of Portugal, Vincent

Key: SS. Ferdinand, Germanus of Paris, HUBERT, Peter, Raymond of Pannafort;—*and book:* St. Petronilla;—*and rosary:* St. Sitha;—*in fish's mouth:* St. Egwin

Keys: *two:* SS. Hippolytus, Maurilius, Riquier; *bunch of:* B.V.M., SS. Genevieve, JAMES THE GREAT, MARTHA, Nothburge

Knife: SS. Agatha, Bartholomew, Christina, Ebba, Peter Martyr

Ladder: SS. Emmeran, John Climacus

Ladle: St. MARTHA

Lamp: SS. FRANCIS, LUCY;—*and book:* St. Hiltrudis

Lance or Spear: *as instrument of martyrdom:* SS. Barbara, Canute, Emmeran, Gerhard, Germanus, Hippolytus, John of Goto, Lambert, Longinus, Matthias, Oswin, THOMAS MM.

Lantern: SS. Gudule, Hugh, Mary of Cabeza

Leopard: *and ox, or lions:* St. Marciana

Lily: SS. Anthony of Padua, Cajetan, Casimir, Catherine of Sweden, Clare, DOMINIC, Joseph, KENELM, Philip Neri, SEBASTIAN, Vincent Ferrer

Lion(s): SS. Adrian, DOROTHEA, Euphemia, Germanus, Ignatius, Jerome, Mark, Prisca

Loom: SS. ANASTASIA, Gudule

Mason's tools: St. Marinus

Nail(s): *as instrument of martyrdom, held or piercing the body:* Alexander, DENYS, Fausta, Gemellus, Julian of Emesa, Pantaleon, Quintin, Severus of Rome, WILLIAM OF NORWICH, MM.

Oar: St. Jude

Organ: St. Cecilia

Ox(en): SS. Blandina, Otto, Frideswide, Fursey, Julitta, Leonard, Lucy, Luke, MEDARD

Padlock: *on lips:* St. John of Nepomuk

Pickaxe: St. Leger

Pig: St. Anthony the Great

Pilgrim's Staff: SS. Dominic, Louis

Pincers: SS. Agatha, Apollonia, LUCY

Plough: SS. Exuperius, Richard

Purse: St. Cyril of Jerusalem; *three:* SS. Brieuc, NICHOLAS

Rats: St. Gertrude of Nivelles

Raven: St. Benedict;—*bringing food:* SS. Erasmus, PAUL THE HERMIT;—*with ring in beak:* SS. Ida, Oswald

Razor: St. Pamphilius

Ring: SS. Barbara, Damascus, Edward

Saw: SS. James the Less, SIMON

Scales: St. Manous; *weighing souls in—:* St. MICHAEL

Scourge: SS. Ambrose, Boniface, Dorotheus, Gervase, Guthlac, Peter Damian

Scythe: SS. Guntilda, Nothburge, Walstan;—*and well:* St. Sidwell

Shears: SS. Agatha, Fortunatus, Marca;—*and bottle:* SS. Cosmas and Damian

Shovel: *bakers':* SS. Aubert, Honorius

Sieve: SS. Benedict, Hippolytus

Spade: St. Fiacre

Sparrow: St. Dominic

Spit: SS. Gengulph, Quentin

Stag(s): SS. Aidan, Eustace, HUBERT, JULIAN

Hospitator, Osyth, Rieul; *ploughing with—:* SS. Kenan, Kentigern

Star: *on or over:* SS. Anastasia, Bernadin, Bruno, Dominic, Humbert, Nicholas of Tolentino, Thomas Aquinas

Swan(2): SS. Cuthbert, Hugh of Grenoble, Kentigern

Sword: *as instrument of martyrdom; piercing head or body:* SS. Boniface, Euphemia, Lucy, Thomas of Canterbury;—*held:* SS. AGNES, Aquila, Prisca, CATHERINE, Irene, JAMES THE GREAT, Paul;—*and chalice:* St. Ewald the Black;—*and club:* St. Arcadius;—*and crosier or dagger:* St. Kilian;—*and hammer:* St. Adrian;—*and stone(s):* SS. Beztert, Pancras;—*and vase:* St. Pantaleon;—*and wheel or book:* St. Catherine MM.

Taper: St. Gudule

Thistle: SS. Caroline, Narcissus

Tongs: SS. Christina, Felician, Martina

Torch: SS. Aidan, Barbara, Dorothea, Eutropia, Irenaeus, MEDARD

Tower: SS. Barbara, Praxedes

Trowel: SS. Winibald, William of Montevergine

Trumpet: St. Vincent Ferrer

Vine: SS. Elpidius, Urban, Urban of Langres

Weavers' Loom: St. Severus of Ravenna

Wheel: SS. Catherine, Euphemia;—*broken:* St. Quentin

Wolf: St. William of Montevergine;—*bringing child:* St. Simpertus;—*bringing goose:* St. Vedast;—*stealing pig:* St. Blaise

Wolfdog: St. Donatus

Woolcomb: St. Blaise

**Sakuntala** (səkun'tələ). The heroine of Kalidasa's great Sanskrit drama *Abhijnanasakuntala.* She was the daughter of a sage, Viswamita, and Menaka, a water-nymph, and was brought up by a hermit. One day King Dushyanta came to the hermitage during a hunt, and persuaded her to marry him; and later, giving her a ring, returned to his throne. A son was born and Sakuntala set out with him to find his father. On the way, while bathing, she lost the ring, and the king did not recognize her owing to enchantment. Subsequently it was found by a fisherman in a fish he had caught, the king recognized his wife, she was publicly proclaimed his queen, and Bharata, his son and heir, became the founder of the glorious race of the Bharatus. Sir William Jones (1746–1794) translated it into English.

**Sakya-Muni** (sahkyəmoo'ni). One of the names of Gautama Siddhartha, the Buddha.

**Salad. A pen'orth of salad oil.** A strapping; a castigation. It was a joke on All Fools' Day (*see* APRIL FOOL) to send one to the saddler's for 'a pen'orth of salad oil'.

The pun is between 'salad oil', and the French *avoir de la salade*, 'to be flogged'. The French *saler* and *salade* are derived from the O.Fr. word for the saddle on which schoolboys were at one time birched. *See also* RICK MOULD.

**Salamander** (sal'əmandə) (Gr. *sala-mandra*, a kind of lizard). The name is now given to a genus of amphibious Urodela (newts etc.), but anciently to a mythical lizard-like monster that was supposed to be able to live in fire, which, however, it quenched by the chill of its body. Pliny refers to this belief (*Nat. Hist.* x, 86; xxix, 23). It was adopted by Paracelsus as the name of the elemental being inhabiting fire (GNOMES being those of the earth, SYLPHS of the air, and UNDINES of the water), and was hence taken over by the ROSICRUCIAN system, from which source Pope introduced salamanders into his *Rape of the Lock* (i, 60).

Francis I of France adopted as his badge a lizard in the midst of flames, with the legend *Nutrisco et extinguo* (I nourish and extinguish). The Italian motto from which it derived was *Nutrisco il buono e spengo il reo* (I nourish the good and extinguish the bad). Fire purifies good metal, but consumes rubbish.

Shakespeare's Falstaff calls Bardolph's nose 'a burning lamp', 'a salamander', and the drink that made such 'a fiery meteor' he calls 'fire'.

I have maintained that salamander of yours with fire any time this two-and-thirty years.
*Henry IV, Pt. I*, III, iii.

**Salii** (sal'iī), or **Salians.** In ancient Rome, a college of twelve priests of MARS traditionally instituted as guardians of the ANCILE. Every year these young patricians paraded the city with song and dance, finishing the day with a banquet, insomuch that *saliares coena* became proverbial for a sumptuous feast. The word *saliens* means dancing.

Nunc est bibendum...
...nunc Saliaribus
Ornare pulvinar Deorum
Tempus est dapibus sodales.
HORACE: I *Odes*, xxxvii, 1–4

**Salmacis.** *See* HERMAPHRODITE.

**Salt. To eat a man's salt.** To partake of his hospitality. Among the Arabs, to eat a man's salt created a sacred bond between host and guest. No one who has eaten of another's salt should speak ill of him or do him an ill turn.

Why dost thou shun the salt? that sacred pledge,
Which, once partaken, blunts the sabre's edge,
Makes even contending tribes in peace unite,
And hated hosts seem brethren to the sight!
BYRON: *The Corsair*, II, iv.

**Spilling salt** was held to be an unlucky omen by the Romans, and the superstition remains, but evil may be averted if he who spills the salt throws a pinch of it over the left shoulder with the right hand. In Leonardo da Vinci's picture of the Last Supper, Judas Iscariot is known by the salt-cellar knocked over accidentally by his arm. Salt was used in sacrifice by the Jews, as well as by the Greeks and Romans. It was an emblem of purity and the sanctifying influence of a holy life on others owing to its preservative quality; also a sign of incorruptibility. It is used for the preparation of Holy Water and it was not uncommon to put salt into a coffin; for it is said that SATAN hates salt. It was long customary to throw a handful of salt on the top of the mash when brewing to keep the witches from it.

**Sampford Ghost.** An uncommonly persistent poltergeist which haunted a thatched house (destroyed by fire *c.* 1942) at Sampford Peverell, Devon, for about three years until 1810. Besides the usual knockings the inmates were beaten, curtains agitated and damaged, levitations occurred, and in one instance an 'unattached arm' flung a folio Greek Testament from a bed into the middle of the room. The Rev. Charles Caleb Colton, rector of the Prior's Portion, Tiverton (credited as author of these freaks), offered £100 to anyone who could explain the matter except on supernatural grounds. No one claimed the reward.

**Sampo.** *See* KALEVALA.

**Sancho Panza** (san'chō pan'zə). The squire of Don QUIXOTE in Cervantes' romance. A short pot-bellied rustic, full of common sense, but without a grain of 'spirituality', he became governor of BARATARIA. He rode upon an ass, Dapple, and was famous for his proverbs. *Panza*, in Spanish, means *paunch*. Hence a *Sancho Panza* as a rough-and-ready, sharp and humorous justice of the peace, an allusion to Sancho, as judge in the isle of Barataria.

**Sanchoniathon** (sangkōnī'əthon). The *Fragments of Sanchoniathon* are the literary remains of a supposed ancient Phoenician philosopher (alleged to have lived before the TROJAN WAR), which are incorporated in the *Phoenician History* by Philo of Byblos (1st and 2nd centuries A.D.), and which were drawn upon by Eusebius (*c.* 260–*c.* 340), the 'Father of Church History'. The name is Greek and may mean 'the whole law of Chon' or alternatively may be a proper name. It is likely that the name was invented by Philo to give ancient authority to his writings.

**Sancy Diamond, The.** A famous diamond (55 carats), said to have once belonged to Charles the Bold of Burgundy, and named after the French ambassador in Constantinople, Nicholas de Harlay, Sieur de Sancy, who, about 1575, bought it for 70,000 francs. Later it was owned by Henri III and Henri IV of France, then by Queen Elizabeth I; James II took it with him in his flight to France in 1688 and sold it to Louis XIV for £25,000. Louis XV wore it at his coronation, but during the French Revolution it was stolen and, in 1828, sold to Prince Paul Demidoff for £80,000. In 1865, it was bought by Sir Jamsetjee Jeejeebhoy, but was on the market again in 1889 and rumoured to have been subsequently acquired by the Tsar of Russia. Its present fate is unknown.

**Sandabar,** or **Sindibad.** Names given to a mediaeval collection of tales much the same as those in the Greek *Syntipas the Philosopher* and the Arabic *Romance of the Seven Viziers* known in Western Europe as *The Seven Sages* (SEVEN WISE MASTERS), and derived from the *Fables of Bidpay*. These names probably result from Hebrew mistransliterations of the Arabic equivalent of Bidpay or Pilpay.

**Sangrado, Dr.** (sangrah'dō). A name applied to an ignorant or 'fossilized' medical practitioner, from the humbug in Le Sage's *Gil Blas* (1715), a tall, meagre, pale man, of very solemn appearance, who weighed every word he uttered and gave an emphasis to his sage 'dicta'. 'His reasoning was geometrical, and his opinions angular.' He prescribed warm water and bleeding for every ailment, for his great theory was that, 'It is a gross error to suppose that blood is necessary for life.'

**Sangrail,** or **Sangreal** (sang·grāl'). The Holy GRAIL. Popular etymology used to explain the word as meaning the real blood of Christ, *sang-real*, or the wine used in the Last Supper; and a tradition arose that part of this wine-blood was preserved by JOSEPH OF ARIMATHEA in the Saint, or Holy Grail.

**Santa Claus.** A contraction of Santa Nikolaus (St. NICHOLAS), the patron saint of German children. His feast-day is 6 December, and the vigil is still held in some places, but for the most part his name is now associated with Christmastide. The custom used to be for someone, on 5 December, to assume the costume of a bishop, and distribute small gifts to 'good children'. The present custom, introduced into England from Germany about 1840, is to put toys and other small presents into a stocking late on Christmas Eve, when the children are asleep, and when they wake on Christmas morn they find at the bedside the gifts brought by Santa Claus, who supposedly travels around in a sleigh pulled by reindeer.

**Sappho** (saf'ō). The Greek poetess of Lesbos, known as 'the Tenth MUSE'. She lived about 600 B.C., and is fabled to have thrown herself into the sea from the Leucadian promontory in consequence of her advances having been rejected by the beautiful youth Phaon.

Pope used the name in his *Moral Essays* (II) for Lady Mary Wortley Montagu.

**Sarsen Stones** (sah'sən). The sandstone boulders of Wiltshire and Berkshire are so called. The early Christian Saxons used the word *Saresyn* (*i.e.* Saracen) as a synonym of pagan or heathen, and as these stones were popularly associated with DRUID worship, they were called *Saresyn* (or heathen) stones. Robert Ricart says of Duke Rollo, 'He was a Saresyn come out of Denmark into France.' In the tin mining areas of Cornwall old attle or rock waste was called *Sarsen* or *Jews' leavings* on the assumption that Saracens, Jews and Phoenicians had once worked there.

**Satan** (sā'tən), in Hebrew, means adversary or enemy, and is traditionally applied to the DEVIL, the personification of evil.

To whom the Arch-enemy
(And thence in heaven called Satan).
MILTON: *Paradise Lost*, Bk. I, 81.

He appears as the SERPENT, tempter of mankind in *Gen*. iii, 1, and the existence of Satan as the centre of evil is part of the teaching of both the Old and New Testament,

But when they have heard, Satan cometh immediately, and taketh away the word that was sown in their hearts.
*Mark* iv, 15.

The name is often used of a tempter or of a person of whom one is expressing abhorrence. Thus the Clown says to Malvolio:

Fie, thou dishonest Satan! I call thee by the most modest terms; for I am one of those gentle ones that will use the devil himself with courtesy.
SHAKESPEARE: *Twelfth Night*, IV, ii.

**Saturn** (sat′ən). A Roman deity, identified with the Greek KRONOS (time). He devoured all his children except JUPITER (air), NEPTUNE (water), and PLUTO (the grave). These Time cannot consume. The reign of Saturn was celebrated by the poets as a 'Golden Age'. According to the old alchemists and astrologers Saturn typified lead, and was a very evil planet to be born under. He was the god of seedtime and harvest and his symbol was a scythe, and he was finally banished from his throne by his son Jupiter.

**Saturn red.** Red lead.

**Saturn's tree.** An alchemist's name for the Tree of DIANA, or Philosopher's Tree.

**Saturnalia.** The ancient Roman festival of SATURN, celebrated on 19 December and eventually prolonged for seven days, was a time of freedom from restraint, merrymaking, and often riot and debauchery. During its continuance public business was suspended, the law courts and schools were closed and no criminals were punished.

**Saturnian.** Pertaining to Saturn; with reference to the 'Golden Age', to the god's sluggishness, or to the baleful influence attributed to him by the astrologers.

Then rose the seed of Chaos and of Night
To blot out order and extinguish light.
Of dull and venal a new world to mould,
And bring Saturnian days of lead and gold.
POPE: *Dunciad*, IV, 13.

**Saturnine.** Grave, phlegmatic, gloomy, dull and glowering. Astrologers affirm that such is the disposition of those who are born under the influence of the leaden planet SATURN.

**Satyr** (sat′ir). One of a body of forest gods or demons who, in classical mythology, were the attendants of BACCHUS. Like the FAUNS, they are represented as having the legs and hind-quarters of a GOAT, budding horns, and goat-like ears, and they were very lascivious.

Hence, the term is applied to a brutish or lustful man; and the psychological condition among males characterized by excessive venereal desire is known as *satyriasis*.

**Saucer. Flying saucers.** Alleged mysterious objects resembling revolving, partially luminous discs that shoot across the sky at a high velocity and at a great height. 'Flying saucers' have been reported on a number of occasions in recent years but their actuality remains as elusive as that of the LOCH NESS MONSTER. *Cp.* UFO.

**Saw.** In Christian art an attribute of St. Simon and St. James the Less, in allusion to the tradition of their being sawn to death.

**Scales.** From time immemorial the scales have been one of the principal attributes of Justice, it being impossible to outweigh even a little right with any quantity of Wrong.

...first the right he put into the scale,
And then the Giant strove with puissance strong
To fill the other scale with so much wrong
But all the wrongs that he therein could lay,
Might not it peise.
SPENSER: *The Faerie Queene*, V, ii, 46.

According to the Koran, at the Judgment Day everyone will be weighed in the scales of the archangel GABRIEL. The good deeds will be put in the scale called 'Light', and the evil ones in the scale called 'Darkness', after which they have to cross the bridge AL-SIRAT, not wider than the edge of a scimitar. The faithful will pass over in safety, but the rest will fall into the dreary realms of Gehenna.

Scales represent the sign of Libra in the ZODIAC; they are also an emblem of Themis as law, order and truth.

In Egyptian myth the soul, at death, was weighed against the feather of truth in the Judgment Hall of OSIRIS.

Christianity has the scales as an emblem of the Archangel MICHAEL.

**Scarab.** A trinket in the form of a dung-beetle, especially *Scarabaeus sacer*. It originated in ancient Egypt as an AMULET, being made of polished or glazed stone, metal or glazed faience, and was perforated lengthwise for suspension. By the XIIIth Dynasty, scarabs became used as seals, worn as pendants, or mounted on signet rings. The insect was supposed to conceal in itself the secret of eternal life, since the scarab was believed to be only of the male sex, hence their use as amulets. They are still the most popular of Egyptian souvenirs.

**Scaramouch** (ska'rəmowch). The English form of Ital. *Scaramuccia* (through Fr. *Scaramouche*), a stock character in old Italian farce, introduced into England soon after 1670. He was a braggart and fool, very valiant in words, but a poltroon, and was usually dressed in a black Spanish costume caricaturing the dons. The Neapolitan actor Tiberior Fiurelli (1608–1694) was surnamed *Scaramouch Fiurelli*. He came to England in 1673, and astonished JOHN BULL with feats of agility. *Cp.* COLUMBINE; HARLEQUIN.

Stout Scaramoucha with rush lance rode in,
And ran a tilt at centaur Arlequin.
    DRYDEN: *Epilogue to the University of Oxford.*

**Scarlet. The Scarlet Woman,** or **Scarlet Whore.** The woman seen by St. John in his vision 'arrayed in purple and scarlet colour', sitting 'upon a scarlet coloured beast, full of names of blasphemy, having seven heads and ten horns', 'drunken with the blood of the saints, and with the blood of the martyrs', upon whose forehead was written 'Mystery, Babylon the Great, The Mother of Harlots and Abominations of The Earth' (*Rev.* xvii, 1–6).

St. John was probably referring to Rome which, at the time he was writing, was 'drunken with the blood of the saints'; some controversial Protestants have applied the words to the Church of Rome, and some Roman Catholics to the Protestant churches generally.

**Will Scarlet.** One of the companions of ROBIN HOOD.

**Scheherazade** (shəher'əzahd). The mouthpiece of the tales related in the ARABIAN NIGHTS, daughter of the grand Vizier of the Indies. The sultan Schahriah, having discovered the infidelity of his sultana, resolved to have a fresh wife every night and have her strangled at daybreak. Scheherazade entreated to become his wife, and so amused him with tales for a thousand and one nights that he revoked his cruel decree, bestowed his affection on her, and called her 'the liberator of the sex'.

I had noticed that the young girl—the story writer, our Scheherazade, as I call her—looked as if she had been crying or lying awake half the night.
    O.W. HOLMES: *The Poet at the Breakfast-table,* ch. iii.

**Schlemihl, Peter** (shlemēl'). The man who sold his shadow to the DEVIL, in Chamisso's tale so called (1814). The name is a synonym for any person who makes a desperate and silly bargain. *Schlemihl* is Yiddish for a clumsy person.

**Sciron** (sī'ron). A robber of Greek legend, slain by THESEUS. He infested the parts about Megara, and forced travellers over the rocks into the sea, where they were devoured by a sea monster.

**Scogan's Jests** (skō'gən). A popular jest-book in the 16th century, said by Andrew Boorde (who published it) to be the work of one John Scogan, reputed to have been court fool to Edward IV. He is referred to (anachronously) by Justice Shallow in *Henry IV, Pt. II*, III, ii, and must not be confused with Henry Scogan (d. 1407), the poet-disciple of Chaucer to whom Ben Jonson alludes:

Scogan? What was he?
Oh, a fine gentleman, and a master of arts
Of Henry the Fourth's times, that made disguises
For the king's sons, and writ in ballad royal
Daintily well.
    *The Fortunate Isles* (1642).

**Scorpio, Scorpion** (skaw'piō). Scorpio is the eighth sign of the ZODIAC, which the sun enters about 24 October. ORION had boasted that he could kill any animal the earth produced. A scorpion was sent to punish his vanity and it stung Orion to death. JUPITER later raised the scorpion to HEAVEN.

Fable has it that scorpions carry with them an oil which is a remedy against their stings. *Cp.* TOAD.

'Tis true, a scorpion's oil is said
To cure the wounds the venom made,
And weapons dress'd with salves restore
And heal the hurts they gave before.
    BUTLER: *Hudibras*, III, ii, 1029.

The oil was extracted from the flesh and given to the sufferer as a medicine; it was also supposed to be very useful to bring away the descending stone of the kidneys. Another belief was that if a scorpion was surrounded by a circle of fire it would sting itself to death with its own tail. Byron, in the *Giaour* (1.422), extracts a simile from the legend:

> The mind that broods o'er guilty woes
> Is like the Scorpion girt by fire;
> One sad and sole relief she knows,
> The sting she nourished for her foes,
> Whose venom never yet was vain,
> Gives but one pang, and cures all pain.

Sumerian myth has scorpions or scorpion-men as guardians of the Gateway of the Sun, the Twin Gates and the Mountains of the East. Scorpions were also associated with *Ishtar* and the Phrygian Sabazius.

In Egyptian lore the scorpion incarnated evil. SET took this form in an attempt to murder the child HORUS whom he stung, but ISIS prayed to RA who sent THOTH to cure the infant god. The scorpion goddess Selket or Selquet is depicted as either a scorpion-headed woman or with a scorpion on her head; she was a protector of the dead. Seven scorpions accompanied Isis in her search for OSIRIS.

The twins, the Dadophori of Mithraism, as representing life and death, the rising and the setting sun, are portrayed as the *Bull* and Scorpion.

In the Old Testament the scorpion typifies the wilderness, drought, desolation and a dreadful scourge (1 *Kings* xii, 11).

**Scratch. Old Scratch.** OLD NICK (*see under* NICK), the DEVIL. From *skratta*, an old Scandinavian word for a GOBLIN or monster (modern Icelandic *skratti*, a devil).

**Scylla** (sil'ə). In Greek legend the name of a daughter of King Nisus of Megara; also a sea monster.

The daughter of Nisus promised to deliver Megara into the hands of her lover, MINOS, and, to effect this, cut off a golden hair on her father's head while he was asleep. Minos despised her for this treachery, and Scylla threw herself from a rock into the sea. Other accounts say she was changed into a lark by the gods and her father into a hawk.

Scylla, the sea monster, was a beautiful NYMPH beloved by GLAUCUS, who applied to CIRCE for a love-potion, but Circe became enamoured of him and metamorphosed her rival into a hideous creature with twelve feet and six heads, each with three rows of teeth. Below the waist her body was made up of hideous monsters, like dogs, which barked unceasingly. She dwelt on the rock of Scylla, opposite CHARYBDIS, on the Italian side of the Straits of Messina and was a terror to ships and sailors. Whenever a ship passed, each of her heads would seize one of the crew.

**Avoiding Scylla, he fell into Charybdis.** *See* CHARYBDIS.

**Between Scylla and Charybdis.** *See* CHARYBDIS.

**To fall from Scylla into Charybdis**—out of the frying-pan into the fire. *See* CHARYBDIS.

**Scythian defiance** (sidh'iən). When DARIUS approached Scythia, an ambassador was sent to his tent with a bird, a frog, a mouse and five arrows, then left without uttering a word. Darius, wondering what was meant, was told by Gobrias it meant this: Either fly away like a bird, hide your head in a hole like a mouse, or swim across the river like a frog, or in five days you will be laid prostrate by the Scythian arrows.

**The Scythian** or **Tartarian Lamb.** *See under* LAMB.

**Sea. The Old Man of the Sea.** *See under* OLD.

**Sea Deities.** In classical myth, besides the fifty NEREIDS, the OCEANIDS, the SIRENS etc., there were numerous deities connected with the sea. Chief among them are: AMPHITRITE; GLAUCUS; Ino (*see* LEUCOTHEA); NEPTUNE; NEREUS and his wife TETHYS; Portumnus (*see* PALAEMON); POSEIDON (the Greek Neptune); PROTEUS; THETIS; TRITON.

**Sea serpent.** A serpentine monster supposed to inhabit the depths of the ocean. Many reports of such a creature have been made by mariners over the centuries but its existence has never been established; thus J. G. Lockhart (*Mysteries of the Sea: The Great Sea-Serpent*) writes: 'We thus conclude with at least three sea-serpents, one in 1857, one in 1875, and one in 1905, for which we have reasonably satisfactory evidence ... Most of the witnesses agree on certain outstanding features; it is a long serpentine creature; it has a series of humps; its head is rather like a horse's; its colour is dark on the top and light below; it appears during the summer months; and unlike the sea monster it is harmless, for it never actually attacked anybody even under provocation'. *Cp.* LOCH NESS MONSTER.

**The Sea-born goddess.** APHRODITE.

**Sebastian, St.** Patron SAINT of archers, martyred in 288. He was bound to a tree and shot at with arrows and finally beaten to death. As the arrows stuck in his body as pins in a pin-cushion, he was also made the patron saint of pin-makers. As he was a captain of the guard, he is the patron saint of soldiers. His feast, coupled with that of St. Fabian, is kept on 20 January.

**The English St. Sebastian.** St. Edmund, the martyr-king of East Anglia (855–870) who is said to have been tied to a tree by the Danes and shot dead with arrows at Hoxne, Suffolk, because he refused to rule as a Danish vassal. His body was taken to the royal manor of Bedricsworth which came to be called St. Edmund's Burgh and his remains, miraculously incorrupt, became the chief relic of the abbey of Bury St. Edmunds.

**Seian Horse, The** (sī'ən). A possession which invariably brought ill luck with it. Hence the Latin proverb *Ille homo habet equum Seianum*. Cneius Seius had an Argive horse, of the breed of Diomed, of a bay colour and surpassing beauty, but it was fatal to its possessor. Seius was put to death by Mark Antony. Its next owner, Cornelius Dolabella, who bought it for 100,000 sesterces, was killed in Syria during the civil wars. Caius Cassius, who next took possession of it, perished after the battle of Philippi by the very sword which stabbed Caesar. Antony had the horse next, and after the battle of Actium slew himself.

Likewise the gold of Tolosa (*see under* GOLD) *and* HARMONIA'S NECKLACE were fatal possessions. *Cp.* NESSUS.

**Selene** (səlē'ni). The moon goddess of Greek mythology, daughter of HYPERION and Theia, corresponding approximately to the Roman DIANA. Selene had 50 daughters by ENDYMION and three by ZEUS, including Erse, the Jew. Selene is represented with a diadem and wings on her shoulders, driving in a chariot drawn by two white horses; Diana is represented with a bow and arrow running after a stag.

**Sellinger's Round.** An old country dance, very popular in Elizabethan times, in which:

the dancers take hands, go round twice and back again; then all set, turn, and repeat; then lead all forward, and back, and repeat; two singles and back, set and turn single and repeat; arms all and repeat.

JOHN PLAYFORD: *The English Dancing Master* (1651).

It is said to be so called either from Sir Thomas Sellynger, buried in St. George's Chapel, Windsor, about 1470, or from Sir Anthony St. Leger, Lord Deputy of Ireland (d.1559).

**Semele** (sem'ili). In Greek mythology, the daughter of 72 CADMUS and HARMONIA. By ZEUS she was the mother of DIONYSUS and was killed by lightning when he granted her request to visit her in his majesty.

**Semiramis** (semir'əmis). In ancient legend, daughter of the goddess Derceto and a young Assyrian. She married Menones, but he hanged himself when NINUS, king of Assyria and founder of Nineveh, demanded Semiramis from him. She forthwith married NINUS who was so enamoured that he resigned the CROWN to her. After this she put him to death, but was herself ultimately slain by her son Ninyas. She is sometimes identified with ISHTAR and her doves. These and other legends accumulated round an Assyrian princess of this name who lived *c.* 800 B.C.

**The Semiramis of the North.** Margaret of Denmark, Sweden and Norway (1353–1412), and Catherine II of Russia (1729–1796) have both been so called.

**Se'nnight.** A week; seven nights. *Fort'night*, fourteen nights. These words are relics of the ancient Celtic custom of beginning the day at sunset, a custom observed by the ancient Greeks, Babylonians, Persians, Syrians and Jews, and by the modern heirs of these peoples. In *Gen.* i, 5, we find the evening precedes the morning: as, 'The evening and the morning were the first day', etc.

He shall live a man forbid:
Weary se'n-nights nine times nine
Shall he dwindle, peak and pine.
SHAKESPEARE: *Macbeth*, I, iii.

**Septentrional Signs** (septen'triōnəl). The first six signs of the ZODIAC, because they belong to the *northern* celestial hemisphere. The north was called the *septentrion* from the seven stars of the Great Bear (Lat. *septem*, seven; *triones*, plough oxen).

**Seraphim.** The highest of the nine choirs of ANGELS, so named from the seraphim of *Is.* vi, 2. The word is probably the same as *saraph*, a serpent, from *saraph*, to burn (in allusion to its bite); and this connection with burning suggested to early Christian interpreters that the seraphim were specially distinguished by the ardency of their zeal and love.

Seraphim is a plural form; the singular, *seraph*, was first used in English by Milton. ABDIEL was,

> The flaming Seraph, fearless, though alone,
> Encompassed round with foes.
> *Paradise Lost*, V, 875.

**Serapis** (se'rəpis). The Ptolemaic form of APIS, an Egyptian deity who, when dead, was honoured under the attributes of OSIRIS and thus became 'osirified Apis' or [O] Sorapis. He was lord of the underworld, and was identified by the Greeks with HADES.

**Serat, Al.** *See* AL-SIRAT.

**Serbonian Bog, The** (sœbō'niən). A great morass, now covered with shifting sand, between the isthmus of Suez, the Mediterranean, and the delta of the Nile. In Strabo's time it was a lake stated by him to be 200 stadia long and 50 broad, and by Pliny to be 150 miles in length. TYPHON was said to dwell at the bottom of it, hence its other name, *Typhon's Breathing Hole*.

> A gulf profound as that Serbonian bog,
> Betwixt Damiata and Mount Cassius old,
> Where armies whole have sunk.
> MILTON: *Paradise Lost*, II, 592.

The term is used figuratively of a mess from which there is no way of extricating oneself.

**Serpent.** The serpent is symbolical of:

(1) Deity, because, says Plutarch, 'it feeds upon its own body; even so all things spring from God, and will be resolved into deity again' (*De Iside et Osiride*, i, 2, p. 5; and *Philo Byblius*).

(2) Eternity, as a corollary of the former. It is represented as forming a circle, holding its tail in its mouth.

(3) Renovation and the healing art. It is said that when old it has the power of growing young again 'like the eagle', by casting its slough, which is done by squeezing itself between two rocks. It was sacred to AESCULAPIUS, and was supposed to have the power of discovering healing herbs. *See* CADUCEUS.

(4) Guardian spirit. It was thus employed by the ancient Greeks and Romans, and not infrequently the figure of a serpent was depicted on their altars.

In the temple of Athena at Athens, a serpent, supposed to be animated by the soul of Erichthonius, was kept in a cage, and called 'the Guardian Spirit of the Temple'.

(5) Wisdom. 'Be ye therefore wise as serpents, and harmless as doves' (*Matt.* x, 16).

(6) Subtlety. 'Now the serpent was more subtil than any beast of the field' (*Gen.* iii, i).

(7) The DEVIL. As the Tempter (*Gen.* iii, 1–6). In early pictures the serpent is sometimes placed under the feet of the Virgin, in allusion to the promise made to Eve after the fall (*Gen.* iii, 15).

In Christian art it is an attribute of St. CECILIA, St. Euphemia, St. PATRICK, and many other SAINTS, either because they trampled on SATAN, or because they miraculously cleared some country of snakes.

Fable has it that the cerastes (horned viper) hides in sand that it may bite the horse's foot and get the rider thrown. In allusion to this belief, Jacob says, 'Dan shall be...an adder in the path, that biteth the horse heels, so that his rider shall fall backward' (*Gen.* xlix, 17). The Bible also tells us that the serpent stops up its ears that it may not be charmed by the charmers, 'charming never so wisely' (*Ps.* lxiii, 4).

Another old idea about snakes was that when attacked they would swallow their young and not eject them until reaching a place of safety.

It was in the form of a serpent, says the legend, that Jupiter AMMON appeared to OLYMPIA and became by her the father of Alexander the Great. *See also* SNAKE.

The Egyptian *uraeus*, the cobra, represented supreme divine and royal power and wisdom, while the coluber depicted SET in his typhonic aspect as the serpent of the mist, the demon of darkness, also the malefic aspect of the midday sun.

Sumero-Semitic myth depicts TAIMAT, 'the footless', as the serpent of darkness who can also be portrayed as a dragon. ISHTAR, as a Great Goddess, has a serpent as an attribute, as had Sabazius, it being his chief emblem. Priestesses of his cult dropped golden snakes through their robes as 'the god through the bosom'. The corn goddess Nidaba had snakes rising from her shoulders. The serpent set up on a pole was worshipped in Canaan and Philistia. The Great Goddess is frequently depicted with serpents, particularly in Crete where she holds a serpent in each hand as protectors of the household and as a phallic symbol, the snake being 'the husband of all women'. It could also restore life to the dead or incarnate the soul of the deceased or of an ancestor. Pet snakes were kept in Greece, Rome and Crete as guardians and as connected with fertility and healing.

The serpent is of great importance in Hindu mythology; it represents creative power and is a manifestation of the Vedic Agni as fire. The cobra is the mount of VISHNU as the cosmic ocean and he sleeps on the coiled serpent of the waters, but the serpent has also an evil aspect which is portrayed as Kaliya, vanquished by KRISHNA who dances on its head. Ahi, 'the throttler' is a three-headed snake killed by INDRA. *See* NAGA.

The serpent can be associated with the Buddha as he once changed himself into a naga to heal the people. At the centre of the Round of Existence the snake represents anger.

Celtic tradition connects the serpent with the healing waters and with the Great Mother Bridget, while the horned serpent is associated with the horned god Cernunnos as fertility.

In Scandinavian myth the Nidhogg, the Dread Biter, is evil as living at the root of the YGGDRASIL and trying to destroy it. The Midgard serpent encircles the world as the all-embracing ocean.

In China the serpent and dragon are largely indistinguishable and have the same symbolism as rain-bringers and creators and the fertilizing power of the waters. The snake is the sixth of the creatures of the Twelve Terrestrial Branches.

As dwelling underground the snake is traditionally at enmity with the solar birds such as the EAGLE and CRANE. This obtains with the Hindu GARUDA BIRD and the NAGAS and is also found on the other side of the world in the Amerindian tradition where it is the enemy of the THUNDER BIRD, but snakes can act as messengers between the people and the underworld. The Great Manitou takes the form of a serpent with horns when it transfixes the TOAD or the Dark Manitou. In Aztec legend the plumed serpent is an attribute of Quetzalcoatl. The snake woman Coatlicue wears a skirt of woven snakes. As with the nagas, the snake can be a culture hero and mytical ancestor.

The serpent as the thirst-quenching rainbow occurs in Indian, Amerindian, Australian and African legend; it is also a sky-hero and creator. In African tribes the snake can be a royal emblem, an incarnation of the dead, or a mythical ancestor. Cambodia was founded on the marriage of a prince to a serpent.

**The old Serpent.** SATAN.

> And he laid hold on the dragon, that old serpent, which is the Devil, and Satan, and bound him a thousand years.
> *Rev.* xx, 2.

**Sea serpent.** *See under* SEA.

**Their ears have been serpent-licked.** They have the gift of foreseeing events, the power of seeing into futurity. This is a Greek superstition. It is said that CASSANDRA and Helenus were gifted with the power of prophecy, because serpents licked their ears while sleeping in the temple of APOLLO.

**To cherish a serpent in your bosom.** To show kindness to one who proves ungrateful. The Greeks say that a husbandman found a frozen serpent, which he put into his bosom. The snake was revived by the warmth, and stung its benefactor. Shakespeare applies the tale to a serpent's egg:

> Therefore think him as a serpent's egg
> Which, hatched, would (as his kind) grow dangerous.
> *Julius Caesar,* II, i.

**Sesame** (ses'əmi). **Open, Sesame!** The password at which the door of the robbers' cave flew open in the tale of *The Forty Thieves* (ARABIAN NIGHTS); hence, a key to a mystery, or anything that acts like magic in obtaining favour, admission, recognition etc.

## Seven

Sesame is an East Indian annual herb, with an oily seed which is used as food, a laxative etc. In Egypt they eat sesame cakes, and the Jews frequently add the seed to their bread.

**Set**, or **Seth.** The Egyptian original of the Greek TYPHON. He was the jealous brother of OSIRIS whom he murdered by tricking him into a coffer, nailing the lid, and having it sealed with molten lead. He was later castrated by HORUS and came to be regarded as the incarnation of evil. He is represented as having the body of a man with a thin curved snout and square-shaped ears, and sometimes with a tail and the body of an animal which has not been identified with any certainty.

**Setebos** (set'ebos). A god or DEVIL worshipped by the Patagonians, and introduced by Shakespeare into his *Tempest* as the god of Sycorax, Caliban's mother.

> His art is of such power,
> It would control my dam's god, Setebos,
> And make a vassal of him.
> *The Tempest*, I, ii.

The cult of Setebos was first known in Europe through Magellan's voyage round the world, 1519–1521.

**Seven.** A mystic or sacred number; it is composed of four and three, which among the Pythagoreans were, and from time immemorial have been, accounted lucky numbers. Among the Babylonians, Egyptians and other ancient peoples there were seven sacred planets; and the Hebrew verb to swear means literally 'to come under the influence of seven things'; thus seven ewe lambs figure in the oath between Abraham and Abimelech at Beersheba (*Gen.* xxi, 28), and Herodotus (III, viii) describes an Arabian oath in which seven stones are smeared with blood.

There are seven days in creation, seven days in the week, seven virtues, seven divisions in the Lord's Prayer, seven ages in the life of man, climacteric years are seven and nine with their multiples by odd numbers, and the seventh son of a seventh son was always held notable.

Among the Hebrews every seventh year was Sabbatical, and seven times seven years was the Jubilee. The three great Jewish feasts lasted seven days, and between the first and second were seven weeks.

Levitical purifications lasted seven days. The number is associated with a variety of occurrences in the Old Testament.

In the *Apocalypse* we have seven churches of Asia, seven candlesticks, seven stars, seven trumpets, seven spirits before the throne of God, seven horns, seven vials, seven plagues, a seven-headed monster, and the Lamb with seven eyes.

The old astrologers and alchemists recognized seven planets, each having its own 'heaven':

> The bodies seven, eek, lo hem heer anoon;
> Sol gold is, and Luna silver we threpe,
> Mars yren, Mercurie quyksilver we clepe;
> Saturnus leed, and Jubitur is tyn;
> And Venus coper, by my fader kyn.
> CHAUCER: *The Canon's Yeoman's Tale*, 472.

**The Seven against Thebes.** The seven Argive heroes (ADRASTUS, Polynices, Tydeus, Amphiaraus, Capaneus, Hippomedon and Parthenopaeus), who, according to Greek legend, made war on Thebes with the object of restoring Polynices (son of OEDIPUS), who had been expelled by his brother Eteocles. All perished except Adrastus, and the brothers slew each other in single combat. The legend is the subject of one of the tragedies of AESCHYLUS. *See* NEMEAN GAMES.

**The Seven Champions.** The mediaeval designation of the national patron saints of England, Scotland, Wales, Ireland, France, Spain and Italy. In 1596 Richard Johnson published a chap-book *The Famous History of the Seven Champions of Christendom.* In this he relates that St. GEORGE of England was seven years imprisoned by the Almidor, the black king of Morocco; St. DENYS of France lived seven years in the form of a hart; St. JAMES of Spain was seven years dumb out of love for a fair Jewess; St. Anthony of Italy, with the other champions, was enchanted into a deep sleep in the Black Castle, and was released by St. George's three sons, who quenched the seven lamps by water from the enchanted fountain; St. Andrew of Scotland delivered six ladies who had lived seven years under the form of white swans; St. PATRICK of Ireland was immured in a cell where he scratched his grave with his own nails; and St. DAVID of Wales slept seven years in the enchanted garden of Ormandine, and was redeemed by St. George.

**The Island of the Seven Cities.** A land of Spanish fable, where seven BISHOPS, who quitted Spain during the dominion of the Moors, founded seven cities. The legend says that many have visited the island, but no one has ever quitted it.

**The Seven Gods of Luck.** In Japanese folklore, Benten, goddess of love; Bishamon, god of war; Daikoku, of wealth; Ebisu, of self-effacement; Fukurokuji and Jojorin, gods of longevity; and Hotei, of joviality.

**The Seven Heavens.** *See under* HEAVEN.

**The Seven Senses.** According to ancient teaching the SOUL of man, or his 'inward holy body' is compounded of seven properties which are under the influence of the seven planets. Fire animates, earth gives the sense of feeling, water gives speech, air gives taste, mist gives sight, flowers give hearing, the south wind gives smelling. Hence the seven senses are animation, feeling, speech, taste, sight, hearing and smelling (*see Ecclesiasticus,* xvii, 5).

**The Seven Sleepers.** Seven Christian youths of Ephesus, according to the legend, who fled during the Diocletian persecution (250) to a cave in Mt. Celion. The cave was walled up by their pursuers and they fell asleep. In the reign of Theodosius II, some 200 years later, they awoke and one of them went into the city for provisions. They fell to sleep again, this time until the resurrection. Their names are given as Constantius, Dionysius, Joannes, Maximianus, Malchus, Martinianus and Serapion. The legend was current in the 6th century and is referred to by Gregory of Tours.

**The Seven Wise Masters.** A collection of oriental tales (*see* SANDABAR) supposed to be told to the king by his advisers. The king's son returned to court after being educated in the seven liberal arts by the Seven Wise Masters. By consulting the STARS, he learned that his life was in danger if he spoke before the elapse of seven days. One of the royal consorts then endeavoured to seduce him without success, whereupon she denounced him to the sovereign and the prince was condemned to death. The Wise Masters, by their tales against women, secured a suspension of the sentence for one day. The woman then told a contrary tale to secure the confirmation of Prince Lucien's punishment. The Wise Masters counteracted this with further tales and so on, until the seventh day, when the prince revealed the truth and his accuser was sentenced to death instead. There are numerous variant versions of these stories, which date from 10th century. *Cp.* SCHEHERAZADE.

**The Seven Wonders of the World.** *See under* WONDER.

**Severn.** *See* SABRINA.

**Shades.** The abode of the departed or HADES; also the spirits or ghosts of the departed.

> Peter Bell excited his spleen to such a degree that he evoked the shades of Pope and Dryden.
> MACAULAY: *Moore's Life of Lord Byron.*

Wine vaults with a bar attached are often known as *shades*. The term originated at Brighton, when the Old Bank in 1819 was turned into a smoking room and bar. There was an entrance by the Pavilion Shades, or Arcade, and the name was soon transferred to the bar.

**Shadow. May your shadow never grow less!** May your prosperity always continue and increase. A phrase of Eastern origin. Fable has it that when those studying the black arts had made certain progress, they were chased through a subterranean hall by the DEVIL. If he caught only their shadow, or part of it, they lost all or part of it, but became first-rate magicians. This would make the expression mean, 'May you escape wholly and entirely from the clutches of the devil', but a more simple explanation is, 'May you never waste away, but always remain healthy and robust.' *See* SCHLEMIHL.

**Shake. To shake hands.** A very old method of salutation and farewell; when one was shaking hands one could not get at one's sword to strike a treacherous blow. When Jehu asked Jehonadab if his 'heart was right' with him, he said, 'If it be, give me thine hand', and Jehonadab gave him his hand (II *Kings* x, 15). NESTOR shook hands with ULYSSES on his return to the Grecian camp with the stolen horses of Rhesus; AENEAS, in the temple of DIDO, sees his lost companions enter, who *avidi conjugere dextras ardebant* (*Aeneid*, I, 514); and Horace, strolling along the Via Sacra, shook hands with an acquaintance: *Arreptaque manu, 'Quid agis dulcissime rerum?'*

**Shakuntala.** *See* SAKUNTALA.

**Shalott, The Lady of** (shəlot'). A maiden in the ARTHURIAN ROMANCES (*see under* ARTHUR), who fell in love with Sir LANCELOT OF THE LAKE, and died because her love was not returned. Tennyson has a poem on the subject; and the story of ELAINE is substantially the same.

**Shamanism** (shah'mənizm). A primitive form of religion, in which it is believed that the world is governed by good and EVIL spirits who can be propitiated through the intervention of a *Shaman*, a priest or sorcerer. The word is Slavonic, the cult being practised by the Samoyeds and other Siberian peoples.

**Shamrock.** The symbol of Ireland, because it was selected by St. PATRICK to illustrate to the Irish the doctrine of the Trinity. According to the elder Pliny no serpent will touch this plant.

**Shandean** (shan'diən). Characteristic of Tristram Shandy or the Shandy family in Sterne's novel, *Tristram Shandy* (9 vols., 1759–1767). Tristram's father, Walter Shandy, is a metaphysical Don QUIXOTE in his way, full of superstitious and idle conceits. He believes in long noses and propitious names, but his son's nose is crushed, and his name becomes Tristram instead of Trismegistus. Tristram's Uncle Toby was wounded at the siege of Namur, and is benevolent and generous, simple as a child, brave as a lion, and gallant as a courtier. His modesty with Widow Wadman and his military tastes are admirable. He is said to be drawn from Sterne's father. The mother was the *beau idéal* of nonentity; and of Tristram himself we hear almost more before he was born than after he had burst upon an astonished world.

**Shanties, Chanties.** Songs of the days of sail sung by a 'shanty man' to help rhythmical action among sailors hauling on ropes, working the capstan etc. The workers joined in the choruses. The word is probably from Fr. *chanter*, to sing. The chorus of one of the most popular runs thus:

Then away, love, away,
Away down Rio.

O fare ye well my pretty young gel,
For we're bound for the Rio Grande.

**Shark.** In Polynesian mythology the shark can embody sacred beings who can appear in either human or shark form, or it can be the incarnation of important people such as chiefs; it can also be a sorcerer's familiar. In some cases the shark is addressed as 'Grandfather'. Hawaii has shark gods and ancestral spirits manifest in shark form.

Some parts of West Africa also hold the shark as sacred and if one is accidentally killed rites of propitiation must be performed. Bones of the shark cast into the sea can become a shark serving the Ocean Spirit.

In ancient Greece shark flesh was a forbidden food at the womens' festival of the Haloa.

**Shedeem.** *See* MAZIKEEN.

**Sheep. Vegetable sheep.** *See* THE VEGETABLE LAMB *under* LAMB.

**Sheer,** or **Shere Thursday.** Maundy Thursday. It is generally supposed to be from M.E. *schere*, clean, *i.e.* free from guilt, from the custom of receiving absolution, or of cleansing the altars on this day. The *Liber Festivalis*, however, says:

Hit is also in English tong 'Schere Thursday', for in owr elde fadur days men wold on y$^t$ day makon scheron hem honest, and dode here hedes ond clypon here berdes and poll here hedes, ond so makon hem honest agen Estur day.

**Sheol** (shē'ōl). *See* HADES.

**Sheppard, Jack** (1702–1724). A notorious thief, son of a carpenter in Smithfield and brought up in Bishopsgate workhouse. He was famous for his prison escapes, especially when he broke out of 'the Castle' of Newgate via the chimney. He was soon afterwards taken and hanged at Tyburn.

'I say, master, did you ever hear tell of Mr Wood's famous 'prentice?'
'What apprentice?' asked the stranger, in surprise.
'Why, Jack Sheppard, the notorious house breaker–him as has robbed half Lunnon to be sure.
W. H. AINSWORTH: *Jack Sheppard*, III, i.

**Shere Thursday.** *See* SHEER.

**Sherlock Holmes.** The most famous figure in detective fiction, the creation of Arthur Conan Doyle (1859–1930). His solutions of crime and mysteries were related in a series of 60 stories that appeared in the *Strand*

*Magazine* between 1891 and 1927. The character was based on Dr. Joseph Bell of the Edinburgh Infirmary, whose methods of deduction suggested a system that Holmes developed into a science—the observation of the minutest details and apparently insignificant circumstances scientifically interpreted. Dr. Watson, Holmes's friend and assistant, was a skit on Doyle himself and Baker Street acquired lasting fame through his writings.

Let me have a report by wire at Baker Street before evening.

And now, Watson, it only remains for us to find out by wire the identity of the cabman.

SIR A. CONAN DOYLE: *The Hound of the Baskervilles*, ch. iv.

**A Sherlock** or **a regular Sherlock.** One who shows an unusual ability in observation and deduction and in solving apparent mysteries; sometimes used derisively. *Sherlock* is also used of a private detective.

**Shield.** The most famous shields in story are the Shield of ACHILLES described by HOMER, of HERCULES described by Hesiod, of AENEAS described by Virgil, and the AEGIS.

Others are that of:

AGAMEMNON, a GORGON.

Amycos (son of POSEIDON), a crayfish, symbol of prudence.

CADMUS and his descendants, a DRAGON, to indicate their descent from the dragon's teeth.

*Eteocles*, a man scaling a wall.

HECTOR, a LION.

IDOMENEUS, a COCK.

*Menelaus*, a SERPENT at his heart; alluding to the elopement of his wife with PARIS.

*Parthenopaeus*, one of the SEVEN AGAINST THEBES, a SPHINX holding a man in its claws.

ULYSSES, a DOLPHIN. Whence he is sometimes called Delphinosemos.

Servius says that in the siege of TROY the Greeks had, as a rule, NEPTUNE on their bucklers, and the Trojans MINERVA.

It was a common custom, after a great victory, for the victorious general to hang his shield on the wall of some temple.

**The clang of shields.** When a Celtic chief doomed a man to death, he struck his shield with the blunt end of his spear by way of notice to the royal BARD to begin his death-song.

Cairbar rises in his arms,

The clang of shields is heard.

OSSIAN: *Temora*, I.

**The Gold and Silver Shield.** A mediaeval allegory tells how two knights coming from opposite directions stopped in sight of a shield suspended from a tree branch, one side of which was gold and the other silver, and disputed about its metal, proceeding from words to blows. Luckily a third knight came up: the point was referred to him, and the disputants were informed that the shield was silver on one side and gold on the other. Hence the sayings, *The other side of the shield, It depends on which side of the shield you are looking at,* etc.

**The Shield of Expectation.** The perfectly plain shield given to a young warrior on his maiden campaign. As he achieved glory, his deeds were recorded or symbolized on it.

**Shipton, Mother.** A prophetess and WITCH of legendary fame first recorded in a pamphlet of 1641, who is said to have foretold the death of Wolsey, Lord Percy and others, and to have predicted the steam-engine and telegraph etc. In 1677 Richard Head brought out a *Life and Death of Mother Shipton.* She was born in a cave at Knaresborough, Yorkshire, in 1488, baptized as Ursula Southiel and married Tony Shipton when she was 24. There is a fake 'Mother Shipton's tomb' at Williton, Somerset.

**Shirt. The shirt of Nessus.** *See* NESSUS.

**Shoe.** It was once thought unlucky to put on the left shoe before the right, or to put either shoe on the wrong foot.

It has long been a custom to throw an old shoe at the bride and bridegroom when they depart from the wedding breakfast or when they go to church to get married. Now it is more usual to tie an old shoe to their car. To throw a shoe after someone is an ancient way of bringing good luck. The custom has been variously interpreted.

In Anglo-Saxon marriages, the father delivered the bride's shoe to the bridegroom who touched her on the head with it to show his authority.

Loosing the shoe (*cp. Josh.* v, 15) is a mark of respect in the East. The Muslim leaves his slippers outside the mosque. In *Deut.* xxv, 5–10, we read that the widow refused by her husband's surviving brother, asserted her independence by 'loosing his shoe'; and in the story of *Ruth* (iv, 7) we are told that it was the custom in exchange to deliver a shoe in token of confirmation. 'A man without sandals' was a proverbial expression among the Jews for a prodigal, from the custom of giving one's sandals in confirmation of a bargain.

Scot (*Discoverie of Witchcraft*, 1584) tells us that 'many will go to bed again if they sneeze before their shoes be on their feet'.

**Another man's shoes.** 'To stand in another man's shoes' is to occupy the place of another. Among the ancient Northmen, when a man adopted a son, the person adopted put on the shoes of the adopter.

In REYNARD THE FOX, Reynard, having turned the tables on Sir Bruin the Bear, asked the queen to let him have the shoes of the disgraced minister; so Bruin's shoes were torn off and put upon the new favourite.

**Shooting stars.** Incandescent meteors shooting across the sky, formerly, like comets, fabled to presage disaster:

A little ere the mightiest Julius fell,
The graves stood tenantless, and the sheeted dead
Did squeak and gibber in the Roman streets;
As stars with trains of fire and dews of blood,
Disasters with the sun.
SHAKESPEARE: *Hamlet*, I, i.

They were called in ancient legends the 'fiery tears of St. Lawrence', because one of the periodic swarms of these meteors is between 9 and 14 August, about the time of St. Lawrence's festival, which is on the 10th. Other periods are from 12 to 14 November, and from 6 to 12 December.

Shooting stars are said by the Arabs to be firebrands hurled by the ANGELS against the inquisitive genii, who are forever clambering up on the constellations to peep into HEAVEN.

**Shoreditch.** The legend that this London district takes its name from Edward IV's mistress, Jane Shore, derives from a ballad in the Pepys' collection, a version of which is given in Percy's *Reliques*:

Thus, weary of my life, at lengthe
I yielded up my vital strength
Within a ditch of loathsome scent,
Where carrion dogs did much frequent:
The which now since my dying daye,
Is Shoreditch called, as writers saye.

It is also suggested that the name comes from *Soerdich*, or *Shordich*, the family who once held the manor, and Bishop Percy says it is 'from its being a common sewer (vulgarly "shore") or drain'; but it is most probably 'the ditch leading to the shore' (of the Thames). According to the old ballad it was in Shoreditch that George Barnwell was led astray:

Good Barnwell, then quoth she,
Do thou to Shoreditch come,
And ask for Mrs. Millwood's house,
Next door unto the Gun.

**Shorne,** or **Schorne, John.** Rector of North Marston, Buckinghamshire (*c.* 1290–1314), in the church of which was once a shrine in his honour. He was renowned for his piety and miraculous powers. He blessed a local well giving it legendary healing properties and also 'conjured the DEVIL into a boot'. His shrine became so frequented by pilgrims that, in 1481, the Dean and Chapter of Windsor, owners of the advowson, with papal permission, removed his shrine and relics to Windsor.

**Shot. Parthian shot.** *See* PARTHIAN.

**Shotten Herring.** A lean, spiritless creature, a Jack-o-Lent, like a herring that has *shot*, or ejected, its spawn. Herrings gutted and dried are likewise so called.

Though they like shotten-herrings are to see,
Yet such tall souldiers of their teeth they be,
That two of them, like greedy cormorants,
Devour more than sixe honest Protestants.
TAYLOR: *Workes*, iii, 5 (1630).

**Shrovetide.** The three days just before the opening of Lent, when people went to confession and afterwards indulged in all sorts of sports and merry-making.

**Shrove Tuesday.** The day before Ash Wednesday; 'Pancake Day'. It used to be the great 'Derby Day' of cock-fighting in England.

Or martyr beat, like Shrovetide cocks, with bats.
PETER PINDAR: *Subjects for Painters: Scene, The Royal Academy*, III.

**Sibyl** (sib'il). A prophetess of classical legend, who was supposed to prophesy under the inspiration of a deity; the name is now applied to any prophetess or woman fortune-teller. There were a number of sibyls, and they had their seats in widely separate parts of the world—Greece, Italy, Babylonia, Egypt etc.

Plato mentions only one, *viz.* the *Erythraean*—identified with AMALTHEA, the *Cumaean* sibyl, who was consulted by AENEAS and accompanied him into HADES and who sold the SIBYLLINE BOOKS to TARQUIN; Martin Capella speaks of two, the *Erythraean* and the *Phrygian*; Aelian of four, the *Erythraean, Samian, Egyptian* and *Sardian*; Varro tells us that there were ten, *viz.* the *Cumaean*, the *Delphic, Egyptian, Erythraean, Hellespontine, Libyan, Persian, Phrygian, Samian* and *Tiburtine*.

How know we but that she may be an eleventh Sibyl or a second Cassandra?
RABELAIS: *Gargantua and Pantagruel*, III, xvi.

The mediaeval monks 'adopted' the sibyls—as they did so much of pagan myth; they made them 12, and gave to each a separate prophecy and distinct emblem:

(1) The *Libyan*: 'The day shall come when men shall see the King of all living things.' *Emblem*, a lighted taper.

(2) The *Samian*: 'The Rich One shall be born of a pure virgin.' *Emblem*, a rose.

(3) The *Cuman*: 'Jesus Christ shall come from heaven, and live and reign in poverty on earth.' *Emblem*, a CROWN.

(4) The *Cumaean*: 'God shall be born of a pure virgin, and hold converse with sinners.' *Emblem*, a cradle.

(5) The *Erythraean*: 'Jesus Christ, Son of God, the Saviour.' *Emblem*, a horn.

(6) The *Persian*: 'Satan shall be overcome by a true prophet.' *Emblem*, a DRAGON under the sibyl's feet, and a lantern.

(7) The *Tiburtine*: 'The Highest shall descend from HEAVEN and a virgin be shown in the valleys of the deserts.' *Emblem*, a dove.

(8) The *Delphic*: 'The Prophet born of the virgin shall be crowned with thorns.' *Emblem*, a crown of thorns.

(9) The *Phrygian*: 'Our Lord shall rise again.' *Emblem*, a banner and a cross.

(10) The *European*: 'A virgin and her Son shall flee into Egypt.' *Emblem*, a sword.

(11) The *Agrippine*: 'Jesus Christ shall be outraged and scourged.' *Emblem*, a whip.

(12) The *Hellespontic*: 'Jesus Christ shall suffer shame upon the cross.' *Emblem*, a T cross.

**Sibylline Books, The.** A collection of oracular utterances preserved in ancient Rome and consulted by the Senate in times of emergency or disaster. According to Livy, there were orginally NINE books offered to TARQUIN by the SIBYL of Cumae but the offer was rejected, and she burnt

three of them. She offered the remaining six at the same price. Again, being refused, she burnt three more. The remaining three were then bought by the King for the original sum.

The three books were preserved in a vault of the temple of JUPITER Capitolinus, and committed to the charge of custodians, ultimately 15 in number. These books were destroyed by fire in 83 B.C. A new collection of verses was made from those preserved in the cities of Greece, Italy and Asia Minor, and deposited in the rebuilt temple. These were transferred to the temple of APOLLO by Augustus in 12 B.C. and were said to have been destroyed by Stilicho (*c.* 405).

**Sibylline Oracles.** A collection of 15 books, 12 of which are extant, of 2nd- and 3rd-century authorship, and written by Jews and Christians in imitation of the SIBYLLINE BOOKS. Their aim was to gain converts to their respective faiths.

**Siege Perilous.** In the cycle of ARTHURIAN ROMANCES a seat at the ROUND TABLE which was kept vacant for him who should accomplish the quest of the Holy GRAIL. For any less a person to sit in it was fatal. At the crown of his achievement Sir GALAHAD took his seat in the Siege Perilous.

**Siegfried** (sēg'frēd), or **Sigurd.** Hero of the first part of the NIBELUNGENLIED. He was the youngest son of Siegmund and Sieglind, King and Queen of the Netherlands.

**Sieve and Shears.** An ancient form of DIVINATION mentioned by Theocritus. The points of the shears were stuck in the wooden rim of the sieve and two persons supported it upright with the tips of their two fingers. Then a verse of the Bible was read aloud, and St. Peter and St. Paul were asked if the guilty person was A, B or C (naming those suspected). When the guilty person was named the sieve would suddenly turn round. This method was also used to tell if a couple would marry, etc.

Searching for things lost with a sieve and shears.
BEN JONSON: *Alchemist*, I, i.

**Sigurd** (sig'uəd). The SIEGFRIED of the Volsunga SAGA, the Scandinavian version of the NIBELUNGENLIED. He falls in love with BRUNHILD but under the influence of a love-potion marries GUDRUN, a union with fateful consequences.

**Silence. Towers of Silence.** The small towers on which the Parsees and Zoroastrians place their dead to be consumed by birds of prey. The bones are picked clean in the course of a day, and are then thrown into a receptacle covered with charcoal.

Parsees do not burn or bury their dead, because they consider a corpse impure, and they will not defile any of the elements. They carry it on a bier to the tower. At the entrance they look their last on the body, and the corpse-bearers carry it within the precincts and lay it down to be devoured by vultures which are constantly on the watch.

**Silenus** (sīlē′nəs). The drunken attendant and nurse of BACCHUS, represented as a fat, jovial old man, always full of liquor, riding an ass.

> Within his car, aloft, young Bacchus stood,
> Trifling his ivy-dart, in dancing mood,
> With sidelong laughing; ...
> And near him rode Silenus on his ass,
> Pelted with flowers as he on did pass
> Tipsily quaffing.
> KEATS: *Endymion*, IV, 209.

**Silver. The Silver Age.** According to Hesiod and the Greek and Roman poets, the second of the AGES of the World; fabled as a period that was voluptuous and godless, and much inferior in simplicity and true happinesss to the Golden Age.

**With silver weapons you may conquer the world.** The Delphic ORACLE to Philip of Macedon, when he went to consult it. Philip, acting on this advice, sat down before a fortress which his staff pronounced to be impregnable. 'You shall see,' said the king, 'how an ass laden with silver will find an entrance.'

**Simon. Simon Magus.** Isidore tells us that Simon Magus died in the reign of Nero, and adds that he had proposed a dispute with Peter and Paul, and had promised to fly up to HEAVEN. He succeeded in rising high into the air, but at the prayers of the two apostles he was cast down to earth by the evil spirits who had enabled him to rise.

Milman, in his *History of Christianity* (ii) tells another story. He says that Simon offered to be buried alive, and declared that he would reappear on the third day. He was actually buried in a deep trench, 'but to this day,' says Hippolytus, 'his disciples have failed to witness his resurrection'.

His followers were known as *Simonians*, and the sin of which he was guilty, *viz.* the trafficking in sacred things, the buying and selling of ecclesiastical offices (*see Acts* viii, 18) is still called *simony*.

**Simon Pure.** The real man, the authentic article etc. In Mrs. Centlivre's *Bold Stroke for a Wife*, a Colonel Feignwell passes himself off for Simon Pure, a Quaker, and wins the heart of Miss Lovely. No sooner does he get the assent of her guardian than the Quaker turns up, and proves beyond a doubt he is the 'real Simon Pure'. In modern usage, a hypocrite, making a great parade of virtue.

**Simple Simon.** A simpleton, a gullible booby; from the character in the well-known anonymous nursery tale, who 'met a pie-man'.

**Simurgh** (simuəg′), **Samurv**, or **Sinamru**. A fabulous creature having affinities with the Arabian ROC and the Indian GARUDA, the Simurgh is half-bird, half-mammal, symbolizing the union of heaven and earth; it suckles its young 'like a bat'. It appears in Persian, Russian and Caucasian tradition and is the bird of the Persian Tree of Life and lives in the land of the sacred Haoma plant whose seeds cure all evil. The Simurgh is prophetic and has magic qualities. One fable said that it lived 1700 years then immolated itself like the PHOENIX.

**Sinbad the Sailor.** The hero of the story of this name in THE ARABIAN NIGHTS ENTERTAINMENTS. He was a wealthy citizen of Baghdad, called 'The Sailor' because of his seven voyages in which, among many adventures, he discovered the ROC's egg and the Valley of Diamonds, and killed the OLD MAN OF THE SEA.

**Sinis** (sī′nis). A Corinthian robber of Greek legend, known as the *Pinebender*, because he used to fasten his victims to two pine-trees bent towards the earth, and then leave them to be rent asunder when the trees were released. He was captured by THESEUS and put to death in the same way.

**Sinister** (Lat. on the left hand). Foreboding of ill; ill-omened. According to AUGURY, birds etc. appearing on the left-hand side forbode ill luck; but on the right-hand side, good luck. Plutarch, following Plato and

Aristotle, gives as the reason that the west (or left side of the augur) was towards the setting or departing sun.

In heraldry it denotes the left side of the shield viewed from the position of its bearer, *i.e.* in illustrations it is the right-hand side.

**Cornix sinistra** (Lat. a crow on the left hand) is a sign of ill luck which belongs to English superstitions as much as to the ancient Roman or Etruscan (Virgil, *Eclogues*, ix, 15).

> That raven on yon left-hand oak
> (Curse on his ill-betiding croak)
> Bodes me no good.
> GAY: *Fable* xxxvii, 27.

**Sinon** (sī'non). The Greek who induced the Trojans to receive the WOODEN HORSE (Virgil, *Aeneid*, II, 102 etc.). Anyone deceiving to betray is called 'a Sinon'.

**Sirat, Al.** *See* AL-SIRAT.

**Siren** (sī'rən). One of the mythical monsters, half woman and half bird, said by Greek poets (*see Odyssey*, XII) to entice seamen by the sweetness of their song to such a degree that the listeners forgot everything and died of hunger (Gr. *sirenes*, entanglers); hence applied to any dangerous, alluring woman.

In Homeric mythology there were but two sirens; later writers name three, viz. PARTHENOPE, Ligea and Leucosia; and the number was still further augmented by others.

ULYSSES escaped their blandishments by filling his companions' ears with wax and lashing himself to the mast of his ship.

> What Song the Syrens sang, or what name Achilles assumed when he hid himself among women, though puzzling questions, are not beyond all conjecture.
> SIR THOS. BROWNE: *Urn Burial*, v.

Plato says there were three kinds of sirens—the *celestial*, the *generative* and the *cathartic*. The first were under the government of JUPITER, the second under that of NEPTUNE, and the third of PLUTO. When the SOUL is in HEAVEN the sirens seek, by harmonic motion, to unite it to the divine life of the celestial host; and when in HADES, to conform it to the infernal regimen; but on earth they produce generation, of which the sea is emblematic (Proclus: *On the Theology of Plato*, Bk. VI).

**Sisyphus** (sis'ifəs) ('The Crafty'). In Greek legend, the son of AEOLUS and husband of MEROPE; in post-Homeric legend, the father of Odysseus (ULYSSES). His punishment in the world of the SHADES was to roll a huge stone up a hill to the top. As it constantly rolled down again just as it reached the summit, his task was everlasting; hence 'a labour of Sisyphus' or 'Sisyphean toil' is an endless, heart-breaking job. The reasons given for this punishment vary. *See* AUTO-LYCUS.

**Sitting Bull** (*c.* 1834–1890). A famous Sioux chief who resisted the governmental policy of reservations for his tribe. He defeated Custer in 1876 and later appeared in Buffalo Bill's show. He was killed while resisting arrest during the Sioux rebellion of 1890.

**Siva or Shiva** (sē'və, shē'və) ('The Blessed One'). Originally the Vedic Rudra, Siva became the third of the Hindu Trimurti. He is the destroyer, but destruction is preliminary to fresh creation. He appears in many shapes and characters. As the male principle Siva is the *shakta* with the phallus as his symbol and his wife Pravati is the shakti with the yoni as her symbol. Siva is also depicted as half-man half-woman. The Dance of Siva is the representation of the five acts of creation, the cosmic dance.

**Sixteen-string Jack.** John Rann, a highwayman (hanged 1774), noted for his foppery. He wore 16 tags, eight at each knee.

**Skanda.** *See* KARTTIKEYA.

**Skeleton. The family skeleton,** or **the skeleton in the cupboard.** Some domestic source of worry or shame which the family conspires to keep to itself; every family is said to have at least one!

The story is that someone without a single care or trouble in the world had to be found. After long and unsuccessful search a lady was discovered who all thought would 'fill the bill'; but to the great surprise of the inquirers, after she had satisfied them on all points and the quest seemed to be achieved, she took them upstairs and there opened a closet which contained a human skeleton. 'I try', said she, 'to keep my trouble to myself, but every night my husband compels me to kiss that skeleton.' She then explained that the skeleton was once her husband's rival, killed in a duel. The expression was given literary use by Thackeray—

> And it is from these that we shall arrive at some particulars regarding the Newcome family, which will show us that they have a skeleton or two in their closets as well as their neighbours.
> *The Newcomes* (1855) ch. lv.

**Skidbladnir** (skid'bladnər). In Scandinavian mythology, the magic ship made by the DWARFS for FREYR. It was big enough to take all the AESIR with their weapons and equipment, yet when not in use could be folded up and carried by Freyr in his pouch. It sailed through both air and water, and went straight to its destination as soon as the sails were hoisted. *Cp.* CARPET.

**Skimmington.** It was an old custom in rural England and Scotland to make an example of nagging wives by forming a ludicrous procession through the village accompanied by rough music to ridicule the offender. A man, mounted on a horse with a distaff in his hand, rode behind the woman with his face to the horse's tail, while the woman beat him about the jowls with a ladle. As the procession passed a house where the woman was paramount the participants gave the threshold a sweep. The event was called *riding the Skimmington*. The origin of the name is uncertain, but in an illustration of 1639 the woman is shown belabouring her husband with a skimming-ladle. Unfaithful husbands were similarly put to scorn. The procession is fully described in Butler's *Hudibras*, II, ii:

> Near whom the Amazon triumphant
> Bestrid her beast, and, on the rump on't,
> Sat face to tail and bum to bum,
> The warrior whilom overcome,
> Arm'd with a spindle and a distaff,
> Which, as he rode, she made him twist off:
> And when he loiter'd, o'er her shoulder
> Chastis'd the reformado soldier.

Scott alludes to it in the *Fortunes of Nigel*, ch. xxi:

> Remember I am none of your husband—and, if I were, you would do well not to forget whose threshold was swept when they last rode the Skimmington upon such another scolding jade as yourself.

For another example see Hardy's *Mayor of Casterbridge*, ch. xxxix, where the *skimmity ride* causes the death of Lucetta Farfrae.

**Sleep. The Sleeper.** EPIMENIDES, the Greek poet, is said to have fallen asleep in a cave when a boy, and not to have waked for 57 years, when he found himself possessed of all wisdom.

In mediaeval legend, stories of those who have gone to sleep and have been—or are to be—awakened after many years are very numerous. Such legends are associated with King ARTHUR, CHARLEMAGNE and BARBAROSSA. *Cp.* also the stories of the SEVEN SLEEPERS of Ephesus, TANNHÄUSER, OGIER THE DANE and RIP VAN WINKLE.

**The Seven Sleepers.** *See under* SEVEN.

**The Sleeper Awakened.** *See* SLY, CHRISTOPHER.

**The Sleeping Beauty.** This charming nursery tale comes from the French *La Belle au Bois Dormant*, by Charles Perrault (1628–1703) (*Contes de ma mère l'Oye*, 1697). The Princess is shut up by enchantment in a castle, where she sleeps a hundred years, during which time an impenetrable wood springs up around. Ultimately she is released by the kiss of a young prince, who marries her.

**Sleepy Hollow.** Any village far removed from the active concerns of the outside world. From Washington Irving's story 'The Legend of Sleepy Hollow' (*Sketch Book*), which deals with a quiet old-world village on the Hudson.

**Slip. Many a slip 'twixt the cup and the lip.** Everything is uncertain till you possess it. *Cp.* ANCAEUS.

**Slope. The slippery slope.** The broad and easy way 'that leadeth to destruction'. *See* AVERNUS.

**Slough of Despond.** A period of, or fit of, great depression. In Bunyan's *Pilgrim's Progress*, Pt. I, it is a deep bog which Christian has to cross in order to get to the Wicket Gate. Help comes to his aid, but Neighbour Pliable turns back.

**Sly, Christopher.** A keeper of bears and a tinker, son of a pedlar, and a sad drunken sot in the *Induction* of *The Taming of the Shrew*. Shakespeare mentions him as a well-known character of Wincot, a hamlet near Stratford-on-Avon, and it is more than probable that in him we have an actual portrait of a contemporary.

Sly is found dead drunk by a lord, who commands his servants to put him to bed, and on his waking to attend upon him like a lord and bamboozle him into the belief that he is a great man; the play is performed for his delectation. The same trick was played by the Caliph Haroun Al-Raschid on ABOU HASSAN, the rich merchant, in *The Sleeper Awakened* (ARABIAN NIGHTS).

**Small. Small-back.** Death. So called because he is usually drawn as a skeleton.
**Small-endians.** *See* BIG-ENDIANS.

**Snail.** As appearing and disappearing, the snail has lunar associations, or it can represent the dawn emerging from the cavern of darkness, or rebirth. It was believed to wear itself away as it moved leaving a trail of slime (*Psalms* lviii, 8), and this track could also be used in divination when recorded on a slate. Hesiod says that the snail indicates the time of harvest when it climbs stalks.

Snails occur in Mayan and Aztec mythology; they are portrayed on stelae and the Mexican moon god Tecciztecatl is enclosed in a snail's shell, while as representing rebirth the snail is depicted on the heads of Aztec gods. The Zuni Indians have a snail clan.
**Snake stones.** Ammonites, from the old belief that these were coiled snakes petrified.

**Snark.** The imaginary animal invented by Lewis Carroll as the subject of his mock-heroic poem *The Hunting of the Snark* (1876). It was most elusive and gave endless trouble, and when eventually the hunters thought they had tracked it down, their quarry proved to be but a Boojum. The name (a 'portmanteau word' of snake and shark) has sometimes been given to the quests of dreamers and visionaries.

It was one of Rossetti's delusions that in *The Hunting of the Snark* Lewis Carroll was caricaturing him.

**Snell, Hannah.** *See* THE FEMALE MARINE *under* MARINE.

**Sneeze.** St. GREGORY has been credited with originating the custom of saying 'God bless you' after sneezing, the story being that he enjoined its use during a pestilence in which sneezing was a mortal symptom. Aristotle, however, mentions a similar custom among the Greeks; and Thucydides tells us that

sneezing was a crisis symptom of the great Athenian plague.

The Romans followed the same custom, their usual exclamation being *Absit omen!* The Parsees hold that sneezing indicates that evil spirits are abroad, and we find similar beliefs in India, Africa, ancient and modern Persia, among the North American Indian tribes etc.

We are told that when the Spaniards arrived in Florida the Cacique sneezed, and all the court lifted up their hands and implored the sun to avert the evil omen. The nursery rhyme says:

If you sneeze on Monday you sneeze for danger;
Sneeze on Tuesday, kiss a stranger,
Sneeze on Wednesday, sneeze for a letter,
Sneeze on Thursday, something better,
Sneeze on Friday, sneeze for sorrow,
Sneeze on Saturday, see your sweetheart tomorrow.

**Snood. The lassie lost her silken snood.** The snood was a ribbon with which a Scots lass braided her hair, and was the emblem of her maiden character. When she married, she changed the snood for the curch or coif; but if she lost the name of virgin before she obtained that of wife, she 'lost her silken snood' and was not privileged to assume the curch.

In more recent times the word has been applied to the net in which women confine their hair.

**Soap. In soaped-pig fashion.** Vague; a method of speaking or writing which always leaves a way of escape. The allusion is to the custom at FAIRS etc., of soaping the tail of a pig before turning it out to be caught by the tail.

He is vague as may be; writing in what is called the 'soaped-pig' fashion.
CARLYLE: *The Diamond Necklace*, ch. iv (*Footnote*).

**Sol** (Lat. *sol*, sun). The Roman SUN god; the sun itself. In Scandinavian mythology Sol was the maiden who drove the chariot of the sun.

The name was given by the alchemists to GOLD and in heraldry it represents *or* (gold).
**Solomon's Carpet.** *See* CARPET.
**Solomon's Ring.** *See under* RING.

**Soma** (sō'mə). An intoxicating drink anciently made, with mystic rites and incantations, from the juice of some Indian plant by the priests, and drunk by the

BRAHMINS as well as offered as libations to their gods. It was fabled to have been brought from HEAVEN by a falcon, or by the daughters of the SUN; and it was itself personified as a god, and represented the MOON. The plant was probably a species of *Asclepias*.

**Song. The Song of Roland.** *See under* ROLAND.

**Sop. To give a sop to Cerberus.** To give a bribe; to quiet a troublesome customer. CERBERUS is PLUTO's three-headed dog, stationed at the gates of the infernal regions. When persons died the Greeks and Romans used to put a cake in their hands as a sop to Cerberus to allow them to pass without molestation.

**Sortes** (saw′tēz) (Lat. *sors, sortis*, chance, lot). A species of DIVINATION performed by selecting passages from a book haphazard. Virgil's *Aeneid* was anciently the favourite work for the purpose. (*Sortes Virgilianae*), but the Bible (*Sortes Biblicae*) has also been in common use.

The method is to open the book at random, and the passage you touch by chance with your finger is the oracular response. Severus consulted Virgil and read these words: 'Forget not thou, O Roman, to rule the people with royal sway.' Gordianus, who reigned only a few days, hit upon this verse: 'Fate only showed him on this earth, and suffered him not to tarry'; and Dr. Wellwood gives an instance respecting Charles I and Lord Falkland. Falkland, to amuse the king, suggested this kind of AUGURY, and the king hit upon IV, 615–20, the gist of which is that 'evil wars would break out, and the king lose his life'. Falkland, to laugh the matter off, said he would show his Majesty how ridiculously the 'lot' would foretell the next fate, and he lighted on XI, 152–81, the lament of Evander for the untimely death of his son Pallas. King Charles soon after mourned over his noble friend who was slain at Newbury (1643).

In Rabelais (III, x), PANURGE consults the *Sortes Virgilianae et Homericae* on the burning question, whether or not he should marry. In Cornelius Agrippa's *De Vanitate Scientiarum*, c. iv, there is a passage violently reprobating the *Sortes*.

**Soul.** The idea of the soul as the immaterial and immortal part of man surviving after death as a ghost or spirit was an ancient and widespread belief. The ancient Egyptians represented it as a bird with a human head. With Aristotle the soul is essentially the vital principle and the Neoplatonists held that it was located in the whole body and in every part. It has also been located in the blood, heart, brain, bowels, liver, kidneys etc.

Muslims say that the souls of the faithful assume the forms of snow-white birds, and nestle under the throne of Allah until the resurrection.

**Sour grapes.** *See* GRAPES.

**Sow. As drunk as David's,** or **Davy's sow.** *See* DAVY'S SOW.
**To send a sow to Minerva.** To 'teach your grandmother to suck eggs' (*see under* EGG), to instruct one more learned in the subject than oneself. From the old Latin proverb, *Sus Minervam docet* (a pig teaching MINERVA); Minerva being the goddess of wisdom.

**Spagyric** (spəji′rik). Pertaining to ALCHEMY; the term seems to have been invented by Paracelsus. Alchemy is 'the spagyric art', and an alchemist a 'spagyrist'.
**Spagyric food.** Cagliostro's name for the ELIXIR of immortal youth.

**Sparrow.** Having marked erotic associations, the sparrow was an attribute of APHRODITE and Lesbia in Greece and was regarded as an aphrodisiac.

There are frequent allusions to the bird in the Old Testament but the name is used vaguely and probably refers to all passerines. In the New Testament the sparrow typifies the humble and worthless—'are not two sparrows sold for a fathing?'. (*Matthew* x, 29) and Christianity continues this significance but also portrays the bird as lewdness and lechery.

**Speaking Heads.** Fables and romance tell of a variety of artificial heads that could speak: among the best known are:

The statue of MEMNON, in Egypt, which uttered musical sounds when the morning sun darted on it.

That of ORPHEUS, at Lesbos, which is said to have predicted the bloody death that terminated the expedition of Cyrus the Great into Scythia.

The head of MINOS, fabled to have been brought by ODIN to Scandinavia, and to have uttered responses.

The BRAZEN HEAD of Roger Bacon, and that of Gerbert, afterwards Pope Sylvester II (10th century).

An earthen head made by Albertus Magnus in the 13th century, which both spoke and moved. Thomas Aquinas broke it, whereupon the mechanist exclaimed: 'There goes the labour of thirty years!'

Alexander's statue of AESCULAPIUS; it was supposed to speak, but Lucian says the sounds were uttered by a concealed man, and conveyed by tubes to the statue.

**Spear.** If a knight kept the point of a spear forward when he entered a strange land, it was a declaration of war; if he carried it on his shoulder with the point behind him, it was a token of friendship. In OSSIAN (*Temora*, I), Cairbar asks if FINGAL comes in peace, to which Morannal replies: 'In peace he comes not, king of Erin, I have seen his forward spear.'

**The spear of Achilles.** *See* ACHILLES' SPEAR.

**Speewah, The.** A mythical cattle station somewhere in Australia where everything is bigger and better than anywhere else in the world. A series of legends comparable only with the adventures of Baron Münchhausen are associated with it.

**Spell** (O.E. *spel*, a saying, fable etc.). Spells as charms and incantations are found the world over in folklore and superstition. They form part of the stock-in-trade of WITCHES, WIZARDS, magicians, sorcerers, GYPSY crones etc., and many FAIRY stories revolve round their use.

The component words of the spells used by mediaeval sorcerers were usually taken from Hebrew, Greek and Latin, but mere gibberish was often employed. *Cp.* ABRACADABRA; ABRAXAS.

**Sphinx** (sfingks). The sphinx of Greek mythology, quite distinct from the Egyptian sphinx, was a monster with the head and breasts of a woman, the body of a dog or LION, the wings of a bird, a SERPENT's tail, and lion's paws. It had a human voice and was said to be the daughter of Orthos and TYPHON (or the CHIMAERA). She inhabited the vicinity of Thebes, setting the inhabitants riddles and devouring those un-

able to find solutions. The Thebans were told by the oracles that she would kill herself if the following riddle was solved:

What goes on four feet, on two feet, and three,
But the more feet it goes on the weaker it be?

It was at length solved by OEDIPUS with the answer that it was a man, who as an infant crawls upon all fours, in manhood goes erect on two feet, and in old age supports his tottering legs with a staff. Thus were the Thebans delivered and this is the riddle of the sphinx.

The Egyptian sphinx was a lion, usually with a Pharaoh's head, symbolizing royal power and came to be associated with 'HORUS in the Horizon' or Harmakhis. The famous Sphinx at Gizeh was hewn out of limestone rock by order of Khephren or Khafre (*c.* 2620 B.C.) and is some 60 ft. high and 180 ft. long.

**Spider.** The spider has a world-wide mythology; as the Great Weaver it is an attribute of all lunar Great Mother goddesses who spin the web of destiny which attaches all people to the weaver, the Cosmic Centre. In Egypt the spider was an emblem of Neith, in Babylon of ISHTAR also of Atargatis and in Greece of ATHENE and the Moirai. The Norse NORNS are also associated with the spinning of fate.

Hindu and Buddhist myth depicts the spider as weaver of the web of illusion, *maya*; it is also a creator as weaving the web of life from its own substance.

Christianity connected the spider with the DEVIL as ensnaring sinners, following the Old Testament symbolism of the web as destruction or as the hypocrite.

The Old Spider holds an important place in Oceanic tradition as the Creator Goddess of the South Pacific. Her son, Young Spider, created fire. The North West monsoon can be represented as a spider, temperamental and unreliable but also beneficial. In Japan Spider Women can ensnare unwary travellers and the Goblin Spider is a shape-shifter who appears in different forms to harm people. The huge spider Tsuchi-Gumo caused trouble in the world until trapped in a cave and smoked to death, since steel could not kill it.

The Australian Aboriginal Great Spider is a sky hero.

Spider is the cosmic creative feminine power in Amerindian myth. She wove the first alphabet after she had woven the dream of the world of phenomena and the web of fate; she was herself created to bring life to the earth, she created plants and animals, giving them all names, and lastly created humans. There is also a trickster spider who is a shape-shifter and who brought culture to the people. Spider can also be a demiurge. Old Spider escaped the FLOOD and was a member of the Animal Council which helped the people Recover the Light. The Trickster spider also appears in Africa among the Ashanti, but is also the Wise One and a divinity, as a trickster he passed with the slave trade over to Jamaica; he is represented as taking on animals, humans and the gods and sometimes being able to outwit even the gods.

There are many old wives' tales about spiders, the most widespread being that they are venomous.

Let thy spiders, that suck up thy venom,
And heavy-gaited toads lie in their way.
SHAKESPEARE: *Richard II*, III, ii.

There may be in the cup
A spider steep'd, and one may drink, depart,
And yet partake no venom.
SHAKESPEARE *The Winter's Tale*, II, i.

During the examination into the murder (1613) of Sir Thomas Overbury, one of the witnesses deposed 'that the countess wished him to get the strongest poison that he could ...'. Accordingly he brought seven great spiders. There are few spiders poisonous to man, but the American Black Widow spider is a notable exception.

Other tales were that fever could be cured by wearing a spider in a nutshell round the neck, and a common cure for jaundice was to swallow a large live house-spider rolled up in butter. In Ireland this was a remedy for ague. A spider on one's clothes was a sign of good luck or that money was coming and the very small spider is called a *money-spider*.

Yet another story was that spiders spin only on dark days.

The subtle spider never spins,
But on dark days, his slimy gins.
S. BUTLER: *On a Nonconformist*, iv, 445.

**Bruce and the spider.** In 1306 Robert Bruce began a resistance to Edward I's domination of Scotland and was crowned King at Scone. The story is that, when in hiding in the island of Rathlin, he noticed a spider try six times to fix its web on a beam in the ceiling. 'Now shall this spider (said Bruce) teach me what I am to do, for I also have failed six times.' The spider made a seventh effort and succeeded. Bruce thereupon left the island (1307), with 300 followers, landed at Carrick, and at midnight surprised the English garrison in Turnberry Castle. His successes steadily grew until, in 1314, he routed the English at the great victory of Bannockburn.

**Frederick the Great and the spider.** While Frederick II was at Sans-Souci, he went into his ante-room to drink a cup of chocolate, but set his cup down to fetch a handkerchief. On his return he found a great spider had fallen from the ceiling into his cup. He called for fresh chocolate and the next moment heard the report of a pistol. The cook had been suborned to poison the chocolate and, supposing he had been found out, shot himself. On the ceiling of the room in Sans-Souci a spider has been painted (according to tradition) in remembrance of this event.

**Mohammed and the spider.** When Mohammed fled from Mecca he hid in a certain cave, with the Koreishites close upon him. Suddenly an acacia in full leaf sprang up at the mouth of the cave, a wood-pigeon had its nest in the branches, and a spider had woven its net between the tree and the cave. When the Koreishites saw this, they felt persuaded that no one could have entered recently, and went on.

**Spirit.** Properly, the breath of life, from Lat. *spiritus* (*spirare*, to breathe, blow):

And the Lord God formed man of the dust of the ground, and breathed into his nostrils the breath of life; and man became a living soul.
*Gen.* ii, 7.

Hence, life or the life principle, the SOUL; a disembodied soul (a ghost or apparition), or an immaterial being that never was supposed to have had a body (sprite), as a GNOME, ELF or FAIRY; also, the temper or disposition of mind as animated by the breath of life, as in *good spirits, high-spirited, a man of spirit.*

The mediaeval physiological notion (adopted from Galen) was that spirit existed in the body in three kinds, *viz.* (1) the *Natural spirit*, the principle of the 'natural functions'—growth, nutrition and generation, said to be a vapour rising from the blood and having its seat in the liver; (2) the *Vital spirit*, which arose in the heart by a mixture of the air breathed in with the natural spirit and supplied the body with heat and life; and (3) the *Animal spirit*, which was responsible for the power of motion and sensation, and for the rational principle generally; this was a modification of the vital spirit, effected in the brain.

The **Elemental spirits** of Paracelsus and the ROSICRUCIANS, *i.e.* those which presided over the four elements, were—the SALAMANDERS (or fire), GNOMES (earth), SYLPHS (air) and UNDINES (water).

*Spirit* also came to mean any volatile agent or essence; and hence, from the alchemists, is still used of solutions in alcohol and of any strong alcoholic liquor. The alchemists named four substances only as 'spirits'—MERCURY, arsenic, sal ammoniac and sulphur.

> The first spirit quyksilver called is:
> The second orpiment; the third y-wis
> Sal armoniac; and the ferth bremstoon.
> CHAUCER: *Canon's Yeoman's Tale*, 102.

**Spiritualism.** The belief that communication between the living and the spirits of the departed can and does take place, usually through the agency of a specially qualified person (a medium) and often by means of rapping, table-turning, or automatic writing; the system, doctrines, practice etc. arising from this belief.

In philosophy, spiritualism—the antithesis of materialism—is the doctrine that the spirit exists as distinct from matter, or as the only reality.

**Spitting for luck.** Spitting was a charm against enchantment among the ancient Greeks and Romans. Pliny says it averted WITCHCRAFT, and availed in giving an enemy a shrewder blow. People sometimes spit for luck on a piece of money given to them or found; boxers spit on their hands, and traders were wont to spit on the first money taken in the day. There are numerous other instances of spitting for luck and it was also common to spit for defiance or as a challenge etc.

**Sprite.** *See* SPIRIT.

**Squirrel.** The squirrel appears in Norse mythology as the Ratatosk, a bringer of rain and snow, but depicted in the YGGDRASIL it typifies spitefulness and mischief-making as it sets the EAGLE and SERPENT at odds with each other. In Celtic lore the squirrel is an emblem of the Irish goddess Medb.

In Central America the squirrel was a sacrificial animal for the Mayan gods. Among Amazonian Indians it is one of the forms that can be taken by Desana, Master of Animals. Southern Amerindian women may not eat squirrels while planting groundnuts as this would cause the crops to dry up. The coming of winter is heralded by catching the first good squirrel.

A general attribute of the squirrel is gathering, planning and hoarding. Christianity uses this as a symbol of greed and avarice.

**Stadium.** This word is from Gr. *stadion*, a length of 600 Greek feet (about 606 English feet), which was the length of the foot-race course at OLYMPIA; hence applied to the race, then the place where it was run. The Olympic stadium had terraced seats along its length and the length of the course was traditionally said to have been fixed by HERCULES.

**Star. His star is in the ascendant.** He is in luck's way; said of a person to whom some good fortune has fallen and who is very prosperous. According to ASTROLOGY, those leading stars which are above the horizon at a person's birth influence his life and fortune; when those stars are in the ASCENDANT, he is strong, healthy and lucky; but when they are in the descendant below the horizon, his stars do not shine on him, he is in the shade and subject to ill fortune. *Cp.* HOUSES, ASTROLOGICAL.

**Stentor** (sten'taw). **The Voice of a Stentor.** A very loud voice. Stentor was a Greek herald in the Trojan war. According to Homer (*Iliad*, V, 783), his voice was as loud as that of 50 men combined; hence *stentorian*, loud-voiced.

**Stir Up Sunday.** The last Sunday after Trinity. So called from the first two words of the collect: 'Stir up, we beseech thee, O Lord, the wills of thy faithful people ...'. It was an old custom to stir the Christmas plum pudding on this day, hence the old schoolboy rhyme, beginning, 'Stir up, we beseech thee, the pudding in the pot.'

**Stockwell Ghost.** A supposed ghost that created a great sensation in Stockwell

(London) in 1772, then a village. The author of the strange noises was Anne Robinson, a servant. *Cp.* COCK LANE GHOST; SAMPFORD GHOST.

**Stone.** Used figuratively when some characteristic - of a stone is implied as, *stone blind, stone cold, stone dead, stone deaf, stone still* etc., as blind, cold, dead, deaf or still as a stone.

> I will not struggle; I will stand stone still.
> SHAKESPEARE: *King John*, IV, i.

In all parts of the world primitive peoples have set up stones, especially those of meteoric origin (fabled to have fallen from HEAVEN), in connection with religious rites. Anaxagoras mentions a stone that fell from JUPITER in Thrace, a description of which is given by Pliny. The Ephesians asserted that their image of DIANA came from Jupiter. The stone at Emessa, in Syria, worshipped as a symbol of the SUN, was a similar meteorite, and there were similar stones at Abydos and Potidaea. At Corinth one was venerated as ZEUS, and Tacitus describes one in Cyprus dedicated to VENUS. The famous BLACK STONE set in the KAABA is also a meteorite.

The great stone circles of Avebury, STONEHENGE and the standing stones of Stenness, are particularly noteworthy examples of the industry and ingenuity of early man, each having their mythological and religious associations. *See also* AETITES; PHILOSOPHER'S STONE; PRECIOUS STONES; TOUCHSTONE; etc.

**Hag-stones.** Flints naturally perforated used in country places as charms against witches, the evil eye etc. They are hung on the key of an outer door, round the neck for luck, on the bed-post to prevent nightmare, on a horse's collar to ward off disease etc.

**The Standing Stones of Stenness,** in Orkney, some 4 miles from Stromness, comprise a Neolithic stone-circle 340 ft. in diameter of which only 13 stones of a probable 60 are still standing, the tallest being 14 ft. high. Scott in a note (*The Pirate*, ch. xxxviii) says 'One of the pillars ... is perforated with a circular hole, through which loving couples are wont to join hands when they take the *Promise of* ODIN.' The *Eyrbyggja Saga* gives an account of the setting apart of the Helga Fels, or Holy Rock, by the pontiff Thorolf for solemn meetings.

**Stone soup,** or **St. Bernard's soup.** The story goes that a beggar asked alms at a lordly mansion, but was told by the servants that they had nothing to give him. 'Sorry for it,' said the man, 'but will you let me boil a little water to make some soup of this stone?' This was so novel a proceeding, that the curiosity of the servants was aroused, and the man was readily furnished with a saucepan, water and a spoon. In he popped the stone, and begged for a little salt and pepper for flavouring. Stirring the water and tasting it, he said it would be the better for any fragments of meat and vegetables they might happen to have. These were supplied, and ultimately he asked for a little ketchup or other sauce. When ready the servants tasted it, and declared that 'stone soup' was excellent.

This story, which was a great favourite in the 16th and 17th centuries, was told with many variations, horseshoes, nails, ram's-horns etc. taking the place of the stone as narrated above.

**To leave no stone unturned.** To spare no trouble, time, expense etc., in endeavouring to accomplish your aim. After the defeat of Mardonius at Plataea (477 B.C.), a report was current that the Persian general had left great treasures in his tent. Polycrates the Theban sought long, but found them not. The ORACLE of Delphi, being consulted, told him 'to leave no stone unturned', and the treasures were discovered.

**Stork.** There was a widespread legend that storks cared for their parents in old age; the belief was corroborated by Aristotle, Pliny and Aelian and appeared in Egypt and in Greece where a law requiring children to care for aged parents took its name from the stork. The bird also represented woman as nourisher, the bringer of life, and was an attribute of HERA/JUNO. Aristotle says that the Thessalonians worshipped the stork which rid them of a plague of snakes.

Storks were believed to be able to appear in human form in other lands on migration, a legend also told of the SWAN.

According to Swedish legend, the stork received its name from flying round the cross of the crucified Redeemer, crying *Styrka! styrka!* (Strengthen, strengthen!).

Lyly in his *Euphues* (1580) says of this bird:

Ladies use their lovers as the stork doth her young ones who pecketh them till they bleed with her bill, and then healeth them with her tongue.

Also:

Constancy is like unto the stork, who wheresoever she fly cometh into no nest but her own.

And:

It fareth with me ... as with the stork, who, when she is least able, carrieth the greatest burden.

It is an old tale to children that babies are brought by storks and they still feature prominently on cards of congratulation to a baby's parents. The origin of this legend is the association between the stork and the creative watery element; the bird fishing in the waters finds embryonic life.

It was also a belief that a stork will kill a snake 'on sight'.

**King Stork.** A tyrant that devours his subjects, and makes them submissive with fear and trembling. The allusion is to the fable of *The Frogs desiring a King. See* A KING LOG *under* LOG.

**Strenia** (strē'niə). A Sabine goddess identified with the Roman Salus, to whom gifts (*strenae*) were taken at the New Year, consisting of figs, dates and honey. The custom is said to have been instituted by the Sabine King Tatius, who entered Rome on New Year's Day and received from some augurs palms cut from the sacred grove dedicated to her. The French *étrenne*, a New Year's gift, is from this goddess.

**Struldbrugs** (strŭld'brŭgz). Wretched inhabitants of Luggnagg (in Swift's *Gulliver's Travels*), who had the privilege of immortality without having eternal vigour, strength and intellect.

**Stygian** (sti'jiən). Infernal, gloomy; pertaining to the river STYX.

At that so sudden blaze the Stygian throng
Bent their aspect.
MILTON: *Paradise Lost*, X, 453.

**Styx** (stiks). The river of Hate (Gr. *stugein*, to hate)—called by Milton 'abhorred Styx, the flood of deadly hate' (*Paradise Lost*, II, 577)—that, according to classical mythology, flowed nine times round the infernal regions. Some say it was a river in ARCADIA whose waters were poisonous and dissolved any vessel put upon them. When a god swore falsely by the Styx, he was made to drink a draught of its water which made

him lie speechless for a year. The river was said to take its name from Styx, the eldest daughter of OCEANUS and TETHYS, and wife of Pallas, by whom she had three daughters, Victory, Strength and Valour. *See* ACHERON; CHARON.

By the black infernal Styx I swear
(That dreadful oath which binds the Thunderer)
'Tis fixed!
POPE: *Thebais of Statius*, I, 411.

**Sub Jove** (Lat.). Under Jove; in the open air. JUPITER is the god of the upper regions of the air, as JUNO is of the lower regions, NEPTUNE of the waters of the sea, VESTA of the earth, CERES of the surface soil, and HADES of the invisible or underworld.

**Succubus** (sŭk'ūbəs) (Med. Lat. masculine form of Late Lat. *succuba*, from *succumbere*, to lie under). A female demon fabled to have sexual relations with sleeping men. *Cp.* INCUBUS.

**Sun.** The source of light and heat, and consequently of life to the whole world; hence regarded as a deity and worshipped as such by all primitive peoples and having a leading place in their mythologies. *Shamash* was the principal sun-god of the Assyrians and Babylonians, MITHRAS of the Persians, RA of the Egyptians, *Tezcatlipoca* (Smoking Mirror) of the Aztecs, HELIOS of the Greeks, known to the Romans as SOL and usually identified with PHOEBUS and APOLLO.

**Sup. To sup with Sir Thomas Gresham.** *See* HUMPHREY.

**Superman.** A hypothetical superior human being of high intellectual and moral attainment, fancied as evolved from the normally existing type. The term (*Übermensch*) was invented by the German philosopher Nietzsche (d. 1900), and was popularized in England by George Bernard Shaw's play, *Man and Superman* (1903).

The wide popularity of the term gave rise to many compounds, such as *super-woman, super-critic, super-tramp, super-Dreadnought,* and *super-tax.*

**Swallow.** The mythology of the swallow is ancient, going back to Babylonian times and the FLOOD legend, the swallow was sent out with the DOVE and RAVEN and returned with the dove. It is an attribute of the Great Mother Nina who could take the form of a swallow. In Egypt it was sacred to ISIS and is referred to in the *Pyramid Text* which calls swallows 'the imperishable northern stars'. They are depicted with the Tree of Life.

Greek myth associated the swallow with the NIGHTINGALE in the escape from Tereus. The swallow was sacred to APHRODITE/VENUS. Spirits of dead children could visit their homes again in the form of a swallow, hence it was unlucky to kill one.

In the Old Testament the swallow is called the 'chatterer' (*Isaiah* xxxviii, 14). Christianity uses it as depicting resurrection and new life. Muslims say it is a holy bird as it makes the pilgrimage to Mecca each year.

The Bestiaries call the swallow the Hirundo and say it has a particularly devout mind, while the Physiologus maintains that the swallow sleeps all winter and wakes in spring. There was an early legend that swallows and swifts hibernated in caves or clefts in the rocks or under water. There was also an ancient belief that they had no feet and they are so portrayed in heraldry with the legs ending in feathers.

According to Scandinavian tradition, this bird hovered over the cross of our Lord, crying *'Svala! svala!'* (Console! console!), whence it was called *svalow* (the bird of consolation).

Aelian says that the swallow was sacred to the PENATES or household gods, and therefore to injure one would be to bring wrath upon your own house. It is still considered a sign of good luck if a swallow or martin builds under the eaves of one's house.

> Perhaps you failed in your foreseeing skill,
> For swallows are unlucky birds to kill.
> DRYDEN: *Hind and Panther*, Pt. III.

Longfellow refers to another old fable regarding this bird:

> Seeking with eager eyes that wondrous stone which the swallow
> Brings from the shore of the sea to restore the sight of its fledglings.
> *Evangeline*, Pt. I, 119.

**One swallow does not make a summer.** You are not to suppose summer has come to stay just because you have seen a swallow; nor that the troubles of life are over because you have surmounted one difficulty. The Greek proverb, 'One swallow does not make a spring', is to be found in Aristotle's *Nicomachaean Ethics* (I, vii, 16).

**Swan.** Zeus took the form of a swan to seduce LEDA and the swan has erotic associations as an emblem of APHRODITE/VENUS and the chariot of Venus can be drawn by swans.

In Hinduism the swan and GOOSE are interchangeable in myth and legend. The Hamsa can be depicted as either, it is the Ham Sa, 'that pair of swans' who depict perfect union, they also portray breath and spirit. BRAHMA has the swan or goose as an attribute and can have one as his mount. Like the Egyptian goose, it was the bird that laid the Cosmic Egg on the waters. Brahma sprang from this Golden Egg. The swan can also be the vehicle of his wife Saraswati, goddess of wisdom, learning and music.

Swan deities are prominent in Celtic tradition, they are solar and associated with the healing waters and sun. Swans can also be shape-shifters, as creatures of water, earth and air they can command all three elements; they can also assume human form but can always be recognized by having a gold or silver chain round the neck. Swans, like STORKS, can take human form on migration. In Norse myth the VALKYRIES could take swan shapes; the nymphs of Serbian legend, the Vila, could become either swans or serpents.

Swans appear in Amerindian lore as workers of the will of the Great Spirit and there is a great white swan which calls up the four winds. The black swan of Australia represents the two sister-wives of the All-Father of the Aboriginals of the Lake Victoria region.

Swans used as figureheads on ships brought good luck since swans do not plunge themselves below the waves.

Cygnus, the Swan star, lives on the River of Heaven, the Milky Way.

The fable that the swan sings beautifully just before it dies is very ancient, but baseless. The only one for which a song of any kind can be claimed is the Whistling Swan (*Cygnus musicus*). The superstition was credited by Plato, Aristotle, Euripides, Cicero, Seneca, Martial etc., and doubted by Pliny and Aelian. Shakespeare refers to it more than once; Emilia, just before she dies, says:

I will play the swan,
And die in music.
>    *Othello*, V, ii.

Spenser speaks of the swan as a bird that sings:

He, were he not with love so ill bedight,
Woulde mount as high, and sing as soote [sweetly]
as Swanne.
>    *Shephearde's Calendar* (October, 89).

Coleridge (*On a Volunteer Singer*), referring to poetasters of the time, gives the old superstition an epigrammatic turn:

Swans sing before they die; 'twere no bad thing
Did certain persons die before they sing.

One Greek legend has it that the soul of APOLLO, the god of music, passed into a swan, hence the Pythagorean fable that the souls of all good poets passed into swans (*see* SWAN OF AVON *below*).

The male swan is called a *cob*, the female, a *pen*; a young swan, a *cygnet*. See *also* FIONNUALA; LEDA; LOHENGRIN.

**The Knight of the Swan.** LOHENGRIN.

**The Order of the Swan.** An order of knighthood founded by Frederick II of Brandenburg in 1440 (and shortly after in Cleves) in honour of the LOHENGRIN legend. It died out in the 16th century but was revived by Frederick William IV of Prussia in 1843. After the arrival of Anne of Cleves in England the *White Swan* was adopted as a PUBLIC-HOUSE SIGN. The badge of the Order was a silver swan surmounted by an image of the Virgin.

**The Swan of Avon.** Shakespeare; so called (Ben Jonson) in allusion to his birthplace at Stratford-upon-Avon and the legend that APOLLO was changed into a swan.

**The Swan with Two Necks.** An old tavern sign, said to be a corruption of 'two nicks' with which the Vintners' Company mark the beaks of their swans. In coaching days, the *Swan with Two Necks* in Lad Lane (now Gresham Street) was the chief London departure point for the North.

**Swan-maidens.** Fairies of northern folklore, who can become maidens or swans at will by means of the *swan shift*, a magic garment of swan's feathers. Many stories are told of how the swan shift was stolen, and the FAIRY was obliged to remain thrall to the thief until rescued by a knight.

**Swan song.** The song fabled to be sung by a dying swan; hence, the last work or appearance of a poet, composer, actor etc.

**Swim. Sink or swim.** No matter what happens; convicted WITCHES were thrown into the water to 'sink or swim'; if they sank they were drowned; if they swam it was clear proof they were in league with the Evil One; so it did not much matter, one way or the other.

**Swithin, St. If it rains on St. Swithin's Day** (15 July), **there will be rain for forty days.**

St. Swithin's day, gif ye do rain, for forty days it
will remain;
St. Swithin's day an ye be fair, for forty days 'twill
rain nae mair.

The legend is that St. Swithin (or Swithun), Bishop of Winchester and adviser of Egbert of Wessex, who died in 862, desired to be buried in the churchyard of the minster, that the 'sweet rain of heaven might fall upon his grave'. At canonization, the monks thought to honour the SAINT by removing his body into the cathedral choir and fixed 15 July 971 for the ceremony, but it rained day after day for 40 days, thereby, according to some, delaying the proceedings. His shrine was destroyed during the Reformation and a new one was dedicated in 1962. Those who hold to this superstition ignore the fact that it is based upon the dating of the Julian Calendar and therefore could not hold for 40 days from the current 15 July which is based on the Gregorian Year.

The St. Swithin of France is St. Gervais (*see also* St. MÉDARD). The rainy saint in Flanders is St. Godeliève; in Germany, the SEVEN SLEEPERS have this attribute.

**Sword.** In the days of chivalry and romance a knight's horse and sword were his two most carefully prized possessions and it was customary to give each a name. Among the most noted of such swords are:

*Balisarda*, ROGERO's sword, made by a
sorceress.
*Balmung*, one of the swords of SIEGFRIED, made
by Wieland.
*Chrysaor* (sword as good as gold), ARTEGAL's
sword in Spenser's *Faerie Queene*.
*Corrouge*. Otuel's sword.
*Courtain* (the short sword), one of the swords of
OGIER THE DANE; *Sauvagine* was the other,
and they both took Munifican three years to
make.
*Durandal*. See ROLAND'S SWORD *under*
ROLAND.
*Flamberge* or *Floberge* (the flame-cutter), the

name of one of CHARLEMAGNE's swords, and also of RINALDO and Maugis.

*Frusberta,* RINALDO's sword.

*Glorious,* OLIVER's sword, which hacked to pieces the nine swords made by Ansias, Galas, and Munifican.

*Gram* (grief), one of the swords of SIEGFRIED.

*Greysteel,* the sword of Koll the Thrall.

*Haute-claire* (very bright), both OLIVER's and Closamont's swords were so called.

*Mimung,* the sword that Wittich lent SIEGFRIED.

*Morglay* (big glaive), Sir BEVIS's sword.

*Nagelring* (nail-ring), Dietrich's sword.

*Philippan,* the sword of Antony, one of the triumvirs.

*Quern-biter* (a foot-breadth), both Haco I and Thoralf Skolinson had a sword of this name.

*Sanglamore* (the big bloody glaive), BRAGGADOCHIO's sword (Spenser's *Faerie Queene*).

*Sauvagine* (the relentless), *see* COURTAIN *above.*

*Tizona,* the CID's sword.

*See also* ANGURVADEL; ARONDIGHT; AZOTH; CALIBURN; Curtana; EXCALIBUR; JOYEUSE; Merveilleuse; ROSSE.

**The Sword of Damocles.** *See* DAMOCLES.

**Sybil.** A perverted spelling of SIBYL, in classical mythology a prophetess, especially the prophetesses of APOLLO (*see* SIBYLLINE BOOKS). George Eliot was known to her friends as *The Sybil.*

**Sylph** (silf). An elemental spirit of air; so named in the Middle Ages by the ROSICRUCIANS and CABBALISTS, from the Greek *silphe,* beetle or larva. *Cp.* SALAMANDER.

Any mortal who has preserved inviolate chastity might enjoy intimate familiarity with these gentle spirits, and deceased coquettes were said to become sylphs, 'and sport and flutter in the fields of air'.

> Whoever, fair and chaste,
> Rejects mankind, is by some sylph embraced.
> POPE: *The Rape of the Lock,* i, 67.

**Symbols of Saints.** *See under* SAINTS.

**Symplegades.** Another name for the CYANEAN ROCKS.

**Syrinx** (sī'ringks). An Arcadian NYMPH of Greek legend. On being pursued by PAN she took refuge in the river Ladon, and prayed to be changed into a reed; the prayer was granted, and of the reed Pan made his pipes. Hence the name is given to the PAN-PIPE, or reed mouth-organ, and also to the vocal organ of birds.

# T

**Table. The Round Table,** or **Table Round.** *See under* ROUND.

**Table-rapping.** The occurrence of knocking sounds on a table without apparent source but coming from the departed, according to spiritualists, who use them as a supposed means of contacting the dead.

**Table-turning.** The turning of tables without the application of mechanical force, which in the early days of SPIRITUALISM was commonly practised at seances, and sank to the level of a parlour trick. It was said by some to be the work of departed spirits, and by others to be due to a force akin to mesmerism.

**Taffy.** A Welshman, from *Davy* (*Dafydd, David*), a common name in Wales; perhaps it is best known among the English from the old rhyme in allusion to the days of border cattle raids.

> Taffy was a Welshman,
> Taffy was a thief,
> Taffy came to my house
> And stole a leg of beef.

**Tages** (tā′jēz). In Etruscan mythology, a mysterious boy with the wisdom of an old man who was ploughed up, or who sprang from the ground, at Tarquinii. He is said to have been the grandson of JUPITER and to have instructed the Etruscans in the art of AUGURY. The latter wrote down his teaching in 12 books, which were known as 'the books of Tages', or 'the Acherontian books'.

**Tail.** According to an old fable lions wipe out their footsteps with their tail, that they may not be tracked.

**Tailed men.** It was an old belief in mediaeval times that such creatures existed and among continentals Englishmen were once reputed to have tails. It was long a saying that the men of Kent were born with tails, as a punishment for the murder of Thomas à Becket.

A *Warwickshire* Man will be known by his Grinn,
as Roman-Catholics imagine a *Kentish* man by
his Tail.

Peter Pindar (*Epistle to the Pope*, 41) fastens the legend on the town of Strood:

> As Becket that good saint, sublimely rode,
> Thoughtless of insult, through the town of Strode,
> What did the mob? Attacked his horse's rump
> And cut the tail, so flowing, to the stump.
> What does the saint? Quoth he, 'For this vile trick
> The town of Strode shall heartily be sick'.
> And lo! by power divine, a curse prevails—
> The babes of Strode are born with horse's tails.

Jews and Cornishmen were also held to have tails, the appendage also being borne by the DEVIL. In the former case from a confusion of *rabbi* with *raboin* or *rabuino*, the devil, from Span. *rabo*, a tail.

**Tale. An old wives' tale.** Legendary lore, or a story usually involving the marvellous, and only accepted by the credulous. George Peele has a play *The Old Wives' Tale* (1595) and Arnold Bennett a novel (1908) of the same title.

**Taliesin** (talies′in). A Welsh BARD of the late 16th century about whom very little is known. The so-called *Book of Taliesin* is of the 13th century and its contents are the work of various authors. The village of Taliesin in Cardiganshire (Powys) is named after him. The story is that Prince Elphin, son of the King of Gwynedd, was given the right to net a certain weir near the mouth of the Dovey once a year, and on this occasion his net was brought ashore without a single salmon in it. While bewailing his constant misfortune, he noticed a leather wallet suspended from the timber of the weir and upon opening it found therein a youth of such lustrous brow that Elphin named him Taliesin (radiant brow). Taliesin brought wonderful prosperity to Elphin and became the greatest of the British bards at the court of King ARTHUR at CAERLEON.

**Talisman.** A charm or magical figure or word, such as the ABRAXAS which is cut on metal or stone under the influence of certain planets; it is supposed to be sympathetic and to communicate to the wearer influence from the planets.

'Know, then, that the medicine to which thou, Sir King, and many one beside, owe their recovery, is a talisman, composed under certain aspects of the heavens, when the Divine Intelligences are most propitious. I am but the poor administrator of its virtues.'
SCOTT: *The Talisman*, xviii.

In order to free a place of vermin, a talisman consisting of the obnoxious creature was made in wax or consecrated metal, in a planetary hour.

Swore you had broke, and robb'd his house,
And stole his talismanic louse.
BUTLER: *Hudibras*, III, i.

The word is the Arabic *tilsam* from late Greek *telesma*, mystery.

**Tammuz.** *See* THAMMUZ.

**Tam-o'-Shanter.** The hero of Burns's poem of that name; the soft hat is so called from him.

**Remember Tam-o'-Shanter's mare.** You may pay too dear for your pleasure, as Meg lost her tail, pulled off by Nannie of the 'Cutty Sark', in Burns's poem.

Think, ye may buy the joys owre dear—
Remember Tam-o'-Shanter's mare.
BURNS: *Tam-o'-Shanter*.

**Tancred** (tang'krid) (d. 1112). One of the chief heroes of the First Crusade, and a leading character in Tasso's *Jerusalem Delivered*. He was the son of Otho the Good and Emma (sister of Robert Guiscard). In the epic he was the greatest of all Christian warriors except RINALDO.

Disraeli's strange romance, *Tancred* (1847), tells of an early-19th-century heir to a dukedom who went on a 'New Crusade' to the Holy Land.

**Tangie.** A water-spirit of the Orkneys appearing as a man covered with seaweed (Dan. *tang*, seaweed) or as a little sea-horse.

**Tannhäuser** (tan'hoizə). A lyrical poet, or Minnesinger of Germany, who flourished in the second half of the 13th century. He led a wandering life, and is said even to have visited the Far East; this fact, together with his *Busslied* (song of repentance), and the general character of his poems, probably gave rise to the legend about him—which first appeared in a 16th-century German ballad. This related how he spends a voluptuous year with VENUS, in the VENUSBERG, a magic land reached through a subterranean cave; at last he obtains leave to visit the upper world, and goes to Pope Urban IV for absolution. 'No', says His Holiness, 'you can no more hope for mercy than this dry staff can be expected to bud again.' Tannhäuser departs in despair; but on the third day the papal staff bursts into blossom; the Pope sends in every direction for Tannhäuser, but the knight is nowhere to be found, for, mercy having been refused, he has returned to end his days in the arms of Venus. *See* ECKHARDT THE FAITHFUL.

Wagner's opera of this name was first produced in 1845.

**Tantalus** (tan'tələs). In Greek mythology, the son of ZEUS and a NYMPH. He was a Lydian king, highly honoured and prosperous; but, because he divulged to mortals the secrets of the gods, he was plunged up to the chin in a river of HADES, a tree hung with clusters of fruit being just above his head. As every time he tried to drink the waters receded from him, and as the fruit was just out of reach, he suffered agony from thirst, hunger and unfulfilled anticipation.

Hence our verb, *to tantalize*, to excite a hope and disappoint it; and hence the name *tantalus* applied to a lock-up spirit chest in which the bottles are visible but un-get-at-able without the key.

**Tara.** The Tibetan Great Mother Goddess Tara is the counterpart of Avalokitesvara; she is the Mother of All Buddhas. Later the two wives of King Srong-tsan-Gompo who introduced Buddhism into Tibet, were revered as incarnations of Tara, one in Nepal as the Green Tara and the other in China as the White Tara.

**Tarot,** or **Tarok Cards.** Italian playing cards, first used in the 14th century and still employed in fortune-telling. The pack originally contained 78 cards: four suits of numeral cards with four coat cards, *i.e.* king, queen, chevalier and valet, and in addition to the four suits 22 *atutti* cards, or trumps, known as *tarots*.

The modern pack contains 54 cards: 32 suit cards, 21 tarots and 1 joker.

**Tarquin** (tah'kwin). The family name of a legendary line of early Roman kings. Tarquinius Priscus, the fifth king of Rome is dated 617–578 B.C. His son, Tarquinius Superbus, was the seventh (and last) king of Rome, and it was his son, Tarquinius Sextus, who committed the rape on Lucretia, in revenge for which the Tarquins were expelled from Rome and a Republic established.

Tarquin is also the name of a 'recreant knight' figuring in the ARTHURIAN ROMANCES.

**Tartarian Lamb.** *See under* LAMB.

**Tartarus.** The infernal regions of classical mythology; used as equivalent to HADES by later writers, but by Homer placed as far beneath Hades as Hades is beneath the earth. It was here that ZEUS confined the TITANS. *Cp.* HELL.

**Tattoo. Beating the devil's tattoo.** *See under* DEVIL (phrases).

**Taurus** (taw'rəs) (Lat. the bull). The second zodiacal constellation, and the second sign of the ZODIAC, which the sun enters about 21 April.

> As bees
> In spring-time, when the sun with Taurus rides,
> Pour forth their populous youth about the hive
> In clusters.
>
> MILTON: *Paradise Lost*, I, 768.

**Tear. St. Lawrence's tears**. *See* SHOOTING STARS.

**Tears of Eos.** The dewdrops of the morning were so called by the Greeks. Eos was the mother of MEMNON, and wept for him every morning.

**Telamones** (teləmō'nēz). Large, sculptured male figures (*cp.* ATLANTES; Caryatides) serving as architectural columns or pilasters. So called from the Greek legendary hero Telamon (father of AJAX) who took part in the Calydonian hunt (*see* CALYDONIAN BOAR *under* BOAR), and the expedition of the ARGONAUTS.

**Telegonus** (tileg'ənəs). The son of ULYSSES and CIRCE, who was sent to find his father. On coming to Ithaca, he began to plunder the fields when Ulysses and TELEMACHUS

appeared in arms to prevent him. Telegonus killed his father, who was unknown to him, with a lance pointed with the spine of a trygon, or sting-ray which Circe had given him. He subsequently married PENELOPE.

**Telemachus** (tilem'əkəs). The only son of ULYSSES and PENELOPE. After the fall of TROY he went, attended by ATHENE in the guise of MENTOR, in quest of his father. He ultimately found him, and the two returned to Ithaca and slew Penelope's suitors.

**Telephus.** *See* ACHILLEA.

**Tell, William.** The legendary national hero of Switzerland whose deeds appear to be an invention of the 15th century and are paralleled in numerous European myths and legends.

The story is that Tell was the champion of the Swiss in the struggle against Albert I (slain 1308), Duke of Austria. Tell refused to salute the cap of Gessler, Albert's tyrannical steward, and for this act of independence was sentenced to shoot with his bow and arrow an apple from the head of his own son. He achieved this feat and Gessler demanded what his second arrow was for, whereupon Tell boldly replied, 'To shoot you with, had I killed my son.' Gessler had him conveyed to Küssnacht castle, but he escaped on the way and later killed Gessler in ambush. A rising followed which established the independence of Switzerland.

The story has been systematically exposed as having no foundation in fact, and similar feats are recorded in the Norse legend of Toki. The popularity of tales of the 'master shot' is evidenced by the stories of Adam Bell, CLYM OF THE CLOUGH, William Cloudesley and EGIL.

**Tendon of Achilles.** *See* ACHILLES TENDON.

**Tenterden. Tenterden steeple was the cause of Goodwin Sands.** A satirical remark when some ridiculous reason is given for a thing. The story, according to one of Latimer's sermons, is that Sir Thomas More, being sent into Kent to ascertain the cause of the Goodwin Sands, called together the oldest inhabitants to ask their opinion. A very old man said, 'I believe Tenterden steeple is the cause,' and went on to explain that in his early days there was no Tenterden steeple, and there were no complaints about the sands. This reason seems ridiculous enough, but the fact seems to be that the Bishops of Rochester applied to the building of Tenterden steeple moneys raised in the county for the purpose of keeping Sandwich haven clear, so that when they found the harbour was getting blocked up there was no money for taking the necessary counter-measures.

**Tenth. The Tenth Muse.** A name given originally to SAPPHO, there being *nine* true MUSES, and afterwards applied to literary women, as Mme de la Garde Deshoulières (1638–1694), Mlle de Scudéry (1607–1701), Queen Christina of Sweden (1626–1689), and the English novelist and essay writer, Hannah More (1745–1833).

**Terpsichore** (tœpsik'əri). One of the nine MUSES of ancient Greece, the Muse of dancing and the dramatic chorus, and later of lyric poetry. Hence *Terpsichorean*, pertaining to dancing. She is usually represented seated, and holding a lyre.

**Testudo** (testū'dō). *See* TORTOISE.

**Tethys** (tē'this). A sea goddess, wife of OCEANUS hence, the sea itself. She was the daughter of URANUS and GAEA, and mother of the Oceanides.

**Teucer** (tū'sə). In the ILIAD, the son of Telamon, and stepbrother of AJAX; he went with the allied Greeks to the siege of TROY, and on his return was banished by his father for not avenging on Odysseus (ULYSSES) the death of his brother.

**Thalestris** (thəles'tris). A queen of the AMAZONS who went with 300 women to meet Alexander the Great, in the hope of raising a race of Alexanders.

**Thalia** (thəli'ə). One of the MUSES who presided over comedy and pastoral poetry. She also favoured rural pursuits and is represented holding a comic mask and a shepherd's crook. Thalia is also the name of one of THE THREE GRACES (*see under* GRACE) or *Charites*.

**Thammuz,** or **Tammuz** (tam'ooz). A Sumerian, Babylonian and Assyrian god who died every year and rose again in the spring. He is identified with the Babylonian MARDUK and the Greek ADONIS. In *Ezek.*

viii, 14, reference is made to the heathen 'women weeping for Tammuz'.

> Thammuz came next behind,
> Whose annual wound in Lebanon allured
> The Syrian damsels to lament his fate
> In amorous ditties all a summer's day,
> While smooth Adonis from his native rock
> Ran purple to the sea, supposed with blood
> Of Thammuz yearly wounded.
> MILTON: *Paradise Lost*, I, 446.

**Thamyris** (tham'iris). A Thracian bard mentioned by Homer (*Iliad*, II, 595). He challenged the MUSES to a trial of skill, and, being overcome in the contest, was deprived by them of his sight and powers of song. He is represented with a broken lyre in his hand.

> Blind Thamyris and blind Maeonides [Homer]
> And Tiresias and Phineus, prophets old.
> MILTON: *Paradise Lost*, III, 35.

**Thanatos.** The Greek personification of death, twin brother of Sleep (*Hypnos*). Hesiod says he was born of Night with no father.

**Thebes. The Seven Against Thebes.** An expedition in Greek legend fabled to have taken place against Thebes of Boeotia before the TROJAN WAR. The Seven were the Argive chiefs ADRASTUS, Polynices, Tydeus, Amphiaraus, Hippomedon, Capancus and Parthenopaeus.

When OEDIPUS abdicated, his two sons agreed to reign alternate years; but at the expiration of the first year, the elder, Eteocles, refused to give up the throne, whereupon Polynices, the younger brother, induced the six chiefs to espouse his cause. The allied army laid siege to Thebes, but without success, and all the heroes perished except Adrastus. Subsequently, seven sons of the chiefs, resolved to avenge their fathers' deaths, marched against the city, took it, and placed Terpander, one of their number on the throne. These are known as the *Epigoni* (Gr. descendants). The Greek tragic poets AESCHYLUS and Euripides dramatized the legend.

**Themis** (thē'mis). A daughter of URANUS and GAEA and a wife of JUPITER, mother of the HORAE and PARCAE. With Jupiter she presides over law and order. She also is protector of hospitality and the oppressed and has oracular powers.

**Theodoric** (thēod'ərik). King of the Ostrogoths (*c.* 454–526), who became celebrated in German legend as Dietrich of Bern, and also has a place in the Norse Romances and the *Nibelungen Saga*. He invaded Italy, slew Odoacer (493), and became sole ruler.

**Thersites** (thœ'sitēz). A deformed, scurrilous officer in the Greek army at the siege of TROY. He was always railing at the chiefs; hence the name is applied to any dastardly, malevolent, impudent railer against the powers that be. ACHILLES felled him to the earth with his fist and killed him.

In Shakespeare's *Troilus and Cressida* (I, iii) he is 'A slave whose gall coins slanders like a mint.'

**Theseus** (thē'ziəs). The chief hero of Attica in ancient Greek legend; son of AEGEUS, and the centre of countless exploits. Among them are the capture of the Marathonian bull, the slaying of the MINOTAUR, his war against the AMAZONS, and the hunting of the CALYDONIAN BOAR (*see under* BOAR). He was eventually murdered by Lycomedes in Scyros. *See* SINIS.

*Theseus* is also the name of the Duke of Athens in Chaucer's *Knight's Tale*. He married Hippolita, and as he returned home with his bride, and Emily her sister, was accosted by a crowd of female suppliants who complained of Creon, King of Thebes. The Duke forthwith set out for Thebes, slew Creon, and took the city by assault. Many captives fell into his hands, amongst whom were the two knights, Palamon and ARCITE.

Shakespeare gives the same name to the Duke of Athens in *A Midsummer Night's Dream*.

**Thetis** (thē'tis). The chief of the NEREIDS of Greek legend. By Peleus she was the mother of ACHILLES.

**Thetis's hair-stone.** A fancy name given to pieces of rock-crystal enclosing hair-like filaments.

**Thief, The Penitent.** *See* DYSMAS.

**Thisbe** (thiz'bi). *See* PYRAMUS.

**Thomas. St. Thomas.** The Apostle who doubted (*John* xx, 25); hence the phrase, **a doubting Thomas,** applied to a sceptic.

The story told of him in the Apocryphal *Acts of St. Thomas* is that he was deputed to go as a missionary to India, and, on refusing, Christ appeared and sold him as a slave to an Indian prince who was visiting Jerusalem. He was taken to India, where he baptized the prince and many others, and was finally martyred at Mylapore.

Another legend has it that Gundaphorus, an Indian king, gave him a large sum of money to build a palace. St. Thomas spent it on the poor, 'thus creating a superb palace in heaven'. On account of this he is the patron SAINT of masons and architects, and his symbol is a builder's square.

Another story is that he once saw a huge beam of timber floating on the sea near the coast, and the king unsuccessfully endeavouring, with men and elephants, to haul it ashore. St. Thomas desired leave to use it in building a church, and, his request being granted, he dragged it easily ashore with a piece of packthread.

His feast day is 3 July (formerly 21 December). His relics are now said to be at Ortona in the Abruzzi.

**Thone,** or **Thonis** (thō'ni, thō'nis). In Greek mythology, the governor of a province of Egypt to which, it is said by post-Homeric poets, PARIS took HELEN, who was given by Polydamnia, wife to Thone, the drug NEPENTHES, to make her forget her sorrows.

> Not that nepenthes which the wife of Thone,
> In Egypt gave to Jove-born Helena
> Is of such power to stir up joy as this.
> MILTON: *Comus*, 675–7.

**Thor** (thaw). Son of WODEN, god of war, and the second god in the PANTHEON of the ancient Scandinavians—their VULCAN, and god of thunder. He had three principal possessions, a Hammer (*Mjollnir*), typifying thunder and lightning, and having the virtue of returning to him after it was thrown; a Belt (*Meginjardir*) which doubled his strength; and Iron Gloves to aid him in throwing his hammer.

He was a god of the household, and of peasants, and was married to Sif, a typical peasant woman. His name is still perpetuated in our THURSDAY, and in a number of place-names such as *Thorsby* (Cumberland), *Torthorwald* (Dumfries), and *Thurso* (Caithness).

**Thoth** (thōth). The Egyptian lunar god, usually with the head of an IBIS but sometimes that of a baboon. His chief centre was Hermapolis (modern Ashmunein) and he was identified with HERMES by the Greeks.

He was the master over writing, languages, laws, annals, calculations etc., and patron of scribes and magicians. He made the Calendar and his control over HIEROGLYPHS and divine words enhanced his magical powers. He acted as secretary of the gods. At the judgment after death he weighed the heart.

**Thousand. Thousand and One Nights.** *See* ARABIAN NIGHTS.

**Three.** Pythagoras calls three the perfect number, expressive of 'beginning, middle and end', wherefore he makes it a symbol of Deity.

A Trinity is by no means confined to the CHRISTIAN creed. The BRAHMINS represent their god with three heads; the world was supposed by the ancients to be under the rule of three gods, *viz.* JUPITER (HEAVEN), NEPTUNE (sea), and PLUTO (HADES). Jove is represented with three-forked lightning, Neptune with a trident, and Pluto with a three-headed dog. The FATES are three, the FURIES three, the Graces three (*see under* GRACE), the Harpies three (*see* HARPY), the SIBYLLINE BOOKS three times three (of which only three survived); the fountain from which HYLAS drew water was presided over by three NYMPHS; the MUSES were three times three; in Scandinavian mythology we hear of 'the Mysterious Three', *viz* 'Har' (High), 'Jafenhar' (Equally High), and 'Thridi' (the third), who sat on three thrones in ASGARD.

Man is threefold (body, mind and spirit); the world is threefold (earth, sea and air); the enemies of man are threefold (the world, the flesh and the DEVIL); the Christian graces are threefold (Faith, Hope and Charity); the Kingdoms of Nature are threefold (animal, vegetable and mineral); the Cardinal colours are three in number (red, yellow and blue), etc. *Cp.* NINE which is three times three.

**The three Musketeers.** Athos, Porthos and Aramis, the three heroes of Dumas's novels *The Three Musketeers*, 1844; *Twenty Years After*, 1845; and *Vicomte de Bragelonne*, 1848–1850. The Musketeers were a mounted guard of gentlemen in the service of the kings of France from 1661 until the Revolution caused their abolition in 1791. They formed two companies, called the Grey and the Black from the colour of their horses. The uniform was scarlet, hence their quarters were known as *La Maison Rouge*. In peacetime the Musketeers formed the king's bodyguard, but in war they fought on foot or on horseback with the army. Their ranks included many Scots, either Jacobite exiles or mere soldiers of fortune.

**Thrones, Principalities and Powers.** According to Dionysius the Areopagite, three of the nine orders of ANGELS. These names or their linguistic counterparts occur frequently in Jewish-Christian writings around New Testament times.

> The host of the heavens and all the holy ones above, and the host of God...all the angels of power, and all the angels of principalities
> *Enoch* vi, 10.

**Thug.** A worshipper of KALI, who practised *thuggee*, the strangling of human victims in the name of religion. Robbery of the victim provided the means of livelihood. They were also called *Phansigars* (Noose operators) from the method employed. Vigorous suppression was begun by Lord William Bentinck in 1828, but the fraternity did not become completely extinct for another 50 years or so.

In common parlance the word is used for any violent 'tough'.

**Thule** (thū′li). The name given by the ancients to an island, or point of land, six days' sail north of Britain, and considered by them to be the extreme northern limit of the world. The name is first found in the account by Polybius (*c.* 150 B.C.) of the voyage made by Pytheas in the late 4th century B.C. Pliny says, 'It is an island in the Northern Ocean discovered by Pytheas, after sailing six days from the Orcades.' Others, like Camden, consider it to be Shetland, in which opinion they agree with Marinus, and the descriptions of Ptolemy and Tacitus; and still others that it was some part of the coast of Norway. The etymology of the word is unknown.

**Ultima Thule.** The end of the world; the last extremity.

> Tibi serviat Ultima Thule.
> VIRGIL: *Georgics*, I, 30.

**Thumb. Tom Thumb.** *see under* TOM.

**Thunder. Thunderbird.** Representing the great forces of nature, the Great Spirit, the thunderbird is an Amerindian mythological creature usually depicted as EAGLE-like. It can be a creator, but at the same time associated with the destructive powers of war. It appears in all North Amerindian culture and is a rain-bringer; the Pacific Indians depict it with a lake on its back. It can eat whales.

The Siberian Giant Eagle has similar properties, its flashing eyes are lightning and its flapping wings the thunder.

Japan has a thunderbird resembling a rook, it flies about during storms and is connected with the destructive powers of nature such as thunder and lightning. It also guards the approaches to the Sky-heaven.

**Thunderbolt.** A missile or mass of heated matter that was formerly supposed to be discharged from thunder-clouds during a storm; used figuratively of an irresistible blow, a sudden and overwhelming shock.

JUPITER was depicted by the ancients as a man seated on a throne, holding a sceptre in his left hand and thunderbolts in his right.

> Be ready, gods, with all your thunderbolts;
> Dash him to pieces!
> SHAKESPEARE: *Julius Caesar*, IV, iii.

The thunderbolt appears in Buddhist tradition as the Dorje of Tibetan Buddhism, the Chinese Ju-i and the Japanese Nyoi. It is also called the Diamond Mace and represents the divine power of the Law, 'the rolling of the Dharma thunder', enlightenment and truth. It is an attribute of the Dhyani Buddhas.

**Thunderday.** *See* THURSDAY.

**Thursday.** The fifth day of the weeek until 1971, now the fourth (*see* SUNDAY). The day of the god THOR, called by the French *jeudi*, that is, Jove's day. Both JOVE and THOR were gods of thunder, and formerly Thursday was sometimes called *Thunderday. See also* MAUNDY THURSDAY.

**Thyestes** (thīes'tēz). Brother of Atreus, and son of PELOPS and HIPPODAMIA. He seduced his brother's wife and also contrived a situation which led to Atreus slaying his own son. By way of revenge, Atreus invited Thyestes to a banquet in which the limbs of two of his sons, slain by Atreus, were served as a dish. Hence a *Thyestean feast*: one at which human flesh is served.

**Thyrsus** (thœ'səs). The staff carried by DIONYSUS and his attendants, topped with a pine cone and decorated with vine and ivy leaves.

**Tiamat** (tiah'mat). The Babylonian Tiamat, usually depicted as a dragon, represented the primordial waters, chaos and darkness. She was the feminine power with Apsu as the masculine; together they gave rise to the gods and the world. Tiamat was defeated by the sun god MARDUK when she led a host of monsters against him; the heavens and earth were created from her dismembered body.

**Tichborne Case.** The most celebrated impersonation case in English law. In March 1853, Roger Charles Tichborne, heir to an ancient Hampshire baronetcy, sailed for Valparaiso, and after travelling a while in S. America embarked on 20 April 1854 in a sailing ship named the *Bella*, bound for Jamaica. The ship went down and nothing more was heard or seen of Roger Tichborne. In October 1865, 'R.C. Richborne' turned up at Wagga Wagga, in Australia, in the person of a man locally known as Tom Castro. On Christmas Day 1866, he landed in England as a claimant to the Tichborne baronetcy, asserting that he was the lost Roger. Lady Tichborne, the real Roger's mother, professed to recognize him, but the family could not be deceived. The case came into the courts where the fellow's claims were proved to be false and he himself identified as Arthur Orton, the son of a Wapping butcher. A further trial for perjury, lasting 188 days, ended in his being sentenced to 14 years' penal servitude.

**Tichborne Dole.** An ancient charity maintained by the Tichborne family, said to have been instituted by Lady Mabel Tichborne in 1150. The legend is that, when dying, she begged her husband to provide for the poor from the produce of the estate and he promised to give the value of the land she could encircle while holding a burning torch. She rose from her deathbed and encompassed 23 acres and prophesied that if the charity were allowed to lapse, seven sons would be born to the family followed by seven daughters and the title would lapse. The dole was stopped after 644 years and the then baronet had seven sons and his heir seven daughters. The third son changed his name to Doughty and revived the dole and escaped the full consequences of the curse. The title became extinct in 1968 with the death of Sir Anthony

Doughty-Tichborne, the fourteenth baronet.

**Tiffany.** A kind of thin silk-like gauze. The word is supposed to be a corruption of *Theophany* (Gr. *theos*, god; *phainein*, to show), the manifestation of God to man, the Epiphany; and the material was so called because it used to be worn at the Twelfth Night (Epiphany) revels.

**Tiger.** The tiger is of great importance in Eastern mythology, often taking the place of the LION as King of the Beasts; it always represents royalty, power and fearlessness. In China the tiger is Lord of the Land Animals and was originally one of the Four Auspicious Creatures, its place being taken later by the KY-LIN. It is the third of the Animals of the Twelve Terrestrial Branches and the emblem of military officers of the Fourth Class, typifying war, might and courage. In this aspect it is *yang* but as portrayed in conflict with the Celestial DRAGON and as nocturnal, the White Tiger becomes *yin*, representing the earth, the West, the region of death, and is the guardian of graves. The Blue Tiger is the East and plant life; the Red Tiger is the South and fire; the Black Tiger is the North and winter, while the Yellow Tiger is the SUN, the Centre. Various deities ride tigers, Chang Tao-ling, the first Pope of popular Taoism, rides a tiger as does the god of wealth and gamblers; the goddess of the wind has a tiger as her mount and the animal also represents ORION in Chinese legend. For an ordinary person to 'ride a tiger' is synonymous with encounters with dangerous powers and situations.

Although the tiger is a mythical animal in Japan it is included in legend; it is credited with a fabulous age of a thousand years and it was adopted as an emblem of the warrior class and of heroes.

Were-tigers appear in Malaysian myth and are particularly dangerous as being able to embody souls of sorcerers and of the dead. The tiger must not be named for fear of attracting it; it is called 'the striped one', 'hairy face', or 'Lord'. Sumatra and Java have a powerful but friendly were-tiger.

The association with the military class also occurs in Indian myth where it is an emblem of the Kshatriyas, the royal and military caste. SIVA and Durga, in their destructive aspect are associated with

tigers, Durga rides one and Siva can be depicted wearing a tiger skin. The tiger god can represent Padma-Sambhava when he appears as a destroyer of demons. Among the Rajputs there is a legend of descent from tigers.

There are two kinds of tigers in heraldry, the heraldic Tigre, a stylized animal since the tiger was unknown in Europe in early times, and the later Royal or Bengal Tiger.

**Tilt. To tilt at windmills.** *See under* WINDMILL.

**Tintagel** (tintaj′əl). The castle on the north coast of Cornwall fabled as King ARTHUR's Castle and according to Geoffrey of Monmouth (*Historia Regum Britanniae*, XIX) the birthplace of King Arthur. The present ruin upon the cliff is of mid-12th century origin.

**Tiphys** (tī′fis). The pilot of the ARGONAUTS, hence a generic name for pilots.

**Tiresias** (tīrē′sias). A Theban of Greek legend, who by accident saw ATHENE bathing, and was therefore struck with blindness by her splashing water in his face. She afterwards repented, and, as she could not restore his sight, conferred on him the power of soothsaying and of understanding the language of birds, giving him a staff with which he could walk as safely as if he had his sight. He found death at last by drinking from the well of Tilphosa.

Another story is that he had been temporarily changed into a woman (for seven years) and was therefore called upon by JUPITER and JUNO to settle an argument as to which of the sexes derived the greatest pleasure from the married state. Tiresias, speaking from experience, declared in favour of the female, whereupon Juno struck him blind.

**Tirynthian** (tirin′thiən). HERCULES is called by Spenser the *Tirynthian Swain* (*Faerie Queene*, VI, xii, 35), and the *Tirynthian Groom* (*Epithalamion*, 329), because he generally resided at Tiryns, an ancient city of Argolis in Greece.

**Tisiphone** (tisif′əni). *See* FURIES.

**Titania** (titah′niə). Wife of OBERON, and Queen of the Fairies. Shakespeare uses the name in his *A Midsummer Night's Dream*.

**Titans** (tī'tənz). In Greek mythology, children of URANUS and GAEA, of enormous size and strength, and typical of lawlessness and the power of force. There were 12, six male (OCEANUS, Coeus, Crius, KRONOS, HYPERION and Japetus or IAPETOS) and six female (Theia, RHEA, THEMIS, MNEMOSYNE, PHOEBE and TETHYS). This is according to Hesiod, but the number is variously given by other writers.

Incited by their mother, they overthrew Uranus and emasculated him, and set up Cronus as king. Cronus was in turn overthrown by his son ZEUS. After the long struggle which some of the Titans carried on against Zeus, they were finally hurled down into TARTARUS. *See* GIANTS' WAR WITH ZEUS.

By Virgil and Ovid the SUN was sometimes surnamed *Titan*; hence Shakespeare's:

And flecked Darkness like a drunkard reels
From forth Day's path and Titan's fiery wheels.
*Romeo and Juliet*, II, iii.

**Tithonus** (tithō'nəs). A beautiful Trojan of Greek legend, brother to Laomedon, and beloved by Eos (AURORA). At his prayer, the goddess granted him immortality, but as he had forgotten to ask for youth and vigour he grew old, and life became insupportable. He now prayed Eos to remove him from the world; this, however, she could not do, but she changed him into a grasshopper.

**Tityus** (tit'iəs). In Greek mythology, a gigantic son of ZEUS and GAEA whose body covered nine acres of land. He tried to defile LATONA, but APOLLO cast him into TARTARUS, where a vulture fed on his liver which grew as fast as it was devoured (*cp.* PROMETHEUS).

**Tiu, Tiw,** or **Tyr** (tē'oo, tiə). In Scandinavian mythology, son of ODIN and a younger brother of THOR. He had his hand bitten off when chaining up the wolf FENRIR. He was identified with MARS, the Roman god of war, and his name is found in our *Tuesday* (Fr. *mardi*). Philologists have generallly equated the name with Gr. ZEUS, Lat. *Deus*, Sansk. *devas*.

**Toad.** The toad was believed to be venomous, being able to spit out poison; Pliny and Aelian maintain this, but there was also a tradition that, like the SERPENT, it carried in its head a precious stone, the Borax, which could act as an antidote to poison. The toad is generally a creature of loathing and can depict evil, but as belonging to the humid principle and as appearing and disappearing, it is lunar and represents resurrection.

The lunar and *yin* aspect is important in Chinese myth as the Three-legged Toad who lives in the moon, its legs depicting the three lunar phases; at lunar eclipses the toad swallows the moon. The creature is also an emblem of the Taoist Immortal Linhai and of Hon Hsien-hsing. Following Chinese tradition, the Japanese Sennin (Genii) Gama is a wizard toad.

In Greek lore the toad is one of the emblems of Sabazius and appears on his Votive Hand.

Celtic myth attributes evil power to the toad and in this aspect it can take the place of a devil, a symbolism which was carried over into Christianity. It was also regarded as a witch's familiar and its poison was part of a witch's brew.

Amerindian legend connects the toad with the Dark Manitou and the powers of darkness which are overcome by the Great Manitou. In Mexico the toad and the toadstool are associated with the sacred mushroom which brings knowledge and insight. There is a mushroom god depicted as sitting under a toadstool.

**Toby.** The dog in the puppet-show of PUNCH AND JUDY. He wears a frill garnished with bells to frighten away the DEVIL from his master.

**Tofana.** *See* AQUA TOFANA.

**Tom Thumb.** Any dwarfish or insignificant person is so called from the tiny hero of the old nursery tale, popular in the 16th century. *The History of Tom Thumb* was published by Richard Johnson in 1621, and there was a similar tale by Perrault, *Le Petit Poucet*, 1697.

Fielding wrote a burlesque (acted 1730) entitled *Tom Thumb the Great*. The American dwarf Charles Sherwood Stratton (1838–1883) was called 'General Tom Thumb' when first exhibited by Phineas T. Barnum. The 'General' was then under 5 years of age and less than 24 inches in height but eventually grew to 40 inches. When at London he was summoned to Buckingham Palace by Queen Victoria and subsequently visited King Louis Philippe in France. He married another American dwarf, Lavinia Warren, in 1863.

**Tortoise.** This animal is frequently taken as the type of plodding persistence—'slow but sure'.

In Hindu myth, the tortoise Chukwa supports the ELEPHANT Maha-pudma, which in its turn supports the world.

The name *tortoise* (Lat. *testudo*) is also given to the ancient Roman protective shelter formed by soldiers with shields overlapping above their heads when attacking a fort.

As the feminine power of the waters the tortoise was an emblem of APHRODITE/VENUS; also of HERMES/MERCURY in Graeco-Roman myth. Pausanias says that it was also sacred to PAN among the Arcadians and that it was prohibited to kill it. There was the legend that, like the OSTRICH, the turtle hatched its eggs 'with looks only'.

In Chinese myth the tortoise also supports the world, its four feet being the four corners of the earth. It is one of the Four Spiritually Endowed, or Auspicious, Creatures and represents the northern regions, the *yin* principle and the element of water. It is the Black Warrior, depicting strength and endurance; it was credited with a great life-span and was therefore a symbol of longevity. In its warrior aspect the tortoise joined the DRAGON on the banners of the imperial army, both represented indestructibility as neither can destroy the other, the tortoise cannot be crushed and the dragon cannot be reached. The tortoise also appears with the CRANE as longevity. The Queen of Heaven, Hsi Wang-mu, can be called the Golden Mother of the Tortoise; it also represents the Great Triad with the dome of its back as the sky, the body as the earth and the lower shell as the waters. The shell is also used in DIVINATION. In Japan the Cosmic Mountain and the abode of the Sennin (the Genii or Immortals of Taoism) are supported by a tortoise.

The tortoise and turtle were not distinguished before the sixteenth century; both appear in Amerindian traditions. For the Sioux the world is a huge tortoise floating on the waters, a myth which also occurs among the Tatars. Another fable is that the earth is supported by four turtles,

but a single tortoise supports the world in Huron tradition; for others the tortoise saved the people from the FLOOD and then carried the new earth on its back. There are various turtle clans and the Pueblos have Turtle Dances in spring and autumn. The animal is associated with both the earth and the waters and is thus a feminine power. The tortoise and turtle can be tricksters, being able to appear and disappear, as a trickster he leads the animals on the war path. Turtles appear on Mayan stelae. For the Aztecs they were a symbol of cowardice and boastfulness, hard outwardly but soft inwardly.

Again representing the feminine to the SERPENT's masculine power, the tortoise is one of the oldest animals of West African mythology. It originated ju-ju and appears in fertility rites. Tortoise also takes on the trickster role but is always outwitted. Like Br'er Rabbit he passed from African to Caribbean lore.

**Achilles and the tortoise.** *See under* ACHILLES.

**The hare and the tortoise.** *See under* HARE.

**Touchstone.** A dark, flinty schist, jasper or basanite (the *Lapis Lydius* of the ancients); so called because GOLD was assayed by comparing the streak made on it by the sample of gold with those made by *touch-needles* of known gold content, after all the streaks had been treated with nitric acid. The needles were made of varying proportions of gold and silver, gold and copper, or of all three metals. Hence the use of *touchstone* as any criterion or standard.

Ovid (*Metamorphoses*, Bk. II, xi) tells us that Battus saw MERCURY steal APOLLO'S oxen, and Mercury gave him a cow to secure his silence, but, being distrustful of the man, changed himself into a peasant, and offered him a cow and an ox if he would tell him where he got the cow. Battus, caught in the trap, told the secret, and Mercury changed him into a touchstone.

Men have a touchstone whereby to try gold; but gold is the touchstone whereby to try men.
FULLER: *The Holy State and the Profane State (The Good Judge).*

Touchstone is the name given to the clown in Shakespeare's *As You Like It*.

**Tournament. The tournament of Tottenham.** A comic romance, given in Percy's

*Reliques.* A number of clowns are introduced, practising warlike games, and making vows like knights of high degree. They tilt on cart-horses, fight with ploughshares and flails, and wear for armour wooden bowls and saucepan-lids.

**Transmigration of Souls.** An ancient belief concerning the transition of the soul after death to another body or substance, usually human or animal; also known as metempsychosis. BRAHMINS and Buddhists accept human descent into plants as well as animals, and the Buddha underwent 550 births in different forms. The ancient Egyptians held to a form of transmigration in which the soul could inhabit another form to allow temporary revisiting the earth.

**Tree. The Tree of Buddha,** or **of Wisdom.** The BO-TREE.

**Tregeagle** (trigā'gl). A kind of Cornish BLUEBEARD who sold his soul to the DEVIL and married and murdered numerous rich heiresses, and whose ghost haunts various parts of Cornwall. His allotted task is to bale out Dozmary Pool on Bodmin Moor with a leaky limpet shell. Hence *to bale out Dozmary Pool with a limpet shell* as a local expression for an impossibility. When the wintry wind howls over the moor, the people say it is Tregeagle roaring, and a child crying lustily is said to be 'roaring worse than Tregeagle'.

**Trident.** In Greek mythology, the three-pronged spear which POSEIDON (Roman NEPTUNE), god of the sea, bore as the symbol of his sovereignty. It has come to be regarded as the emblem of sea power and as such is borne by Britannia. In gladiatorial combats in Rome, the trident was used by the Retiarius, whose skill lay in entangling his opponent in a net, and then despatching him with his trident.

**Trigon** (trī'gon). In ASTROLOGY, the junction of three signs. The ZODIAC is partitioned into four trigons, named respectively after the four elements: the *watery* trigon includes CANCER, SCORPIO and Pisces; the *fiery*, ARIES, Leo and SAGITTARIUS; the *earthly*, TAURUS, Virgo (*see* VIRGIN) and CAPRICORN; and the *airy*, GEMINI, LIBRA and AQUARIUS.

**Trine** (Lat. *trinus*, threefold). In ASTROLOGY, a planet distant from another one-third of the circle is said to be in trine; one-fourth, it is in square; one-sixth or two signs, it is in sextile; but when one-half distant, it is said to be 'opposite'.

> In sextile, square, and trine, and opposite
> Of noxious efficacy.
> MILTON: *Paradise Lost,* X, 659.

Planets distant from each other six signs or half a circle have opposite influences, and are therefore opposed to each other.

**Triptolemus** (triptol'imǝs). A Greek hero and demi-god who was born at Eleusis and was taught the arts of agriculture by CERES. He established the ELEUSINIAN MYSTERIES and festivals.

**Trismegistus** (trismǝjis'tǝs). *See* HERMETIC ART.

**Tristram** Sir (Tristam, Tristan, or **Tristem**). A hero of mediaeval romance whose exploits, though originally unconnected with it, became attached to the ARTHURIAN cycle, he himself being named as one of the KNIGHTS of the ROUND TABLE. There are many versions of his story, which is, roughly, that he was cured of a wound by Iseult, or YSOLDE, daughter of the king of Ireland, and on his return to Cornwall told his uncle, King MARK, of the beautiful princess. Mark sent him to solicit her hand in marriage, and was accepted. Tristram escorted her to England, but on the way they both unknowingly partook of a magic potion and became irretrievably enamoured of each other. Iseult married the king, and on Mark's discovering their liaison Tristram fled to Brittany and married Iseult, daughter of the Duke of Brittany. Wounded by a poisoned weapon, he sent for Iseult of Ireland to come and heal him. The vessel in which she was to come had orders to hoist a white sail if she was on board, otherwise a black sail. Tristram's wife, seeing the vessel approach, told her husband, from jealousy, that it bore a black sail. In despair Tristram died; Iseult of Ireland, arriving too late, killed herself.

The name was originally *Drystan*, from the Pictish name *Drostan*, and the initial was changed to *T* apparently to connect it with Lat. *tristis*, sad. Wagner's opera *Tristan and Isolde* was first produced in 1865.

**Triton.** Son of POSEIDON and AMPHITRITE, represented as a fish with a human head. It is this sea-god that makes the roaring of the ocean by blowing through his shell. He can also be depicted as holding POSEIDON's trident. Sometimes Tritons appear in the plural in literature.

**A Triton among the minnows.** A great man among a host of inferiors.

**Troglodytes** (Gr. *trogle*, cave; *duein*, to go into). A name given by the ancient Greeks to races of uncivilized men who dwelt in caves or holes in the ground. Strabo mentions troglodytes in Syria and Arabia, and Pliny (v, 8) asserts that they fed on serpents. The best-known were those of southern Egypt and Ethiopia. The term is applied to other cave-dwellers, and, figuratively, to those who dwell in seclusion.

In ornithology, wrens, which mostly build their nests in holes, are named *troglodytes*.

**Troilus.** The prince of chivalry, one of the sons of PRIAM, killed by ACHILLES in the TROJAN WAR.

The loves of Troilus and CRESSIDA, celebrated by Chaucer and Shakespeare, form no part of the old classic tale. This story appears for the first time in the *Roman de Troie* by the 12th century Trouvère Benoit de Ste. More. Guido delle Colonne included it in his *Historia Trojana* (1287), it thence passed to Boccaccio, whose *Il Filostrato* (1338)—where Pandarus first appears— was the basis of Chaucer's *Troilus and Criseyde*.

**As true as Troilus.** Troilus is meant by Shakespeare to be the type of constancy, and Cressida the type of female inconstancy.

> After all comparisons of truth...
> 'As true as Troilus' shall crown up the verse.
> And sanctify the numbers.
> *Troilus and Cressida*, III, ii.

**Trojan. Trojan Horse.** *See* WOODEN HORSE OF TROY.

**Trojan War.** The legendary war sung by Homer in the ILIAD as having been waged for ten years by the confederated Greeks against the men of TROY and their allies, in consequence of PARIS, son of PRIAM, the Trojan king, having carried off HELEN, wife of MENELAUS. The last year of the siege is the subject of the *Iliad*; the burning of Troy and the flight of AENEAS is told by Virgil in his AENEID.

There is no doubt that the story of the siege of Troy, much doubted in the 19th century, has a historical basis and probably took place during the 13th and 12th centuries B.C.

**He is a regular Trojan.** A fine fellow, with courage and spirit, who works very hard, usually at some uncongenial task, indeed, doing more than could be expected of him. The Trojans in Homer's ILIAD and Virgil's AENEID are described as truthful, brave, patriotic and confiding.

> There they say right, and like true Trojans.
> BUTLER: *Hudibras*, I, i.

**Trolls.** In Icelandic myth, malignant one-eyed giants; in Scandinavian folklore, mischievous DWARFS, some cunning and treacherous, some fair and good to men, akin to the Scottish BROWNIE. They were wonderfully skilled in working metals and lived in the hills, and had a propensity for stealing, even carrying off women and children. They were especially averse to noise, from a recollection of the time when THOR used to be forever flinging his hammer after them.

**Trophonius** (trŏfō'niəs). An architect, celebrated in Greek legend as the builder of the Temple of Apollo at DELPHI. After his death he was deified, and had an ORACLE in a cave near Lebadeia, Boeotia, which was so awe-inspiring that those who entered and consulted the oracle never smiled again. Hence a melancholy or habitually terrified man was said to have visited the cave of *Trophonius*.

**Trows,** or **Drows.** DWARFS of Orkney and Shetland mythology, similar to the Scandinavian TROLLS. There are land-trows and sea-trows. 'Trow tak' thee' is a phrase still used by the island women when angry with their children.

> When I hung around the neck that gifted chain, which all in our isles know was wrought by no earthly artist, but by the Drows, in the secret recesses of their caverns, thou wert then but fifteen years old.
> SCOTT: *The Pirate*, ch. x.

**Troy.** The fortress city of Homer's ILIAD in the extreme north-west corner of Asia Minor overlooking the strait of the Dardanelles; also the land of Troy or the *Troad*, with Ilium as its chief city.

**The siege of Troy.** *See* ACHILLES; ILIAD; HELEN; TROJAN WAR; ULYSSES; WOODEN HORSE OF TROY (*under* HORSE), etc.

**Trygon.** *See* TELEGONUS.

**Tuatha De Danann** (too'əthə dā dah'nən).
A legendary race of superhuman heroes
which invaded Ireland, overthrew the
Firbolgs and Fomors, and were themselves
overthrown by the MILESIANS, who later
worshipped them as gods.

**Tuck, Friar.** *See* FRIAR TUCK.

**Tuneful Nine, The.** The nine MUSES.

> When thy young Muse invok'd the tuneful Nine,
> To say how Louis did not pass the Rhine,
> What Work had we with Wageninghen, Arnheim,
> Places that could not be reduced to Rhime?
> PRIOR: *Letter to Boileau Despréaux*, l.18
> (1704).

**Turkey.** The turkey was a sacred bird in the
Mayan, Toltec and Aztec traditions, being
the 'Jewelled Fowl', the 'Great Xolotl'. The
turkey and the DOG were both domesticated
in early Central and South American
societies and were also sacrificial animals.
The turkey represented self-sacrifice and
caring for others in Amerindian lore and
was called the 'give-away'. There was a
Turkey Dance at the New Fire Festival of
the Creek Indians.

In the seventeenth century the turkey
became the traditional food for Thanksgiving Day in North America, commemorating
the first harvest feast of the Pilgrim
Fathers, in 1621, when they ate four wild
turkeys. From America the turkey was introduced into England and became the
Christmas Day fare, largely replacing the
traditional goose or beef.

**Turpin.** Archbishop of Rheims, who appears
in several CHANSONS DE GESTE as a friend
and companion of CHARLEMAGNE. He was
formerly supposed to be the writer of the
*Historia de vita Caroli et Rolandi*. In the
*Chanson de Roland* Turpin dies with the
hero and is buried with him. He is most
likely the same as Tilpin, archbishop of
Rheims in the 8th century (*c.* 753–*c.* 800).
**Dick Turpin** (1705–1739). The 'King of
the Road' was born at the Bell Inn, Hemp-
stead, Essex, and apprenticed to a butcher
at Whitechapel at the age of 16. He soon
became a footpad to supplement his earn-
ings and, after his marriage in 1728, set up
as a butcher in Essex. He took to stocking
his shop with stolen cattle and sheep and,
on discovery, joined a gang of smugglers
near Canvey Island and there turned to

housebreaking with Gregory's Gang in
Epping Forest. In 1735 he became a highwayman working around the south of
London, and in 1736 began his partnership
with Tom King; his effrontery became a
public legend as did his activities in Epping
Forest and Hounslow Heath. After the
death of King in 1737, he shifted to Lincolnshire and thence to Yorkshire where he was
finally apprehended and hanged at the
Mount, outside the walls of York. The
legend of Black BESS and the ride to York
derives from Harrison Ainsworth's *Rookwood* (1834) although that of the ride has
historical precedents.

> And the fame of Dick Turpin had been something
> less
> If he'd ne'er rode to York on his bonnie Black
> Bess.
> ELIZA COOK: *Black Bess*.

**Tutankhamun's Curse.** *See under* CURSE.

**Tutivillus,** or **Titivil** (tūtivil'əs). The
demon of mediaeval legend who collects all
the words skipped over or mutilated by
priests in the celebration of the Mass.
These scraps or shreds he deposits in that
pit which is said to be paved with 'good intentions' never brought to effect.

**Tweedledum and Tweedledee.** Names invented by John Byrom (1692–1763) to satir-
ize two quarrelling schools of musicians
between whom the real difference was
negligible. Hence used of people whose
persons or opinions are 'as like as two
peas'.

> Some say compared to Bononcini
> That mynheer Handel's but a ninny;
> Others aver that he to Handel
> Is scarcely fit to hold a candle.
> Strange all this difference should be
> 'Twixt Tweedledum and Tweedledee.
> J. BYROM: *Feud between Handel and Bononcini*.

The Duke of Marlborough and most of the
nobility took the side of G. B. Bononcini (d.
*c.* 1752), but the Prince of Wales, with
Pope and Arbuthnot, was for Handel.

Lewis Carroll uses the names for two fat
little men in his *Through the Looking-Glass*.

**Twilight of the Gods.** *See* RAGNAROK.

**Twins, The.** *See* GEMINI.

**Twitcher, Jemmy.** A cunning, treacherous
highwayman in Gay's *Beggar's Opera*. The
name was given about 1765, in a poem by
Gray, to John, Lord Sandwich (1718–1792),

noted for his liaison with Miss Ray, who was shot by the Rev. 'Captain' Hackman out of jealousy.

**Twm Shon Catti** (toom shon kat'i). A kind of Welsh ROBIN HOOD who was born about 1530. He is mentioned in George Borrow's *Wild Wales*. There are many tales of his exploits and he is said to have eventually married an heiress and ended up as a squire and magistrate.

**Two.** The evil principle of Pythagoras. Accordingly the second day of the second month of the year was sacred to PLUTO, and was esteemed unlucky.

**Tylwyth Teg** (tŭl'with tāg) (Welsh *tylwyth*, family; *teg*, fair). The fairies of Welsh folklore, friendly but mischievous, who live in caves and on the mountains, who communicate by signs and never speak. They are versed in country lore, but if they touch iron, vanish away.

**Typhoeus** (tīfē'əs), or **Typhon** (tī'fon). A monster of Greek mythology, son of GAEA and TARTARUS, with a hundred heads, each with a terrible voice. He made war on ZEUS, who killed him with a THUNDERBOLT. According to one legend, he lies buried under Mount ETNA. By ECHIDNA he fathered ORTHOS, CERBERUS, the Lernaean HYDRA, the CHIMAERA, the Theban SPHINX and the NEMEAN LION. *See* SET.

**Tyr.** *See* TIU.

# U

**UFO** Unidentified flying object; the name given to objects claimed to have been sighted in the sky such as FLYING SAUCERS (*see under* SAUCER) etc., or picked up on radar screens, the exact nature of which is uncertain. Study and observation of UFOs is termed *ufology* by enthusiasts.

**Ugly Duckling.** An unpromising child who develops into a beautiful or handsome adult; also anything of an unprepossessing character that may change with time into something attractive. The expression is taken from Hans Andersen's story of the *Ugly Duckling* that endured many embarrassments but grew into a beautiful swan.

**Ultima Thule.** *See under* THULE.

**Ultor** (ŭl'taw) (Lat. the Avenger). A title given to MARS when, after defeating the murderers of Julius Caesar at Philippi, Augustus built a temple to him in the Forum at Rome.

**Ulysses,** or **Odysseus** (ū'lisēz, ōdis'iəs) ('the hater'). A mythical king of Ithaca, a small rocky island of Greece, one of the leading chieftains of the Greeks in Homer's ILIAD, and the hero of his ODYSSEY, represented by Homer as wise, eloquent, and full of artifices.

According to Virgil, it was he who suggested the device of the WOODEN HORSE (*see under* HORSE) through which TROY was ultimately taken. *See* TELEGONUS.

**Ulysses' Bow.** Only ULYSSES could draw his own bow, and he could shoot an arrow through 12 rings. By this sign PENELOPE recognized her husband after an absence of 20 years. He was also recognized by his dog, Argus.

The bow was prophetic. It belonged at one time to Eurytus of Oechalia.

**Uncle. Old Uncle Tom Cobleigh.** The last named of the seven village worthies who borrowed Tom Pearce's grey mare on which to ride to Widecombe Fair and whose names form the refrain of the famous ballad of that name which has become as much the county song of Devon as 'D'ye ken John Peel' is of Cumberland.

> When the wind whistles cold on the moor of a night,
> All along, down along, out along lee,
> Tom Pearce's old mare doth appear gashly white,
> Wi' Bill Brewer, Jan Stewer, Peter Gurney, Peter Davy, Dan'l Whidden, Harry Hawk, Old Uncle Tom Cobleigh and all,
> Old Uncle Tom Cobleigh and all.

**Uncle Remus** (rē'məs). The old plantation negro whose quaint and proverbial wisdom, and stories of Br'er Rabbit and BR'ER FOX, were related by Joel Chandler Harris (1848–1908) in *Uncle Remus, his Songs and Sayings* (1880), and *Nights with Uncle Remus* (1883).

**Undine** (ŭn'dēn). One of the elemental spirits of Paracelsus, the spirit of the waters. She was created without a soul; but had this privilege, that by marrying a mortal and bearing him a child she obtained a soul, and with it all the pains and penalties of the human race. She is the subject of a tale (*Undine*, 1811) by Friedrich de la Motte Fouqué (1777–1843). *Cp.* SYLPH.

**Unicorn** (Lat. *unum cornu*, one horn). A mythical and heraldic animal, represented by mediaeval writers as having the legs of a buck, the tail of a LION, the head and body of a HORSE, and a single horn, white at the base, black in the middle and red at the tip, in the middle of its forehead. The body is white, the head red and eyes blue. The earliest author that describes it is Ctesias (400 B.C.); the mediaeval notions concerning it are well summarized in the following extract:

> The unicorn has but one horn in the middle of its forehead. It is the only animal that ventures to attack the elephant; and so sharp is the nail of its foot, that with one blow it can rip the belly of the beast. Hunters can catch the unicorn only by

placing a young virgin in his haunts. No sooner does he see the damsel, than he runs towards her, and lies down at her feet, and so suffers himself to be captured by the hunters. The unicorn represents Jesus Christ, who took on Him our nature in the virgin's womb, was betrayed by the Jews and delivered into the hands of Pontius Pilate. Its one horn signifies the Gospel of Truth.
*Le Bestiaire Divin de Guillaume, Clerc de Normandie* (13th century).

Another popular belief was that the unicorn by dipping its horn into a liquid could detect whether or not it contained poison. In the designs for gold and silver plate made for the Emperor Rudolph II by Ottavio Strada is a cup on which a unicorn stands as if to assay the liquid.

The supporters of the old royal Arms of Scotland are two Unicorns; when James VI of Scotland came to reign over England (1603) he brought one of the Unicorns with him, and with it supplanted the RED DRAGON which, as representing Wales, was one of the supporters of the English shield, the other being the Lion.

The animosity which existed between the lion and the unicorn referred to by Spenser in his *Faerie Queene* (II, v, 10):

Like as a lyon, whose imperiall powre
A prowd rebellious unicorn defyes—

is allegorical of that which once existed between England and Scotland.

It also represents the conflict between the solar and lunar powers, depicted by the golden lion and the white unicorn, and all the pairs of opposites.

The mythology of, and belief in, the unicorn is worldwide and the animal has been depicted in paintings and sculptures from the East to the West from early times, but accounts differ greatly as to its size and temperament. In size it varied from a KID to a GAZELLE, a HORSE, or an ELEPHANT and in temperament it differed from the gentle and playful to the fierce and violent. Its horn also varied from a matter of inches to four feet in length. Caesar says the unicorn was the size of a bull but shaped like a stag, while Aelian. says it resembled a mature horse.

One of the oldest forms of the unicorn is the Chinese KY-LIN, a fabulous animal, one of the Four Spiritually Endowed or Auspicious Creatures which embody the Five Elements and is also a union of the *yin-yang* powers, the Ky being the masculine and *yang*, the Lin the *yin* and feminine. It was said to have appeared to the legendary Fü Hsi about the year 3000 B.C., coming up out of the Yellow River. Its appearance announced the birth or death of some great figure, such as the death of the Yellow Emperor and the birth of Confucius. It was a gentle creature, never striking with its horn; it symbolized longevity and all that was desirable or virtuous. Although the Ky-lin was a fabulous creature, travellers in Tibet said the unicorn actually occurred there in great numbers. The Abbé Huc, in the nineteenth century, said: 'The unicorn really exists in Tibet' where it was known as the Serou, or as the Kere in Mongolia. Genghis Khan was said to have seen one but in more modern times a British Major Latta, in 1820, said that beyond doubt the unicorn existed in Tibet and was called the Tso'po.

Graeco-Roman myth used the unicorn as an attribute of all virgin, lunar goddesses and the CHARIOT of ARTEMIS/DIANA was drawn by eight unicorns.

Arab tradition said that the unicorn appeared in the Temple of Mecca and Ethiopia had unicorns which were 'ferocious beasts, impossible to capture'.

Unicorn legend pervaded mediaeval literature as a fabulous creature, but accounts continued to occur of people seeing the traditional animal also in the West, where it was reported in Florida in 1564 and on the Canadian border in 1673.

There was a tradition that the unicorn existed in early times but perished in the FLOOD.

**Driving unicorn.** Two wheelers and one leader. The leader is the one horn.


**Uranus** (ū'rənəs). In Greek mythology, the personification of HEAVEN, son and husband of GAEA (Earth), and father of the TITANS, the CYCLOPS etc. He hated his children and confined them in the body of Earth who begged them to avenge her, and his son KRONOS unmanned him with a sickle and dethroned him.

**The planet Uranus** was discovered in 1781 by Herschel, and named by him *Georgium Sidus* in honour of George III. Its five satellites are named *Ariel, Umbriel, Titania, Oberon* and *Miranda*.

293

**Uriel** (ū'riəl). One of the seven ARCHANGELS of rabbinical angelology, sent by God to answer the questions of Esdras (II *Esdras* iv). In Milton's *Paradise Lost* (III, 690) he is the 'Regent of the Sun', and 'sharpest-sighted spirit of all in HEAVEN'.

**Urim and Thummim** (ū'rim, thŭm'im). Sacred LOTS of unknown nature used for DIVINATION by the ancient Hebrews as a means of ascertaining the will of God. They are mentioned in *Exod.* xxviii, 30; *Deut.* xxxiii, 8; I *Sam.* xxviii, 6; *Ezra* ii, 63, etc., but fell out of use as more spiritual conceptions of the Deity developed and there is no mention of them after the time of David.

**Ursula, St.** A 5th-century British princess, according to legend, who went with 11,000 virgins on a pilgrimage to Rome and was massacred with all her companions by the Huns at Cologne. One explanation of the story is that *Undecimilla* (mistaken for *unecim millia*, 11,000) was one of Ursula's companions.

**Utgard** (oot'gahd). In Scandinavian mythology, the abode of the giants, where Utgard-LOKI had his castle.

**Utopia.** Nowhere (Gr. *ou*, not; *topos*, a place). The name given by Sir Thomas More to the imaginary island in his political romance of the same name (1516), where everything is perfect—the laws, the morals, the politics etc., and in which the evils of existing laws etc. are shown by contrast.

Hence *Utopian*, applied to any idealistic but impractical scheme.

Rabelais (Bk. II, ch. xxiv) sends PANTA-GRUEL and his companions to Utopia, where they find the citizens of its capital, Amaurote, most hospitable.

# V

**Vagitanus.** *See* BABES, PROTECTING DEITIES OF.

**Valentine, St.** A priest of Rome who was imprisoned for succouring persecuted Christians. He became a convert and, although he is supposed to have restored the sight of the gaoler's blind daughter, he was clubbed to death (*c.* 270). His day is 14 February, as is that of St. Valentine, bishop of Terni, who was martyred a few years later. There are several other saints of this name.

The ancient custom of choosing *Valentines* has only accidental relation to either SAINT, being essentially a relic of the old Roman *Lupercalia* (*see* LUPERCAL), or from association with the mating season of birds. It was marked by the giving of presents and nowadays by the sending of a card on which CUPIDS, transfixed hearts etc. are depicted.

Chaucer refers to this in his *Assembly of Fowls* (310):

For this was on Saint Valentine's Day,
When ev'ry fowl cometh to choose her make,

and Shakespeare (*Midsummer Night's Dream*, IV, i) has:

Good morrow, friends! St. Valentine is past;
Begin these wood-birds but to couple now?

**Valentine and Orson.** An old French ROMANCE connected with the Carolingian cycle.

The heroes, from whom it is named, were the twin sons of Bellisant, sister of King Pepin, and Alexander, and were born in a forest near Orléans. Orson (Fr. *ourson*, a little bear) was carried off by a bear and became a wild man and the terror of France. While the mother was searching for him, Valentine was carried off by his uncle, the King. The brothers had many adventures and Orson was reclaimed by Valentine. Orson married Fezon, daughter

of Duke Savary of Aquitaine, and Valentine, Clerimond, sister of the Green Knight.

**Valhalla** (valhal'ə). In Scandinavian mythology, the hall in the celestial regions whither the souls of heroes slain in battle were borne by the VALKYRIES, to spend eternity in joy and feasting (*valr*, the slain, and *hall*).

Hence the name is applied to buildings, such as Westminster Abbey, used as the last resting-place of a nation's great men.

**Valkyries** (valkiə'riz). (Old Norse, the choosers of the slain). The nine (or seven, or twelve) handmaidens of ODIN, who, mounted on swift horses and holding drawn swords, rushed into the *mêlée* of battle and selected those destined to death. These heroes they conducted to VALHALLA, where they waited upon them and served them with mead and ale in the skulls of the vanquished.

**Vamana** (vah'manə). *See* AVATAR.

**Vampire.** A fabulous being, supposed to be the ghost of a heretic, criminal etc., who returned from the grave in the guise of a monstrous bat to suck the blood of sleeping persons who usually became vampires themselves. The only way to destroy them was to drive a stake through their body. The superstition is essentially Slavonic.

But first on earth, as vampire sent,
Thy corse shall from its tomb be rent,
Then ghastly haunt thy native place
And suck the blood of all thy race.
BYRON: *The Giaour*, 755.

The word is applied to one who preys upon his fellows—a 'blood-sucker'.

One of the classic horror stories, Bram Stoker's *Dracula* (1897), centres on vampirism. The Dracula of Transylvanian legend appears to originate from Vlad V of Wallachia (1456–1476), known as Vlad the Impaler, although he was not a vampire. It is suggested that Stoker's Count Dracula was a composite figure derived from Vlad the Impaler and the Countess Báthori, who was arrested in 1610 for murdering girls. It was her habit to wash in the blood of her several hundred girl victims in order to maintain her skin in a youthful condition. The name comes from Vlad's membership of the Order of the Dragon, although *dracul* in Romanian also means *devil*.

**Vanir** (vah'niə). A Scandinavian race of gods of peaceful and benevolent functions in contrast to the AESIR, who were essentially warriors. Among them were Njörd, FREYR, and FREYJA.

**Vanity Fair.** In Bunyan's *Pilgrim's Progress*, a fair established by BEELZEBUB, Apollyon and Legion, in the town of Vanity, and lasting all the year round. Here were sold houses, lands, trades, places, honours, preferments, titles, countries, kingdoms, lusts, pleasures and delights of all sorts.

Thackeray adopted the name for the title of his novel (1847) satirizing the weaknesses and follies of human nature.

**Varaha.** *See* AVATAR.

**Varuna** (va'runə). In Hindu mythology, the brother of Mitra, one of the ADITYAS. Varuna shines at night and is linked with the MOON. He is represented as a white man riding on a sea monster, is the witness of everything, orders the seasons and controls the rains. Mitra is linked with the sun and shines or sees by day.

The moon is the kingdom of the dead, over which, with YAMA, Varuna rules.

**Venus.** The Roman goddess of beauty and sensual love, identified with APHRODITE, in some accounts said to have sprung from the foam of the sea, in others to have been the daughter of JUPITER and DIONE, a NYMPH. VULCAN was her husband, but she had amours with MARS and many other gods and demigods. By MERCURY she was the mother of CUPID, and by the hero Anchises, the mother of AENEAS, through whom she was regarded by the Romans as the foundress of their race. Her chief festival is 1 April. *See* VENUS VERTICORDIA, *below*.

Her name is given to the second planet from the SUN (*see* HESPERUS), and in ASTROLOGY 'signifiethe white men or browne ... joyfull, laughter, liberall, pleasers, dauncers, entertayners of women, players, perfumers, musitions, messengers of love'.

Venus loveth ryot and dispence.
CHAUCER: *Wife of Bath's Prol.*, 700.

By the alchemists *copper* was designated *Venus*, probably because mirrors were anciently made of copper. A mirror is still the astronomical symbol of the planet Venus.

The best cast at dice (three sixes) used to be called *Venus*, and the worst (three aces), *Canis* (dog); hence the phrase, 'His Venus has turned out a whelp' equivalent to, 'all his swans are geese'.

**Venus Anadyomene.** VENUS rising from the sea, accompanied by dolphins. The name is given to the famous lost painting by APELLES, and to that by Botticelli in the Accademia delle Belle Arti at Florence.

**Venus Callipyge** (Gr., with the beautiful buttocks). The name given to a late Greek statue in the Museo Nazionale at Naples. There is no real ground for connecting the statue with VENUS.

**Venus de' Medici.** A famous statue, since 1860 in the Uffizi Gallery, Florence, ranking as a canon of female beauty. It is supposed to date from the time of AUGUSTUS, and was dug up in the 17th century in the villa of Hadrian, near Tivoli, in 11 pieces. It was kept in the Medici Palace at Rome till its removal to Florence by Cosimo III.

**Venus Genetrix** (Lat., she that has borne). VENUS worshipped as a symbol of marriage and motherhood. Caesar erected a temple to Venus Genetrix in the Forum at Rome and there are several statues of this name. She is represented as raising her light drapery and holding an apple, the emblem of fecundity.

**Venus of Cnidus.** The nude statue of Praxiteles, purchased by the ancient Cnidians, who refused to part with it, although Nicomedes, king of Bithynia, offered to pay off their national debt as its price. It was subsequently removed to Constantinople, and perished in the great fire during the reign of Justinian (A.D. 532); but an ancient reproduction is in the Vatican.

**Venus of Milo,** or **Melos.** This statue, with three of HERMES, was discovered by the French admiral Dumond d'Urville in Milo or Melos, one of the Greek islands. It dates from the 2nd century B.C. and is probably the finest single work of ancient art extant. It is now in the Louvre.

**Venus Verticordia.** One of the surnames of VENUS because she was invoked to 'turn the hearts' of women to virtue and chastity (Lat. *vertere*, to turn; *cor, cordis*, heart).

**Venus Victrix.** VENUS, as goddess of victory, represented on numerous Roman coins.

**Venus's Fly-trap.** A plant (*Dionaea muscipula*) which feeds on insects, and is found in Carolina.

**Venus's girdle.** The CESTUS.

**Venus's hair.** The maidenhair fern, *Adiantum capillus-Veneris*.

**Venus's hair-stone,** or **pencil.** Rock-crystal or quartz penetrated by acicular crystals of rutile which show through as hair-like filaments.

**Venus's Looking-glass** (*Specularia hybrida*). A rare small plant growing in the south and east of England on chalky soil. It has blue or purple flowers.

**Venusberg.** The Hörselberg, or mountain of delight and love, situated between Eisenach and Gotha, in the caverns of which, according to mediaeval German legend, the Lady Venus held her court. Human visitors were sometimes allowed in, such as Thomas of Ercildoune and TANNHÄUSER, but they ran the risk of eternal perdition. ECKHARDT the Faithful sat outside to warn them against entering.

**Verbena.** *See* VERVAIN.

**Vertumnus** (vœtŭm′nəs). The ancient Roman god of the seasons, and the deity presiding over gardens and orchards. He was the husband of POMONA. 12 August was his festival.

**Vervain** (vœ′văn). Called 'holy herb', from its use in ancient rites. Also called 'pigeons' grass', 'Juno's tears', and 'simpler's joy'. *Verbena* is its botanical name. *See* HERBA SACRA.

**Vesta.** The virgin goddess of the hearth in Roman mythology, corresponding to the Greek Hestia, one of the 12 great Olympians. She was custodian of the sacred fire brought by AENEAS from TROY, which was never permitted to go out lest a national calamity should follow.

**Vestals.** The six spotless virgins who tended the sacred fire brought by AENEAS from TROY, and preserved by the state in a sanctuary in the Forum at Rome. They were chosen by lot from maidens between the ages of six and ten and served under strict discipline for 30 years, after which they were free to marry, although few took this step. In the event of their losing their virginity they were buried alive.

The word *vestal* has been figuratively applied by poets to any woman of spotless chastity. Shakespeare bestowed the epithet on Elizabeth I.

A fair vestal enthroned by the west.
*A Midsummer Night's Dream*, II, i.

**Veto** (Lat. I forbid). Louis XVI and Marie Antoinette were called *Monsieur* and *Madame Veto* by the Republicans, because the Constituent Assembly (1791) allowed the king to have the power, which he abused, of putting his veto upon any decree submitted to him.

**Vidar** (vē′dah). In Scandinavian mythology, a son of ODIN, noted for his taciturnity and fearless destruction of FENRIR.

**Vinalia** (vinā′liə). Roman wine festivals in honour of JUPITER and also associated with VENUS as a goddess of vineyards. The first such festival was held on 23 April when the wine of the previous season was broached and the second on 19 August when the vintage began (Lat. *vinalis*, pertaining to wine).

**Viraj.** *See* MANU.

**Virgo** (Lat. Virgin). One of the ancient constellations and the sixth sign of the ZODIAC (23 August–22 September). The constellation is the metamorphosis of ASTRAEA. *See also* ICARIUS.

**Vishnu** (vish′noo). The Preserver; the second in the Hindu TRIMURTI, though worshipped by many Hindus as the supreme deity. He originally appears as sun-god. He is beneficent to man and has ten incarnations, the ninth being as the Buddha, while the tenth is to come when he will appear in his final incarnation as KALKI, the White Horse, on which he will come from the sky and will establish the new age of rebirth when all wrongs will be righted. (*See* AVATAR.) He is usually represented as four-armed and carrying a mace, a conch-shell, a disc and a LOTUS, and often riding the EAGLE Garuda. His wife is LAKSHMI, born from the sea.

**Vitus, St.** (vī'təs). A Sicilian youth who was martyred with Modestus, his tutor, and Crescentia, his nurse, during the Diocletian persecution, *c*. 303.

**St. Vitus's Dance.** In Germany in the 17th century it was believed that good health for the year could be secured by anyone who danced before a statue of St. VITUS on his feast-day; such dancing to excess is said to have come to be confused with chorea, hence its name, *St. Vitus's Dance*, the SAINT being invoked against it.

**Vixere fortes ante Agamemnona.** *See under* AGAMEMNON.

**Volund** (vō'lund). *See* WAYLAND.

**Voodoo,** or **Voodooism.** A mixture of superstition, magic, WITCHCRAFT, serpent-worship etc., derived from African rites and some Christian beliefs. It still survives among some Negro groups in Haiti, and other parts of the West Indies and the Americas.

The name is said to have been first given to it by missionaries, from Fr. *Vaudois*, a Waldensian, as these were accused of sorcery; but Sir Richard Burton derived it from *vodun*, a dialect form of Ashanti *obosum*, a fetish or tutelary spirit. *Cp*. OBEAH.

**Vulcan.** A son of JUPITER and JUNO, and GOD of fire, and the working of metals, and patron of handicraftsmen in metals, identified with the Gr. Hephaestus, and called also MULCIBER, *i.e.* the softener.

His workshops were under Mount ETNA and other volcanoes where the CYCLOPS assisted him in forging thunderbolts for JOVE. It is said that he took the part of Juno against Jupiter who hurled him out of HEAVEN. He was nine days in falling and was saved by the people of Lemnos from crashing to earth, but one leg was broken, hence his lameness. VENUS was his wife and, in consequence of her amour with MARS, he came to be regarded as the special patron of cuckolds. He was the father of CUPID and the Cecrops, and created PANDORA from clay.

**Vulcanist.** One who supports the Vulcanian or Plutonian theory, which ascribes the changes on the Earth's surface to the agency of fire. These theorists say the earth was once in a state of igneous fusion, and that the crust has gradually cooled down to its present temperature. *Cp*. NEPTUNIAN.

**Vulture.** There was an early belief that all vultures were either parthenogenic or female, if the latter the male was a HAWK. Vultures represented maternal instinct and caring and there was a legend that the mother fed the young on her own blood; this was later said also of the PELICAN.

The Egyptian High Priest Horapollo said: 'The vulture is the type of merciful man because if food cannot be obtained for its young it opens its thigh and permits them to partake of its blood.' The bird is an emblem of ISIS, who once took this form, and is also sacred to Mat as goddess of maternity; she can be depicted as vulture-headed or with a vulture headdress. HATHOR can also be vulture-headed and Nekhabet of Southern Egypt sometimes appears as a vulture. The bird was known as 'Pharaoh's Hen', representing the feminine principle associated with the SCARAB as the male.

In Graeco-Roman myth the vulture is associated with PALLAS, ARES/MARS and APOLLO and is the mount of KRONOS/SATURN. HERCULES slew the vulture which tore the liver of PROMETHEUS and the bird was sacred to him. HARPIES were represented as having the body of a vulture with the head and breast of a woman.

There was a legend that the vulture, like the EAGLE, did not lay eggs but gave birth to fully-fledged live young. Aelian says that sweet perfume kills vultures and that myrrh and pomegranates are also fatal. The claw of a vulture, like the horn of a UNICORN, detects the presence of poison in food or drink.

Zoroastrianism uses the vulture in funeral rites as cleaning the corpses in the *Towers of Silence* and it is called the 'Compassionate Purifier'.

The Griffin Vulture was a royal emblem on the standards of Assyrian and Persian armies. There was an Arabian vulture god Nasr. In West Africa the vulture Fene-Ma-So is the Bird of the Sky, the King of the Birds.

# W

**Wagoner.** *See* BOÖTES.

**Wagtail.** In Indian mythology the wagtail bears a holy caste mark and is a prophetic bird used in DIVINATION; the direction from which it appears and its proximity to other objects are of import, near a LOTUS, ELEPHANT, HORSE, COW or SERPENT it is propitious, by bones, ashes or refuse it bodes ill.

In Japan wagtails are sacred to Izanagi and Izanami who were instructed in love by them and they are an attribute of the divine pair. Ainu legend says that the earth was originally a sterile quagmire but the Creator sent wagtails down to beat the earth with their wings and tails until it became hardened and elevated in places so that the water drained off and the land became suitable for the people. The water-wagtail is the CUPID of the Ainu myth and its feathers and bones are love charms.

**Walhalla.** *See* VALHALLA.

**Walpurgis Night** (valpuə'gis). The eve of MAY DAY, when the witch-world was supposed to hold high revelry under its chief, the DEVIL, on certain high places, particularly the Brocken, the highest point of the Harz Mountains. Walpurgis was an English nun who went as a missionary to Germany and became abbess of Heidenheim (d. *c.* 788). Her day is 1 May, hence her coincidental association with the rites of an earlier pagan festival.

**Walpurgis oil.** A bituminous kind of oil exuding from the rock at Eichstatt in which the relics of St. Walpurgis were deposited. It was supposed to have miraculous healing and curative properties.

**Wandering Jew, The.** The central figure of the widespread later-mediaeval legend which tells of a Jew who insulted or spurned Christ when He was bearing the cross to Calvary, and was condemned to wander over the face of the earth till Judgment Day.

The usual form of the legend says that he was Ahasuerus, a cobbler, who refused to allow Christ to rest at his door, saying, 'Get off! Away with you, away!' Our Lord replied, 'Truly I go away, and that quickly, but tarry thou till I come.'

An earlier tradition has it that the Wandering Jew was Cartaphilus, the door-keeper of the judgment hall in the service of Pontius Pilate. He struck our Lord as he led Him forth, saying, 'Go on faster, Jesus'; whereupon the Man of Sorrows replied, 'I am going, but thou shalt tarry till I come again.' (*Chronicle of St. Alban's Abbey*, 1228). The same Chronicle, continued by Matthew Paris, tells us that Cartaphilus was baptized by Ananias, and received the name of Joseph. At the end of every hundred years he falls into a trance, and wakes up a young man about 30.

In German legend he is associated with John Buttadaeus, seen at Antwerp in the 13th century, again in the 15th, and the third time in the 16th. His last appearance was in 1774 at Brussels. In the French version he is named Isaac Laquedom or Lakedion; another story has it that he was Salathiel ben-Sadi, who appeared and disappeared towards the close of the 16th century at Venice, in so sudden a manner as to attract the notice of all Europe; and another connects him with the WILD HUNTSMAN.

> 'I'll rest, sayd hee, but thou shalt walke;'
> So doth this wandring Jew
> From place to place, but cannot rest
> For seeing countries newe.
> PERCY: *Reliques* (*The Wandering Jew*).

There are several plants called *The Wandering Jew*.

**Wantley, The Dragon of.** An old story, preserved in Percy's *Reliques*, tells of this monster who was slain by More of More Hall. He procured a suit of armour studded with spikes, and kicked the DRAGON in the backside, where alone it was vulnerable. Percy says the Dragon stands for a greedy renter of the Tithes of the Wortley family who attempted to take the tithes in kind from the parishioners and More was the man who conducted the suit against him. There are other theories. Wantley is Wharncliffe in Yorkshire.

**Warlock.** An evil spirit; a WIZARD. O.E. *waerloga*, a traitor, one who breaks his word.

**Warrior Queen, The.** BOADICEA.

**Wayland Smith.** The English form of the Scandinavian Volund (Ger. *Wieland*), a wonderful and supernatural smith and lord of the elves (*see* ELF), a kind of VULCAN. The legend is found in the Edda and is alluded to in BEOWULF. He was bound apprentice to Mimir, the smith. King Nidung cut the sinews in his feet in order to retain his services but he eventually flew away in a feather robe which had been first tested out by his brother EGIL. The legend has much in common with that of DAEDALUS.

Tradition has placed his forge in a megalithic monument known as *Wayland Smith's Cave* near the WHITE HORSE in Berkshire, where it was said that if a traveller tied up his horse there, left sixpence for fee, and retired from sight, he would find the horse shod on his return.

Neither the tradition of Alfred's Victory, or of the celebrated Pusey Horn, are better preserved in Berkshire than the wild legend of Wayland Smith.

SCOTT: *Kenilworth*, ch. xiii.

**Weasel.** The weasel was sacred in Egypt and Aelian says that the Thebans worshipped it, but in China it was one of the dreaded Five Animals which can bewitch people.

Among the Amerindians the weasel is a creature of stealth, ingenuity and insight; it can hear everything that is said and can detect the inner meanings. It was the weasel that foretold the coming of the white men and the disaster they would bring. There are short-tailed and long-tailed weasels who are siblings.

The weasel and the COCK are the only creatures capable of killing the BASILISK who is afraid of them.

The flesh of the weasel, salted,

powdered and drunk in wine was a cure for snake bite.

**Web. The Web of Life.** The destiny of an individual from the cradle to the grave. An allusion to the three FATES who, according to Roman mythology, spin the thread of life, the pattern being the events which are to occur.

**Wedding Finger.** The fourth finger of the left hand. Macrobius says the thumb is too busy to be set apart, the forefinger and little finger are only half protected, the middle finger is called *medicus*, and is too opprobrious for the purpose of honour, so the only finger left is the *pronubus*.

Aulus Gellius tells us that Appianus asserts in his Egyptian books that a very delicate nerve runs from the fourth finger on the left hand to the heart, on which account this finger is used for the marriage ring.

The finger on which the ring [the wedding-ring] is to be worn is the fourth finger on the left hand, next unto the little finger; because by the received opinion of the learned ... in ripping up and anatomising men's bodies, there is a vein of blood, called *vena amoris*, which passeth from that finger to the heart.

HENRY SWINBURNE: *Treaties of Spousals* (1680).

In the Roman Catholic Church, the thumb and next two fingers represent the Trinity; thus the bridegroom says, 'In the name of the Father,' and touches the thumb; 'in the name of the Son,' and touches the index finger; and 'in the name of the Holy Ghost,' and he touches the long or third finger; with the word 'Amen' he then puts the ring on the fourth finger and leaves it there. In some countries the wedding ring is worn on the right hand; this was the custom generally in England until the end of the 16th century, and among Roman Catholics until much later.

In the Hereford, York and Salisbury missals, the ring is directed to be put first on the thumb, then on the index finger, then on the long finger, and lastly on the ring-finger, *quia in illo digito est quaedam vena procedens usque ad cor*.

**Weeping.** A notion long prevailed in this country that it augured ill for future married happiness if the bride did not weep profusely at the wedding.

As no WITCH could shed more than three tears, and those from her left eye only, a copious flow of tears gave assurance to the husband that the lady had not 'plighted her troth' to SATAN, and was no witch.

**Werewolf, or Werwolf.** A 'man-wolf' (O.E. *wer*, man), *i.e.* a man who, according to ancient superstition, was turned—or could at will turn himself—into a WOLF (the *loupgarou* of France). It had the appetite of a wolf, and roamed about at night devouring infants and sometimes exhuming corpses. Its skin was proof against shot or steel, unless the weapon had been blessed in a chapel dedicated to St. HUBERT.

Ovid tells the story of LYCAON, King of ARCADIA, turned into a wolf because he tested the divinity of JUPITER by serving up to him a 'hash of human flesh'; Herodotus describes the Neuri as having the power of assuming once a year the shape of wolves; Pliny relates that one of the family of ANTAEUS was chosen annually, by lot, to be transformed into a wolf, in which shape he continued for nine years; and St. PATRICK, we are told, converted Vereticus, King of Wales, into a wolf.

Hence the term *lycanthropy* (Gr. *lukos*, wolf; *anthropos*, man) for this supposed transformation and for the form of insanity in which the subject exhibits depraved animal traits.

Tigers, hyenas and leopards had the same associations in other parts of the world, and after the disappearance of the wolf in England WITCHES were commonly 'transformed' into cats.

**Whale.** The whale, like the TORTOISE, is one of the animals said to support the earth. Arabic tradition says that the earth rests on the back of a whale and that earthquakes are caused by its movements. Russia has the same myth and in Slav lore four whales support the world. There is also a legend that the back of the whale could be mistaken for an island and that sailors would land on it and light fires to cook food; feeling the heat the whale could plunge under the waves and the sailors would drown. This story occurs in *The Arabian Nights* and is also used by the Physiologus and the Bestiaries to illustrate the DEVIL luring people to destruction.

The Belly-of-the-Whale myth of Jonah in the Bible is typical of the initiation rites of death and rebirth. The jaws of the whale are the Gates of Hell. Origen says that great whales represent violent passions and criminal impulses. The belly theme occurs among the Innuits (Eskimos) in the myth of RAVEN as trickster. There are northern whale festivals and there is a Killer Whale clan.

In Norse legend whales have magic powers and can be the mount of witches.

**Wheel. The wheel of Fortune.** Fortuna, the goddess, is represented on ancient monuments with a wheel in her hand, emblematical of her inconstancy.

> Though fortune's malice overthrow my state,
> My mind exceeds the compass of her wheel.
> SHAKESPEARE: Henry VI, *Pt. III*, iv, iii.

*See also* PRAYING-WHEEL, *below*.

**Whetstone.** *See* ACCIUS NAEVIUS.
**Lying for the whetstone.** Said of a person who is grossly exaggerating or falsifying a statement. One of the Whitsun amusements of our forefathers was the lie-wage or lie-match; he who could tell the greatest lie was rewarded with a whetstone to sharpen his wit. The nature of these contests may be illustrated by the following: one of the combatants declared he could see a fly on the top of a church steeple; the other replied, 'Oh, yes, I saw him wink his eye.'

**White. White Lady.** A kind of spectre, the appearance of which generally forebodes death in the house. It is a relic of Teutonic mythology, representing HULDA or BERCHTA, the goddess who received the SOULS of maidens and young children. She is dressed in white and carries a bunch of keys at her side.

The first recorded instance of this apparition was in the 15th century, and the name given to the lady is Bertha von Rosenberg. She last appeared, it is said, in 1879. German legend says that when the castle of Neuhaus, Bohemia, was being built a white lady appeared and promised the workmen a sweep soup and a carp on the completion of the castle. In remembrance thereof, these dainties were for long given to the poor on MAUNDY THURSDAY.

In Normandy the White Ladies lurk in ravines, fords, bridges etc., and ask the wayfarer to dance, and if refused fling him into a ditch. The most famous of these ladies are *La Dame d'Aprigny*, who used to occupy the site of the Rue St. Quentin, at Bayeux, and *La Dame Abonde*.

The *White Lady of Avenel*, in Scott's *The Monastery*, is based upon these legends.

**White magic.** Sorcery in which the DEVIL is not invoked and plays no part, as distinct from *black* magic.

**White witch.** One who practises WHITE MAGIC only.

**Whittington, Dick.** According to the popular legend and PANTOMIME story, a poor boy who made his way to London when he heard that the streets were paved with gold and silver. He found shelter as a scullion in the house of a rich merchant who permitted each of his servants to partake in sending a cargo of merchandise to Barbary. Dick sent his CAT, but subsequently ran away owing to ill-treatment below stairs. He was recalled by Bow Bells seeming to say:

Turn again Whittington
Thrice Lord Mayor of London.

He returned to find his cat had been purchased for a vast sum by the King of Barbary, who was much plagued by rats and mice. He married his master's daughter Alice, prospered exceedingly, and became thrice Lord Mayor.

In fact, he was the youngest son of Sir William Whittington of Pauntley in Gloucestershire and duly became a mercer of London, having married Alice, the daughter of Sir Ivo Fitzwaryn. He became very wealthy, the richest merchant of his day, and was made Lord Mayor of London in 1397–1398, 1406–1407, and 1419–1420. He died in 1423 leaving his vast wealth for charitable and public purposes.

The part of the cat in the story has been carefully explained: that he traded in coals brought to London in *cats* (a type of sailing-vessel), and that it is a confusion with Fr. *achat*, 'purchase' (a term then used for trading at a profit). Whatever be the truth, Dick Whittington and his cat are now inseparables.

**Wieland.** *See* WAYLAND SMITH.

**Wiggen tree.** *See* ROWAN.

**Wild. Wild Boy.** *See* GAZELLE BOY.

**The Wild Huntsman.** A spectral hunter of mediaeval legend, who with a pack of spectral dogs frequents certain forests and occasionally appears to mortals. It takes numerous forms in Germany, France and England, and the wild huntsman is often identified with various heroes of national legend. In England, there is notably Herne the Hunter, one-time keeper in Windsor Forest. Shakespeare says he 'walks' in winter-time, about midnight, blasts trees and takes cattle. He wears horns and rattles a chain (*Merry Wives of Windsor*, IV, iv). Herne is also featured in Harrison Ainsworth's *Windsor Castle*. *See* HERNE OAK *under* OAK.

There is a Midnight Hunter of Dartmoor accompanied by the WISH HOUNDS. *Cp.* GABRIEL'S HOUNDS; MAUTHE DOG.

The Wild Hunt also rides through the air on stormy nights or, in Norse legend, on New Year's Eve. The object of the hunt varies from lost souls to visionary animals of the hunt such as a wild BOAR, white HORSE, white breasted maiden, or NYMPHS. The Norse and Teutonic Wild Hunt was led by ODIN/WODEN, the original Wild Huntsman, or by the Erl King. The hunt was an omen of death. The hunt can also be led by various sinister characters such as Herod or Cain, though King ARTHUR was also said to ride with a pack.

An English tradition was that a little black DOG could be left behind, cowering and whining on the hearth and, unless exorcized, it had to be fed for a year.

**Will-o'-the-wisp.** *See* IGNIS FATUUS.

**William. St. William of Norwich** (1132–1144). A tanner's apprentice of Norwich, alleged to have been crucified and murdered by Jews during the Passover. It was said at the time that it was part of Jewish ritual to sacrifice a Christian every year. (*See* Drayton's *Poly-Olbion*, song xxiv.)

**William Tell.** *See* TELL.

**Winchester.** Identified by Malory and other old writers with the CAMELOT of ARTHURIAN ROMANCE. It was King Alfred's capital. *See also* SWITHIN.

**Wind.** According to classical mythology, the north, south, east and west winds (BOREAS, *Notus*, EURUS and ZEPHYRUS) were under the rule of AEOLUS, who kept them confined in a cave on Mount Haemus, Thrace. Other strong winds of a more destructive nature were the brood of TYPHOEUS.

The story says that Aeolus gave ULYSSES a bag tied with a silver string, in which were all the hurtful and unfavourable winds, so that he might arrive home without being delayed by tempests. His crew, however, opened the bag in the belief that it contained treasure, the winds escaped, and a terrible storm at once arose, driving the vessel out of its course and back to the island of Aeolus.

*Aquilo* is another Latin name for the north wind, as *Auster* is of the south and FAVONIUS of the west. *Thrascias* is a north-north-west wind and *Libs* a west-south-west wind, *Caurus* or *Corus* a north-west wind (also personified as *Argestes*), *Volturnus* a south-east wind and *Africus* and *Afer ventus* a south-west wind.

> Boreas and Caecias, and Argestes loud,
> And Thrascias rend the woods, and seas upturn...
> Notus and Afer, black with thunderous clouds,
> From Serraliona; thwart of these, as fierce,
> Forth rush...Eurus and Zephyr...
> Sirocco and Libecchio.
> MILTON: *Paradise Lost*, X, 699–706.

**Wine of Ape.** In Chaucer's Prologue to the *Manciple's Tale*, the Manciple says, 'I trow that ye have drunken wine of ape'—*i.e.* wine to make you foolishly drunk; in French *vin de singe*. According to Rabbinical tradition SATAN came to Noah when he was planting vines, and slew a *lamb*, a *lion*, a *pig* and an *ape*, to teach Noah that man, in turn, reveals the characteristics of all four according to the amount of liquor consumed.

**Winkle, Rip Van.** *See* RIP VAN WINKLE.

**Wise Men of Gotham.** *See* GOTHAM.

**Wish. Wish Hounds,** or **Yell Hounds.** Spectral hounds that hunt the wildest parts of Dartmoor on moonless nights, urged on by the 'Midnight Hunter of the Moor' on his huge horse which breathes fire and flame. The baying of these hounds, held by some to be headless, if heard, spells death to the hearer within the year. The Abbot's Way, an ancient track across the southern part of the moor, is said to be their favourite path. *See* WILD HUNTSMAN.

**Wishing Cap.** *See* FORTUNATUS.

**Witchcraft.** (O.E. *wiccian*, to practise sorcery). Belief in witchcraft, prevalent into the 18th century and later, was a legacy from pagan times and is found in the Bible

(*see* WITCH OF ENDOR). DIVINATION of all kinds was a fundamental aspect of witchcraft. Even St. Augustine believed in it; in 1258, Pope Alexander IV instructed the Inquisition to deal with witchcraft when allied to heresy and Innocent VIII's celebrated bull (*Summis Desiderantes*, 1484) encouraged the Inquisition to severe measures against witches. Countless people suffered death from this superstition, especially old women. Witchcraft was made a felony in England in 1542, causing death by witchcraft became a capital offence in 1563, and in the same year witchcraft became subject to the death penalty in Scotland.

Witch-hunting was a particular pastime of 17th-century Presbyterians until after the Restoration. The notorious 'witch-finder' Matthew Hopkins travelled through the eastern counties in the 1640s to hunt out witches and is said to have hanged 60 in one year in Essex alone. In 1647 he was tested by his own methods; when cast into the river, he floated, and so was hanged as a WIZARD.

The last trial for witchcraft in England occurred in 1712, and in Scotland in 1722. English and Scottish laws against witchcraft were repealed in 1736.

**Witch balls.** The popular name for the lustred glass globes in use since the 16th century as domestic ornaments. They mirror in miniature the contents of a room, and the name is probably a fanciful corruption of *watch* ball. The inside of the ball was usually coated with a preparation largely made up of mercury. It was also said that they could be carried on a stick over the shoulder to see if a witch were following.

**The Witch of Endor.** The woman who had 'a familiar spirit' through whom Saul sought communication with the dead Samuel. She brought Samuel up 'out of the earth' (a classic case of NECROMANCY) having first secured a promise from Saul that he would take no action against her as a witch (*see* I *Sam.* xxviii).

**The Witch of Wookey.** *See* WOOKEY HOLE.

**Witches' Sabbath.** A midnight meeting of witches, demons etc., supposed to have been held annually. Mediaeval devotees of the witchcraft cult held sabbaths at Candlemas, Roodmas, Lammas and ALL HALLOWS' EVE, and their celebrations lasted until dawn. The rites were led by the

'Coven', a group of 12 members and one DEVIL.

**Witch-hunting.** In political usage it denotes the searching out and exposure of opponents alleged to be disloyal to the State, often amounting to persecution.

**Witchen.** *See* ROWAN.

**Wivern** (wī'vœn). A fabulous creature of heraldry consisting of a winged DRAGON ending in a barbed, serpent's tail.

**Wizard.** A magician, one adept in the black arts; the male counterpart of a WITCH. It is derived from *wise*.

*Wizard* is popularly used to express admiration etc., as, *a wizard performance*, a wonderful performance; *absolutely wizard*, absolutely splendid.

**Wolf.** The wolf can appear in either an evil or beneficent guise in mythology; in its malefic form it is associated with destruction, death and gods of the dead: as a totem animal or protector it is venerated and worshipped.

The Egyptian god Upuat or Ap-uat is depicted either as a wolf or wolf- or jackal-headed, he was also Khenti Amenti, associated with OSIRIS as Lord of the Dead, he was a psychopomp, conducting souls through the Gates of the West at death and also guiding the barque of the sun.

There was a cult of the wolf in ARCADIA and Plato and Pausanias speak of the rites of ZEUS Lycaeus in which the animal was sacrificed and eaten and its essence absorbed by the devotees who became one with it and called themselves 'Lukoi'. Aelian says that the wolf was worshipped by the Delphians and associated with APOLLO and there was a bronze image of a wolf at DELPHI. The animal was also sacred to ARES/MARS and Silvanus. In the legend of the founding of Rome, the twins Romulus and Remus were suckled by a wolf and the animal appeared prominently in Roman art and gave its name to the LUPERCALIA. The Latin 'lupa', the she-wolf represented a prostitute and the wolf's lair, the 'lupanar', was a brothel. Pliny and Plato recount the myth that if a wolf is seen by a man with its mouth shut it loses the power of opening it again, but if the wolf sees the man first with his mouth shut he loses his voice. The myth was carried over into the Physiologus and the Bestiaries.

Both Hinduism and Zoroastrianism hold the wolf as evil. In the former it represents darkness and evil and the Asvins rescue the QUAIL of the day from the wolf of the night, while in the latter it is the legionary of AHRIMAN and is the 'flatterer, the deadly wolf', depicting also the evil in human nature.

The Bible represents the wolf as destructive (*Jeremiah* v, 6) and as dishonesty and bloodshed (*Ezekiel* xxii, 27; *Zephaniah* iii, 3); and Christianity associates it with the DEVIL and 'ravening wolves' depict false prophets. The wolf is also associated with stiff-necked people as it was believed the animal could not turn its neck. St Francis tamed the wolf Gubbio and it is one of his emblems.

Celtic and Irish legend portray the wolf as a helpful animal, having much in common with the DOG. Deities and heroes could manifest as wolves and in Celtic art Cernunnos, as Lord of the Animals, is accompanied by a wolf among other animals. An Irish tribe claimed descent from a wolf and Cormac, King of Ireland, like Romulus and Remus, was suckled by a wolf.

The wolf appears in a dual role in Teutonic and Norse myth, it is a bringer of victory as ridden by ODIN/WODEN, but the FENRIS wolf or Fenrir, is the epitome of evil and one of the monsters created by LOKI. He was captured but will return at RAGNAROK and will be vanquished ultimately by VIDAR. Two wolves, Sköll and Hati, accompanying Odin, depict repulsion and hatred and they incessantly pursue the sun and moon in an attempt to plunge the world into darkness. Wolves are ridden across the sky by the VALKYRIES. Wolf-headed men appear in Norse art.

Amerindian culture has numerous, wolf tribes and clans; the animal is associated with Sirius, the Dog Star, the home of the gods, and is a path-finder and teacher. It is an ally of the moon and has psychic powers. The soul of a hunter can pass into the realm of wolves and some tribes claim descent from wolves who are culture heroes or brothers of the hero, while the Innuits (Eskimos) have a Great Wolf Amarok.

Wolves can appear as were-animals and in Armenian legend can be a form taken by witches and warlocks who can also ride wolves. *See* WEREWOLF.

**To cry 'Wolf!'** To give a false alarm. The

allusion is to the fable of the shepherd lad who so often called 'Wolf!' merely to make fun of the neighbours, that when at last the wolf came no one would believe him. This fable appears in almost every nation the world over.

**Wonder. The Seven Wonders of the World.** In the ancient world:
The Pyramids of Egypt.
The HANGING GARDENS OF BABYLON.
The Tomb of Mausolus (Mausoleum).
The Temple of DIANA at Ephesus.
The COLOSSUS of Rhodes.
The Statue of JUPITER by Phidias.
The Pharos of Alexandria.
A later list gives:
The Coliseum of Rome.
The Catacombs of Alexandria.
The Great Wall of China.
Stonehenge.
The Leaning Tower of Pisa.
The Porcelain Tower of Nanking.
The Mosque of San Sophia at Constantinople (Istanbul).

**Wood. The Wooden Horse.** *See under* HORSE.

**Woodpecker.** The woodpecker can be a form taken by ZEUS/JUPITER and was also sacred ARES/MARS as representing war; it was also an attribute of Silvanus, Tiora and Triptolemus. A woodpecker watched over and fed the infant ROMULUS and Remus while the WOLF suckled them.

The red mark on the bird signifies fire in Indo-European myth, as does its tapping and striking on wood. It is the Aryan bird of the storm clouds and depicts war and sudden attack.

The war association also occurs in Amerindian tradition and the woodpecker is the totem animal of the Omaha tribe.

The Bestiaries call the bird the Picus and it represents DIVINATION as used by Picus, son of SATURN. Christianity equates the woodpecker with the DEVIL and heretics. In England it is called the Yaffle and is a rain prophet.

There was a tradition that the woodpecker and the QUAIL are at enmity.

**Wookey Hole.** A famous cavern near Wells in Somerset, which has given rise to numerous legends. *Wicked as the Witch of Wookey* is an old local simile. Her repulsiveness led to her directing her spells against 'the youth of either sex' as well as blasting every plant and blistering every flock. She was turned into a stone by a 'lerned wight' from 'Glaston' but left her curse behind, since the girls of Wookey found 'that men are wondrous scant'.

Here's beauty, wit and sense combin'd,
With all that's good and virtuous join'd
Yet hardly one gallant.
PERCY: *Reliques* (*The Witch of Wookey*).

**Worm.** The word was formerly used of DRAGONS and great SERPENTS, especially those of Teutonic and old Norse legend; it is now figuratively applied to miserable, grovelling creatures; also to the ligament under a dog's tongue.

**Wormwood.** The common name for the aromatic herbs of the genus *Artemisia*, especially *A. absinthium*, from which absinthe and vermouth are concocted. Culpeper recommends it as a specific against worms. It is said to have been so called because this plant, according to legend, sprang up in the track of the SERPENT as it writhed along the ground when driven out of PARADISE. The word is also used figuratively to denote bitterness or its cause.

**Wren.** The wren is known as the King of the Birds, a title which, according to Teutonic legend, it gained by deceit in a contest. It was decided that the bird which flew nearest the sun should be king. The EAGLE naturally reached the highest point but the wren had hidden itself on the eagle's back and so was nearer the sun.

The wren has an ambivalent significance, being on the one hand a WITCHES' bird, yet its feathers are a charm against witchcraft, and on the other hand the wren can take the place of the DOVE as Spirit.

In Celtic lore the wren is prophetic and omens were read from the direction from which it called. It is the Druidic King of the Birds and was sacred to TALIESIN as it was also to the Greek Triptolemus.

Although generally it is unlucky to kill a wren there was a earlier ceremony of hunting the wren on St. Stephen's Day, 26 December, though the origin of the hunt rose from an ancient pre-Christian rite. Ritually-dressed hunters killed a wren, hung it on a pole, and went in procession, demanding largesse, then burying the wren in the churchyard. A different origin for the hunt was seen in the Norse Yule legend when a SIREN who lured men into the sea was hunted but escaped in the form of a wren; it returned once a year and was hunted and killed.

In Brittany the killing of a wren brought disaster to the flocks and the killer would be either struck by lightning or his fingers would drop off. Anyone touching the young in the nest would be stricken by the Fire of St. Lawrence rash.

In Scotland the bird was the Lady of Heaven's Hen and it was extremely unlucky to kill one.

The wren is lucky in Japan and the Ainus, when out hunting, salute it as a tiny god which brought fire from heaven.

**Wyvern.** A mythical creature, the wyvern, from the Saxon 'wyvere', a SERPENT, is a DRAGON with wings and a serpentine body, but it has only two legs, formed like talons. It is frequently seen in heraldry and represents war, pestilence, envy and viciousness. Depicted without wings it is the Lindworm.

# X

**Xanthus,** or **Xanthos** (zan'thəs) (Gr. reddish-yellow). ACHILLES' wonderful HORSE, brother of Balios, Achilles' other horse, and offspring of ZEPHYRUS and the harpy, Podarge. Being chid by his master for leaving PATROCLUS on the field of battle, Xanthus turned his head reproachfully, and told Achilles that he also would soon be numbered with the dead, not from any fault of his horse, but by the decree of inexorable destiny (*Iliad*, xix).

*Xanthus* is also the ancient name of the Scamander, and of a city on its banks. Aelian and Pliny say that HOMER called the Scamander 'Xanthos', or the 'Gold-red river', because it coloured with such a tinge the fleeces of sheep washed in its waters. Others maintain that it was so called because a Greek hero of this name defeated a body of TROJANS on its banks, and pushed half of them into the stream.

**Xerxes** (zœ'ksēz). A Greek way of writing the Persian *Ksathra* or *Kshatra*. Xerxes I, the great Xerxes, King of Persia (485–465

B.C.), is identical with the Ahasuerus of the Bible.

When Xerxes invaded Greece he constructed a pontoon bridge across the Dardanelles, which was swept away by the force of the waves; this so enraged the Persian despot that he 'inflicted 300 lashes on the rebellious sea, and cast chains of iron across it'. This story is a Greek myth, founded on the peculiar construction of Xerxes' second bridge, which consisted of 300 boats, lashed by iron chains to two ships serving as supporters.

Another story tells us that when he reviewed his enormous army before starting for Greece, he wept at the thought of the slaughter about to take place. 'Of all this multitude, who shall say how many will return?'

**Ximena** (zimē'nə). The CID's bride.

**Xylomancy** (zī'lōmansi). A form of DIVINATION using twigs, rods etc. (Gr. *xylon*, wood; *manteia*, prophecy).

# Y

**Yahoo** (yah'hoo). Swift's name, in *Gulliver's Travels*, for brutes with human forms and vicious propensities. They are subject to the HOUYHNHNMS, the horses with human reason. Hence applied to coarse, brutish or degraded persons.

**Yale.** An interesting and unique form of the ANTELOPE is seen in the yale, a heraldic animal appearing on the arms of John, Duke of Bedford, in association with his earldom of Kendal and later adopted by Lady Margaret Beaufort, mother of King Henry VII. It is the only version of the antelope depicted with curved horns branching in opposite directions. The arms may be seen on the oriel of the Master's Lodge and the Great Gate of Christ's College, Cambridge.

**Yama.** In Hindu mythology, the first of the dead, born from the SUN, judge of men and king of the dead. His kingdom is the PARADISE for the worthy where friends and relations are reunited. His twin sister is called Yami and he is usually represented as four-armed and riding a buffalo.

**Yell Hounds.** *See* WISH HOUNDS.

**Yellow-hammer.** A bunting with yellowish head, neck and breast (O.E. *amore*; Ger. *Ammer*, a bunting). The tradition is that the bird fluttered about the CROSS, and got its plumage stained with the Blood; by way of punishment its eggs were doomed ever after to bear marks of blood. Because the bird was 'cursed', boys were taught that it was right and proper to destroy its eggs.

**Yeti.** Tibetan name for the ABOMINABLE SNOWMAN.

**Yggdrasil** (ig'drəsil). The world tree of Scandinavian mythology that, with its roots and branches, binds together HEAVEN, earth and HELL. It is an ash, and is evergreen, and at the root is a fountain of wonderful virtues. In the tree, which drops honey, sit an EAGLE, a SQUIRREL and four stags. It is the tree of life and knowledge, and of time and space.

**Ymir** (ē'miə). The primaeval being of Scandinavian mythology, father of all the GIANTS. He was nourished by the four milky streams which flowed from the cow Audhumla. From his body the world was created and his skull became the vault of the heavens.

**Yoga** (yō'gə). A practice of Hindu philosophy, the withdrawal of the physical senses from external objects. Adepts in yoga are able to hold their breath for protracted periods and do other things in apparent contravention of natural requirements. Hypnotism and self-mortification are part of the cult. Union with the Deity became its object (Sans. *yoga*, union, devotion). A *yogi* is one who practises yoga.

**Ysolde (Yseult, Isolde** etc.) (ēsol'də, ēsoolt'). The name of two heroines of ARTHURIAN ROMANCE, *Ysolde the Fair*, daughter of the king of Ireland, wife of King MARK and lover of TRISTRAM, the other *Ysolde of the White Hands* or *Ysolde of Brittany*.

**Yuga.** One of the four ages of the world into which, according to Hindu cosmogony, mundane time is divided.

**Yule log,** or **Yule clog.** A great log of wood formerly laid across the hearth with great ceremony on Christmas Eve and lit with a brand from the previous year's log. There followed drinking and merriment.

# Z

**Zadkiel** (zad'kiəl). In Rabbinical angelology, the ANGEL of the planet JUPITER. The name was adopted as a pseudonym by the astrologer Richard James Morrison (1795–1874), a naval lieutenant, author of the *Herald of Astrology* (1831), continued as **Zadkiel's Almanack.**

**Zany** (zā'ni). The buffoon who mimicked the clown in the Commedia dell'Arte; hence, a simpleton, one who 'acts the goat'. The name is the Ital. *zanni*, a buffoon, a familiar form of *Giovanni* (*i.e.* John).

> For indeed,
> He's like the zani to a tumbler
> That tries tricks after him to make men laugh.
> JONSON: *Every Man out of his Humour*, IV, i.

**Zem Zem.** The sacred well near the KAABA at Mecca. According to Arab tradition, this is the very well that was shown to Hagar when Ishmael was perishing of thirst.

**Zen.** A Japanese Buddhist sect which believes that the ultimate truth is greater than words and is therefore not to be wholly found in the sacred writings, but must be sought through the 'inner light' and self-mastery. It originated in the 6th century in China.

**Zephyr** (zef'ər). **Zephyrus.** In classical mythology, the west wind, son of Astraeus and AURORA, and lover of Flora, identified with the Roman FAVONIUS; hence, any soft, gentle wind.

> Fair laughs the Morn and soft the Zephyr blows,
> While proudly riding o'er the azure realm
> In gallant trim the gilded vessel goes;
> Youth on the prow, and Pleasure at the helm.
> GRAY: *The Bard*, 71.

**Zeus** (zūs). The Greek equivalent of JUPITER. The root meaning of the word is 'bright'.

**Zodiac** (Gr. *zodiakos*, pertaining to animals; from *zoon*, an animal). The imaginary belt or zone of the heavens, extending about eight degrees each side of the Ecliptic, which the SUN traverses annually.

**Signs of the Zodiac.** The zodiac was divided by the ancients into 12 equal parts, proceeding from west to east, each part of 30 degrees, and distinguished by a sign; these originally corresponded to the zodiacal constellations bearing the same names, but now, through the precession of the equinoxes, they coincide with the constellations bearing the names next in order.

Beginning with ARIES, we have first six on the north side and six on the south side of the Equator; beginning with CAPRICORNUS, we have six ascending and then six descending signs—*i.e.* six which ascend higher and higher towards the north, and six which descend lower and lower towards the south. The six northern signs are: *Aries* (the ram), TAURUS (the bull), GEMINI (the twins), spring signs; CANCER (the crab), *Leo* (the lion), VIRGO (the virgin), summer signs. The six southern are: LIBRA (the balance), SCORPIO (the scorpion), SAGITTARIUS (the archer), autumn signs; *Capricornus* (the goat), AQUARIUS (the water-bearer), and *Pisces* (the fishes), winter signs.

> Our vernal signs the RAM begins,
> Then comes the BULL, in May the TWINS;
> The CRAB in June, next LEO shines,
> And VIRGO ends the northern signs.
> The BALANCE brings autumnal fruits,
> The SCORPION stings, the ARCHER shoots;
> December's GOAT brings wintry blast,
> AQUARIUS rain, the FISH come last.
> E.C.B.

The Egyptian Denderah depicts the northern constellations at the centre surrounded by the signs of the Zodiac, but CAPRICORN is portrayed as a GOAT with a FISH tail and the SCARAB replaces CANCER. The Arabian Zodiac is represented by a fruit tree with twelve branches on which the stars appear as fruits.

The Zodiac of the Hindus, the *Rasi chakra*, or Wheel of the Signs, has the Sun Chariot at the centre, surrounded by the planetary deities, with the outer circle having the signs in the Egyptian order.

The Chinese Zodiac has the signs of the Twelve Terrestrial Branches with the Beasts of the Constellations under the branches of the Year Tree, they are the RAT, OX, TIGER, HARE, DRAGON, SNAKE, HORSE, GOAT, MONKEY, COCK, DOG, BOAR, comprising six wild and six domestic animals, six *yin* and six *yang*.

The Islamic Zodiac has six northern and wet with six southern and dry signs. ARIES, LEO, SAGITTARIUS represent the East, fire, the hot and dry; TAURUS, VIRGO, CAPRICORNUS, the South, the earth, cold and dry; GEMINI, LIBRA, AQUARIUS, the West, air, the hot and wet; CANCER, SCORPIO, PISCES, the North, water, the cold and wet.

The Inca Zodiac agrees largely with the signs now in use; the inner circle has the signs for the twenty weekday names.

**Zoilus.** A Greek rhetorician of the 4th century B.C., a literary THERSITES, shrewd, witty, and spiteful, nicknamed *Homeromastix* (Homer's scourge), because he mercilessly assailed the epics of HOMER, and called the companions of ULYSSES in the island of CIRCE 'weeping porkers'. He also attacked PLATO and ISOCRATES. His name is applied to a spiteful and carping critic. *See* THRACIAN DOG *under* DOG.

**Zombie.** The python god of certain West African tribes. Its worship was carried to the West Indies with the slave trade, and still somewhat covertly survives in VOODOO ceremonies in Haiti and some of the Southern States of the USA.

The word *zombie* is also applied to an alleged dead body brought to life in a more or less cataleptic or automaton state by Voodoo magic; also, colloquially, to a half-wit or thick-head.